Frommer's

Hawaii day BY day

1st Edition

by Jeanette Foster

WILEY
Wiley Publishing, Inc.

> Hawaiians were the world's first surfers, and the sport was once considered a deeply spiritual art.

Contents

PAGE 73

PAGE 202

PAGE 85

PAGE 456

PAGE 396

PAGE 346

PAGE 14

PAGE 288

PAGE 470

PUBLISHED BY
Wiley Publishing, Inc.
111 River St., Hoboken, NJ 07030-5774

ISBN 978-0-470-45025-3

Frommer's®

Editorial by Frommer's

EDITOR
Christine Ryan

PHOTO EDITOR
Cherie Cincilla

CARTOGRAPHER
Andrew Dolan

CAPTIONS
Mike Hammer

COVER PHOTO RESEARCH
Richard Fox

SIDESHOW MEDIA

Produced by Sideshow Media

PUBLISHER
Dan Tucker

MANAGING EDITOR
Megan McFarland

PROJECT EDITOR
Alicia Mills

PHOTO RESEARCHERS
John Martin, Paula Trotto

DESIGN
Kevin Smith, And Smith LLC

SPOTLIGHT FEATURE DESIGN
Em Dash Design LLC

For information on our other products and services or to obtain technical support, please contact our Customer Care Department within the U.S. at 800/762-2974, outside the U.S. at 317/572-3993 or fax 317/572-4002.

Wiley also publishes its books in a variety of electronic formats. Some content that appears in print may not be available in electronic formats.

MANUFACTURED IN CHINA

5 4 3 2

How to Use This Guide

The Day by Day guides present a series of itineraries that take you from place to place. The itineraries are organized by time (The Best of the Big Island in 1 Week), by region (Central Oahu & the North Shore), by town (Kona), and by special interest (Romantic Maui). You can follow these itineraries to the letter, or customize your own based on the information we provide. Within the tours, we suggest cafes, bars, or restaurants where you can take a break. Each of these stops is marked with a coffee-cup icon. In each chapter, we provide detailed hotel and restaurant reviews so you can select the places that are right for you.

The hotels, restaurants, and attractions listed in this guide have been ranked for quality, value, service, amenities, and special features using a **star-rating system.** Hotels, restaurants, attractions, shopping, and nightlife are rated on a scale of zero stars (recommended) to three stars (exceptional). In addition to the star-rating system, we also use a kids icon to point out the best bets for families.

The following **abbreviations** are used for credit cards:

AE American Express
V Visa
MC MasterCard
DISC Discover
DC Diners Club

A Note on Prices

Frommer's lists exact prices in local currency. Currency conversions fluctuate, so before departing consult a currency exchange website such as **www.oanda.com/convert/classic** to check up-to-the-minute conversion rates.

In the "Take a Break" and "Best Bets" sections of this book, we have used a system of dollar signs to show a range of costs for 1 night in a hotel (the price of a double-occupancy room) or the cost of an entree at a restaurant. Use the following table to decipher the dollar signs:

COST	HOTELS	RESTAURANTS
$	under $100	under $10
$$	$100–$200	$10–$20
$$$	$200–$300	$20–$30
$$$$	$300–$400	$30–$40
$$$$$	over $400	over $40

How to Contact Us

In researching this book, we discovered many wonderful places—hotels, restaurants, shops, and more. We're sure you'll find others. Please tell us about them, so we can share the information with your fellow travelers in upcoming editions. If you were disappointed with a recommendation, we'd love to know that, too. Please email us at frommersfeedback@wiley.com or write to:

Frommer's Hawaii Day by Day, 1st Edition
Wiley Publishing, Inc.
111 River Street
Hoboken, NJ 07030-5774

Travel Resources at Frommers.com

Frommer's travel resources don't end with this guide. **Frommers.com** has travel information on more than 4,000 destinations. We update features regularly, giving you access to the most current trip-planning information and the best airfare, lodging, and car-rental bargains. You can also listen to podcasts, connect with other Frommers.com members through our active reader forums, share your travel photos, read blogs from guidebook editors and fellow travelers, and much more.

An Additional Note

Please be advised that travel information is subject to change at any time—and this is especially true of prices. We suggest that you write or call ahead for confirmation when making your travel plans. The authors, editors, and publisher cannot be held responsible for the experiences of readers while traveling. Your safety is important to us, so we encourage you to stay alert and be aware of your surroundings.

About the Author

A resident of the Big Island, **Jeanette Foster** has skied the slopes of Mauna Kea—during a Fourth of July ski meet, no less—and gone scuba diving with manta rays off the Kona Coast. A prolific writer widely published in travel, sports, and adventure magazines, she's also the editor of *Zagat's Survey to Hawaii's Top Restaurants.* In addition to writing this guide, Jeanette is the author of *Frommer's Hawaii; Frommer's Maui; Frommer's Kauai; Frommer's Hawaii with Kids; Frommer's Portable Big Island; Frommer's Honolulu, Waikiki & Oahu; Frommer's Maui Day by Day;* and *Frommer's Honolulu & Oahu Day by Day.*

Acknowledgments

Special thanks to Priscilla Life, the world's best researcher.

About the Contributing Photographers

Marco Garcia, a Honolulu-based photographer, specializes in people and assignment photography. His photographs have appeared in national and international magazines, newspapers, advertisements, and websites. **Carla McGrew Jalbert** has an M.A. in Instructional Technology and is an experienced wedding and portrait photographer. **Kristin Mills** has been photographing professionally since 2005. Mostly, she loves taking pictures of people—kids, weddings, sports, and candids. **Dana Nadeau**, owner of Garden Island Photography (www.gardenislandphotography.com), has lived on Kauai for more than twenty years. **Bruce Omori**, a Big Island native, is a professional photographer based in Hilo, Hawaii. Best known for stunning lava imagery, his work has appeared globally in newspapers, magazines, and websites such as *National Geographic*, the *Los Angeles Times*, MSNBC, and *Time*. **Ryan Siphers** graduated from the world-renowned Brooks Institute in Santa Barbara, California, in 2006 with a B.A. in Industrial Scientific Photography. He has lived and worked in Hawaii ever since, specializing in architecture, travel, lifestyle, and food photography.

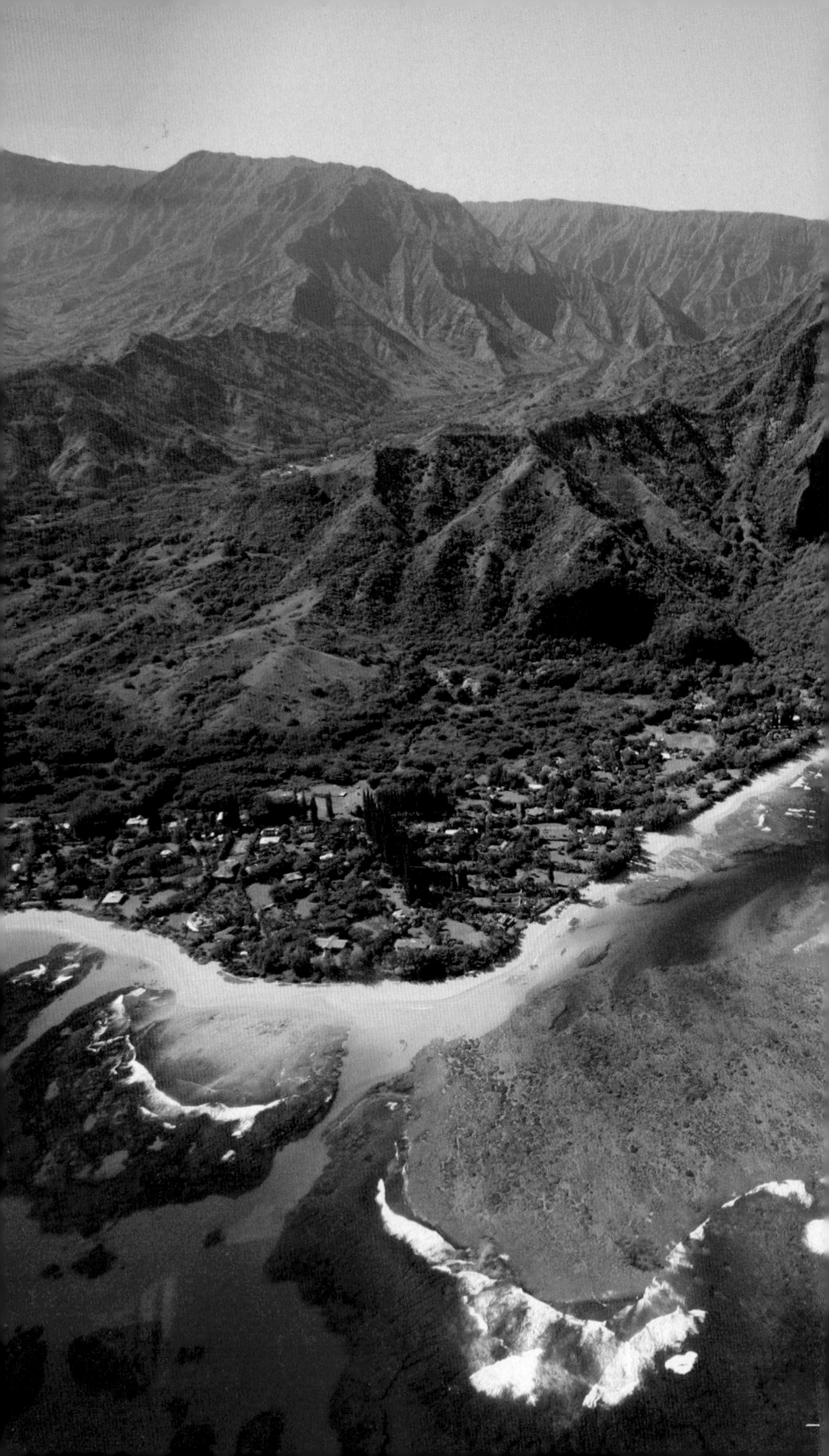

1 The Best of Hawaii

My Favorite Hawaii Moments

3 Feeling history come alive at Pearl Harbor

1 Watching North Shore's big waves

My Favorite Small Towns

2 Haleiwa

The Best Hiking & Camping

6 Diamond Head Crater

Hawaii's Best Snorkeling & Diving

7 Hanauma Bay

Hawaii's Best Adventures in the Ocean

5 Submarine rides

Hawaii's Best Lodging

5 Halekulani

5 Royal Hawaiian

Hawaii's Best Dining Experiences

4 Alan Wong's Restaurant

4 Chef Mavro Restaurant

5 Sansei Seafood Restaurant & Sushi Bar

The Best of Oahu

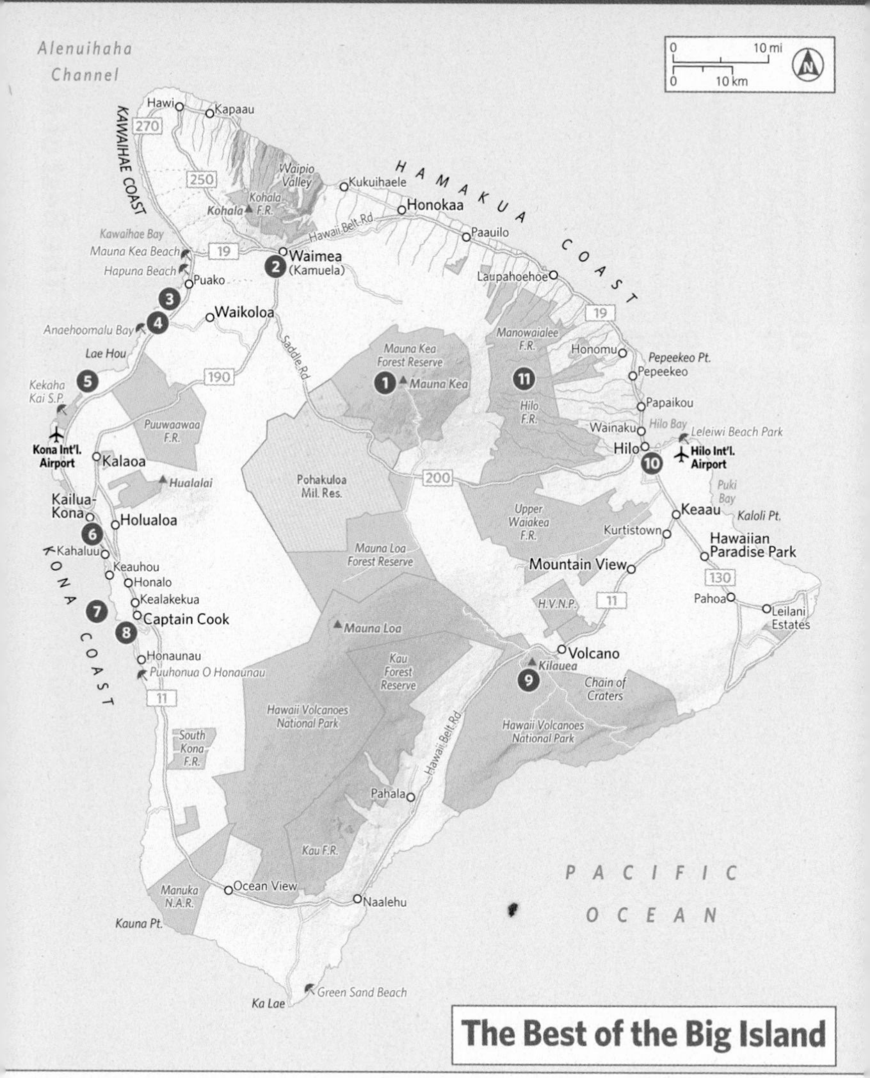

The Best of the Big Island

My Favorite Hawaii Moments

1 Seeing the sunset atop Mauna Kea

9 Devastation Trail, Hawaii Volcanoes National Park

My Favorite Small Towns

10 Hilo

The Best Hiking & Camping

9 Devastation Trail, Hawaii Volcanoes National Park

Hawaii's Best Adventures on Land

11 Birding at Hakalau Forest National Wildlife Refuge

Hawaii's Best Snorkeling & Diving

8 Kealakekua Bay

Hawaii's Best Adventures in the Ocean

7 Sport fishing off the Kona Coast

Hawaii's Best Lodging

5 Four Seasons Resort Hualalai at Historic Kaupulehu

6 Kona Tiki Hotel

Hawaii's Best Dining Experiences

3 Brown's Beach House

2 Merriman's

4 Sansei Seafood Restaurant & Sushi Bar

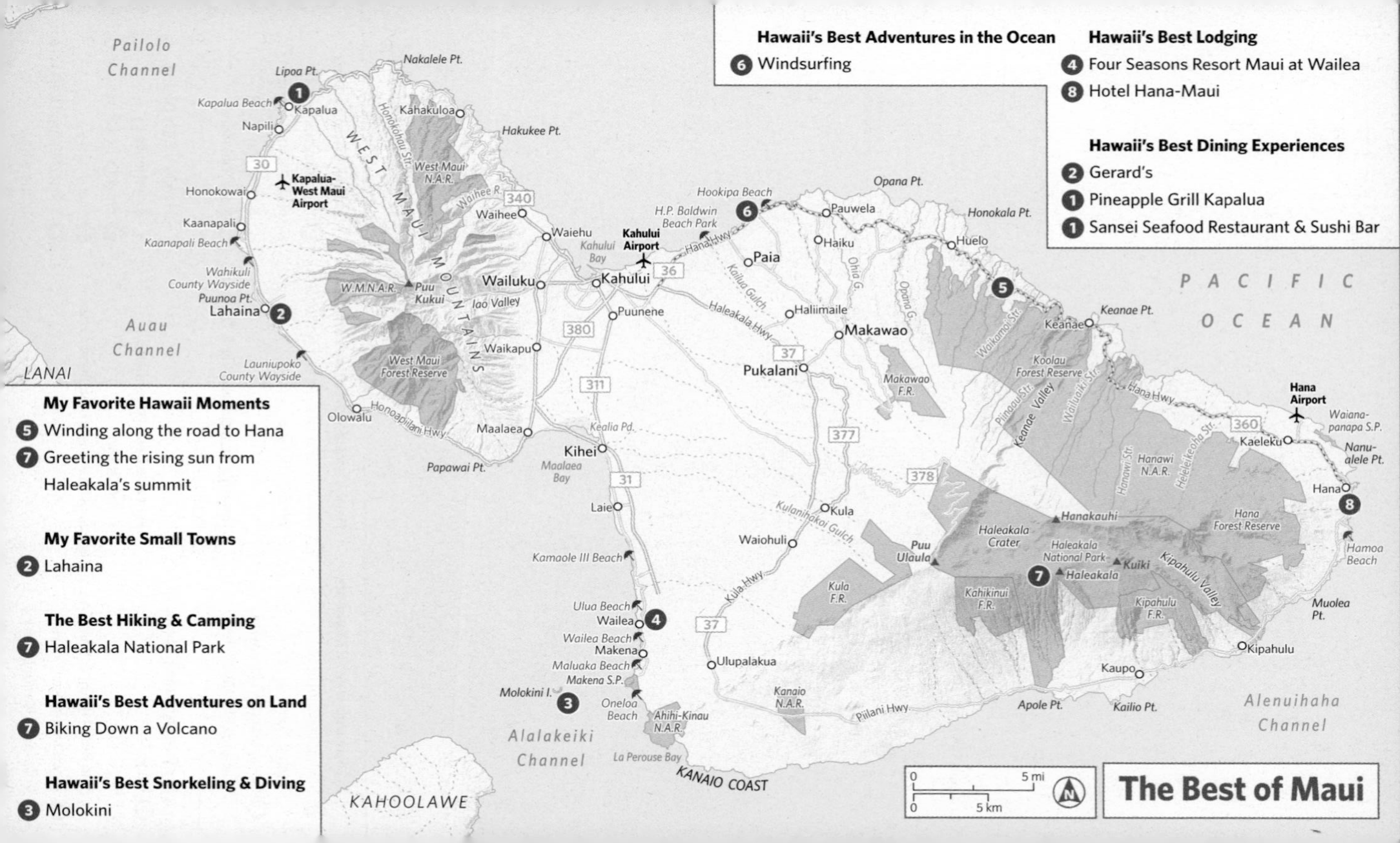
The Best of Maui
Hawaii's Best Adventures in the Ocean
6 Windsurfing
Hawaii's Best Lodging
4 Four Seasons Resort Maui at Wailea
8 Hotel Hana-Maui
Hawaii's Best Dining Experiences
2 Gerard's
1 Pineapple Grill Kapalua
1 Sansei Seafood Restaurant & Sushi Bar
My Favorite Hawaii Moments
5 Winding along the road to Hana
7 Greeting the rising sun from Haleakala's summit
My Favorite Small Towns
2 Lahaina
The Best Hiking & Camping
7 Haleakala National Park
Hawaii's Best Adventures on Land
7 Biking Down a Volcano
Hawaii's Best Snorkeling & Diving
3 Molokini
Pailolo Channel
Auau Channel
LANAI
Alalakeiki Channel
KAHOOLAWE
Alenuihaha Channel
PACIFIC OCEAN
KANAIO COAST
Lipoa Pt.
Nakalele Pt.
Kapalua Beach
Kapalua
Napili
Honokowai
Kaanapali
Kaanapali Beach
Wahikuli County Wayside
Puunoa Pt.
Lahaina
Launiupoko County Wayside
Olowalu
Honoapiilani Hwy.
Kapalua-West Maui Airport
WEST MAUI MOUNTAINS
Honokohau Str.
Kahakuloa
Hakukee Pt.
West Maui N.A.R.
Waihee R.
Waihee
Waiehu
W.M.N.A.R.
Puu Kukui
Iao Valley
West Maui Forest Reserve
Wailuku
Waikapu
Maalaea
Papawai Pt.
Kahului Bay
Kahului Airport
Kahului
Puunene
Kealia Pd.
Kihei
Maalaea Bay
Laie
Kamaole III Beach
Ulua Beach
Wailea
Wailea Beach
Makena
Maluaka Beach
Makena S.P.
Molokini I.
Oneloa Beach
Ahihi-Kinau N.A.R.
La Perouse Bay
H.P. Baldwin Beach Park
Hookipa Beach
Hana Hwy.
Paia
Kailua Gulch
Pauwela
Haiku
Ohia G.
Opana G.
Opana Pt.
Haliimaile
Haleakala Hwy.
Makawao
Pukalani
Makawao F.R.
Huelo
Honokala Pt.
Waikamoi Str.
Keanae
Keanae Pt.
Koolau Forest Reserve
Piinaau Str.
Keanae Valley
Wailuaiki Str.
Hanawi Str.
Hanawi N.A.R.
Heleleikeoha Str.
Hana Airport
Waianapanapa S.P.
Kaeleku
Nanualele Pt.
Hana
Hamoa Beach
Hana Forest Reserve
Muolea Pt.
Kipahulu
Kipahulu Valley
Kipahulu F.R.
Kaupo
Kailio Pt.
Apole Pt.
Hanakauhi
Haleakala Crater
Haleakala National Park
Kuiki
Haleakala
Kahikinui F.R.
Puu Ulaula
Kula
Kulanihakoi Gulch
Waiohuli
Kula F.R.
Kula Hwy.
Ulupalakua
Kanaio N.A.R.
Piilani Hwy.
30
340
36
380
311
31
37
377
378
360
0 5 mi
0 5 km

The Best of Molokai

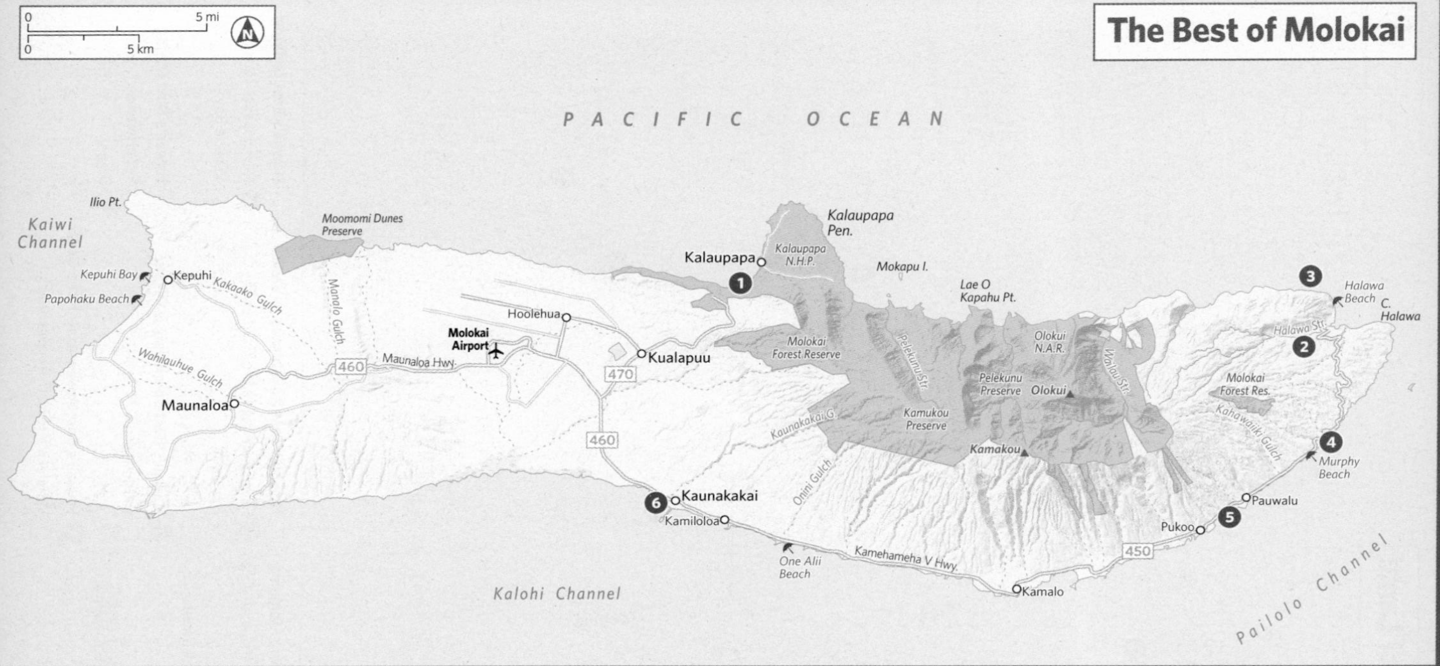

My Favorite Hawaii Moments

1 Riding a mule to Kalaupapa

My Favorite Small Towns

6 Kaunakakai

The Best Hiking & Camping

2 Halawa Valley

Hawaii's Best Adventures on Land

1 Riding a mule into a leper colony

Hawaii's Best Snorkeling & Diving

4 Murphy (Kumimi) Beach

Hawaii's Best Adventures in the Ocean

3 Kayaking along the north shore

Hawaii's Best Lodging

5 Aloha Beach House

The Best of Lanai

Polihua Beach ① — Keanapapa Pt.

Shipwreck Beach ↗

Auau Channel

②

Kanepuu Hwy.

Keomuku Rd.

Maunalei Gulch

Hauola Gulch

Hauola Gulch

Lanai City ○ ③ ④

Lanaihale ▲

Lopa Gulch

Kaumalapau Hwy.

Manele Rd.

✈ **Lanai Airport**

440

440

Palawai Basin

Kaumalapau Har.

Palaoa Pt.

Hulopoe Beach ↗ ⑤ Manele Bay

⑥

⑦

Kealaikahiki Channel

P A C I F I C

O C E A N

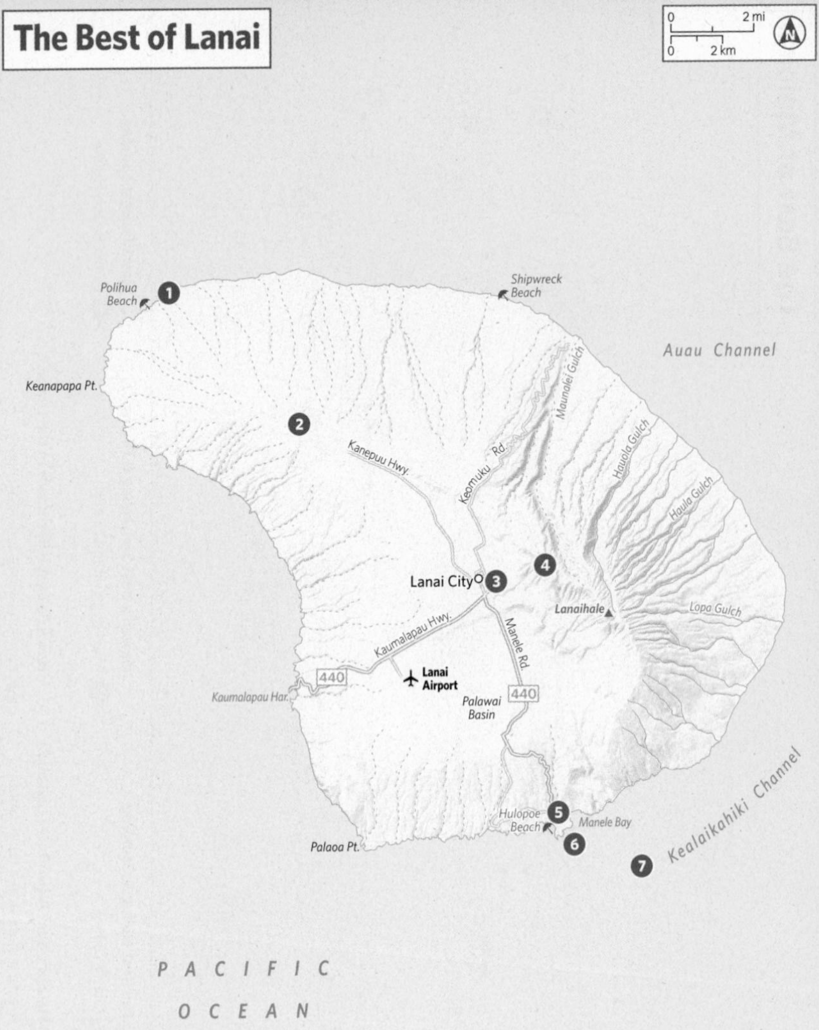

My Favorite Hawaii Moments
⑥ Taking a day trip to Lanai

My Favorite Small Towns
③ Lanai City

The Best Hiking & Camping
④ Munro Trail

Hawaii's Best Adventures on Land
② Four-wheeling to the Garden of the Gods

Hawaii's Best Snorkeling & Diving
⑦ Cathedrals I & II

Hawaii's Best Adventures in the Ocean
① Whale-watching from the beach

Hawaii's Best Lodging
⑤ Four Seasons Resort at Manele Bay

Hawaii's Best Dining Experiences
⑤ Ihilani

My Favorite Hawaii Moments

5 Taking a helicopter tour of Kauai

The Best Hiking & Camping

1 Waimea Canyon Trail

Hawaii's Best Adventures on Land

3,7 Horseback riding to remote beaches

Hawaii's Best Snorkeling & Diving

2 Oceanarium

Hawaii's Best Adventures in the Ocean

2,6 Surfing

Hawaii's Best Lodging

6 Grand Hyatt Kauai Resort & Spa

4 Kauai Country Inn

Hawaii's Best Dining Experiences

6 The Beach House

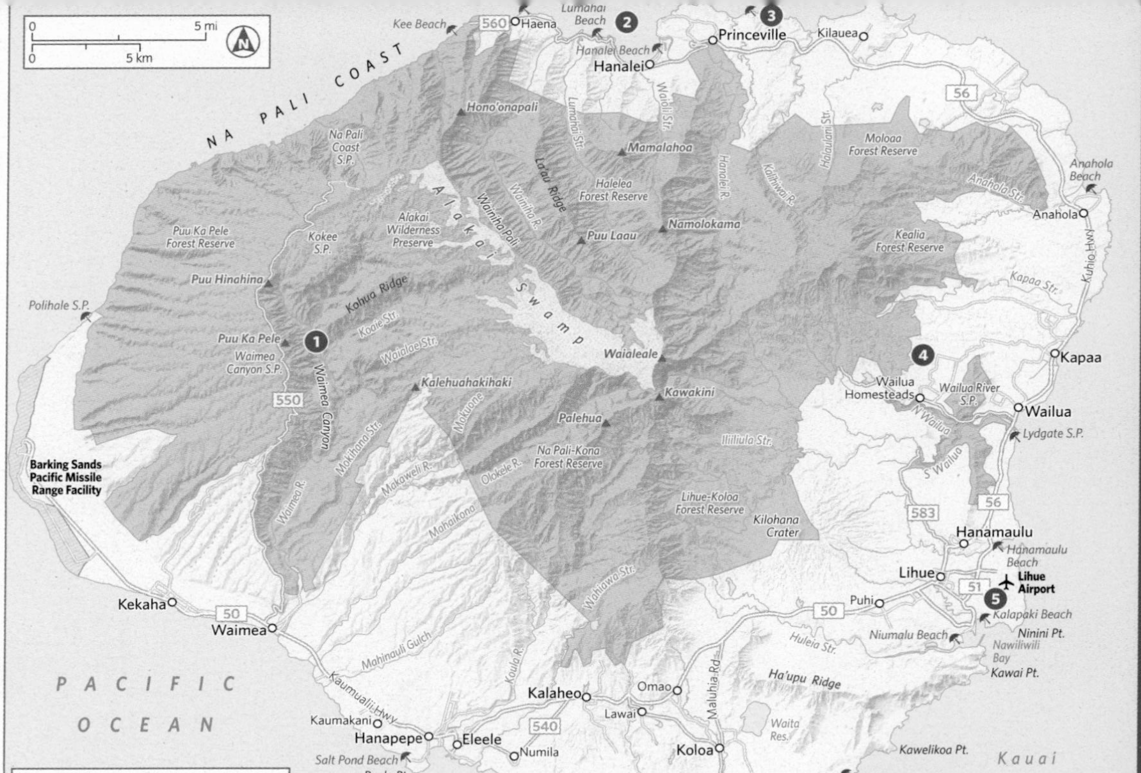

The Best of Kauai

> PAGE 1 *It'll cost big bucks, but a Blue Hawaii helicopter tour will buy eye-popping views of Kauai's spectacular North Shore.* THIS PAGE *Oahu offers the world's raddest surfing, from the treacherous Pipeline to the 50-foot walls of water in Waimea Bay.*

My Favorite Hawaii Moments

Feeling history come alive at Pearl Harbor, Oahu. The United States could turn its back on World War II no longer after December 7, 1941, when Japanese warplanes bombed Pearl Harbor. Standing on the deck of the USS *Arizona* Memorial—the eternal tomb for the 1,177 sailors and Marines trapped below when the battleship sank in just 9 minutes—is a moving experience you'll never forget. Also in Pearl Harbor, you can visit the USS *Missouri* Memorial, where World War II came to an end. The Japanese signed their surrender on the deck of this 58,000-ton battleship on September 2, 1945. Map p 2, ❸. See p 119–20, ❶ to ❸.

Watching North Shore's big waves, Oahu. Just an hour's drive from Honolulu, the North Shore is another world: a pastoral, rural setting with magnificent beaches and a slower way of life. During the winter months, stop and watch the professionals surf the monster waves. Map p 2, ❶. See p 126.

Seeing the sunset atop Mauna Kea, Big Island. The Hawaiians thought the gods lived on Mauna Kea, the world's tallest mountain at 33,476 feet when measured from the ocean's floor. Don't miss the opportunity to see the sun sink into the Pacific and watch the stars slowly come out of the inky black sky. The summit is so clear that the world's largest telescopes are located here. Map p 3, ❶. See p 53, ㉝.

Watching a volcano erupt, Big Island. Some call the 3-decades-long eruption of Kilauea the Eighth Wonder of the World. It's an awe-inspiring sight at any time, but especially dramatic at night, when you can watch the glowing red lava snake down the side of the island and explode into the ocean. Map p 3, ❾. See p 233, ⓮.

Winding along the road to Hana, Maui. The Hana Highway is much more than a way to get from point A to point B. Stop along the way to plunge into icy mountain ponds filled by cascading waterfalls; gaze upon vistas of waves pummeling soaring ocean cliffs; inhale the sweet aroma of blooming ginger; and take a walk back in time, catching a glimpse of what Hawaii looked like before concrete condos and fast-food joints washed ashore. Map p 4, ❺. See p 342.

Greeting the rising sun from Haleakala's summit, Maui. Bundle up in warm clothing, fill a thermos full of hot java, and drive up to the summit to watch the sky turn from inky black to muted charcoal as a small sliver of orange forms on the horizon. Standing at 10,000 feet, breathing in the rarefied air, and watching the first rays of light streak across the sky is a mystical experience of the highest magnitude. Map p 4, ❼. See p 355, ❼.

Riding a mule to Kalaupapa, Molokai. Even if you have only 1 day to spend on Molokai, spend it on a mule. The Molokai Mule Ride trek from "topside" Molokai to the Kalaupapa National Historic Park (Father Damien's world-famous leper colony) is a once-in-a-lifetime adventure. The cliffs are taller than 300-story skyscrapers, and the narrow 3-mile trail includes 26 dizzying switchbacks, but Buzzy Sproat has never lost one of his trustworthy mules (or any riders) on the difficult trail. The mules make the trek daily, rain or shine. Map p 5, ❶. See p 419, ❼.

Taking a day trip to Lanai. From Lahaina, in Maui, take the Expeditions Lahaina/Lanai Passenger Ferry from Maui over to the island of Lanai and rent a four-wheel-drive jeep on your own. It's a two-for-one island experience: Board in Lahaina Harbor and admire Maui from offshore, then get off at Lanai and go snorkeling in the clear waters, tour the tiny former plantation island, and catch the last ferry home. Map p 6, ❻. See p 58, ❸.

Taking a helicopter tour of Kauai. Don't leave Kauai without seeing it from a helicopter. It's expensive but worth the splurge. You can take home memories of the thrilling ride up and over the Kalalau Valley on Kauai's wild North Shore and into the 5,200-foot vertical temple of Mount Waialeale, the most sacred place on the island and the wettest spot on earth. Map p 7, ❺. See p 520.

My Favorite Small Towns

> *Hilo's quaint streets, Victorian architecture, and banyan-lined bay make it one of my favorite places to visit on the Big Island.*

Haleiwa, Oahu. The North Shore is the Hawaii of Hollywood—giant waves, surfers galore, tropical jungles, waterfalls, and mysterious Hawaiian temples. If you're looking for a quieter vacation that's closer to nature, the North Shore is your place. The artsy little beach town of Haleiwa and the surrounding shoreline seem a world away from Waikiki. The North Shore boasts good restaurants, shopping, and cultural activities—but here they come with the quiet of country living. Bed-and-breakfasts are the most common accommodations, but there's one first-class hotel and some vacation rentals as well. Be forewarned: It's an hour's drive to Honolulu and Waikiki, and it's about twice as rainy on the North Shore as in Honolulu. Map p 2, 2. See p 128, 4.

Hilo, Big Island. When the sun shines in Hilo, it's one of the most beautiful tropical cities in the Pacific. Hawaii's largest metropolis after Honolulu is a quaint, misty, flower-filled city of Victorian houses overlooking a half-moon bay, with a restored historic downtown and a clear view of Mauna Loa's often snowcapped peak. Hilo catches everyone's eye until it rains—it rains a lot in Hilo, and when it rains, it pours. Map p 3, 10.

Lahaina, Maui. This old seaport is a tame version of its former self, a raucous whaling town where sailors swaggered ashore in search of women and grog. Today the village teems with restaurants, T-shirt shops, and galleries, and parts of it are downright tacky, but there's still lots of real history to be found. Lahaina is a great place to stay; accommodations include a few old hotels, quaint bed-and-breakfasts, and a handful of oceanfront condos. Map p 4, 2. See p 328.

Kaunakakai, Molokai. Kaunakakai is the closest thing Molokai has to a business district. Friendly Isle Realty and Friendly Isle Travel offer islanders dream homes and vacations; Rabang's Filipino Food posts bad checks in the window; antlered deer-head trophies guard the grocery aisles at Misaki's Market; and Kanemitsu's, the town's legendary bakery, churns out fresh loaves of onion-cheese bread daily. Once an ancient canoe landing, Kaunakakai was the royal summer residence of King Kamehameha V. The port town bustled when pineapple and sugar were king, but those days, too, are gone. With its Old West–style storefronts laid out in a 3-block grid on a flat, dusty plain, Kaunakakai is a town from the past. Map p 5, 6. See p 422.

Lanai City, Lanai. The only town on this island (pop. 3,200) sits at 1,645 feet above sea level. Built in 1924, this plantation village is a tidy grid of quaint tin-roofed cottages in bright pastels, with tropical gardens of banana, lilikoi, and papaya. Many of the residents are Filipino immigrants who worked the pineapple fields. Their clapboard homes, now worth $500,000 or more, are excellent examples of historic preservation; the whole town looks like it's been kept under a bell jar. Map p 6, 3. See p 450, 5.

Hawaii's Best Hiking & Camping

Diamond Head Crater, Oahu. This is a moderate, but steep, walk to the summit of the 750-foot volcanic cone, Hawaii's most famous landmark. A climb to the top rewards you with a 360-degree view of the island. The 1.4-mile round-trip takes about 1½ hours. Map p 2, ❻. See p 144.

Devastation Trail, Hawaii Volcanoes National Park, Big Island. Up on the rim of Kilauea Iki Crater, you can see what an erupting volcano did to a once-flourishing ohia forest. The scorched earth with its ghostly tree skeletons stands in sharp contrast to the rest of the lush forest. Everyone can take this half-mile hike on a paved path across the eerie bed of black cinders. Map p 3, ❾. See p 240.

Haleakala National Park, Maui. Hiking into Maui's dormant volcano is really the best way to see it. The terrain inside the wilderness area of the volcano, which ranges from burnt-red cinder cones to ebony-black lava flows, is simply spectacular. The best route takes in two trails: head into the crater along Sliding Sands Trail, which begins on the rim at 9,800 feet and descends into the belly of the beast, to the valley floor at 6,600 feet, and back out along Halemauu Trail. Hardy hikers can consider making the 11-mile one-way descent, which takes 9 hours, and the equally long return ascent in 1 day. The rest of us will need to extend this steep but wonderful hike to 2 days. Map p 4, ❼. See p 360.

Halawa Valley, Molokai. Of the five great valleys of Molokai, only Halawa, with its two waterfalls, golden beach, sleepy lagoon, great surf, and offshore island, is easily accessible. An easy hike will take you from the ocean to the foot of a waterfall. Map p 5, ❷. See p 427.

Munro Trail, Lanai. This tough, 11-mile round-trip, uphill climb through the groves of Norfolk Island pines is a lung-buster, but if you reach the top, you'll be rewarded with a breathtaking view of Molokai, Maui, Kahoolawe, the peaks of the Big Island, and—on a really clear day—Oahu in the distance. Figure on 7 hours of hiking. The trail follows Lanai's ancient caldera rim, ending up at the island's highest point, Lanaihale. Map p 6, ❹. See p 458.

> *Hikers can climb 11 miles into a dormant volcano on Maui's Sliding Sands Trail in Haleakala National Park.*

Waimea Canyon Trail, Kauai. You want to hike Hawaii's Grand Canyon, but you don't think you have time? Take the Canyon Trail to the east rim for a breathtaking view into the 3,000-foot-deep canyon. The 3.5-mile round-trip takes 2 to 3 hours and leads to Waipoo Falls and back. Map p 7, ❶. See p 508.

Hawaii's Best Adventures on Land

> *See waterfalls spill from spectacular 300-foot cliffs along Molokai's remote Kalaupapa Trail.*

Birding at Hakalau Forest National Wildlife Refuge, the Big Island. Native Hawaiian birds are few—and dwindling. But Hawaii still offers extraordinary birding for anyone nimble enough to traverse tough, mucky landscape. And the best birding is on the Big Island; birders the world over come here hoping to see three Hawaiian birds, in particular: akiapolaau, a woodpecker wannabe with a war club–like head; nukupuu, an elusive little yellow bird with a curved beak, one of the crown jewels of Hawaiian birding; and alala, the critically endangered Hawaiian crow that's now almost impossible to see in the wild. Hakalau Forest National Wildlife Refuge is the first national wildlife refuge established solely for forest bird management. It's on the eastern slope of Mauna Kea, above the Hamakua Coast. Map p 3, 11. See p 250.

Biking down a volcano, Maui. It's not even close to dawn, but here you are, rubbing your eyes awake, riding in a van up the long, dark road to the top of Maui's sleeping volcano. It's colder than you ever thought possible for a tropical island. The air is thin. You stomp your chilly feet while you wait, sipping hot coffee. Then comes the sun, exploding over the yawning Haleakala Crater, which is big enough to swallow Manhattan whole—it's a mystical moment you won't soon forget, imprinted on a palette of dawn colors. Now you know why Hawaiians named it the House of the Sun. But there's no time to linger: Decked out in your screaming yellow parka, you mount your steed and test its most important feature—the brakes—because you're about to coast 37 miles down a 10,000-foot volcano. Map p 4, 7. See p 366.

Riding a mule into a leper colony, Molokai. Don't pass up the opportunity to see this hauntingly beautiful peninsula. Buzzy Sproat's mules go up and down the 3-mile Kalaupapa Trail to Molokai's famous leper colony. The views are breathtaking: You'll see the world's highest sea cliffs (over 300 stories tall) and waterfalls plunging thousands of feet into the ocean. If you're afraid of heights, catch the views from the Kalaupapa Lookout, in Palaau Park. Map p 5, 1. See p 419, 7.

Four-wheeling to the Garden of the Gods, Lanai. Hop on a four-wheel-drive vehicle and head out on the dirt road that leads out of Lanai City, through the now uncultivated pineapple fields, to the Garden of the Gods, on Lanai's north shore. Take the time to explore this rugged, barren, beautiful place, full of rocks strewn by volcanic forces and shaped by the elements into a variety of shapes and colors—brilliant reds, oranges, ochers, and yellows. Ancient Hawaiians considered this desolate, windswept place an entirely supernatural phenomenon. Scientists, however, have other, less colorful explanations. Some call the area an "ongoing posterosional event"; others say it's just "plain and simple badlands." Go early in the morning when the light casts eerie shadows on the mysterious lava formations. Map p 6, 2. See p 449, 2.

Horseback riding to remote and hidden beaches, Kauai. Only in Kauai can you ride a horse across the wide-open pastures of a working ranch under volcanic peaks and rein up near a waterfall pool. No wonder Kauai's *paniolo* (cowboys) smile and sing so much. It's worth your time and money just to get out to this seldom-seen part of Kauai. Map p 7, 3 & 7. See p 521.

> *Hawaii's rapidly disappearing native bird species remain very visible in the wildlife refuge on the Big Island.*

> *You can bike 37 miles straight toward the center of the earth in Maui's massive Haleakala Crater.*

Hawaii's Best Snorkeling & Diving

> *Molokini's crescent-shaped crater is teeming with exotic marine life—and therefore snorkelers and divers too.*

Hanauma Bay, Oahu. Oahu's most popular snorkeling spot is a curved, 2,000-foot gold-sand beach packed elbow-to-elbow with people year-round. Part of an old crater that fell into the sea, the bay's shallow shoreline water and abundant marine life are the main attractions to snorkelers. A shallow reef outside the bay protects the inside from surf rolling in, making the waters in the bay very calm. Hanauma Bay is a conservation district; you may look at but not touch or take any marine life here. Feeding the fish is also prohibited. Map p 2, 7. See p 159.

Kealakekua Bay, Big Island. Probably the best snorkeling for all levels can be found in Kealakekua Bay. The calm waters of this underwater preserve teem with a wealth of marine life. Coral heads, lava tubes, and underwater caves all provide an excellent habitat for Hawaii's vast array of tropical fish, making mile-wide Kealakekua the Big Island's best accessible spot for snorkeling and diving. Without looking very hard, you can see octopi, free-swimming moray eels, parrotfish, and goatfish; once in a while, a pod of spinner dolphins streaks across the bay. Map p 3, 8. See p 208.

Molokini, Maui. This marine life park is one of Hawaii's top dive and snorkel spots. This crescent-shaped crater has three tiers of diving: a 35-foot plateau inside the crater basin (used by beginning divers and snorkelers), a wall sloping to 70 feet just beyond the inside plateau, and a sheer wall on the outside and back-side of the crater that plunges 350 feet. This underwater park is very popular thanks to calm, clear, protected waters and an abundance of marine life, from manta rays to clouds of yellow butterflyfish. Map p 4, 3. See p 374.

Murphy (Kumimi) Beach, Molokai. Just don your gear and head for one of the best beaches for snorkeling on the East End, where you'll find lots of exotic tropical fish, including long-nosed butterflyfish, saddle wrasses, and convict tangs. Map p 5, 4. See p 424.

Cathedrals I and II, Lanai. Just off the south shore, two of Hawaii's best-known dive spots are found in Lanai's clear waters. The sun lights up an underwater grotto like a magnificent church, hence the name—some scuba divers claim it is a near-religious experience. Snorkeling is terrific at nearby Hulopoe Beach. Map p 6, 7. See p 459.

Oceanarium, Kauai. Northwest of Hanalei Bay, offshore you'll find a kaleidoscopic marine world in a horseshoe-shaped cove. From the rare (long-handed spiny lobsters) to the more common (taape, conger eels, and nudibranchs), the resident population is one of the more diverse on the island. The topography, which features pinnacles, ridges, and archways, is covered with cup corals, black-coral trees, and nooks and crannies enough for a dozen dives. Snorkelers will be happy at nearby Hanalei Bay. Map p 7, 2.

Hawaii's Best Adventures in the Ocean

> *Windsurfers from around the world blow into Hookipa Beach in Paia for the stiff breeze and rolling waves.*

Submarine rides, Oahu. For a Jules Verne–type experience, plunge 100 feet under the sea in a state-of-the-art, high-tech submarine. You'll meet swarms of vibrant tropical fish up close and personal as they flutter through the deep blue waters off Waikiki. Map p 2, ❺. See p 160.

Sport fishing off the Kona Coast, Big Island. If you want to catch fish, it doesn't get any better than the Kona Coast, known internationally as the marlin capital of the world. Big-game fish, including gigantic blue marlin and other Pacific billfish, tuna, mahimahi, sailfish, swordfish, ono (also known as wahoo), and ulua (giant trevallies) roam the waters. When anglers here catch marlin that weigh 1,000 pounds or more, they call them *granders;* there's even a "wall of fame" on Kailua-Kona's Waterfront Row, honoring 40 anglers who've nailed more than 20 tons of fighting fish. Nearly 100 charter boats with professional captains and crews offer fishing charters out of Keauhou, Kawaihae, Honokohau, and Kailua Bay harbors. Map p 3, ❼. See p 258.

Windsurfing, Maui. Maui has Hawaii's best windsurfing beaches. In winter windsurfers from around the world flock to the town of Paia to ride the waves. Hookipa Beach, known all over the globe for its brisk winds and excellent waves, is the site of several world-championship contests. Map p 4, ❻. See p 377.

Kayaking along the north shore, Molokai. This is the Hawaii of your dreams: waterfalls thundering down sheer cliffs, remote sand beaches, miles of tropical vegetation, and the wind whispering in your ear. The best times to go are late March and early April, or in summer, especially August to September, when the normally galloping ocean lies down flat. Beginners should stick to kayaking the East End, where schools of tropical fish will tempt you to stop and snorkel every few feet. Map p 5, ❸. See p 430.

Whale-watching from the beach, Lanai. Polihua Beach, Lanai's largest white-sand beach, is a great spot to look for whales in season (Nov–Mar). The beach generally is not safe for swimming (strong currents) and it can be windy here, but it most likely will be deserted and you'll have a great view of Molokai in the distance. Map p 6, ❶. See p 454.

Surfing Hawaii's waves, Kauai. Hanalei Bay's winter surf is the most popular on the island, but it's for experts only. Poipu Beach is an excellent spot to learn to surf; the waves are small and—best of all—nobody laughs when you wipe out. Map p 7, ❷ & ❻. See p 525.

Hawaii's Best Lodging

> *The Spanish-style Royal Hawaiian Hotel is known as the Pink Palace of the Pacific and is Waikiki's most iconic landmark.*

kids **Halekulani, Oahu.** My favorite hotel in all Hawaii, this is the ultimate heavenly Hawaii luxury accommodation, spread over 5 acres of prime Waikiki beachfront. Some 90% of the large rooms face the ocean and have top-drawer amenities to match. The best Waikiki has to offer. Map p 2, ❺. See p 189.

kids **Royal Hawaiian, Oahu.** The symbol of Waikiki, this flamingo-pink oasis, nestled in tropical gardens, offers rooms in the 1927 historic wing (my pick, with carved wooden doors, four-poster canopy beds, flowered wallpaper, and period furniture) as well as modern oceanfront towers. The sun, the beach, the aroma of flowers—it's the perfect honeymoon location. The beach outside is the best in Waikiki for sunbathing (perfect slant to the sand). Map p 2, ❺. See p 192.

kids **Four Seasons Resort Hualalai at Historic Kaupulehu, Big Island.** This is a great place to relax in the lap of luxury. Low-rise clusters of oceanview villas nestle between the sea and the greens of a new golf course, with three seaside swimming pools and a snorkeling pond. It looks more like a 2-story town house project than a resort hotel. Map p 3, ❺. See p 283.

Kona Tiki Hotel, Big Island. Located right on the ocean, away from the hustle and bustle of downtown Kailua-Kona, this is one of the best budget deals in Hawaii. All of the rooms are tastefully decorated and feature private lanais overlooking the ocean. Although it's called a hotel, this small family-run operation is more like a large B&B, with lots of aloha and plenty of friendly conversation at the morning breakfast buffet around the pool. Map p 3, ❻. See p 287.

kids **Four Seasons Resort Maui at Wailea, Maui.** If money's no object, this is the place to spend it. This modern version of a Hawaiian palace by the sea sits on a glorious beach and inhabits its own world, thanks to an open courtyard of pools and gardens. First-rate amenities, attentive service, lots of kid-friendly touches, and a fabulous spa. Come here to be spoiled. Map p 4, ❹. See p 399.

Hotel Hana-Maui, Maui. The atmosphere, the landscape, and the culture of old Hawaii set in 21st-century accommodations. The hotel sits on 66 rolling seaside acres, with an excellent spa and access to one of the best beaches in Hana. Map p 4, ❽. See p 400.

> *A top spa, championship links, and four-star restaurants are just some of the lures of the lush Grand Hyatt Kauai.*

Aloha Beach House, Molokai. This Hawaiian-style beach house sits right on the white-sand beach of Waialua on the lush East End. Perfect for families, this impeccably decorated, two-bedroom, 1,600-square-foot beach house has hardwood floors and a huge open living/dining/kitchen area that opens out to an old-fashioned porch. Fully equipped, from the complete kitchen to beach toys. Map p 5, ❺. See p 441.

Four Seasons Resort Lanai at Manele Bay, Lanai. Located on a sun-washed southern bluff overlooking Hulopoe Beach, one of Hawaii's best stretches of golden sand, this U-shaped hotel steps down the hillside to the pool and the beach. Most of the spacious, airy rooms open to a breathtaking view of the big blue Pacific. Map p 6, ❺. See p 465.

Grand Hyatt Kauai Resort & Spa, Kauai. This is one of Hawaii's best luxury hotels and one of the top-ranked tropical resorts in *Condé Nast Traveler*'s annual readers' poll. The 4-story resort, built into the oceanside bluffs, spreads over 50 acres that overlook Shipwreck Beach. The $250-million Hyatt uses the island architecture of the mid-1920s to recapture the old Hawaii of the Matson Line steamship era. Map p 7, ❻. See p 545.

Kauai Country Inn, Kauai. This old-fashioned country inn is a slice of paradise on 2 acres, about a 20-minute drive from the beach. Each suite is uniquely decorated in Hawaiian Art Deco with a touch of humor, complete with hardwood floors, private baths, kitchen or kitchenette, and your own computer with Wi-Fi connection. Everything is top-drawer, from the "rain" shower head in the bathroom to the subzero refrigerator. Map p 7, ❹. See p 547.

Hawaii's Best Dining Experiences

> *Ihilani melds Italian and island cuisine, resulting in one of Lanai's top gourmet restaurants.*

Alan Wong's Restaurant, Oahu. James Beard Award-winner chef Alan Wong, worshiped by foodies across the state, serves brilliantly creative and irresistibly cutting-edge cuisine in a casual, sometimes noisy, room that is always packed. Map p 2, ❹. See p 177.

Chef Mavro, Oahu. If you have only 1 night on Oahu, splurge on this intimate dining experience by James Beard Award-winner chef George Mavro. An inspired menu (poached fresh fish with sago-coconut nage, thai herbs, limu, and lime froth) with perfect wine pairings in a very non-touristy neighborhood. Map p 2, ❹. See p 177.

Sansei Seafood Restaurant & Sushi Bar, Oahu, Big Island, and Maui. Don't miss perpetual award-winner D. K. Kodama's statewide restaurants, known not only for their extensive menus but also for Kodama's outrageous sushi creations: seared foie gras nigiri sushi (duck liver lightly seared over sushi rice, with caramelized onion and ripe mango) or the wonderful mango crab salad hand roll (mango, blue crab, greens, and peanuts with a sweet Thai chili vinaigrette). Oahu, map p 2, ❺, review p 185; Big Island, map p 3, ❹, review p 278; and Maui, map p 4, ❶, review p 396.

Brown's Beach House, Big Island. The spectacular beachfront setting complements a menu that features Big Island cuisine with a flare (kiawe-grilled fresh island catch with tomato fondue). The perfect choice for a sunset dinner. Map p 3, ❸. See p 270.

Merriman's, Big Island. Merriman's is a premier Hawaiian culinary attraction. Order anything from Chinese short ribs to a goat-cheese-and-eggplant sandwich for lunch; at dinner, choose from the signature wok-charred ahi, kung pao shrimp, lamb from nearby Kahua Ranch, and a noteworthy vegetarian selection. Map p 3, ❷. See p 275.

Gerard's, Maui. Chef Gerard Reversade (a frequent winner of the Wine Spectator Award of Excellence) is at the helm of this creative French cuisine in the elegant setting of an old Victorian house, with excellent service. Map p 4, ❷. See p 392.

Pineapple Grill Kapalua, Maui. If you have only 1 night to eat on the island of Maui, this is the place. Executive Chef Joey Macadangdang is a genius at combining Asian/Filipino ingredients into culinary masterpieces. The dining room overlooks the rolling hills of the Kapalua Golf Course. Map p 4, ❶. See p 396.

Ihilani, Lanai. Overlooking the resort and the ocean beyond, this classy traditional Italian restaurant serves a range of well-prepared dishes, from inspiring risottos (Puna goat cheese with pine nuts) to fresh fish (ahi caponata with eggplant), veal, chicken, and beef. Map p 6, ❺. See p 463.

The Beach House, Kauai. This is the best special-occasion restaurant on Kauai and the premier spot for sunset drinks, appetizers, and dinner—a treat for all the senses. The oceanfront room is large, accented with oversize sliding-glass doors, with old Hawaii regional favorites on the menu. Map p 7, ❻. See p 535.

> *ABOVE Brown's Beach House on the Big Island is a sunset dining destination. BELOW Sushi's the star at Oahu's Sansei Seafood Restaurant & Sushi Bar.*

2

Strategies for Seeing Hawaii

Strategies for Seeing Hawaii

There really is just one cardinal rule to enjoying a Hawaiian vacation: relax—you are in Hawaii. Don't focus on seeing everything, but take the time to actually experience the island. If you are so busy rushing to do everything, you won't feel the magic of the island through your senses. In this chapter I have several suggestions for making the most out of your time in these enchanted isles.

Tip #1. Go in the off season. Not only will you save a bundle of money, but there will be fewer people, you'll get better service and more attention, the beaches will be less crowded, and you'll be able to get into your favorite restaurants. I've always had to laugh that it is called the "off season" because it's the best time to come to Hawaii. Most people either want to come when it is cold in the U.S. Mainland (Dec–Mar) or during summer vacation (June–Sept). The so-called "off season," September to mid-December and April to June, is when the weather is at its best (not too hot, not too rainy).

Tip #2. To get the best deals, do some research. In this book, I'll give you my favorite picks of hotels, restaurants, activities, and airlines, but use that as a starting point. Get online and check out airfares, hotels, and package deals (airfare plus accommodations and sometimes car rental; for more on finding a good package deal, see the Savvy Traveler appendix). Find out what prices everyone is offering before you book.

Fly Direct

If possible, fly nonstop and direct to the island of your choice (see p 587 for a list of airlines with direct flights from the U.S. Mainland to various islands). Not only is it easier, but it will save you time. Not flying direct means getting off one plane and transferring to another—and perhaps going through the fun-filled security procedures (and taking off your shoes) again, checking in, and waiting (sometimes up to 2 hr.) for your flight.

Tip #3. Think about how you want to spend your vacation. Is this a lie-on-the-beach vacation or a get-up-early-and-do-an-adventure-every-day vacation? Or a combination? My favorite part of a trip is planning the trip (months in advance). I love looking at all the options available for things to do and places to stay. I read everything I can on everything from restaurants to best shopping opportunities. If you are traveling with your sweetie, be sure you have a plan that makes both parties happy (perhaps plenty of golfing plus lots of shopping). If you are bringing your family, make sure that everyone gets in on the planning—it makes for a vacation that everyone can enjoy.

Tip #4. Remember you are on vacation. Don't jam-pack your days from the time you get up until you drop off to sleep at night. This is Hawaii, so stop and smell the plumerias. Allow time to just relax. And don't forget that you most likely will arrive jet-lagged, so ease into your vacation, and allow time on your first day to just lounge around the beach or the hotel swimming pool—exposure to sunlight can help reset your internal clock.

Tip #5. Allow plenty of time to get around the island. If you look at the map, the islands look small, like you could just zip from one side of an island to the other. Not true—it can take half a day to get from one side of some of the islands to the other. Don't forget to allow for rush-hour traffic from 6 to 9am and 3 to 6pm (even in paradise, people have to work). Plan accordingly, sleep in late, and get on the road after the traffic has cleared out. Hawaii's roads are not as user-friendly as those on the mainland; 50 miles of road does not necessarily mean an hour of driving. In the case of the Hana Highway, it can mean several hours.

Tip #6. Rent a car. Only the island of Oahu (where Honolulu and Waikiki are located) has a public bus service, TheBus. However, TheBus will not allow you to bring luggage aboard (everything must fit under your seat), and the bus schedule will slow you way down, eating into your precious vacation time. So rent a car, but plan to get out of it as much as possible. Don't just "view" the island from the car window, get out and breathe in the tropical aroma, fill up on those views, and listen to the sounds of the tropics.

Tip #7. If your visit is short, stay in one place. Don't waste your precious vacation checking in and out of several hotels. Pick a resort area that appeals to you, or if you will be zipping all over the island, choose a central location. Staying in one place not only saves time but may also save you money; many hotels and resorts offer lower prices for extended stays.

Tip #8. Pick the key activity of the day and plan accordingly. To maximize your time, decide what you really want to do that day, then plan all other activities in the same geographical area. For example, if you really want to go golfing at one end of the island, pick a beach in the same area for the afternoon or other activities in the area and plan dinner nearby. That way you won't have to track back and forth across the island.

Tip #9. Remember you are on the island of aloha. Honolulu is not the U.S. Mainland. The islander's way of life is very different. Slow down (what are you in such a rush for?—you're on vacation). Smile and say, "Aloha." It's what the local residents do. Ask them, "Howzit?" (the local expression for how are you). When they ask, you say, "Couldn't be better—I'm in Hawaii!" Wave at everyone, you'll feel better, they'll feel better. Laugh a lot, even if things aren't going as planned—hey, you're in paradise, how bad can it be?

> *PAGE 20 Ancient volcanic explosions gave birth to the world's highest sea cliffs on rugged Molokai's undeveloped North Shore. THIS PAGE Take advantage of the glassy oceans around Oahu in spring and summer and explore the shore by kayak.*

Tip #10. Use this book as a reference, not a concrete plan. You will not hurt my feelings if you don't follow every single tour and do absolutely everything I suggest in the itinerary. In fact, you will have a better time if you pick and choose the tours you want to take and the things you want to do. This book is filled with suggestions only.

One Island per Week, Please!

Visitors who have traveled to places like the Caribbean think they should pack their vacation with as many Hawaiian Islands as they can. Please, do not do this. With the exception of the islands that make up Maui County (Maui, Molokai, and Lanai), the islands are not located close to each other. Jumping from one island to another will eat up a day of your valuable time as you pack up, check out of your hotel, drive to the airport, return your car, check in for your flight, wait in the security line, wait for your plane, fly to another island, then do the whole thing in reverse—get a rental car, drive to your accommodation, check in, etc. A good rule of thumb is one island per week. Not sure which island is for you? Check out the suggested itineraries in chapter 3 to help you decide.

3 The Best All-Hawaii Itineraries

The Best of Oahu in 1 Week

If possible, stay on Oahu for at least a week, so you can take in the sights at a slow, leisurely, island-style pace. You'll have time to see all the major sights, plus explore the enchanting underwater world at Hanauma Bay and Sea Life Park, delve into Hawaiian history and culture, visit the art world, do some shopping, and spend some time lazing at the beach.

> PREVIOUS PAGE *South Shore waves aren't so nasty, but Diamond Head's perfect sets make Waikiki Beach a jewel of the surfing world.* THIS PAGE *The protected beach of Hanauma Bay offers unparalleled snorkeling and scuba diving with spectacular marine life and coral.*

START Waikiki. **FINISH** Ala Moana Shopping Center. **TRIP LENGTH** 1 week and 218 miles.

Day 1

1 ★★★ kids **Waikiki Beach.** You will never forget your first steps onto the powdery sands of this world-famous beach. If you are just off the plane, plan to spread your towel on the beach, relax, take in the smell of the salt air and feel the warmth on your skin. Be careful with your first day in the sun—put on plenty of sunscreen and don't spend more than an hour on the beach. For details on this magical beach and the options for ocean activities here, see p 143.

Walk down Waikiki Beach toward Diamond Head. If you are unable to walk to the Aquarium, you can catch TheBus 20 anywhere on Kalakaua Ave. and get off at the Aquarium.

2 ★★ kids **Waikiki Aquarium.** Half of Hawaii is its underwater world, and this is the best place to explore it without getting wet. This small, but fabulous, aquarium houses some 3,000 animals representing more than 500 species—everything from translucent jellyfish to lumbering turtles to endangered Hawaiian monk seals, and even sharks. My favorite things to see are the chambered nautilus (nature's submarine and inspiration for Jules Verne's *20,000 Leagues Under the Sea)*, the Edge of the Reef exhibit (a 7,500-gallon outdoor exhibit where you see reef fish up close and personal), and the Mahimahi Hatchery (where these delicious eating fish are raised from egg to adult). ⏲ 2½ hr.; arrive early on weekends before the crowds come. 2777 Kalakaua Ave. (in Kapiolani Park). ☎ 808/923-9741. www.waquarium.org. Admission: $9 adults,

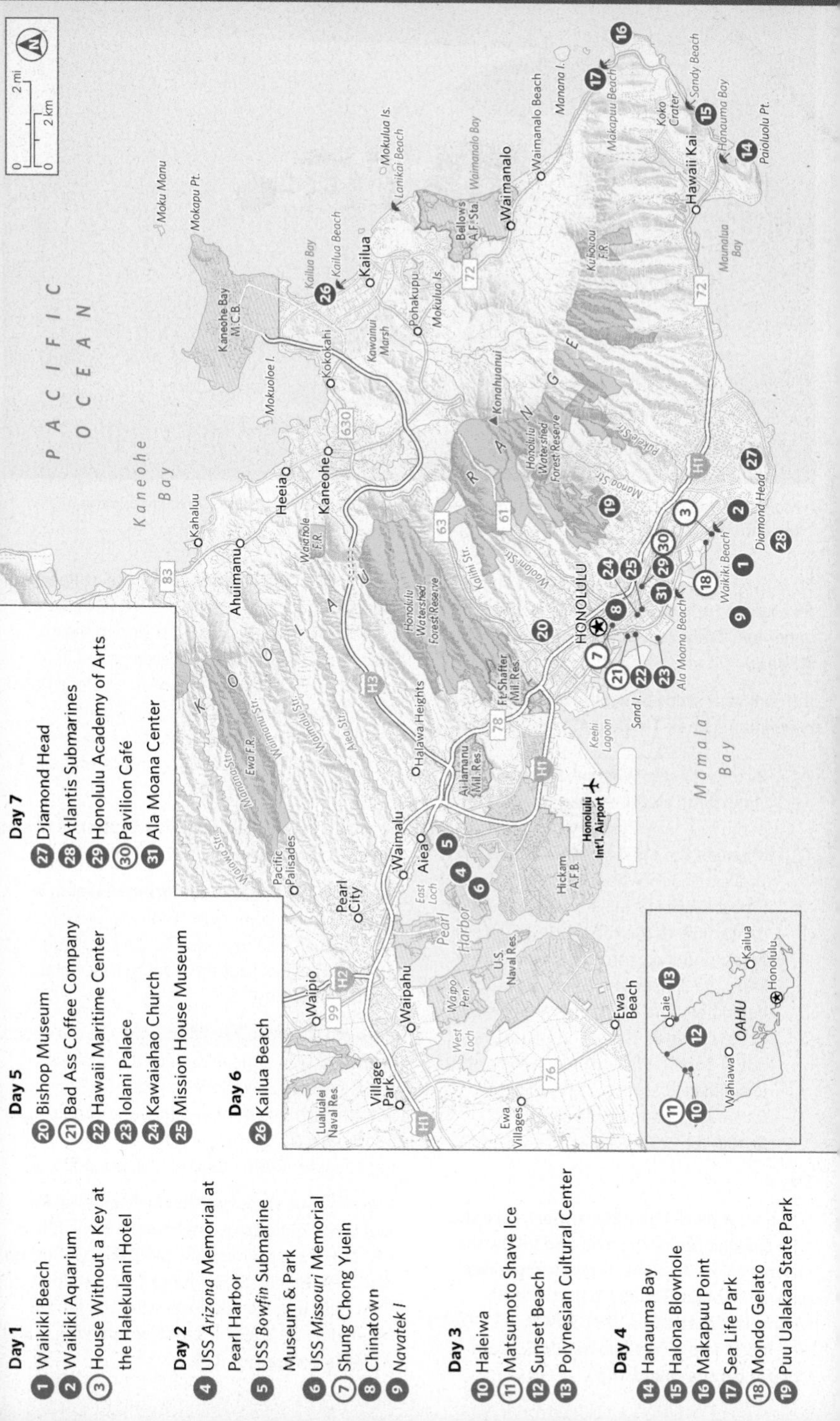
Day 1
1 Waikiki Beach
2 Waikiki Aquarium
3 House Without a Key at the Halekulani Hotel
Day 2
4 USS Arizona Memorial at Pearl Harbor
5 USS Bowfin Submarine Museum & Park
6 USS Missouri Memorial
7 Shung Chong Yuein
8 Chinatown
9 Navatek I
Day 3
10 Haleiwa
11 Matsumoto Shave Ice
12 Sunset Beach
13 Polynesian Cultural Center
Day 4
14 Hanauma Bay
15 Halona Blowhole
16 Makapuu Point
17 Sea Life Park
18 Mondo Gelato
19 Puu Ualakaa State Park
Day 5
20 Bishop Museum
21 Bad Ass Coffee Company
22 Hawaii Maritime Center
23 Iolani Palace
24 Kawaiahao Church
25 Mission House Museum
Day 6
26 Kailua Beach
Day 7
27 Diamond Head
28 Atlantis Submarines
29 Honolulu Academy of Arts
30 Pavilion Café
31 Ala Moana Center
PACIFIC OCEAN
Kaneohe Bay
Mamala Bay
HONOLULU
Kailua
Kaneohe
Waimanalo
Hawaii Kai
Pearl Harbor
Honolulu Int'l. Airport
Diamond Head
Waikiki Beach
Ala Moana Beach
Kailua Beach
Lanikai Beach
Makapuu Beach
Sandy Beach
Hanauma Bay
Waimanalo Beach
OAHU
Laie
Wahiawa
0 2 mi
0 2 km

> *More than 500 species of aquatic creatures, from sharks to sea turtles, keep your eyes underwater at the Waikiki Aquarium.*

$6 active military, seniors, and college students, $4 children 13-17, $2 children 5-12, children 4 and under free. Daily 9am-5pm (last ticket sold at 4:30pm).

Retrace your steps down Waikiki Beach to Halekulani Hotel. TheBus: 42.

③ ★★★ **House Without a Key at the Halekulani Hotel.** As the sun gets lower in the sky, take a break with a libation at one of the most beautiful hotels on Waikiki Beach, where you can watch the former Miss Hawaii, Kanoelehua Miller, dance hula to the riffs of Hawaiian steel guitar under a century-old kiawe tree. With the sunset and ocean glowing behind her and Diamond Head visible in the distance, the scene is straight out of Somerset Maugham—romantic, evocative, nostalgic. 2199 Kalia Rd. (Diamond Head side of Lewers St.). ☎ 808/923-2311. $$$.

Day 2

Drive west on H-1 past the airport; take the USS *Arizona* Memorial exit, and follow the green-and-white signs; there's ample free parking. Or take TheBus 20; or *Arizona* Memorial Shuttle Bus VIP (☎808/839-0911), which picks up at Waikiki hotels 6:50am-1pm ($9 per person round-trip).

❹ ★★★ kids **USS *Arizona* Memorial at Pearl Harbor.** Unfortunately, no trip to Honolulu would be complete without a visit to the Memorial, where 1,177 U.S. sailors died in a bombing attack by the Japanese on December 7, 1941. Get there early, preferably by the 7:30am opening—otherwise face long lines (waits up to 2 hr.). Plan on spending at least 3 hours here. See p 119, ❶.

If you are a real history buff, an option is to see the next two museums, right next door.

❺ ★ kids **USS *Bowfin* Submarine Museum & Park.** This is a great opportunity to see what life is like on a submarine. Plus the museum has an impressive collection of submarine-related artifacts. See p 119, ❷.

❻ ★ kids **USS *Missouri* Memorial.** On the deck of this 58,000-ton battleship (the last one the Navy built), World War II came to an end with the signing of the Japanese surrender on September 2, 1945. Definitely take the tour to get a feel for this historic vessel. See p 120, ❸.

Retrace your steps on Arizona Memorial Rd., and turn right onto Kamehameha Hwy. (Hwy. 99) to H-1 east (Honolulu/Waikiki). Get off on exit 21-A, Bishop St. Turn right on Bishop St., then right again on Beretania St. and left on Maunakea St. Look for on-street parking in the 2 blocks before Hotel St.

> *Step on the deck where the Japanese surrendered and World War II ended at Pearl Harbor's USS* Missouri *Memorial.*

⑦ ★ kids **Shung Chong Yuein.** Before you start your tour of Chinatown, take a break at this shop for delicious Asian pastries, such as moon cakes and almond cookies, all at very reasonable prices. The shop also has a wide selection of dried and sugared candies (ginger, pineapple, lotus root) that make great gifts for friends back home. 1027 Maunakea St. (near Hotel St.). ☎ 808/531-1983. $.

8 ★★ kids **Chinatown.** Plan to spend the rest of the day in this exotic part of Honolulu. Colorful open markets, Buddhist temples, a waterside walkway, and plenty of tempting restaurants will keep you occupied for hours. See p 122.

Continue down Maunakea St., turn left on N. King St., then right on Nuuanu Ave. Make a slight left on Nimitz Hwy. (Hwy. 92). Look for the sign for Pier 6 just after Aloha Tower, and turn right. TheBus: 56.

9 ★ kids ***Navatek 1.*** Say aloha to the sun from the ocean on this sunset dinner cruise. See p 96, 9.

Day 3

Take H-1 west out of Waikiki to the H-2 north exit (exit 8A) toward Mililani/Wahiwa. After 7 miles, H-2 becomes Kamehameha Hwy. (Hwy. 80). Look for the turnoff to Haleiwa town. TheBus: 19, transfer to 52.

10 ★★★ kids **Haleiwa.** Start your day in this funky former plantation town. See p 128, 4.

⑪ ★ kids **Matsumoto Shave Ice.** Cool off with a sweet treat from Matsumoto's. See p 97, ⑪.

Continue down Kamehameha Hwy. for about 6½ miles. TheBus: 52.

12 ★★★ kids **Sunset Beach.** During the summer months, this is a safe beach for swimming. During the winter, it's best to just sit and watch the big-wave surfers. See p 143.

Drive another 12 miles down Kamehameha Hwy. to the town of Laie. TheBus: 52, which is renamed 55 at Turtle Bay Resort.

13 ★★ kids **Polynesian Cultural Center.** Finish up the day at this living museum of Polynesia. Stay for a show, but skip the luau. See p 97, 13.

Day 4

From Waikiki, take H-1 east, which becomes the Kalanianaole Hwy. Look for the Koko Head Regional Park on the left; the beach is on the right (ocean side). Avoid the crowds by going early, about 8am, on a weekday morning; once the parking lot's full, you're out of luck. The Hanauma Bay Shuttle Bus runs from Waikiki to Hanauma Bay every ½ hour from 8:45am to 1pm. You can catch it at any city bus stop in Waikiki. It returns every hour from noon to 4pm.

> *Take a stroll through Honolulu's Chinatown, packed with authentic atmosphere and offerings, and forget you're in the United States.*

14 ★★★ kids **Hanauma Bay.** Spend the morning at Oahu's best snorkeling beach. ***Note:*** The beach is closed on Tuesdays to give the fish a day off. See p 140.

Continue to drive east on Kalanianaole Hwy. Stop at mile marker (MM) 11.

15 kids **Halona Blowhole.** Stop here to see one of Mother Nature's unique creations: The surf funnels through a hole in the rocks, creating an explosion of water and a distinct moaning sound. Look out to sea from Halona over Sandy Beach and across the 26-mile gulf to neighboring Molokai and the faint triangular shadow of Lanai on the far horizon. Be sure to obey all the signs to stay away from the blowhole. ⏱ 15 min. Kalanianaole Hwy. (Hwy. 72) at around MM 11.

Continue to drive east on Kalanianaole Hwy. Look for the Makapuu Point sign and park in the lot.

16 kids **Makapuu Point.** From the parking lot, follow the trail to the top of this 647-foot-high cliff not only to see the lighthouse (which once signaled safe passage for steamship passengers arriving from San Francisco but now brightens Oahu's south coast for passing tankers, fishing boats, and sailors) but also for the heart-stopping panoramic vista. ⏱ 20–30 min.

Continue east on Kalanianaole Hwy. TheBus: 58.

17 ★ kids **Sea Life Park.** This 62-acre ocean theme park is one of the island's top attractions, with marine animal shows, exhibits, and displays. Don't miss the Hawaiian reef tank full of tropical fish; a "touch" pool, where you can touch a real sea cucumber; and a bird sanctuary, where you can see birds like the red-footed booby and the frigate bird. See p 101, 18.

Continue on Kalanianaole Hwy. (Hwy. 72), turn left on Pali Hwy. (Hwy. 61), then take H-1 east to Waikiki. TheBus: 58.

---

18 kids **Mondo Gelato.** Take a break and cool off with a real Italian-style gelato (Italian ice cream) and other gelato products like sorbetto or yogurt gelato.

Out of the more than 100 flavors, my favorite is the papaya sorbetto. Waikiki Beach Walk, 226 Lewers St. (at Kalia St.). ☎ 808/926-6961. $.

From Waikiki, take Ala Wai Blvd. to McCully St., turn right, and drive mauka (inland) beyond the H-1 on-ramps to Wilder St. Turn left and go to Makiki St. Turn right and continue onward and upward about 3 miles.

(19) ★ **Puu Ualakaa State Park.** My favorite sunset view of Honolulu is from a 1,048-foot-high hill named for sweet potatoes. Actually, the poetic Hawaiian name means "rolling sweet potato hill"—early planters used gravity to harvest their crops. The panorama is sweeping and majestic. On a clear day, which is almost every day, you can see from Diamond Head to the Waianae Range, almost the length of Oahu. At night, several scenic overlooks provide romantic spots for young lovers who like to smooch under the stars with the city lights at their feet. It's a top-of-the-world experience—the view, that is. ⏱ 15–20 min. At the end of Round Top Dr. Daily 7am–6:45pm (to 7:45pm in summer). No bus service.

Day 5

Take Ala Wai Blvd. out of Waikiki. Turn right at Kalakaua Ave., then left on S. Beretania St. and right at Piikoi St. Make a left on Lunalilo St., and bear left onto H-1 west. Take exit 20B, which puts you on Halona St. Turn right at Houghtailing St. and then left onto Bernice St. TheBus: 2.

(20) ★★★ kids **Bishop Museum.** If you are the least bit curious about what ancient Hawaii was like, this is a must stop. Not only does this multibuilding museum have the world's greatest collection of natural and cultural artifacts from Hawaii and the Pacific, but recently it has added a terrific new 16,500-square-foot Science Adventure Center, specializing in volcanology (walk inside an erupting volcano) and oceanography (interactive exhibits on the ocean). In the Hawaiian Hall, you can venture back in history and see what Hawaii and the culture was like before Westerners arrived. Don't miss my faves: the weekday ★**hula performances,** at 11am and 2pm, and the terrific show in the planetarium, **Explorers of Polynesia,** at 3:30pm daily. ⏱ 3–4 hr.; 1525 Bernice St., just off Kalihi St. (aka Likelike Hwy.). ☎ 808/847-3511. www.bishopmuseum.org. Admission $16 adults, $13 children 4–12 and seniors. Wed–Mon 9am–5pm.

> *Sunsets on Haleiwa's North Shore serve up Hawaii's official credentials as a Pacific Paradise.*

Turn right out of the parking lot onto Bernice St., left at Kapalama Ave., and right again on N. School St. Make a right on Liliha St., a left on N. King St., and a right on River St. Turn left on Nimitz Hwy. and then right at Aloha Tower Dr. Bus: City Express A.

(21) **Bad Ass Coffee Company.** Take a break at this gourmet Hawaiian coffee shop. I recommend a cup of delicious Kona, but they also offer java from Molokai, Kauai, and Maui. Aloha Tower Marketplace, 1 Aloha Tower Dr. ☎ 808/524-0888. $.

> *Live Hawaiian music is one of the draws of a* Navatek *dinner cruise.*

Walk toward Diamond Head along the waterfront.

22 ★★ kids **Hawaii Maritime Center.** As we went to press, the Bishop Museum, owner of the Hawaii Maritime Center, "temporarily" closed operations here "due to adverse economic conditions." Please call Bishop Museum (☎ 808/846-3511) to see if the Hawaii Maritime Center has reopened by the time you visit. If it has, it is well worth a couple of hours of your time to learn the story of Hawaii's rich maritime past. See p 102, 21.

Walk mauka (inland) up Bishop St., right on S. King St., and left on Richards St.

23 ★ kids **Iolani Palace.** Hawaii is the only state in the U.S. to have a royal palace. Once the site of a *heiau* (temple), Iolani Palace took 3 years and $350,000 to complete in 1882, with all the modern conveniences for its time (electric lights were installed here 4 years before they were in the White House). It was also in this palace that Queen Liliuokalani was overthrown and placed under house arrest for 9 months. The territorial and then the state governments used the palace until 1968. At that point, the palace was in shambles; it has since undergone a $7-million overhaul to restore it to its former glory. Admission options include the Grand Tour, a 90-minute docent-led tour that covers the state apartments, private quarters, and basement galleries; the 50-minute Audio Tour, which covers the same areas as the Grand Tour but is self-guided; or the Galleries Tour, a self-guided tour of the basement galleries only, where you'll see the crown jewels, ancient feathered cloaks, royal china, and more.
⏱ 1–2hr. At S. King and Richards sts. ☎ 808/522-0832. Grand Tour $20 adults, $5 children 5–12; Audio Tour $12 adults, $5 children; Gallery Tour $6 adults, $3 children. Children under 5 free, but only allowed in the basement galleries. Tues–Sat 9am–4:30pm (last Grand Tour at 11:15am; last Audio Tour at 3pm).

Continue to walk toward Diamond Head on S. King St. to Punchbowl St.

24 ★ **Kawaiahao Church.** When the missionaries came to Hawaii, the first thing they did was build churches. Four thatched-grass churches had been built on this site before the Rev. Hiram Bingham began building what he considered a "real" church—a New England-style congregational structure with Gothic influences. Between 1837 and 1842, the building of the church required some 14,000 giant coral slabs (some weighing more than 1,000 lb.). Hawaiian divers raped the reefs, digging out huge chunks of coral and causing irreparable environmental damage. Kawaiahao, Hawaii's oldest church, has been the site of numerous historical events, such as a speech made by King Kamehameha III in 1843, an excerpt from which became Hawaii's state motto (*Ua mau ke ea o ka aina i ka pono,* which translates as "The life of the land is preserved in righteousness"). The clock tower in the church, which was donated by King Kamehameha III and installed in 1850, continues to tick today. Don't sit in the pews in the back, marked with kahili feathers and velvet cushions; they are still reserved for the descendants of royalty. 957 Punchbowl St. (at King St.). ☎ 808/522-1333. Free admission (donations appreciated). Mon–Fri 8am–4pm; Sun services in Hawaiian 9am.

Continue in the Diamond Head direction on S. King St.

25 **Mission Houses Museum.** The original buildings of the Sandwich Islands Mission Headquarters still stand, and tours are often led by descendants of the original missionaries to Hawaii. The missionaries brought their own prefab houses along with them when they came around Cape Horn from Boston in 1819. The Frame House was designed for New England winters and had small windows. (It must have been stiflingly hot inside.) Finished in 1921, it is Hawaii's oldest wooden structure. The missionaries believed that the best way to spread the Lord's message to the Hawaiians was to learn their language, and then to print literature for them to read. So it was the missionaries who gave the Hawaiians a written language. ⌚ 1 hr. 553 S. King St. (at Kawaiahao St.). ☎ 808/531-0481. www.missionhouses.org. $10 adults, $6 students (age 6–college). Tues–Sat 10am–4pm.

> ABOVE *The original prefab Mission House brought from New England by Western evangelists in 1819 still stands as a museum.* BELOW *Oahu's surf and sand lure play-loving pilgrims from every corner of the planet.*

> *Diamond Head's towering volcano offers breathtaking sights of the surf pounding the beach 760 feet below.*

> *Oahu's windward Kailua Beach is the island's unofficial watersports capital, with quality kayaking and windsurfing.*

To get back to Waikiki, pick up your car at Aloha Tower Marketplace, and turn right on Nimitz Hwy., which becomes Ala Moana Blvd. and leads into Waikiki. TheBus: 13.

Day 6

Take H-1 west to exit 21B (Pali Hwy. north). Pali Hwy. (Hwy. 61) becomes the Kalanianaole Hwy., which becomes Kailua Rd. Veer to the right onto Kuulei Rd. Then turn right on Kalahelo Ave., which becomes Kawailoa Rd., and follow it to the beach. TheBus: 8 or 19, transfer to 57.

26 ★★★ kids **Kailua Beach.** Spend the entire day at one of Oahu's most fabulous beaches on the windward side of the island. You can just veg out in the sand or try your hand at kayaking to the tiny isles offshore. See p 140.

Day 7

Drive to the intersection of Diamond Head Rd. and 18th Ave. Follow the road through the tunnel (which is closed 6pm–6am), and park in the lot. TheBus: 58 (from the Ala Moana Shopping Center).

27 ★ kids **Diamond Head.** On your last day, get a bird's-eye view of the island from atop this 760-foot extinct volcano. See p 144.

> *Atlantis Submarines takes you on an otherworldly high-tech trip under the crystal clear surf off Oahu.*

Retrace your steps back to Waikiki.

㉘ ★★★ kids **Atlantis Submarines.** You've seen Oahu from the top. Now plunge beneath the waves and see it from underwater in this high-tech submarine. See p 160.

Follow Ala Moana Blvd. in the ewa (west) direction, make a right on Ward Ave., and another right on Kinau St. to the parking lot. TheBus: 2.

㉙ ★★ kids **Honolulu Academy of Arts.** After feasting on the beauty of the island in the morning, now feed your soul with the incredible art and cultural collection of one of Hawaii's most prestigious galleries. The state's only general fine-arts museum features one of the top Asian art collections in the country. Also on exhibit are American and European masters and prehistoric works of Mayan, Greek, and Hawaiian art. The museum's award-winning architecture is a paragon of graciousness, featuring magnificent courtyards, lily ponds, and sensitively designed galleries. ⏱ 2–3 hr. 900 S. Beretania St. (at Ward Ave.). ☎ 808/532-8700, or 808/532-8701 for recording. www.honoluluacademy.org. $10 adults; $5 students, seniors, and military personnel; children under 12 free. Tues–Sat 10am–4:30pm, Sun 1–5pm; tours Tues–Sat 10:15am, 11am, and 1:15pm and Sun 1:15pm.

Undiscovered Oahu

For a trip that is "off the beaten path," take 3 days and visit the parts of the island that not many visitors stop to see: Chinatown and South and Windward Oahu. Spend day 1 following the "A Stroll Through Chinatown" tour starting on p 122. On days 2 and 3 follow the "Southern Oahu & the Windward Coast" tour starting on p 132.

㉚ ★★ **Pavilion Café.** Take a break at this intimate cafe, which is shaded by a 70-year-old monkeypod tree and faces a landscaped garden with a rushing waterfall and sculptures by Jun Kaneko. Sip a glass of merlot or enjoy a chocolate-walnut tart with a cup of green tea. Honolulu Academy of Art, 900 Beretania St. ☎ 808/532-8734. $$.

Turn left, toward the ocean, on Ward Ave., and another left on Ala Moana Blvd. TheBus: 3.

㉛ ★★ **Ala Moana Center.** Spend your last few hours on the island wandering through Hawaii's largest shopping center looking for souvenirs and gifts for your friends and relatives back home. See p 173.

The Best of Oahu in 2 Weeks

Two weeks on Oahu is perfect—enough time to see all the sites and experience the true flavor of Hawaii, with plenty of time to relax and really enjoy your vacation. For the first week, follow the suggestions in the "Best of Oahu in 1 Week" tour starting on p 26. Below starts the second week of your holiday, when you can explore a tropical rainforest, see more incredible beaches, sail on the windward side, have a day of retail therapy, discover Hawaii's nightlife, and even take in a luau.

START & FINISH Waikiki. **TRIP LENGTH** 2 weeks and 467 miles.

Day 8

Walk in the Diamond Head direction down Kalakaua Ave. TheBus: 20.

SITE GUIDE PAGE 39

32 ★★ kids **Kapiolani Park.** Spend a lazy day just a coconut's throw from the high-rise concrete jungle of Waikiki in this 133-acre grassy park donated to the people by King David Kalakaua in 1877. He asked that the park be named after his beloved wife, Queen Kapiolani, and he celebrated the opening of this vast grassy area with a free concert and "high stakes" horse races (the king loved gambling) on the new horse-racing oval he had built below Diamond Head. These days, people come to the park to listen to music, watch ethnic dancing, exercise, enjoy team sports, take long meditative walks, picnic, buy art, smell the roses, and just relax. Spreading banyans, huge monkeypod trees, blooming royal poincianas, and swaying ironwoods dot the grassy park. Throughout the open spaces are jogging paths, tennis courts, soccer and cricket fields, and even an archery range. Allow at least an hour each for walking around the park, wandering around the zoo,

> *The 130-year-old Kapiolani Park is a sports and picnic paradise on a lush 133 acres.*

Day 8
- 32 Kapiolani Park
- 33 Kumu Kahua Theatre

Day 9
- 34 North Shore Beaches
- 35 Society of Seven

Day 10
- 36 Manoa Falls hike
- 37 Andy's Sandwiches & Smoothies
- 38 Ihilani Spa
- 39 Paradise Cove Luau

Day 11
- 40 Captain Bob's Adventure Cruises
- 41 The Magic of Polynesia

Day 12
- 42 Contemporary Museum
- 43 Contemporary Museum Café
- 44 Hawaii State Art Museum
- 45 Foster Botanical Garden
- 46 Honolulu Symphony Orchestra/Hawaii Opera Theatre

Day 13
- 47 Shopping the Aloha Flea Market
- 48 Waikele Premium Outlets
- 49 Royal Hawaiian Shopping Center

Day 14
- 50 Island Seaplane Service
- 51 Aloha Tower Observation Deck
- 52 Don Ho's Island Grill

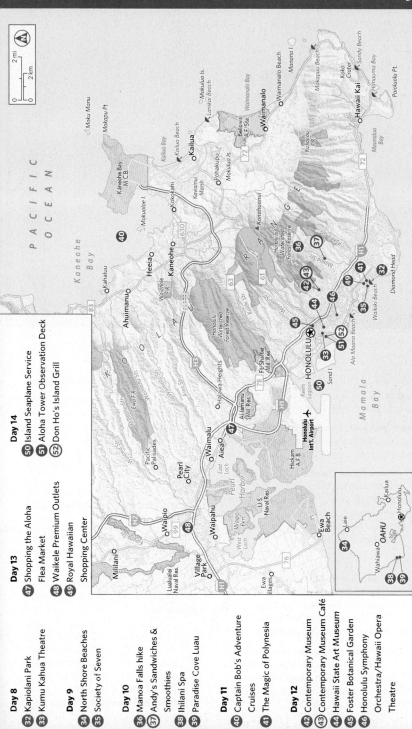

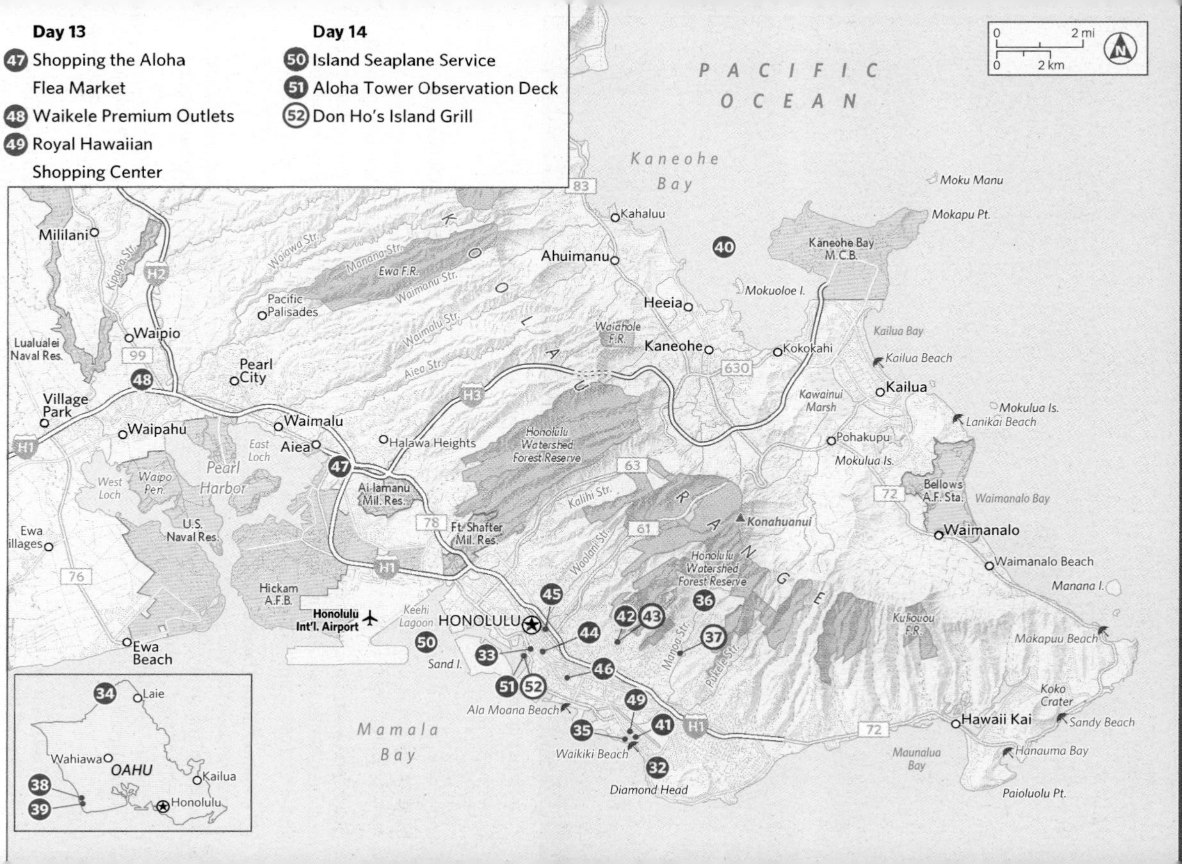

> *Sunbathers on beautiful Banzai Beach can watch the surfers take on notorious Pipeline curls.*

and exploring the aquarium, plus all the time you want for the beach. Come on a Wednesday if you want to visit the People's Open Market.

Head ewa (west) on Ala Moana Blvd., which becomes Nimitz Hwy. Turn right on Bethel St. and left on Merchant St. Bus: City Express B.

33 ★ **Kumu Kahua Theatre.** For an intimate glimpse of island life, this tiny (100 seats) theater produces plays, often written by residents, that deal with today's cultural experience in Hawaii. 2-3 hr. 46 Merchant St. ☎ 808/536-4441. www.kumukahua.org. Tickets $13.

Day 9

Take H-1 west out of Waikiki, then take the H-2 north exit (exit 8A) toward Mililani/Wahiawa. After 7 miles H-2 becomes Kamehameha Hwy. (Hwy. 80). Look for the turnoff to Haleiwa town. TheBus: 19, then transfer to 52.

34 ★★★ kids **North Shore Beaches.** Spend the day beaching. Start with breakfast in Haleiwa and stops at North Shore's best beaches: Waimea, Pupukea, Sunset, and Banzai. See "Oahu Beaches A to Z" on p 138.

Retrace your route back to Waikiki.

35 ★ **Society of Seven.** This nightclub act, which is a blend of skits, Broadway hits, popular music, and costumed musical acts, is so popular it has been playing for more than 30 years in a town where most shows barely make it 1. See p 201.

Day 10

Take Manoa Rd. past Lyon Arboretum and park in the residential area below Paradise Park. TheBus: 5.

36 ★ kids **Manoa Falls Hike.** Just 15 minutes from Waikiki you can be in a tropical rainforest. See p 147.

Retrace your route back down Manoa Rd., turn left on Oahu Ave., then left again on E. Manoa Rd.

---

37 ★ kids **Andy's Sandwiches & Smoothies.** This neighborhood fixture is a terrific place to stop for a smoothie and a healthy snack after your hike (try the mango muffins). 2904 E. Manoa Rd., opposite Manoa Marketplace. ☎ 808/988-6161. $.

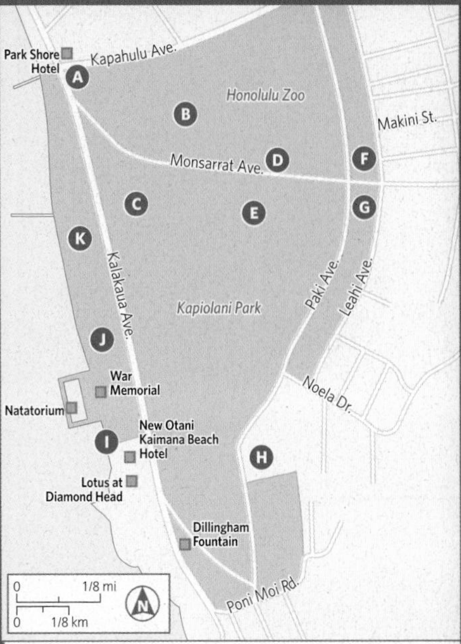

32 Kapiolani Park

Start at the intersection of Kalakaua and Kapahulu avenues, at the A **Kapiolani Park Kiosk.** Pick up information on upcoming events at the various sites within the park, as well as a park map. The best time to see the 42-acre B **Honolulu Zoo** (p 98, 1) is as soon as the gates open—the animals are more active then. If you're lucky, you may be able to catch a show at the C **Kapiolani Park Bandstand.** Stop by D **Art Mart** (The Artists of Oahu Exhibit) to chat up some local artisans and check out their work. Prices here are considerably lower than the prices you'll see in galleries. The open-air E **Waikiki Shell** hosts numerous musical shows, from the Honolulu Symphony to traditional Hawaiian music. At the F **Queen Kapiolani Garden** you'll see a range of hibiscus plants and dozens of varieties of roses, including the somewhat rare Hawaiian rose. If it's Wednesday morning (10–11am), swing through the G **People's Open Market** (pictured above) to buy fresh produce and flowers. Tennis fans can hit some balls for free at the H **Diamond Head Tennis Courts** (limit your play to 45 min. if someone's waiting for a court). Open for play during daylight hours 7 days a week. I **Sans Souci Beach** (next to the New Otani Kaimana Beach Hotel) is one of the best swimming beaches in Waikiki. Facilities include outdoor showers and a lifeguard. Try to save time for the J **Waikiki Aquarium** (p 26, 2), home to the only living chambered nautilus born in captivity. Finish up the day relaxing on the stretch of grassy lawn alongside K **Kapiolani Beach Park,** one of the best-kept secrets of Waikiki. It's much, much less crowded than Waikiki Beach, plus it has adjacent grassy lawns, barbecue areas, picnic tables, restrooms, and showers. The swimming is good here year-round. The middle section of the beach park, in front of the pavilion, is known as Queen's Beach or Queen's Surf and is popular with the gay community.

> *Hike to Oahu's majestic Manoa Falls, which spills 150 feet from a rocky cliff into a glistening tropical pool.*

From E. Manoa Rd., drive toward the ocean and get on H-1 west. Stay on H-1 until it ends and becomes Farrington Hwy. Take the Ko Olina exit, and turn left on Aliinui Dr., then turn right on Olani St. No bus service.

38 ★★★ **Ihilani Spa.** Spend the rest of the day being pampered at an oasis by the sea. This free-standing, 35,000-square-foot luxury facility is dedicated to the traditional spa definition of "health by water." The modern, multistoried spa, filled with floor-to-ceiling glass looking out on green tropical plants, combines Hawaiian products with traditional therapies to produce some of the best water treatments in the state. You'll also find a fitness center, tennis courts, and a bevy of aerobic and stretching classes. ⏲ 1-2 hr. JW Marriott Ihilani Resort, 92-1001 Olani St., Kapolei. ☎ 808/679-0079. www.ihilani.com.

Retrace your route to Aliinui Dr.

39 **Paradise Cove Luau.** While you are out in Ko Olina, experience a luau. Don't expect an intimate affair, as Paradise Cove generally has some 600 to 800 guests a night. In fact, you're getting more than just a luau—the small thatched village feels more like a Hawaiian theme park, with Hawaiian games, craft demonstrations, and a beautiful shoreline looking out over what is usually a storybook sunset. Tahitian dance and ancient and modern hula make this a fun-filled evening for those spirited enough to join in. The food is not breathtaking, and features both luau cuisine (Hawaiian kalua pork, lomi salmon, poi, and coconut pudding and cake) and American fare (salads, rice, pineapple, chicken, etc.). ⏲ 3½ hr. 92-1089 Aliinui Dr., Ko Olina. ☎ 808/842-5911. www.paradisecovehawaii.com. Packages $80–$137 for adults. Nightly 5–9pm.

Retrace your route back to H-1, then take H-1 into Waikiki.

Day 11

Take Captain Bob's shuttle from Waikiki (it's included in the price of the following cruise).

40 ★ kids **Captain Bob's Adventure Cruises.** Spend the day on the water seeing the majestic Windward Coast the way it should be seen—from a boat. Captain Bob will take you on a 4-hour, lazy-day sail of Kaneohe Bay aboard his 42-foot catamaran, which skims across the almost always calm water above the shallow coral reef, lands at the disappearing sandbar Ahu o Laka, and takes you past two small islands to snorkel spots full of tropical fish and, sometimes, turtles. See p 154.

41 ★ kids **The Magic of Polynesia.** Finish off your day at one of Waikiki's best dinner shows. See p 200.

Day 12

Take McCully St. out of Waikiki, then turn left on Dole St. and right on Punahou St. Turn left on Nehoa St., right on Makiki St., then left on Makiki Heights Dr. TheBus: 4, then about a ¾-mile walk up Makiki Heights Dr.

42 ★ **Contemporary Museum.** Start your day of culture and the arts at this incredible, elegant former home that not only features cutting-edge art but also has inspiring views of Honolulu and Waikiki. ⏱ 1½–2 hr. 2411 Makiki Heights Dr. (near Mott-Smith Dr.). ☎ 808/526-0232. www.tcmhi.org. Tickets $8 adults, $6 seniors and students, children 12 and under free (the third Thurs of each month is free). Tues–Sat 10–4pm, Sun noon–4pm.

43 ★ **Contemporary Museum Café.** After you have nourished your soul, take a break at this relaxing, intimate cafe. I recommend the crostini of the day (baguette toasts with a savory topping) or the sinfully delicious flourless chocolate cake and either a just-brewed latte or a fresh lemonade. Contemporary Museum, 2411 Makiki Heights Dr. (near Mott-Smith Dr.). ☎ 808/523-3362. www.tcmhi.org. $$.

Continue up Makiki Heights Dr. Keep straight when the road becomes Mott-Smith Dr. Turn left to stay on Mott-Smith Dr. Make a right onto Nehoa St., then make a slight right onto Prospect St. Turn left at Ward Ave. and then right onto S. Beretania St. Make a left on Richards St. and then a slight right on S. Hotel St. Park on the street.

44 ★★ **Hawaii State Art Museum.** This historic building was once the Royal Hawaiian Hotel, built in 1872 during the reign of King Kamehameha V. All of the 360 works on display were created by artists who live in Hawaii. The pieces were all purchased by the state thanks to a 1967 law that says that 1% of the cost of state buildings must be used to acquire works of art. Nearly 4 decades later, the state has amassed some 5,000 pieces. ⏱ 2–3 hr. 250 S. Hotel St. (at Richards St.). ☎ 808/586-0900. www.state.hi.us/sfca. Free admission. Tues–Sat 10am–4pm. Also the first Fri of every month 5–9pm.

> *ABOVE Up to 800 guests pack the raucous Paradise Cove Luau for torch-lit Tahitian hula dancing and a Polynesian pig roast. BELOW Foster Botanical Garden is a lush tropical oasis amid Honolulu's city streets.*

> *Hula lessons are just one of the many activities available at the massive, open-air Royal Hawaiian Shopping Center.*

Continue down Hotel St. and turn right on Alakea St. Next block turn left on Beretania St. Make a right on Nuuanu Ave. and then a left on N. Vineyard Blvd.

45 **Foster Botanical Garden.** The giant trees that tower over the main terrace of this leafy oasis were planted in the 1850s by William Hillebrand, a German physician and botanist, on royal land leased from Queen Emma. Today this 14-acre public garden, on the north side of Chinatown, is a living museum of plants, some rare and endangered, collected from the tropical regions of the world. Of special interest are 26 "Exceptional Trees" protected by state law, a large palm collection, a primitive cycad garden, and a hybrid orchid collection. ⏲ 2–3 hr. 50 N. Vineyard Blvd. (at Nuuanu Ave.). ☎ 808/522-7066. www.co.honolulu.hi.us/parks/. Admission $5 adults, $1 children 6–12. Daily 9am–4pm; guided tours Mon–Sat 1pm (reservations recommended).

Take Ala Moana Blvd. to Ward Ave., and turn right. Turn left on King St. for the entrance to the parking lot. TheBus: 2 or 13.

46 **Honolulu Symphony Orchestra/Hawaii Opera Theatre.** Complete your day of culture with either a visit to the Symphony, which performs from September to May, or the Opera, which takes the stage from January to March. See the "Symphony, Opera & Dance Performances" section starting on p 201.

Day 13

For directions to all the shopping areas below, see "Honolulu & Waikiki Shopping A to Z," starting on p 165.

47 kids **Shopping the Aloha Flea Market.** More than just bargain shopping, this giant outdoor bazaar is an adventure full of strange food, odd goods, and incredible bargains. Nobody ever leaves this place empty-handed—or without having had lots of fun. See p 169.

48 **Waikele Premium Outlets.** The second stop on your bargain hunting day is at these two discount outlets. This is retail therapy at frugal prices. Just say the word *Waikele* and my eyes glaze over. So many shops, so little time! See p 174.

49 **Royal Hawaiian Shopping Center.** You've seen the bargains. Now it's time to wander in luxury at this newly renovated, 293,000-square-foot open-air mall (17,000 sq. ft. larger than before) with 110 stores, restaurants, and entertainment on 4 levels. See p 174.

Day 14

I suggest taking Island Seaplane's complimentary van from your hotel in Waikiki. They will even drop you at the Aloha Tower on your way back.

50 ★★ kids **Island Seaplane Service.** Spend your last day seeing why Oahu was the island of kings—and the only way to do it is from a plane. You'll never forget the sound of the slap of the waves as the seaplane skims across the water and then effortlessly lifts into the air. See the box "See World War II History from the Air," p 121.

51 ★ kids **Aloha Tower Observation Deck.** When it was built in 1926, this 10-story building was the tallest in the islands. It welcomed thousands of visitors who arrived in Hawaii via boat. In the 1920s and 1930s, "Boat Day," the arrival of a passenger ship, became a festive celebration shared by the whole community. Take in the panoramic view of Honolulu and Waikiki before you bid the island aloha.

---

52 kids **Don Ho's Island Grill.** Raise a glass of good cheer to your fabulous vacation as you look out over Honolulu Harbor. Order the Molokai Seafood Martini, with *he'e* (squid) poke, lomi salmon, and seared ahi (tuna) served in a martini glass, and start planning your next trip to Hawaii. See p 198.

> ABOVE *Once the tallest structure in Hawaii, the Aloha Tower still offers one of the best views of Honolulu and Waikiki.* BELOW *Catch a performance of the Honolulu Symphony Orchestra or Hawaii Opera Theatre at the Neal Blaisdell Center.*

The Best of the Big Island in 1 Week

The Big Island of Hawaii—the island that lends its name to the entire 1,500-mile-long Hawaiian archipelago—is where Mother Nature pulled out all the stops. Simply put, it's spectacular. The Big Island has it all: fiery volcanoes and sparkling waterfalls, black-lava deserts and snowcapped mountain peaks, tropical rainforests and alpine meadows, a glacial lake and miles of golden-, black-, and even green-sand beaches. It looks like the inside of a barbecue pit on one side and a lush jungle on the other. A week is barely enough time on this huge island (it's twice the size of all the others combined), but this tour covers the highlights.

START Kealakekua Bay. **FINISH** Kailua-Kona. **TRIP LENGTH** 1 week and 446 miles.

Days 1-3

❶-⓯. See "The Best of the Big Island in 3 Days," p 208.

Day 4

From Hilo take Hwy. 19 north. Just after MM 7, turn right (toward the ocean) on Scenic Dr., and continue for just over 1 mile to:

⓰ ★★ **Hawaii Tropical Botanical Garden.** More than 1,800 species of tropical plants thrive in this little-known Eden by the sea. The 40-acre garden, nestled between the crashing surf and a thundering waterfall, has the world's largest selection of tropical plants growing in a natural environment, including torch gingers (which tower on 12-ft. stalks), a banyan canyon, an orchid garden, a banana grove, a bromeliad hill, and a golden bamboo grove, which rattles like a jungle drum in the trade winds. Some

> *The icy peaks that cap Mauna Kea's towering volcanic summit sparkle as the sun rises over the Big Island.*

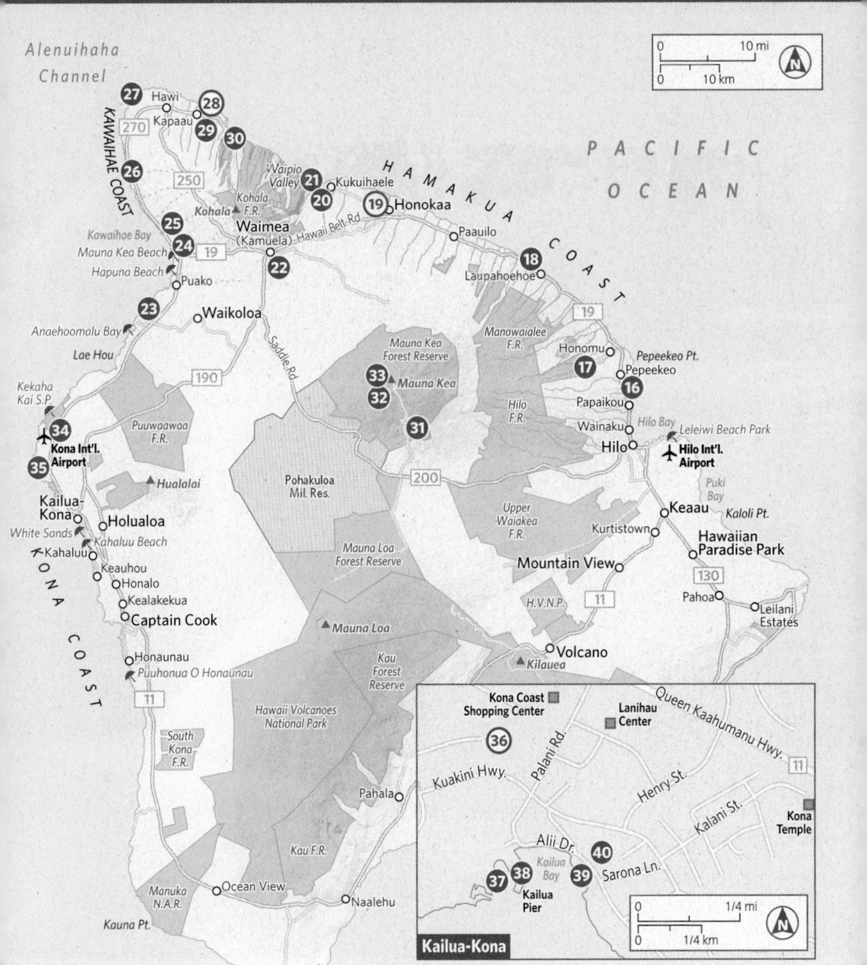

Day 4

16 Hawaii Tropical Botanical Garden
17 Akaka Falls
18 Laupahoehoe Beach Park
19 Simply Natural
20 Waipio Valley Lookout
21 Waipio Valley
22 Parker Ranch

Day 5

23 Puako Petroglyph Archaeological District
24 Puukohola Heiau National Historic Site
25 Pua Mau Place
26 Lapakahi State Historical Park
27 Mo'okini Luakini Heiau
28 Kohala Rainbow Café
29 The Original King Kamehameha Statue
30 Pololu Valley Lookout

Day 6

31 Onizuka Visitor Information Station
32 Lake Waiau
33 Mauna Kea Summit

Day 7

34 Ellison S. Onizuka Space Center
35 Natural Energy Laboratory of Hawaii Authority (NELHA)
36 Kona Brewing Co. & Brewpub
37 Kamehameha's Compound at Kamakahonu Bay
38 Kailua Pier
39 Hulihee Palace
40 Mokuaikaua Church

> *Enjoy a bit of peace, quiet, and solitude at Hawaii Tropical Botanical Garden.*

endangered Hawaiian specimens, such as the rare *Gardenia remyi,* are flourishing in this habitat. The gardens are seldom crowded; you can wander around by yourself all day. ⌚ 1–2 hr. Off Hwy. 19 on the 4-mile Scenic Dr., Onomea Bay (8 miles north of Hilo). ☎ 808/964-5233. www.htbg.com. Admission $15 adults, $5 children 6–16, free for children 5 and under. Daily 9am–5pm (last entry at 4pm).

Continue on Scenic Dr. back to Hwy. 19, and turn right. At MM 13, turn left at the sign for Honomu onto Akaka Falls Rd. A little more than 3½ miles later, the road ends at Akaka Falls State Park.

17 ★★★ kids **Akaka Falls.** See one of Hawaii's most scenic waterfalls via an easy 1-mile paved loop through a rainforest, past bamboo and ginger, and down to an observation point. You'll have a perfect view of 442-foot Akaka and nearby Kahuna Falls, which is a mere 100-footer. Keep your eyes peeled for rainbows. The noise you hear is the sound of the coqui frog, a nonnative frog from Puerto Rico that has become a pest on the Big Island. ⌚ ½–1 hr. On Hwy. 19, Honomu (8 miles north of Hilo). Turn left at Honomu and head 3½ miles inland on Akaka Falls Rd. (Hwy. 220).

> *Akaka Falls is easily accessible by a step trail that runs along its right shoulder down into the gorge.*

Retrace your route to Hwy. 19, and turn left. Continue for 14 miles to just after MM 27, and turn right (toward the ocean) at the sign for:

18 ★ **Laupahoehoe Beach Park.** This idyllic place holds a grim reminder of nature's fury. In 1946 a tidal wave swept across the village that once stood on this lava-leaf (that's what *Laupahoehoe* means) peninsula and claimed the lives of 20 students and 4 teachers. A memorial in this pretty little park recalls the tragedy. The land here ends in black sea stacks that resemble tombstones. It's not a place for swimming, but the views are spectacular. ◷ 10–20 min. Laupahoehoe Point exit off Hwy. 19.

Retrace your steps to Hwy. 19, and turn right. Just past MM 42, turn right (toward the ocean) onto Hwy. 240, which goes through the town of Honokaa (where Hwy. 240 is called Mamane St.).

19 ★ kids **Simply Natural.** Stop at this charming deli with its friendly staff, wholesome food, and vintage interior. Don't be fooled by the unpretentiousness of the place—the food is fabulous. See p 279.

Continue west on Mamane St. (which is also Hwy. 240) another 7 miles to the end. Park in the parking lot. Do NOT attempt to drive into the valley without a four-wheel-drive vehicle.

20 ★★★ kids **Waipio Valley Lookout.** Not only is this an incredibly awe-inspiring site, but it also is the birthplace of the kings of Hawaii. Just don't try to drive a car without four-wheel drive into the valley. Trust me. See p 223, 11.

21 ★★ kids **Waipio Valley.** Options for visiting this lush tropical valley include a guided shuttle tour and a ride in a mule-drawn surrey. See "How to Get into Waipio Valley," p 223.

> *Pua Mau Place's botanical gardens flower along the slopes of the Kohala Mountains.*

Retrace your route back to Hwy. 19, turn right, and drive about 12 miles into the town of Waimea (also known as Kamuela). After MM 57, look for the Parker Ranch Center on your left between Pukalani and Lindsey rds. Allow 20 to 30 minutes for the drive.

22 ★ kids **Parker Ranch.** The *paniolo* (cowboy) tradition began here in 1809, when John Parker, a 19-year-old New England sailor, jumped ship and rounded up wild cows for King Kamehameha. There's some evidence that Hawaiian cowboys were the first to be taught by the great Spanish horsemen, the *vaqueros;* they were cowboying 40 years before their counterparts in California, Texas, and the Pacific Northwest. The Parker Ranch, after six generations of cowboys, is smaller today than in its glory, but it is still a working ranch. Some 12 cowboys work 250 horses and more than 30,000 head of cattle on 175,000 acres. If you are interested, there is a 4-hour tour of Parker Ranch, which explores the 160-plus years of history and operations at Hawaii's oldest working cattle ranch. Guests visit historical and operational areas of Parker Ranch, many not open to the general public, while learning about the saga of the Parker family and the history of its cowboys. The tour is $135 and leaves from Parker Ranch Store. You can also tour two historic homes on the ranch. In 1989 the late Richard Smart—a sixth-generation heir—opened his 8,000-square-foot yellow Victorian home, Puuopelu, to art lovers. The French Regency gallery here includes original works by Renoir, Degas, Dufy, Corot, Utrillo, and Pissarro. Next door is Mana Hale, a little New England saltbox built from koa wood 140 years ago. Cost is $9 per person. ⌚ **1-4 hr. Parker Ranch Store, in the Parker Ranch Center, Hwy. 19 (btw. Pukalani and Lindsey rds), Waimea. ☎ 808/885-7655. www.parkerranch.com. Mon-Sat 9am-5pm.**

Trip Tip

Spend the night either in Waimea or on the Kohala Coast; see p 280 for our lodging recommendations.

Day 5

From Waimea continue west on Hwy. 19. At MM 67, turn left (south) and continue on Hwy. 19. After 6 miles down the road, look for the sign to Mauna Lani Resort just after MM 73. Turn right into the resort on Mauna Lani Dr. At the roundabout turn right (toward the Fairmont Orchid) on Kaniku Dr. Just before you reach the Fairmont Orchid, look for a sign on the left directing you to:

23 ★ kids **Puako Petroglyph Archaeological District.** The Hawaiian petroglyphs are a great enigma of the Pacific—no one knows who made them or why. They appear at 135 different sites on 6 inhabited islands, but most of them are found on the Big Island. At first glance, the huge slate of pahoehoe lava looks like any other smooth black slate of lava on the seacoast of the Big Island—until gradually, in slanting rays of the sun, a wonderful cast of characters leaps to life before your eyes. You might see dancers and paddlers, fishermen and chiefs, hundreds of marchers all in a

> *The Big Island's mysterious petroglyphs tell visual stories of its rich history.*

row. Pictures of the tools of daily life are everywhere: fish hooks, spears, poi pounders, canoes. The most common representations are family groups. There are also post-European-contact petroglyphs of ships, anchors, horses, and guns. The largest concentration of these stone symbols in the Pacific lies within this 233-acre site. Don't miss this 1.5-mile Malama Trail. Go in the early morning or late afternoon, when it's cool, to see the 3,000 designs that have been identified here. ⏱ 30 min. Kaniku Dr., Mauna Lani Resort.

Retrace your steps back to Hwy. 19, and turn left, retracing your route. At the intersection of Hwy. 19 and Hwy. 270, turn left (toward the ocean) onto Hwy. 270. Look on the left for the entry sign to:

24 ★★★ kids **Puukohola *Heiau* National Historic Site.** This seacoast temple, called "the Hill of the Whale," is the single most imposing and dramatic structure of the ancient Hawaiians. It was built by Kamehameha I from 1790 to 1791. The temple stands 224 feet long by 100 feet wide, with three narrow terraces on the sea-side and an amphitheater from which to view canoes. Kamehameha built this temple after a prophet told him he would conquer and unite the islands if he did so; 4 years later, he fulfilled his kingly goal. The site includes an interactive visitor center, the house of John Young, a trusted advisor of Kamehameha, and, offshore, the submerged ruins of Hale O Ka Puni, a shrine dedicated to the shark gods. ⏱ 1 hr. Hwy. 270, near Kawaihae Harbor. ☎ 808/882-7218. www.nps.gov/puhe. Free admission. Daily 7:30am-4pm. The visitor center is on Hwy. 270; the *heiau* is a short walk away. The trail is closed when it's too windy, so call ahead if you're in doubt.

Return to Hwy. 270 and turn left. Just past MM 6 look on your right for the entry to Kohala Estates, and turn right on Ala Kahua Dr. Go ½ mile up the hill to the gate at a lava rock wall.

25 kids **Pua Mau Place.** Perched on the sun-kissed western slopes of the Kohala Mountains and dotted with deep, craggy ravines lies one of Hawaii's most unusual botanical gardens, Pua Mau Place, a 45-acre oasis with breathtaking views of both the ocean and the majestic mountains. It's dedicated to plants that are "ever blooming," an expansive collection of continuously flowering tropical flowers, trees, and shrubs. The gardens also have an aviary of exotic birds and a unique hibiscus maze planted with some 200 varieties of hibiscus. This is a great place for families (children are invited to feed the birds in the aviary). Visitors can take the self-guided tour (along with a

booklet filled with the names and descriptions of all the plants) along mulched pathways meandering through the gardens, where every plant is clearly marked. ⏲ 1-2 hr. 10 Ala Kahua, Kawaihae. ☎ 808/882-0888. www.puamau.com. Admission $10 adults, $8 seniors and students, children 12 and under free. Daily 9am–4pm. Located off Hwy. 270 on Ala Kahua Dr. (in Kohala Estates), just north of Kawaihae.

Retrace your route back to Hwy. 270, and turn right, heading north. Continue about 7½ miles to just after MM 13, and look on your left (ocean side) for the sign to turn into:

26 ★ kids **Lapakahi State Historical Park.** This 14th-century fishing village, on a hot, dry, dusty stretch of coast, offers a glimpse into the lifestyle of the ancients. Lapakahi is the best-preserved fishing village in Hawaii. Take the self-guided 1-mile loop trail past stone platforms, fish shrines, rock shelters, salt pans, and restored *hale* (houses) to a coral-sand beach and the deep-blue sea (good snorkeling). Wear good hiking shoes or tennies; it's a hearty 45-minute walk. Go early in the morning or late in the afternoon to beat the heat. ⏲ 1 hr. Hwy. 270, Mahukona. ☎ 808/889-5566. www.hawaiistateparks.org/parks. Free admission. Daily 8am–4pm.

If you have called ahead and it is a "working" Saturday, then proceed to the next stop, the Mo'okini *Heiau*. If not, skip this next stop. IT IS NOT OPEN TO THE PUBLIC unless it is a working Saturday and you have made a reservation. This is a very sacred Hawaiian place, so please be respectful and do not go unless you have a reservation. From Lapakahi get back on Hwy. 270, and turn left. Just after MM 18, turn left at the Old Coast Guard Rd., and then turn right on the Old Railroad Right of Way.

27 ★★ kids **Mo'okini Luakini *Heiau*.** This 1,500-year-old temple, once used by kings to pray and offer human sacrifices, is Hawaii's oldest, largest, and most sacred religious site (and now a national historic landmark). The massive 3-story stone temple, dedicated to Ku, the Hawaiian god of war, was erected in A.D. 480; each stone is said to have been passed hand to hand from Pololu Valley, 14 miles away, by 18,000 men who worked from sunset to sunrise. Kamehameha, born nearby under Halley's comet, sought spiritual guidance here before embarking on his campaign to unite

> *The Pololu Valley Lookout offers unparalleled vistas of the towering jade-green cliffs of the Hamakua Coast.*

Climbing the World's Tallest Mountain

The summit of Mauna Kea, the world's tallest mountain if measured from its base on the ocean floor, is the best place on earth for astronomical observations because its mid-Pacific site is near the Equator and because it enjoys clear, pollution-free skies and pitch-black nights with no urban light to interfere. That's why Mauna Kea is home to the world's largest telescope; but the star-gazing from here is fantastic even with the naked eye.

Always check the weather and Mauna Kea road conditions before you head out (☎ 808/969-3218). Dress warmly; the temperatures drop into the 30s (around 0°C) after dark. Drink as much liquid as possible, avoiding alcohol and coffee, in the 36 hours surrounding your trip to avoid dehydration. Don't go within 24 hours of scuba diving—you could get the bends. Pregnant women and anyone under 13 or with a heart condition or lung ailment are advised to stay below. Once you're at the top, don't overexert yourself; it's bad for your heart. Take it easy up here.

If you'd rather not go it alone to the top, you can caravan up as part of a **free summit tour,** offered Saturday and Sunday at 1pm from the visitor center (returns at 5pm). You must be 16 or older and in good health (no cardiopulmonary problems), not be pregnant, and have a four-wheel-drive vehicle. The tours explain the development of the facilities on Mauna Kea and include a walking tour of an observatory at 13,796 feet. Call ☎ 808/961-2180 if you'd like to participate.

Another **telescope tour** is offered, free, during the day, by the Subaru Telescope (☎ 808/934-5056; www.subarutelescope.org). You must book the 40-minute tour a week in advance, as they offer only 9 tours a week: Tuesday through Thursday, at 10:30am, 11:30am, and 1:30pm, on a first-to-sign-up basis. The Subaru Telescope is one of 13 world-class telescopes on the summit of Mauna Kea. You will need a four-wheel-drive vehicle to make the trip. It is recommended that you stop for at least 30 minutes at the Onizuka Visitor Center at 9,000 feet to acclimate.

Mauna Kea Summit Adventures offers a 7- to 8-hour luxury adventure to the summit that includes an extensively trained guide who discusses the geography, geology, natural history, and Hawaiian culture along the way; dinner (gourmet sandwiches and vegetarian onion soup); heavy, arctic-style hooded parkas and gloves; a sunset view from the summit; and star-gazing. The cost for this celestial adventure is $197 including tax (get a 15% discount if you book online at www.maunakea.com 2 weeks in advance). For more information, call ☎ 888/322-2366 or 808/322-2366, or go to www.maunakea.com.

Trip Tip

Spend the night at one of the hotels on the Kohala Coast. See p 280 for our recommendations.

Hawaii. You can see the temple only on the third Saturday of every month, when volunteers pull weeds and clean up property surrounding the temple. If you'd like to help out, call the Mo'okini Preservation Foundation, on Oahu (☎ 808/373-8000). You must call ahead to visit the temple. **On the north shore, near Upolu Point Airport.**

Back on Hwy. 270, turn left, and drive about 5 miles. After passing through the town of Hawi and into the town of Kapaau, just after MM 23, look to your left. Across the street from the King Kamehameha statue and the Civic Center is:

---

(28) kids **Kohala Rainbow Café.** Stop by this tiny eatery and enjoy a cold drink, ice cream, a smoothie, or a yummy dessert. There are a few seats outdoors next to a striking mural. Hwy. 270, Kapaau, across the street from the King Kamehameha statue. ☎ 808/889-0099. $.

(29) ★★ kids **The Original King Kamehameha Statue.** Here stands King Kamehameha the Great, right arm outstretched, left arm holding a spear, as if guarding the seniors who have turned a century-old New England–style courthouse into an airy center for their golden years. The center is worth a stop just to meet the town elders, who are quick to point out the local sights, hand you a free *Guide to Historic North Kohala,* and give you a brief tour of the courthouse, whose walls are covered with the faces of innocent-looking local boys killed in World War II, Korea, and Vietnam. But the statue's the main attraction here. There's one just like it in Honolulu, across the street from Iolani Palace, but this is the original: an 8-foot, 6-inch bronze by Thomas R. Gould, a Boston sculptor. It was cast in Europe in 1880 but was lost at sea on its way to Hawaii. A sea captain eventually recovered the statue, which was placed here, near Kamehameha's Kohala birthplace, in 1912. Kamehameha was born in 1750, became ruler of Hawaii in 1810, and died in Kailua-Kona in 1819. His burial site remains a mystery. ⏱ 10 min. Hwy. 270, Kapaau.

Continue north on Hwy. 270 for about 5½ miles to the end of the road.

(30) ★★★ kids **Pololu Valley Lookout.** At this end-of-the-road scenic lookout, you can gaze at the vertical jade-green cliffs of the Hamakua Coast and two islets offshore. The view may look familiar once you get here—it often appears on travel posters. Linger if you can; adventurous travelers can take a switchback trail (a good 45-min. hike) to a secluded black-sand beach at the mouth of a wild valley once planted in taro; bring water and bug spray. ⏱ 15–20 min. At the end of Hwy. 270, Makapala.

Day 6

From the Kohala Coast take Hwy. 19 north to the intersection of Hwy. 19 and Hwy. 270, just below Kawaihae. Turn right, and continue on Hwy. 19 into Waimea. At the intersection of Hwy. 19 and Hwy. 190 turn right onto Hwy. 190. Outside of Wailea look for the sign saying SADDLE ROAD (Hwy. 200), and turn left on Saddle Rd. It's about an hour from Waimea to the visitor center and another 30 to 45 minutes from the visitor center to the summit. From the turnoff onto Saddle Rd., it's about 19 miles to Mauna Kea State Recreation Area, a good place to stop and stretch your legs. Go another 9 miles down Saddle Rd. to the unmarked Summit Rd. turnoff, at MM 28 (about 9,300 ft.), across from the Hunter's Check-in Station. People usually start getting lightheaded after the 9,600-foot marker (about 6¼ miles up Summit Rd.), the site of the visitor center (also the last place for a bathroom stop). Allow 1½ to 2 hours from a Kohala Coast hotel to the visitor center.

(31) **Onizuka Visitor Information Station.** The station is named in memory of Hawaii's fallen astronaut, Ellison Onizuka, a native of the Big Island and a victim of the *Challenger* explosion. Every night from 6 to 10pm, you can do some serious star-gazing from the Onizuka Visitor Information Station. There's a free lecture at 6pm, followed by a video, a question-and-answer session, and your chance to peer through 11-inch, 14-inch, and 16-inch telescopes. Bring a snack and, if you've got them, your own telescope or binoculars, along

> *Mauna Kea mountain's clear, pollution-free skies and its proximity to the Equator make it one of the world's best star-gazing spots.*

with a flashlight (with a red filter). Dress for 30° to 40°F (-1° to 4°C) temperatures, but call for the weather report first (☎ 808/961-5582). Families are welcome. ⏲ 1–3 hr. ☎ 808/961-2180. www.ifa.hawaii.edu/info/vis. Daily 9am–10pm.

On the final approach to the summit area, once you are on the blacktop road, go about 200 yards to the major switchback. Just after MM 6, park at Parking Area 2. The trail head to Lake Waiau is across the road, though the lake is not visible from this point. Cross and walk down the road until you see a signpost marking the beginning of the ½-mile trail that goes down to the lake about 200 feet across the lava. Follow the base of the big cinder cone on your left; you should have the summit of Mauna Loa in view directly ahead as you walk.

32 **Lake Waiau.** Inside a cinder cone just below the summit is Lake Waiau, the only glacial lake in the mid-Pacific, and at 13,020 feet above sea level, one of the highest lakes in the world. The lake never dries up, even though it gets only 15 inches of rain a year and sits in porous lava where there are no springs. Nobody quite knows what to make of this, but scientists suspect the lake is replenished by snowmelt and permafrost from submerged lava tubes. ⏲ 30 min.

Trip Tip

Day 6 is devoted to exploring Mauna Kea, the Big Island's highest peak. You'll need a four-wheel-drive vehicle to climb to the peak, Observatory Hill. A standard car will get you as far as the visitor center, but check your rental agreement before you go; some agencies prohibit you from taking your car on the Saddle Road, which is narrow and rutted and has a soft shoulder.

Continue up Summit Rd. to the end, and park in the parking lot.

33 **Mauna Kea Summit.** Up here, 11 nations, including Japan, France, and Canada, have set up peerless infrared telescopes to look into deep space. Among them sits the Keck Telescope, the world's largest. Developed by the University of California and the California Institute of Technology, it's 8 stories high, weighs 150 tons,

> A mecca for skiiers and snowboarders, Mauna Kea towers above the clouds at sunset.

and has a 33-foot-diameter mirror made of 36 perfectly attuned hexagon mirrors, like a fly's eye, rather than one conventional lens. Also at the summit, up a narrow footpath, is a cairn of rocks; from it, you can see across the Pacific Ocean in a 360-degree view that's beyond words and pictures. When it's socked in, you get a surreal look at the summits of Mauna Loa and Maui's Haleakala poking through the puffy white cumulus clouds beneath your feet. ⏱ 1 hr. Plan to arrive at the summit at sunset so you have a fantastic sunset view and get to watch the stars come out. End of Summit Rd.

Day 7

From the Kohala resorts take Hwy. 19 south to MM 93, and turn right (toward the ocean) at the sign for Kona Airport. At the stop sign turn right, and park in the airport lot. Ellison S. Onizuka Space Center is across the street from the parking lot by the airport terminals.

34 kids **Ellison S. Onizuka Space Center.** This small museum has a real moon rock and memorabilia in honor of Big Island–born astronaut Ellison Onizuka, who died in the 1986 *Challenger* space shuttle disaster. Displays include a gravity well, which illustrates orbital motion, and an interactive rocket-propulsion exhibit,

More on Mauna Kea

One of the best books on Mauna Kea, written by Onizuka Visitor Information Station manager David Byrne and Big Island writer Leslie Lang, is *Mauna Kea: A Guide to Hawaii's Sacred Mountain* (☎ 866/900-BOOK (900-2665); www.bookshawaii.net). The book covers everything from the cultural history of the sacred mountain to its natural history, including great insights on the scientific value of the dormant volcano.

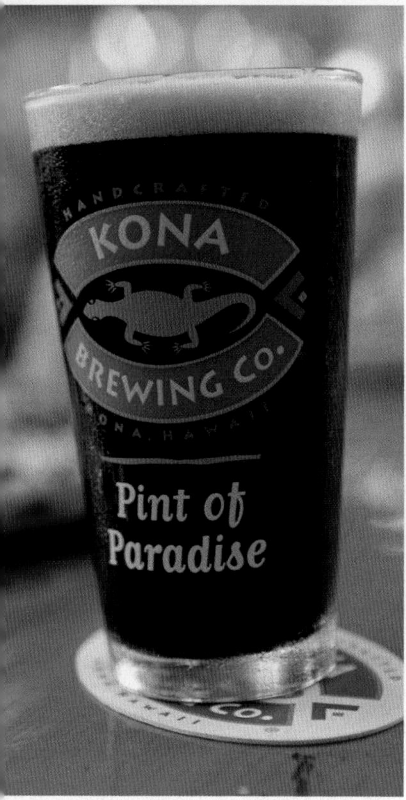

> *Hawaii's own Kona Brewing Co. & Brewpub serves up 124,000 gallons of South Pacific suds a year.*

where you can launch your own miniature space shuttle. 1 hr. At Kona International Airport, Kailua-Kona. ☎ 808/329-3441. www.hawaiimuseums.org. Admission $3 adults and seniors, $1 children 12 and under. Daily 8:30am–4:30pm. Parking in airport lot $2 per hour.

From the airport return to Hwy. 19, and turn right. Just past MM 94 turn right, and drive nearly to the end of the road.

35 **Natural Energy Laboratory of Hawaii Authority (NELHA).** Technology buffs should consider a visit to NELHA, where the hot tropical sun, in combination with a complex pumping system that brings 42°F (6°C) ocean water from 2,000 feet deep up to land, is used to develop innovations in agriculture, aquaculture, and ocean conservation. The interesting 90-minute tour takes in all areas of the high-tech ocean science and technology park, including the seawater delivery system, the energy-conversion process, and some of the park's more interesting tenants, from Maine lobsters to giant clams. There is also an abalone farm tour (which lasts another hour); a tasting can be added on to the tour for an additional $25. 1½–2½ hr. 73-4460 Queen Kaahumanu Hwy. (at MM 94), Kailua-Kona. ☎ 808/329-8073. www.nelha.org. Public presentation tours $8 adults, children 8 and under free. Mon, Tues, Wed, Thurs 10am; reservations required.

Retrace your route back to Hwy. 19, turn right, drive about 7 miles to Kailua-Kona, and turn left at Palani Rd. At the second stoplight on Palani Rd., turn right (north) on Kuakini Hwy., drive approximately ½ mile to the first stop sign, Kaiwi St., and turn right. Take your first right on Pawai Place and follow it until it ends at the brewery parking lot. Watch for directional signs along the way.

36 **Kona Brewing Co. & Brewpub.** Take a break at this microbrewery—the first of its kind on the Big Island. Spoon and Pops, a father-and-son duo from Oregon, brought their brewing talents here and now produce about 25 barrels (about 124,000 gal.) per year. Drop by any time during their business hours and take a quick, informal tour of the brewery, after which you get to taste the product. A brewpub on the property serves gourmet pizza, salads, and fresh-brewed Hawaiian ales. 75-5629 Kuakini Hwy., Kailua-Kona. ☎ 808/334-BREW (334-2739). www.konabrewingco.com. Free tours and tastings. Tours Mon–Fri 10:30am and 3pm. $.

Retrace your route back out to Kaiwi St., turn left (toward the ocean), then left again at the four-way stop onto Kuakini Hwy. At the light turn right onto Palani St. Go ½ block, and turn into the parking lot at King Kamehameha's Kona Beach Hotel.

37 ★★ kids **Kamehameha's Compound at Kamakahonu Bay.** On the ocean side of the Kona Beach Hotel is a restored area of deep spiritual meaning to Hawaiians. This was the spot that King Kamehameha the Great chose to retreat to in 1812 after conquering the Hawaiian Islands. He stayed until his death in 1819. The king built a

> *Kamehameha's historic Compound at Kamakahonu Bay is the site where Hawaiians first recognized the rights of women.*

temple, Ahuena *Heiau,* and used it as a gathering place for his *kahuna* (priests) to counsel him on governing his people in times of peace. In 1820 it was on this sacred ground that Kamehameha's son Liholiho, as king, sat down to eat with his mother, Keopuolani, and Kamehameha's principal queen, Kaahumanu, thus breaking the ancient *kapu* (taboo) against eating with women; this act established a new order in the Hawaiian kingdom. The temple grounds are now just a third of their original size but still impressive. You're free to come and wander the grounds, envisioning the days when King Kamehameha appealed to the gods to help him rule with the spirit of humanity's highest nature. ⏱ 1 hr. On the grounds of King Kamehameha's Kona Beach Hotel, 75-5660 Palani Rd., Kailua-Kona. ☎ 808/329-2911. www.konabeachhotel.com. Free admission. Daily 9am–4pm.

Leave your car parked in King Kamehameha's Kona Beach Hotel parking lot, and walk from the historical grounds across the street to the Kailua Pier.

38 Kailua Pier. This is action central for water adventures. Fishing charters, snorkel cruises, and party boats all come and go here. Stop by around 4pm, when the captains weigh in with the catch of the day, usually huge marlin—the record-setters often come in here. It's also a great place to watch the sunset. ⏱ 15–20 min. On the waterfront outside King Kamehameha's Kona Beach Hotel, Kailua-Kona. ☎ 808/329-7494.

Keep your car in the parking lot, and continue on foot from the pier, where you will turn right and walk along the ocean, making a right on Alii Dr. Continue on Alii Dr. to the first building on the ocean side of the street.

39 ★★ Hulihee Palace. This 2-story New England–style mansion of lava rock and coral mortar, built in 1838 by the Big Island's governor, John Adams Kuakini, overlooks the harbor at Kailua-Kona. The largest, most elegant residence on the island when it was erected, Hulihee became a home to Hawaii's royalty, making it the other royal palace in the United States (the most famous being Oahu's Iolani Palace). Now run by Daughters of Hawaii, it features many 19th-century mementos and gorgeous koa furniture. You'll get lots of background and royal lore on

> *Built in 1820, Mokuaikaua Church is the oldest Christian place of worship on the islands.*

the guided tour. No photography is allowed. There was some damage to this historic structure in the 2006 earthquake, but by the time you read this, it should be repaired. The palace hosts 12 Hawaiian music and hula concerts a year, each dedicated to a Hawaiian monarch, at 4pm on the last Sunday of the month (except June and Dec, when the performances are held in conjunction with King Kamehameha Day and Christmas). ⏱ 1 hr. 75-5718 Alii Dr., Kailua-Kona. ☎ 808/329-1877. www.daughtersofhawaii.com. Admission $6 adults, $4 seniors, $1 children. Daily 9am–4pm. Tours held throughout the day (arrive at least an hour before closing).

Walk across the street.

40 Mokuaikaua Church. This is the oldest Christian church in Hawaii. It's constructed of lava stones, but its architecture is New England–style all the way. The 112-foot steeple is still the tallest man-made structure in Kailua-Kona. ⏱ 15 min. 75-5713 Alii Dr., Kailua-Kona. ☎ 808/329-0655. www.mokuaikaua.org.

> *The uniquely Hawaiian Hulihee Palace is a 2-story New England mansion forged from local lava rock and sea coral.*

The Best of Maui in 1 Week

This weeklong itinerary expands the 3-day tour on p 302.

I've added a few of my favorites to round out the week: sailing to the island of Lanai; seeing the sharks and other ocean creatures at the Maui Ocean Center; and spending your last day either catching a few rays, being pampered in a spa, or shopping. Remember: You are on vacation, so take time to stop and smell the plumerias. To avoid unnecessary driving I'd suggest staying in West Maui the first 3 nights, in Hana the next 2 nights, and in South Maui the last night.

> *Protected from winds and currents by the high rocks of the bay shore, Kapalua's calm waters are ideal for swimmers of any ability.*

Travel Tip

West Maui is the area from Lahaina north, including Kaanapali, Honokowai, Kahana, Napili, and Kapalua. South Maui includes Kihei, Wailea, and Makena.

START Kapalua Beach. **FINISH** Iao Valley. **TRIP LENGTH** 1 week and 247 miles.

Day 1

1 ★★★ **Kapalua Beach,** and **2** **Lahaina.** See Day 1 in "The Best of Maui in 3 Days," p 302.

Day 2

Go south on Hwy. 30 to Lahaina. Turn right at the light on Dickenson St. Look for the Republic Parking sign on the right side of the street. Allow 30 minutes from Kapalua and 15 minutes from Kaanapali.

3 ★★★ **Lanai.** You'll likely wake up early on your first day in Hawaii, so take advantage of it and get out on the water early with **Trilogy** (p 372), my favorite sailing-snorkeling trip in Hawaii. You'll spend the day (breakfast and lunch included) sailing to the island of Lanai, snorkeling, and touring the island. The trip departs from and returns to Lahaina. Plus you still have the afternoon to go shopping for souvenirs or take a nap. For dinner, I'd book a table on the roof at sunset at the **Lahaina Store Grille and Oyster Bar** (p 395), followed by the drama/dance/music show **'Ulalena** (p 407).

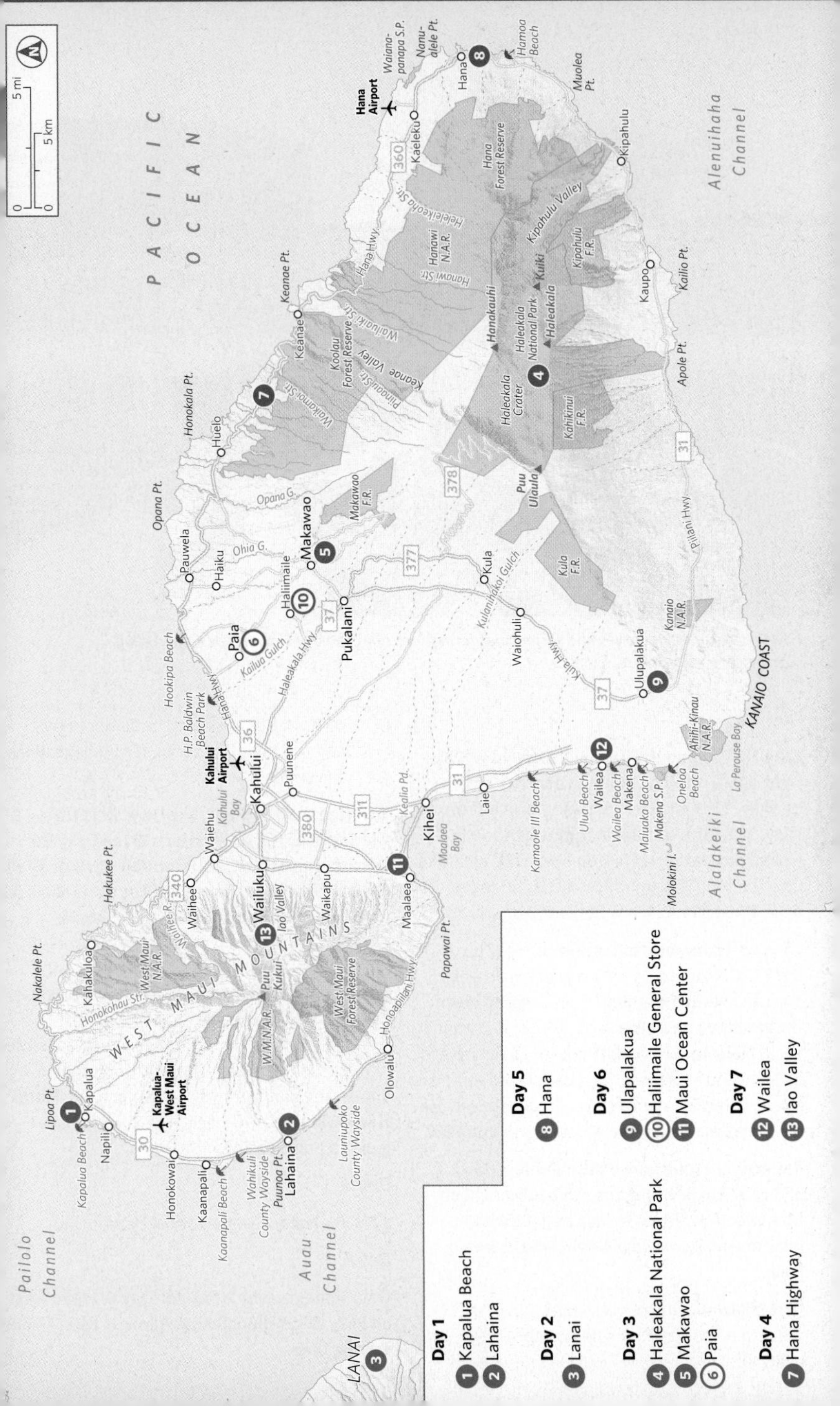
Day 1
1 Kapalua Beach
2 Lahaina
Day 2
3 Lanai
Day 3
4 Haleakala National Park
5 Makawao
6 Paia
Day 4
7 Hana Highway
Day 5
8 Hana
Day 6
9 Ulapalakua
10 Haliimaile General Store
11 Maui Ocean Center
Day 7
12 Wailea
13 Iao Valley
PACIFIC OCEAN
Pailolo Channel
Auau Channel
Alalakeiki Channel
Alenuihaha Channel
LANAI
WEST MAUI MOUNTAINS
KANAIO COAST
Kapalua-West Maui Airport
Kahului Airport
Hana Airport
Kapalua
Napili
Honokowai
Kaanapali
Lahaina
Olowalu
Kahakuloa
Waihee
Waiehu
Wailuku
Waikapu
Maalaea
Kahului
Puunene
Kihei
Laie
Wailea
Makena
Paia
Haliimaile
Makawao
Pukalani
Haiku
Pauwela
Huelo
Keanae
Kula
Waiohuli
Ulupalakua
Kaupo
Kipahulu
Kaeleku
Hana
Haleakala National Park
Haleakala Crater
Hana Forest Reserve
Koolau Forest Reserve
West Maui Forest Reserve
Kipahulu Valley
Iao Valley
Hana Hwy
Haleakala Hwy
Kula Hwy
Piilani Hwy
Honoapiilani Hwy
30
36
37
31
311
340
360
377
378
380
5 mi
5 km

> *Maui's crystal-clear coves and surreal lava formations offer some of Hawaii's best snorkeling and sightseeing opportunities.*

Day 3

Take Hwy. 30 south. Turn right on Hwy. 380, right again on Hwy. 36, then another right on Hwy. 37. Just after Pukalani, turn left on Hwy. 377. Turn left again at the sign to the Haleakala National Park on Hwy. 378 and take it to the top. The summit is 40 to 50 miles from West Maui. Allow at least 2 hours.

4 ★★★ **Haleakala National Park.** Head up to the 10,000-foot (dormant) volcano, Haleakala. You can **hike in the crater** (p 360), **speed down the mountain on a bicycle** (p 366), or just wander about **Haleakala National Park.** You don't have to be at the top for sunrise, but I have to tell you—it is a near-religious experience you'll never forget. See the "Haleakala National Park" tour starting on p 352.

Retrace your route down the mountain (Hwy. 378 to 377 to 37), and turn right at the light on Makawao Ave. To get to Paia from Makawao, head downhill on Baldwin Ave., which ends in Paia.

5 **Makawao.** On your way back down the mountain, stop and tour this cowboy town. See p 318, 11.

6 **Paia.** Plan on lunch or dinner in this colorful town. For dining recommendations, see p 388.

To return to West Maui, take Hwy. 30 north toward Kahului Airport, and turn left on Dairy Rd., which becomes Hwy. 380. Turn left on Hwy. 30 all the way to Lahaina/Kaanapali. The trip is about 30 to 40 miles and takes at least 1 to 1½ hours.

Day 4

7 ★★★ **Hana Highway.** Plan to take the entire day to drive the 50 miles to Hana on this 1½-lane twisting road, and then spend a couple of nights in this wonderful town. Splurge on dinner and stay at my favorite place, the **Hotel Hana-Maui** (p 400). See "The Road to Hana" tour starting on p 342.

Day 5

8 ★★★ **Hana.** See the tour of Hana, p 346.

Day 6

Get on the road by 10am for Day 6. Head west on Hwy. 31 to Ulupalakua. Allow at least 1 hour driving time.

9 Ulupalakua. Visit Maui's only winery at **Ulupalakua Ranch.** See p 341, 4.

After Ulupalakua, Hwy. 31 is called Hwy. 37. Turn right on Haliimaile Rd.; the restaurant is in the town of Haliimaile. The drive takes 30 to 40 minutes.

---

10 **Haliimaile General Store.** Heading down Haleakala Mountain, stop for lunch in the middle of the pineapple fields at this haven for Hawaii Regional Cuisine fans. See p 392.

Get back on Hwy. 37, and turn right, heading downhill. Turn left at the stoplight at the intersection of Hwy. 36 and then left again on Dairy Rd., which becomes Hwy. 380. When the road ends, turn left on Hwy. 30. The left turn to Maalaea comes up in less than a mile. The Maui Ocean Center is at the entrance to the village. The drive will take about 30 to 40 minutes.

11 Maui Ocean Center. Spend the afternoon checking out the marine life, especially the sharks. I'd suggest that, since tomorrow's itinerary is Wailea and the beach, you spend the night in Wailea. My lodging recommendations start on p 398. See p 308, 7.

Day 7

To get to South Maui from Maalaea, turn right on Hwy. 30 and then right again on Hwy. 31. To get to Wailea Beach from South Maui (allow 15 min. from the north end of Kihei), take Hwy. 31 south, which ends on Wailea Iki Dr. At the stop sign (note the Shops at Wailea straight ahead), turn left on Wailea Alanui Rd., and look for the blue shoreline access sign, which will take you to a public parking lot.

12 Wailea. Spend your last day on Maui catching some rays or snorkeling with the tropical fish. I never pass up an opportunity to go to my favorite beach in South Maui, **Wailea Beach,** fronting the Four Seasons Maui and the Grand Wailea resorts (you don't have to stay at these resorts to use the beach). Depending on how much time you have on your final day, you can relax on the beach, be pampered in a spa at either of these hotels (see the box "Relax, Breathe Deep & Say Spaaah" on p 325), and/or shop at the nearby **Shops at Wailea** (p 386). See p 333, 4.

> *The spectacular natural beauty of the winding 50-mile Hana Highway makes driving a destination in itself.*

To go from Wailea Beach to Iao Valley, head north on Hwy. 31, and turn right on Hwy. 30. In the town of Wailuku, turn left at the light onto Main St., which becomes Iao Valley Rd. and ends at Iao Valley State Park. The 8-mile trip will take about 30 to 40 minutes across the island.

13 Iao Valley. If you have a late flight, you might want to check out this historic area on your way back to the airport. See p 336, 2.

The Best Multi-Island Itineraries

Because moving interisland is not easy in Hawaii, a good rule of thumb is to visit one island per week, with the exception of travel in Maui County (which encompasses Maui, Molokai, and Lanai). If you have the luxury of spending 2 weeks in Hawaii, spend a week on Oahu, following the 1-week tour in this chapter, then follow my 1-week tour of Maui, which includes a day trip to see Lanai. If you have 3 weeks, go to Oahu for a week, then follow the 2-week Maui itinerary in this chapter, which includes day trips to Lanai and Molokai.

The Best of Maui in 2 Weeks

Two weeks on Maui separates the visitors from the adventurers and gives you the time to really get to know this exotic isle. You'll see everything we cover in the 1-week tour, plus you'll take a ferry to Molokai and ride a mule into the dramatic Kalaupapa Peninsula, see Maui from the air in a helicopter, drive around the back-side of Maui, snorkel in the old volcanic crater of Molokini, tour Maui's farms, and kayak off historic Makena. To cut back on excess driving, plan to spend 6 nights in West Maui, 2 nights in Hana, and 5 nights in South Maui.

START Kapalua Beach. **FINISH** Kihei. **TRIP LENGTH** 2 weeks and 538 miles.

Day 1

To get to Kapalua Beach from Lahaina/Kaanapali, take Hwy. 30 north to Kapalua. Go left at the Kapalua Resort sign on Office Rd. and follow it to the end. Turn left on Honoapiilani Rd. and right (toward the ocean) at the beach access sign next door to the Napili Kai condominium.

❶ ★★★ **Kapalua Beach.** See Day 1 in "The Best of Maui in 3 Days" (p 302).

> *The spectacular colors of sunrise at The Kalahaku Overlook in Haleakala National Park.*

Day 2

Go south on Hwy. 30 to Lahaina. Turn right at the light on Dickenson St. Look for the Republic Parking sign on the right side of the street. Allow 30 minutes from Kapalua and 15 minutes from Kaanapali.

❷ ★★★ **Lanai.** Don't miss this opportunity to sail 9 miles across the channel to the island of Lanai. See (p 58) ❸.

Day 3

Turn right on Hwy. 30 to Lahaina.

❸ ★★ **Lahaina.** Plan to arrive in this historic town early, before the crowds. I'd recommend

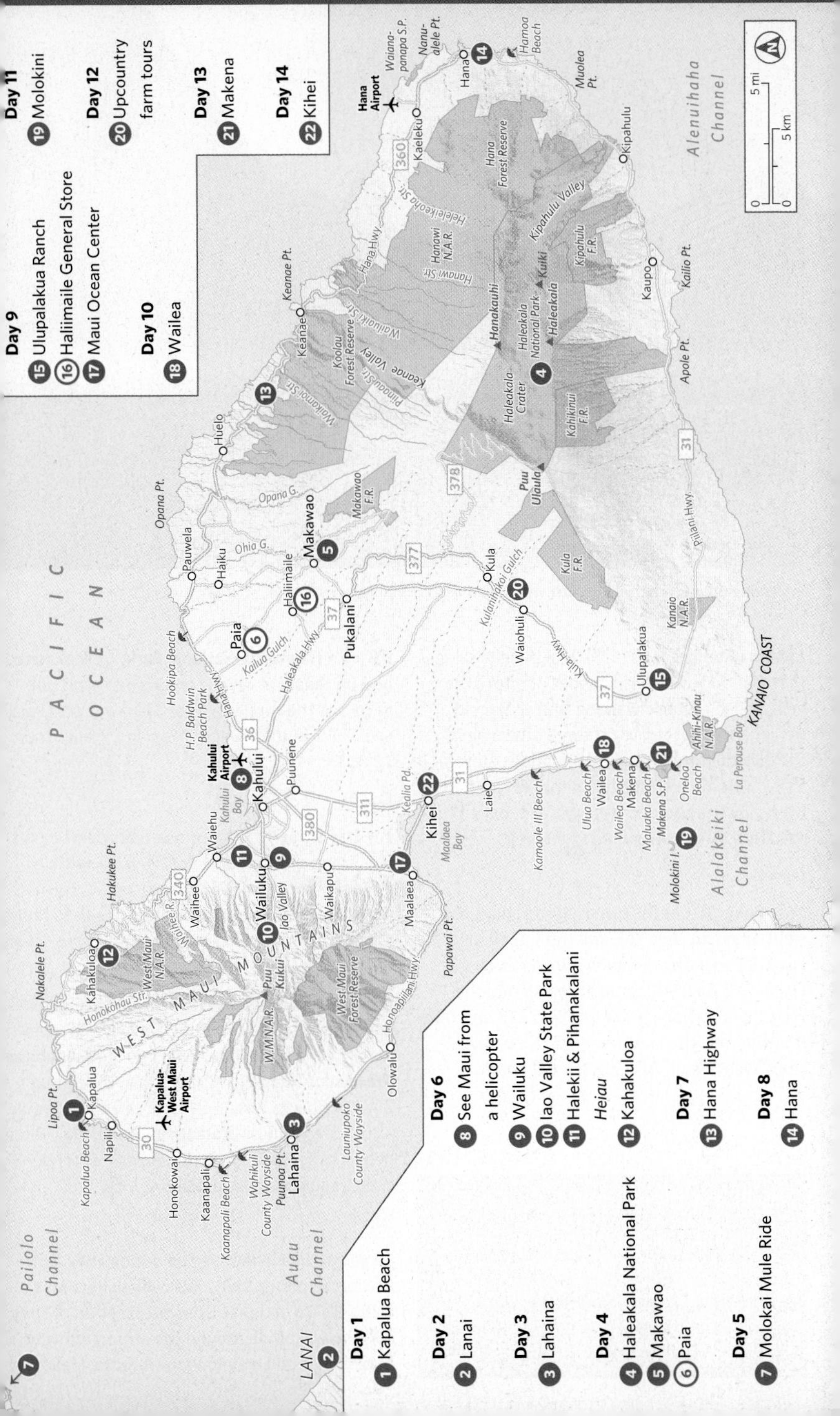
Day 1
1 Kapalua Beach
Day 2
2 Lanai
Day 3
3 Lahaina
Day 4
4 Haleakala National Park
5 Makawao
6 Paia
Day 5
7 Molokai Mule Ride
Day 6
8 See Maui from a helicopter
9 Wailuku
10 Iao Valley State Park
11 Halekii & Pihanakalani Heiau
12 Kahakuloa
Day 7
13 Hana Highway
Day 8
14 Hana
Day 9
15 Ulupalakua Ranch
16 Haliimaile General Store
17 Maui Ocean Center
Day 10
18 Wailea
Day 11
19 Molokini
Day 12
20 Upcountry farm tours
Day 13
21 Makena
Day 14
22 Kihei
PACIFIC OCEAN
Pailolo Channel
Auau Channel
Alalakeiki Channel
Alenuihaha Channel
LANAI
WEST MAUI MOUNTAINS
Kapalua-West Maui Airport
Kahului Airport
Hana Airport
Lipoa Pt.
Kapalua
Kapalua Beach
Napili
Honokowai
Kaanapali
Kaanapali Beach
Wahikuli County Wayside
Puunoa Pt.
Lahaina
Launiupoko County Wayside
Olowalu
Honoapiilani Hwy.
Papawai Pt.
Maalaea
Nakalele Pt.
Honokohau Str.
Kahakuloa
West Maui N.A.R.
W.M.N.A.R.
Puu Kukui
West Maui Forest Reserve
Hakukee Pt.
Waihee
Waihee R.
Waiehu
Wailuku
Iao Valley
Waikapu
Kahului
Kahului Bay
Puunene
Maalaea Bay
Kihei
Kealia Pd.
Laie
Kamaole III Beach
Ulua Beach
Wailea
Wailea Beach
Makena
Maluaka Beach
Makena S.P.
Oneloa Beach
Molokini I.
La Perouse Bay
Ahihi-Kinau N.A.R.
KANAIO COAST
H.P. Baldwin Beach Park
Hookipa Beach
Paia
Kailua Gulch
Haleakala Hwy.
Haliimaile
Pukalani
Pauwela
Haiku
Ohia G.
Opana Pt.
Opana G.
Makawao
Makawao F.R.
Huelo
Waikamoi Str.
Keanae
Keanae Pt.
Keanae Valley
Koolau Forest Reserve
Piinaau Str.
Wailuaiki Str.
Hana Hwy.
Hanawi Str.
Hanawi N.A.R.
Heleleikeoha Str.
Kaeleku
Waianapanapa S.P.
Nanualele Pt.
Hana
Hamoa Beach
Muolea Pt.
Hana Forest Reserve
Kipahulu Valley
Kipahulu F.R.
Kipahulu
Kaupo
Kailio Pt.
Apole Pt.
Hanakauhi
Kuiki
Haleakala
Haleakala National Park
Haleakala Crater
Kahikinui F.R.
Puu Ulaula
Kula
Kula F.R.
Kulaniihakoi Gulch
Waiohuli
Kula Hwy.
Ulupalakua
Kanaio N.A.R.
Piilani Hwy.
30
340
380
311
31
36
37
377
378
360
5 mi
5 km

> *Quaint native structures contrast with the majestic mountains of Iao Valley in West Maui.*

Lahaina Coolers (see p 394) for a big breakfast, then put on your walking shoes and take the self-guided **historic walking tour** of the old town on p 328. Plan to do some browsing in the **quaint stores** (recommendations start on p 378), watch the surfers skim the waves in front of the library, and pop over to Kaanapali to the **Whalers Village Museum** (p 314, ❷).

Day 4

Take Hwy. 30 south. Turn right on Hwy. 380, right again on Hwy. 36, and right again on Hwy. 37. Just after Pukalani, turn left on Hwy. 377. Turn left again at the sign to the Haleakala National Park on Hwy. 378 and take it to the top. The summit is 40 to 50 miles from West Maui. Allow at least 2 hours.

Travel Tip: Rush Hour

Yes, Virginia, Maui has "rush hour"—from 7 to 9am and from 4 to 6pm, when the roads can be jampacked, bumper-to-bumper. It's not a fun way to spend your vacation, so do your best to plan your day to avoid it.

❹ ★★★ **Haleakala National Park,** ❺ **Makawao, and** ⑥ **Paia.** For details on exploring this volcano and the rural towns of Makawao and Paia, see Day 3 in the "Best of Maui in 1 Week" tour (p 60).

Day 5

For Day 5's ferry ride from Lahaina Harbor to the island of Molokai, take Hwy. 30 south to Lahaina. At the light at Dickenson St., turn right. Park, and walk toward the ocean to Front St., and after the library, turn toward the ocean to the harbor.

❼ ★★★ **Molokai Mule Ride.** If you have a spare day or two, head over to the "Friendly Isle" to experience the **Mule Ride** down into the **Kalaupapa Peninsula.** This adventure will take you through 26 switchbacks on a 1,600-foot cliff and give you a chance to tour the **Kalaupapa Peninsula,** where people suffering from leprosy have lived for decades. Book in advance. See p 419, ❼.

Day 6

To get to the Heliport, head out on Hwy. 30, and turn right on Hwy. 380, which becomes Dairy Rd. Turn right at the intersection of Hwy. 30. You will circle around the airport runway. Make a left on Leleipio Place into the Heliport.

> *Native fruits and flowers are plentiful for purchase along the scenic, winding road to Hana.*

8 ★★★ **See Maui from a Helicopter.** Lifting off straight up in the air and then floating over Maui in a helicopter will give you an entirely different perspective of the island. Of all the helicopter companies, my favorite is **Blue Hawaiian** (p 367) for the most comfortable, informative, and fun tour in the air.

Retrace your steps back to Hwy. 37. Continue on Hwy. 37 to where it merges with Hwy. 36. Follow Hwy. 36 until it merges with Hwy. 32 (Kaahumanu Ave.), which will take you into Wailuku (the street changes its name to Main St. in Wailuku).

9 **Wailuku.** Take some time to explore old Wailuku town, wandering through the shops and stopping at the Bailey House Museum, on west Main St. See p 338.

Continue on Main St., which changes its name to Iao Valley Rd., to the end, where you will be in Iao Valley.

10 **Iao Valley State Park.** See p 336, 2.

From here, retrace your route back to Main St. Make a left on Market St., then a right on Mill St., which ends at Lower Main St. Turn left and then left again on to Waiheu Beach Rd. (Hwy. 340). Go left on Kuhio Place, and then take your first left on Hea Place, and go to the end of the street.

Buckle Up or Pay Up!

Under Hawaiian law, everyone in the car must wear a seat belt or be subject to a ticket with a stiff fine. Don't forget to get car seats for the kids—you can rent them from your car rental agency.

11 **Halekii and Pihanakalani *Heiau.*** See p 316, 4.

If you aren't too tired, return to West Maui, but drive around the "back way," via the Kahekili Hwy. Get here by retracing your route back to Waiheu Beach Rd. (Hwy. 340) and turning left. When the road ends, make a right on Kahekili Hwy. (Hwy. 340).

12 **Kahakuloa.** Stop to spend a little time at this ancient village, about 12 miles after you turn on Kahekili Highway. (Hwy. 340). See p 316, 4.

Continue on to Lahaina, another 21 miles away.

> Cheese fans will eat up the Surfing Goat Dairy tour, where you can sample the finest local fromage.

Day 7

To reach Hana Hwy. from Lahaina/Kaanapali, take Hwy. 30 south to Hwy. 380 and turn right (east). In Kahului, Hwy. 380 becomes Dairy Rd. Turn right (east) on Hwy. 36.

13 ★★★ **Hana Highway.** Don't miss Maui's famous road with some 600 curves and 50 bridges. See "The Road to Hana" tour starting on p 342.

Day 8

14 ★★★ **Hana.** Maui's garden of lush, tropical Eden. See the "Hana" tour starting on p 346.

Day 9

Get on the road by 10am for Day 9. Head west on Hwy. 31 to Ulupalakua. Allow at least 1 hour driving time.

15 **Ulupalakua.** Continue driving around the island, past Kaupo and up to the Ulupalakua Ranch. See p 341, 4.

After Ulupalakua, Hwy. 31 becomes Hwy. 37. Turn right on Haliimaile Rd. The restaurant is in the town of Haliimaile. The drive takes 30 to 40 minutes.

16 **Haliimaile General Store.** Heading down Haleakala Mountain, stop for lunch in the middle of the pineapple fields at this haven for Hawaii Regional Cuisine fans. See p 392.

17 **Maui Ocean Center.** See p 308, 7.

Day 10

To get to South Maui from Maalaea, turn right on Hwy. 30 and then right again on Hwy. 31. To get to Wailea Beach from South Maui (allow 15 minutes from the north end of Kihei), take Hwy. 31 south, which ends on Wailea Iki Dr. At the stop sign (note the Shops at Wailea straight ahead), turn left on Wailea Alanui Rd., and look for the blue shoreline access sign, which will take you to a public parking lot.

18 **Wailea.** Spend the day catching some rays or snorkeling with the tropical fish. I never pass up an opportunity to go to my favorite beach in South Maui, **Wailea Beach,** fronting the Four Seasons Maui and the Grand Wailea resorts (you don't have to stay at these resorts to use the beach). You can also choose to be on the beach, being pampered in a spa at either of these hotels (see the box "Relax, Breathe Deep & Say Spaaah" on p 325), or to shop at the nearby **Shops at Wailea** (p 386). See p 333, 4.

Day 11

Day 11's boat trip to Molokini departs from Maalaea Harbor. Travel on Hwy. 31 north, and turn left on Hwy. 30. The left turn exit to Maalaea comes up within a mile.

19 ★★★ **Molokini.** Take a day to see the fish inside the **Molokini Crater.** Go in the morning before the wind comes up. If it's whale season and you're lucky, you may spot whales on the way over or back. I never pass up an opportunity to go with **Trilogy**—they're the best (see p 372).

Day 12

Depending on traffic, allow at least an hour to drive from South Maui to Alii Kula Lavender Farm. Take Hwy. 31 north to Hwy. 311, and turn right. At the light at Hwy. 380, turn right on Dairy Rd. Turn right onto Hwy. 37 and follow it up the mountain to Kula. Take the second left after Rice Park onto Kekaulike Ave. Drive about ¼ mile, rounding a bend and taking a quick right up Waipoli Rd.

From the lavender farm to the Surfing Goat Dairy, retrace your route to the Kula Hwy. About 3 miles on Kula Hwy., make a left down Omaopio Rd. In about 3 miles you'll see the farm sign on the left.

20 **Up-Country Farm Tours.** Plan at least one off-the-beaten-path tour while you're on Maui. For a really exotic tour, with great food, take the **Garden and Culinary Tour of the Alii Kula Lavender Farm** (p 323, ④), which includes a tour of the farm and lunch made with lavender products. Cheese aficionados will love the **Surfing Goat Dairy** tour (p 323, ❸) and the sampling of their cheeses.

Day 13

To get to Makena Beach, take Hwy. 31 south, which ends at Wailea Ike Dr. Turn right onto Wailea Ike Dr., then turn left at the intersection onto Wailea Alanui Rd., which becomes Makena Alanui Rd. Turn right on Makena Rd. to Makena Bay. From there to La Pérouse Bay, continue on Makena Rd. until it ends, and then take off on foot for a couple of miles to reach the bay.

21 **Makena.** Kayaking is so easy that you will be paddling away within a few minutes of lessons. One of the best kayak places is in **Makena**—it's calm, the water is so clear you can see the fish, and you are protected from the wind. See **Makena Kayak Tours** (p 370). After a couple of hours of kayaking and snorkeling, stop for a picnic lunch at **Makena Landing** (p 370), then explore the area. If you still have some energy to spare, hike over to Ahihi-Kinau National Monument and **La Pérouse Bay** (p 332, ❶), along the rugged shoreline.

> *A Trilogy sail/snorkel tour is a great way to get out on the water and explore Maui's oceanic world.*

Day 14

Head north on S Kihei Rd.

22 **Kihei.** Your last day on Maui can be spent beach-hopping the 5 miles of white-sand beaches that line the town of Kihei (see p 334, ❻). After 13 days of exploring Maui, spend your last day doing what you love best: beachcombing, snorkeling, shopping, or whatever your favorite Maui activity is. Pick up a lei (at the K-Mart on Dairy Rd., right before the airport) before you go to the airport so you will have a little bit of Maui with you as you say aloha.

Look for the Flashing Blue Light

No, not the flashing blue lights on a police car but the flashing strobe lights on 12-foot poles—these are emergency call boxes, programmed to call 911 as soon as you pick up the handset. There are 29 emergency call boxes on Maui's highways and in remote areas.

Undiscovered Maui

Maui, which has been named the number-one island in the world by numerous travel magazines, doesn't have too many "undiscovered" places, but it does have several sites that most visitors miss. This 3-day itinerary takes you to a couple of unusual Up-country farms, a far-flung beach, two ancient temples, a drive on a seldom-used road, and a quaint Hawaiian village.

> *Kayaking rentals, lessons, and tours are as abundant as water throughout Makena.*

START Kula, Upcountry Maui. **FINISH** Wailuku. **TRIP LENGTH** 3 days and 58 miles.

Day 1

Depending on traffic, allow at least 1 hour to drive from South Maui to the Alii Kula Lavender Farm. Take Hwy. 31 north to Hwy. 311, and turn right. At the light on Hwy. 380, turn right on Dairy Rd. Turn right onto Hwy. 37, and follow it up the mountain to Kula. Take the second left after Rice Park onto Kekaulike Ave. Drive about ¼ mile, and after you round the bend, take a quick right up Waipoli Rd.

From the lavender farm to the Surfing Goat Dairy, retrace your route to the Kula Highway. About 3 miles on the Kula Highway, make a left down Omaopio Road. In about 3 miles you'll see the farm sign on the left.

❶ **Up-Country Farm Tours.** Plan at least one off-the-beaten-path tour while you're on Maui. For a really exotic tour, with great food, take the **Garden and Culinary Tour of the Alii Kula Lavender Farm** (p 323, ④), which includes a tour of the farm and lunch made with lavender products. Cheese aficionados will love the **Surfing Goat Dairy** tour (p 323, ❸), which includes a sampling of their cheeses.

Day 2

To get to Makena Beach take Hwy. 31 south, which ends at Wailea Ike Dr. Turn right on Wailea Ike Dr., and then turn left at the intersection onto Wailea Alanui Rd., which becomes Makena Alanui Rd. Turn right on Makena Rd. to Makena Bay. From there to La Pérouse Bay, continue on Makena Rd. until it ends, and then take off on foot for a couple of miles to reach the bay.

❷ **Makena.** Spend your day kayaking and hiking, with a break for a picnic lunch. See p 333, ❸.

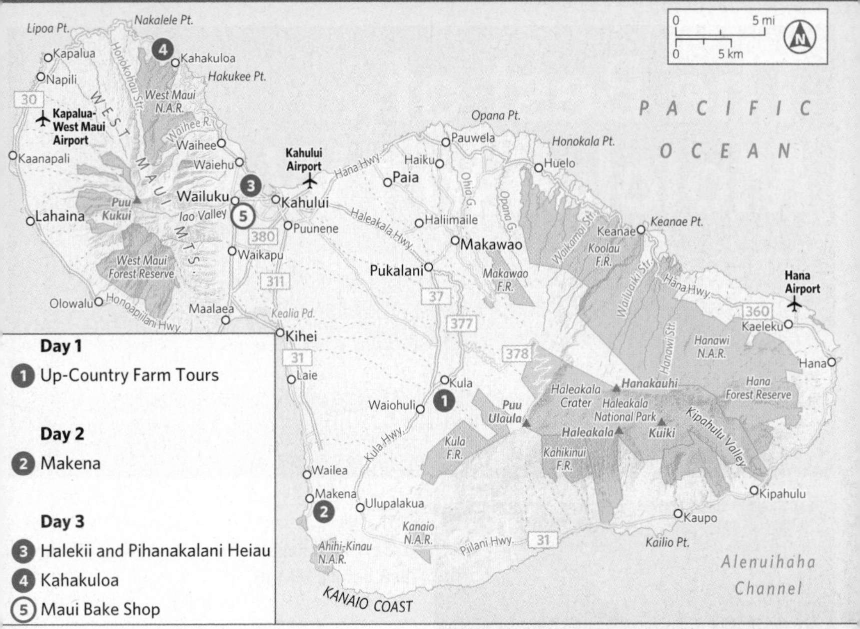

Day 3

Head north on South Kihei Rd. (Hwy. 31) to Hwy. 311 and turn right. Turn right on Hwy. 380, left on Hwy. 36, left on Hwy. 32, and right on Hwy. 340. After you have passed the Wailuku Industrial Park, turn left on Kuhio Place, go 3 blocks, and then turn left on Hea Place. Drive to the end of the road.

❸ **Halekii and Pihanakalani *Heiau*.** These ancient temples give you a taste of history and a breathtaking view. See p 316, ❹.

Return to Hwy. 340. After the town of Waihee, the road narrows and becomes very winding. Continue to Kahakuloa village, which is after MM 15.

❹ **Kahakuloa.** At this picturesque village, with a dozen weather-worn houses, a church with a red-tile roof, and vivid green taro patches, life hasn't changed much during the past few decades.

From the *heiau* to Wailuku, retrace your steps on Hwy. 340. Just after the Wailuku Industrial Park, turn right on Lower Main St., which becomes East Main. Veer to the right at the fork to Waiale Dr. to stay on East Main St. Turn right on Market St., go 1 block, turn left on Vineyard St., and then go 1 more block to the Maui Bake Shop.

> *End your garden and culinary tour of the beautiful Alii Kula Lavendar Farm with a sumptuous lunch made from the farm's lavender products.*

⑤ **Maui Bake Shop.** Resist the temptation to buy the great-smelling breads, baked in one of Maui's oldest brick ovens, installed in 1935; bypass the sumptuous fresh-fruit gâteaux, puff pastries, and dozens of other baked goods and confections; and head for my favorite: white-chocolate macadamia nut cheesecake. See p 316.

The Best of Molokai in 1 Week

Only 38 miles from end to end and just 10 miles wide, Molokai stands like a big green wedge in the blue Pacific. This long, narrow island is like yin and yang: On the West End of the island is a flat, austere, arid desert; on the East End is a lush, green, tropical Eden. Three volcanic eruptions formed Molokai; the last produced the island's "thumb"—a peninsula jutting out of the steep cliffs of the north shore like a punctuation mark on the island's geological story.

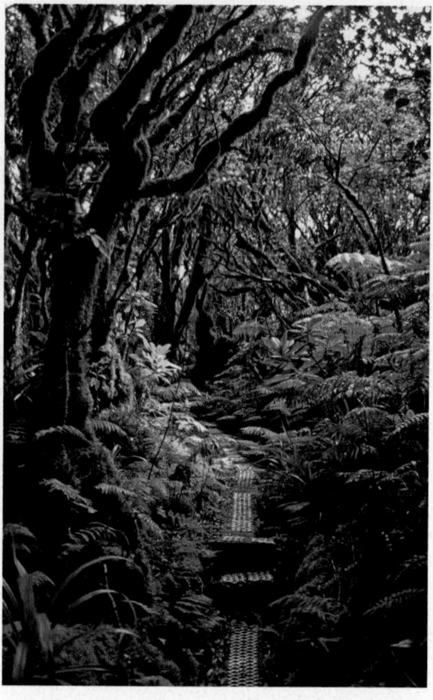

> *Stroll through exotic native vegetation on the beautiful Pepeopae boardwalk trail, which runs through Molokai's Kamakou Preserve.*

START Kaunakakai. **FINISH** Kawaaloa Bay, North Shore. **TRIP LENGTH** 1 week and 174 miles.

Days 1–3

1–16. Follow "The Best of Molokai in 3 Days" tour starting on p 416.

Day 4

From Kaunakakai head east on Hwy. 450 until just before MM 16.

(17) **Mana'e Goods and Grindz.** Before you hit the beach, get a takeout lunch from this quick-stop market/lunch counter. It's nothing fancy, and that's what I love about it. Near mile marker 16 in the Pukoo area en route to the East End, this tiny store appears like a mirage, complete with large parking area and picnic tables. The place serves omelets, Portuguese sausage, and other breakfast specials (brunch is very popular), then segues into sandwiches, salads, mahimahi plates, and varied over-the-counter lunch offerings, served on paper plates with plastic utensils. Favorites include the mahimahi plate lunch, the chicken katsu, and the Mexican plate, each one with a tried-and-true home-cooked flavor. There are daily specials, ethnic dishes, and some vegetarian options, as well as burgers (including a killer veggie burger), saimin, and legendary desserts. Made-on-Maui Roselani ice cream is a featured attraction. A Molokai treasure, this is the only grocery store on the East End. Hwy. 450, near MM 16, Pukoo. ☎ 808/558-8498. $.

Return to Hwy. 450, and continue east to MM 20. Look for the sandy beach between MM 20 and MM 21.

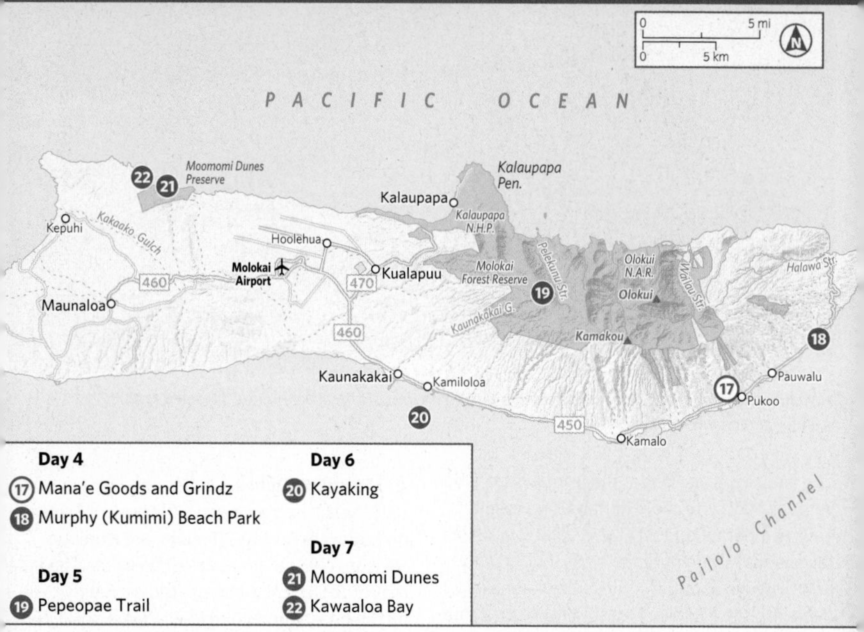

18 ★ kids **Murphy (Kumimi) Beach Park.** This beach, between mile markers 20 and 21 off Kamehameha V Hwy., is a great place to spend the afternoon. The reef here is easily reachable, and the waters are calm year-round. In 1970 the Molokai Jaycees wanted to create a sandy beach park with a good swimming area for the children of the East End. They chose a section known as Kumimi Beach, which was owned by the Pu'u o Hoku Ranch. The beach was a dump—literally. The ranch owner, George Murphy, gave his permission to use the site as a park, and the Jaycees cleaned it up and built three small pavilions, adding picnic tables and barbecue grills. Officially, the park is called the George Murphy Beach Park (shortened to Murphy Beach Park), but some old-timers still call it Kumimi Beach, and, just to make things really confusing, some people call it Jaycees Park. No matter what you call it, this small park is shaded by ironwood trees that line a white-sand beach. It's generally a very safe swimming area. On calm days snorkeling and diving are great outside the reef. Fishermen also frequently come here to look for papio and other island fish. ⏲ 3–5 hr., **Hwy. 450, btw. MM 20 and MM 21, Waialua.**

Take Hwy. 450 west back to Kaunakakai.

Day 5

To get to the trail head, you'll need a four-wheel-drive vehicle. Take Hwy. 460 west from Kaunakakai for 3½ miles, and turn right before the Manawainui Bridge onto the unmarked Molokai Forest Reserve Rd. (sorry, there aren't any signs). The pavement ends at the cemetery; continue on the dirt road. After about 2 to 2½ miles, you'll see a sign telling you that you are now in the Molokai Forest Reserve. At the Waikolu Lookout and picnic area, which is just over 9 miles on the Molokai Forest Reserve Rd., sign in at the box near the entrance. Continue on the road for another 5 miles to a fork in the road with the sign PUU KOLEKOLE pointing to the right side of the fork. Do not turn right; instead, continue straight at the fork, which leads to the clearly marked trail head. The drive will take about 45 minutes.

19 ★★ **Pepeopae Trail.** Molokai's most awesome hike takes you back a few million years. On the cloud-draped trail (actually a boardwalk across the bog), you'll see mosses, sedges, native violets, knee-high ancient ohia, and lichens that evolved in total isolation over eons. Eerie, intermittent mists blowing in and out will give you an idea of this island at its creation. The narrow boardwalk, built by volunteers, protects the

> *Molokai's Moomomi Dunes have yielded amazing discoveries of ancient burial sites and rare, endangered plant species.*

bog and keeps you out of the primal ooze. Don't venture off it; you could damage this fragile environment or get lost. The 3-mile round-trip takes about 90 minutes to hike—but first you have to drive about 20 miles from Kaunakakai, deep into the Molokai Forest Reserve on a four-wheel-drive-only road. ⏱ 8 hr. Plan a full day for this outing. Better yet, go on a guided nature hike with the Nature Conservancy of Hawaii, which guards this unusual ecosystem. For information, write to the Nature Conservancy at 1116 Smith St., Suite 201, Honolulu, HI 96817. No permit is required for this easy hike. Call ahead (☎ 808/537-4508 or 808/553-5236; www.nature.org) to check on the condition of the ungraded, four-wheel-drive-only, red-dirt road that leads to the trail head and to let people know that you'll be up there.

Day 6

20 ★★ Kayaking from Kaunakakai to Kamalo. Sign up with Molokai Outdoors for their easy "downwind" kayak tour. Beginners to advanced kayakers can enjoy paddling 6 miles "downwind" along the stretch of pristine reef offshore. If conditions permit, the tour stops for snorkeling. Cost is $89, plus an additional $10 if you want lunch, and includes all equipment (kayak, life vests, and snorkel gear). ⏱ 4-6 hr. ☎ 877/553-4477 or 808/553-4477; www.molokai-outdoors.com.

Day 7

Take Hwy. 460 (Mauna Loa Hwy.) from Kaunakakai. Turn right onto Hwy. 470, and follow it to Kualapuu. At Kualapuu turn left on Hwy. 480 and go through Hoolehua village; it's 3 miles to the bay.

21 Moomomi Dunes. Undisturbed for centuries, the 920-acre preserve Moomomi Dunes, on Molokai's northwest shore, are a unique treasure chest of great scientific value. The area may look like just a pile of sand as you fly over on the final approach to Hoolehua Airport, but Moomomi Dunes is much more than that. Archaeologists have found adz quarries, ancient Hawaiian burial sites, and shelter caves; botanists have identified five endangered plant species; and marine biologists are finding evidence that endangered green sea turtles are coming out from the waters once again to lay eggs here. The greatest discovery, however, belongs to Smithsonian Institute ornithologists, who have found bones of prehistoric birds—some of them flightless—that existed nowhere else on earth. Accessible by jeep trails that thread downhill to the shore, this wild coast is buffeted by strong afternoon breezes. It's hot, dry, and windy, so take water, sunscreen, and a windbreaker. ⏱ 3-4 hr. Plan in advance: Sign up for the monthly guided nature tours led by the Nature Conservancy of Hawaii; call ☎ 808/553-5236 or 808/524-0779 for an exact schedule and details.

Proceed on foot to the left. After about a 20-minute walk, you'll see a fabulous golden-sand beach.

22 Kawaaloa Bay. You'll most likely have this golden-sand beach all to yourself. ***Warning:*** Due to the rough seas, stay out of the water. Walk the beach instead; this is the perfect place to say aloha to Molokai. ⏱ 1-2 hr. North Shore.

> *An arresting aerial view of Molokai's rugged North Shore cliffs, the highest sea cliffs in the world.*

The Best of Lanai in 3 Days

Three days is ideal for Lanai. It gives you the opportunity to explore the island one day, relax on the beach the next, and then indulge in your favorite adventure: either hiking, some of the best scuba diving and snorkeling in the state, or golfing.

> You may have the surf to yourself on Lanai's often-deserted Polihua Beach.

START & FINISH Lanai City. **TRIP LENGTH** 3 days and 85 miles.

Day 1

Leave Lanai City heading north on Lanai Ave. and then right to Hwy. 430 (Keomuku Hwy.). Turn left on Polihua Rd., just behind the stables and before the tennis courts (look for the rock sign GARDENS OF THE GODS). The next 26 miles are dirt jeep trails and will take 60 to 75 minutes all the way down to the beach.

❶ ★★ kids **Polihua Beach.** Lanai's largest white-sand beach is a great spot to begin the journey. The beach generally is not safe for swimming (strong currents) and it can be windy here, but it most likely will be deserted and you'll have a great view of Molokai in the distance. So many

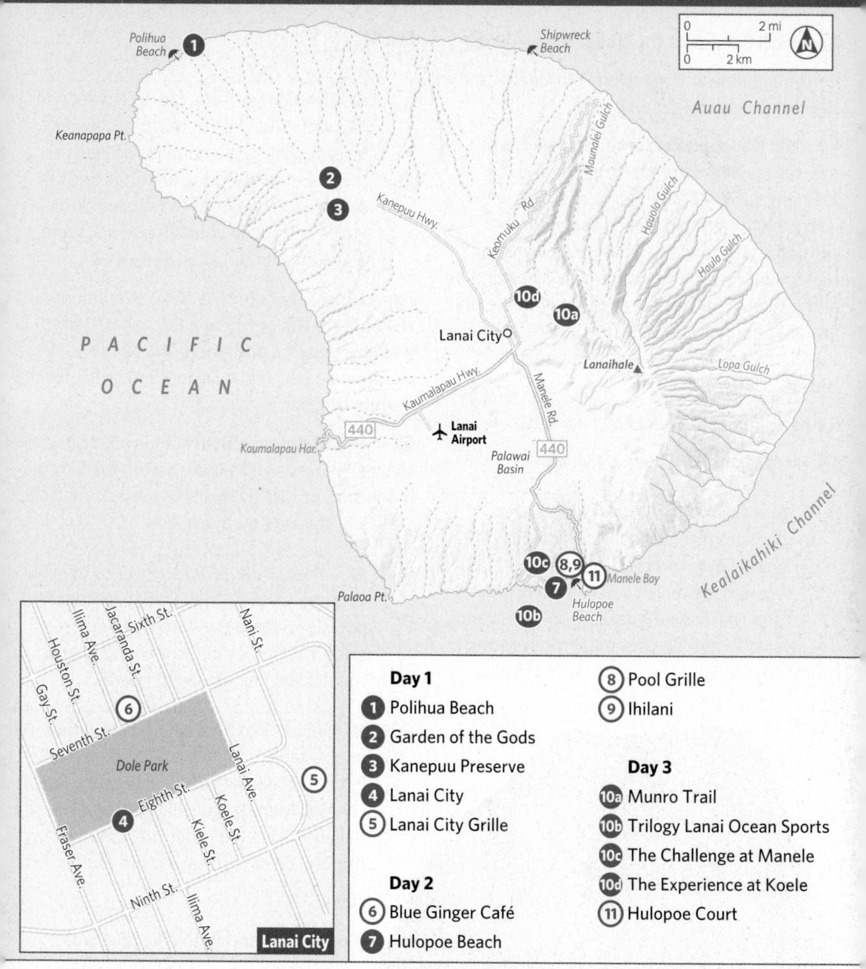

sea turtles once hauled themselves out of the water to lay their eggs in the sunbaked sand on Lanai's northwestern shore that Hawaiians named the beach here *Polihua,* or "egg nest." Although the endangered green sea turtles are making a comeback, they're seldom seen here now. You're more likely to spot an offshore whale (in season) or the perennial litter that washes up onto this deserted beach. There are no facilities, so bring water and sunscreen. Relax for a couple of hours, eat lunch, and walk the beach looking for treasure.

Retrace your route back on Polihua Rd. for about 12 miles and 45 minutes.

Travel Tips

See the box on p 450 for information on getting to and around Lanai. Generally you will not need a car if you are staying at one of the two resorts or at the Hotel Lanai (they provide shuttle bus service), but exploring Lanai's many back roads is a fantastic opportunity to go four-wheeling. Make sure to grab a picnic lunch from **Pele's Other Garden** (p 464) before you head out of Lanai City.

2 ★★ kids **Garden of the Gods.** See p 449, **2**.

Continue another 5 miles on Polihua Rd. to the sign for Kanepuu Preserve.

3 ★ kids **Kanepuu Preserve.** Stop and take this self-guided nature trail, about a 10- to 15-minute walk through eight stations, with interpretive signs explaining the natural or cultural significance of what you're seeing. Kanepuu is one of the last remaining examples of the type of forest that once covered the dry lowlands throughout the state. There are some 49 plant species here that are found only in Hawaii. ⏱ 15 min.

Retrace your route back to Lanai City.

4 ★★ kids **Lanai City.** See p 450, **5**.

---

⑤ ★ **Lanai City Grille.** Plan to have dinner in this old-fashioned country lodge dining room in the Hotel Lanai. I recommend a dish you will get only on Lanai: pan-seared, caught-on-the-island venison, served over mushroom risotto. See p 464.

Day 2

---

⑥ **Blue Ginger Cafe.** Start your second day with breakfast at this tiny cafe. My favorite dish is the homemade French toast. Get a refill on your coffee and sit outside on the porch and chat with the locals; introduce yourself and ask them questions about Lanai. See p 462.

From Lanai City take Hwy. 440 (Kaumalapau Hwy.). Turn left at Manele Rd., where Hwy. 440 continues. Continue to the end to Hulopoe Beach. Allow 30 to 35 minutes for the 11-mile trip.

7 ★★★ kids **Hulopoe Beach.** Plan a lazy day at the beach. Get a good book, watch the kids play in the surf, or take a long, slow walk around the crescent-shaped bay. See p 454.

---

⑧ ★ **Pool Grille.** Wander over to the Four Seasons Lanai at Manele Bay for lunch poolside, where the yummy calamari salad with crispy chow mein noodles is "onolicious," as we say in Hawaii.

---

⑨ **Ihilani.** Plan on a splurge for dinner—book a table here to watch the sun sink into the ocean, at the Four Seasons Resort Lanai at Manele Bay, followed by exquisite Italian cuisine (I'd order the Kona lobster risotto). Be sure to save room for dessert.

Day 3

For those wanting to hike or drive the Munro Trail, it begins at Lanai Cemetery along Keomoku Rd. (Hwy. 430). If you are interested in taking the Trilogy sail-snorkel, the boat leaves from Manele Boat Harbor. From Lanai City, take Hwy. 440 (Kaumalapau Hwy.) and continue to the end of the road. Allow 30 to 35 minutes for the trip. The Experience at Koele Golf Course is next door to the Lodge at Koele in Lanai City; and the Challenge at Manele is next door to the Four Seasons Resort Lanai at Manele Bay.

> *Strewn with natural rock sculptures, Lanai's Garden of the Gods is a breathtaking testimony to the art of nature.*

> Hulopoe Beach is a lazy and relaxing destination for families looking for a laid-back day in the sun.

> Sip on a tropical concoction at the Lanai City Grill.

⑩ **Adventures on Land or Water.** On your third day, if it hasn't been raining and the ground is dry, do a little exploring. Here are a few options: The truly ambitious can spend the day (plan on at least 7 hr.) climbing to the top of Lanai at Lanai-hale on the ★★★ Ⓐ **Munro Trail** (p 458). This tough, 11-mile (round-trip) uphill climb through groves of Norfolk Island pines begins at Lanai Cemetery along Keomoku Road (Hwy. 430). It's a lung-buster, but the views from the top are worth the effort. If you'd rather go out on (or into) the water, contact Ⓑ ★★★ kids **Trilogy Lanai Ocean Sports** (☎ 888/MAUI-800 (628-4800); www.visitlanai.com) about their sailing-snorkeling, whale-watching, or scuba trips. Golfers can head for either Ⓒ ★★★ **The Challenge at Manele** (p 456), a target-style, desert-links course designed by Jack Nicklaus, or Ⓓ ★★ **The Experience at Koele** (p 456), a traditional par-72 course designed by Greg Norman.

⑪ **Hulopoe Court.** Have dinner at this restaurant in the Four Seasons Resort Lanai at Manele Bay. See p 463.

The Best of Kauai in 1 Week

Hawaii's oldest island, ringed with white-sand beaches, is small and easy to circumnavigate in a week. But there are so many wonderful things to do and see that you may find yourself wishing you had more time.

> *Rocky bluffs surround peaceful beaches on the Na Pali Coast, which you can only reach by helicopter, boat, or a brutal 22-mile hike.*

START Lihue. **FINISH** Kokee State Park. **TRIP LENGTH** 1 week and 106 miles.

Day 1

1-6 See Day 1 of "The Best of Kauai in 3 Days," p 472.

Day 2

7 ★★★ **Waimea Canyon.** Take some time to hike "The Grand Canyon of the Pacific." See p 492, 9.

8 kids **Russian Fort Elizabeth State Historical Park.** Take a self-guided tour through the ruins of this star-shaped fort. See p 491, 4.

Day 3

9 **Kokee State Park Trails.** If you aren't too sore from hiking in Waimea Canyon, head back up the mountain another 16 miles up the hill from the Waimea Canyon Lookout, where at 4,000 feet lie wonderful forest trails. See p 509.

Day 2
- 7 Waimea Canyon
- 8 Russian Fort Elizabeth State Historical Park

Day 3
- 9 Kokee State Park Trails
- 10 Kokee Lodge

Day 4
- 11 Kukuiula Small Boat Harbor
- 12 The Beach House

Day 5
- 13 Polihale State Park

Day 6
- 14 Na Pali Coast

Day 7
- 15 Kilauea Point National Wildlife Refuge
- 16 Kilauea Fish Market
- 17 Na Aina Kai Botanical Gardens

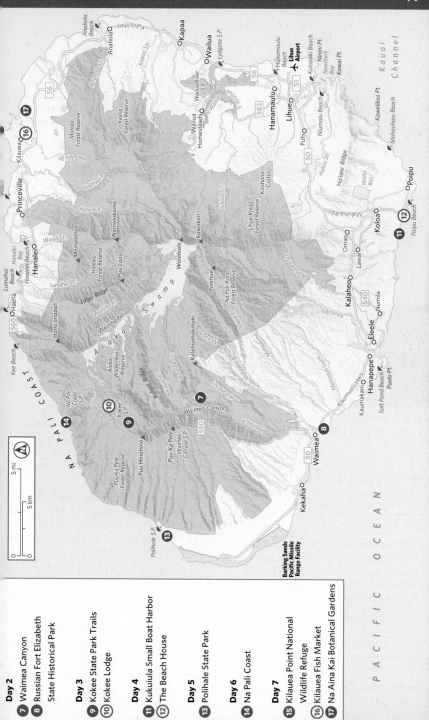

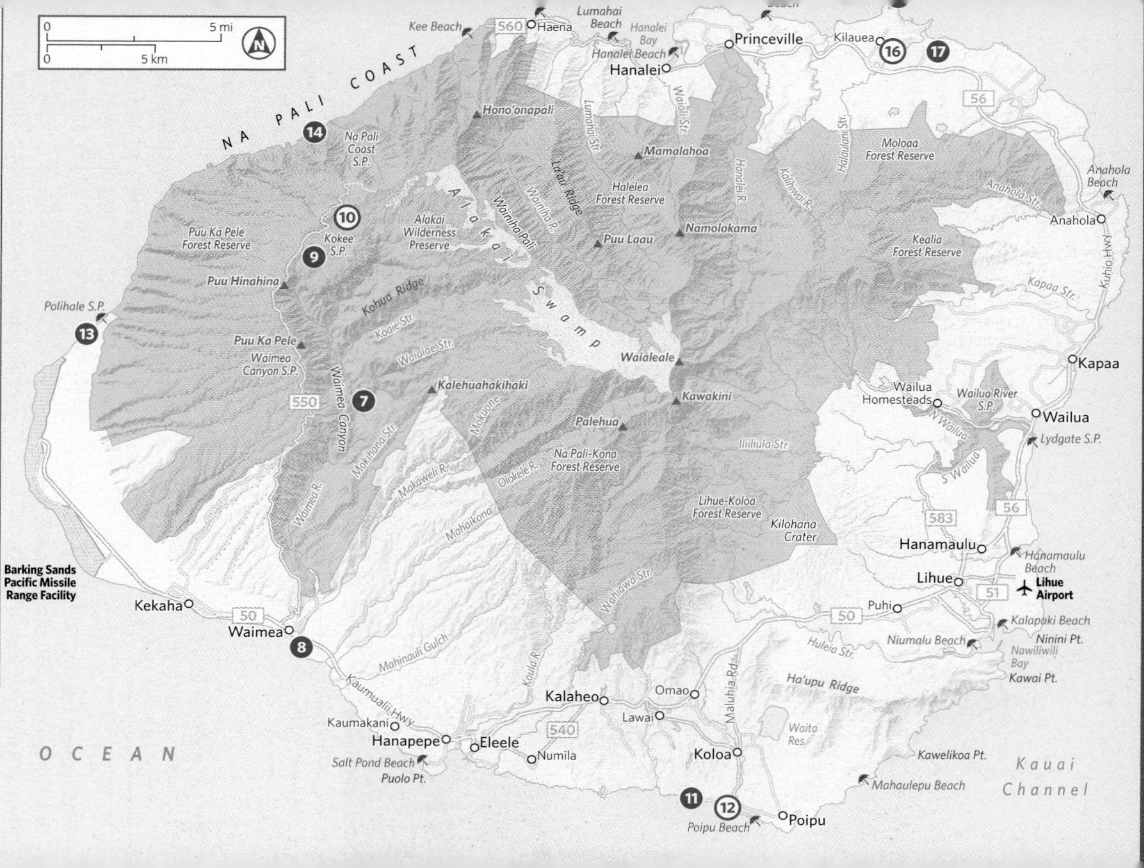

> *Share the surf with beautiful locals (and local creatures) on the unspoiled shores in western Kauai.*

⑩ **Kokee Lodge.** Stop for a warm drink and a quick snack at this quaint cafe in the state park. See p 548.

Day 4

Continue east on Hwy. 50 for 16 miles, then turn right on Hwy. 530 (Koloa Rd.). At Koloa town turn right on Poipu Rd. (Hwy. 520). When the road forks, veer right onto Lawai Rd., then go about 1½ miles to:

⓫ **Kukuiula Small Boat Harbor.** After a day in the mountains, it's time to head to the beach again. If you like sailing and snorkeling, book a **sail-snorkel tour** out of the Kukuiula Small Boat Harbor. See p 522.

Retrace your route back on Lawai Rd. Go about ¾ of a mile.

⑫ **The Beach House.** Stop for sunset drinks and pupu or stay for a fabulous dinner. See p 535.

Day 5

⓭ **Polihale State Park.** Spend the day at Kauai's largest beach and be sure to check out the "barking" sands at **Barking Sands Beach.** See p 505.

Day 6

⓮ **Na Pali Coast.** One of Hawaii's most spectacular natural attractions is Kauai's Na Pali Coast. Unless you're willing to make an arduous 22-mile hike (see p 515), there are only two ways to see it: by helicopter (see p 520) or by boat. Picture yourself cruising the rugged Na Pali coastline in a 42-foot ketch-rigged yacht under full sail, watching the sunset as you enjoy a tropical cocktail, or speeding through the aquamarine water in a 40-foot trimaran as porpoises play off the bow. When the Pacific humpback whales make their annual visit to Hawaii from December to March, they swim right by Kauai. In season, most boats on Kauai—including sail- and power-boats—combine whale-watching with their regular adventures. See "Sailing," p 522.

Day 7

From the south, take Hwy. 56 out of Lihue north to Kilauea, after MM 23. Turn right at the sign for Kilauea, then take the first left on to Kilauea Rd. (also known as Lighthouse Rd.), and follow it all the way to the end at the ocean and the entry for:

⓯ **Kilauea Point National Wildlife Refuge.** This 200-acre habitat is for the birds—Hawaii's ocean birds, that is. Bring a picnic, join a guided hike, or just wander through the fairyland of the wilderness area. ½–1 hr.

Retrace your route back about a mile to:

⑯ **Kilauea Fish Market.** Stop for a snack at this roadside cafe. See p 540.

Continue on Kilauea Rd. to the highway and turn left. Just after MM 22, turn left (toward the ocean) on Wailapa Rd. and follow it to the end.

⓱ ★★★ kids **Na Aina Kai Botanical Gardens.** Finish up the day with a visit to this magical, off-the-beaten-path garden. See p 476 ❹.

> *The 20-mile River of the Great Sacred Spirit flows into Opaekaa Falls deep in the lush hills of Wailua River State Park.*

The Best of Kauai in 2 Weeks

Two weeks on Kauai is perfect. It allows you to see everything at a much slower pace with plenty of relaxation and lazy beach days. I'd suggest adding lots of naps, vegging out on the beach, and stopping to smell all the exotic flowers. For your first week on the island, follow the "Best of Kauai in 1 Week" tour starting on p 78. This tour starts on Day 8 of your visit.

> *Rugged Kauai may be best seen on horseback; many tours will take you to hidden falls and beaches.*

START Kilaeua **FINISH** Lihue.
TRIP LENGTH 2 weeks and 310 miles.

Day 8

From Kilauea continue south on Hwy. 56 for 17 miles. At MM 6 is:

⑱ **Wailua Beach.** This beach, which features Hawaiian historical and cultural sites, is also a great place to just sit under a palm tree and figure out how you can move here permanently. See p 506.

From Wailua Beach continue south on Hwy. 56 to the stoplight and turn right onto Kuamoo Rd. (Hwy. 580). Continue up the hill, for just over 4 miles. ¼ mile past MM 4, turn left on Kaholalele Rd. and go 1 block to the end of the road. The information center is at 107 Kaholalele. Park on Temple Lane.

⑲ **San Marga Iraivan Temple.** Believe it or not, a sacred Hindu temple is being carved out of rocks from India on the banks of the Wailua River. This temple is being built to last

Day 8
18 Wailua Beach
19 San Marga Iraivan Temple

Day 9
20 Tubing
21 Zipline

Day 10
22 Kayaking
23 Horseback Riding

Day 11
24 ANARA Spa

Day 12
25 Poipu Beach
26 Brennecke's Beach Broiler

Day 13
27 Kapaa

Day 14
28 Lihue

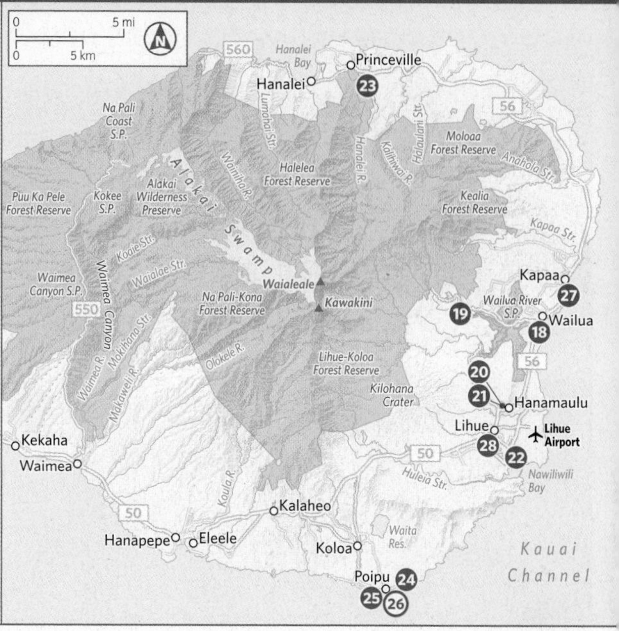

"a thousand years or more," on the 458-acre site of the Saiva Siddhanta Church monastery. In the making for years now and not expected to be completed until 2010, the Chola-style temple is the result of a vision by the late Satguru Sivaya Subramuniyaswami, known to his followers as Gurudeva, the founder of the church and its monastery. He specifically selected this site in 1970, recognizing that the Hawaiians also felt the spiritual power of this place. The Hawaiians called it *pihanakalani,* "where heaven touches the earth." See "Make a Pilgrimage to a Hindu Temple," p 497.

Day 9

From the San Marga Iraivan Temple, retrace your route back down Kaholalele Rd. Turn right on Kuamoo Rd. (Hwy. 580). Turn right on Kuhio Hwy. (Hwy. 56) and drive for 3 miles. When the road forks, continue on Hwy. 56 (veer to the right). The Kauai Backcountry office (where all tours leave from) is about a mile down the road at 3-4131 Kuhio Hwy. (Hwy. 56) in Hanamaulu.

20 **Tubing Adventure.** Sign up with Kauai Backcountry Adventures for a chance to float down the former sugarcane irrigation flumes. See p 527.

21 **Zip-Line Adventure.** This is the latest offering from Outfitters Kauai: You fly through the air tethered to a cable, skipping over treetops. See p 521.

Day 10

To get to Kauai Water Ski & Surf Co., turn left on Kuhio Hwy. (Hwy. 56) in Hanamaulu, continuing on Hwy. 56 at the fork. Just after MM 6, look for the Kinipopo Shopping Village on the ocean side of the highway.

22 **Kayak Tour.** See Kauai from the ocean, where you will skim over the ocean's (or a river's) surface coming eyeball-to-eyeball with turtles, flyingfish, and other marine creatures. See p 524.

23 **Horseback Riding Tour.** In the afternoon, view Kauai from the vantage point of a horse's back. There are a variety of different types of tours, from riding along secluded beaches to trekking back to hidden waterfalls. See p 521.

Day 11

From Lihue, take Hwy. 50 west. Just before MM 7, turn left at Hwy. 520. Take 520 to the Poipu-Koloa Bypass Rd. (Ala Kinoiki St.), and turn left. When the road ends, turn left onto Poipu Rd. In less than a mile turn right into the Grand Hyatt Kauai Resort & Spa, 1571 Poipu Rd.

> ANARA Spa's opulence and exotic treatments make it a mandatory destination for lovers of luxury.

(24) **ANARA Spa.** Relax at the best spa on Kauai. Try something new—maybe a traditional Hawaiian lomilomi massage or an ayurvedic massage (once given only to royalty for rejuvenation). Do nothing but lie around and relax. Order room service or get takeout for dinner. 1571 Poipu Rd. ☎ 800/55-HYATT (554-9288) or 808/742-1234. www.anaraspa.com.

Day 12

From the Grand Hyatt Resprt Spa retrace your steps to Poipu Rd., heading west. Turn left on Ho'owili Rd. and follow it to the end. Park in the parking lot and walk across the street to:

(25) **Poipu Beach Park.** Spend a day in the water snorkeling and eyeballing the tropical reef fish. See p 505.

(26) **Brennecke's Beach Broiler.** Grab a snack (nachos, calamari) or go for one of the gourmet burgers at this classic beach burger joint just across the street from Poipu Beach. See p 535.

Day 13

From Poipu retrace your route from Ho'owili Rd., turning right on Poipu Rd. and left on the Poipu-Koloa Bypass Rd. (Ala Kinoiki St.). When the road ends, turn right on Hwy. 520 and drive to the end. At Hwy. 50 turn right. In Lihue the highway is renamed Hwy. 56; continue on it to Kapaa.

(27) **Kapaa.** Get out the list of people you must buy gifts for and spend the day shopping in this quaint village. For our list of great places to shop, great buys, and ideas on what to take home, see p 530.

Day 14

From Kapaa retrace your steps on Hwy. 56 back to Lihue.

(28) **Lihue.** Spend your last day in Lihue. It's close to the airport, and there are plenty of things to do. See the tour "Lihue & Environs," starting on p 482, for ideas. I particularly recommend the Kauai Museum (p 484, (5)) and Kilohana (p 482, (1)).

> *End your Kauai Backcountry Adventures tour with a splash at a natural swimming hole.*

4
Oahu

My 16 Favorite Oahu Moments

The island of Oahu is filled with so many magical moments: the orange glow as the sun rises behind the outline of Diamond Head, the silvery reflection of the moon on the inky black waters of Waikiki at night, the intoxicating smell of plumeria flowers in the air, the quiet whisper of bamboo dancing in the breeze. A few more of my personal favorite Honolulu moments are described below.

> PREVIOUS PAGE *Brave bathers take a leap of faith off the rocky bluffs of Waimea Bay.* THIS PAGE *Boat cruises off the Waikiki shore offer spectacular views of the city's skyline.*

1 **Seeing Waikiki offshore.** If you think Waikiki is beautiful, wait until you see it from a boat. I strongly urge you to either take a boat cruise during the day (if you are prone to seasickness, try the ultrasmooth *Navatek 1* cruise) or, for the more romantically inclined, take a sunset cruise and watch the sun go down and the lights of Waikiki and Honolulu come up. See p 154.

2 **Experiencing a turning point in America's history: the bombing of Pearl Harbor.** I guarantee that you will never forget your reaction when you step on the deck of the USS *Arizona* Memorial at Pearl Harbor and look down at the dark oil oozing like dripping blood from the ship underneath. The full impact of that fateful day (December 7, 1941, when the 608-foot *Arizona* sank in just 9 minutes after being bombed during the Japanese air raid) wil

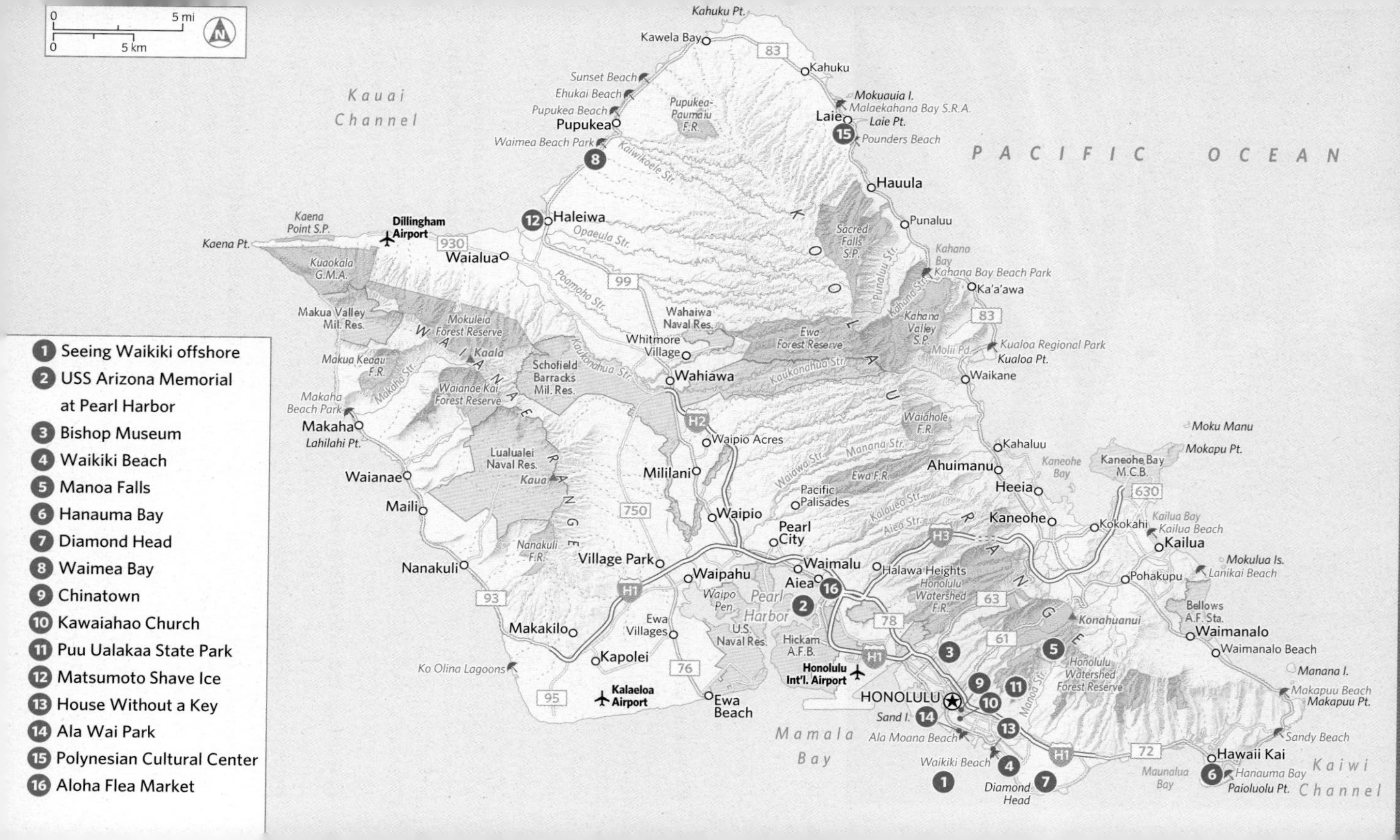

1. Seeing Waikiki offshore
2. USS Arizona Memorial at Pearl Harbor
3. Bishop Museum
4. Waikiki Beach
5. Manoa Falls
6. Hanauma Bay
7. Diamond Head
8. Waimea Bay
9. Chinatown
10. Kawaiahao Church
11. Puu Ualakaa State Park
12. Matsumoto Shave Ice
13. House Without a Key
14. Ala Wai Park
15. Polynesian Cultural Center
16. Aloha Flea Market

> *Surfers shred the traffic as they commute to the famous waves of Waikiki Beach.*

no longer seem like something from a book—it will be very real. See p 119, ①.

③ **Walking back in history.** People always ask me: "Where do I see the real Hawaii?" I send them to the Bishop Museum. Don't think dreary rooms with stuff crowded into cases; think living history, as in experiencing goose bumps as a deep booming voice breaks into Hawaiian chant when you enter the Hawaiian Hall or excitement as you watch a live performance of traditional hula. Created by a Hawaiian princess in 1899, not only is it *the* repository for Hawaiian cultural artifacts, but it also has a new Science Adventure Center, where you can step into the interior of an erupting volcano. See p 31, ⑳.

④ **Getting a tan on Waikiki Beach.** I've soaked up rays all over the globe, but nothing compares to the special experience of being kissed by the sun and serenaded by the sound of the tumbling surf as you lie on the soft sand of this world-famous beach. My favorite place to put my beach mat is directly in front of the big pink Royal Hawaiian Hotel (where the angle of the beach is perfect for sunning). It's also a great spot for people-watching. Get here early; by midday it's towel-to-towel. See p 143.

⑤ **Venturing into a rainforest.** Immerse yourself in a place where colorful birds flit among giant ferns and hanging vines, while misty sunbeams filter through a thick canopy of towering tropical trees that shelters all below in cool shadows. It's just a short hike, less than a mile, to a freshwater pool and waterfall. The emerald world of the Manoa Falls trail is a true Eden, and it's just 15 minutes from bustling Waikiki. See p 147.

⑥ **Snorkeling among the rainbow-colored fish in the warm waters of Hanauma Bay.** I love this underwater park, once a volcanic crater, because it's teeming with tropical fish and bordered by a 2,000-foot gold-sand beach. Plus, the bay's shallow water (10 ft. in places) is perfect for neophyte snorkelers. ***Tip:*** Arrive early to beat the crowds—and don't forget that the bay is closed on Tuesday. See p 140.

⑦ **Hiking to the top of Diamond Head.** See Waikiki and Honolulu from the top of Hawaii's most famous landmark. Nearly everyone can hike this 1.4-mile round-trip, which goes up to the top of the 750-foot volcanic cone, where you have a 360-degree view of Oahu. Allow an hour for the trip up and back, and don't forget your camera. See p 144.

> Just 15 minutes from Waikiki, a short hike along the Manoa Falls Trail takes you into a lush tropical rainforest.

8 Watching the North Shore's big waves. When monstrous waves—some 30 feet tall—steamroll into Waimea Bay (Nov–Mar), I head out to the North Shore for an amazing show: watching the best surfers in the world paddle out to challenge these freight trains. It's shocking to see how small they appear in the lip of the giant waves. My favorite part is feeling those waves when they break on the shore—the ground actually shakes, and everyone on the beach is covered with salt-spray mist. An unforgettable experience that won't cost you a dime. See p 143.

9 Buying a lei in Chinatown. I love dipping into the cultural sights and exotic experiences to be had in Honolulu's Chinatown. Wander through this several-square-block area with its jumble of Asian shops offering herbs, Chinese groceries, and acupuncture services. Be sure to check out the lei sellers on Maunakea Street (near N. Hotel St.), where Hawaii's finest leis go for as little as $5. See p 122.

> Chinatown's Maunakea Street brims with vendors selling everything from herbs to acupuncture services to beautiful leis.

10 Attending a Hawaiian-language church service. On Sunday, I head over to the historic Kawaiahao Church, built in 1842 (considered to be the Westminster Abbey of Hawaii), for the service (which is in Hawaiian) and the Hawaiian music. You can practically feel the presence of the Hawaiian monarchy, many of whom were crowned in this building. See p 33, 24.

11 Basking in the best sunset you'll ever see. Anyone can stand on the beach and watch the sun set, but my favorite viewing point for saying *aloha-oe* to Sol is from a 1,048-foot hill named after a sweet potato. It's more romantic than it

> *Visitors sway to steel guitar and hula music at the Hawaii slack key guitar festival.*

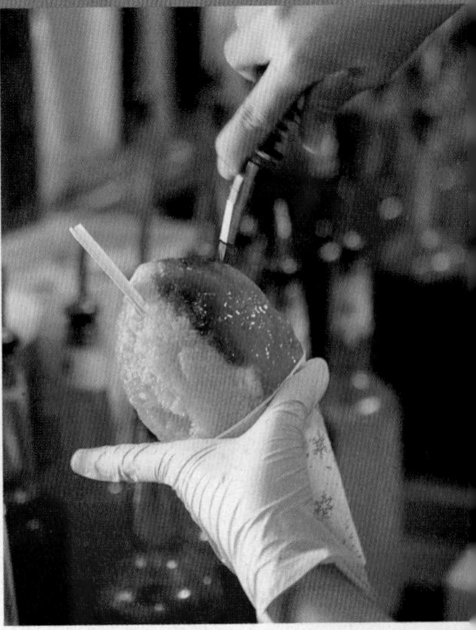

> *Head to Matsumoto's in Haleiwa for delicious shaved ices drenched in exotic flavors like guava and coconut.*

sounds—Puu Ualakaa State Park, at the end of Round Top Drive, translates into "rolling sweet potato hill" (early planters used gravity to harvest their crops). This majestic view of the sunset is not to be missed. See p 31, ⑲.

⑫ **Ordering a shave ice in a tropical flavor you can hardly pronounce.** I think you can actually taste the islands by slurping "shave ice." It's similar to a snow cone, but the ice is actually shaved and then covered with an exotic flavor poured over the top. My favorite is *li hing mui* (lee hing *moo*-ee), or preserved plum, with sweet Japanese adzuki beans hidden inside. This taste of tropical paradise goes for less than $1.50 at Matsumoto Shave Ice in Haleiwa. See p 97, ⑪.

⑬ **Listening to the soothing sounds of Hawaiian music.** Just before sunset, I head for the huge banyan tree at The Veranda in the Westin Moana Surfrider, Waikiki, order a libation, and sway to live Hawaiian music. Another quintessential sunset oasis is Halekulani's House Without a Key, a sophisticated oceanfront lounge with wonderful hula and steel guitar music, a great view of Diamond Head, and the best mai tais on the island. See p 28.

⑭ **Discovering the ancient Hawaiian sport of canoe paddling.** For something you most likely will see only in Hawaii, find a comfortable spot at Ala Wai Park, next to the canal, and watch hundreds of canoe paddlers re-create this centuries-old sport of taking traditional Hawaiian canoes out to sea. Or try it yourself off Waikiki Beach. See p 584.

⑮ **Immersing yourself at the Polynesian Cultural Center.** Even though I have traveled throughout the Pacific, I still love spending a day at the Polynesian Cultural Center, a kind of living museum of Polynesia. Here you can see firsthand the lifestyles, songs, dance, costumes and architecture of seven Pacific islands or archipelagos—Fiji, New Zealand, Marquesas, Samoa, Tahiti, Tonga, and Hawaii—in the re-created villages scattered throughout a 42-acre lagoon park. See p 97, ⑬.

⑯ **Finding a bargain at the Aloha Flea Market.** I come here more for entertainment than pure shopping. Just $1 will get you into this all-day show at the Aloha Stadium parking lot, where more than 1,000 vendors sell everything from junk to jewels. Half the fun is talking to the vendors and listening to their stories. Serious shoppers go early for the best deals. See p 169.

Getting Married in Paradise

Hawaii is a great place for a wedding. Not only does the entire island exude romance and natural beauty, but after the ceremony, you're only a few steps away from the perfect honeymoon.

More than 20,000 marriages are performed each year on the islands, and nearly half of the couples married here are from somewhere else. This booming business has spawned dozens of companies that can help you organize a long-distance event and stage an unforgettable wedding.

The easiest way to plan your wedding is to let someone else handle it at the resort or hotel where you'll be staying. Most resorts and hotels have wedding coordinators who can plan everything from a simple, (relatively) low-cost wedding to an extravaganza that people will talk about for years. Remember that resorts can be pricey—be frank with your wedding coordinator if you want to keep costs down. You don't have to use a coordinator: You can also plan your own island wedding, even from afar, and not spend a fortune doing it.

You will need a marriage license. On Oahu, contact the **Marriage License Office,** Room 101 (1st floor) of the Health Department Building, 1250 Punchbowl St. (corner of Beretania and Punchbowl sts.), ☎ 808/586-4545; hawaii.gov/health/vital-records/vital-records/marriage/index.html or e-mail vr-info@doh.hawaii.gov. On Maui, contact **Marriage License Office,** State Department of Health Building, 54 S. High St., Wailuku, HI 96793 (☎ 808/984-8210; hawaii.gov/health/vital-records/vital-records/marriage/index.html). Once in Hawaii, the prospective bride and groom must go together to the marriage-licensing agent to get a license. A license costs $60 and is good for 30 days. The only requirements for a marriage license are that both parties are 15 years of age or older (couples 15–17 years old must have proof of age, written consent of both parents, and the written approval of the judge of the family court) and are not more closely related than first cousins.

The Best of Oahu in 3 Days

There is more to Oahu than just Honolulu or Waikiki; it's an entire island. It's best to spend at least a week exploring, but it is possible to see the highlights of this romantic isle in just 3 days. Each day starts and finishes in Waikiki, which like most urban cities has traffic congestion, especially during rush hour, so allow plenty of driving time. On this tour you'll see the best Waikiki has to offer: Pearl Harbor, the Bishop Museum, Chinatown, and the North Shore.

> *The ancient Hawaiian sport of canoe paddling comes to life during race season, when hundreds of paddlers take to the open water.*

START & FINISH Waikiki.
TRIP LENGTH 3 days and 109 miles.

Day 1

❶ ★★★ kids **Waikiki Beach,** ❷ ★★ kids **Waikiki Aquarium,** and ③ ★★★ **House Without a Key at the Halekulani Hotel.** For details, see Day 1 in "The Best of Oahu in 1 Week," p 26, ❶-❸.

More of Oahu

See chapter 3 for my suggested 1- and 2-week Oahu itineraries.

Day 2

Drive west on H-1 past the airport; take the USS *Arizona* Memorial exit and follow the green-and-white signs. There's ample free parking. TheBus: 20.

❹ ★★★ kids **USS *Arizona* Memorial at Pearl Harbor,** ❺ ★ kids **USS *Bowfin* Submarine Museum & Park,** and ❻ ★ kids **USS *Missouri* Memorial.** Start off your day viewing wartime Honolulu in the morning. See p 119, ❶-❸.

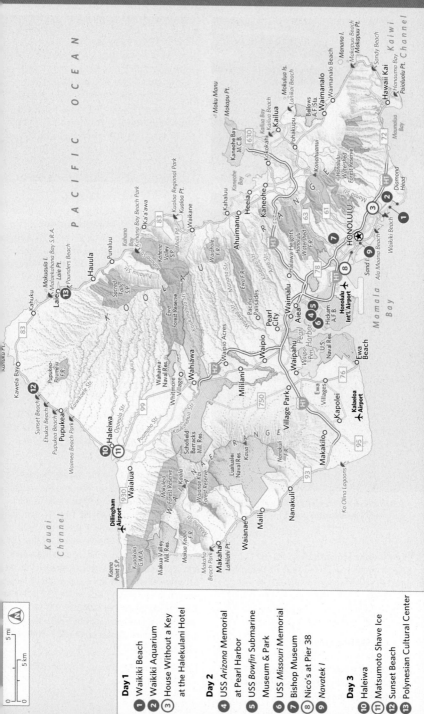

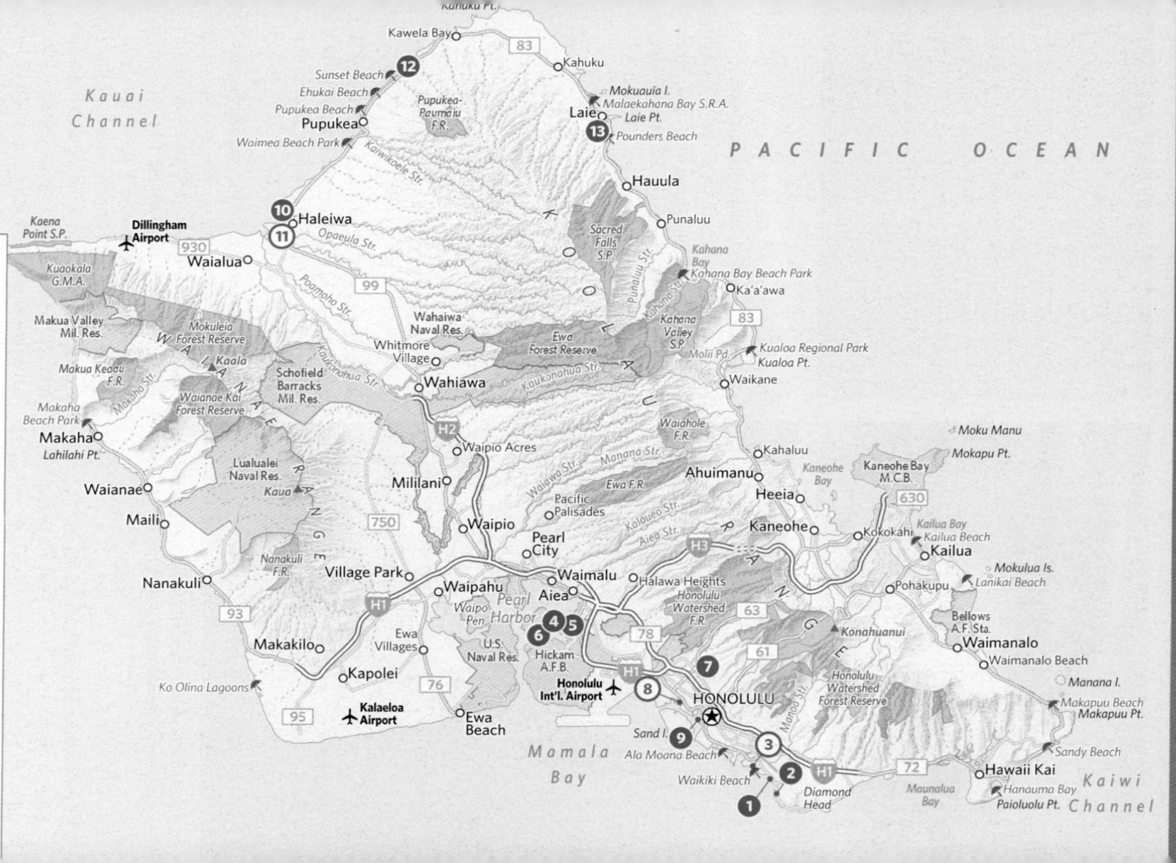

Day 1

1. Waikiki Beach
2. Waikiki Aquarium
3. House Without a Key at the Halekulani Hotel

Day 2

4. USS *Arizona* Memorial at Pearl Harbor
5. USS *Bowfin* Submarine Museum & Park
6. USS *Missouri* Memorial
7. Bishop Museum
8. Nico's at Pier 38
9. *Navatek I*

Day 3

10. Haleiwa
11. Matsumoto Shave Ice
12. Sunset Beach
13. Polynesian Cultural Center

> *Even the license plates tell the story of what's on everybody's minds on the busy streets of Haleiwa.*

From Arizona Memorial Rd. turn right on Kamehameha Hwy. (Hwy. 99). Take the ramp onto H-1 east toward Honolulu. Take exit 20A (Likelike Hwy. exit). Turn left on Kalihi St. (Hwy. 63) to Bernice St., and turn right. TheBus: 40, transfer to City Express B.

7 ★★★ kids **Bishop Museum.** This entrancing museum may be the highlight of your trip. Find out everything you've always wanted to know about Hawaii, from grass shacks to how a volcano works. See p 31, 20.

Travel Tip

Don't max out your days. You're in Hawaii—which means you should allow some time to do nothing but relax. Ease into your vacation. Due to jet lag, you'll probably be tired your first day, and hitting the pillow at 8 or 9pm might sound good. Don't be surprised if you wake up your first morning in Hawaii before the sun comes up. Your internal clock might still be set 2 to 6 hours earlier than Hawaii.

Turn right from the Bishop Museum parking lot onto Bernice St. and right again on Houghtailing St., which becomes Waiaskamilo Rd. Turn left on Dillingham Blvd. and right on Alakawa St. into the Honolulu Harbor Pier area. Watch for signs to Nico's. TheBus: 7, transfer to 19 or 20.

8 ★★ kids **Nico's at Pier 38.** This gourmet French restaurant serves fresh island fish at frugal lunch prices: You can get a takeout lunch of furikake-panseared ahi with the addicting ginger-garlic-cilantro dip, plus greens or macaroni salad, for only $8.75. See p 183.

Retrace your route to Nimitz Hwy. (Hwy. 92), and make a right toward Waikiki. Look for the sign for Pier 6 (just after Aloha Tower) and turn right. TheBus: 19 or 20.

9 ★ kids ***Navatek 1.*** On the *Navatek* Sunset Dinner Cruise, watch the sun sink into the waters of the Pacific, then turn and face land as the lights of Waikiki slowly blink. This 140-foot-long SWATH (Small Waterplane Area Twin Hull) vessel rests on twin torpedo-like hulls that cut through the water so you don't bob like a cork and spill your mai tai (or get seasick). If you go between January and April, you might be lucky enough to see a humpback whale. ⏱ 2 hr. Aloha Tower Marketplace, Pier 6. ☎ 808/973-1311. www.hawaiiactive.com/oahu-activities/oahu-navatek-dinnercruise.html. Dinner cruises $89–$149 adults, $53–$92 children 2–11.

Take a right on Ala Moana Blvd. and follow it into Waikiki. TheBus: 19 or 20.

Day 3

Take H-1 west out of Waikiki to the H-2 north exit (exit 8A) toward Mililani/Wahiwa. After 7 miles H-2 becomes Kamehameha Hwy. (Hwy. 80). Look for the turnoff to Haleiwa town. TheBus: 19, transfer to 52.

10 ★★★ kids **Haleiwa.** Start your day touring this famous North Shore surfing town. See p 128, 4.

---

11 ★ kids **Matsumoto Shave Ice.** For a tropical taste of the islands, stop at this nearly 50-year-old shop where Hawaii's rendition of a snow cone is served. The ice is shaved instead of crushed, giving it a unique texture. My favorite of the rainbow of flavors available is the *li hing mui* (pronounced lee hing *moo*-ee), which is preserved plum with a mixture of Chinese spices, sugar, and salt. 66-087 Kamehameha Hwy., Haleiwa. ☎ 808/637-4827. $.

Continue down Kamehameha Hwy. for about 6½ miles. TheBus: 52.

12 ★★★ kids **Sunset Beach.** During the summer months, this is a safe beach for swimming. During the winter, it's best to just sit and watch the big-wave surfers. See p 143.

Drive another 11½ miles down Kamehameha Hwy. to the town of Laie. TheBus: 52, which is renamed 55 at Turtle Bay Resort.

13 ★★ kids **Polynesian Cultural Center.** This living museum of Polynesia features the lifestyles, songs, dance, costumes, and architecture of seven Pacific islands or archipelagos—Fiji, New Zealand, Marquesas, Samoa, Tahiti, Tonga, and Hawaii—in the re-created villages scattered throughout the 42-acre lagoon park. I recommend traveling through this museum via canoe on a man-made freshwater lagoon. Each village is "inhabited" by native students from Polynesia who attend Hawaii's Brigham Young University. The park, which is operated by the Mormon Church, also features a variety of stage shows celebrating the music, dance, history, and culture of Polynesia. Stay for the show, but skip the luau. ⏱ 4–6 hr. Get there when the doors open to avoid the crowds. 55-370 Kamehameha Hwy., Laie. ☎ 800/367-7060, 808/293-3333, or 808/923-2911. www.polynesia.com. Admission $60 adults, $45 children 5–11. Admission, IMAX, luau, and nightly show $120 adults, $85 children. Ambassador VIP (deluxe) tour $225 adults, $175 children. Mon–Sat 12–9pm.

> *Views of a Hawaiian sunset and the twinkling Honolulu skyline make the* Navatek *dinner cruise doubly appetizing.*

Continue along Kamehameha Hwy. (Hwy. 83), which follows the windward coastline for about 22 miles. Look for the sign for the Likelike Hwy. (Hwy. 63). From Likelike Hwy. take the Kalihi St./H-1 exit. Take H-1 to Waikiki. TheBus: 55, transfer to 19 or 20.

It's Sure Not New York City

Unfortunately Honolulu does not have convenient public transportation, which is why I strongly recommend that you rent a car. If that is not possible, I have added how to get around using Honolulu's public bus system, called TheBus, which costs $2. But TheBus is set up for Hawaii residents and not tourists carrying coolers, beach mats, beach toys, and other things to the beach (all carry-ons must fit under the bus seat). Some destinations may be extremely complicated, requiring several bus transfers, or TheBus may not stop right in front of your destination. Before you set out, always call **TheBus** (☎ 808/848-5555 or 808/296-1818 for recorded information) or check out www.thebus.org.

Honolulu & Oahu with Kids

If you have enough trouble getting your kids out of the house in the morning, dragging them thousands of miles away may seem like an insurmountable challenge. But family travel can be immensely rewarding, giving you new ways of seeing the world through smaller pairs of eyes. The following itinerary gives you the nuts and bolts you need to plan an affordable, safe, and fun family vacation.

> *Rafters happily brave the eye of the Tornado at the popular Wet 'n' Wild water park.*

START & FINISH Waikiki.
TRIP LENGTH 1 week and 196 miles.

Day 1

From Waikiki, take Kalakaua Ave. through Waikiki and turn left on Kapahulu Ave. Look for the zoo parking on the right.

❶ ★★ **Honolulu Zoo.** If the kids aren't too tired, head for this 43-acre municipal zoo, where my favorite section is the 10-acre African Savannah, with more than 40 African critters roaming around in the open. Special programs include the "Honolulu Zoo by Twilight Tour," which offers a behind-the-scenes look into the lives of the zoo's nocturnal residents; "Snooze in the Zoo," which is an overnight program complete with pizza, a

Travel Tip

For hotel, dining, and shopping recommendations, see p 186 (hotels), p 176 (restaurants), and p 164 (shopping).

Day 1
1 Honolulu Zoo
2 Cold Stone Creamery
3 Waikiki Aquarium
4 Waikiki Beach

Day 2
5 Haleiwa
6 Matsumoto Shave Ice
7 Sunset Beach
8 Polynesian Cultural Center

Day 3
9 USS *Arizona* Memorial at Pearl Harbor
10 USS *Bowfin* Submarine Museum & Park
11 USS *Missouri* Memorial
12 Sam Choy's Breakfast, Lunch, Crab & Big Aloha Brewery
13 Chinatown
14 *Navatek 1*

Day 4
15 Hanauma Bay
16 Halona Blowhole
17 Makapuu Point
18 Sea Life Park

Day 5
19 Bishop Museum
20 Bad Ass Coffee Company
21 Hawaii Maritime Museum
22 Iolani Palace

Day 6
23 Wet 'n' Wild

Day 7
24 Hawaii Children's Discovery Center
25 Big City Diner
26 Diamond Head
27 Atlantis Submarines

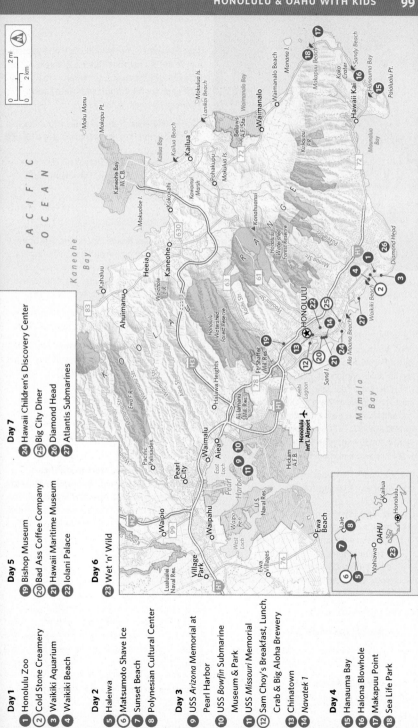

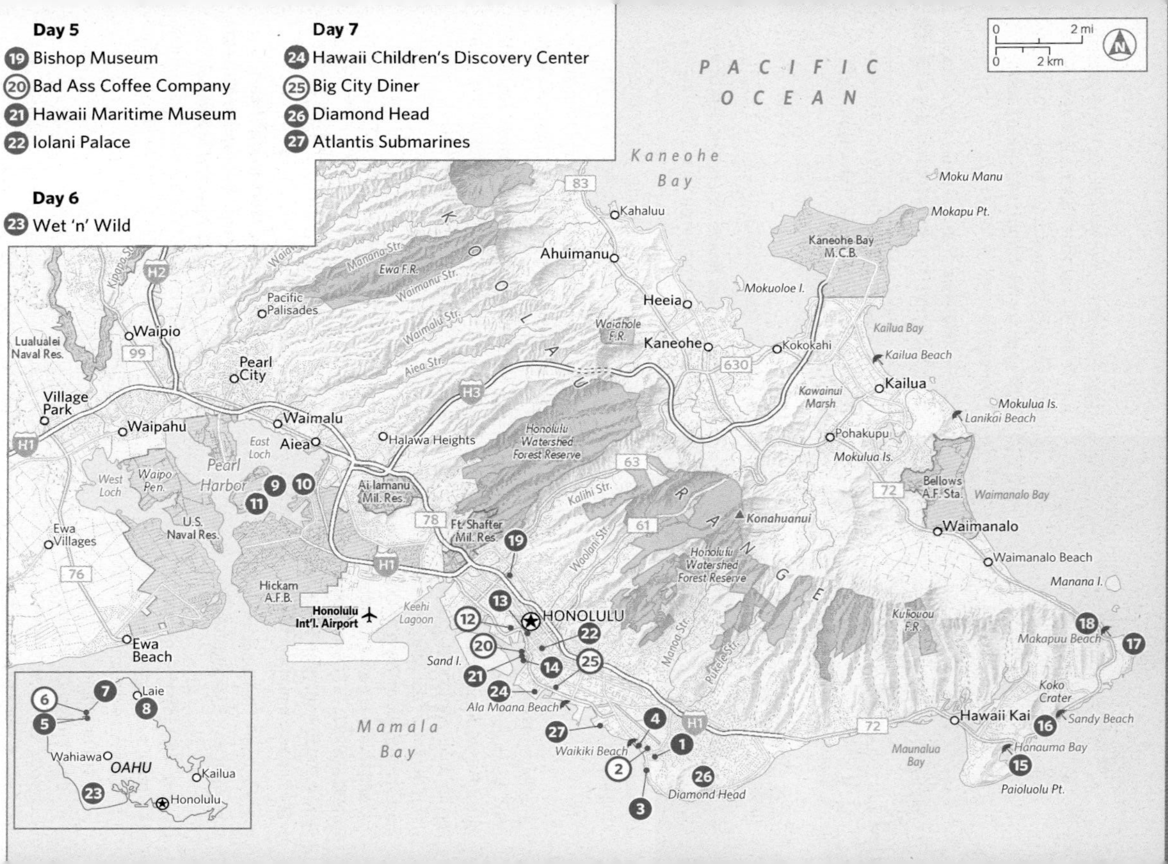

> *Hawaiian history and culture come to life at the Polynesian Cultural Center in Honolulu.*

campfire, and breakfast; and "Star Gazing at the Zoo," which combines an evening tour of the zoo with an exploration of the night sky. Contact the zoo for dates and prices. ⏱ 2–3 hr. Best time to visit is as soon as the gates open; the animals are most active in the morning. 151 Kapahulu Ave. (btw. Paki and Kalakaua aves.), at entrance to Kapiolani Park. ☎ 808/971-7171. www.honoluluzoo.org. Daily 9am–4:30pm. Admission $8 adults, $1 children 6–12, children 5 and under free. Family pass $25.

Retrace your steps back to Kapahulu Ave., and turn right on Kalakaua Ave. for 1 block.

② **Cold Stone Creamery.** It's not cheap, but it's close, it's air-conditioned, and it does have dreamy ice cream with about a zillion toppings to choose from (I love their brownies). ResortQuest Waikiki Beach Hotel, 2570 Kalakaua Ave. (at Paoakalani St.). ☎ 808/923-1656. $.

Backtrack on Kalakaua Ave.

❸ ★★ **Waikiki Aquarium**. See p 26, ❷.

Walk ewa (west) along the beach until you find a spot you like.

❹ ★★★ **Waikiki Beach.** Finish off your day with some fun in the sun. See p 143.

Day 2

Take H-1 west out of Waikiki to the H-2 north exit (exit 8A) toward Mililani/Wahiwa. After 7 miles H-2 becomes Kamehameha Hwy. (Hwy. 80). Look for the turnoff to Haleiwa town. TheBus: 19, transfer to 52.

❺ ★★★ **Haleiwa.** Start your day exploring this famous North Shore surfing town. See p 128, ❹.

⑥ ★ **Matsumoto Shave Ice.** Take time out for a cool, sweet Hawaiian treat. See p 97, ⓫.

Continue down Kamehamaha Hwy. for about 6½ miles. TheBus: 52.

❼ ★★★ **Sunset Beach.** Spend the rest of the morning playing on Sunset Beach. During the summer months, this is a safe beach for swimming. During the winter, it's best to just sit and watch the big-wave surfers. See p 143.

Drive another 12 miles down Kamehameha Hwy. to the town of Laie. TheBus: 52, transfer to 55.

❽ ★★ **Polynesian Cultural Center.** Spend the rest of the afternoon and evening at this "living museum" of Polynesia. See p 97, ⓭.

Day 3

Drive west on H-1 past the airport. Take the USS *Arizona* Memorial exit and follow the green-and-white signs. There's ample free parking. TheBus: 20.

❾ ★★★ **USS *Arizona* Memorial at Pearl Harbor,** ❿ ★ **USS *Bowfin* Submarine Museum & Park,** and ⓫ ★ **USS *Missouri* Memorial.** For a trip back in history, take the kids to see these three powerful memorials to World War II. See p 119, ❶-❸.

From Arizona Memorial Rd. turn right on Kamehameha Hwy. (Hwy. 99). Take the ramp onto H-1 east toward Honolulu. Take exit 20A and turn right (toward the ocean on Kalihi St., which is also Likelike Hwy.). Take Kalihi down to Nimitz Hwy. The road will split, with eastbound traffic on one side and westbound traffic across a divider. You have to drive past Sam Choy's and turn left (toward the mountain) on Kuhahi St., then make an immediate left back on Nimitz Hwy. to get to the entrance of the restaurant.

⑫ **Sam Choy's Breakfast, Lunch, Crab & Big Aloha Brewery.** Take a break at chef/restaurateur Sam Choy's crab house, which features gigantic meals (fried poke, Cajun seared ahi) with unusual decor (like the sampan boat in the middle of the 11,000-sq.-ft. restaurant) and several varieties of Big Aloha beer, brewed on-site. I'd suggest a sweet snack: the home-made chocolate brownie with a scoop of ice cream, topped off with chocolate sauce, macadamia nuts, whipped cream, and a cherry (just $7). See p 184.

Turn left on Nimitz Hwy., right on Pacific St., right on Iwilei Rd., and right again on N. King St., which will bring you into the heart of Chinatown. TheBus: 20.

⑬ ★★ **Chinatown.** Plan to spend several hours in this exotic part of Honolulu. Colorful, open markets, Buddhist temples, waterside walkway, and plenty of tempting restaurants will keep you occupied for hours. See p 122.

Trace your route back to N. King St., then turn left toward Waikiki. Turn right on Nuuanu Ave., then make a slight left on Nimitz Hwy. (Hwy. 92). Look for the sign for Pier 6, just after Aloha Tower, and turn right. TheBus: 56.

⑭ ★ ***Navatek 1.*** Say aloha to the day from the ocean on a sunset dinner cruise. See p 96, ❾.

Day 4

From Waikiki, take H-1 east, which becomes the Kalanianaole Hwy. Look for the Koko Head Regional Park on the left; the beach is on the right (ocean side). Avoid the crowds by going early, about 8am, on a weekday morning; once the parking lot's full, you're out of luck. The Hanauma Bay Shuttle Bus runs from Waikiki to Hanauma Bay every half-hour from 8:45am to 1pm. You can catch it at any city bus stop in Waikiki. It returns every hour from noon to 4pm.

⑮ ★★★ **Hanauma Bay.** Spend the morning at Oahu's best snorkeling beach—just don't go on Tuesday, when it's closed. See p 140.

Continue to drive east on Kalanianaole Hwy. Look for MM 11.

⑯ **Halona Blowhole.** Kids will enjoy this natural wonder—a blowhole that spouts ocean water up to 30 feet high. See p 30, ⑮.

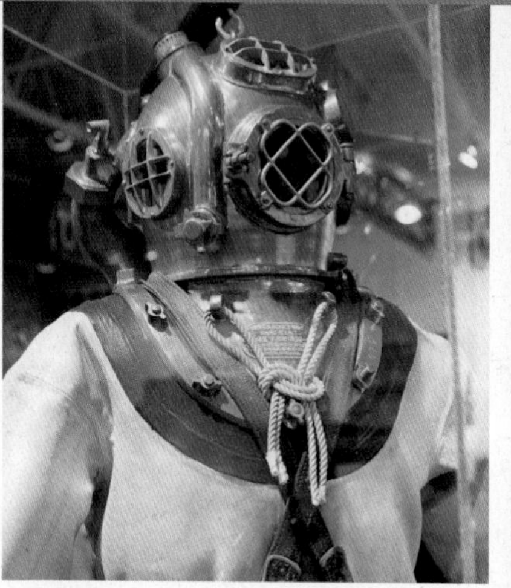

> *The USS* Bowfin *Submarine Museum brings World War II history to life.*

Continue to drive east on Kalanianaole Hwy., looking for the sign for Makapuu Point.

⑰ **Makapuu Point.** The kids will love hiking out to this 647-foot-high cliff and still-functioning lighthouse. See p 30, ⑯.

Continue east on Kalanianaole Hwy. TheBus: 58.

⑱ ★ **Sea Life Park.** This 62-acre ocean theme park, located in East Oahu, is one of the island's top attractions. Come here to swim with dolphins, get up close to sea lions, or just relax and watch the marine mammal shows. My favorite stops are the stingray lagoon (where you can get a good look at these normally shy creatures) and the sea turtle lagoon, which also doubles as a breeding sanctuary for the endangered Hawaiian green sea turtle. There's also a Hawaiian reef tank full of tropical fish; a touch pool, where you can touch a real sea cucumber (commonly found in tide pools); and a bird sanctuary, where you can see birds like the red-footed booby and the frigate bird. The chief curiosity, though, is the world's only "wholphin"—a cross between a false killer whale and an Atlantic bottle-nosed dolphin. On-site, marine biologists operate a recovery center for endangered marine life. During your visit, you may be able to see rehabilitated Hawaiian monk seals and seabirds. ⏲ 2–4 hr. 41-202 Kalanianaole Hwy. (at Makapuu Point). ☎ 808/259-7933. www.sealifeparkhawaii.com. Admission $29 adults, $19 children 3–11. Daily 10:30am–5pm. Parking $3.

> *Swim with dolphins, feed sea lions, or marvel at majestic stingrays in Honolulu's 62-acre Sea Life Park.*

Continue on Kalanianaole Hwy. (Hwy. 72), turn left on Pali Hwy. (Hwy. 61), then take H-1 east to Waikiki. TheBus: 58.

Day 5

Take Ala Wai Blvd. out of Waikiki. Turn right at Kalakaua Ave., then left on S. Beretania St. and right at Piikoi St. Make a left onto Lunalilo St., and bear left onto H-1 west. Take exit 20B, which puts you on Haloma St. Turn right at Houghtailing St. and then left onto Bernice St. TheBus: 2.

⑲ ★★★ **Bishop Museum.** This entrancing museum may be the highlight of your trip. Exhibits cover everything you've always wanted to know about Hawaii, from grass shacks to how a volcano works. See p 31, ⑳.

Turn right out of the parking lot onto Bernice St., left at Kapalama Ave., and right again on N. School St. Make a right on Liliha St., a left on N. King St., and right on River St. Turn left on Nimitz Hwy. and then right at Aloha Tower Dr. Bus: City Express A.

⑳ **Bad Ass Coffee Company.** Stop for a cup of joe made from beans grown right here in Hawaii. See p 31, ㉑.

Leave your car at Aloha Tower, and walk toward Diamond Head along the waterfront.

㉑ ★★ **Hawaii Maritime Center.** As we went to press, the Bishop Museum, owner of the Hawaii Maritime Center, "temporarily" closed operations here "due to adverse economic conditions." Please call the Bishop Museum (☎ 808/846-3511) to see if the Hawaii Maritime Center has reopened by the time you visit. If it has, it is well worth a couple of hours of your time to learn the story of Hawaii's rich maritime past. Pier 7 (next to Aloha Tower).

Walk mauka (inland) up Bishop St., right on S. King St., and left on Richards St.

㉒ ★ **Iolani Palace.** Highlights for kids here include the Throne Room, which has glittering chandeliers, carved mirrors, gilded cornices, and elegant satin drapes—like something out of a fairy tale. Also a hit with kids (at least those with a penchant for the gross and macabre) is Kamehameha the Great's temple drum, which was carved from a coconut tree and inlaid with real human teeth. See p 32, ㉓.

To get back to Waikiki, pick up your car at Aloha Tower Marketplace and turn right on Nimitz Hwy., which becomes Ala Moana Blvd. and leads into Waikiki. TheBus: 13.

Day 6

Take H-1 west to exit 1 (Campbell Industrial Park). Make an immediate left turn to Farrington Hwy., and you will see the park on your left. Bus: City Express B, transfer to Country Express C.

㉓ ★ **Wet 'n' Wild.** Kids love this 29-acre water-theme amusement park, which opened in spring 1999 with some $14 million in attractions (it was formerly called Hawaiian Waters Adventure Park). Plan to spend the day. Highlights are a football field–size wave pool for bodysurfing, two 65-foot-high free-fall slides, two water toboggan bullet slides, inner tube slides, body flume slides, a continuous river for floating inner tubes, and separate pools for adults, teens, and children. In addition, there are restaurants, Hawaiian performances, and shops. ⏱ All day. 400 Farrington Hwy. (at Kalaeloa Blvd.), Kapolei. ☎ 808/674-9283. www.hawaiianwaters.com. Admission $40 adults, $17 seniors, $30 children 3–11, children under 3 free. Hours vary, but generally the park is open daily 10:30am–4 or 5pm in peak season (summer); during off-peak season 10:30am–3:30 or 4pm; closed some weekdays.

Day 7

Take Ala Moana Blvd. out of Waikiki. Turn left on Koula St., then right on Olomehani, and right again on Ohe St. TheBus: 42 from Ala Moana Center.

㉔ ★★ **Hawaii Children's Discovery Center.** Perfect for children ages 2 to 13, this center's 37,000 square feet of color, motion, and activities will entertain them for hours with hands-on exhibits and interactive stations. Where else can you can play volleyball with a robot or put on sparkling costumes from India or dress up as a purple octopus? Lots of summer classes and activities range from playing with clay to painting (most of them invite adults to participate, too). ⏱ 2 hr. 111 Ohe St. (at Olomehane St.), Honolulu. ☎ 808/524-5437; www.discoverycenterhawaii.org. Admission $10 adults, $6.75 ages 1–17, children under 1 free. Tues–Fri 9am–1pm; Sat–Sun 10am–3pm.

Retrace your route back to Ala Moana Blvd., and turn right toward Waikiki. Make a left on Ward Ave. and a right on Auahi St. TheBus: 56.

㉕ **Big City Diner.** Take a break and let the kids order the "World's Smallest Sundae" from the kids menu. They can dig into vanilla ice cream, Hershey's chocolate syrup, whipped cream, and a cherry for just $2.79, while you enjoy the homemade brownie pie. Ward Center, 1060 Auahi St. ☎ 808/591-8891. $.

Go back to Ala Moana Blvd. and turn left toward Waikiki. Turn right on Kalakaua Ave., then right on Diamond Head Rd. Just after 18th Ave., turn left into the Diamond Head Crater parking lot. TheBus: 3.

㉖ ★ **Diamond Head.** On your last day get a bird's-eye view of the island from atop this 760-foot extinct volcano. See p 144.

Retrace your steps back to Waikiki.

㉗ ★★★ **Atlantis Submarines.** Once you've gotten a bird's-eye view of Oahu, plunge beneath the waves and see it from underwater in this high-tech submarine. See p 160.

> *Book a ride with Atlantis Submarines and even the non-swimmers in your group can explore Oahu's underwater world.*

Oahu History & Culture

Spend a week seeing Oahu's sacred places, from ancient Hawaiian sites to the spot where members of royalty were born. Go back to the days of missionaries and old plantations and to World War II, when Pearl Harbor was attacked.

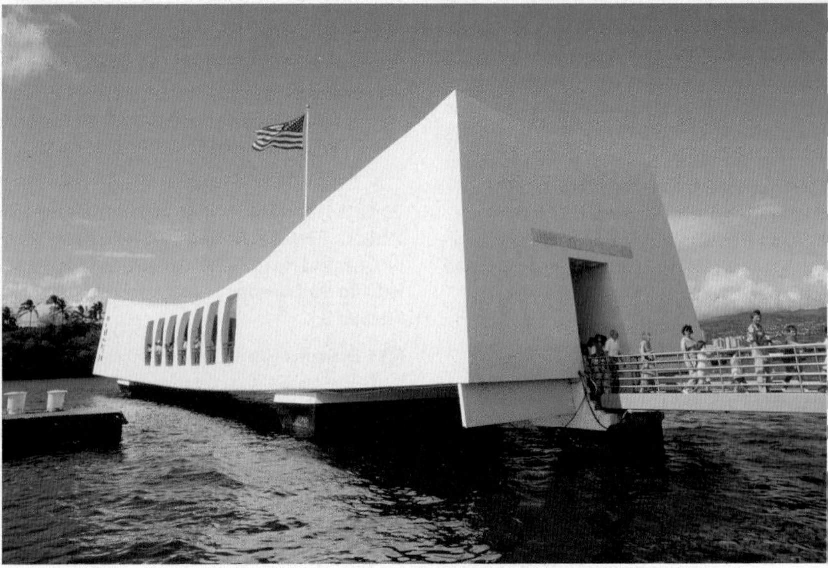

> *No historical tour of Oahu would be complete without a visit to the USS* Arizona *Memorial at Pearl Harbor.*

START & FINISH Waikiki.
TRIP LENGTH 1 week and 69 miles.

Day 1

❶ ★★ kids **Waikiki Historic Trail.** To get an overview of Waikiki's history, take this 4.5-mile walk, with stops marked by 6-foot-tall surfboards explaining the history of today's favorite resort area. See p 110 for a full description of the trail.

Day 2

Take Ala Wai Blvd. out of Waikiki. Turn right at Kalakaua Ave., then left on S. Beretania St. and right at Piikoi St. Make a left onto Lunalilo St., and bear left onto H-1 west. Take exit 20B, which puts you on Haloma St. Turn right at Houghtailing St., and then left onto Bernice St. TheBus: 2.

❷ ★★★ kids **Bishop Museum.** Take the entire day to see this entrancing museum (which could be the highlight of your trip). See p 31, ⓴.

Day 3

Drive west on H-1 past the airport. Take the USS *Arizona* Memorial exit and follow the green-and-white signs. There's ample free parking. TheBus: 20.

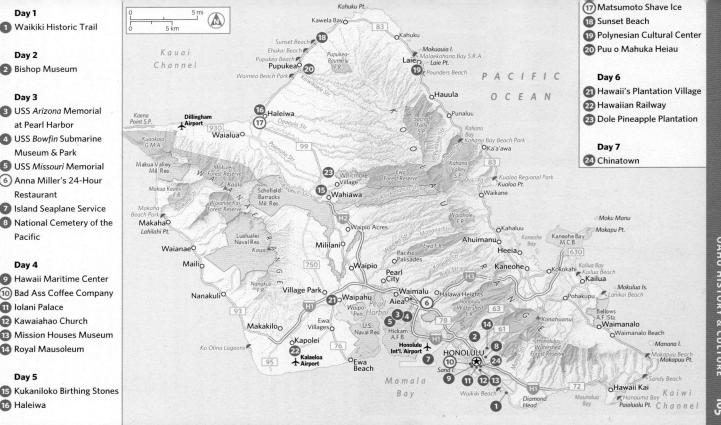

Day 1

1. Waikiki Historic Trail

Day 2

2. Bishop Museum

Day 3

3. USS *Arizona* Memorial at Pearl Harbor
4. USS *Bowfin* Submarine Museum & Park
5. USS *Missouri* Memorial
6. Anna Miller's 24-Hour Restaurant
7. Island Seaplane Service
8. National Cemetery of the Pacific

Day 4

9. Hawaii Maritime Center
10. Bad Ass Coffee Company
11. Iolani Palace
12. Kawaiahao Church
13. Mission Houses Museum
14. Royal Mausoleum

Day 5

15. Kukaniloko Birthing Stones
16. Haleiwa
17. Matsumoto Shave Ice
18. Sunset Beach
19. Polynesian Cultural Center
20. Puu o Mahuka Heiau

Day 6

21. Hawaii's Plantation Village
22. Hawaiian Railway
23. Dole Pineapple Plantation

Day 7

24. Chinatown

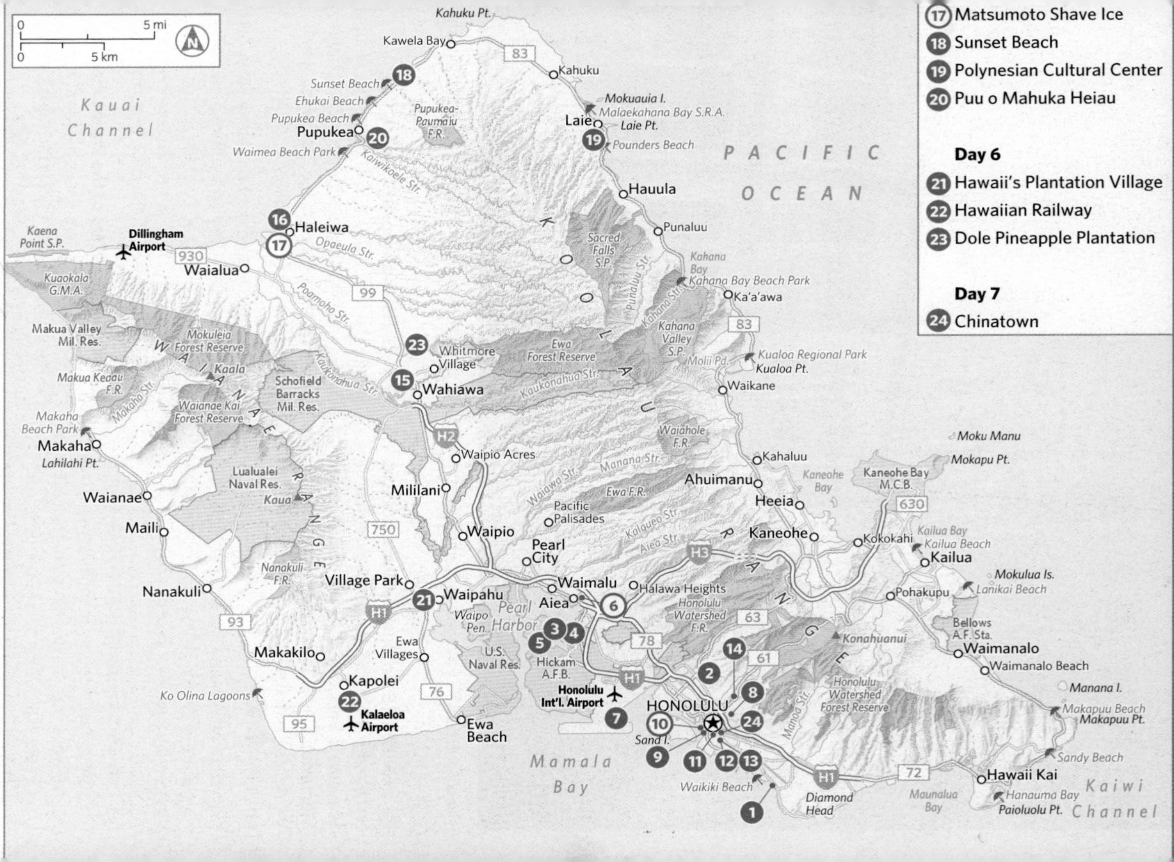

> Iolani is America's only royal palace and recently received a $7 million renovation to restore its former majesty.

❸ ★★★ kids **USS *Arizona* Memorial at Pearl Harbor,** ❹ ★ kids **USS *Bowfin* Submarine Museum & Park,** and ❺ ★ kids **USS *Missouri* Memorial.** These three powerful memorials to World War II make for a moving experience. See p 119, ❶-❸.

Turn right on Arizona Rd. and then left on Kamehameha Hwy. (Hwy. 99). Turn right on Kaonohi St. Bus: City Express A.

⑥ ★ kids **Anna Miller's 24-Hour Restaurant.** Just a couple of miles away is this always-busy casual dining restaurant in Pearlridge, which serves the best fresh strawberry pie on the island (with a generous helping of fluffy whipped cream). Pearlridge Centre, 98-115 Kaonohi St. (Kamehameha Hwy.). ☎ 808/487-2421. $.

Turn left on Kamehameha Hwy. (Hwy. 99) and merge onto Hwy. 78 east. Take exit 3 toward the airport, which puts you on Puuloa Rd. and becomes Lagoon Dr.

❼ ★★ kids **Island Seaplane Service.** To get a feel for the fateful day in 1941 that propelled the U.S. into the war, sign up for the unforgettable tour of the entire island. See "See World War II History from the Air," p 121.

From Lagoon Dr. turn right on Nimitz Hwy. Take H-1 east, exit 21A (Pali Hwy.). Turn right on Kuakini St., then left on Lusitana St. Turn right on Concordia St., then left on Puowaina Dr. to the end of the road. TheBus: 62, transfer to 6.

❽ **National Cemetery of the Pacific.** End the day seeing the consequences of war at the National Cemetery of the Pacific (also known as "the Punchbowl"). See p 121, ❺.

Day 4

From Aloha Tower Marketplace, walk toward Diamond Head along the waterfront.

❾ ★★ kids **Hawaii Maritime Center.** As we went to press, the Bishop Museum, owner of the Hawaii Maritime Center, "temporarily" closed operations here "due to adverse economic conditions." Please call the Bishop

> *The Hawaii Maritime Center takes visitors on a fascinating tour of the islands' rich nautical history (call first to see if it's open during your visit).*

Museum (☎ 808/846-3511) to see if the Hawaii Maritime Center has reopened by the time you visit. If it has, it is well worth a couple of hours of your time to learn the story of Hawaii's rich maritime past. Pier 7 (next to Aloha Tower).

Retrace your steps back to the Aloha Tower Marketplace.

---

(10) **Bad Ass Coffee Company.** Try a cup of Kona for a perfect pick-me-up. See p 31, (21).

Walk up Bishop St. to King St. and make a right. At Richards St. turn left.

(11) ★ kids **Iolani Palace.** If you want to really understand Hawaii, I suggest taking the Grand Tour of this royal palace, built by King David Kalakaua in 1882. Ogle the crown jewels, ancient feather cloaks, and royal china, and see how Hawaii's *alii* (royalty) lived. See p 32, (23).

Continue to walk toward Diamond Head on S. King St. to Punchbowl St.

(12) ★ **Kawaiahao Church.** Don't miss the crowning achievement of the first missionaries in Hawaii—the first permanent stone church, complete with bell tower and colonial colonnade. See p 33, (24).

Continue in the Diamond Head direction on S. King St.

(13) **Mission Houses Museum.** See what life was like for the 19th-century American Protestant missionaries. See p 33, (25).

Retrace your steps to your car at the Aloha Tower. Drive in the Diamond Head direction on Nimitz Hwy. and turn left on Alakea St. Turn left on Beretania St., right on Punchbowl St., and get on the Pali Hwy. north. Exit at Wylolie St., and turn left on Nuuana Ave. TheBus: 4.

(14) **Royal Mausoleum.** In the cool uplands of Nuuanu, on a 3¾-acre patch of sacred land dedicated in 1865, is the final resting place of King Kalakaua, Queen Kapiolani, and 16 other Hawaiian royals. Only the Hawaiian flag flies over this grave, a remnant of the kingdom. ⏲ 1 hr. 2261 Nuuanu Ave. (btw. Wyllie and Judd sts.). ☎ 808/536-7602. Free admission. Mon–Fri 8am–4:30pm.

Take Nuuanu Ave. down to Nimitz Hwy., which becomes Ala Moana Blvd. and takes you back to Waikiki. TheBus: 4.

Day 5

Take H-1 west out of Waikiki to the H-2 north exit (exit 8A) toward Mililani/Wahiwa. After 7 miles H-2 becomes Kamehameha Hwy. (Hwy. 80). Look for the sign between Wahiawa and Haleiwa, on Plantation Rd., opposite the road to Whitmore Village. No bus.

> *Get to know Hawaii's most recognizable export product at the Dole Pineapple Plantation. Kids love the maze and the train tour.*

15 Kukaniloko Birthing Stones. Women of ancient Hawaii gave birth to potential *alii* (royalty) at this sacred site. See p 127, 2.

Continue on Hwy. 80 to Haleiwa. To get from Sunset Beach to Polynesian Cultural Center, continue down Kamehameha Hwy. for 6½ miles.

16 ★★★ kids **Haleiwa,** ☕ 17 ★ kids **Matsumoto Shave Ice, 18** ★★★ kids **Sunset Beach** (the famous surfing site), and **19** ★★ kids **Polynesian Cultural Center.** See p 97, 10–13.

Retrace your route back to Haleiwa. Take Pupukea Rd. mauka (inland) at Foodland, and drive less than a mile up a switchback road. TheBus: 52, then walk up Pupukea Rd.

20 ★ kids **Puu o Mahuka *Heiau.*** Go at sunset to feel the *mana* (sacred spirit) of this 18th-century *heiau,* known as the "hill of escape." Sitting on a 5-acre, 300-foot bluff overlooking Waimea Bay and 25 miles of Oahu's wave-lashed North Coast, this sacrificial temple (the largest on Oahu) appears as a huge rectangle of rocks (170 ft. x 575 ft.), with an altar often covered by the flower and fruit offerings of native Hawaiians. ***Warning:*** Never walk, climb on, or even touch the rocks at a *heaiu.* ⏱ 30 min. Pupukea Rd.

Day 6

Take H-1 west to the Waikele-Waipahu exit (exit 7); get in the left lane and turn left on Paiwa St. At the fifth light, turn right onto Waipahu St. After the second light, turn left. TheBus: 58, transfer to 43.

21 kids **Hawaii's Plantation Village.** The tour of this restored 50-acre village offers a glimpse back in time to when sugar planters shaped the land, economy, and culture of Hawaii. From 1852, when the first contract laborers arrived here from China, to 1947, when the plantation era ended, more than 400,000 men, women, and children from China, Japan, Portugal, Puerto Rico, Korea, and the Philippines came to work the sugarcane fields. ⏱ 1½ hr. Waipahu Cultural Garden Park, 94-695 Waipahu St. (at Waipahu Depot Rd.), Waipahu. ☎ 808/677-0110. www.hawaiiplantationvillage.org. Admission (including escorted tour) $13 adults, $10 seniors, $7 military personnel, $5 children 4–11, children 3 and under free. Mon–Sat 10am–2pm.

Take Farrington Hwy. to Fort Weaver Rd. (Hwy. 76) toward Ewa Beach. Turn right on Renton Rd.

> *An 18th-century sacrificial temple, or* heiau, *Puu O Mahuka sits on a 300-foot cliff overlooking Waimea Bay.*

22 kids **Hawaiian Railway.** Between 1890 and 1947, the chief mode of transportation for Oahu's sugar mills was the Oahu Railway and Land Co.'s narrow-gauge trains. The line carried not only equipment, raw sugar, and supplies but also passengers from one side of the island to the other. You can relive those days every Sunday with a narrated ride through Ko Olina Resort and out to Makaha. On the second Sunday of the month, you can ride on the nearly 100-year-old, custom-built, parlor-observation car ($20; no kids under 13). ⏱ 2 hr. 91-1001 Renton Rd., Ewa Beach. ☎ 808/681-5461. www.hawaiianrailway.com. Admission $10 adults, $7 seniors and children 2-12. Departures Sun 1 and 3pm.

Backtrack to Fort Weaver Rd. and take H-1 east (toward Honolulu). Take exit 8B on the left and merge onto H-2 north (Miilani/Wahiawa). Take exit 8 onto Kamehameha Hwy. TheBus: 44, transfer to 42, transfer to 62, transfer to 53.

23 kids **Dole Pineapple Plantation.** Concluding this day of Plantation Hawaii, this agricultural exhibit/retail area is a modern pineapple plantation with a few adventures for kids. See p 128, 3.

Retrace your route back on Kamehameha Hwy. to H-1, then take H-1 to Waikiki. TheBus: 52, transfer to City Express B.

Day 7

Start at N. Hotel and Maunakea sts.; to avoid the parking problems, take TheBus 2 or 20. If you insist on driving, take Ala Moana Blvd. and turn right on Smith St. Make a left on Beretania St. and a left again at Maunakea St. The city parking garage is on the ewa (west) side of Maunakea, between N. Hotel and N. King sts.

24 ★★ kids **Chinatown.** Plan to spend the entire day in this exotic part of Honolulu. Colorful open markets, Buddhist temples, a waterside walkway, and plenty of tempting restaurants will keep you occupied for hours. See p 122.

Historic Waikiki

Take a few hours to walk through history and experience Waikiki before Westerners came to its shores. This tour describes each of the Waikiki Historic Trail Markers (6-foot-tall surfboards) that explain the history of Hawaii's most popular resort area.

START Kapiolani Avenue (near Monsarrat Ave.). **FINISH** King Kalakaua Statue, Kalakaua and Kuhio avenues. **TRIP LENGTH** 3 hours and ½ mile.

1 The Beaches of Waikiki. In ancient times there were two *heiau* (temples) in this area covering Sans Souci and Queen's Surf beaches and all of Kapiolani Park. One was Kupalaha, located on the shoreline at Queen's Beach and thought to be part of the Papa'ena'ena Heiau, where Kamehameha I made the last human sacrifice in Waikiki. The other, Makahuna, near Diamond Head, was dedicated to Kanaloa, the god of the ocean. Kalakaua Ave. (near the Natatorium, close to Monsarrat Ave.).

Walk away from Diamond Head to the Groin at Kapahulu Ave.

2 Kapahulu Groin. Waikiki has always been a popular surfing site. Near here, on the slopes of Diamond Head, a *heiau* (temple) was dedicated to *he'e nalu* (surfing), and the priests there were responsible for announcing the surfing conditions to the village below by flying a kite. Kalakaua and Kapahulu aves.

Turn mauka (toward the mountains) up Kapahulu Ave. to Ala Wai Blvd.

3 Ala Wai/Liliuokalani Estate. This was the site of the estate of Queen Liliuokalani, Hawaii's last monarch, who was overthrown by the U.S. government in 1893. She had two homes here: *Paoakalani* ("royal perfume"), located where the canal now stands, and *Kealohilani* ("the brightness of heaven"), located opposite Kuhio Beach. Kapahulu Ave. and Ala Wai Blvd.

Continue in the ewa (west) direction on Ala Wai Blvd. and turn left on Paoakalani Ave. Walk down to the beach.

4 Kuhio Beach Park. This beach park is named in honor of Prince Jonah Kalanianaole, Hawaii's second delegate to the U.S. Congress (1902–22). He successfully got the passage of the Homes Commission Act, giving native Hawaiians some 200,000 acres of land. His home, *Pualeilani* ("flower from the wreath of heaven"), which was located on the beach here, was given to the city upon his death. 2453 Kalakaua Ave. (btw. Kealohilani and Liliuokalani sts.).

Continue walking in the ewa (west) direction down Kalakaua Ave.

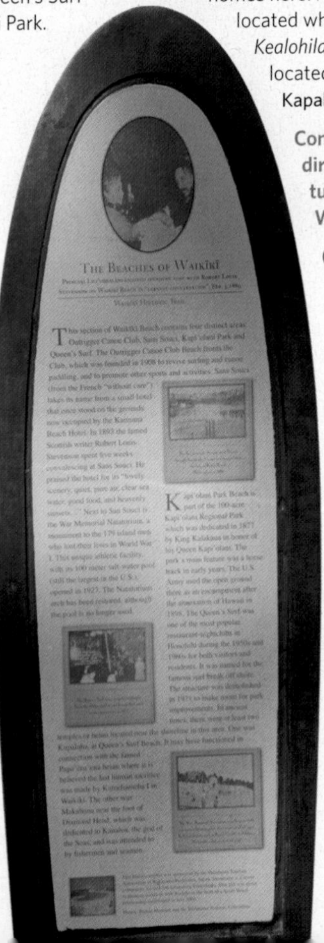

> *Six-foot surfboards act as markers and offer the details of Hawaii's past along Waikiki's historic walking trail.*

1 The Beaches of Waikiki
2 Kapahulu Groin
3 Ala Wai/Liliuokalani Estate
4 Kuhio Beach Park
5 Duke Kahanamoku Statue
6 Wizard Stones of Kapaemahu
7 King's Village
8 Rock Island Café
9 Aina Hau Park Triangle
10 International Marketplace Banyan Tree
11 Banyan Tree, Westin Moana Hotel
12 Duke's, Outrigger Waikiki on the Beach
13 Royal Hawaiian Hotel
14 Outrigger Reef Hotel
15 U.S. Army Museum
16 Kalia Road
17 Paoa Park
18 Lappert's Ice Cream
19 Ilikai Hotel
20 Ala Moana Park
21 Ala Wai Canal
22 Fort DeRussy
23 King Kalakaua Statue

> *Duke's overlooks the spot where legendary surf champion Duke Kahanamoku won his first competition.*

5 **Duke Kahanamoku Statue.** Olympic swimming champion, internationally known surfer, movie actor, and Hawaii's ambassador of Aloha, Duke Paoa Kahanamoku, born August 24, 1980, won three gold medals, two silvers, and a bronze in four Olympics. He introduced surfing to Europe, Australia, and the East Coast of the U.S. and appeared in movies from 1925–1933. There's no surfboard marker; just the statue of Duke. Kalakaua Ave. (btw. Liliuokalani and Uluniu sts.).

Continue walking in the ewa (west) direction down Kalakaua Ave.

6 **Wizard Stones of Kapaemahu.** According to legend, four healers from Tahiti (Kapaemahu, Kahaloa, Kapuni, and Kinohi) came to Hawaii in perhaps the 15th-century. Before they left, they transferred their healing powers into stones that were located in Kaimuki, 2 miles away. No one knows how the 8-ton stones got to Waikiki. Diamond Head side of the Waikiki Police Sub-Station, 2405 Kalakaua Ave.

At Kaiulani Ave. turn toward the mountain to Koa Ave.

7 **King's Village.** This is the site of the 2-story home of King David Kalakaua (1836–1891), which was surrounded by towering coconut trees. The king loved dancing and revived the hula tradition, which the missionaries had just about succeeded in stamping out. He also loved to give parties and earned the nickname "The Merrie Monarch." The official name for the block-long shopping center that stands here today is King's Village, but everyone calls it King's Alley. 131 Kaiulani Ave. (btw. Koa Ave. and Prince Edward St.).

Inside King's Village.

8 kids **Rock Island Café.** Order a cherry coke at this nostalgic soda fountain filled with memorabilia from when "Elvis was the King, Marilyn was Queen, and they both drank Coca-Cola." King's Village. 131 Kaiulani Ave. (btw. Koa Ave. and Prince Edward St.). ☎ 808/923-8033. $.

Continue mauka (inland) on Kaiulani Ave. to Prince Edward St.

9 **Aina Hau Park Triangle.** This tiny park was once part of the palm-tree-lined grand entrance to the 10-acre estate of Governor Archibald Scott Cleghorn and his wife, Hawaiian Chieftess Miriam Kapili Likelike. Miriam was a composer (like her sister, Liliuokalani, and her brother, Kalakaua) and wrote the song "Ainahau" ("land of the hau tree") to describe

the estate of 3 lily ponds, 500 coconut trees, 14 varieties of hibiscus, 8 different kinds of mango, and a giant banyan tree. The huge, 2-story Victorian house stood between present-day Cleghorn and Tusitala streets, 2 blocks away. Kaiulani/Kuhio aves.

Turn left on Kuhio Ave. and enter the International Marketplace.

⑩ **International Marketplace Banyan Tree.** At one time this area fronted the Apuakehau Stream and was the summer home of King William Kanaina Lunalilo (1835–1874), who was the first elected king of Hawaii. The Hawaiians called him *ke alii lokomaikai,* or "the kind chief." His reign was only 1 year and 25 days; he died due to poor health. Duke's Lane (btw. Kuhio and Kalakua aves.).

Walk through the International Marketplace, toward the ocean. At Kalakaua Ave. cross the street.

⑪ **Banyan Tree, Westin Moana Hotel.** The first hotels in Waikiki were just bathhouses that offered rooms for overnight stays. The first oceanfront hotel, the Park Beach, was a home converted into a hotel with ten rooms, one bathroom, and one telephone. Then the Moana Hotel opened its doors on March 11, 1901, with 4 stories (the tallest structure in Hawaii) and 75 rooms (with a bathroom and a telephone in each room). What put Waikiki on the map was Harry Owens and Webley Edwards's radio show, "Hawaii Calls," which started in 1935. At the peak of the show's popularity, in 1952, it was broadcast to 750 stations around the globe. 2365 Kalakaua Ave. (near Kaiulani Ave.).

Next door, on the ewa (west) side:

⑫ **Duke's, Outrigger Waikiki on the Beach.** The outside lanai of Duke's Canoe Club in this hotel was once where the Apuakehau ("basket of dew"), which flowed through the middle of Waikiki, emptied into the ocean. *Paradise of the Pacific* magazine described the river as flowing through "taro patches, rice and banana fields ... with canoes gliding along the shining surface ... and women and children catching shrimp in long narrow baskets, often stopping to eat a few." 3553 Kalakaua Ave. (across the street from Duke's Lane and Kaiulani Ave.).

Continue down Kalakaua Ave. in the ewa (west) direction. Turn toward the ocean at Royal Hawaiian Ave.

⑬ **Royal Hawaiian Hotel.** At one time, this area, known then as Helumoa, was a royal coconut grove filled with 10,000 coconut trees, first planted in the 16th-century by Chief Kakuhihewa. Later Kamehameha I camped here before his conquest of Oahu, and after winning battles in Nuuanu, he made Waikiki the capital of the Hawaiian Islands. In 1927, the Royal Hawaii Hotel (dubbed the "Pink Palace") opened with 400 rooms. It cost $5 million to build. 2365 Kalakaua Ave. (Royal Hawaiian Ave.). ☎ 808/922-3111.

Retrace your steps back to Kalakaua Ave. and turn left. Turn left (toward the ocean) at Lewers St. Turn right at Kalia Rd.

⑭ **Outrigger Reef Hotel.** Waikiki is known today for its incredible beauty, but in the olden days, Waikiki was known by the Hawaiians as

> *This Waikiki statue honors Hawaii's only Olympic swimming champ and the Babe Ruth of surfing, Duke Kahanamoku.*

> *Diners enjoy the atmosphere under a massive banyan tree outside Waikiki's Moana Surfrider, renowned for its opulent splendor for more than 100 years.*

a powerful place of healing. Very successful *kahuna la'au lapa'au* (medical physicians) lived in this area, and the royal families often came here to convalesce. The beach starting where the Halekulani Hotel is today to the Outrigger Reef was called Kawehewehe ("removal") because if you bathed in the waters out front, your illness would be removed. 2169 Kalia Rd. (Lewers St.). ☎ 808/923-3111.

⑮ **U.S. Army Museum.** The grounds where the museum stands today were once the 3-acre estate and villa of Chung Afong, Hawaii's first Chinese millionaire and a member of King David Kalakaua's privy council. Afong arrived in Honolulu in 1849 and in just 6 years had made a fortune in retailing, real estate, sugar, rice, and opium (he had the only government license to sell it). In 1904 the U.S. Army Corps of Engineers bought the property for $28,000 to defend Honolulu Harbor. On December 7, 1976, it became a museum. Ft. DeRussy, near Saratoga and Kalia rds. ☎ 808/955-9552.

Continue in the ewa (west) direction on Kalia Rd.

⑯ **Kalia Road.** In 1897, Fort DeRussy, from Kalia Road mauka (mountainside) some 13 acres, was the largest fishpond in Waikiki. Called Ka'ihikapu, this pond (like the hundreds of others in Waikiki) functioned as a "royal icebox" where *'ama'ama* (mullet) and *awa* (milkfish) were raised in brackish water. Hawaiians have lots of legends about fishponds, which they believed were protected by *mo'o* (lizards) that could grow to 12–30 feet long. In 1908, it took the U.S. military more than 250,000 cubic yards of landfill and 1 year to cover Ka'ihikapu. Kalia Rd. (btw. Saratoga Rd. and Ala Moana Blvd.) mauka (mountainside) to Kalakaua Ave.

Continue in the ewa (west) direction on Kalia Rd.

⑰ **Paoa Park.** The 20 acres where the Hilton Hawaiian Village stands today was once home to Olympic champion Duke Kahanamoku's mother's family, the Paoas. Duke's grandfather, Ho'olae Paoa, was a descendant of royal chiefs and got the land from King Kamehameha III in the Great Mahele of 1848 (which allowed the king, chiefs, and commoners to claim private title to lands and for the first time allowed foreigners to own land in Hawaii). Kalia Rd. (bordered by Paoa Rd. and Ala Moana Ave.).

Walk inside the Hilton Hawaiian Village to the Rainbow Bazaar.

> *The Wizard Stones of Kapaemahu are said to contain the powers of four 16-century Tahitian healers.*

(18) **Lappert's Ice Cream.** Before you leave the Hilton Hawaiian Village, take an ice cream break at this local shop, where they have some 33 different flavors, including my favorite, Kona coffee. Rainbow Bazaar, Hilton Hawaiian Village, 2005 Kalia Rd. (Ala Moana Blvd.). ☎ 808/943-0256. $.

Make a left on Ala Moana Blvd.

(19) **Ilikai Hotel.** Waikiki's third stream, Pi'inaio, once emptied into the ocean where the outside lanai is today. However, unlike the other two streams (Kuekkaunahi and Apuakehau), Pi'inaio was a muddy delta area with several smaller streams pouring in. It was also a very productive fishing area, filled with reef fish, crab, shrimp, lobster, octopus, eel, and limu (seaweed). Today Waikiki is nearly fished out. 1777 Ala Moana Blvd. (at Hobron Lane).

Continue west down Ala Moana Blvd. After you cross the bridge, look for the marker on the corner of Atkinson Dr. at the entrance to the park.

(20) **Ala Moana Park.** In the late 1800s, Chinese farmers had moved into Waikiki and converted the area of the park and shopping center into duck ponds. In 1931, the City and County of

> *Kuhio Beach Park, one of the string of beaches that form Waikiki Beach, offers beachgoers the quickest access to the Waikiki shoreline.*

> *Evidence of American might in the Pacific still stands guard at the U.S. Army Museum near Honolulu Harbor.*

Honolulu wanted to clean up the waterfront and built a park here. In 1959, the 50 acres across the street opened as one of the largest shopping centers in the U.S. Ala Moana Blvd. (at Atkinson Dr.); the marker is located at the Diamond Head corner of the entrance to the park.

Turn right toward the mountains on Atkinson Dr. Bear right on Kapiolani Blvd. The convention center is on the corner of Kapiolani Blvd. and Kalakaua Ave.

21 **Ala Wai Canal.** At the turn of the 20th-century, people on Oahu were not very happy with Waikiki. The smelly duck farms, coupled with the zillions of mosquitoes from the stagnant swamplands, did not make it a pretty picture. Work began on the Ala Wai ("fresh water") Canal in 1922 and was completed in 1928. Once the canal had drained the wetlands, the taro and rice fields dried up and the duck farms and fishponds disappeared. 1801 Kalakaua Ave. (Ala Wai Canal); the marker is on the Ala Wai Canal side of the convention center.

Continue in the Diamond Head direction down Kalakaua Ave. to the park on the corner of Ala Moana Blvd.

22 **Fort DeRussy.** This green recreational area was named after Brigadier General Rene E. DeRussy, Corps of Engineers, who served in the American-British War of 1812. All of Fort DeRussy and all the land from here to the foothills of Manoa Valley was planted in taro for centuries. By 1870, the demand for taro had diminished, and the Chinese farmers began planting rice in the former taro fields. Marker is near the corner of Ala Moana Blvd. and Kalakaua Ave.

Continue in the Diamond Head direction on Kalakaua Ave. to the intersection of Kuhio Ave.

23 **King Kalakaua Statue.** Next to Kamehameha I, King David Kalakaua is Hawaii's best-known king and certainly lived up to his nickname: The Merrie Monarch. He was born to royal parents in 1836, raised in the court of King Kamehameha IV, and elected to the position of king in 1874, after King William Lunalilo died. During his 17-year reign he restored Hawaii's rapidly fading culture of chanting, music, and hula (which had been banned by the missionaries for years). He was also forced to sign what has been termed the "Bayonet Constitution," which restricted his royal powers, in 1887. In 1890, he sailed to California for medical treatment and died in San Francisco due to a mild stroke, kidney failure, and cirrhosis. No marker (yet); statue is at the intersection of Kuhio and Kalakaua aves.

Touring Honolulu from a Trolley Car

It's fun to ride the 34-seat, open-air, motorized **Waikiki Trolley** (☎ 800/824-8804 or 808/593-2822; www.waikikitrolley.com), which looks like a San Francisco cable car. The trolley loops around Waikiki and downtown Honolulu, stopping every 40 minutes at 12 key places like Iolani Palace, Chinatown, the State Capitol, King Kamehameha's Statue, the Mission Houses Museum, the Aloha Tower, the Honolulu Academy of Arts, Fisherman's Wharf, and Restaurant Row. The driver provides commentary along the way. Stops on the new 2-hour, fully narrated Ocean Coast Line of the southeast side of Oahu include Sea Life Park, Diamond Head, and Waikiki Beach. A 1-day trolley pass—which costs $30 for adults, $20 for seniors over 62, and $14 for kids ages 4 to 11—allows you to jump on and off all day long (8:30am-5:30pm). Four-day passes cost $48 for adults, $28 for seniors, and $20 for kids 4 to 11.

Wartime Honolulu

On December 7, 1941, Hawaii's historic "day of infamy," Pearl Harbor was bombed by the Japanese, and the United States entered World War II. Honolulu is rich with history of the war years, and this 1-day tour covers the highlights.

> *Experience what World War II was like under the surface at the USS* Bowfin *Submarine Museum & Park at Pearl Harbor.*

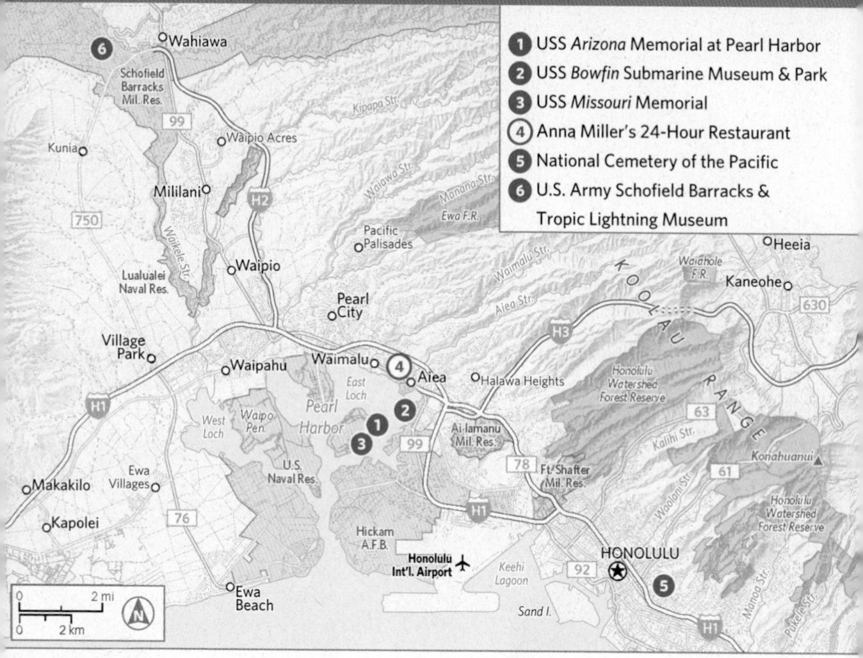

START & FINISH Waikiki.
TRIP LENGTH 1 day and 73 miles.

Drive west on H-1 past the airport. Take the USS *Arizona* Memorial exit and follow the green-and-white signs. There's ample free parking. TheBus: 20.

1 ★★★ kids **USS *Arizona* Memorial at Pearl Harbor.** The number-one attraction on Oahu is this memorial to the December 7, 1941, Japanese air raid that plunged the U.S. into World War II. The 608-foot battleship sank in 9 minutes without firing a shot, taking 1,177 sailors and Marines to their deaths. A visit to this memorial is one you'll never forget. The deck of the ship lies 6 feet below the surface of the sea. Oil still oozes slowly up from the *Arizona*'s engine room to stain the harbor's calm, blue water; some say the ship still weeps for its lost crew. Today a free U.S. Navy launch takes visitors to the *Arizona*. I highly recommend getting the ★★★ **Audio Tour,** which will make the trip even more meaningful. The tour (on an MP3 player) is about 2½ hours long and is like having your own personal park ranger as your guide; the $5 fee is worth every nickel. ***Note:*** Due to increased security measures visitors cannot carry purses, handbags, fanny packs, backpacks, camera bags (but you can carry your camera or video camera with you), diaper bags, or other items that offer concealment on the boat. However, there is a storage facility to store carry-on-size items (no bigger than 30 x 30 x 8 in.), for a fee. ⏱ 3 hr. Go first thing in the morning to avoid the huge crowds; waits of 1–3 hr. are common. ☎ 808/422-0561 (recorded info), or 808/422-2771. www.nps.gov/usar. Free admission. Daily 7am–5pm (programs run 7:45am–3pm). Children under 12 should be accompanied by an adult. Shirts and closed-toed shoes required; no swimsuits or flip-flops allowed (shorts are okay). Wheelchairs gladly accommodated.

2 ★ kids **USS *Bowfin* Submarine Museum & Park.** This is a great opportunity to see what life is like on a submarine. You can go below deck of this famous submarine—nicknamed the "Pearl Harbor Avenger" for its successful attacks on the Japanese—and see how the 80-man crew lived during wartime. The *Bowfin* museum has an impressive collection of

> *World War II veterans salute their fallen comrades at the USS* Arizona *Memorial at Pearl Harbor.*

Travel Tip

The *Arizona* Memorial Shuttle Bus VIP (☎ 808/839-0911) picks up at Waikiki hotels from 6:50am to 1pm ($9 per person round-trip).

submarine-related artifacts. The Waterfront Memorial honors submariners lost during World War II. ⏱ 1 hr.; 11 Arizona Memorial Rd. (next to the USS *Arizona* Memorial Visitor Center). ☎ 808/423-1341. www.bowfin.org. Admission $10 adults, $7 active-duty military personnel and seniors, $4 children 4–12 (children under 4 are not permitted for safety reasons). Daily 8am–5pm.

3 ★ kids **USS *Missouri* Memorial.** On the deck of this 58,000-ton battleship (the last one the Navy built), World War II came to an end with the signing of the Japanese surrender on September 2, 1945. I recommend taking the tour, which begins at the visitor center. Guests are shuttled to Ford Island on military-style buses while listening to a 1940s-style radio program (complete with news clips, wartime commercials, and music). Once on the ship, guests watch an informational film and are then free to explore on their own or take a guided tour. Highlights of this massive (more than 200-ft. tall) battleship include the forecastle (or *fo'c's'le,* in Navy talk), where the 30,000-pound anchors are "dropped" on 1,080 feet of anchor chain; the 16-inch guns (each 65 ft. long and weighing 116 tons), which can accurately fire a 2,700-pound shell some 23 miles in 50 seconds; and the spot where the Instrument of Surrender was signed as Douglas MacArthur, Chester Nimitz, and "Bull" Halsey looked on. ⏱ 1½ hr. 11 Arizona Memorial Rd. ☎ 808/423-2263. www.ussmissouri.com. Admission $16 adults, $8 children 4–12. Guided tours: $23–$45 adults, $15–$20 children (admission included). Daily 9am–5pm; guided tours 9am–4pm. Check in at the visitor center of the USS *Bowfin* Memorial.

Turn right on Arizona Memorial Rd. and then left on Kamehameha Hwy. (Hwy. 99). Turn right on Kaonohi St. Bus: City Express A.

④ ★ kids **Anna Miller's 24-Hour Restaurant.** Don't miss the fresh strawberry pie, my favorite on the island. See p 106, ⑥.

Turn left on Kamehameha Hwy. (Hwy. 99) and merge on Hwy. 78 east, which merges into H-1 east. Take exit 21A (Pali Hwy.). Turn left on Pali Hwy., right on School St., left on Lusitana St., then right on Puowaina Dr. Stay right on Puowaina Dr. to the end of the road. TheBus: 62, transfer to 6.

❺ ★ **National Cemetery of the Pacific.** The National Cemetery of the Pacific (also known as "the Punchbowl") is an ash-and-lava tuff cone that exploded about 150,000 years ago—like Diamond Head, only smaller. Early Hawaiians called it Puowaina, or "hill of sacrifice." The old crater is a burial ground for 35,000 victims of three American wars in Asia and the Pacific: World War II, Korea, and Vietnam. Among the graves, you'll find many unmarked ones with the date December 7, 1941, carved in stone. ⏱ 1 hr. Punchbowl Crater, 2177 Puowaina Dr. (at the end of the road). ☎ 808/541-1434. Free admission. Daily 8am–5:30pm (Mar–Sept to 6:30pm).

Backtrack on Puowaina Dr., then turn left on Lusitana St. Go right on School St., then take H-1 west to H-2 north, which becomes Hwy. 99. Turn left on Kunia Rd., then right on Lyman Rd. (through the gate), right on Flagler Rd., and left on Waianae Ave. Museum is in Building 361. TheBus: 6, transfer to 52, transfer to 72.

❻ kids **U.S. Army Schofield Barracks & Tropic Lightning Museum.** With its broad palm-lined boulevards and Art Deco buildings, this old Army cavalry post is still the largest operated by the U.S. Army outside the continental United States. You can no longer visit the barracks themselves, but the history of Schofield Barracks and the 25th Infantry Division is told in the small Tropic Lightning Museum. Displays range from a 1917 bunker exhibit to a replica of Vietnam's infamous Cu Chi tunnels. ⏱ 1½ hr. Schofield Barracks, Building 361, Waianae Ave. ☎ 808/655-0497. Free admission. Tues–Sun 1–4pm.

> *The crater that hosts National Cemetery of the Pacific, called "the Punchbowl," is the resting place for 35,000 American war casualties.*

Retrace your route back to H-2 South, then take H-1 into Waikiki.

See World War II History from the Air

For a unique perspective on Oahu's historical sites, I highly recommend the **Island Seaplane Service's** (☎ 808/836-6273; www.islandseaplane.com) 1-hour tour of the island. You leave on your historic journey from a floating dock in the protected waters of Keehi Lagoon. There's nothing quite like feeling the slap of the waves as the plane skims across the water and then effortlessly lifts into the air. The tour ($250) gives you aerial views of several notable landmarks (Waikiki Beach, Diamond Head Crater, Chinaman's Hat) and returns across the island over Hawaii's historic wartime sites: Schofield Barracks and the Pearl Harbor memorials.

Through
wn

atown is a mix of Asian cultures, re tangy spices rule the cuisine, open-air markets have kept out the minimalls, and the way to good health is through acupuncture and herbalists.

START & FINISH North Hotel and Maunakea streets. **TRIP LENGTH** 2 hours (more if you like to browse).

To avoid the parking problems, take TheBus 2 or 20. If you drive, take Ala Moana Blvd. and turn right on Smith St. Make a left on Beretania St. and a left again at Maunakea St. The city parking garage is on the ewa (west) side of Maunakea St., between N. Hotel and N. King sts.

1 ★ kids **Hotel Street.** During World War II, Hotel Street was synonymous with good times. Pool halls and beer parlors lined the blocks, and prostitutes were plentiful. Nowadays the more nefarious establishments have been replaced with small shops, from art galleries to specialty boutiques. As you wander up and down this street, browsing the shops, head to the intersection with Smith Street. On the Diamond Head (east) side of Smith, you'll notice stones in the sidewalk; they were taken from the sandalwood ships, which came to Hawaii empty of cargo except for these stones, which were used as ballast on the trip over. The stones were removed, and the ships' hulls were filled with sandalwood for the return to the mainland. Hotel St., from Maunakea St. to Bethel St.

From Hotel St., head back to Maunakea St. and turn toward the ocean.

2 kids **Bank of Hawaii.** This unusual-looking bank is not the conservative edifice you'd expect—it's guarded by two fire-breathing-dragon statues. 101 N. King St. (Maunakea St.). ☎ 808/532-2480.

Turn right onto King St. (Maunakea St.).

3 ★ kids **Yat Tung Chow Noodle Factory.** The delicious, delicate noodles that star in numerous Asian dishes are made here, ranging from threadlike noodles (literally no thicker than embroidery thread) to fat udon. There aren't any tours of the factory, but you can look through the window and watch as dough is fed into rollers at one end of the noodle machines; perfectly cut noodles emerge at the other end. 150 N. King St. (Maunakea St.). ☎ 808/531-7982. Mon–Sat 6am–3pm.

> *The former Shinto Temple that is home to Chinatown's Izumo Taishakyo Mission Cultural Hall (and this statue) is also believed to host a deity.*

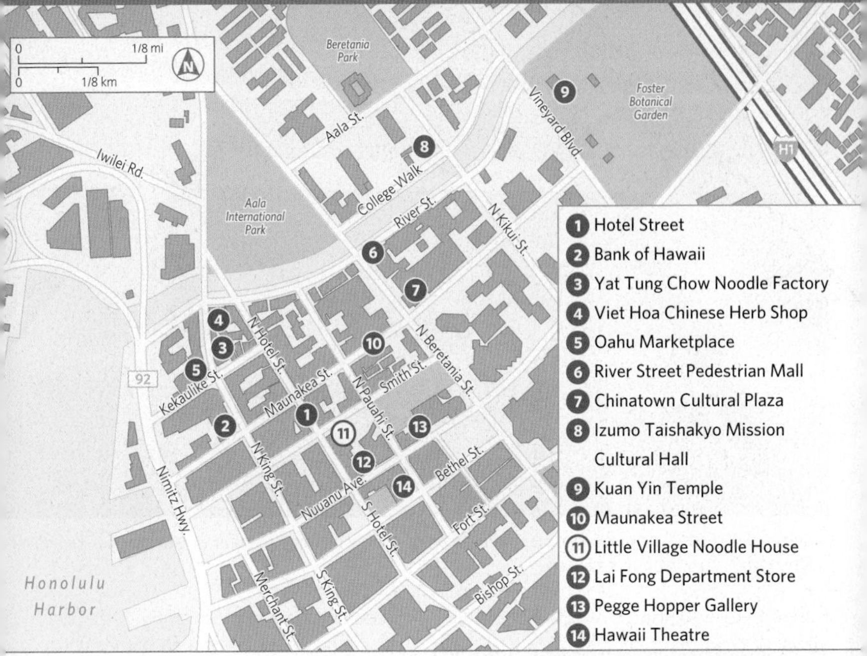

4 kids **Viet Hoa Chinese Herb Shop.** Here Chinese herbalists act as both doctors and dispensers of herbs. There's a wall of tiny drawers all labeled in Chinese characters. The herbalist quickly pulls from the drawers various objects that range from dried flowers and ground-up roots to such exotics as mashed antelope antler. The patient then takes the concoction home to brew into a strong tea. 162 N. King St. (Maunakea St.). ☎ 808/523-5499. Mon–Sat 8:30am–5pm; Sun 8:30am–2pm.

Cross to the south side of King St., where, just west of Kekaulike St., you'll come to the most-visited part of Chinatown, the open-air market.

5 ★★ kids **Oahu Marketplace.** Those interested in Asian cooking will find all the necessary ingredients here, including pigs' heads, poultry (some still squawking), fresh octopus, salted jellyfish, pungent fish sauce, fresh herbs, and thousand-year-old eggs. The friendly vendors are happy to give instructions on how to prepare these exotic treats. The market has been at this spot since 1904. N. King & Kekaulike sts. Daily 6am–6pm.

> *A wide variety of beautiful leis dangle seductively in shops on Chinatown's Maunakea St.*

> *Chinatown's first inhabitants were plantation laborers who set up small shops and restaurants around River Street when their contracts were up.*

Follow King St. to River St. and turn right.

6 kids **River Street Pedestrian Mall.** The statue of Chinese revolutionary leader Sun Yat-sen marks the beginning of this wide mall, which borders the Nuuanu Stream. Shade trees, park benches, and tables where seniors gather to play mah-jongg and checkers line the mall. There are plenty of takeout restaurants along River Street if you'd like to eat lunch outdoors. If you're up early (5:30am in summer and 6am in winter), you'll see seniors practicing tai chi. N. Beretania St. to Vineyard Blvd.

7 ★ kids **Chinatown Cultural Plaza.** This modern complex is filled with shops featuring everything from tailors to calligraphers (most somewhat more expensive than their street-side counterparts), as well as numerous restaurants, Asian magazine vendors, and even a small post office for those who want to mail cards home with the "Chinatown" postmark. The best feature of the plaza is the **Moongate Stage** in the center, the site of many cultural presentations, especially around the Chinese New Year. 100 N. Beretania St. (Vineyard Blvd.). ☎ 808/521-4934.

Continue up the River Street Mall and cross the Nuuanu Stream via the bridge at Kukui St.

8 kids **Izumo Taishakyo Mission Cultural Hall.** This small wooden Shinto shrine, built in 1923, houses a male deity (look for the X-shaped crosses on the top). Members of the faith ring the bell out front as an act of purification when they come to pray. Inside the temple is a 100-pound sack of rice, symbolizing good health. 215 N. Kukui St. (Kukui St.). ☎ 808/538-7778.

Walk a block toward the mountains to Vineyard Blvd. Cross back over Nuuanu Stream, past the entrance of Foster Botanical Gardens.

9 kids **Kuan Yin Temple.** This Buddhist temple, painted in a brilliant red with a green ceramic-tiled roof, is dedicated to Kuan Yin Bodhisattva, the goddess of mercy, whose statue towers in the prayer hall. The temple is still a house of worship, so enter with respect and leave your shoes outside. You may see people burning paper "money" for prosperity and good luck or leaving flowers and fruits at the altar (gifts to the goddess). A common offering is the pomelo, a grapefruitlike fruit that's a fertility symbol as well as a gift, indicating a request for the blessing of children. 170 N. Vineyard Blvd. ☎ 808/533-6361.

Continue down Vineyard Blvd. and then turn right (toward the ocean) on:

10 ★★ kids **Maunakea Street.** Numerous lei shops line this colorful street, where the air is heavy with the aroma of flowers being woven into beautiful treasures. Not only is this the best place in all of Hawaii to get a deal on leis,

but the size, color, and design of the leis made here are exceptional. Btw. Beretania and King sts.

Turn left on King St. and then left on Smith St.

---

(11) ☕ ★★ kids **Little Village Noodle House.** Take a break with some exotic desserts at this wonderful Chinese neighborhood eatery. Kids love the almond float (sweet almond-flavored Jello, served with fruit cocktail topping). My pick is the steamed sweet buns (get the adzuki bean filling for an unusual treat). See p 183.

Continue up Smith St. (with the ocean to your back) to Hotel St., turn right toward Diamond Head (east), and then right (toward the ocean) on Nuuanu Ave. to:

(12) ★ **Lai Fong Department Store.** Before you enter this classic Chinatown store, owned by the same family for more than 80 years, check out the sidewalks on Nuuanu Avenue—they're made of granite blocks used as ballast by ships that brought tea from China to Hawaii in the 1800s. Walking into Lai Fong is like stepping back in time. The old store sells everything from precious antiques to god-awful knick-knacks to rare Hawaiian postcards from the early 1900s—but it has built its reputation on its fabulous selection of Chinese silks, brocades, and custom dresses. 1118 Nuuanu Ave. (Hotel St.). ☎ 808/537-3497. Mon–Sat 9am–7:30pm.

(13) ★ **Pegge Hopper Gallery.** One of Hawaii's best-known artists, famous for her colorful paintings of beautiful Hawaiian women. 1164 Nuuanu Ave. (btw. Hotel and Pauahi sts.). ☎ 808/524-1160. Tues–Fri 11am–4pm, Sat 11am–3pm.

At Pauahi St., turn toward Diamond Head and walk up to Bethel St.

(14) ★★★ kids **Hawaii Theatre.** This restored 1920 Art Deco theater is a work of art in itself. It hosts a variety of programs, from the Hawaii International Film Festival to Hawaiian concerts. 1130 Bethel St. (at Pauahi St.). ☎ 808/528-0506.

Turn right onto Bethel St. and walk toward the ocean. Turn right again onto Hotel St., which will lead you back to where you started.

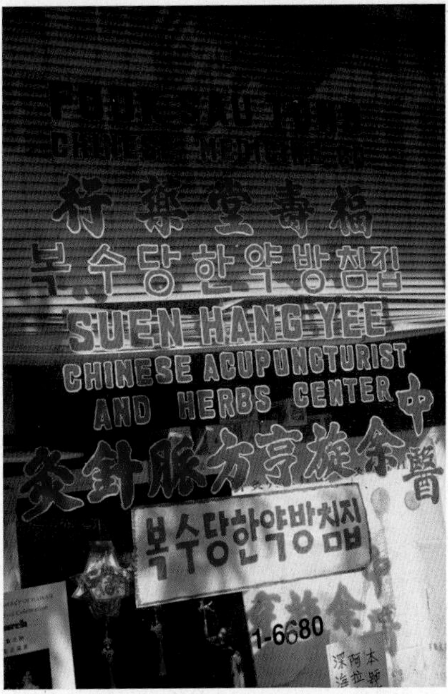

> ABOVE *Chinatown is the perfect place to sample authentic dim sum.* BELOW *Chinese herbalists will diagnose your ills and send you off with a packet of herbs to brew into a tea.*

Central Oahu & the North Shore

In Hawaii, half the fun is getting there, and that's especially true of a drive through the center of the island to the famous North Shore. If you can afford the splurge, rent a bright, shiny convertible and tan as you go. Majestic sandalwood trees once covered the central plains before the Hawaiian chiefs ordered them cut down. Now tract homes, malls, and factory outlets have taken their place. Beyond that is the North Shore and Haleiwa, a quaint, turn-of-the-20th-century sugar plantation town turned surfer outpost. Art galleries, restaurants, and shops that sell hand-decorated clothing, jewelry, and sports gear line the streets.

> *A former sugar plantation town, Haleiwa blends the quaint customs and lifestyle of old Hawaii with a modern surf culture.*

START & FINISH Waikiki. **TRIP LENGTH** 3 days and 95 miles.

Day 1

Take H-1 west to H-2 north, which becomes Hwy. 99. Turn left on Kunia Rd., then right on Lyman Rd. (through the gate), right on Flagler Rd., and left on Waianae Ave. The museum is in Bldg. 361. TheBus: 6, transfer to 52, transfer to 72.

1 kids **U.S. Army Schofield Barracks & Tropic Lightning Museum.** With its broad palm-lined boulevards and Art Deco buildings, this old Army cavalry post is still the largest operated by the U.S. Army outside the continental United States. See p 121, 6.

Retrace your route back to Hwy. 99, make a right at the next intersection to stay on Hwy. 99, then another right at Whitemore Ave. The stones are about ½ mile down this road on the left before the intersecton of Kamehameha Hwy. (Hwy. 80). TheBus: 52.

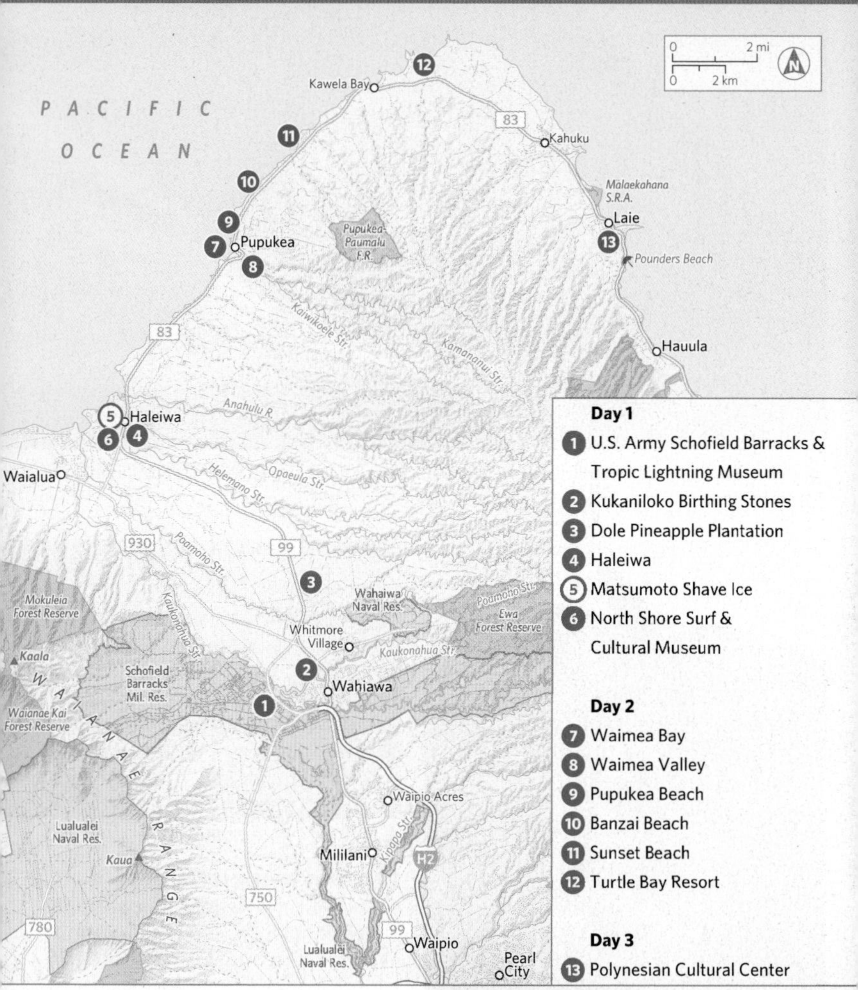

2 Kukaniloko Birthing Stones. This is the most sacred site in central Oahu. Two rows of 18 lava rocks once flanked a central stone, where women of ancient Hawaii gave birth to potential *alii* (royalty). Used by Oahu's *alii* for generations of births, the *pohaku* (rocks), many in bowl-like shapes, now lie strewn in a grove of trees that stands in a pineapple field here. Some think the site may also have served ancient astronomers—like a Hawaiian Stonehenge. Look for the two interpretive signs, one explaining why this was chosen as a birth site and the other telling how the stones were used to aid in the birth process. ⏱ 30 min. Whitemore Ave. (btw. Hwy. 99 and Hwy. 80).

> *Many Hawaiian royals were born at Kukaniloko. Birth rituals involved the presence of 48 chiefs and ceremonial cutting of the umbilical cord in a nearby heiau (now destroyed).*

> *Haleiwa is ground zero for thrilling winter "Big Wave Surfing" tournaments where competitors ride monster swells up to 50 feet. high.*

> *The Dole Pineapple Plantation offers a 22-minute locomotive ride (popular with kids) and a self-guided tour.*

Make a left on Kamehameha Hwy. (Hwy. 80), then a right at the intersection on Hwy. 99 (also called Kamehameha Hwy.). TheBus: 52.

Where to Stay & Dine

See dining recommendations starting on p 176 and lodging on p 186. My top picks: Luxurious Turtle Bay Resort (p 193) is one of the best places on Oahu to get away from it all. And if you're looking for a special-occasion restaurant, book a table at 21 Degrees North (p 185), the Turtle Bay Resort's signature restaurant.

3 kids **Dole Pineapple Plantation.** Your kids will love this rest stop with pineapples, pineapple history, pineapple trinkets, and pineapple juice, plus an agricultural exhibit/retail area which features a host of things for kids: a maze, a single-engine diesel locomotive that takes a 22-minute tour around the plantation's grounds, and a self-guided Plantation Garden Tour through the various crops that have been grown on Oahu's North Shore. 1-2hr. 64-1550 Kamehameha Hwy. (☎ 808/621-8408. www.dole-plantation.com. Fees vary with tour, but range from $4–$7.75 adults, $3.25–$5.75 children. Daily 9:30am–5pm.

Continue on Kamehameha Hwy. TheBus: 52.

4 ★★★ kids **Haleiwa.** Only 34 miles from Waikiki is Haleiwa, the funky ex-sugar plantation town that's the world capital of big-wave surfing. This beach town really comes alive in

> *Sunset Beach is a safe haven for swimmers in calmer summer months but is best left to Big Wave surfers in the winter.*

winter, when waves rise up, light rain falls, and temperatures dip into the 70s; then, it seems, every surfer in the world is here to see and be seen. Officially designated a historic cultural and scenic district, Haleiwa thrives in a time warp recalling the turn of the 20th-century, when it was founded by sugar baron Benjamin Dillingham, who built a 30-mile railroad to link his Honolulu and North Shore plantations in 1899. He opened a Victorian hotel overlooking Kaiaka Bay and named it Haleiwa, or "house of the Iwa," the tropical seabird often seen here. The hotel and railroad are gone, but Haleiwa, which was rediscovered in the late 1960s by hippies, resonates with rare rustic charm. Tofu, not taro, is a staple of the local diet. Arts and crafts, boutiques, and burger stands line both sides of the town. There's also a busy fishing harbor full of charter boats. ⌚ **2-3 hr.**

⑤ ★★ kids **Matsumoto Shave Ice.** Since 1951, this small humble shop operated by the Matsumoto family has served a popular rendition of the Hawaii-style snow cone flavored with tropical tastes. See p 97, ⑪.

6 kids **North Shore Surf & Cultural Museum.** Even if you've never set foot on a surfboard, you'll want to visit Oahu's only surf museum to learn the history of this Hawaiian sport of kings. This collection of memorabilia traces the evolution of surfboards from an enormous weathered redwood board made in the 1930s to the modern-day equivalent—a light, sleek, racy, foam-and-fiberglass board. Other items include classic 1950s surf-meet posters, 1960s surf-music album covers, old beach movie posters, historical photos, and trophies won by surfing's greatest. ⌚ **30 min. North Shore Marketplace, 66-250 Kamehameha Hwy. (behind Kentucky Fried Chicken), Haleiwa. ☎ 808/637-8888. www.captainrick.com/surf_museum.htm. Free admission. Tues-Sun noon-5pm.**

Day 2

From Haleiwa, continue on Kamehameha Hwy. TheBus: 52.

7 ★★ kids **Waimea Bay.** From November to March, monstrous waves—some 30 feet tall—roll into Waimea. When they break on the shore, covering everyone on the beach with

North Shore's Best Spa

The Zen-like **Spa Luana,** located at the Turtle Bay Resort, not only faces the ocean but actually has a thatched-hut treatment room on the ocean, plus a meditation waiting area, an outdoor workout area, and a complete fitness center. Best of all, you can book a room on the second floor and use the private elevator reserved for guests getting spa treatments. 57-091 Kamehameha Hwy. (at Kuhuku Dr.). ☎ 800/203-3650 or 808/293-6000.

> *The down-home North Shore Surf & Cultural Museum traces the rich history of Hawaii's native sport.*

> *Matsumoto Shave Ice shop has been serving up local tropical-flavored treats to lines of customers since 1951.*

salty mist, the ground actually shakes. The best surfers in the world paddle out to challenge these freight trains. It's amazing to see how small they appear in the lip of the giant waves. See p 143.

Turn toward the mountain on Waimea Valley Rd.

8 ★ kids **Waimea Valley.** For nearly 3 decades, Waimea Falls Park hosted visitors to the 1,875-acre park (home to some 6,000 species of plants and trees) and activity center (from cliff diving and hula performances to kayaking and ATV tours). In 2008 the Office of Hawaiian Affairs took over and formed a new nonprofit corporation, Hi'ipaka, to run the park, with the emphasis on perpetuating and sharing the "living Hawaiian culture." As we went to press, the new corporation was just taking over and had plans to have authentic hula performances and demonstrations of native Hawaiian crafts. The public is invited to hike the trails, wander through, and spend a day in this quiet oasis. ⏱ 2–3 hr. 59-864 Kamehameha Hwy. ☎ 808/638-7766. www.waimeavalley.org. Admission $10 adults, $5 children 4–12 and seniors. Daily 10am–5:30pm.

Continue on Kamehameha Hwy. to get to the next three beaches. Pick one and stay a while, or do a little beach-hopping and visit them all. TheBus: 52.

9 ★ kids **Pupukea Beach.** This 80-acre beach park, excellent for snorkeling and diving, is a Marine Life Conservation District with strict rules about taking marine life, sand, coral, shells, and rocks. See p 142.

Continue on Kamehameha Hwy. Access is via Ehukai Beach Park, off Kamehameha Hwy., on Ke Nui Rd. in Pupukea. TheBus: 52

10 ★ kids **Banzai Beach.** In the winter, this is a very popular beach with surfers, surf fans, curious residents, and visitors; it's less crowded in the summer months. See p 138.

Continue on Kamehameha Hwy. TheBus: 52.

11 ★★ kids **Sunset Beach.** If it's winter, just people-watch on this sandy beach, as the waves are huge here. But during the summer it is a safe swimming beach. See p 143.

Continue on Kamehameha Hwy. TheBus: 52.

⑫ ★★★ kids **Turtle Bay Resort.** The resort is spectacular: An hour's drive from Waikiki but eons away in its country feeling. Sitting on 808 acres, this place is loaded with activities and 5 miles of shoreline with secluded white-sand coves. Even if you don't stay here, check out the beach activities, golf, horseback riding, tennis, and spa. 57-091 Kamehameha Hwy., Kahuku Dr., ☎ 808/293-6000. www.turtlebayresort.com. See p 193.

Day 3

From Turtle Bay Resort, continue on Kamehameha Hwy. TheBus: 55.

⑬ ★ kids **Polynesian Cultural Center.** Visit the islands of the Pacific in a single day. See p 97, ⑬.

Continue on Kamehameha Hwy. Turn right on Likelike Hwy. Take the Kalihi St./H-1 exit and continue on H-1 to Waikiki. TheBus: 55, transfer to City Express B.

The Shrimp Trucks

Maybe it's a Hawaii thing, but the best, sweetest, most juicy shrimp you are ever going to eat will be from a shrimp truck on Oahu's North Shore. Several trucks line up around the entry to Haleiwa, just off the Kamehameha Highway, but my two favorites are: **Giovanni's Original White Shrimp Truck** (pictured above) and **Holy Smokes: Hawaiian Meats and Seafood.**

Giovanni's (usually parked across the street from Haleiwa Senior Housing; ☎ 808/293-1839) claims to be the first shrimp truck to serve the delicious aquaculture shrimp farmed in the surrounding area. The menu is simple, and most items are priced at $12: spicy, garlic, or lemon-and-butter shrimp. The battered white truck has picnic tables under the awning outside, so you can munch away right there.

The other truck parked in the same area, Holy Smokes, has a bit more of an extensive menu. In addition to the famous shrimp, they also have pork spareribs ($8.95), smoked chicken ($7.95), and a steak plate ($10.95).

The trucks are usually in place before noon and stay until about sunset. Depending on how much shrimp you can down, expect to spend no more than $12 per person.

Southern Oahu & the Windward Coast

From the high-rises of Waikiki, venture to the arid south shore and lush windward side. The landscape on the south side is reminiscent of a moonscape, with prickly cacti onshore and, in winter, spouting whales cavorting in the water. Some call it the South Shore, others Sandy's (after the mile-long beach here), but Hawaiians call it *Ka Iwi*, which means "the bone"—a tribute to the bone-cracking shore breaks along this coastline, popular with body boarders. The south gives way to the lush Windward Coast, where lots of rain keeps the vegetation green, and a string of white-sand cove beaches promise a great outing.

> *The Kahala Hotel's beautiful crescent beach and lagoon combine with fine dining and a luxurious spa to make the ultimate Hawaiian hideaway.*

START & FINISH Waikiki.
TRIP LENGTH 2 days and 85 miles.

Day 1

From Waikiki, head out Kalakaua Ave. to Poni Moi Rd. and turn left. Turn right on Diamond Head Rd., which becomes Kahala Ave., then go to the end of the street. TheBus: 14.

1 ★★ kids **Kahala Hotel & Resort.** Stop by and check out this lush, tropical resort where the grounds include an 800-foot crescent-shaped beach and a 26,000-square-foot lagoon (home to two bottle-nosed dolphins, sea turtles, and tropical fish), great dining, and a fabulous spa. 1 hr. 5000 Kahala Ave. (next to the Waialae Country Club). ☎ 800/367-2525 or 808/739-8888. See p 137.

Retrace Kahala Ave., turn right on Kealaolu Ave., and slight right at Waialae Ave., which becomes Kalanianaole Hwy. Right at Hanauma

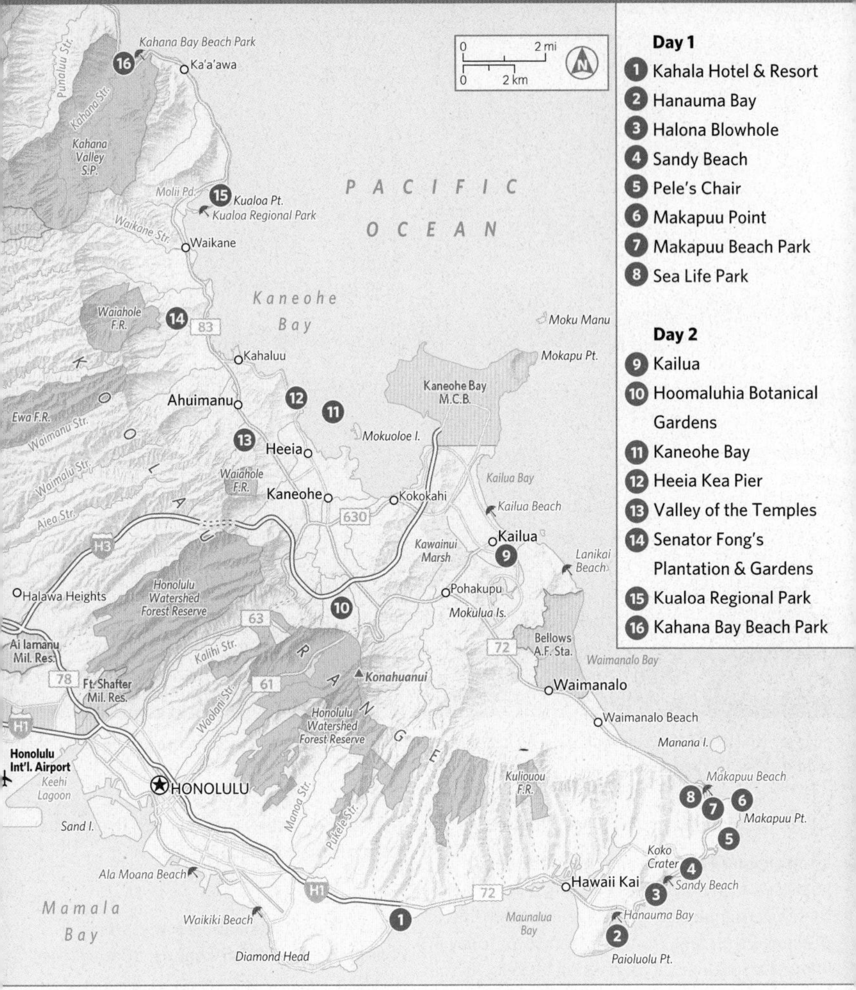

Bay. To get the bus you have to walk nearly a mile to Kilauea Ave. and Makaiwa St., then take TheBus 22.

2 ★★★ kids **Hanauma Bay.** This marine preserve is a great place to stop for a swim; you'll find the friendliest fish on the island here. ***A reminder:*** The beach park is closed on Tuesdays. See p 140.

Continue about a mile down Kalanianaole Hwy. (Hwy. 72) to around MM 11. TheBus: 58.

3 **Halona Blowhole.** Stop at this scenic lookout for the view and the unusual ocean blowhole. See p 30, **15**.

Continue about ½ mile down Kalanianaole Hwy. TheBus: 58.

4 ★ **Sandy Beach.** Oahu's most dangerous beach—it's the only one with an ambulance always standing by to whisk injured wave catchers to the hospital. Body boarders love it. I suggest you just sit on the sand and watch. See p 142.

Continue on Kalanianaole Hwy. TheBus: 58.

5 **Pele's Chair.** Just after you leave Sandy's, look out to sea for this famous formation, which from a distance looks like a mighty throne. It's believed to be the fire goddess's last resting place on Oahu before she flew off to continue her work on other islands. ⏲ A few minutes.

> *At the foot of the Koolau Mountains, Kailua is rated one of the islands' two best beaches and an affordable alternative to Waikiki.*

Continue on Kalanianaole Hwy. TheBus: 58.

❻ **Makapuu Point.** As you round the bend, you'll see a 647-foot-high hill, with a lighthouse that once signaled safe passage for steamship passengers arriving from San Francisco. Today it lights the south coast for passing tankers, fishing boats, and sailors. You can take a short hike up here for a spectacular vista. Park in the lot and follow the well-marked trail. ⏱ 20–30 min.

Continue on Kalanianaole Hwy. TheBus: 58.

❼ **Makapuu Beach Park.** In summer, the ocean here is as gentle as a Jacuzzi, and swimming and diving are perfect; come winter, however, Makapuu is hit with big pounding waves that are ideal for expert bodysurfers but too dangerous for regular swimmers. See p 142.

Cross Kalanianaole Hwy. TheBus: 58.

❽ ★ kids **Sea Life Park.** This 62-acre ocean theme park is one of the island's top attractions. Swim with dolphins, get up close to the sea lions, or just relax and watch the marine mammal shows. See p 101, ⓲.

Day 2

Continue on Kalanianaole Hwy., which changes to Kailua Rd. TheBus: 58, transfer to 57.

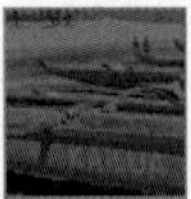

SITE GUIDE PAGE 135

❾ **Kailua.** The biggest little beach town in Hawaii, Kailua sits at the foot of the sheer green Koolau mountain range on a great bay with two of Hawaii's best beaches, Kailua and Lanikai. The town itself is a funky low-rise cluster of timeworn shops and homes; million-dollar houses sit next to tarpaper shacks, antiques shops, and bed-and-breakfasts. Kailua has become the B&B capital of Hawaii and an affordable alternative to Waikiki. With the prevailing trade winds whipping up a cooling breeze, Kailua attracts windsurfers from around the world.

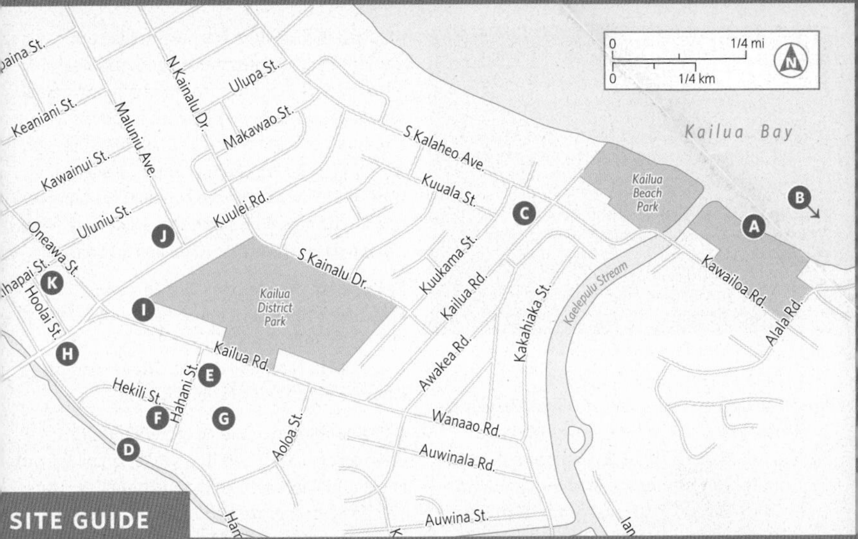

SITE GUIDE

9 Kailua

Hawaii's biggest beach town has 50,000 residents and two special beaches: A **Kailua Beach** (p 140) and B **Lanikai Beach** (p 141). Kailua is a 2-mile-long, wide golden strand with dunes, palm trees, panoramic views, and offshore islets that are home to seabirds and every type of ocean activity you can think of. Lanikai's crystal-clear lagoon is like a giant saltwater swimming pool. Too gorgeous to be real, this is one of Hawaii's postcard-perfect beaches, and it's generally quiet and uncrowded to boot. Take Kailua Road to the T intersection at Kalaheo Drive. Turn right on South Kalaheo Drive to get to Kailua Beach and Lanikai Beach. If you're interested in watersports, your first stop should be C **Kailua Sailboards & Kayaks** (130 Kailua Rd.), which offers rentals, lessons, a guided kayak tour, and snorkeling and surfing equipment. The oldest and most established windsurfing business in Hawaii is D **Naish Hawaii/ Naish Windsurfing Hawaii** (155-A Hamakua Dr.), which offers sales, rentals (windsurfing and kitesurfing), advice, and recommendations on instructors for lessons. Divers should head to E **Aaron's Dive Shop** (307 Hahani St.), which offers boat and beach dive excursions off the coast. For surfboard rentals (no lessons), head to F **Kimo's Surf Hut** (151 Hekili St.), where you can admire Kimo's personal collection of vintage surfboards lovingly displayed on the walls of the shop. The best place to pick up some takeout or a picnic lunch is G **Don Quijote** (345 Hahani St.). Choose from sushi, Korean kalbi, pizza, Chinese food, bento lunches, and wonderful fresh produce. Had enough of the sun and surf? My favorite shops in Kailua are H **Heritage Antiques & Gifts** (767 Kailua Rd.), known for its selection of Tiffany-style lamps; I **BookEnds** (600 Kailua Rd.), the quintessential neighborhood bookstore, with more than 60,000 new and used titles to choose from; and J **Alii Antiques of Kailua II** (9-A Maluniu Ave.), tops for vintage Hawaiiana. Don't leave town without a stop at K **Agnes' Portuguese Bake Shop,** an old-fashioned tea shop with the best baked goods in Kailua.

Where to Stay & Dine

See lodging recommendations starting on p 186 and dining starting on p 176. My top hotel pick is the Kahala Hotel & Resort (p 191), which offers the peace and serenity of a neighbor-island resort just a 10-minute drive from the conveniences of Waikiki. My top dining pick is Hoku's (p 181), the hotel's upscale dining room, which combines European finesse with an island touch.

From Kalaheo Ave. and Kuulei Rd., drive along Kuulei to Oneawa St. and turn right. Turn left at Mokapu Blvd., which becomes Mokapu Saddle Rd. Make a slight left on Kaneohe Bay Dr., turn left on Kamehameha Hwy. and right on Luluku Rd. Bus: 70, transfer to 57, transfer to 65, and walk 1 mile.

⑩ ★ kids **Hoomaluhia Botanical Gardens.** If you've had enough time at the beach, stop by this 400-acre botanical garden, the perfect place for a picnic or hike. Its name means "a peaceful refuge," and that's exactly what the Army Corps of Engineers created when they installed a flood-control project here, which

> *Hoomaluhia Botanical Gardens has 400 acres of beautiful tropical flowers along with a 32-acre freshwater lake.*

resulted in a 32-acre freshwater lake and garden. The gardens feature geographical groupings of plantings from the major tropical regions around the world, with a special emphasis on native Hawaiian plants. ⏱ 2–3 hr. 45-680 Luluku Rd. (visitor center), Kaneohe. ☎ 808/233-7323. www.co.honolulu.hi.us/parks/hbg/hmbg.htm. Free admission. Daily 9am–4pm. Guided nature hikes Sat 10am and Sun 1pm.

Retrace your route back to Kamehamaha Hwy., turn right, and immediately get on H-3 east. Take the Kaneohe Bay Dr. exit. Drive down Kaneohe Bay Dr., then right on Kamehameha Hwy. No bus service.

⑪ **Kaneohe Bay.** Take an incredibly scenic drive around Kaneohe Bay, which is spiked with islets and lined with gold-sand beaches. The bay has a barrier reef and four tiny islets, one of which is known as Moku o Loe, or Coconut Island. Don't be surprised if it looks familiar—it appeared in *Gilligan's Island.* ⏱ 15 min.

Turn right out on Heeia Kea Pier off Kamehameha Hwy.

⑫ **Heeia Kea Pier.** This old fishing pier juts onto Kaneohe Bay, making it a great place to view the bay. You can also take a snorkel cruise from here, or sail out to a sandbar in the middle of the bay for an incredible view of Oahu. ⏱ 30 min.

Retrace your route on Kamehameha Hwy. Turn right at Haiku Rd., right at Kahekili Hwy. (Hwy. 83), then left at Valley of the Temples. TheBus: 65.

⑬ **Valley of the Temples.** This famous site is stalked by wild peacocks and about 700 curious people a day, who come to see the 9-foot meditation Buddha, 2 acres of ponds full of more than 10,000 Japanese koi carp, and a replica of Japan's 900-year-old Byodo in the Temple of Equality. A 3-ton brass temple bell brings good luck to those who can ring it. ⏱ 1 hr. 47-200 Kahekili Hwy. (across the street from Temple Valley Shopping Center). ☎ 808/239-8811. Admission $2 adults, $1 children under 12 and seniors 65 and over. Daily 8:30am–4:30pm.

Continue on Kahekili Hwy., which becomes Kamehameha Hwy. Turn left on Pulama Rd. TheBus: 65, transfer to 55, and a 1-mile walk uphill.

> *This replica of a 900-year-old Japanese temple was built in Valley of the Temples in 1968 to commemorate the 100th anniversary of the arrival of Hawaii's first Japanese immigrants.*

⑭ kids **Senator Fong's Plantation & Gardens.** Sen. Hiram Fong, the first Chinese-American elected to the U.S. Senate, served 17 years before retiring to this 725-acre tropical garden years ago. The landscape you see today is relatively the same as what early Polynesians saw hundreds of years ago, with forests of kukui, hala, koa, and ohia-'ai (mountain apple). Ti and pili grasses still cover the slopes. ⏱ 1 hr. 47-285 Pulama Rd., Kaneohe. ☎ 808/239-6775. www.fonggarden.net. Admission $15 adults, $13 seniors, $9 children 5-12, with 1-hr. guided nature walk. Daily 10am-2pm.

Turn left on Kamehameha Hwy. for 1 mile. TheBus: 55.

⑮ ★★ kids **Kualoa Regional Park.** This 150-acre coconut palm-fringed peninsula is the biggest beach park on the windward side and one of Hawaii's most scenic. The long, narrow, white-sand beach is perfect for swimming, walking, beachcombing, kite flying, or just sun-bathing. See p 141.

Continue on Kamehameha Hwy. about 10 miles. TheBus: 55.

⑯ ★★ kids **Kahana Bay Beach Park.** This white-sand, crescent-shaped beach features a picture-postcard backdrop: a huge jungle-cloaked valley with dramatic, jagged cliffs. The bay's calm water and shallow, sandy bottom make it a safe swimming area for children. See p 140.

Retrace your route on Kamehameha Hwy. to Kahekili Hwy. Turn right on Likelike Hwy. Take the Kahili St./H-1 exit. Merge onto H-1 and continue into Waikiki. TheBus: 55, transfer to City Express B.

Southern Oahu's Best Spa

The Kahala Hotel & Resort has taken the concept of spa as a journey into relaxation to a new level with **Spa Suites at the Kahala** (5000 Kahala Ave., next to the Waialae Country Club; ☎ 808/739-8938), which has converted former garden guest rooms into individual personal spa treatment rooms. Each has a glass-enclosed shower, private changing area, infinity-edge deep soaking Jacuzzi tub, and personal relaxation area. No detail is overlooked, from the warm foot bath when you arrive to the refreshing hot tea served on your personal enclosed garden lanai after your relaxation treatment.

Oahu Beaches A to Z

★★ kids **Ala Moana Beach Park** WAIKIKI
The gold-sand Ala Moana ("by the sea") stretches for more than a mile along Honolulu's coast between downtown and Waikiki. This 76-acre midtown beach park, with spreading lawns shaded by banyans and palms, is one of the island's most popular playgrounds. It has a man-made beach, as well as its own lagoon, yacht harbor, tennis courts, music pavilion, bathhouses, picnic tables, and enough wide-open green spaces to accommodate four million visitors a year. The water is calm almost year-round, protected by black lava rocks set offshore. There's a large parking lot as well as metered street parking. 1200 Ala Moana Blvd. (btw. Kamakee St. and Atkinson Dr.).

★ **Banzai/Pipeline/Ehukai Beach Park** NORTH SHORE There are three separate areas, but since the sandy beach is continuous with only one sign, EHUKAI BEACH PARK, most people think of it as one beach park. Located near Pupukea, **Ehukai Beach Park** is 1 acre of grass with a parking lot, great for winter surfing and summer swimming. The park also provides access to Pipeline and Banzai. **Pipeline** is about 100 yards to the left of Ehukai Beach Park. When the winter surf rolls in and hits the shallow coral shelf, the waves that quickly form are steep—so steep, in fact, that the crest of the wave falls forward, forming a near-perfect tube, or "pipeline." Surfers have tried for years to master Pipeline; many have wiped out. Just west of Pipeline is the area surfers call **Banzai Beach.** The Japanese word *banzai* means "10,000 years"; it's given as a toast or as a battle charge, meaning "go for it." In the late 1950s, filmmaker Bruce Brown was shooting one of the first surf movies ever made, *Surf Safari,* when he saw a bodysurfer ride a huge wave. Brown yelled "Banzai!" and the name stuck. In the winter, this is a very popular beach with surfers and surf fans. It's less crowded in the summer months. Ehukai Beach Park, 59-337 Ke Nui Rd. (off Kamehameha Hwy.). Pupukea. TheBus: 52.

> *World-famous Waikiki Beach packs a lot of activity into just 1½ miles. Visitors flock here to swim, surf, snorkel, canoe, dive, sail, and just relax in the sun.*

Oahu Beaches A to Z

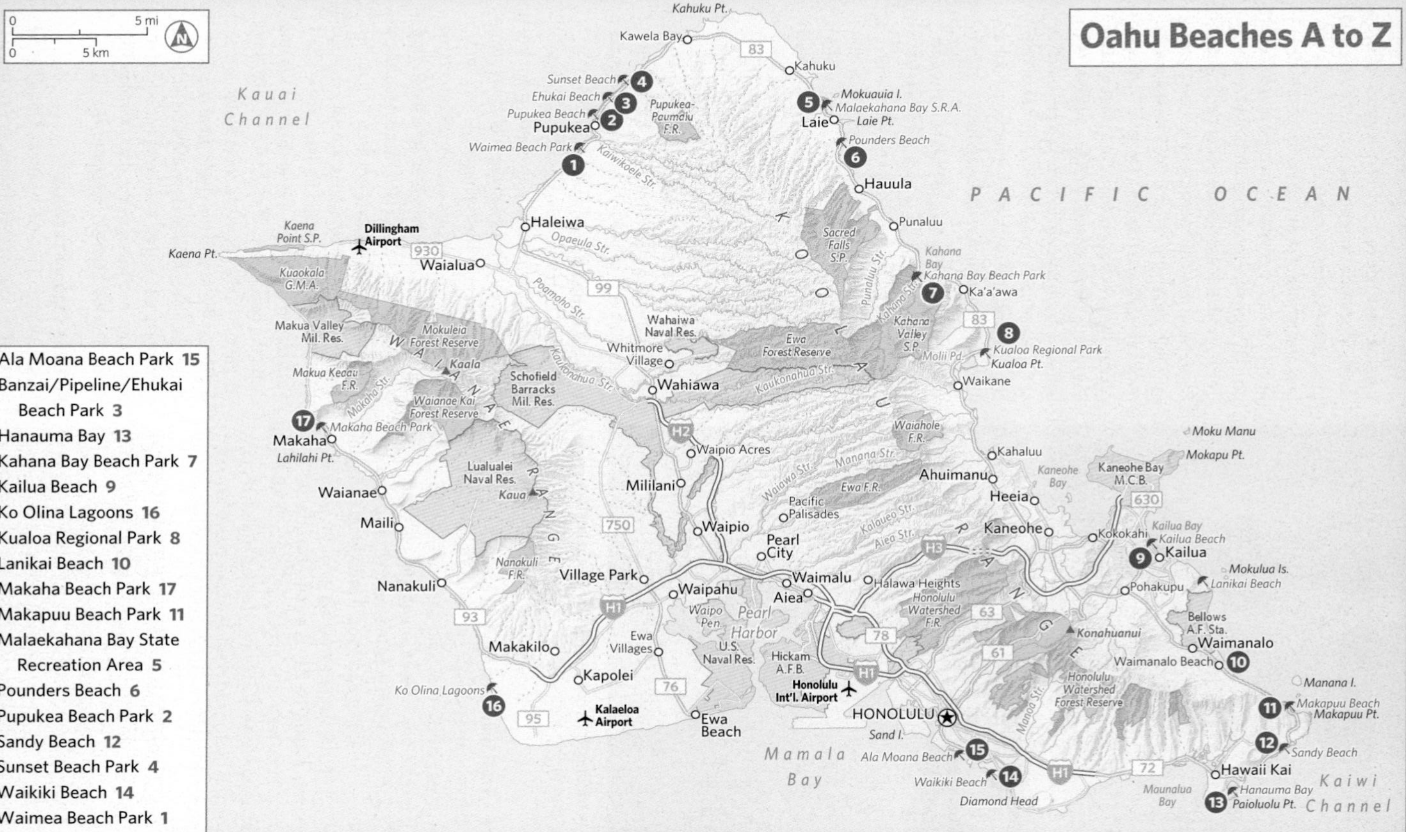

- Ala Moana Beach Park 15
- Banzai/Pipeline/Ehukai Beach Park 3
- Hanauma Bay 13
- Kahana Bay Beach Park 7
- Kailua Beach 9
- Ko Olina Lagoons 16
- Kualoa Regional Park 8
- Lanikai Beach 10
- Makaha Beach Park 17
- Makapuu Beach Park 11
- Malaekahana Bay State Recreation Area 5
- Pounders Beach 6
- Pupukea Beach Park 2
- Sandy Beach 12
- Sunset Beach Park 4
- Waikiki Beach 14
- Waimea Beach Park 1

> *Kahana Bay's calm waters make it a popular swimming spot.*

★★★ kids **Hanauma Bay** KOKO HEAD
Oahu's most popular snorkeling spot is a small, curved, 2,000-foot gold-sand beach that is packed elbow-to-elbow with people year-round. This good-looking beach is also popular for sun-bathing and people-watching. Outside the bay, the deeper water is great for scuba diving. Hanauma Bay is a conservation district—you may look at but not touch or take any marine life here. Feeding the fish is also prohibited. A motorized tram will take you down the steep road to the beach (50¢). Facilities include parking, restrooms, a pavilion, a grass volleyball court, lifeguards, barbecues, picnic tables, and food concessions. Alcohol is prohibited in the park; no smoking past the visitor center. Expect to pay $1 per vehicle to park and a $5 per person entrance fee (children 12 and under are free). Avoid the crowds by going early, about 8am, on a weekday morning; once the parking lot's full, you're out of luck. 7455 Kalanianaole Hwy. (at Hanauma Bay Rd.). Or, take TheBus to escape the parking problem: The Hanauma Bay Shuttle runs from Waikiki to Hanauma Bay every half-hour from 8:45am to 1pm; you can catch it at the Ala Moana Hotel, the Ilikai Hotel, or any city bus stop. It returns every hour from noon to 4:30pm. Hanauma Bay is closed Tues.

A Word of Warning

Wherever you are on Oahu, remember that you're in an urban area. Never leave valuables in your car. Thefts do occur at Oahu's beaches, and locked cars are not a deterrent.

★★ kids **Kahana Bay Beach Park** WINDWARD
This white-sand, crescent-shaped beach is backed by a huge jungle-cloaked valley with dramatic, jagged cliffs and is protected by ironwood and kamani trees. The bay's calm water and shallow, sandy bottom make it a safe swimming area for children. The surrounding park has picnic areas, camping, and hiking trails. The wide sand-bottom channel that runs through the park and out to Kahana Bay is one of the largest on Oahu—it's perfect for kayakers. Locals come here on weekends, so weekdays are less crowded. 52-222 Kamehameha Hwy., Kahana. TheBus: 55.

★★★ kids **Kailua Beach** WINDWARD
Windward Oahu's premier beach is a 2-mile-long, wide golden strand with dunes, palm trees, panoramic views, and offshore islets that are home to seabirds. The swimming is excellent, and the azure waters are usually decorated with bright sails; this is Oahu's premier windsurfing beach as well. It's also a favorite spot to sail catamarans, bodysurf the gentle waves, or paddle a kayak. Water conditions are quite safe, especially at the mouth of Kaelepulu Stream, where toddlers play in the freshwater shallows at the middle of the beach park. The water's usually about 78°F (26°C), the views are spectacular, and the setting, at the foot of the sheer, green Koolaus, is idyllic. Facilities include lifeguards, picnic tables, barbecues, restrooms, a volleyball court, a public boat ramp, and free parking. 450 Kawailoa Rd., Kailua. TheBus: 56 or 57, transfer to 70.

Ko Olina Lagoons LEEWARD
The developer of the 640-acre Ko Olina Resort has created four white-sand lagoons to make the

> *Oahu's Sandy Beach offers a saltwater playground for swimmers and boogie boarders.*

rocky shoreline more attractive and accessible. Nearly circular, the man-made lagoons offer calm, shallow waters and a powdery white-sand beach bordered by a broad grassy lawn. No lifeguards are present, but the generally tranquil waters are great for swimming, perfect for kids, and offer some snorkeling opportunities around the boulders at the entrance to the lagoons. Two lagoons have restrooms, and there's plenty of public parking. Off Aliinui Dr. (btw. Olani and Mauloa Place), Ko Olina Resort. No bus.

★★ kids Kualoa Regional Park WINDWARD
This 150-acre coconut palm–fringed peninsula is the biggest beach park on the windward side and one of Hawaii's most scenic. The park has a broad grassy lawn and a long, narrow, white-sand beach ideal for swimming, walking, beachcombing, kite flying, or just sun-bathing. Picnic and camping areas are available, too. The waters are shallow and safe for swimming year-round, and at low tide, you can swim or wade out to the islet of Mokolii (popularly known as Chinaman's Hat), which has a small sandy beach and is a bird preserve—so don't spook the red-footed boobies. Lifeguards are on duty. Less crowded on weekdays. 49-600 Kamehameha Hwy., Kualoa. TheBus: 55.

★★ Lanikai Beach WINDWARD
Gold-sand Lanikai's crystal-clear lagoon is like a giant saltwater swimming pool—one of Hawaii's best spots for swimming. The beach is a mile long and narrow in places, but the sand is soft and onshore trade winds make this an excellent place for sailing and windsurfing. Kayakers often paddle out to the two tiny offshore Mokulua islands, which are seabird sanctuaries. Sun worshipers: Arrive in the morning—the Koolau Mountains block the afternoon rays. Mokulua Dr., Kailua. TheBus: 56 or 57, transfer to 70.

Makaha Beach Park LEEWARD
When surf's up here, it's spectacular: Monstrous waves pound the beach from October through

Staying Safe in the Water

From 1999 to 2004, the number of drownings of nonresidents in Hawaii more than doubled, from 18 deaths to 40. Below are some tips to keep in mind when swimming in Hawaii's gorgeous waters:

- Never swim alone.
- Always supervise children in the water.
- Always swim at beaches with lifeguards.
- Know your limits—don't swim out too far.
- Read the posted warning signs before you enter the water.
- Call a lifeguard or 911 if you see someone in distress.

> *Koko Head's sandy beach at Hanauma Bay draws swimmers with its 15- to 20-foot waves and reputation for Hawaii's best bodysurfing.*

April. Nearly a mile long, this half-moon, gold-sand beach is tucked between 231-foot Lahilahi Point, which locals call Black Rock, and Kepuhi Point, a toe of the Waianae mountain range. Summer is the best time to hit this beach—the waves are small, the sand abundant, and the water safe for swimming. Children hug the shore on the north side of the beach, near the lifeguard stand, while surfers dodge the rocks and divers seek an offshore channel full of big fish. Facilities include restrooms, lifeguards, and parking. **84-369 Farrington Hwy. (near Kili Dr.), Waianae. TheBus: 51.**

★ **Makapuu Beach Park** WINDWARD
Hawaii's most famous bodysurfing beach is a beautiful 1,000-foot-long, gold-sand beach cupped in the stark black Koolau cliffs. In summer, the ocean here is as gentle as a Jacuzzi, and swimming and diving are perfect; come winter, however, Makapuu is hit with big pounding waves that are ideal for expert bodysurfers but too dangerous for regular swimmers. Small boards—3 feet or less with no skeg (bottom fin)—are permitted; regular board surfing is banned by state law. Facilities include restrooms, lifeguards, barbecue grills, picnic tables, and parking. **41-095 Kalanianaole Hwy. (across the street from Sea Life Park), Waimanalo. TheBus: 57 or 58.**

★★★ kids **Malaekahana Bay State Recreation Area** NORTH SHORE This almost mile-long white-sand crescent lives up to just about everyone's image of the perfect Hawaiian beach. It's excellent for swimming, and at low tide you can wade offshore to Goat Island, a sanctuary for seabirds and turtles. Facilities include restrooms, barbecue grills, picnic tables, outdoor showers, and parking. **Kamehameha Hwy. (Hwy. 83), 2 miles north of the Polynesian Cultural Center. TheBus: 52.**

Pounders Beach NORTH SHORE
This wide beach, extending a quarter-mile between two points, has easy access from the highway and is very popular on weekends. At the west end of the beach, the waters are usually calm and safe for swimming in summer. However, at the opposite end, near the limestone cliffs, there's a shore break that can be dangerous for inexperienced bodysurfers; there, the bottom drops off abruptly, causing strong rip currents. Go on a weekday morning to have the beach to yourself. **Kamehameha Hwy., about ½ mile south of the Polynesian Cultural Center, Laie. TheBus: 55.**

★ **Pupukea Beach Park** NORTH SHORE
This 80-acre beach park, very popular for snorkeling and diving, is a Marine Life Conservation District with strict rules about taking marine life, sand, coral, shells, and rocks. Swimming, diving, and snorkeling are best from May to October, when the water is calm; nevertheless, watch out for surges. In the winter, when currents form and waves roll in, this area is very dangerous, even in the tide pools; a lifeguard is never present in this area. Summers are packed with visitors weekdays and weekends (local dive operators take their clients here). In the winter, it's nearly empty during the week. **59-727 Kamehameha Hwy. (Pupukea Rd.), Pupukea. TheBus: 52.**

★ **Sandy Beach** KOKO HEAD
Sandy Beach is one of the best bodysurfing beaches on Oahu; it's also one of the most dangerous. It's better to just stand and watch the daredevils literally risk their necks at this 1,200-foot-long gold-sand beach that's pounded by wild waves and haunted by a dangerous shore break and strong backwash. Weak swimmers and children should definitely stay out of the water here; Sandy Beach's heroic lifeguards make more rescues in a year than those at any other beach

> *Waimea Beach Park is a popular summer swimming spot, but watch out in winter, when waves up to 50 feet high pummel the shore.*

on Oahu. Visitors, easily fooled by experienced bodysurfers who make wave-riding look easy, often fall victim to the bone-crunching waves. Lifeguards post flags to alert beachgoers to the day's surf: Green means safe, yellow caution, and red indicates very dangerous water conditions; always check the flags before you dive in. Facilities include restrooms and parking. Go weekdays to avoid the crowds, weekends to catch the bodysurfers in action. 8800 Kalanianaole Hwy. (about 2 miles east of Hanauma Bay). TheBus: 22.

★★ **Sunset Beach Park** NORTH SHORE
Surfers around the world know this famous site for its spectacular winter surf—the waves can be huge thundering peaks reaching 15 to 20 feet. During the winter surf season (Sept–Apr), swimming is very dangerous here, due to the alongshore currents and powerful rip currents. The only safe time to swim is during the calm summer months. People-watching is great on the wide sandy beach, but don't go too near the water when the lifeguards have posted the red warning flags. To avoid the crowds, go midweek. 59-100 Kamehameha Hwy. (near Paumalu Place). TheBus: 52.

★★★ kids **Waikiki Beach** WAIKIKI
No beach anywhere is so widely known or so universally sought after as this narrow, 1½-mile-long crescent of imported sand (from Molokai) at the foot of a string of high-rise hotels. Home to the world's longest-running beach party, Waikiki attracts nearly five million visitors a year from every corner of the planet. Waikiki is actually a string of beaches that extends from **Sans Souci State Recreational Area,** near Diamond Head to the east, to **Duke Kahanamoku Beach,** in front of the Hilton Hawaiian Village Beach Resort & Spa, to the west. Great stretches along Waikiki include **Kuhio Beach,** next to the Westin Moana Surfrider, which provides the quickest access to the Waikiki shoreline; the stretch in front of the Royal Hawaiian Hotel, known as **Grey's Beach,** which is canted so it catches the rays perfectly; and **Sans Souci,** the small popular beach in front of the New Otani Kaimana Beach Hotel that's locally known as "Dig Me" Beach because of all the gorgeous bods who strut their stuff here. Waikiki is fabulous for swimming, board- and body-surfing, outrigger canoeing, diving, sailing, snorkeling, and pole fishing. Every imaginable type of marine equipment is available for rent here. Facilities include showers, lifeguards, restrooms, grills, picnic tables, and pavilions at the **Queen's Surf** end of the beach (at Kapiolani Park, between the zoo and the aquarium). Stretching from Ala Wai Yacht Harbor to Diamond Head Park. TheBus: 19 or 20.

★★ **Waimea Beach Park** NORTH SHORE
This deep, sandy bowl has gentle summer waves that are excellent for swimming, snorkeling, and bodysurfing. To one side of the bay is a huge rock that local kids like to climb up and dive from. The scene is much different in winter, when waves pound the narrow bay, sometimes rising to 50 feet high. When the surf's really up, very strong currents and shore breaks sweep the bay—and it seems like everyone on Oahu drives out to Waimea to get a look at the monster waves and those who ride them. Weekends are great for watching the surfers; to avoid the crowds, go on weekdays. Facilities include lifeguards, restrooms, showers, parking, and nearby restaurants and shops in Haleiwa town. 51-031 Kamehameha Hwy., Waimea. TheBus: 52.

Oahu's Best Hiking & Camping

Hawaii's great outdoors offers oceanfront camping, hiking in a tropical rainforest, and scenic views that will be imprinted in your memory forever. Just a couple of warnings: If you plan to camp, bring your own gear (no one on Oahu rents it), and if you plan to go hiking, take a (fully charged) cellphone, in case of emergency.

> *You have to pay a $1 fee to climb the 1.4 miles to the top of Diamond Head, but the view from the 750-foot summit is priceless.*

★★★ kids **Diamond Head Crater**
Hiking. This is a moderate, but steep, walk to the summit of the 750-foot volcanic cone, Hawaii's most famous landmark, with a reward of a 360-degree view of the island. The 1.4-mile round-trip takes about 1½ hours. The entry fee is $1. Wear decent shoes (rubber-soled tennies are fine), and take a flashlight (you'll walk through several dark tunnels), binoculars (for better viewing at the top), water, a hat to protect you from the sun, and a camera. You might want to put all your gear in a pack to leave your hands free for the climb. Go early, preferably just after the 6:30am opening, before the midday sun starts beating down. Monsarrat and 18th aves. TheBus: 58.

★ kids **Hoomaluhia Botanical Gardens**
Hiking & Camping. This relatively unknown windward side camping area, outside Kaneohe, is a real find. *Hoomaluhia* means "peace and tranquility," an apt description for this 400-acre lush botanical garden with rare plants and craggy cliffs in the background. It's hard to

Hiking

Diamond Head Crater **5**
Hoomaluhia Botanical Gardens **3**
Kahana Bay Beach Park **2**
Makapuu Lighthouse Trail **4**
Makiki Valley–Tantalus–
 Round Top-Nuuanu
 Valley Trails **7**
Manoa Falls Trail **6**

Camping

Hoomaluhia Botanical Gardens **3**
Kahana Bay Beach Park **2**
Malaekahana Bay State
 Recreation Area **1**

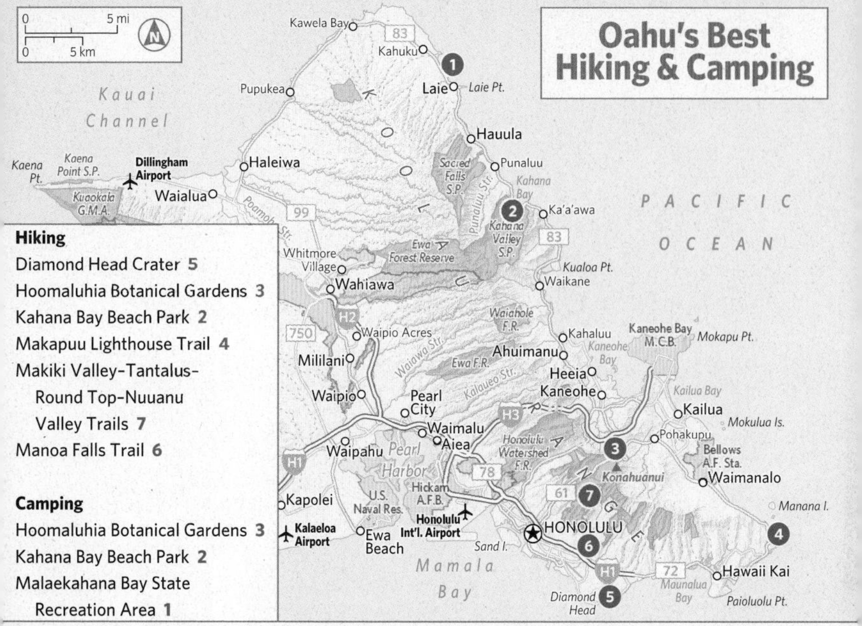

Twilight Warning

When planning sunset activities, be aware that Hawaii, like other places close to the Equator, has a very short (5–10 min.) twilight period after the sun sets. After that, it's dark. If you hike out to watch the sunset, be sure you can make it back quickly, or take a flashlight.

Safe Hiking & Camping

Water might be everywhere in Hawaii, but more than likely it isn't safe to drink. Most stream water must be treated because it is probably contaminated with the bacterium *Leptospira,* which is found in freshwater streams throughout the state and enters the body through breaks in the skin or through the mucous membranes. It produces flulike symptoms and can be fatal. Firewood isn't always available, so it's a good idea to carry a small, light backpacking stove, which you can use both to boil water and to cook meals. Make sure that your drinking water is safe by vigorously boiling it. If boiling is not an option, use tablets with hydroperiodide; portable water filters will not screen out *Leptospira.* Remember, the island is not crime-free: Never leave your valuables (wallet, airline ticket, and so on) unprotected. Carry a day pack if you have a campsite, and never camp alone. Some more do's and don'ts: Do bury personal waste away from streams, don't eat unknown fruit, and do carry out your trash.

believe you're just a half-hour from downtown Honolulu. A 32-acre lake sits in the middle of the scenic park (no swimming or boating is allowed, though), and there are numerous hiking trails. The visitor center can suggest a host of activities, ranging from guided walks to demonstrations of ancient Hawaiian plant use. Facilities include a tent-camp area, restrooms, cold showers, dishwashing stations, picnic tables, grills, and water. Permits are free, but you have to get here before 3pm Friday, when the office closes for the weekend. Stays are limited to Friday, Saturday, and Sunday nights. **Hoomaluhia Botanical Gardens,** 45–680 Luluku Rd. (at Kamehameha Hwy.), Kaneohe. ☎ 808/233-7323. TheBus: 55.

> *Adventurers re-energize themselves aside the soothing and spectacular Manoa Falls.*

★★ kids Kahana Bay Beach Park

Camping. Under Tahiti-like cliffs, with a beautiful gold-sand crescent beach framed by pine needle casuarina trees, Kahana Bay Beach Park is a place of serene beauty. You can swim, bodysurf, fish, hike, and picnic, or just sit and listen to the trade winds whistle through the beach pines. Both tent and vehicle camping are allowed at this oceanside oasis. Facilities include restrooms, picnic tables, drinking water, public phones, and a boat-launching ramp. See "Camping Permits," p 147.

Hiking. Spectacular views of this verdant valley and a few swimming holes are the rewards of a 4.5-mile loop trail above the beach. The downsides to this 2- to 3-hour, somewhat ardent adventure are mosquitoes (clouds of them) and some thrashing about in dense forest, with a bit of navigation required along the not-always-marked trail. The trail starts behind the visitor center at the Kahana Valley State Park. 52-222 Kamehameha Hwy. btw. Kaaawa and Kahana. TheBus: 55.

★ kids Makapuu Lighthouse Trail

Hiking. It's a little precarious at times, but anyone in reasonably good shape can handle this 45-minute (one-way) hike, which winds around the 646-foot-high sea bluff to the lighthouse. The rewards are the views: the entire Windward Coast, across the azure Pacific and out to Manana (Rabbit) Island. Kalanianaole Hwy. (½ mile down the road from the Hawaii Kai Golf Course), past Sandy Beach. TheBus: 57 or 58.

★★ Makiki Valley–Tantalus–Round Top–Nuuanu Valley Trails

Hiking. This is the starting place for some of Oahu's best hiking trails—miles of trails converge through the area. The draws here are the breathtaking views, historic remains, and incredible vegetation. Stop at the Hawaii Nature Center, by the trail head, for information and maps on hiking. 2131 Makiki Heights Dr., Honolulu. ☎ 808/955-0100. Mon–Fri 8am–4:30pm. TheBus: 4.

★★★ kids Malaekahana Bay State Recreation Area

Camping. This beautiful beach camping site has a mile-long gold-sand beach. Facilities include picnic tables, restrooms, showers, sinks, drinking water, and a phone. See "Camping Permits," below. Kamehameha Hwy. btw. Laie and Kahuku. TheBus: 55.

★★ kids Manoa Falls Trail

Hiking. This easy .75-mile (one-way) hike is terrific for families. It takes less than an hour to reach idyllic Manoa Falls. The often-muddy trail follows Waihi Stream and meanders through the forest reserve past guavas, mountain apples, and wild ginger. The forest is moist and humid and is inhabited by giant bloodthirsty mosquitoes, so bring repellent. If it has rained recently, stay on the trail and step carefully, as it can be very slippery (and it's a long way down if you slide off the side). The trail head is marked by a footbridge. End of Manoa Rd., past Lyon Arboretum. TheBus: 5.

> Hikers make their way to the top of Diamond Head.

Camping Permits

There is no camping on Wednesday and Thursday in both county and state parks. You must get a camping permit for all camping in all parks. Camping in Honolulu County Parks (like **Kualoa Regional Park,** p 141) is free but limited to 5 days. To get a permit, contact Honolulu Department of Parks and Recreation, 650 S. King St., Honolulu, HI 96713 (☎ 808/523-4525; www.co.honolulu.hi.us/parks). Camping in state parks (like **Kahana Bay Beach Park** and **Malaekahana Bay State Recreation Area**) requires a $5-per-night permit and is limited to 5 nights. Permits can be obtained at any state parks office, including the Department of Land and Natural Resources, State Parks Division, P.O. Box 621, Honolulu, HI 96809 (☎ 808/587-0300; information at www.hawaiistateparks.org/parks/oahu) or download the permit (http://www.hawaiistateparks.org/pdf/parkpermit.pdf).

Oahu's Best Golf Courses

Oahu has nearly three dozen golf courses, ranging from bare-bones municipal courses to exclusive country club courses with membership fees running to six figures a year. Below are the best of a great bunch. You should know that the windward courses play much differently than the leeward courses. On the windward side, the prevailing winds blow from the ocean to shore, and the grain direction of the greens tends to run the same way—from the ocean to the mountains. Leeward golf courses have the opposite tendency: The winds usually blow from the mountains to the ocean, with the grain direction of the greens corresponding.

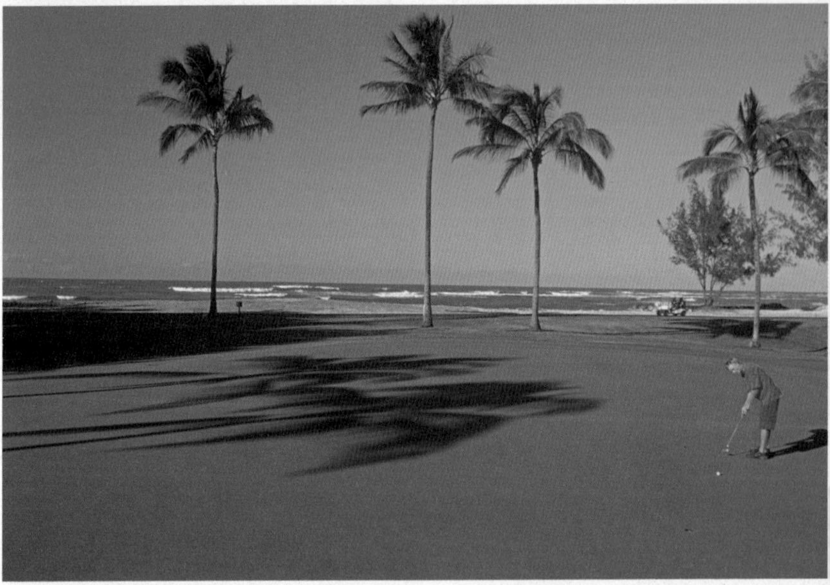

> *Hawaii's spectacular vistas and championship quality courses provide golfers with their own slice of paradise at Turtle Bay Resort.*

Ala Wai Municipal Golf Course. The *Guinness Book of World Records* lists this as the busiest golf course in the world; some 500 rounds a day are played on this 18-hole municipal course within walking distance of Waikiki's hotels. It is a challenge to get a tee time (you can book only 3 days in advance). Ala Wai has a flat layout and is less windy than most Oahu courses, but pay attention because some holes are not as easy as you may think. 404 Kapahulu Ave., Waikiki. ☎ 808/733-7387 (golf course), or 808/296-2000 tee time reservations. www.co.honolulu.hi.us/des/golf/alawai.htm. Greens fees: $42; twilight rate $21. TheBus: 19, 20, or 22.

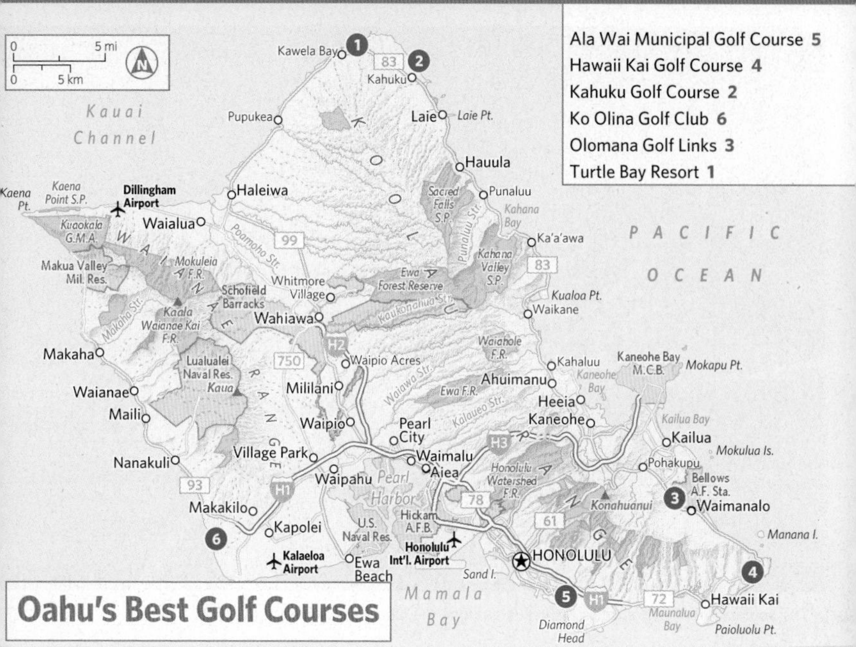

Hawaii Kai Golf Course. This is actually two golf courses in one. The par-72, 6,222-yard **Hawaii Kai Championship Golf Course** is moderately challenging, with scenic vistas. The course is forgiving to high-handicap golfers, although it does have a few surprises. The par-3 **Hawaii Kai Executive Golf Course** is fun for beginners and those just getting back in the game after a few years. The course has lots of hills and valleys, with no water hazards and only a few sand traps. Facilities include lockers. **8902 Kalanianaole Hwy., Honolulu. ☎ 808/395-2358. www.hawaiikaigolf.com. Greens fees: Champion Course $100 ($90 early-bird Internet special; book 7 days in advance) Mon–Fri, $110 ($100 when booked on Internet) Sat–Sun; twilight rate $70; Executive Course $37 Mon–Fri, $42 Sat–Sun. TheBus: 58.**

Kahuku Golf Course. This 9-hole budget golf course is a bit funky: no club rentals, no clubhouse, and no facilities other than a few pull carts that disappear with the first handful of golfers. But a round at this scenic oceanside course amid the tranquility of the North Shore is quite an experience. Duffers will love the ease of this recreational course, and weight watchers will be happy to walk the gently sloping greens. Don't forget to bring your camera for the views. No reservations are taken; tee times are first-come, first-served, and with plenty of retirees happy to sit and wait, the competition is fierce for early tee times. Bring your own clubs and call ahead to check the weather. **56-501 Kamehameha Hwy., Kahuku. ☎ 808/293-5842. Greens fees: $10 for 9 holes. TheBus: 55.**

★★★ **Ko Olina Golf Club.** The Ted Robinson-designed course (6,867-yard, par-72) has rolling fairways and elevated tee and water features. The signature hole—the 12th, a par-3—has an elevated tee that sits on a rock garden with a cascading waterfall. At the 18th hole, you'll see and hear water all around you—seven pools begin on the right side of the fairway and slope down to a lake. Book in advance; this course is crowded all the time. Facilities include driving range, locker rooms, Jacuzzi, steam rooms, and a restaurant and bar. Lessons are available. **92-1220 Aliinui Dr., Kapolei. ☎ 808/676-5309. www.koolinagolf.com. Greens fees: $179 ($159 for Ihilani Resort guests); twilight rate (after 1pm in winter and 2pm in summer) $119**

> *The popular Ala Wai golf course is nestled among the high-rises of bustling Waikiki.*

($99 for guests). Men and women are asked to wear a collared shirt. No bus service.

Olomana Golf Links. Low-handicap golfers may not find this gorgeous course difficult, but the striking views of the craggy Koolau mountain ridge alone are worth the fees. The par-72, 6,326-yard course is popular with locals and visitors alike. The course starts off a bit hilly on the front 9 but flattens out by the back 9, where there are some tricky water hazards. This course is very, very green; the rain gods bless it regularly with brief passing showers. You can spot the regular players here—they all carry umbrellas, wait patiently for the squalls to pass, and then resume play. Facilities include driving range, practice greens, club rental, pro shop, and restaurant. 41-1801 Kalanianaole Hwy., Waimanalo. ☎ 808/259-7926. www.olomanagolflinks.com. Greens fees: $95; twilight rate $80 (after 1:30pm). TheBus: 57.

★★ **Turtle Bay Resort.** This North Shore resort is home to two of Hawaii's top golf courses: the 18-hole **Arnold Palmer Course** (formerly the Links at Kuilima) and the par-71, 6,200-yard **George Fazio Course.** Palmer's is the most challenging, and the front 9 (rolling terrain, only a few trees, and lots of wind) plays like a British Isles course. The back 9 has narrower, tree-lined fairways and water. Fazio's is a more forgiving course, without all the water hazards and bunkers of the Palmer course. Facilities include pro shop, driving range, putting and chipping green, and snack bar. Weekdays are best for tee times. 57-049 Kamehameha Hwy., Kahuku. ☎ 808/293-8574 or 808/293-9094. www.turtlebayresort.com. Greens fees: Palmer Course $195 (Turtle Bay guests $155); Fazio Course $160 (guests $135). TheBus: 52 or 55.

Golfing on a Budget

Oahu's golf courses tend to be crowded, so I suggest that you go midweek if you can. Also, most island courses have twilight rates that offer substantial discounts, so if you're willing to tee off in the afternoon (usually btw. 1 and 3pm) you'll save a bundle.

For last-minute and discount tee times, call **Stand-by Golf** (☎ 888/645-BOOK; www.standbygolf.com), which offers discounted tee times for same-day or next-day golfing. Call between 7am and 11pm for a guaranteed tee time with up to 50% off greens fees.

> *Book well in advance to play at the popular Ko Olina Golf Club, known for its elevated tees and abundant water features.*

Oahu Adventures on Land

Honolulu isn't just sparkling ocean water and rainbow-colored fish, it is also the land of adventure—bicycling back in history to an ancient terraced taro field, soaring through the air in silence in a glider, galloping along a deserted sandy beach, or even leaping from a plane and floating to earth in a tandem skydiving escapade.

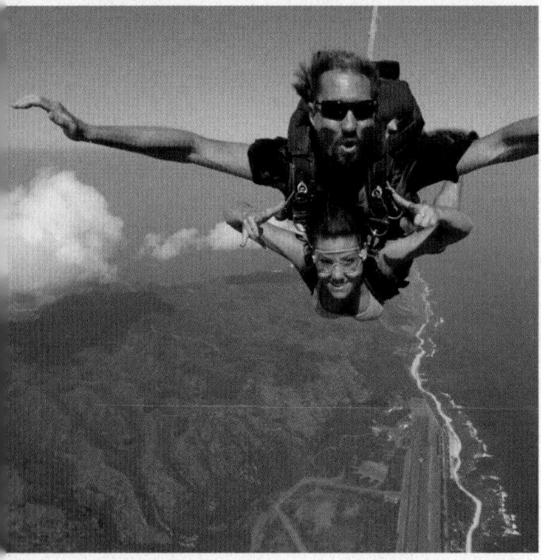

> *Get the ultimate adrenaline rush on a tandem jump with SkyDive Hawaii.*

Bicycling

Bike Hawaii. Get off the street and get dirty with an off-road, guided mountain bike tour through the 1,000-acre Kaaawa Valley on Oahu's northeast shore. The tour is the same site as the annual 24 Hours of Hell Mountain Bike Race, where you will follow dirt roads and single track through verdant tropical landscape dotted with mountain streams. ☎ 877/682-7433 or 808/734-4214. www.bikehawaii.com. Adults $120, children 13 and under $76 (includes mountain bike, van transportation, helmet, lunch, snacks, water bottle, and guide).

Glider Rides

Honolulu Soaring. Imagine soaring through silence on gossamer-like wings, a panoramic view of Oahu below you. A glider ride is an unforgettable experience, and it's available at Dillingham Air Field, in Mokuleia, on Oahu's North Shore. The glider is towed behind a plane, and at the proper altitude, the tow is dropped and you (and the glider pilot) are left to soar in the thermals. Dillingham Air Field, Mokuleia. ☎ 808/677-0207. www.honolulusoaring.com. From $60 for 10 min.

Horseback Riding

★ kids **Happy Trails Hawaii.** This small operation welcomes families (kids as young as 6 are okay) on these guided trail rides on a hilltop above Pupukea Beach and overlooking Waimea Valley. Happy Trails Hawaii, 59-231 Pupukea Rd. ☎ 808/638-RIDE (638-7433). www.happytrailshawaii.com. From $68 for 1½-hr rides.

★ **Turtle Bay Resort.** You can gallop along a deserted North Shore beach with spectacular ocean views and through a forest of ironwood trees, or take a romantic evening ride at sunset

Biking on Your Own

Bicycling is a great way to see Oahu, and most streets here have bike lanes. For information on bikeways and maps, contact the **Honolulu City and County Bicycle Coordinator** (☎ 808/527-5044; www.co.honolulu.hi.us/dts/bikeway/maps.htm).

If you're in Waikiki, you can rent a bike for as little as $10 for a half-day and $20 for 24 hours at **Big Kahuna Rentals,** 407 Seaside Ave. (☎ 808/924-2736; www.bigkahunarentals.com/sntmainbikes.htm).

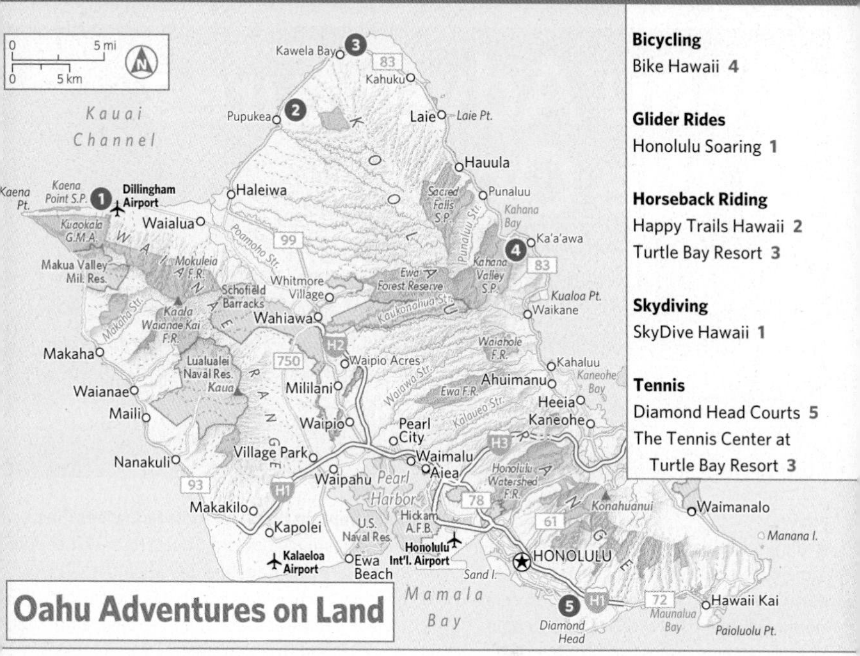

Oahu Adventures on Land

with your sweetheart. Turtle Bay Resort 57-091 Kamehameha Hwy., Kahuku. ☎ 808/293-8811. www.turtlebayresort.com. TheBus: 52 or 55. Beach rides (45 min.) $75 adults, $55 children 7-12 (they must be at least 4 ft. 4 in. tall); sunset rides $90.

Skydiving

SkyDive Hawaii. Dangerous, but also a once-in-a-lifetime experience: Leap from a plane and float to earth in a tandem jump (where you're strapped to an expert who wears a chute big enough for both of you). 68-760 Farrington Hwy., Waialua. ☎ 808/637-9700. www.hawaiiskydiving.com. $225.

Tennis

Diamond Head Courts. Oahu has 181 free public tennis courts, but these are the closest to Waikiki. The courts are available on a first-come, first-served basis; playing time is limited to 45 minutes if others are waiting. 3908 Paki Ave. (across from Kapiolani Park). ☎ 808/971-7150.

The Tennis Center at Turtle Bay Resort. Two of the eight Plexipave courts here are lit for night play. Facilities include instruction, rental equipment, player matchup, and even a ball machine. You must reserve the night courts in advance; they're very popular. 57-091 Kamehameha Hwy., Kahuku. ☎ 808/293-6024. www.turtlebayresort.com. TheBus: 52 or 55). Court time: $10 per person (complimentary for guests); equipment rental $8; lessons $35 for 30 min. and $70 for 1 hr.

Rolling through Waikiki on a Segway

One of my favorite ways to tour Waikiki is on a Segway Personal Transporter. It just takes a few minutes to get the hang of this contraption, which works through a series of high-tech stabilization mechanisms that read the motion of your body to turn or go forward or backward. It's a lot of fun—think back to the first time you rode your bicycle and the incredible freedom of zipping through space. **Glide Ride Tours and Rentals,** located in the Hawaii Tapa Tower of the Hilton Hawaiian Village Beach Resort & Spa, 2005 Kalia Rd., Honolulu. (☎ 808/941-3151; www.segwayofhawaii.com), will instruct you on the Segway (they make sure that you are fully competent before you leave their training area), and then take you on a series of tours ($125 per person to a 3-hour tour of Waikiki, Kapiolani Park, and Diamond Head).

Oahu Adventures in the Ocean

To really appreciate Oahu, you need to get off the land and get on the sea. Plunge beneath the waves with scuba gear to really see the Neptunian world. Or skip across the water in a sailing charter. Or challenge yourself by battling a 1,000-pound marlin in the sport of big game fishing. Or slowly glide over the water in a kayak, or get into the water and ride the waves bodysurfing, board surfing, or windsurfing. Whatever ocean adventure thrills you, you will find it here.

Boating

A funny thing happens to people when they come to Hawaii: Maybe it's the salt air, the warm tropical nights, or the blue Hawaiian moonlight, but otherwise-rational people who have never set foot on a boat in their life suddenly want to go out to sea. You can opt for a "booze cruise," jammed with loud, rum-soaked strangers, or you can sail on one of these special yachts, all of which will take you out **whale-watching** in season (roughly Jan–Apr).

★ kids **Captain Bob's Adventure Cruises.** See the majestic Windward Coast the way it should be seen—from Kaneohe Bay aboard a 42-foot catamaran, which skims across the almost-always calm water above the shallow coral reef. You'll land at the disappearing sandbar Ahu o Laka and visit snorkel spots full of tropical fish and, sometimes, turtles. Kaneohe Bay. ☎ 808/942-5077. $80 adults, $60 children 3–14, children under 3 free. TheBus: 55 or 56.

> *Adventurers flip for Hawaii's endless opportunities to surf, dive, kayak, sail, or simply swim in the world's most famous surf.*

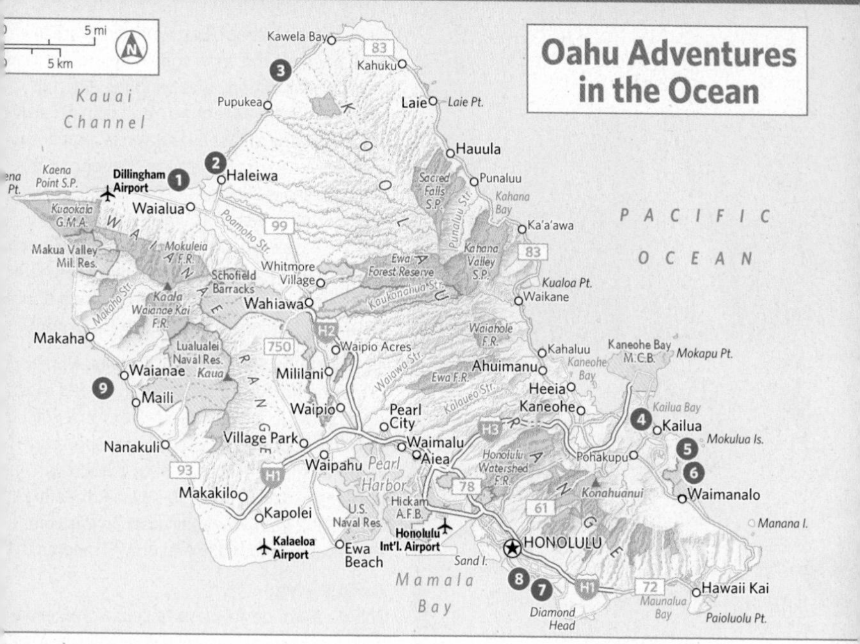

Body Boarding & Bodysurfing
Bellows Field Beach Park **6**
Kailua Beach **4**
Waikiki Beach **7**

Ocean Kayaking
Lanikai Beach **5**
Kailua Beach **4**

Sportfishing
Kewalo Basin **8**

Scuba Diving
Kahuna Canyon (Mokuleia) **1**
Wreck of the *Mahi* (Waianae) **9**

Submarine Rides
Atlantis Submarines **7**

Surfing
North Shore **3**
Waikiki **7**

Windsurfing and Kitesurfing
Haleiwa **2**
Kailua Beach **4**

★ ***Navatek 1.*** The 140-foot-long *Navatek I* isn't ʼen called a boat; it's actually a SWATH (Small /aterplane Area Twin Hull) vessel. It's the noothest ride in Waikiki. In fact, *Navatek 1* is ɪe only dinner cruise ship to receive U.S. Coast uard certification to travel beyond Diamond ead. They offer both lunch and sunset dinner uises and during the whale season (roughly n-Apr), you get whales to boot. Both cruises clude live Hawaiian music. Aloha Tower arketplace, Pier 6, c/o Hawaiian Cruises Ltd. 808/973-1311. www.hawaiiactive.com/activities/ ahu-navatek-dinnercruise.html. Dinner cruises 39–$149 adults, $53–$92 children 2–12; lunch uises $65 adults, $33 children 2–11. TheBus: 8, 19, 0, 55, 56, or 57.

kids **Wild Side Tours.** Sail on a 42-foot catamaran to a snorkel spot in the calm waters off the Waianae coast, where you'll likely see turtles and perhaps even spinner dolphins. In the winter, you may spot humpback whales on the morning cruise, which also includes continental breakfast and other refreshments, plus snorkel gear, instruction, and flotation device. Waianae Boat Harbor, Waianae. ☎ 808/306-7273. www.sailhawaii.com. Morning sail/snorkel $105 (ages 6 and up, not recommended for younger children). MC, V. Check in 7:30am, tour 8am–noon. TheBus: 19 or 20, transfer to 40 or 40A.

> *Kailua Beach attracts body boarders and swimmers, but the challenging, strong winds bring just as many sailors to its shores.*

Body Boarding, Boogie Boarding & Bodysurfing

Riding the waves without a board and becoming one with the rolling water is a way of life in Hawaii. Some bodysurfers just rely on their hands to ride the waves; others use a hand board, boogie board, or body board. Both bodysurfing and body boarding require a pair of open-heeled swim fins to help propel you through the water. Good places to learn to body board are in the small waves of **Waikiki Beach** (p 143) and **Kailua Beach** (p 140) and **Bellows Field Beach Park,** off Kalanianaole Hwy. (Hwy. 72, Hughs Rd.) in Waimanalo, which is open to the public on weekends (noon Fri–midnight Sun and holidays). TheBus: 57.

Ocean Kayaking

Gliding silently over the water, propelled by a paddle, seeing Oahu from the sea the way the early Hawaiians did—that's what ocean kayaking is all about. Early mornings are alway[s] best, because the wind comes up around 11am, making seas choppy and paddling difficult. For a wonderful adventure, rent a kayak, arrive at **Lanikai Beach** just as the sun is appearing, and paddle across the emerald lagoon to the pyramid-shaped islands called Mokulua—it's an experience you won't forget. Another favorite kayak-launching area is **Kailua Beach.** Kayak equipment rental starts at $10 an hour for a single kayak, and $16 an hour for a doubl[e] kayak. See "Where to Rent Beach Toys," p 160.

★★ kids **Kailua Sailboards & Kayaks.** First-time kayakers can learn a lot with the guided tour, which is designed for the novice. You'll get lunch, all equipment, lessons, transportation from Waikiki hotels, and about 2 hours of kayaking in Kailua Bay. 130 Kailua Rd., Kailua. ☎ 808/262-2555. www.kailuasailboards.com. 4-hr. excursion tour $89 adults, $75 children 8–1[2]

Scuba Diving

Oahu is a wonderful place to scuba dive, especially for those interested in wreck diving. One o[f] the more famous wrecks in Hawaii is the ***Mahi,*** a 185-foot former minesweeper easily accessible just south of Waianae. Abundant marine life makes this a great place to shoot photos—schools of lemon butterflyfish and taape (bluelined snapper) are so comfortable with divers and photographers that they practically pose. Eagle rays, green sea turtles, manta rays, and white-tipped sharks occasionally cruise by as well, and eels peer out from the wreck.

For nonwreck diving, one of the best dive spots in summer is **Kahuna Canyon.** In Hawaiian, *kahuna* means "priest," "wise man," or "sorcerer," and this massive amphitheater, located near Mokuleia, is a perfect example of something a sorcerer might conjure up. Walls rising from the ocean floor create the illusion of an underwater Grand Canyon. Inside the amphitheater, crabs, octopi, slippers, and spiny lobsters abound (be aware that taking them in summer is illegal), and giant trevally, parrotfish, and unicorn-fish congregate as well. Outside the amphitheater, you're likely to see an occasional shark in the distance.

Because Oahu's greatest dives are offshore your best bet is to book a two-tank dive from a dive boat. Hawaii's oldest and largest outfitter is **Aaron's Dive Shop,** 307 Hahani St., Kailua.

Get a new perspective of Oahu when you explore the shoreline from a kayak. Guided tours are typically beginner-friendly and include free lessons.

☎ 808/262-2333; www.hawaii-scuba.com). A two-tank boat dive costs $125 (including ransportation from the Kailua shop). **Dive ahu,** 1085 Ala Moana Blvd., Waikiki (☎ 808/ 22-3483; www.diveoahu.com) has two-tank oat dives for $129. **Surf-N-Sea,** 62-595 amehameha Hwy., Haleiwa (☎ 808/637- 887; www.surfnsea.com) has two-tank oat dives for $135.

SNORKEL GUIDE PAGE 159

Snorkeling

Snorkeling is a huge attraction in Waikiki and around the island—and almost anyone can do it. All you need are a mask, a snorkel, fins, and some basic swimming skills. Floating over underwater worlds through colorful clouds of tropical fish is like a dream. In many places all you have to do is wade into the water and look down. If you've never snorkeled before, most resorts and

Experiencing Jaws: Up Close & Personal

You're 4 miles out from land, surrounded by open ocean. Suddenly, from out of the blue depths, a shape emerges: the sleek, pale shadow of a 6-foot-long gray reef shark, followed quickly by a couple of 10-foot-long Galapagos sharks. Within a couple of heartbeats, you are surrounded by sharks on all sides. Do you panic? No, you paid $120 to be in the midst of these jaws of the deep. And of course, you have a 6x6x10-foot aluminum shark cage separating you from all those teeth. It happens every day at **North Shore Shark Adventures** (☎ 808/228-5900; www.hawaiisharkadventures.com). Depending on the sea conditions and the weather, snorkelers can stay in the cage as long as they wish, with the sharks just inches away. The shark cage, connected to a boat with wire line, holds up to four snorkelers (it's comfortable with two but pretty snug at full capacity). You can also stay on the boat and view the sharks from a more respectable distance for just $60. The more adventurous, down in the cage with just thin aluminum separating them from the sharks, are sure to create a memory they won't forget.

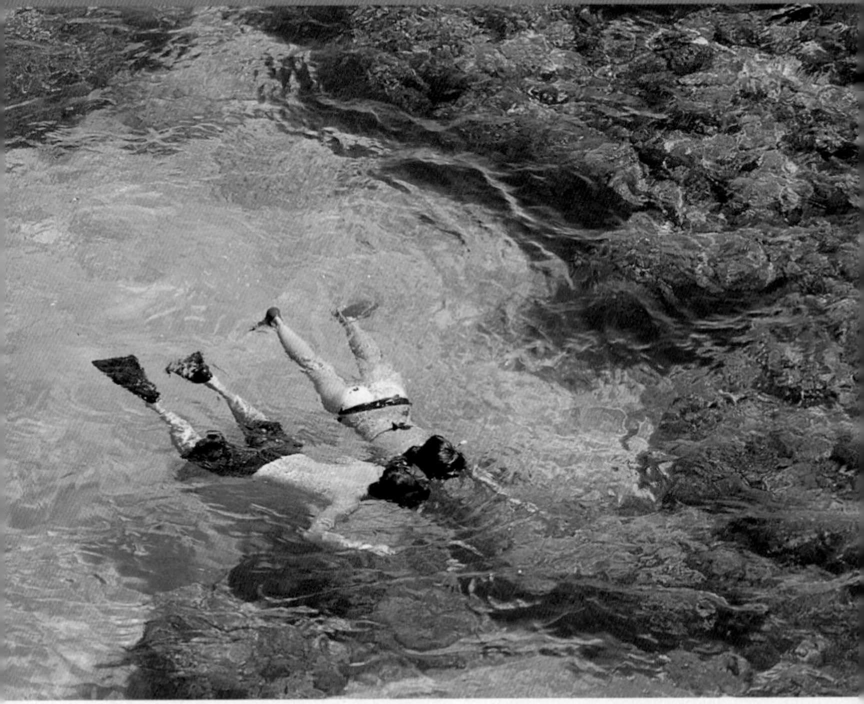

> *You can go eyeball-to-eyeball with exotic sea life while snorkeling in crystal clear Hanauma Bay.*

excursion boats offer instruction, but it's plenty easy to figure it out for yourself.

If you want to rent beach toys (snorkeling equipment, boogie boards, surfboards, kayaks, and more), check out the following rental shops: **Snorkel Bob's,** on the way to Hanauma Bay at 700 Kapahulu Ave. (at Date St.), Honolulu (☎ 808/735-7944; www.snorkelbob.com); and **Aloha Beach Service,** in the Westin Moana Surfrider Hotel, 2365 Kalakaua Ave. (☎ 808/922-3111, ext. 2341), in Waikiki. On Oahu's windward side, try **Kailua Sailboards & Kayaks,** 130 Kailua Rd., a block from the Kailua Beach Park (☎ 808/262-2555; www.kailuasailboards.com). On the North Shore, get equipment from **Surf-N-Sea,** 62-595 Kamehameha Hwy., Haleiwa (☎ 808/637-9887; www.surfnsea.com).

Sport Fishing

Marlin (as big as 1,200 lb.), tuna, ono, and mahimahi await the baited hook in Hawaii's coastal and channel waters. No license is required. Just book a sport fishing vessel out of **Kewalo Basin,** the main location for charter fishing boats on Oahu, located between Honolulu International Airport and Waikiki (Ala Moana Blvd. at Ward Ave.). TheBus: 19 or 20. When the fish are biting, the captains display the catch of the day in the afternoon.

Sportfish Hawaii. This sport fishing booking agency helps match you with the best fishing boat. Every vessel they book has been inspected and must meet rigorous criteria to guarantee that you will have a great time. ☎ 877/388-1376 or 808/396-2607; www.sportfishhawaii.com. $812–$932 for a full-day exclusive charter (you, plus five friends, get the entire boat to yourself); from $717 for a half-day exclusive; from $191 for a full-day share charter (you share the boat with five other people).

Diving on Your Own

A great resource for diving on your own is the University of Hawaii Sea Grant's ***Dive Hawaii Guide,*** www.hawaiiscubadiving.com, which describes nearly every dive site on the various Hawaiian Islands, including Oahu.

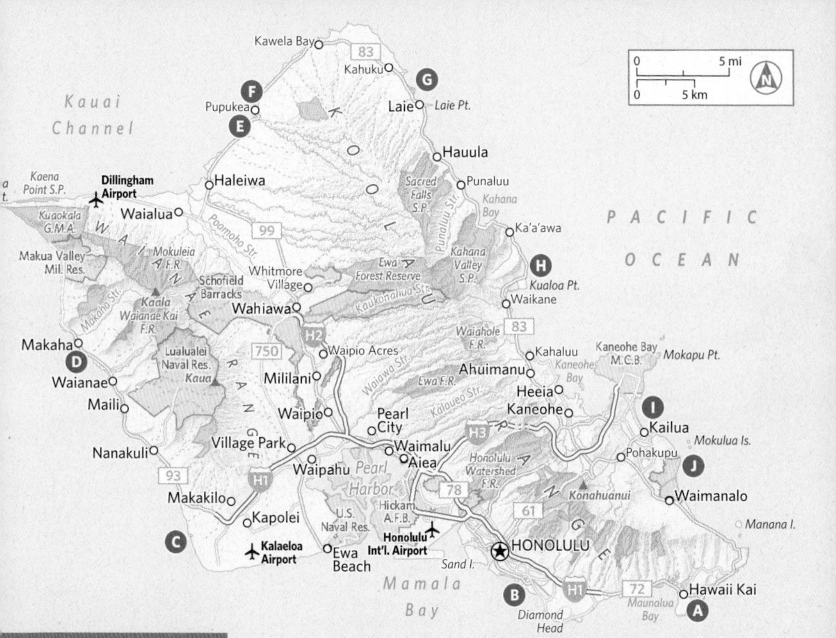

SNORKEL GUIDE

Oahu's Best Snorkeling

Oahu's most popular snorkeling spot is **A Hanauma Bay** (p 140). Part of an old crater that fell into the sea, the bay's shallow shoreline water and abundant marine life are the main attractions to snorkelers. My favorite snorkeling spot along **B Waikiki Beach** (p 143) is Queen's Beach. I usually get in the water behind the Waikiki Aquarium and snorkel up to the Natatorium and back. There's great snorkeling at **C Ko Olina Lagoons** (p 140) around the boulders at the entrance to each lagoon. During the summer, the waters at **D Makaha Beach Park** (p 141) are clear and filled with a range of sealife (including turtles). Plus the arches and tunnels just 40 feet down make great habitats for reef fish. The gentle summer waves at **E Waimea Beach Park** (p 143) allow access to great snorkeling around the rocks and reef. Stay out of the water in winter. The two snorkeling areas at **F Pupukea Beach Park** (p 142) are Shark's Cove (which is *not* named for an abundance of sharks) and, at the southern end, Three Tables (named for the three flat sections of reef visible at low tide). Snorkeling is best from May to October, when the water is calm. At **G Malaekahana Bay State Recreation Area** (p 142), you'll find the best snorkeling in the rocky areas around either of the two points (Makahoa Point and Kalanai Point) that define this bay. **H Kualoa Regional Park** (p 141) has some good snorkeling areas in the sandy waters offshore. **I Kailua Beach** (p 140) offers great snorkeling (along with a host of other ocean activities), with safe water conditions most of the year. **J Lanikai Beach** (p 141), one of Hawaii's best spots for snorkeling, has a crystal-clear lagoon that has so many fish you'll think you're in a giant saltwater aquarium. The reef extends out for about a half-mile, with snorkeling along the entire length.

> *Marlins literally jump out of the ocean with sport fishermen in hot pursuit.*

> *Surfing lessons for kids and adults are available throughout Oahu, but it's hard to beat learning to hang ten on Waikiki Beach.*

Submarine Rides

★ **Atlantis Submarines.** Here's your chance to play Jules Verne and experience the underwater world from the comfort of a submarine, which will take you on an adventure below the surface in high-tech comfort. The

Where to Rent Beach Toys

If you want to rent beach toys (snorkeling equipment, boogie boards, surfboards, kayaks, and more), check out the following rental shops: **Snorkel Bob's,** on the way to Hanauma Bay at 700 Kapahulu Ave. (at Date St.), Honolulu (☎ 808/735-7944; www.snorkelbob.com); and **Aloha Beach Service,** in the Westin Moana Surfrider Hotel, 2365 Kalakaua Ave. (☎ 808/922-3111, ext. 2341), in Waikiki. On Oahu's windward side, try **Kailua Sailboards & Kayaks,** 130 Kailua Rd., a block from the Kailua Beach Park (☎ 808/262-2555; www.kailuasailboards.com). On the North Shore, get equipment from **Surf-N-Sea,** 62-595 Kamehameha Hwy., Haleiwa (☎ 808/637-9887; www.surfnsea.com).

Even non-swimmers can explore Hawaii's underwater world on an Atlantis Submarine tour.

ntire trip is narrated as you watch tropical sh and sunken ships just outside the sub; if wimming's not your thing, this is a great way o see Hawaii's spectacular sea life. **Shuttle oats to the sub leave from the Hilton Hawaiian 'illage Pier. ☎ 800/548-6262 or 808/973-9811; ww.atlantisadventures.com/hawaii.cfm. $95 dults, $45 kids 12 and under (children must be at east 36 in. tall). *Tip:* Book online for discounts.**

urfing

he ancient Hawaiian sport of *hee nalu* (wave iding) is probably the sport most people picture hen they think of the islands. In summer, when e water's warm and there's a soft breeze in the ir, the south swell comes up. It's surf season in Vaikiki, the best place on Oahu to learn how to urf. For lessons, go early to **Aloha Beach Serice,** next to the Moana Surfrider, 2365 Kalakaua ve. (☎ 808/922-3111). Lessons are $30 an hour nd rentals $10 for the first hour, $5 for every our after that. On the North Shore, contact the **lans Hedemann Surf School** at the Turtle Bay esort (☎ 808/924-7778; www.hhsurf.com). ledemann has been a champion surfer for some 4 years. Lessons start at $75 an hour.

Windsurfing and Kitesurfing

Windward Oahu's **Kailua Beach** is the home of champion and pioneer windsurfer Robbie Naish; it's also the best place to learn to windsurf. The oldest and most established windsurfing business in Hawaii is **Naish Hawaii/Naish Windsurfing Hawaii,** 155-A Hamakua Dr., Kailua (☎ 800/767-6068 or 808/262-6068; www.naish.com). Private lessons start at $75 for a 90-minute sesson; beginner equipment rents for $40 for 4 hours, $45 for 8 hours. Kite board rentals cost $25 for a half-day, $30 for a full day. Another option is **Kailua Sailboards & Kayaks,** 130 Kailua Rd., Kailua (☎ 808/262-2555; www.kailuasailboards.com). Group lessons cost $89 per person for 3 hours; private lessons cost $109. Prices include all gear, hotel pick-up, and lunch.

Surf's Up!

To find out where the waves are, call the **Surf News Network Surfline** (☎ 808/596-SURF) to get the latest surf conditions.

SURFING

Sport of Kings and Commoners

BY MEGAN McFARLAND

IN CONTRAST to the Hollywood stereotype of surfing as the pastime of teenyboppers, underachievers, and California rich kids, surfing originated in Hawaii centuries ago as a deeply spiritual art, intimately tied to culture and religion. Surfing was required training for Hawaiian chiefs and was used to resolve conflicts; rituals and *kapu* (taboos) surrounded every aspect of the practice, from praying for good surf to building a surfboard. Polynesians came to the Hawaiian Islands in the fourth century A.D., bringing with them their *paipo* (belly) boards and exceptional water navigation skills. But the art of surfing—standing upright on a wave-borne board—is thought to be a uniquely Hawaiian invention. In ancient times, prior to the arrival of Europeans in the late-eighteenth century, two kinds of surfboards existed: the long *olo*, for chiefs and noblemen (*alii*), and the shorter *alaia*, for commoners, who were strictly forbidden from using the *olo* and surfing in the zones reserved for the *alii*.

Surfing History

1779	1820	1866	1890	1905	1907	1908
First written description of surfing by a Westerner, Lieutenant James King, commander of Captain Cook's HMS *Discovery*.	First Christian missionaries arrive from England, imposing Christian moral rules on Hawaiian customs, including surfing.	Mark Twain visits Hawaii, describing surfing in his book *Roughing It*: "I tried surf-bathing once, subsequently, but made a failure of it."	**DUKE PAOA KAHANAMOKU** is born (d. 1968). A great surfer and Olympic gold medal swimmer, Duke became a lifelong ambassador for surfing.	Hawaiians found the informal *Hui Nalu* ("Club of the Waves") surf club on Waikiki, revitalizing native interest in surfing.	Waikiki beach boy George Freeth is invited to California to demonstrate, "wave-riding."	The Hawaiian Outrigger Canoe Club is established—the first modern clu[b] dedicated to wave-riding and outrigger canoeing.

Aloha 'Aina, Aloha Kai
Love the Land, Love the Sea

Surfing On Screen In Hawaii

RIDE THE WILD SURF 1964
Young heartthrobs Fabian and Tab Hunter starred in this epitome of 1960s teenage surf flicks; shot at Waimea Bay on the North Shore.

BLUE CRUSH 2002
Real-life surfers joined actress Kate Bosworth in this "girl-power" film about female surfers on Oahu. Filmed on and around Sunset Beach, with amazing surfing sequences.

RIDING GIANTS 2004
A stunning documentary on the history of surfing and big-wave surfers; *Surfer* magazine called this film "one of the best surf movies ever made."

Hawaii's Most Famous Surfing Beaches

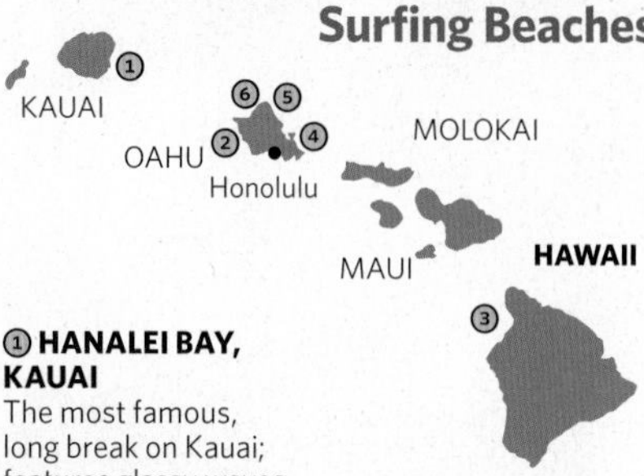

① HANALEI BAY, KAUAI
The most famous, long break on Kauai; features glassy waves sheltered by the surrounding mountains.

② DIAMOND HEAD LIGHTHOUSE, OAHU
Protected from trade winds by Diamond Head, this reef picks up most south swells and is the best surfing area on the South Shore.

③ KE'EI, KEALAKEKUA BAY, BIG ISLAND
In this huge bay the best waves are found at the southern end.

④ SUNSET BEACH, OAHU *(NORTH SHORE)*
The sand quickly turns to rock behind Sunset Beach, which generates extremely fast waves.

⑤ BANZAI/PIPELINE, OAHU *(NORTH SHORE)*
One of the world's most challenging surf beaches.

⑥ WAIMEA BAY, OAHU *(NORTH SHORE)*
Legendary winter big-wave spot.

Surfing Lingo

BRAH Used by native Hawaiians: a surfer friend.

DA KINE Could mean anything—but in surfing, it's associated with something good or genuine: "That wave was da kine, brah!"

GUN A long, thin surfboard ranging from 6 to 10 feet, for big-wave riding.

MULLERING A major, painful wipeout.

STICK Surfboard.

SHUBEE A tourist who dresses like a surfer but has never surfed.

STOKED Describes the feeling after an awesome ride; or a state of mind: a happy surfer.

DUDE Considered retro slang by most. Refers to anyone you're talking to, specifically a fellow surfer.

Honolulu & Waikiki Shopping Best Bets

Best Alohawear
Bailey's Antiques & Aloha Shirts, 517 Kapahulu Ave. (p 165).

Best Antiques
Antique Alley, 1347 Kapiolani Blvd. (p 168).

Best Place to Browse
Native Books Na Mea Hawaii, 1050 Ala Moana Blvd. (p 173).

Best Cookies
Yama's Fish Market, 2332 Young St. (p 172).

Best Exotic Foods
Asian Grocery, 1319 Beretania St. (p 170).

Best Fashion Deals
The Ultimate You, 449 Kapahulu Ave. (p 170).

Best Gifts
Nohea Gallery, 1050 Ala Moana Blvd. (p 173).

Best Hawaii Artist
Pegge Hopper Gallery, 1164 Nuuanu Ave. (p 168).

Best Hawaiian Books
Rainbow Books and Records, 1010 University Ave. (p 169).

> *Head straight to Local Motion for some of the coolest T-shirts on the island.*

Best Hawaiian CDs
Shop Pacifica, 1525 Bernice St. (p 173).

Best Hawaiian Memorabilia
Hula Supply Center, 2346 S. King St. (p 172).

Best Place for a Lei
Cindy's Lei Shoppe, 1034 Maunakea St. (p 172).

Best Made-in-Hawaii Products
It's Chili in Hawaii, 2080 S. King St. (p 171).

Best Shopping Center
Ala Moana Center, 1450 Ala Moana Blvd. (p 173).

Best Shopping-as-Entertainment
Honolulu Fish Auction, Pier 38, 1131 N. Nimitz Hwy. (p 172).

Best Sinfully Delicious Bakery
Honolulu Chocolate Co., 1200 Ala Moana Blvd. (p 170).

Best Sushi Takeout
Sushi Company, 1111 McCully St. (p 172).

Best T-Shirts
Local Motion, 2250 Kalakaua Ave. (p 175).

Best Wine & Liquor
Fujioka's Wine Merchants, 2919 Kapiolani Blvd. (p 170).

Honolulu & Waikiki Shopping A to Z

Alohawear

★ Avanti Fashion WAIKIKI
This leading retro aloha shirt label turns out stunning, hip, and nostalgic silk shirts and dresses in authentic 1930s to 1950s fabric patterns. 2164 Kalakaua Ave. (at Kuhio St.). ☎ 808/924-3232. www.avantishirts.com. AE, DC, DISC, MC, V. TheBus: 19 or 20. Map p 167.

★★ Bailey's Antiques & Aloha Shirts KAPAHULU
Honolulu's largest selection (thousands) of vintage, secondhand, and nearly new aloha shirts and other collectibles fill this eclectic emporium, as well as old ballgowns, feather boas, fur stoles, leather jackets, 1930s dresses, and scads of other garments from Hollywood movie costume. 517 Kapahulu Ave. (at Castle St.). ☎ 808/734-7628. www.alohashirts.com. DISC, MC, V. TheBus: 13 or 14. Map p 167.

★ kids Hilo Hattie IWILEI, ALA MOANA
Hawaii's largest manufacturer of Hawaiian fashions has become "hip" in the last few years with inexpensive silk aloha shirts as well as brand-name aloha shirts like Tommy Bahama and the store's own Hilo Hattie label. 700 N. Nimitz Hwy. (at Pacific St.) ☎ 808/535-6500; and Ala Moana Center 1450 Ala Moana Blvd. (at Piikoi) ☎ 808/973-3266. TheBus: 19 or 20. www.hilohattie.com. AE, DISC, MC, V. Map p 166.

Macy's ALA MOANA
If it's alohawear, Macy's has it. The extensive aloha shirt and muumuu departments here feature every label you can conjure, with a selection—in all price ranges—that changes with the times. Ala Moana Center, 1450 Ala Moana Blvd. (at Atkinson Dr.). ☎ 808/941-2345. www.macys.com. AE, DISC, MC, V. TheBus: 19 or 20. Map p 166.

Reyn's ALA MOANA
Reyn's used to be a prosaic line but has stepped up its selection of women's and men's alohawear with contemporary fabric prints and stylings, appealing to a trendier clientele. Ala

> Oahu shopping opportunities include everything from kitschy souvenirs to fine art.

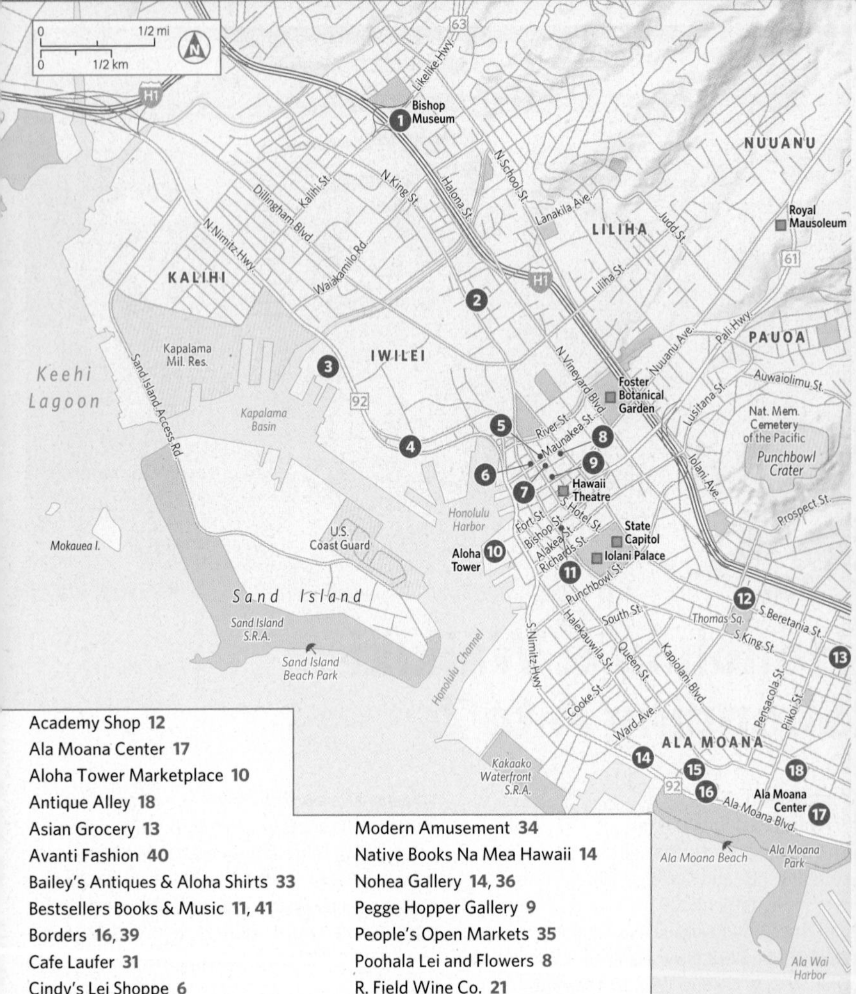

Academy Shop 12
Ala Moana Center 17
Aloha Tower Marketplace 10
Antique Alley 18
Asian Grocery 13
Avanti Fashion 40
Bailey's Antiques & Aloha Shirts 33
Bestsellers Books & Music 11, 41
Borders 16, 39
Cafe Laufer 31
Cindy's Lei Shoppe 6
Contemporary Museum Gift Shop 22
DFS Galleria 37
Don Quijote 20
Foodland 21
Fujioka's Wine Merchants 29
Gallery at Ward Centre 16
Hawaiian Island Creations 17
Hilo Hattie 4, 17
Honolulu Chocolate Co. 16
Honolulu Fish Auction 3
Hula Supply Center 27
It's Chili in Hawaii 24
Kicks 19
Local Motion 38
Macy's 17
Maunakea Marketplace Food Court 5
Modern Amusement 34
Native Books Na Mea Hawaii 14
Nohea Gallery 14, 36
Pegge Hopper Gallery 9
People's Open Markets 35
Poohala Lei and Flowers 8
R. Field Wine Co. 21
Rainbow Books and Records 28
Rainforest Plantes et Fleurs 30
Ramsay Galleries 7
Reyn's 17
Royal Hawaiian Shopping Center 39
Rudy's Flowers 25
Sconees 32
Shop Pacifica 1
Sushi Company 23
T. Fujii Japanese Antiques 30
Tamashiro Market 2
The Ultimate You 34
Ward Centre 16
Ward Entertainment Center 15
Ward Warehouse 14
Yama's Fish Market 26

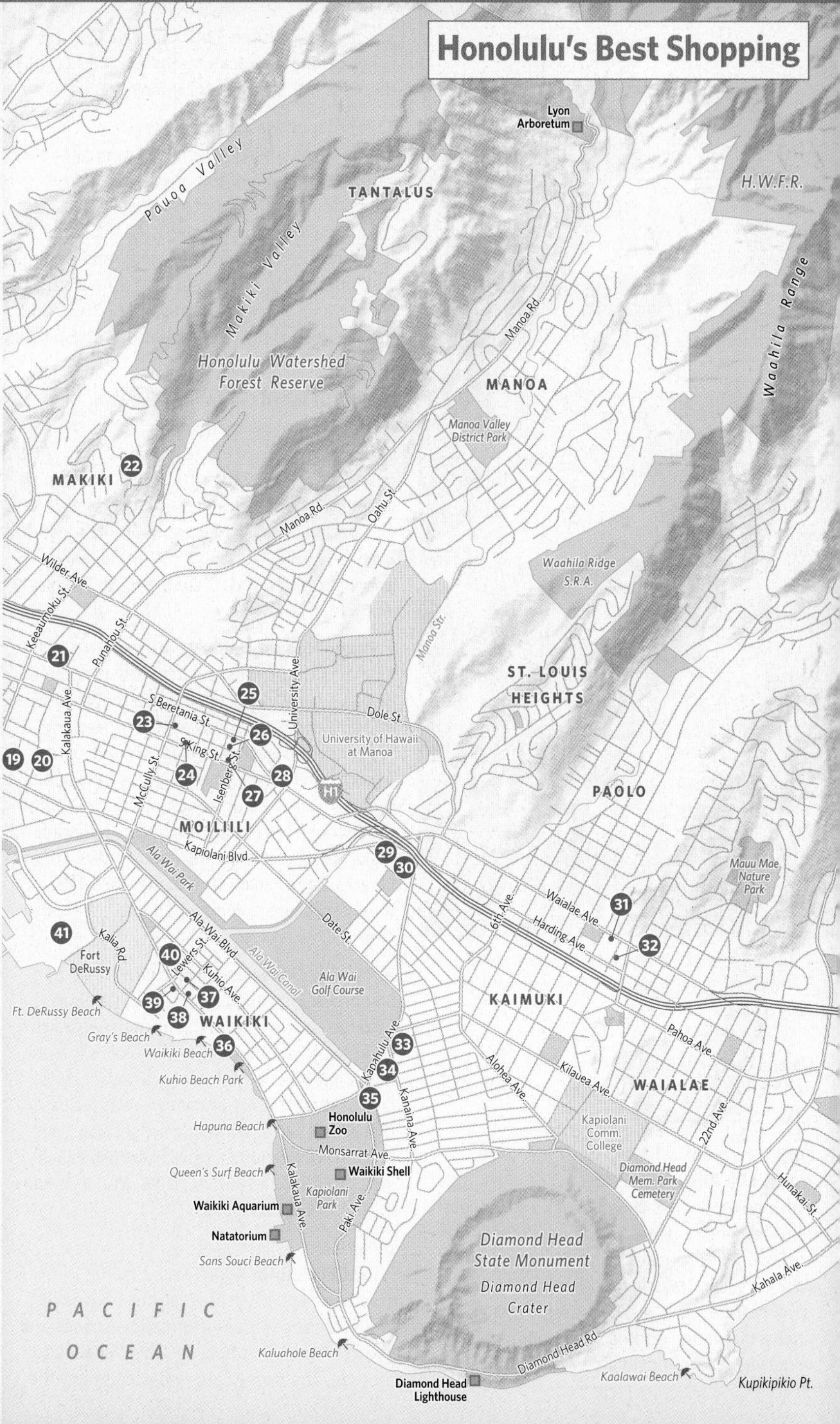
Honolulu's Best Shopping
Lyon Arboretum
H.W.F.R.
TANTALUS
Pauoa Valley
Makiki Valley
Honolulu Watershed Forest Reserve
Manoa Rd.
MANOA
Manoa Valley District Park
Waahila Range
MAKIKI
Oahu St.
Wilder Ave.
Waahila Ridge S.R.A.
Keeaumoku St.
Punahou St.
Manoa Str.
University Ave.
ST. LOUIS HEIGHTS
S Beretania St.
Dole St.
S King St.
University of Hawaii at Manoa
Kalakaua Ave.
McCully St.
Isenberg St.
H1
PAOLO
MOILIILI
Kapiolani Blvd.
Ala Wai Park
Mauu Mae Nature Park
Waialae Ave.
Ala Wai Blvd.
Date St.
6th Ave.
Harding Ave.
Kalia Rd.
Fort DeRussy
Lewers St.
Kuhio Ave.
Ala Wai Canal
Ala Wai Golf Course
KAIMUKI
Ft. DeRussy Beach
WAIKIKI
Gray's Beach
Waikiki Beach
Kapahulu Ave.
Pahoa Ave.
Kuhio Beach Park
Alohea Ave.
Kilauea Ave.
WAIALAE
Kanaina Ave.
Honolulu Zoo
Hapuna Beach
22nd Ave.
Kapiolani Comm. College
Monsarrat Ave.
Queen's Surf Beach
Waikiki Shell
Diamond Head Mem. Park Cemetery
Hunakai St.
Kalakaua Ave.
Kapiolani Park
Waikiki Aquarium
Paki Ave.
Natatorium
Diamond Head State Monument
Sans Souci Beach
Diamond Head Crater
Kahala Ave.
PACIFIC OCEAN
Kaluahole Beach
Diamond Head Rd.
Kaalawai Beach
Kupikipikio Pt.
Diamond Head Lighthouse
19
20
21
22
23
24
25
26
27
28
29
30
31
32
33
34
35
36
37
38
39
40
41

> *Bailey's Antiques & Aloha Shirts offers the Islands' largest selection of second-hand clothing with a local flavor.*

Moana Center, 1450 Ala Moana Blvd. (at Piikoi). ☎ 808/949-5929. AE, DC, DISC, MC, V. TheBus: 19 or 20. Map p 166.

Antiques & Collectibles

★ **Antique Alley** KAKAAKO
This narrow shop is chockablock with collections ranging from old Hawaiian artifacts and surfing and hula nostalgia to estate jewelry, antique silver, Hawaiian bottles, collectible toys, pottery, cameras, Depression-era glass, linens, plantation photos and ephemera, and a wide selection of nostalgic items from Hawaii and across America. 1347 Kapiolani Blvd. (at Piikoi; behind America's Mattress). ☎ 808/941-8551. AE, MC, V. TheBus: 2. Map p 166.

T. Fujii Japanese Antiques MOILIILI
This is a long-standing icon in Hawaii's antiques world and an impeccable source for *ukiyo-e* prints, scrolls, obis, Imari porcelain, tansus, tea-ceremony bowls, and screens, as well as contemporary ceramics from Mashiko and Kasama, with prices from $25 to $18,000. 1016-B Kapahulu Ave. (King St. and H-1). ☎ 808/732-7860. www.tfujiiantiques.com. MC, V. TheBus: 14. Map p 167.

Art

Gallery at Ward Centre ALA MOANA
A cooperative gallery of Oahu artists, the gallery features fine works in all media, including paper, clay, scratchboard, oils, watercolors, collages, woodblocks, lithographs, glass, jewelry, and more. Ward Centre, 1200 Ala Moana Blvd. (at Auahi St.). ☎ 808/597-8034. www.gwcfineart.com. AE, DC, DISC, MC, V. TheBus: 19 or 20. Map p 166.

★ **Pegge Hopper Gallery** CHINATOWN
One of Hawaii's most popular artists, Hopper displays her widely collected paintings (usually of Hawaiian women with broad, strong features) in her attractive gallery, which has become quite the gathering place for exhibits ranging from Tibetan sand-painting by saffron-robed monks to the most avant-garde printmaking in the islands. 1164 Nuuanu Ave. (btw. Beretania and Pauahi sts.). ☎ 808/524-1160. www.peggehopper.com. AE, DC, MC, V. TheBus: 19 or 20. Map p 166.

★ **Ramsay Galleries** CHINATOWN
Nationally known quill-and-ink artist Ramsay, who has drawn everything from the Plaza Hotel in New York to most of Honolulu's historic buildings, maintains a vital monthly show schedule featuring her own work as well as that of her fellow Hawaiian artists. Tan Sing Building, 1128 Smith St. (btw. Hotel and Pauahi sts.). ☎ 808/537-2787. AE, DISC, MC, V. TheBus: 2, 3, 12, or 13. Map p 166.

Bakeries

★ kids **Cafe Laufer** WAIALAE
This small cheerful cafe features frilly decor and sublime pastries—from apple scones and linzertortes to fruit flan, decadent chocolate mousse, and carrot cake—to accompany the

latte and espresso. 3565 Waialae Ave. (at 11th Ave.). ☎ 808/735-7717. www.cafelaufer.com. AE, DISC, MC, V. No bus. Map p 167.

Foodland KAKAAKO
This grocery store flies in dough from Los Angeles's famous La Brea bakery and bakes it fresh at this location, so you can pick up fresh-from-the-oven organic wheat, rosemary-olive oil, roasted garlic, potato-dill, and other spectacular breads. 1460 S. Beretania St. (btw. Kalakaua Ave. and Makiki St.). ☎ 808/949-4654. www.foodland.com. AE, DISC, MC, V. TheBus: 2. Map p 167.

Sconees WAIALAE
Formerly Bea's Pies, this unique bakery has fantastic scones, yummy pumpkin-custard pies, and tempting Danishes. 1117 12th Ave. (at Harding). ☎ 808/734-4024. No credit cards. No bus. Map p 167.

Bargains

★★★ **Aloha Flea Market** AIEA
More than just bargain shopping (although there are plenty of bargains to be found here), this giant outdoor bazaar is an adventure full of strange food and odd goods and is heaven for bargain hunters. Nobody leaves empty-handed—or without having had lots of fun. Go early for the best deals. Bring $1 for the entry fee (kids 11 and under are free). Open Wednesday, Saturday, and Sunday from 6am to 3pm. Aloha Stadium, 99–500 Salt Lake Blvd., Aiea. ☎ 808/486-6704. No credit cards. No bus.

Bookstores

★ **Bestsellers Books & Music** DOWNTOWN/WAIKIKI Hawaii's largest independent bookstore has a complete selection of nonfiction and fiction titles with an emphasis on Hawaiian books and music. 1001 Bishop St. (at Hotel St.). ☎ 808/528-2378. TheBus: 4. Also at the Hilton Hawaiian Village, 2005 Kalia Rd. (at Ala Moana Blvd.). ☎ 808/953-2378. TheBus: 19 or 20. AE, MC, V. Map p 166 and p 167.

Borders WAIKIKI/ALA MOANA
Borders is a beehive of literary activity, with weekly signings, prominent local and mainland musicians at least monthly, and special events almost daily that make this store a major Honolulu attraction. 2201 Kalakaua Ave. (btw. Royal Hawaiian and Seaside aves.). ☎ 808/922-4154. TheBus: 19 or 20. Also at the Ward Centre, 1200 Ala Moana Blvd. (at Auahi St.). ☎ 808/591-8995. www.bordersstores.com. AE, DC, DISC, MC, V. TheBus: 19 or 20. Map p 166 and p 167.

> *Don't leave the Island before tasting mouth-watering homemade delicacies at Honolulu Chocolate Company.*

★ **Rainbow Books and Records** MOILIILI
A little weird but totally lovable, especially among students and eccentrics (and insatiable readers), this tiny bookstore is notable for its selection of popular fiction, records, and Hawaii-themed books, secondhand and reduced. 1010 University Ave. (at King St.). ☎ 808/955-7994. www.rainbowbookshawaii.com. AE, DISC, MC, V. TheBus: 4. Map p 167.

> *Get free samples of the Island's hottest food every Saturday night at It's Chili in Hawaii, which offers spicy sauces from around the world.*

Consignment Shops

★★ The Ultimate You WAIKIKI
At this resale boutique, the clothes are relatively current (fashion of the last 2 years) and not always cheap, but they're always 50% to 90% off retail. You might see clothes from Escada, Chanel, Prada, Gianfranco Ferre, Donna Karan, Yves St. Laurent, Armani, Ralph Lauren, Laura Ashley, and Ann Taylor on the racks. 449 Kapahulu Ave. (at Ala Wai Blvd.). ☎ 808/681-6784. www.theultimateyou.com. DISC, MC, V. TheBus: 2. Map p 167.

Edibles

★ Asian Grocery KAKAAKO
A great stop for foodies, this shop supplies many of Honolulu's Thai, Vietnamese, Chinese, Indonesian, and Filipino restaurants with authentic spices, rice, noodles, produce, sauces, herbs, and other adventurous ingredients. 1319 S. Beretania St. (btw. Piikoi and Keeaumoku sts.). ☎ 808/593-8440. MC, V. TheBus: 2. Map p 166.

Don Quijote KAKAAKO
You can find everything at this huge emporium, ranging from takeout sushi, Korean *kal bi*, pizza, Chinese food, flowers, and Mrs. Fields cookies to Kau navel oranges, macadamia nuts, Kona coffee, Chinese taro, and other Hawaii products. Open 24 hours. 801 Kaheka St. (at Kahunu St.). ☎ 808/973-4800. AE, DISC, MC, V. TheBus: 2. Map p 167.

Fujioka's Wine Merchants MOILIILI
Oenophiles flock here for a mouthwatering selection of wines (excellent Italian wines), single-malt Scotches, and affordable, farm-raised caviar—food and libations for all occasions. Market City Shopping Center, 2919 Kapiolani Blvd. (at S. King St.), lower level. ☎ 808/739-9463. AE, DC, DISC, MC, V. TheBus: 14. Map p 167.

★★ Honolulu Chocolate Co. ALA MOANA
Life's greatest pleasures are dispensed here with abandon: expensive gourmet chocolates made in Honolulu, Italian and Hawaiian biscotti, boulder-size caramel and pecan turtles, truffles, and my favorites—macadamia nut clusters dipped in dark chocolate (heavenly). Ward Centre, 1200 Ala Moana Blvd. (at Auahi St.). ☎ 808/591-2997. www.honoluluchocolate.com. AE, DC, MC, V. TheBus: 19 or 20. Map p 166.

★★ **It's Chili in Hawaii** MCCULLY
This is *the* oasis for chili-heads, a house of heat with endorphins aplenty and good food to accompany the hot sauces from around the world, including a fabulous selection of made-in-Hawaii products. Every Saturday free samples of green-chili stew are dished up to go with the generous hot-sauce tastings. 2080 S. King St., Suite 105 (btw. McCully and Wiliwili sts.). ☎ 808/945-7070. MC, V. TheBus: 6. Map p 167.

Maunakea Marketplace Food Court CHINATOWN
Hungry patrons line up for everything from pizza and plate lunches to quick, authentic, and inexpensive Vietnamese, Thai, Italian, Chinese, Japanese, and Filipino dishes. The best seafood fried rice comes from the woks of **Malee Thai/ Vietnamese Cuisine**—it's perfectly flavored, with morsels of fish, squid, and shrimp. **Tandoori Chicken Cafe** serves a fount of Indian culinary pleasures, from curries and jasmine-chicken rice balls to spiced rounds of curried potatoes and a wonderful lentil dal. **Masa's** serves bento and Japanese dishes, such as miso eggplant, that are famous. You'll find the best dessert around at **Pho Lau,** which serves haupia (coconut pudding), tapioca, and taro in individual baskets made of pandanus. Join in the spirit of discovery at the produce stalls (pungent odors, fish heads, and chicken feet on counters—not for the squeamish). Vendors sell everything from fresh ahi and whole snapper to yams and taro, seaweed, and fresh fruits and vegetables. 1120 Maunakea St. (btw. N. Hotel and Pauahi sts.), Chinatown. ☎ 808/524-3409. No credit cards. TheBus: 2. Map p 166.

★ **People's Open Markets** WAIKIKI
Truck farmers from all over the island bring their produce to Oahu's neighborhoods in regularly scheduled, city-sponsored open markets, held Monday through Saturday at various locations. Paki and Monsarrat aves. ☎ 808/522-7088; http://www.honolulu.gov/parks/programs/pom/index1.htm. Map p 167.

R. Field Wine Co. KAKAAKO
Richard Field—oenophile, gourmet, and cigar aficionado—moved his wine shop and thriving gourmet store into this grocery store, offering all manner of epicurean delights, including wines and single-malt Scotches. Foodland Super

> *Peruse a wide array of Hawaiian books and products at Native Books Na Mea in Ward Warehouse on Ala Moana Blvd.*

Market, 1460 S. Beretania St. (btw. Kalakaua Ave. and Makiki St.). ☎ 808/596-9463. AE, DISC, MC, V. TheBus: 2. Map p 167.

★ **Sushi Company** MCCULLY
Skip the sushi bar and pick up some takeout at this small, incredible sushi store that sells fast-food sushi of non-fast-food quality, at great prices. 1111 McCully St. (btw. King and Beretania sts.). ☎ 808/947-5411. No credit cards. TheBus: 6. Map p 167.

Fashion

Kicks KAKAAKO
Attention sneaker aficionados, collectors, and those looking for shoes as a fashion statement: This is your store. You'll find limited editions and classic footwear by Nike and Adidas, as well as trendy clothing lines. 1530 Makaloa St. (btw. Keeaumoku and Amana sts.). ☎ 808/941-9191. www.kickshawaii.com. AE, DISC, MC, V. TheBus: 13. Map p 167.

Modern Amusement KAPAHULU
One of only four MA stores in the world, the appeal here is to the artsy type or nonconformist surfers, skateboarders, and clubbers (and Japanese tourists) looking for both sophisticated surf-wear and classic club outfits. 449 Kapahulu Ave., Suite 102 (btw. Ala Wai Blvd. and Kanaina Ave.). ☎ 808/738-2769. AE, DC, DISC, MC, V. TheBus: 13. Map p 167.

Fish Markets

★★ kids **Honolulu Fish Auction** IWILEI
If you want to experience the high drama of fish-buying, head to this auction at the United Fishing Agency, where fishermen bring their fresh catch in at 5:30am (sharp) Monday through Saturday, and buyers bid on a variety of fish, from fat tuna to weird-looking hapupu. Pier 38, 1131 N. Nimitz Hwy. ☎ 808/536-2148. No credit cards. TheBus: 42. Map p 166.

★ **Tamashiro Market** IWILEI
Good service and the most extensive selection of fresh fish in Honolulu has made this the granddaddy of fish markets, where you will find everything from live lobsters and crabs to glistening fresh slabs of ahi to *onaga* and *ehu* (whole or filets). 802 N. King St. (btw. Palama St. and Austin Lane), Kalihi. ☎ 808/841-8047. MC, V. TheBus: 42. Map p 166.

Yama's Fish Market MOILIILI
Known for its inexpensive fresh fish, tasty poke, lomi salmon, and many varieties of prepared seafood, Yama's also has a variety of prepared foods and bakery items (their chocolate-chip and mac-nut cookies are peerless). 2332 Young St. (Hoawa Lane). ☎ 808/941-9994. www.yamasfishmarket.com. DISC, DC, MC, V. TheBus: 6. Map p 167.

Flowers & Leis

★ kids **Cindy's Lei Shoppe** CHINATOWN
I love this lei shop because it always has unusual leis, such as feather dendrobiums, firecracker combinations, and everyday favorites like ginger, tuberose, orchid, and pikake. I also love its "curb service": You phone in your order and pick up your lei curbside, a great convenience on this busy street. 1034 Maunakea St. (at Hotel St.). ☎ 808/536-6538. MC, V. TheBus: 2. Map p 166.

Poohala Lei and Flowers CHINATOWN
If you are looking for a worthy selection of the classics at fair prices, this is the shop. 69 N. Beretania St. (btw. Smith and Maunakea sts.). ☎ 808/537-3011. MC, V. TheBus: 19 or 20. Map p 166.

★ **Rainforest Plantes et Fleurs** KAPAHULU
Come to Rainforest for a special-occasion designer bouquet or lei. Custom-designed leis and special arrangements come with cards in Hawaiian (with English translations). Kilohana Square, 1016 Kapahulu Ave. (btw. H-1 and Kehei Place). ☎ 808/591-9999. AE, DC, DISC, MC, V. No bus. Map p 167.

Rudy's Flowers MOILIILI
The best prices on roses, Micronesian ginger leis, and a variety of cut blooms. 2357 S. Beretania St. (at Isenburg St.). ☎ 808/944-8844. www.rudysflowers.com. AE, DISC, MC, V. TheBus: 6. Map p 167.

Hawaiiana Gifts

★ kids **Hula Supply Center** MOILIILI
Hawaiiana meets kitsch in this shop's marvelous selection of souvenirs and memorabilia of Hawaii, including Day-Glo cellophane skirts, bamboo nose flutes, T-shirts, hula drums, shell leis, feathered rattle gourds, lauhala accessories, fiber mats, and a wide assortment of pareu fabrics. 2338 and 2346 S. King St. (at Isenberg St.). ☎ 808/941-0100. www.hulasupplycenter.com. MC, V. TheBus: 6. Map p 167.

★★★ kids **Native Books Na Mea Hawaii** ALA MOANA This is a browser's paradise, featuring a variety of Hawaiian items, from musical instruments to calabashes, jewelry, leis, books, contemporary Hawaiian clothing, Hawaiian food products, and other high-quality gift items. Ward Warehouse, 1050 Ala Moana Blvd. (at Ward Ave.). ☎ 808/596-8885. www.nativebookshawaii.com. AE, DISC, MC, V. TheBus: 19 or 20. Map p 166.

★★★ kids **Nohea Gallery** ALA MOANA/WAIKIKI A fine showcase for contemporary Hawaii art, Nohea celebrates the islands with thoughtful, attractive selections like pit-fired raku, finely turned wood vessels, jewelry, handblown glass, paintings, prints, fabrics (including Hawaiian-quilt cushions), and furniture. Ward Warehouse, 1050 Ala Moana Blvd. (at Ward Ave.). ☎ 808/596-0074. Also at Westin Moana Surfrider Hotel, 2365 Kalakaua Ave. (at Kaiulani Ave.). ☎ 808/923-6644. TheBus: 19 or 20. www.noheagallery.com. AE, DC, DISC, MC, V. Map p 166 & 167.

Museum Stores

★ kids **Academy Shop** KAKAAKO The place to go for art books, jewelry, basketry, ethnic fabrics, native crafts from all over the world, posters, and fiber vessels and accessories. Honolulu Academy of Arts, 900 S. Beretania St. (at Ward Ave.). ☎ 808/532-8703. www.honoluluacademy.org. AE, DISC, MC, V. TheBus: 2 or 13, or City Express B. Map p 166.

★ **Contemporary Museum Gift Shop** MAKIKI HEIGHTS I love the glammy selection of jewelry and novelties such as twisted-wire wall hangings at this browser-friendly shop. You'll also find cards and stationery, books, home accessories, and gift items made by artists from Hawaii and across the country. 2411 Makiki Heights Rd. (btw. Round Top and Mott-Smith drives). ☎ 808/523-3447. www.tcmhi.org. AE. DC, DISC, MC, V. No bus. Map p 167.

★★ kids **Shop Pacifica** KALIHI Plan to spend time browsing through the local crafts (terrific Niihau shell leis), lauhala and Cook Island woven products, Hawaiian music tapes and CDs, pareu, and a vast selection of Hawaii-themed books that anchor this gift shop. Bishop Museum, 1525 Bernice St. (btw. Kalihi St. and Kapalama Ave.). ☎ 808/848-4158. www.bishopmuseum.org. AE, DC, DISC, MC, V. TheBus: 2. Map p 166.

> *Fine-crafted flowered leis and custom orders keep the customers coming back to Cindy's Lei Shoppe on Manaukea Street.*

Shopping Centers

★★ kids **Ala Moana Center** ALA MOANA Nearly 400 shops and restaurants sprawled over several blocks make this Hawaii's largest shopping center catering to every imaginable need, from over-the-top upscale (**Neiman Marcus, Tiffany,** and **Chanel**), to mainland chains (**The Gap, Banana Republic, DKNY,** and **Old Navy**), to department stores **(Macy's, Sears),** to practical services, such as banks, a foreign-exchange service **(Travelex),** a post office, several optical companies (including 1-hr. service by **LensCrafters**), and a handful of smaller locally owned stores **(Islands' Best, Splash! Hawaii).** The buzzing **food court** serves up everything from Cajun food, ramen, pizza, plate lunches, vegetarian fare, green tea and fruit freezes (like frozen yogurt), panini, and countless other treats. 1450 Ala Moana Blvd. (btw. Kaheka and Piikoi sts.). ☎ 808/955-9517. www.alamoanacenter.com. AE, DC, DISC, MC, V. TheBus: 8, 19, or 20. Map p 166.

> *At the Royal Hawaiian Shopping Center, you can pick up anything from a ukulele to a pair of Ferragamos.*

Aloha Tower Marketplace HONOLULU HARBOR
Dining and shopping prospects abound here: **Hawaiian Pacific Crafts, Hawaiian Ukulele Company, Sunglass King, Don Ho's Island Grill, Chai's Island Bistro,** and **Gordon Biersch Brewery Restaurant.** 1 Aloha Tower Dr. (at Bishop St.). ☎ 808/528-5700, www.alohatower.com. AE, DC, DISC, MC, V. TheBus: 19 or 20. Map p 166.

DFS Galleria WAIKIKI
"Boat days" is the theme at this Waikiki emporium, a three-floor extravaganza of shops ranging from the superluxe (like **Chloe** and **Coach**) to the very touristy, with great Hawaiian food products **(Big Island Candies),** aloha shirt and T-shirt shops, surf and skate equipment, a terrific Hawaiian music department, and a labyrinth of fashionable stores thrown in to complete the retail experience. 330 Royal Hawaiian Ave. (at Kalakaua Ave.). ☎ 808/931-2655, www.dfsgalleria.com. AE, DC, MC, V. TheBus: 19 or 20. Map p 167.

★ **Royal Hawaiian Shopping Center** WAIKIKI
After 2 years and $84 million in remodeling and renovations, a larger upscale shopping center opened in 2007 with new shops, restaurants, nightclub and theater, entry porte-cochere, and even a garden grove of 70 coconut trees with entertainment area. In all you'll find 110 stores, restaurants, and entertainment on four levels: everything from **Hilo Hattie** to **Cartier, Hermès,** and **Salvatore Ferragamo.** 2201 Kalakaua Ave. (at Royal Hawaiian Ave.). ☎ 808/922-0588. www.shopwaikiki.com. AE, DC, DISC, MC, V. TheBus: 19 or 20. Map p 167.

Waikele Premium Outlets WAIKELE
There are two sections to this sprawling discount shopping mecca: the **Waikele Premium Outlets,** some 51 retailers offering designer and name-brand merchandise **(Saks Fifth Avenue, Barneys),** and the **Waikele Value Center** across the street, with another 25 stores, more practical than fashion-oriented **(Eagle Hardware, Sports Authority).** The 64-acre complex has made discount shopping a travel pursuit in itself, with bargains on everything from perfumes, luggage, and hardware to sporting goods, fashions, vitamins, and china. 94-790 Lumiaina St., Waikele (about 20 miles from Waikiki). ☎ 808/676-5656. www.premiumoutlets.com/waikele.

> *Delicious fruits and vegetables are brought from all over the islands to the People's Open Markets in Honolulu.*

★ kids **Ward Centre** ALA MOANA
Great restaurants **(Kakaako Kitchen, Kua Aina)** and shops **(Crazy Shirts Factory Outlet, Paper Roses, Honolulu Chocolate Co., The Gallery,** and **Borders)** make this a popular place, bustling with browsers. 1200 Ala Moana Blvd. (at Kamakee St.). ☎ 808/591-8411. www.victoriaward.com. AE, DC, DISC, MC, V. TheBus: 19 or 20. Map p 166.

kids **Ward Entertainment Center** ALA MOANA
This is the place for eating, drinking, and entertainment: everything from a 16-movie megaplex to eateries **(Dave & Buster's, Buca di Beppo,** and **Cold Stone Creamery),** retail therapy **(Nordstrom Rack, Office Depot,** and **Pier 1 Imports),** and the ubiquitous **Starbucks Coffee.** At the corner of Auahi and Kamakee sts. ☎ 808/591-8411. www.victoriaward.com. AE, DC, DISC, MC, V. TheBus: 19 or 20. Map p 166.

★ kids **Ward Warehouse** ALA MOANA
Older than its sister properties (see above), Ward Warehouse remains a popular stop for dining **(Old Spaghetti Factory, Honolulu Cookie Company)** and shopping **(Native Books & Beautiful Things, Nohea Gallery).** 1050 Ala Moana Blvd. (at Ward Ave.). ☎ 808/591-8411. www.victoriaward.com. AE, DC, DISC, MC, V. TheBus: 19 or 20. Map p 166.

T-Shirts

Hawaiian Island Creations ALA MOANA
This super-cool surf shop offers sunglasses, sun lotions, surf-wear, surfboards, skateboards, and accessories galore. Ala Moana Center, 1450 Ala Moana Blvd. (btw. Piikoi and Kaheka sts.). ☎ 808/973-6780. www.hicsurf.com. AE, DISC, MC, V. TheBus: 19 or 20. Map p 166.

★ kids **Local Motion** WAIKIKI
The icon of surfers and skateboarders, both professionals and wannabes, has everything from surfboards, T-shirts, aloha- and casual-wear to countless accessories for life in the sun. Waikiki Shopping Plaza, 2250 Kalakaua Ave. (btw. Seaside and Royal Hawaiian aves.). ☎ 808/924-4406. www.localmotionhawaii.com. AE, DISC, MC, V. TheBus: 19 or 20. Map p 167.

Oahu Restaurant Best Bets

Best Breakfast
Hula Grill Waikiki $$ 2335 Kalakaua Ave. (p 181).

Best Buffets
Prince Court $$$ 100 Holomoana St. (p 184).

Best Burger
Kua Aina $ 1116 Auahi St. (p 182).

Best Chinese
Little Village Noodle House $ 1113 Smith St. (p 183).

Best Dim Sum
Legend Seafood Restaurant $ 100 N. Beretania St. (p 182).

Best for Families
Kaka'ako Kitchen $ 1200 Ala Moana Blvd. (p 182).

Best French/Vietnamese
Duc's Bistro $$$ 1188 Maunakea St. (p 180).

Best Hawaii Regional Cuisine
Alan Wong's Restaurant $$$$ 1857 S. King St. (p 177).

Best Meals under $10
Nico's at Pier 38 $ 1133 N. Nimitz Hwy. (p 183).

> *Kua Aina offers an appetizing menu of delicacies including this burger, which carries the reputation of "Best on the Island."*

Best for Meat Lovers
d.k. Steakhouse $$$ 2552 Kalakaua Ave. (p 180).

Best Restaurant Open Late
Eggs 'n Things $ 1911-B Kalakaua Ave. (p 181).

Most Romantic
La Mer $$$$$ 2199 Kalia Rd. (p 182).

Best Splurge
Chef Mavro Restaurant $$$$$ 1969 S. King St. (p 177).

Best Sunday Brunch
Orchids $$$$ 2199 Kalia Rd. (p 184).

Best Sunset Views
Duke's $$$ 2335 Kalakaua Ave. (p 180).

Best Sushi
Sansei Seafood Restaurant & Sushi Bar $$$ 2552 Kalakaua Ave. (p 185).

Best Tapas
Hiroshi Eurasian Tapas $$ 500 Ala Moana Blvd. (p 181).

Most Trendy
Town $$ 3435 Waialae Ave. (p 185).

Best View of Waikiki
Hau Tree Lanai $$$ 2863 Kalakaua Ave. (p 181).

Oahu Restaurants A to Z

★★★ **Alan Wong's Restaurant** MCCULLY *HAWAII REGIONAL CUISINE* James Beard Award-winner chef Alan Wong, worshiped by foodies across the state, serves brilliantly creative and irresistibly cutting-edge cuisine (think ginger-crusted onaga) in a casual, sometimes noisy room that is always packed. Book in advance. 1857 S. King St. (btw. Kalakaua Ave. and McCully St.). ☎ 808/949-2526. Entrees $35–$52; 5-course sampling menu $75 ($105 with wine); chef's 7-course tasting menu $95 ($135 with wine). AE, DC, MC, V. Dinner daily. TheBus: 13. Map p 179.

★ **Assaggio** KAILUA *ITALIAN* The affordable prices, attentive service, and winning menu items have attracted loyal fans of this neighborhood bistro. You can choose linguine, fettuccine, or ziti with 10 different sauces in small or regular portions for any of the extensive list of seafood or chicken dishes. 354 Uluniu St. (at Aulike St.). ☎ 808/261-2772. Entrees $10–$25. AE, DC, DISC, MC, V. Lunch Mon–Fri, dinner daily. Map p 181.

> *Mariposa offers Pacific and American dishes in a bright and airy environment overlooking Ala Moana Park.*

★★ **Bali by the Sea** WAIKIKI *CONTINENTAL/PACIFIC RIM* Get a window seat at sunset for oceanfront dining on such dishes as herb-infused rack of lamb, Kona lobster, and a host of mouthwatering desserts. Come Friday to see the 7:30pm fireworks. Hilton Hawaiian Village, 2005 Kalia Rd. (Ala Moana Blvd.). ☎ 808/941-2254. Entrees $29.50–$58. AE, DC, DISC, MC, V. Dinner Mon–Sat. TheBus: 19 or 20. Map p 179.

★ kids **Cafe Haleiwa** NORTH SHORE *MEXICAN* Haleiwa's legendary breakfast joint is a big hit with surfers, urban gentry with weekend country homes, reclusive artists, and anyone who loves generous servings of home-cooked food in a Formica-casual setting. 66-460 Kamehameha Hwy. (near Paalaa Rd.). ☎ 808/637-5516. Main courses $6–$11. AE, MC, V. Breakfast and lunch daily. Map p 180.

★★★ **Chef Mavro** MCCULLY *PROVENÇAL/HAWAII REGIONAL CUISINE* If you have only one night on Oahu, splurge at this intimate dining experience in a non-touristy neighborhood. James Beard Award-winner chef George Mavro's inspired menu (roast pork with apple quinoa; poached fresh fish with sago-coconut nage, thai herbs, limu, and lime

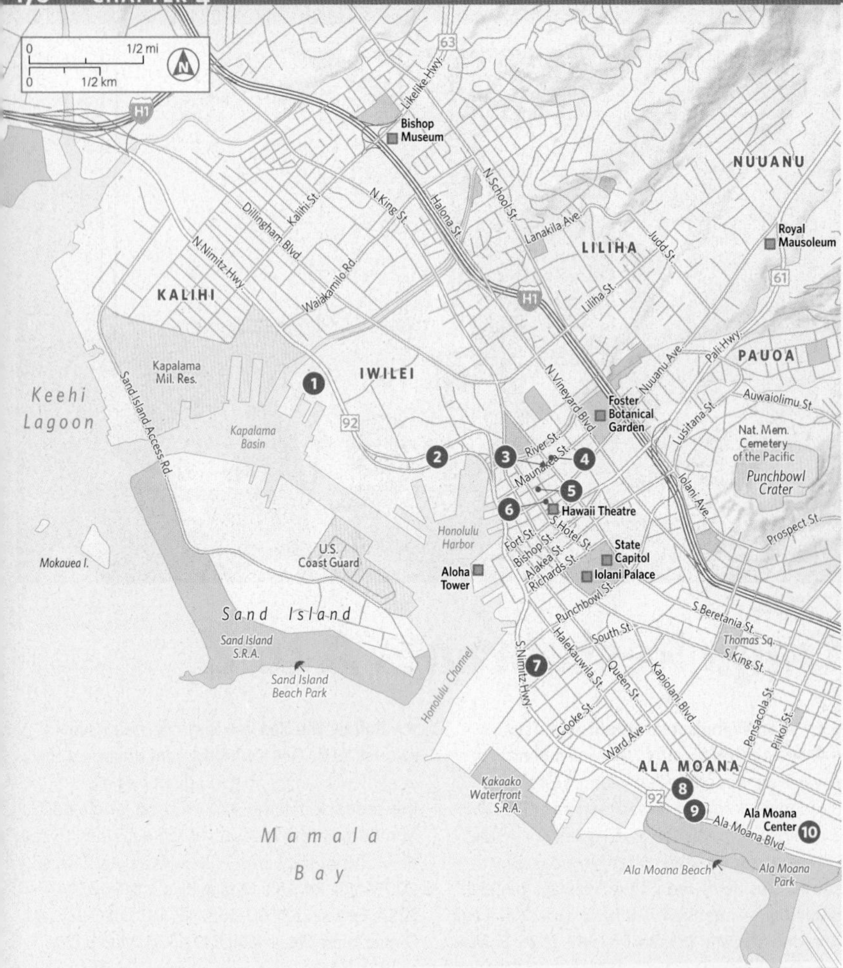

Honolulu's Best Restaurants

Alan Wong's Restaurant **11**
Bali by the Sea **15**
Chef Mavro **12**
d.k. Steakhouse **18**
Diamond Head Grill **20**
Duc's Bistro **3**
Duke's **17**
Eggs 'n Things **14**
Hau Tree Lanai **19**
Hiroshi Eurasian Tapas **7**
Hula Grill Waikiki **17**
Indigo Eurasian Cuisine **6**
Kaka'ako Kitchen **9**
Kua Aina **8**
La Mer **16**
Legend Seafood Restaurant **4**
Little Village Noodle House **5**
Mariposa **10**
Michel's **21**
Nico's at Pier 38 **1**
Orchids **16**
The Pineapple Room **10**
Prince Court **13**
Sam Choy's Breakfast, Lunch Crab & Big Aloha Brewery **2**
Sansei Seafood Restaurant & Sushi Bar **18**
3660 on the Rise **24**
Town **22**
12th Avenue Grill **23**

Manoa Falls
Lyon Arboretum
H.W.F.R.
Pauoa Valley
TANTALUS
Makiki Valley
Waahila Range
Manoa Rd.
Honolulu Watershed Forest Reserve
MANOA
Manoa Valley District Park
MAKIKI
Manoa Rd.
Oahu St.
Waahila Ridge S.R.A.
Wilder Ave.
Keeaumoku St.
Punahou St.
University Ave.
Manoa Str.
ST. LOUIS HEIGHTS
Kalakaua Ave.
S.Beretania St.
Dole St.
University of Hawaii at Manoa
S.King St.
McCully St.
Isenberg St.
H1
PAOLO
MOILIILI
Kapiolani Blvd.
Ala Wai Park
Waialae Ave.
Mauu Mae Nature Park
Date St.
Ala Wai Blvd.
6th Ave.
Kalia Rd.
Lewers St.
Harding Ave.
Fort DeRussy
Kuhio Ave.
Ala Wai Canal
Ala Wai Golf Course
KAIMUKI
Ft. DeRussy Beach
WAIKIKI
Pahoa Ave.
Gray's Beach
Waikiki Beach
Kapahulu Ave.
Kanaina Ave.
Alohea Ave.
Kilauea Ave.
WAIALAE
Kuhio Beach Park
22nd Ave.
Honolulu Zoo
Kapiolani Comm. College
Hapuna Beach
Monsarrat Ave.
Diamond Head Mem. Park Cemetery
Queen's Surf Beach
Waikiki Shell
Hunakai St.
Kalakaua Ave.
Kapiolani Park
Waikiki Aquarium
Paki Ave.
Natatorium
Diamond Head State Monument
Sans Souci Beach
Kahala Ave.
Diamond Head Crater
PACIFIC OCEAN
Kaluahole Beach
Diamond Head Rd.
Kaalawai Beach
Diamond Head Lighthouse
Kupikipikio Pt.
11
12
13
14
15
16
17
18
19
20
21
22
23
24

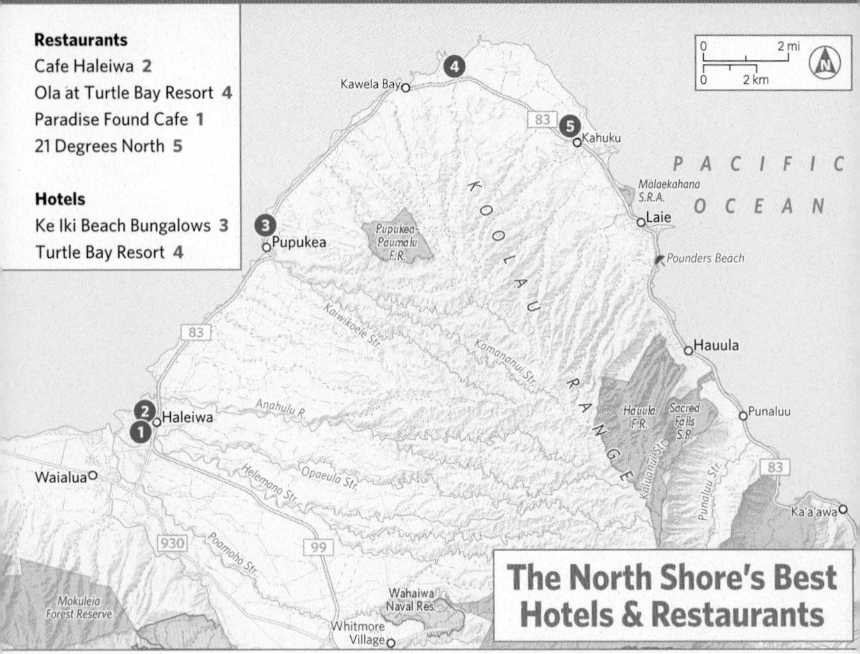

froth) comes with perfect wine pairings. 1969 S. King St. (McCully St.). ☎ 808/944-4714. Prix fixe $65–$150 ($98–$154 with wine pairings). AE, DC, DISC, MC, V. Tues–Sun 6–9:30pm. TheBus: 13, transfer to 1. Map p 179.

★ **d.k Steakhouse** WAIKIKI *STEAK*
Attention carnivores: This is the ultimate steakhouse for the 21st-century at very reasonable prices (especially for Waikiki). Book an outside table on the lanai to enjoy the sunset over Waikiki Beach. Waikiki Beach Marriott Resort, 2552 Kalakaua Ave. (Ohua Ave.). ☎ 808/931-6280. Entrees $25–$62. AE, DISC, MC, V. Daily 5:30–10pm. TheBus: 19 or 20. Map p 179.

★ **Diamond Head Grill** WAIKIKI *ECLECTIC*
Three good reasons to dine here: new executive chef Eric Sakai's unusual menu (from lobster ravioli to pork chops with risotto); sinful desserts; and a place to party—after 10pm on Friday and Saturday, it becomes a hot nightspot. West Honolulu, 2885 Kalakaua Ave. (across from Kapiolani Park). ☎ 808/922-3734. Entrees $15–$30. AE, DC, DISC, MC, V. Dinner daily. TheBus: 19 or 20. Map p 179.

★★ **Duc's Bistro** CHINATOWN *FRENCH/VIETNAMESE* Dine on Honolulu's best French-Vietnamese cuisine (from seafood spring rolls to steak au poivre) in a quietly elegant restaurant that features live music nightly. 1188 Maunakea St. (Beretania St.). ☎ 808/531-6325. Entrees: $13–$22 lunch, $20–$50 dinner. AE, DC, DISC, MC, V. Mon–Fri 11:00am–2pm; Mon–Sat 5–10pm. TheBus: 19 or 20. Map p 178.

The Ultimate Room Service Menu

Room Service in Paradise (☎ 808/941-DINE; www.941-dine.com) delivers almost a dozen different cuisines from oodles of restaurants to your hotel room. All you do is select a restaurant and order what you want (see the online menu or pick up one of its magazines in various Waikiki locations). There's a $6.75 delivery charge in Waikiki (more in outlying areas).

★ kids **Duke's** WAIKIKI *STEAK/SEAFOOD*
This open-air dining room (outfitted in surfing memorabilia), overlooking Waikiki Beach, is the best spot to watch the sunset (with Hawaiian musicians serenading in the background), as you debate over a menu ranging from burgers to fresh fish. Outrigger Waikiki on the Beach,

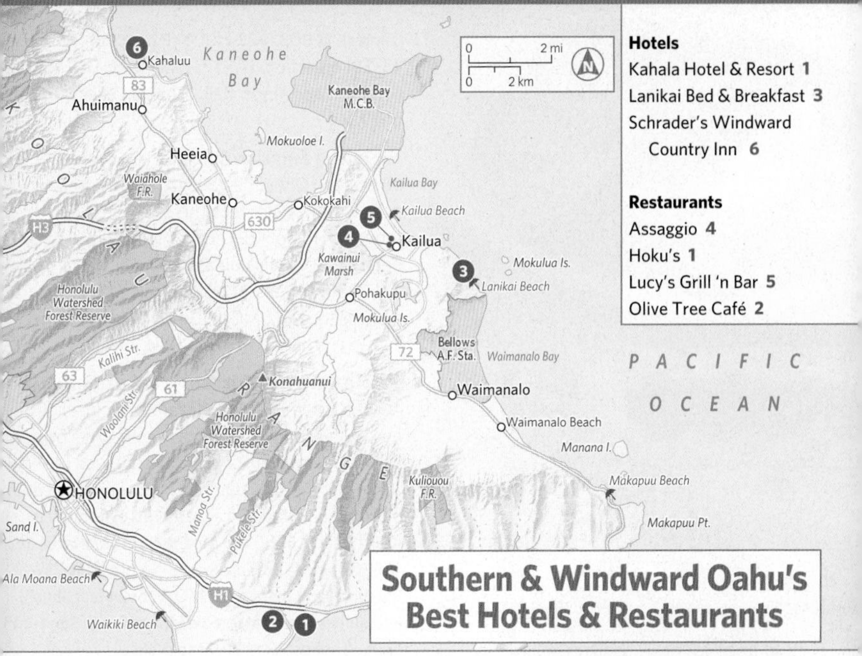

Southern & Windward Oahu's Best Hotels & Restaurants

2335 Kalakaua Ave. (next door to Royal Hawaiian Shopping Center). ☎ 808/922-2268. Entrees $18–$38. AE, DC, DISC, MC, V. Breakfast, lunch, and dinner daily. TheBus: 19 or 20. Map p 179.

★ kids **Eggs 'n Things** WAIKIKI *BREAKFAST* This popular breakfast-only eatery is famous for its huge plates of food and its all-night hours on weekends. 1911-B Kalakaua Ave. (at Ala Moana Blvd.). ☎ 808/949-0820. Entrees $7–$12. No credit cards. Mon–Wed 6am–2pm; Thurs–Sun 11pm–2pm the next day. TheBus: 19 or 20. Map p 179.

★ kids **Hau Tree Lanai** WAIKIKI *PACIFIC RIM* Located under a giant hau tree right on the beach (just a few yards from the waves), this informal eatery has the best view of Waikiki Beach. Breakfast is my favorite—especially the taro pancakes. New Otani Kaimana Beach Hotel, 2863 Kalakaua Ave. (across from Kapiolani Park). ☎ 808/921-7066. Entrees $18–$39. AE, DC, DISC, MC, V. Breakfast, lunch, and dinner daily. TheBus: 19 or 20. Map p 179.

★ **Hiroshi Eurasian Tapas** RESTAURANT ROW *EURO-ASIAN FUSION* My pick for the best tapas (small plates), with such choices as truffled crab cake and kampachi carpaccio. Go with as many people as possible so you can sample more items. Restaurant Row, 500 Ala Moana Blvd. (btw. Punchbowl and South sts.). ☎ 808/533-HIRO (533-4476). Tapas $7–$22. AE, DISC, MC, V. Dinner daily. TheBus: 19 or 20. Map p 178.

★★★ **Hoku's** KAHALA *HAWAII REGIONAL CUISINE* Elegant without being stuffy, and creative without being overwrought, the upscale dining room of the Kahala Hotel & Resort combines European finesse with an island touch, with dishes like steamed whole fresh fish, pan-seared foie gras, rack of lamb, ahi steak, and the full range of East-West specialties. Sunday brunch is not to be missed. Kahala Hotel, 5000 Kahala Ave. (end of street). ☎ 808/739-8780. Entrees $32–$94. AE, DC, DISC, MC, V. Dinner daily, brunch Sun. Map (above).

★★ kids **Hula Grill Waikiki** WAIKIKI *HAWAII REGIONAL CUISINE* This is the best place for breakfast in Waikiki: Not only does this oceanside bistro have a terrific ocean view (clear to Diamond Head), but the food is fabulous (crab cake eggs Benedict, Maui-pineapple and coconut pancakes). Good value, too. Outrigger Waikiki on the Beach, 2335 Kalakaua Ave. (next to Royal Hawaiian Shopping

Center). ☎ 808/923-HULA (923-4852). Entrees: $5–$14 breakfast, $17–$33 dinner. AE, DC, MC, V. Breakfast and dinner daily. TheBus: 19 or 20. Map p 179.

★★ **Indigo Eurasian Cuisine** CHINATOWN *EURASIAN* Dine in the elegant indoor setting or in a tropical garden. The East-West menu ranges from pot stickers to plum-glazed baby-back ribs. 1121 Nuuanu Ave. (Pauahi St.). ☎ 808/521-2900. Entrees: $17–$24 lunch, $23–$37 dinner. DC, DISC, MC, V. Lunch Tues–Fri, dinner Tues–Sat. TheBus: 19 or 20. Map p 178.

★★ kids **Kaka'ako Kitchen** HONOLULU *GOURMET PLATE LUNCHES* Bring the family for local home-style cooking at budget prices. It's owned by chef Russell Siu, of 3660 On the Rise (see p 185), so it's great value for the money. The catch: Styrofoam plates and a warehouse ambience. Ward Centre, 1200 Ala Moana Blvd. (Kamakee St.). ☎ 808/596-7488. Entrees: $5–$8 breakfast, $7–$13 lunch and dinner. AE, MC, V. Breakfast, lunch, and dinner Mon–Sat; breakfast and lunch Sun (until 5pm). TheBus: 19 or 20. Map p 178.

★ kids **Kua Aina** HONOLULU *AMERICAN* I recommend skipping the long lines for a seat at this branch of the popular North Shore burger and sandwich joint. Instead, call ahead for take-out and go to the beach. Ward Village, 1116 Auahi St. (Kamakee St.). ☎ 808/591-9133. Sandwiches and burgers $6–$8.50. No credit cards. Lunch and dinner daily. TheBus: 19 or 20. Map p 178.

★★★ **La Mer** WAIKIKI *NEOCLASSIC FRENCH* This oceanfront bastion of haute cuisine is the place to go for a romantic evening. Michelin award-winner chef Yves Garnier prepares classic French dishes with fresh island ingredients, such as hamachi with pistachio, shrimp on black risotto, and scallops with ratatouille served with a saffron sauce. Halekulani Hotel, 2199 Kalia Rd. (Lewers St.). ☎ 808/923-2311. 3-course prix fixe $90; 4-course $120; 5-course $135; 9-course $150. AE, DC, MC, V. Dinner daily. TheBus: 19 or 20. Map p 179.

★ kids **Legend Seafood Restaurant** CHINATOWN *DIM SUM/SEAFOOD* This is my favorite dim sum eatery. It's not fancy, but who cares with the creative dim sum coming out of the kitchen

> *TOP TO BOTTOM* *Assaggio; Bali By The Sea; Duc's Bistro; d.k Steakhouse.*

(ranging from deep-fried taro puffs to prawn dumplings). The clientele are mainly Chinese-speaking diners, so you know it's authentic. Chinese Cultural Plaza, 100 N. Beretania St. (Maunakea St.). ☎ 808/532-1868. Dim sum under $16. AE, DC, MC, V. Mon–Fri 10:30am–2pm and 5:30–10pm; Sat–Sun 8am–2pm and 5:30–10pm. TheBus: 19 or 20. Map p 178.

★★ kids **Little Village Noodle House** CHINATOWN *CHINESE* My pick for the best Chinese food served "simple and healthy" (its motto) is this tiny neighborhood restaurant with helpful waitstaff and even parking in the back (unheard of in Chinatown). Try the honey-walnut shrimp or the garlic eggplant. The menu includes Northern, Canton, and Hong Kong–style dishes. 1113 Smith St. (btw. King and Pauahi sts.). ☎ 808/545-3008. Entrees under $13. AE, DISC, MC, V. Lunch and dinner daily. TheBus: 19 or 20. Map p 178.

★★ kids **Lucy's Grill 'n Bar** KAILUA *HAWAII REGIONAL CUISINE* This is one of Kailua's most popular restaurants, not just because of the open-air bar and the outdoor lanai seating but also because of the terrific food. Try the Szechuan-spiced jumbo tiger prawns with black-bean cream and penne pasta or the lemon grass–crusted scallops with yellow Thai curry. 33 Aulike St. (at Kuulei Rd.). ☎ 808/230-8188. Entrees $14–$28. MC, V. Dinner daily. Map p 181.

★★ kids **Mariposa** ALA MOANA *AMERICAN HERITAGE* High ceilings inside and outside tables with views of Ala Moana Park pair beautifully with a menu of Pacific and American specialties (from a king crab, shrimp, and mussel risotto to pan-roasted Hawaiian snapper). At lunch, order the signature starter: the popover with *poha* (gooseberry) butter. Neiman Marcus, Ala Moana Center, 1450 Ala Moana Blvd. (Piikoi St.). ☎ 808/951-3420. Entrees: $15–$27 lunch, $25–$58 dinner. AE, DC, MC, V. Lunch and dinner daily. TheBus: 19 or 20. Map p 178.

★★ **Michel's** WAIKIKI *FRENCH/HAWAII REGIONAL CUISINE* One side of this 45-year-old classic French restaurant opens to the ocean view (get there for sunset), but the food is the real draw. Tuxedo-clad waiters serve classic French cuisine with an island infusion (lobster bisque, steak Diane, and a Caesar salad made at your table) in an elegantly casual atmosphere. Colony Surf Hotel, 2895 Kalakaua Ave. (across from Kapiolani Park). ☎ 808/923-6552. Entrees $36–$49. AE, DC, DISC, MC, V. Dinner daily. TheBus: 19 or 20. Map p 179.

> *Duke's packs 'em in for authentic atmosphere recalling Hawaii's greatest hero, as well as a full board of tropical libations.*

★★ kids **Nico's at Pier 38** IWILEI *FRESH FISH* I never miss a chance to eat at this tiny takeout place, which serves up island-style gourmet French cuisine in Styrofoam takeout containers at frugal prices. My favorite is the furikake-pan-seared ahi with an addicting ginger-garlic-cilantro dip, served with greens or macaroni salad for $8.75. Pier 38, 1133 N. Nimitz Hwy. (Alakawa St.). ☎ 808/540-1377. www.nicospier38.com. Entrees: $2.45–$7.35 breakfast, $6.55–$8.80 lunch. Breakfast and lunch Mon–Sat. TheBus: 19 or 20. Map p 178.

★★ kids **Ola at Turtle Bay Resort** NORTH SHORE *ISLAND STYLE CUISINE & SEAFOOD* The location (literally on the beach), the view (lapping waves), the romantic atmosphere (tiki torches at sunset), and the food (slow-poached

> *The popular 3660 On the Rise provides out-of-this world delicacies at reasonable prices.*

salmon, fisherman's stew, kiawe smoked beef tenderloin) make this open-air eatery one of the best on the North Shore. **Turtle Bay Resort, 57-091 Kamehameha Hwy. (at Kuhuku Dr). ☎ 808/293-0801. Entrees: $9–$16 lunch, $17–$53 dinner. AE, DC, DISC, MC, V. Lunch Sun–Thurs; dinner daily. TheBus: 52 or 55. Map p 180.**

★★ kids **Olive Tree Café** KAHALA *GREEK/EASTERN MEDITERRANEAN* This hip hole-in-the-wall eatery serves up divine Greek fare at budget-friendly prices—it's my top pick for a meal under $20. There are umbrella tables outside and a few seats indoors, and you order and pay at the counter. Winners include mussel ceviche, creamy, tender chicken saffron, and a generous Greek salad. **4614 Kilauea Ave., across from Kahala Mall. ☎ 808/737-0303. Entrees $8–$15. No credit cards. Dinner daily. Map p 181.**

★★★ kids **Orchids** WAIKIKI *INTERNATIONAL/SEAFOOD* This is the best Sunday brunch in Hawaii, with an outstanding array of dishes, from popovers to sushi to an omelet station. Excellent food in an extraordinary setting (right on Waikiki Beach). **Halekulani Hotel, 2199 Kalia Rd. (Lewers St.). ☎ 808/923-2311. Dinner entrees $24–$58; 3-course chef's prix-fixe dinner $57; Sunday brunch $50. AE, DC, MC, V. Breakfast, lunch, and dinner daily (brunch Sun). TheBus: 19 or 20. Map p 179.**

kids **Paradise Found Cafe** NORTH SHORE *VEGETARIAN* This tiny, "pure" vegetarian hole in the wall offers organic, healthy breakfast and lunch to eat in or take out. **66-443 Kamehameha Hwy. (near Paalaa Rd.). ☎ 808/637-4540. All items less than $12. No credit cards. Breakfast and lunch daily. Map p 180.**

★★ kids **The Pineapple Room** ALA MOANA *HAWAII REGIONAL CUISINE* Culinary icon chef Alan Wong's bistro features gustatory masterpieces that will probably leave you wanting to come back to try breakfast, lunch, and dinner, just to see what else he will present. Expect anything from *moi* (served whole and steamed Chinese-style) to apple curry-glazed pork chops with pumpkin and mascarpone puree and mango chutney. **Macy's, 1450 Ala Moana Blvd. (Piikoi St.). ☎ 808/945-6573. Lunch entrees $16–$20; prix-fixe lunch $29; dinner entrees $28–$38; sampling dinner $75. AE, DC, MC, V. Breakfast Sat–Sun, lunch and dinner daily. TheBus: 19 or 20. Map p 178.**

★ kids **Prince Court** WAIKIKI *CONTEMPORARY ISLAND CUISINE* Floor-to-ceiling windows, sunny views of the harbor, and top-notch buffets are Prince Court's attractions. I especially recommend the Friday and Saturday seafood buffets with sushi, Vietnamese pho, crab, oysters, shrimp, scallops, and even prime rib. **Hawaii Prince Hotel Waikiki, 100 Holomoana St. (Ala Moana Blvd.). ☎ 808/944-4494. Entrees $18–$28; breakfast buffet $21; weekend brunch $35; luncheon buffet $25; dinner buffet $43. AE, DC, MC, V. Breakfast, lunch, and dinner daily (brunch Sat–Sun). TheBus: 19 or 20. Map p 179.**

kids **Sam Choy's Breakfast, Lunch, Crab & Big Aloha Brewery** IWILEI *ISLAND CUISINE/SEAFOOD* Chef/restaurateur Sam Choy's crab house features gigantic meals (fried poke, Cajun seared ahi) and several varieties of Big

Aloha beer, brewed on-site. The unusual decor includes a sampan boat smack in the middle of the restaurant. 580 Nimitz Hwy. (btw. Pacific and Kukahi sts.). ☎ 808/545-7979. Entrees: $5–$13 breakfast, $9–$40 lunch, $19–$45 dinner. AE, DC, DISC, MC, V. Breakfast, lunch, and dinner daily. TheBus: 19 or 20. Map p 178.

★★ **Sansei Seafood Restaurant & Sushi Bar** WAIKIKI *SUSHI/ASIAN–PACIFIC RIM* Perpetual award-winner D. K. Kodama's Waikiki restaurant earns fans not only for its extensive menu but also for Kodama's outrageous sushi creations (he's my favorite sushi chef). Examples include seared foie gras nigiri sushi (duck liver lightly seared over sushi rice with caramelized onion and ripe mango) or the wonderful mango crab salad hand roll (mango, blue crab, greens, and peanuts with a sweet Thai-chili vinaigrette). Waikiki Beach Marriott Resort, 2552 Kalakaua Ave. (Paoakalani Ave.). ☎ 808/931-6286. Sushi $6.50–$18; entrees $19–$43. AE, DISC, MC, V. Dinner daily. TheBus: 19 or 20. Map p 179.

★★★ **3660 On the Rise** KAIMUKI *EURO-ISLAND* In his elegant 200-seat restaurant, chef Russell Siu adds Asian and local touches to the basics: rack of lamb with macadamia nuts, filets of catfish in *ponzu* (a Japanese sauce), and seared ahi salad with grilled shiitake mushrooms. Save room for the warm chocolate cake. 3660 Waialae Ave. (Koko Head Ave.). ☎ 808/737-1177. Entrees $25–$45; prix fixe $40. AE, DC, DISC, MC, V. Dinner Tues–Sun. No bus. Map p 179.

★ **Town** KAIMUKI *CONTEMPORARY ITALIAN* The latest hip restaurant along Waialae's miracle mile of "in" spots is a surprisingly delicious place to eat. Dine on ahi tartar on risotto cakes or outstanding gnocchi in a metro high-tech atmosphere (highly polished concrete floors, stainless steel tables, and incredibly uncomfortable chairs). Lunches consist of sandwiches, salads, and pastas, and the recently added breakfast menu includes frittata of the day, eggs, and wonderful baked goods. 3435 Waialae Ave. (at Ninth St.). ☎ 808/735-5900. Entrees $3.75–$6.50 breakfast, $8–$14 lunch, $16–$26 dinner. AE, MC, V. Breakfast Mon–Thurs, lunch and dinner Mon–Sat. No bus. Map p 179.

★ kids **12th Avenue Grill** KAIMUKI *RETRO-AMERICAN* All 14 tables in this tiny, upscale neighborhood diner are packed every night with people hungry for good ol' American food but a little more sophisticated than what mom used to make. Try gourmet macaroni and smoked parmesan cheese, smoked trout, or grilled pork chop with apple chutney. 1145-C 12th Ave. (at Waialae Ave.). ☎ 808/732-9469. Small plates $6–$11; large plates $19–$32. MC, V. Dinner Mon–Sat. No bus. Map p 179.

> *The view is nearly as appetizing as the four-star menu at Hoku's Restaurant in Kahala.*

★★★ kids **21 Degrees North** NORTH SHORE *PACIFIC RIM CUISINE* The signature restaurant at Turtle Bay Resort serves up contemporary island cuisine made fresh and interesting with unusual combinations like crab-crusted Hawaiian sea bass, salmon with Molokai mashed sweet potatoes, and roasted Peking duck with an orange and soy glaze. Floor-to-ceiling windows overlook the North Shore's famous rolling surf. 57-091 Kamehameha Hwy. (at Kuhuku Dr.). ☎ 808/293-8811. Entrees $29–$42. AE, DC, DISC, MC, V. Dinner Tues–Sat. TheBus: 52 or 55. Map p 180.

Oahu Hotel Best Bets

Most Romantic
Royal Hawaiian $$$$ 2259 Kalakaua Ave. (p 92)

Most Historic
Moana Surfrider, A Westin Resort $$$$ 2365 Kalakaua Ave. (p 191).

Most Luxurious
Halekulani $$$$$ 2199 Kalia Rd. (p 189) .

Best Moderately Priced
Ilima Hotel $$ 445 Nohonani St. (p 190).

Best Budget Hotel
Royal Grove Hotel $ 151 Uluniu Ave. (p 192).

Best for Kids
Embassy Suites Hotel–Waikiki Beach Walk $$$ 201 Beach Walk (p 189).

Best Value
The Breakers $$ 250 Beach Walk (p 188).

Hippest Hotel
Waikiki Parc $$$ 2233 Helumoa Rd. (p 193).

Best View of Waikiki Beach
Hilton Hawaiian Village Beach Resort & Spa $$$$ 2005 Kalia Rd. (p 190).

Best View of Ala Wai Harbor
Hawaii Prince Hotel Waikiki $$$ 100 Holomoana St. (p 189).

Best View of Ft. DeRussy Park
Outrigger Luana Waikiki $$$$ 2045 Kalakaua Ave. (p 191).

Most Hawaiian
Hawaiiana Hotel $$ 260 Beach Walk (p 189).

Most Serene
Ke Iki Beach Bungalows $$$ 59-579 Ke Iki Rd. (p 191).

Best Hi-Tech Gadgets
Hotel Renew $$$ 129 Paoakalani Ave. (p 190).

Best Hidden Gem
New Otani Kaimana Beach Hotel $$$ 2863 Kalakaua Ave. (p 191).

Best Boutique
DoubleTree Alana Hotel Waikiki $$$ 1956 Ala Moana Blvd. (p 188).

Best Family Condo
Outrigger Waikiki Shore Condominium $$$$ 2161 Kalia Rd. (p 192).

> *The Royal Hawaiian is a symbol of Hawaiian luxury with carved doors, oceanfront towers, and an elegant pink pastel exterior.*

Waikiki's Best Hotels

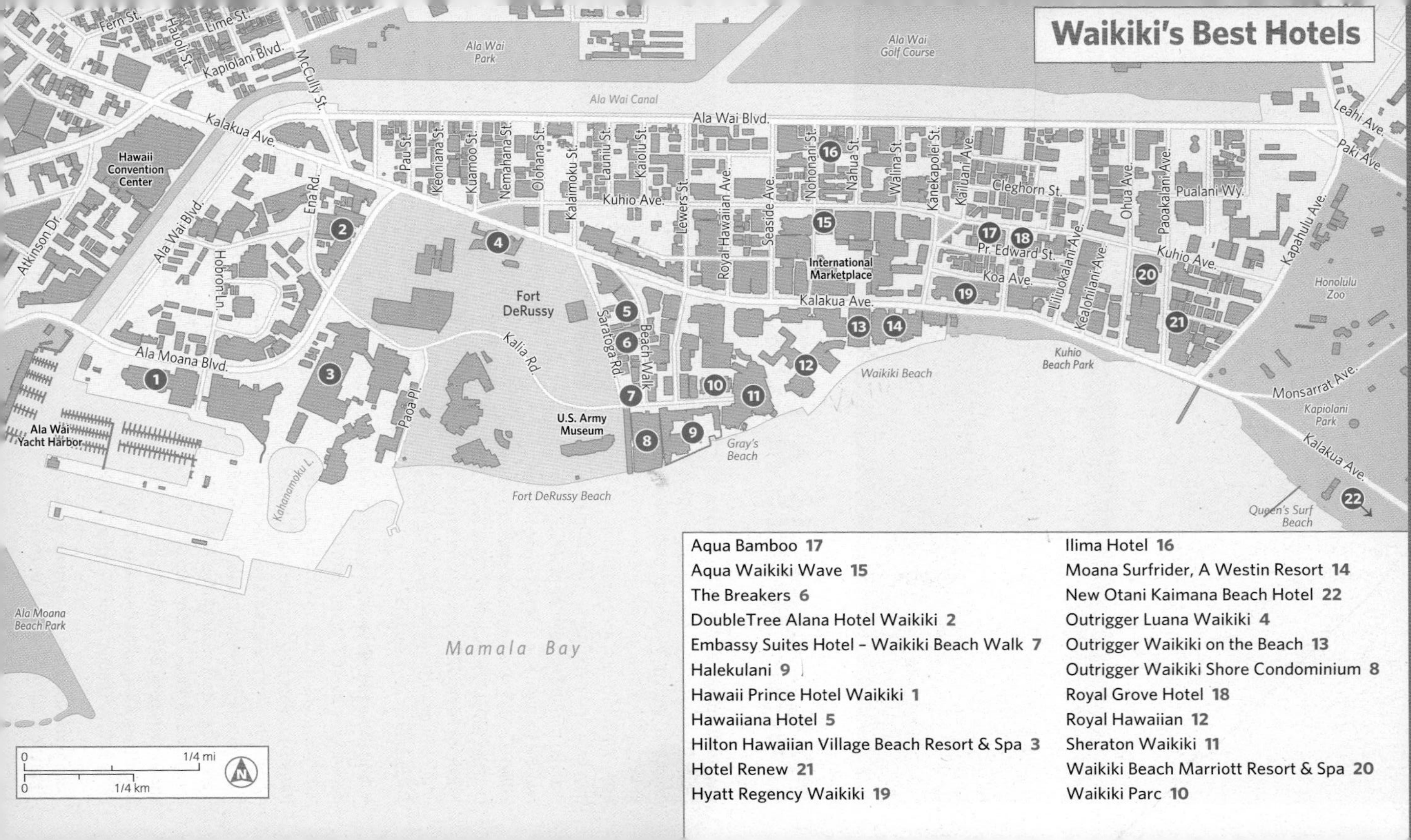

Aqua Bamboo 17
Aqua Waikiki Wave 15
The Breakers 6
DoubleTree Alana Hotel Waikiki 2
Embassy Suites Hotel – Waikiki Beach Walk 7
Halekulani 9
Hawaii Prince Hotel Waikiki 1
Hawaiiana Hotel 5
Hilton Hawaiian Village Beach Resort & Spa 3
Hotel Renew 21
Hyatt Regency Waikiki 19
Ilima Hotel 16
Moana Surfrider, A Westin Resort 14
New Otani Kaimana Beach Hotel 22
Outrigger Luana Waikiki 4
Outrigger Waikiki on the Beach 13
Outrigger Waikiki Shore Condominium 8
Royal Grove Hotel 18
Royal Hawaiian 12
Sheraton Waikiki 11
Waikiki Beach Marriott Resort & Spa 20
Waikiki Parc 10

Oahu Hotels A to Z

★ Aqua Bamboo MID-WAIKIKI MAUKA
I love the intimacy of this boutique hotel, decorated with an Asian flair (with kitchenettes or kitchens). Other pluses: location a block from Waikiki Beach, free breakfast, spa on property, and personal service. Minus: not enough parking for all rooms. 2425 Kuhio Ave. (at Kaiulani Ave.). ☎ 800/367-5004 or 808/922-7777. www.aquaresorts.com. 90 units. Doubles $195–$210; studio doubles $220–$250; 1-bedroom from $280; luxury suites from $420; with continental breakfast. AE, DISC, MC, V. TheBus: 19 or 20. Map p 187.

★ Aqua Waikiki Wave MID-WAIKIKI MAUKA
Recently renovated rooms with hip decor, flatscreen TVs, and free Wi-Fi have put this formerly dreary hotel on the map. Located in a not-very-hip neighborhood next door to International Marketplace, about a 10-minute walk to the beach. 2299 Kuhio Ave. (at Duke's Lane). ☎ 866/406-2782 or 808.922-1262. www.aquaresorts.com. 247 units. Doubles $156–$175; suites from $184; with continental breakfast. AE, DISC, MC, V. TheBus: 19 or 20. Map p 187.

> *The Halekulani offers the ultimate in luxury plus a prime Waikiki beachfront location.*

North Shore & Windward Hotels

For maps of hotels on the North Shore, Southern Oahu, and the Windward Coast, see p 180 and p 181.

★ kids The Breakers MID-WAIKIKI MAKAI
One of Waikiki's best deals: This 2-story 1950s budget hotel is a terrific buy for a family (kitchenette in all rooms) and just a 2-minute walk to the beach, numerous restaurants, and shopping. Expect comfortable budget accommodations with tropical accents. 250 Beach Walk (btw. Kalakaua Ave. and Kalia Rd.). ☎ 800/426-0494 or 808/923-3181. www.breakers-hawaii.com. 64 units. Doubles $125–$135; studio $185. AE, DC, MC, V. TheBus: 19 or 20. Map p 187.

★ DoubleTree Alana Hotel Waikiki EWA
This boutique hotel (operated by the Hilton Hawaiian Village) is a welcome oasis of small but comfortable rooms and offers the amenitie of a more luxurious hotel at affordable prices. Great location, too: Waikiki Beach is a 10-minute walk away, and the convention center is about a 7-minute walk. 1956 Ala

The DoubleTree Alana Hotel Waikiki is a boutique inn with small but elegant rooms at affordable rates.

Moana Blvd. (near Kalakaua Ave.). ☎ 800/222-TREE (222-8733) or 808/941-7275. www.doubletree.com. 317 units. Doubles $189–$349. AE, DC, DISC, MC, V. TheBus: 19 or 20. Map p 187.

★★★ kids **Embassy Suites Hotel–Waikiki Beach Walk** MID-WAIKIKI MAKAI Opened in 2007, this ultra-luxurious one- and two-bedroom hotel chain, famous for its complimentary "cooked to order" breakfast and evening cocktail reception, has a great location just 1 block from the beach. Waikiki Beach Walk provides plenty of shops and restaurants on property as well. Prices may seem high, but it pencils out to a deal for families. 201 Beach Walk (at Kalia Rd.). ☎ 800/EMBASSY (362-2779) or 808/921-2345. www.waikikibeach.embassysuites.com. 421 suites. Doubles: $169–$394 1-bedroom, $479–$529 2-bedroom; with breakfast. AE, DC, DISC, MC, V. TheBus: 19 or 20. Map p 187.

★★★ kids **Halekulani** MID-WAIKIKI MAKAI This is my favorite hotel in all Hawaii; the ultimate heavenly Hawaii luxury accommodation, spread over 5 acres of prime Waikiki beachfront. Some 90% of the large rooms (620 sq. ft.) face the ocean, and all have furnished lanais and top-drawer amenities. The best Waikiki has to offer. 2199 Kalia Rd. (at Lewers St.). ☎ 800/367-2343 or 808/923-2311. www.halekulani.com. 455 units. Doubles $445–$555. AE, DC, MC, V. TheBus: 19 or 20. Map p 187.

★★ **Hawaii Prince Hotel Waikiki** EWA For a vacation with a view and the feel of a palace, stay in these striking, 33-story, twin high-tech towers, where service is a priority. All bedrooms face the Ala Wai Yacht Harbor, with floor-to-ceiling sliding-glass windows (sorry, no lanais). The higher the floor, the higher the price. Ala Moana Center is a 10-minute walk away and Waikiki's beaches are just a 5-minute walk. 100 Holomoana St. (just across Ala Wai Canal Bridge). ☎ 800/321-OAHU (321-6248) or 808/956-1111. www.princeresortshawaii.com. 521 units. Doubles $229–$314. AE, DC, DISC, MC, V. TheBus: 19 or 20. Map p 187.

★ kids **Hawaiiana Hotel** MID-WAIKIKI MAKAI This older hotel, with a 1950s feel, offers plenty of aloha spirit to its loyal guests at great prices. The concrete, hollow-tiled guest rooms have kitchenettes and two beds—great for families. The hotel is about a block from the beach and within walking distance of Waikiki shopping and nightlife. 260 Beach Walk (near Kalakaua Ave.). ☎ 800/367-5122 or 808/923-3811. www.hawaiianahotelatwaikiki.com. 95 units. Doubles $125–$215. AE, DC, DISC, MC, V. TheBus: 19 or 20. Map p 187.

Waikiki Neighborhoods

The neighborhoods in Waikiki can be divided up into four districts: **Ewa** (the western end of Waikiki from Ala Wai Canal to Fort DeRussy Park), **Mid-Waikiki Makai** (from the ocean up to Kalakaua Ave. and from Fort DeRussy Park to Kaiulani St.), **Mid-Waikiki Mauka** (mountain side of Kalakaua Ave. to Ala Wai Blvd. and from Kalaimoku St. to Kaiulani St.), and **Diamond Head** (from the ocean to Ala Wai Blvd. and from Kaiulani to Diamond Head).

> *A room at the Royal Hawaiian.*

★★ kids **Hilton Hawaiian Village Beach Resort & Spa** EWA Sprawling over 20 acres, this is Waikiki's biggest resort—with tropical gardens dotted with exotic wildlife (flamingos, peacocks, and even penguins), award-winning restaurants (including Bali by the Sea, p 177), 100 different shops, a secluded lagoon, two minigolf courses, and a gorgeous stretch of Waikiki Beach. A wide choice of accommodations, from simple to ultradeluxe, are housed in five towers. 2005 Kalia Rd. (at Ala Moana Blvd.). ☎ 800/HILTONS (445-8667) or 808/949-4321. www.hiltonhawaiianvillage.com. 2,860 units. Doubles $279–$429. AE, DISC, MC, V. TheBus: 19 or 20. Map p 187.

★★ **Hotel Renew** DIAMOND HEAD This boutique is a gem among aging Waikiki hotels: an oasis of tranquility and excellent taste in a sea of schlock. True to its name, Hotel Renew recently underwent several millions dollars' worth of renovations—every single surface was redone. The result is a quiet, Zen-like decor, just a block from the beach, with complimentary gourmet breakfast, lots of hi-tech gadgets, and a free fitness center and yoga classes. 129 Paoakalani Ave. (at Lemon Rd.). ☎ 866-406-2782 or 808/687-7700. www.hotelrenew.com. 70 units. Doubles $183–$289. AE, DC, MC, V. TheBus: 19 or 20. Map p 187.

★ kids **Hyatt Regency Waikiki** DIAMOND HEAD This is one of Waikiki's largest hotels, with two 40-story towers covering nearly an entire city block, located across the street from Waikiki Beach. The location is great, there's a good children's program, and guest rooms are large and luxuriously furnished, but I find it too big and too impersonal, with service to match. 2424 Kalakaua Ave. (btw. Kaiulani St. and Uluniu Ave.). ☎ 800/233-1234 or 808/923-1234. www.waikiki.hyatt.com. 1,230 units. Doubles $270–$510. AE, DC, DISC, MC, V. TheBus: 19 or 20. Map p 187.

★ kids **Ilima Hotel** MID-WAIKIKI MAUKA Local residents frequent this 17-story, condo-style hotel that offers value for your money: huge rooms (with full kitchen), walking distance to restaurants and shops, and low prices. The only two caveats: It's a 15-minute hike to the beach, and there aren't any ocean views. 445 Nohonani St. (near Ala Wai Blvd.). ☎ 800/801-9366 or 808/923-1877. www.HotelWaikiki.com. 99 units. Doubles: $135–$185, 1-bedroom (rate for 4) $169–$219, 2-bedroom (rate for 4, sleeps 6) $245–$285, 3-bedroom (rate for 6, sleeps 8) $375–$395. AE, DC, DISC, MC, V. TheBus: 19 or 20. Map p 187.

★★ kids **Kahala Hotel & Resort** KAHALA Located in one of Oahu's most prestigious residential areas, the Kahala offers elegant guest rooms and the peace and serenity of a neighbor-island resort, with the conveniences of Waikiki just a 10-minute drive away. The lush, tropical grounds include an 800-foot crescent-shaped beach and a 26,000-square-foot lagoon (home to two bottle-nosed dolphins, sea turtles, and tropical fish). Activities range from Hawaiian cultural programs to daily dolphin-education talks by a trainer from Sea Life Park. 5000 Kahala Ave. (next to the Waialae Country Club). ☎ 800/367-2525 or 808/739-8888. www.kahalaresort.com. 343 units. Doubles: $395–$820; suite from $1,600. AE, DC, DISC, MC, V. Map p 181.

★ kids **Ke Iki Beach Bungalows** NORTH SHORE This collection of studio, one-, and two-bedroom cottages, located on a 200-foot stretch of beautiful white-sand beach, is affordable and perfect for families. All units have full kitchens and their own barbecue areas. 59-579 Ke Iki Rd. (off Kamehameha Hwy.). ☎ 866/638-8229 or 808/638-8829. www.keikibeach.com. 11 units. Doubles: $145–$215 studio and 1-bedroom, $165–$230 2-bedroom. AE, MC, V. TheBus: 52. Map p 180.

★ **Lanikai Bed & Breakfast** LANIKAI Choose from a 1,000-square-foot 2-bedroom apartment, or a 540-square-foot honeymooner's studio in this B&B tucked away in a swank beach community. They also have a booking agency to help you with other B&B and vacation rentals nearby. 1277 Mokulua Dr. (btw. Onekea and Aala drs.). ☎ 800/258-7895 or 808/261-7895. www.lanikaibb.com. 2 units. Doubles $160–$185. Map p 181.

★★ kids **Moana Surfrider, A Westin Resort** MID-WAIKIKI MAKAI Old Hawaii reigns here. I recommend staying in the historic Banyan Wing, where rooms are modern replicas of

> *Sign up for a slice of old Hawaii in the Banyan Wing of the Moana Surfrider, where each room is a modern replica of Waikiki's first hotel.*

Waikiki's first hotel (built in 1901). Outside is a prime stretch of beach and an oceanfront courtyard centered around a 100-year-old banyan tree, where there's live music in the evenings. 2365 Kalakaua Ave. (across from Kaiulani St.). ☎ 800/325-3535 or 808/922-3111. www.moana-surfrider.com. 793 units. Doubles $299–$675. AE, DC, MC, V. TheBus: 19 or 20. Map p 187.

★ kids **New Otani Kaimana Beach Hotel** DIAMOND HEAD This is one of Waikiki's best-kept secrets: a boutique hotel nestled on the beach at the foot of Diamond Head, with Kapiolani Park just across the street. Skip the inexpensive, teeny-tiny, barely-room-for-two rooms and go for the park-view studios with kitchen. 2863 Kalakaua Ave. (near Waikiki Aquarium, across from Kapiolani Park). ☎ 800/356-8264 or 808/923-1555. www.kaimana.com. 124 units. Doubles $144–$395. AE, DC, DISC, MC, V. TheBus: 19 or 20. Map p 187.

★ kids **Outrigger Luana Waikiki** EWA ***Families take note:*** This mid-size hotel offers studios with kitchenettes and one-bedrooms with full kitchens. You also get terrific views of Fort DeRussy Park and the ocean in the distance. 2045 Kalakaua Ave. (at Kuhio Ave.). ☎ 800/OUTRIGGER (688-7444) or 808/955-6000. www.outrigger.com. 205 units. Doubles: $265–$295, 1-bedroom $385–$485, 2-bedroom $615. AE, DC, DISC, MC, V. TheBus: 19 or 20. Map p 187.

Outrigger Waikiki on the Beach MID-WAIKIKI MAKAI I'd pick this Outrigger to stay in: Not only does it have an excellent location on Waikiki Beach, but with $20 million invested into guest room renovations and upgrades (oversize Jacuzzi bathtubs with ocean views in some rooms), coupled with the great dining (Duke's and Hula Grill, see p 180 and p 181), it offers more for the money. 2335 Kalakaua Ave. (btw. the Royal Hawaiian Shopping Center and the Sheraton Moana Surfrider). ☎ 800/OUTRIGGER (688-7444) or 808/923-0711. www.outrigger.com. 525 units. Doubles $239–$649. AE, DC, DISC, MC, V. TheBus: 19 or 20. Map p 187.

★★ kids **Outrigger Waikiki Shore Condominium** MID-WAIKIKI MAKAI One of the few condominiums on Waikiki Beach offers guests a terrific location (right on the beach, close to shopping and restaurants), a spectacular panoramic view, daily maid service, and fully equipped kitchens. 2161 Kalia Rd. (at Saratoga Rd.). ☎ 800/OUTRIGGER (688-7444) or 808/922-3871. www.outrigger.com. 168 units. Studio $305, 1-bedroom $355–$485, 2-bedroom $505–$695. AE, DC, DISC, MC, V. TheBus: 19 or 20. Map p 187.

★ kids **Royal Grove Hotel** DIAMOND HEAD This is a great bargain for frugal travelers and families; the budget accommodations are no-frills (along the lines of a Motel 6), but the family-owned hotel has genuine aloha for all the guests, and Waikiki Beach is a 3-minute walk away. 151 Uluniu Ave. (btw. Prince Edward and Kuhio aves.). ☎ 808/923-7691. www.royalgrovehotel.com. 85 units. Doubles: $67 1-bedroom $90. AE, DC, DISC, MC, V. TheBus: 19 or 20. Map p 187.

★★ kids **Royal Hawaiian** MID-WAIKIKI MAKAI The symbol of Waikiki, this flamingo-pink oasis nestled in tropical gardens, offers rooms in both the 1927 historic wing (my favorites, with carved wooden doors, four-poster canopy beds flowered wallpaper, and period furniture) as well as modern oceanfront towers. The beach outside is the best in Waikiki for sun-bathing. 2259 Kalakaua Ave. (at Royal Hawaiian Ave.). ☎ 800/325-3535 or 808/923-7311. www.sheraton.com. 527 units. Doubles $299–$745. AE, MC, V. TheBus: 19 or 20. Map p 187.

kids **Schrader's Windward Country Inn** KANEOHE Despite the name, the ambience here is more motel than "country inn," but Schrader's offers a great buy for families. Nestled in the tranquil, tropical setting on Kaneohe Bay, the complex is made up of aging cottage-style motels and a collection of older homes, all with cooking facilities. ***Tip:*** When booking, ask for a unit with a lanai; that way you'll end up with at least a partial view of the bay. 47-039 Lihikai Dr. (off Kamehameha Hwy.). ☎ 800/735-5071 or 808/239-5711. www.hawaiiscene.com/schrader. 20 units. 1-bedroom $72–$143, 2-bedroom for 4 $127–$215, 3-bedroom for 6 $226–$358, 4-bedroom for 8 $446–$501; with continental breakfast. AE, DC, DISC, MC, V. Map p 181.

> *The beachside pool at the Kahala Hotel & Resort offers luxurious serenity just a 10-minute ride from Waikiki.*

> *Just 100 yards from the beach, the Waikiki Parc has recently been renovated with a modern design and amenities for a younger clientele.*

★ kids **Sheraton Waikiki** MID-WAIKIKI MAKAI It's hard to get a bad room here: the hotel sits right on Waikiki Beach, with a whopping 1,200 oceanview units and 650 rooms overlooking Diamond Head. However, this is a megahotel, with two 30-story towers and an immense lobby. It's a frequent favorite of conventions and can be crowded, noisy, and overwhelming (not to mention the long wait at the bank of nearly a dozen elevators). 2255 Kalakaua Ave. (at Royal Hawaiian Ave.). ☎ 800/325-3535 or 808/922-4422. www.sheraton.com. 1,852 units. Doubles $285–$605. AE, DC, DISC, MC, V. TheBus: 19 or 20. Map p 187.

★★★ kids **Turtle Bay Resort** NORTH SHORE The resort is spectacular—an hour's drive from Waikiki but eons away in its country feeling. Sitting on 808 acres, this place is loaded with activities and has 5 miles of shoreline with secluded white-sand coves. Even if you don't stay here, check out the beach activities, golf, horseback riding, tennis, and the best spa on the North Shore. 57-091 Kamehameha Hwy. (at Kuhuku Dr.). ☎ 800/203-3650 or 808/293-6000. www.turtlebayresort.com. 443 units. Doubles $340–$432; cottage $703–$774; suite from $500; villa from $888. AE, DC, DISC, MC, V. TheBus: 52 or 55. Map p 180.

kids **Waikiki Beach Marriott Resort & Spa** DIAMOND HEAD Pluses: It's across the street from the beach, has renovated rooms, and boasts great restaurants (Sansei Seafood Restaurant and Sushi Bar and d.k Steakhouse, see p 180 and p 185). The minus: Rack rates are way too high—check their website for 40% off. 2552 Kalakaua Ave. (at Ohua Ave.). ☎ 800/848-8110 or 808/922-6611. www.marriottwaikiki.com. 1,310 units. Doubles $340–$560. AE, DC, DISC, MC, V. TheBus: 19 or 20. Map p 187.

★★ **Waikiki Parc** MID-WAIKIKI MAKAI Recently redesigned and renovated, especially for the 20s and 30s crowd, this "hidden" luxury hotel (operated by the Halekulani) offers lots of bonuses: It's just 100 yards from the beach, has modern hi-tech rooms, hosts frequent wine-party receptions, and offers first-class service. 2233 Helumoa Rd. (at Lewers St.). ☎ 800/422-0450 or 808/921-7272. www.waikikiparchotel.com. 297 units. Doubles $173–$415. AE, DC, MC, V. TheBus: 19 or 20. Map p 187.

Oahu Nightlife & Entertainment Best Bets

Best Place to Celebrate St. Patrick's Day
Murphy's Bar & Grill, 2 Merchant St. (p 195).

Best for Hawaiian Music
House Without a Key, Halekulani Hotel. 2199 Kalia Rd. (p 199).

Best Club for Jazz
Indigo's, 1121 Nuuanu Ave. (p 195).

Best Club for Concerts
Pipeline, 805 Pohukaina St. (p 195).

Most Romantic Place for Sunset
The Veranda, Westin Moana Surfrider, 2365 Kalakaua Ave. (p 199).

Best Place to People-Watch at Sunset
Duke's Canoe Club, Outrigger Waikiki on the Beach Hotel, 2335 Kalakaua Ave. (p 199).

Best Luau
Royal Hawaiian Hotel, 2259 Kalakaua Ave. (p 199).

Best Performing Arts Center
Neal Blaisdell Center, 777 Ward Ave (p 201).

Best for Outdoor Concerts
Waikiki Shell, 2805 Monsarrat Ave. (p 201).

Best for Film Buffs
The Movie Museum, 3566 Harding Ave. (p 198).

Best Magic Show
The Magic of Polynesia, Ohana Waikiki Beachcomber, 2300 Kalakaua Ave. (p 200).

Best Musical Show
Society of Seven, 2335 Kalakaua Ave. (p 201).

Most Historic Theater
Hawaii Theatre, 1130 Bethel St. (p 201).

Best Place to See Locally Written and Produced Plays
Kumu Kahua Theatre, 46 Merchant St. (p 201).

> *Monday nights at the Royal Hawaiian are reserved for the traditional and raucous luau with native dancers, music, and delicacies.*

Oahu Nightlife & Entertainment A to Z

Bars & Cocktail Lounges

Aaron's Atop the Ala Moana ALA MOANA
For the more mature set: Take in the best view in town (from the 36th floor of the hotel), watch the Honolulu city lights wrap around the room, and cha-cha-cha to the vertigo! There's live music and dancing nightly, a lengthy dinner menu, and an appetizer menu nightly from 5pm. In the Ala Moana Hotel, 410 Atkinson Dr. (next to the Ala Moana Shopping Center). ☎ 808/955-4466. No cover, no minimum. TheBus: 19 or 20. Map p 197.

★ **Gordon Biersch Brewery Restaurant** ALOHA TOWER A new stage area allows diners to swing to jazz, blues, and island riffs. 1 Aloha Tower Dr., on the waterfront btw. piers 8 and 11, Honolulu Harbor (at Bishop St.). ☎ 808/599-4877. www.gordonbiersch.com. No cover, no minimum. No bus. Map p 196.

★ **Murphy's Bar & Grill** DOWNTOWN
One of Honolulu's most popular downtown ale houses and media haunts. Over a dozen beers on tap, including (of course) Murphy's and Guinness. 2 Merchant St. (at Nuuanu Ave.). ☎ 808/531-0422. www.gomurphys.com. No cover, no minimum. TheBus: 19 or 20. Map p 196.

Club Scene

★★ **Indigo's** CHINATOWN
This Chinatown spot serves sizzling food during the day, turns to cool jazz in the early evening, and progresses to late-night DJs spinning Top 40, disco, rock, funk, and more. 1121 Nuuanu Ave. (btw. Hotel and Pauahi sts.). ☎ 808/521-2900. www.indigo-hawaii.com. No cover, no minimum. TheBus: 13. Map p 196.

★ **Pipeline** KAKAAKO
This huge club/concert venue has dancing, darts, pool, and a sports bar with larger-than-life TV screens. Patrons here tend to be younger (you can get in at 18 years old) and are dressed to go clubbing. 805 Pohukaina St. (btw.

> *The Brothers Cazimero became local legends through regular Wednesday-night shows at Chai's Island Bistro at the Aloha Tower Marketplace.*

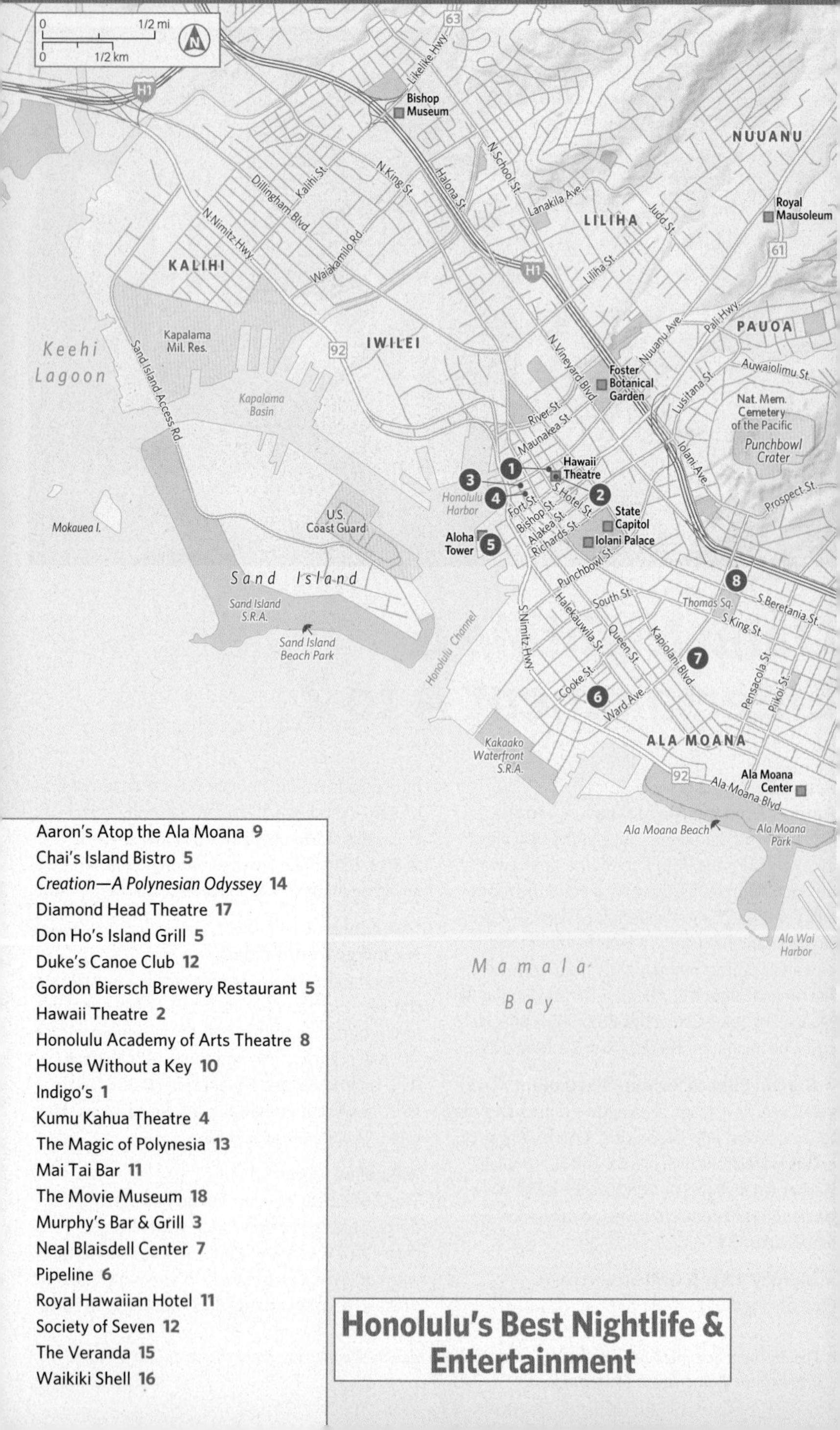

Honolulu's Best Nightlife & Entertainment

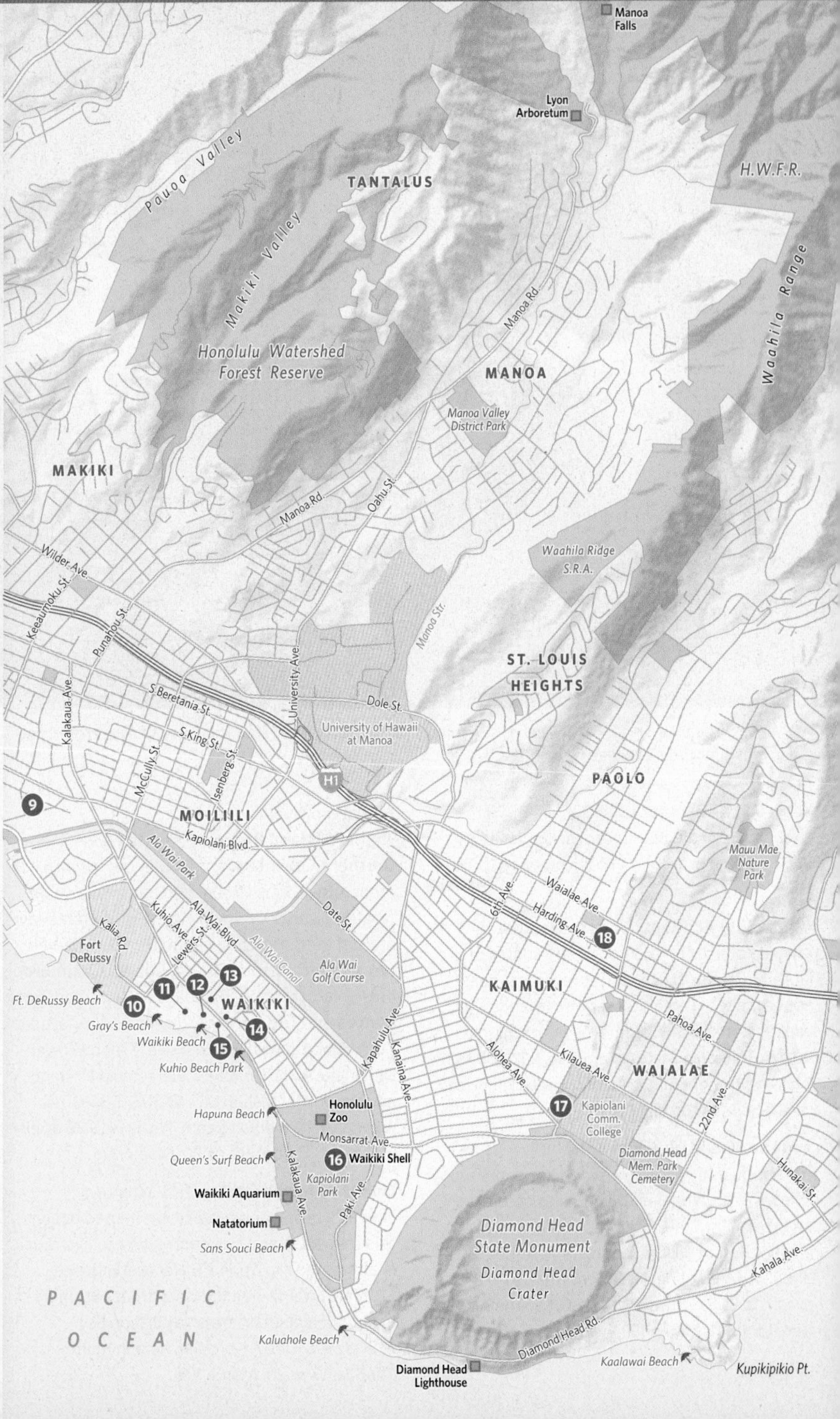
Manoa Falls
Lyon Arboretum
H.W.F.R.
TANTALUS
Pauoa Valley
Makiki Valley
Waahila Range
Manoa Rd.
Honolulu Watershed Forest Reserve
MANOA
Manoa Valley District Park
MAKIKI
Manoa Rd.
Oahu St.
Wilder Ave.
Waahila Ridge S.R.A.
Keeaumoku St.
Punahou St.
University Ave.
Manoa Str.
ST. LOUIS HEIGHTS
S Beretania St.
Dole St.
Kalakaua Ave.
S King St.
University of Hawaii at Manoa
McCully St.
Isenberg St.
H1
PAOLO
9
MOILIILI
Kapiolani Blvd.
Ala Wai Park
Mauu Mae Nature Park
6th Ave.
Waialae Ave.
Date St.
Kuhio Ave.
Ala Wai Blvd.
Harding Ave.
18
Kalia Rd.
Lewers St.
Ala Wai Canal
Fort DeRussy
Ala Wai Golf Course
13
11
12
KAIMUKI
Ft. DeRussy Beach
10
WAIKIKI
Gray's Beach
14
Pahoa Ave.
Waikiki Beach
15
Alohea Ave.
Kapahulu Ave.
Kanaina Ave.
Kilauea Ave.
WAIALAE
Kuhio Beach Park
22nd Ave.
17
Kapiolani Comm. College
Hapuna Beach
Honolulu Zoo
Monsarrat Ave.
Diamond Head Mem. Park Cemetery
Queen's Surf Beach
16
Waikiki Shell
Hunakai St.
Kapiolani Park
Waikiki Aquarium
Kalakaua Ave.
Paki Ave.
Natatorium
Diamond Head State Monument
Sans Souci Beach
Diamond Head Crater
Kahala Ave.
PACIFIC
OCEAN
Kaluahole Beach
Diamond Head Rd.
Kaalawai Beach
Kupikipikio Pt.
Diamond Head Lighthouse

> *The hugely popular Society of Seven has served up a menu of Broadway show tunes, comedy sketches, and pop music for three decades.*

Koula and Kamani sts.). ☎ 808/589-1999. www.pipelinecafe.net. Cover charge usually $1-$5; concerts around $15. No bus. Map p 196.

Film

★ Honolulu Academy of Arts Theatre KAKAAKO This is the film-as-art center of Honolulu, offering special screenings, guest appearances, and cultural performances, as well as noteworthy programs in the visual arts. 900 S. Beretania St. (at Ward Ave.). ☎ 808/532-8700. www.honoluluacademy.org. Ticket prices vary. TheBus: 2 or 13. Map p 196.

★★ The Movie Museum KAIMUKI Film buffs and esoteric movie-lovers can enjoy special screenings as they recline comfortably on brown vinyl, stuffed recliners or rent from a collection of 3,000 vintage and hard-to-find films. 3566 Harding Ave. (btw. 11th and 12th aves.). ☎ 808/735-8771. Tickets $5. TheBus: 22, transfer to 14. Map p 197.

Hawaiian Music

★ Chai's Island Bistro ALOHA TOWER **Brothers Cazimero** remain one of Hawaii's most gifted duos (Robert on bass; Roland on 12-string guitar), appearing every Wednesday at 7pm at this leading venue for Hawaiian entertainment. Also at Chai's: **Robert Cazimero** plays piano solo on Tuesdays at 7pm, and **Jerry Santos** and **Olomana** perform on Mondays at 7pm. Aloha Tower Marketplace, 1 Aloha Tower Dr., on the waterfront btw. piers 8 and 11, Honolulu Harbor (at Bishop St.). ☎ 808/585-0011. www.chaisislandbistro.com. No cover, $25 drink minimum. TheBus: 19 or 20. Map p 196.

Don Ho's Island Grill ALOHA TOWER Hawaii's best-known musician helped design this relaxed island bar/eatery, where live music is always on tap. Aloha Tower Marketplace, 1 Aloha Tower Dr., on the waterfront btw. piers 8 and 11, Honolulu Harbor (at Bishop St.). ☎ 808/528-0807. No cover, no minimum. TheBus: 19 or 20. Map p 196.

★★ Duke's Canoe Club WAIKIKI
The outside Barefoot Bar is perfect for sipping a tropical drink, watching the waves and sunset, and listening to music. It can get crowded, so get there early. Hawaii sunset music is usually from 4 to 6pm on weekends, and there's live entertainment nightly from 10pm to midnight. Outrigger Waikiki on the Beach Hotel, 2335 Kalakaua Ave. (btw. Duke's Lane and Kaiulani Ave.). ☎ 808/922-2268. www.dukeswaikiki.com. No cover, no minimum. TheBus: 19 or 20. Map p 197.

★★★ House Without a Key WAIKIKI
This is my favorite place to relax at sunset. Watch the breathtaking Kanoelehua Miller dance hula to the riffs of Hawaiian steel-pedal guitar under a century-old kiawe tree with the sunset and ocean glowing behind her—a romantic, evocative, nostalgic scene. It doesn't hurt, either, that the Halekulani happens to make the best mai tais in the world. This place has the after-dinner hours covered, too, with light jazz by local artists from 10:15pm to midnight nightly. Halekulani Hotel, 2199 Kalia Rd. (at Lewers St.). ☎ 808/923-2311. www.halekulani.com. No cover, no minimum. TheBus: 19 or 20. Map p 197.

Mai Tai Bar WAIKIKI
This circular bar, right down at beach level, features live Hawaiian music nightly. Royal Hawaiian Hotel, 2259 Kalakaua Ave. (at Seaside Ave.). ☎ 808/923-7311. www.royal-hawaiian.com. Music 4:30–10:30pm nightly. No cover, 1-drink minimum. TheBus: 19 or 20. Map p 197.

★★ The Veranda WAIKIKI
Enjoy a romantic evening sitting on the back porch of this historic hotel, overlooking an islet-size canopy of banyan trees, as you watch the sun set and sip a drink to the sounds of live Hawaiian music playing softly in the background. You'll be in good company; Robert Louis Stevenson once loved to linger here. Westin Moana Surfrider, 2365 Kalakaua Ave. (btw. Duke's Lane and Kaiulani Ave.). ☎ 808/922-3111. www.moana-surfrider.com/dining-and-entertaintment/the-veranda. No cover, 2-drink minimum. TheBus: 19 or 20. Map p 197.

Luaus

Royal Hawaiian Hotel WAIKIKI
Waikiki's only oceanfront luau features a variety of traditional Hawaiian as well as continental American dishes: roasted kalua pork,

> *The best way to start off an evening on Oahu is with a tropical drink and a sunset view.*

Arts with Aloha

Art lovers now have a wonderful new resource: a 44-page brochure offering an overview of the music, theater, history, and visual arts of Oahu. The free brochure, which includes a map, phone numbers, websites, and more, is put out by Arts with Aloha, representing 11 major Honolulu cultural organizations. You can download it from www.artswithaloha.com; send a legal-size, self-addressed, stamped envelope to Arts with Aloha, c/o Honolulu Academy of Arts, 900 S. Beretania St., Honolulu, HI 96822; or call the 24-hour hot line at ☎ 808/532-8713.

> *House Without a Key is the perfect place to sip a mai tai, watch the sunset, and listen to the soft strains of Hawaiian music.*

Comedy Tonight

The best way to see comedy in Waikiki, since the comics seem to move round a lot, is to check their websites. The best in comedy acts are: **Andy Bumatai** (www.andybumatai.com), **Augie T** (www.augietulba.com), and **Frank Delima** (www.frankdelima.com). All three perform "local" stand-up sketches that will give you insight into local residents and have you screaming with laughter.

mahimahi, teriyaki steak, poi, sweet potatoes, rice, vegetables, haupia (coconut pudding), and a selection of desserts. Entertainment includes songs and dances from Hawaii and other Polynesian island nations. Royal Hawaiian Hotel, 2259 Kalakaua Ave. (at Seaside Ave.). ☎ 888/808-4668. www.best-luaus.com. Mon 5:30pm. Adults $95, children 5–12 $53. AE, DISC, MC, V. TheBus: 19 or 20. Map p 197.

Shows

★ kids **Creation—A Polynesian Odyssey**
WAIKIKI Don't miss this theatrical journey of fire dancing, special effects, illusions, hula, and Polynesian dances from Hawaii and the South Pacific. Sheraton Princess Kaiulani, Ainahau Showroom, 120 Kaiulani Ave. (at Kalakaua Ave.). ☎ 808/931-4600. www.princess-kaiulani.com. Shows 7:20pm Tues and Thurs–Sun. $85–$135 with dinner; $49 with just cocktails; $64–$100 children 5–12. TheBus: 19 or 20. Map p 197.

★ kids **The Magic of Polynesia** WAIKIKI
This is not your typical dinner theater. This stage show combines magic, illusions, and Polynesian dance, song, and chant. International Magician Society's Merlin award-winner master illusionist John Hirokawa performs amazing magic with a pinch of pyrotechnics, lasers, and other special effects thrown in. Ohana Waikiki Beachcomber, 2300 Kalakaua Ave. (at Duke's Lane). ☎ 808/971-

4321. www.robertshawaii.com. 8pm show nightly. Dinner $85 adults, $57 children 4–11. TheBus: 19 or 20. Map p 197.

★ **Society of Seven** WAIKIKI
This nightclub act (a blend of skits, Broadway hits, popular music, and costumed musical acts) is into its third decade, which is no small feat. Outrigger Waikiki on the Beach, 2335 Kalakaua Ave. (btw. Duke's Lane and Kaiulani Ave.). ☎ 808/922-6408. www.outriggeractivities.com. Shows 8:30pm Wed–Sat. Show with dinner $52 adults, $43 children 5–20; show with cocktails only $37 adults, $24 children. TheBus: 19 or 20. Map p 197.

Symphony, Opera & Dance Performances

★★ **Neal Blaisdell Center** KAKAAKO
Hawaii's premier performance center for the best in entertaining. This arena/concert hall/exhibition building can be divided into a 2,175-seat concert hall or an 8,805-seat arena, serving everyone from symphonygoers to punk rockers. Playing here from September to May is the **Honolulu Symphony Orchestra** (☎ 808/524-0815; www.honolulusymphony.com). Then from January to March, the highly successful **Hawaii Opera Theatre** takes to the stage with hits like *La Bohème, Carmen, Turandot, Romeo and Juliet, Rigoletto,* and *Aïda*. Also performing at this concert hall are Hawaii's four ballet companies: **Hawaii Ballet Theatre, Ballet Hawaii, Hawaii State Ballet,** and **Honolulu Dance Theatre.** 777 Ward Ave. (btw. Kapiolani Ave. and King St.). ☎ 808/591-2211. www.blaisdellcenter.com. TheBus: 19 or 20. Map p 196.

★★ kids **Waikiki Shell** WAIKIKI
This outdoor venue in the middle of Kapiolani Park allows concertgoers to watch the sunset and see the stars come out before the concert begins. A range of performers, from Hawaiian to jazz musicians, have graced this stage. 2805 Monsarrat Ave. (btw. Kalakaua and Paki aves.). ☎ 808/527-5400. www.waikikishell.com. TheBus: 19 or 20. Map p 197.

Theater

★ **Diamond Head Theatre** DIAMOND HEAD
Hawaii's oldest theater (since 1915), this community theater produces a variety of performances, from musicals to comedies to classical dramas. 520 Makapu'u Ave. (at Alohea Ave.). ☎ 808/733-0277. www.diamondheadtheatre.com. Tickets $12–$42. TheBus: 58. Map p 197.

★★★ **Hawaii Theatre** CHINATOWN
Audiences have stomped to the big off-Broadway percussion hit *Stomp* and have enjoyed the talent of *Tap Dogs*, Momix, the Jim Nabors Christmas show, the Hawaii International Jazz Festival, the American Repertory Dance Company, barbershop quartets, and John Ka'imikaua's halau—all here. The neoclassical Beaux Arts landmark features a 1922 dome, 1,400 plush seats, a hydraulically elevated organ, and gilt galore. 1130 Bethel St. (btw. Hotel and Pauahi sts.). ☎ 808/528-0506. www.hawaiitheatre.com. Ticket prices vary. TheBus: 2 or 13. Map p 196.

★★ **Kumu Kahua Theatre** DOWNTOWN
For an intimate glimpse at island life, take in a show at Kumu Kahua. This tiny theater (100 seats) produces plays dealing with today's cultural experience in Hawaii, often written by residents. 46 Merchant St. (at N. Bethel St.). ☎ 808/536-4441. www.kumukahua.org. Tickets $16. Bus: City Express B. Map p 196.

Get Down with ARTafterDark

The last Friday of every month (except Nov and Dec) the place to be after the sun goes down is the **Honolulu Academy of Arts' ARTafterDark** (☎ 808/532-6091; www.artafterdark.org), a *pau-hana* (after-work) mixer in the art museum, at 900 S. Beretania St., that brings residents and visitors together around a theme combining art with food, music, and dancing. In addition to the exhibits in the gallery, ARTafterDark also features visual and live performances. Last year the themes ranged from "Plant Rice"—rice- and sake-tastings, rice dishes, and Asian beers with live Asian fusion music and a tour of the *Art of Rice* exhibit—to " '80s Night," "Turkish Delights," "Cool Nights, Hot Jazz, and Blues," and "Havana Heat."

The entry fee is $7. The party gets going about 6pm and lasts to 9pm, the crowd ranges from 20s to 50s, and the dress is everything from jeans and T-shirts to designer cocktail party attire.

5 The Big Island

My 16 Favorite Big Island Moments

The Big Island really is big, and not just in size (although it is twice the size of all the other islands combined) but also in things to do and see. The volcano goddess, Pele, has been erupting continually for nearly 2½ decades, adding even more land to the island. In addition to the new terrain that Pele has added, there are historical sites to see, world-renowned telescopes to stargaze through, underwater treasures to discover, local cuisine (and that famous Kona coffee) to savor, and rainbows to admire. Here are my favorite Big Island moments.

> PREVIOUS PAGE *The Big Island's best-known attraction is Hawaii Volcanoes National Park, where you can witness Pele's spectacular natural fireworks.* THIS PAGE *Akaka Falls, about 11 miles north of Hilo.*

1 **Creeping up to the ooze.** Since Kilauea's ongoing eruption began in 1983, lava has been bubbling and oozing in a mild-mannered way that lets you walk right up to the creeping flow for an up-close encounter. See p 228.

2 **Going underwater at Kealakekua Bay.** The islands have lots of extraordinary snorkel and dive sites, but none is so easily accessible as mile-wide Kealakekua Bay, an uncrowded marine preserve on the South Kona Coast. Here you can swim with dolphins, sea turtles, and every species of tropical fish that calls Hawaii's waters home. See p 208, 1.

3 **Discovering Old Hawaii at Puuhonua O Honaunau National Historical Park.** Protected by a huge rock wall, this sacred Honaunau site was once a refuge for ancient Hawaiian warriors. Today you can walk the consecrated grounds and glimpse a former way of life in a partially restored 16th-century village, complete with thatched huts, canoes, forbidding idols, and a temple that holds the bones of 23 Hawaiian chiefs. See p 210, 3.

4 **Stargazing from Mauna Kea.** A jacket, beach mat, and binoculars are all you need to enjoy every star and planet in this ultraclean atmosphere, where the visibility is so keen that 11 nations have set up telescopes (including the world's two largest) to probe deep space. See p 52, 31, and p 51.

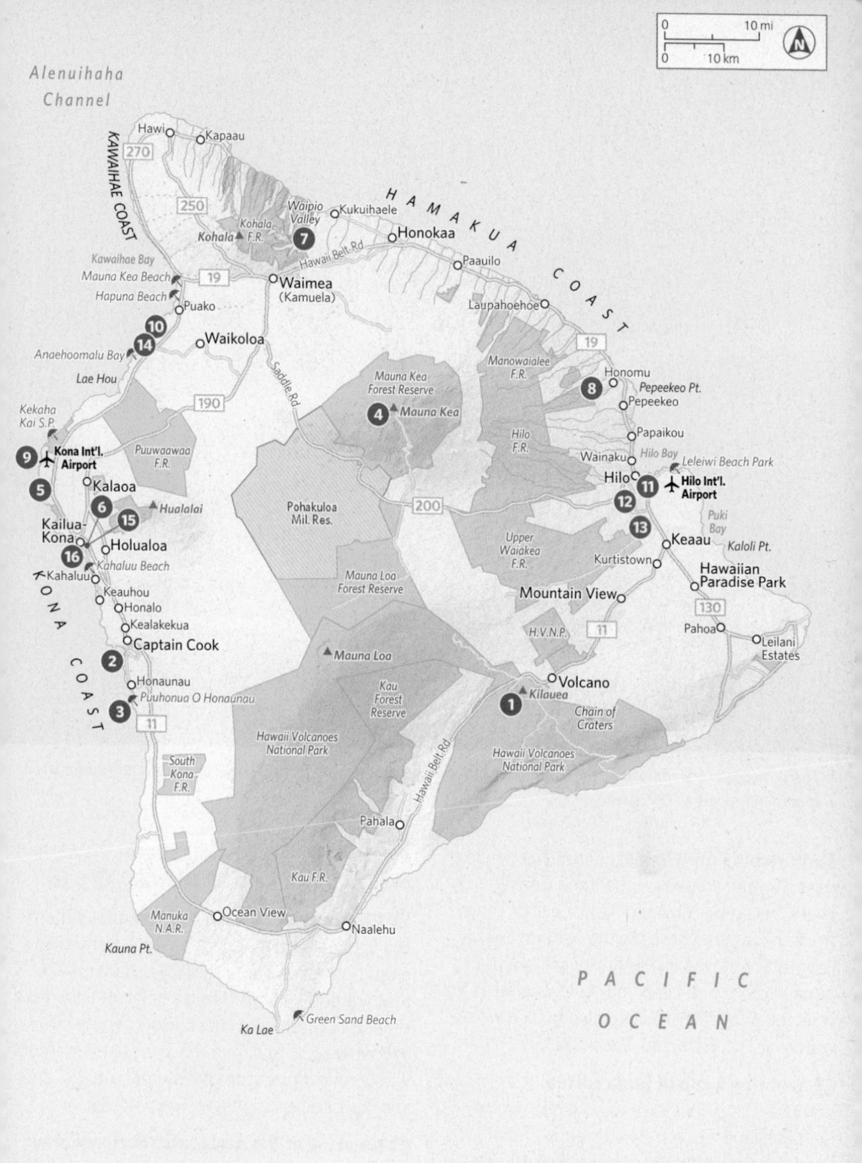

1. Hawaii Volcanoes National Park
2. Going underwater at Kealakekua Bay
3. Puuhonua O Honaunau National Historical Park
4. Stargazing from Mauna Kea
5. Watching for whales
6. Savoring a cup of Kona coffee
7. Hanging out in Waipio Valley
8. Chasing rainbows at Akaka Falls
9. Gawking at the day's catch in Honokohau Harbor
10. Puako Petroglyph Archaeological District
11. Shopping at the Hilo Farmers Market
12. Imiloa: the Astronomy Center of Hawaii
13. Panaewa Rainforest Zoo
14. Twilight at Kalahuipua'a
15. Home Tours Hawaii
16. Riding a submarine

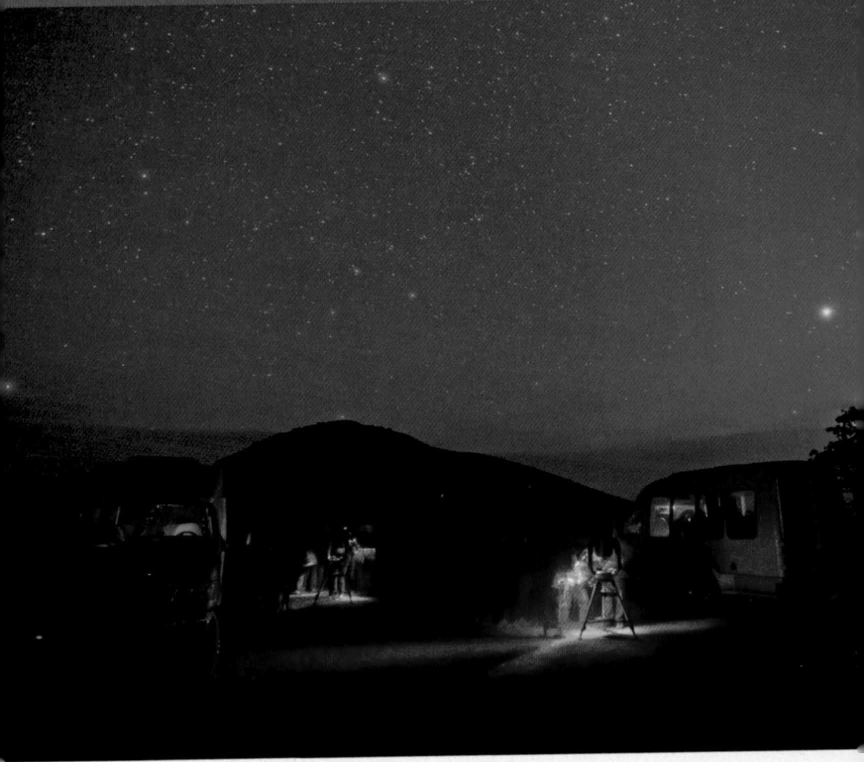

> *The atmosphere is so crisp at the summit of Mauna Kea that people from all over the world gather for a spectacular view of the stars.*

5 **Watching for whales.** Humpback whales pass through waters off the Kona Coast every December through April. To spot them from shore, head down to the Natural Energy Laboratory of Hawaii Authority just south of Kona Airport, and keep your eyes peeled as you walk the shoreline. You can also book a whale-watching trip in season. See p 252.

6 **Savoring a cup of Kona coffee.** It's just one of those things you have to do while you're on the Big Island. For a truly authentic cup of java, head upcountry to where several small cafes buy green coffee beans from local farmers, roast and grind them, and pour you the freshest cup of coffee you've ever had. See "Kona Coffee Craze!," p 270.

7 **Hanging out in Waipio Valley.** Pack a picnic and head for this gorgeously lush valley that time forgot. Delve deep into the jungle on foot, comb the black-sand beach, or just laze the day away by a babbling stream, the tail end of a 1,000-foot waterfall. See p 223, 11 & 12.

8 **Chasing rainbows at Akaka Falls.** When the light is right, a perfect prism is formed and a rainbow leaps out of this spectacular 442-foot waterfall, about 11 miles north of Hilo. Take time to roam through the surrounding rainforest, where you're sure to have close encounters with exotic birds, aromatic plumeria trees, and shocking-red torch ginger. See p 46, 17.

9 **Gawking at the day's catch in Honokohau Harbor.** Every afternoon between 4 and 5pm, local fishermen pull into the fuel dock to weigh in their big-game fish: 1,000-pound blue marlins, 150-pound yellowfin tunas, and plenty of scale-tipping mahimahi, ono (also known as wahoo), and others. Sit in the bleachers and check out these magnificent creatures.

10 **Hunting for petroglyphs.** The majority of Hawaii's ancient rock carvings are found in

> *Humpbacks literally leap through Kona's clear waters, offering some of the world's most abundant whale-watching possibilities.*

the 233-acre Puako Petroglyph Archaeological District, near Mauna Lani Resort. The best time to go looking is in the cool early morning or late afternoon. There are more than 3,000 petroglyphs in this area alone. See p 48, ㉓.

⑪ **Shopping at Hilo Farmers Market.** For a handful of dollars, you can buy a pound of rambutan (a sweet Indonesian fruit), a bouquet of tropical orchids, and a couple of tasty foot-long Hawaiian laulau (pork, chicken, or fish steamed in ti leaves). But be sure to arrive early (the market opens at sunrise) because many of the 200 or so vendors quickly sell out. See p 265.

⑫ **Seeing the stars from both sides.** The Imiloa Astronomy Center of Hawaii is an incredible museum/planetarium that looks at the stars from the Western astronomer's viewpoint as well as from the native Hawaiian's outlook. Some 300 exhibits fill the 12,000-square-foot gallery, and there's a state-of-the-art digital projection system in the planetarium. See p 213, ⑭.

⑬ **Going eyeball-to-eyeball with a Sumatran tiger.** The Panaewa Rainforest Zoo, the only outdoor rainforest zoo in the U.S., has 50 species of animals from rainforests all over the globe. See p 217, ⑦.

⑭ **Listening to Old Hawaiian music.** Once a month, on the Saturday night closest to the full moon, Hawaiian cultural expert Daniel Akaka, Jr., revives a bit of Hawaii's past with Twilight at Kalahuipua'a, a cultural celebration where the public is invited to sit on lawn chairs and towels on the shoreline as Danny "talks story" with his guests. See p 294.

⑮ **Seeing what it's like to live in Hawaii.** "Go local" for a day with the Home Tours Hawaii tour of how people really live in Hawaii. Not only do you get an inside look at local residents' homes (from a handmade coffee cottage to a luxury estate), but throughout the tour, tour leader chef Ann Sutherland serves a mouthwatering progressive brunch made exclusively of locally grown products. You'll even get a goodie bag of Hawaii products to take home with you. www.hometourshawaii.com.

⑯ **Riding a submarine.** If you aren't a swimmer, or if you have young children, take the *Atlantis* 48-passenger submarine some 120 feet down below the surface; it's like something out of a Jules Verne novel. You'll view this Neptunian-world from the comfort of your padded chair and never have to get wet. See p 258.

The Best of the Big Island in 3 Days

The Big Island of Hawaii—the island that lends its name to the entire 1,500-mile-long Hawaiian archipelago—is where Mother Nature pulled out all the stops. Simply put, it's spectacular. The Big Island has it all: fiery volcanoes and sparkling waterfalls, black-lava deserts and snowcapped mountain peaks, tropical rainforests and alpine meadows, a glacial lake and miles of golden-, black-, and even green-sand beaches. The Big Island has an unmatched diversity of terrain and climate. A 50-mile drive will take you from snowy winter to sultry summer, through landscape that looks like the inside of a barbecue pit on one side and a lush jungle on the other.

> *The Thurston Lava Tube features a perfect tunnel that was created by searing hot lava flows just a few hundred years ago.*

START Kailua-Kona. **FINISH** Hilo. **TRIP LENGTH** 3 days and 261 miles.

From Kailua Kona, take Queen Kaahumanu Hwy. (Hwy. 19 which turns into Hwy. 11) south. After about 5 miles, turn right (toward the ocean) at King Kamehameha III Rd. Turn left on Alii Dr., then right on Keleiopapa Rd., and follow it to Keauhou Bay, where you'll find parking.

Day 1

1 Kealakekua Bay. Since you most likely will be up early your first day in Hawaii (and still on mainland time), take advantage of it and book a morning sailing/snorkeling tour on the *Fair Wind* (p 254) to Kealakekua Bay, a marine life preserve. Spend the morning floating in a rainbowed sea of fish and enjoy a terrific lunch onboard the sailing catamaran. ⌚ 3–4 hr.

Retrace your steps back to Hwy. 11. Turn right (south), and continue about 9 miles down the road. About a mile past the Kealakekua Ranch Shopping Center, look on the right (ocean side) for the Coffee Shack.

2 ★ kids **The Coffee Shack.** After a day on the water, take a break at this informal bistro with a deck framed by ferns, palms, and banana and avocado trees. Here's your chance to try the famous Kona coffee and nibble on homemade poi bread, lemon bars, or carrot cake. Worth a stop just for the views. Hwy. 11, 1 mile south of Captain Cook. ☎ 808/328-9555. $-$$.

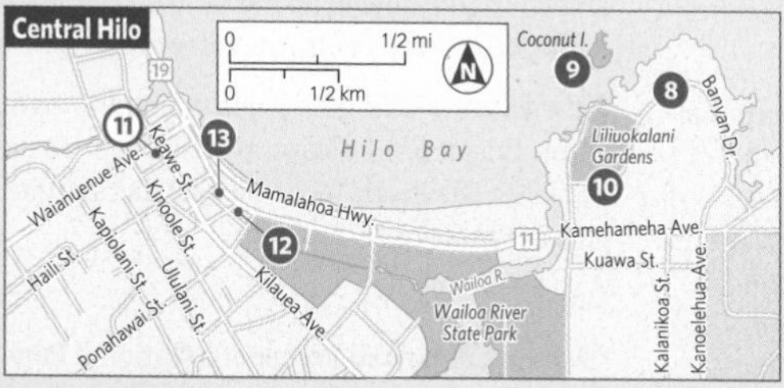

Day 1

1. Kealakekua Bay
2. The Coffee Shack
3. Puuhonua O Honaunau National Historical Park
4. South Point: Land's End
5. Volcano Village

Day 2

6. Hawaii Volcanoes National Park

Day 3

7. Rainbow Falls
8. Banyan Drive
9. Coconut Island
10. Liliuokalani Garden
11. Bears' Coffee
12. Hilo Farmers Market
13. Mokupapapa Discovery Center
14. Imiloa Astronomy Center of Hawaii
15. Imiloa Sky Garden Restaurant

> *Legend has it the glistening 80-foot Rainbow Falls that cascade into a natural pool hide the home of Hina, the goddess mother of Maui.*

Continue south on Hwy. 11 for about 4 miles. At MM 104, look for the sign on the highway directing you to turn right to Puuhonua O Honaunau National Historical Park (also known as the City of Refuge). Follow the road for 3½ miles to the signposted park entrance on your left.

3 ★★★ kids **Puuhonua O Honaunau National Historical Park.** With its fierce, haunting idols, this sacred site on the black-lava Kona Coast certainly looks forbidding. To ancient Hawaiians, however, Puuhonua O Honaunau served as a 16th-century place of refuge, providing sanctuary for defeated warriors and *kapu* (taboo) violators. A great rock wall—1,000 feet long, 10 feet high, and 17 feet thick—defines the refuge where Hawaiians found safety. On the wall's north end is Hale O Keawe *Heiau,* which holds the bones of 23 Hawaiian chiefs. Other archaeological finds include burial sites, old trails, and a portion of an ancient village. On a self-guided tour of the 180-acre site—which has been restored to its precontact state—you can see and learn about reconstructed thatched huts, canoes, and idols, and feel the *mana* (power) of old Hawaii. ⏱ 1-2 hr. Hwy. 160 (off Hwy. 11 at MM 104), Honaunau. ☎ 808/328-2288. www.nps.gov/puho. Admission $5 per vehicle, good for 7 days. Visitor center daily 8am-5pm; park daily 7am-8pm.

Big Island Facts

The Big Island is the largest island in the Hawaiian chain (4,038 sq. miles—about the size of Connecticut), the youngest (800,000 years old), and the least-populated (with 30 people per sq. mile). It has the highest peaks in the Pacific, the most volcanoes of any Hawaiian island, and the newest land on earth.

Return to Hwy. 11, turn right, and continue south for about 34 miles. Just past MM 70 is the turnoff to Land's End. Turn right and continue 11 miles to the end of the road.

4 ★★★ kids **South Point: Land's End.** At the end of 11 miles of bad road that peters out at Kaulana Bay, in the lee of a jagged, black-lava point, you'll find Land's End—the southernmost point in the United States. From the tip (beware of the big waves that lash the shore if you walk out there), the nearest continental landfall is Antarctica, 7,500 miles away. ⏱ 30 min. End of South Point Rd.

Retrace your route back to Hwy. 11. Turn right and continue, now in an easterly direction, for about 42 miles to Volcano Village.

5 ★ **Volcano Village.** Plan to spend the night in this quaint artsy village at 4,000 feet above sea level. See dining recommendations starting on p 266; lodging on p 280.

Day 2

6 ★★★ kids **Hawaii Volcanoes National Park.** Spend the day exploring this natural wonder. See p 228.

Spend the night in Volcano Village.

> *Enjoy beautiful views of Hilo Bay and Mauna Kea from Coconut Island.*

Day 3

From Volcano Village take Hwy. 11 toward Hilo. Allow at least 1 hour for the drive. Turn left onto E. Puainako St., then right onto Komohana St. Turn left onto Waianuenue Ave., then right onto Rainbow Dr.

7 ★ kids **Rainbow Falls.** Go in the morning, around 9 or 10am, just as the sun comes over the mango trees, to see Rainbow Falls at its best. The 80-foot falls spill into a big round natural pool surrounded by wild ginger. According to legend, Hina, the mother of the demigod, Maui, lives in the cave behind the falls. Unfortunately, swimming in the pool is no longer allowed. ⏱ 10–20 min. Rainbow Dr., just off Waianuenue Ave.

Turn left back onto Waianuenue Ave. Turn right on Komohana St., then left on Ponahawai St. Turn right on Kamehameha Ave., then left on Banyan Dr.

More of the Big Island

See chapter 3 for my suggested 1-week Big Island itinerary.

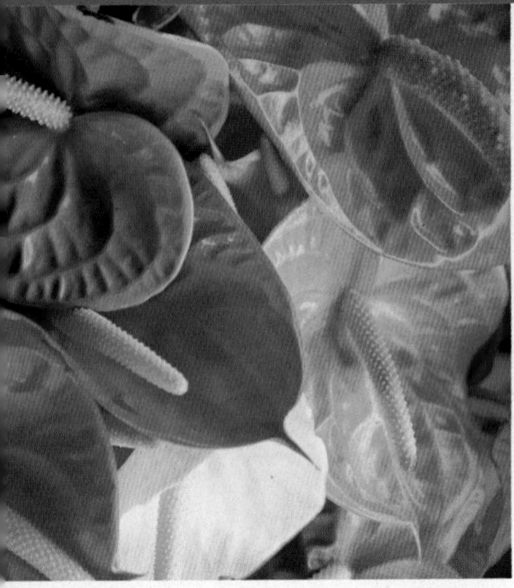

> *You'll find a spectacular assortment of flowers, fruits, and vegetables at the Farmers Market on Hilo's Kamehameha Avenue.*

8 ★★ **Banyan Drive.** This lane lined with old banyan trees curves along the waterfront to the Hilo Bay hotels. Most of the trees were planted in the mid-1930s by memorable visitors like Cecil B. DeMille (who was here in 1933 filming *Four Frightened People*), Babe Ruth (his tree is in front of Hilo Hawaiian Hotel), King George V, Amelia Earhart, and other celebrities whose fleeting fame didn't last as long as the trees themselves. ⏱ 20-30 min.

Park in front of the Naniloa Hotel, 93 Banyan Dr., and walk across the short concrete bridge to:

9 **Coconut Island.** This tiny island offers one of the best views of Mauna Kea. See p 217, 9.

Cross Banyan Dr. from the Naniloa Hotel to the large park:

10 ★★ kids **Liliuokalani Garden.** This is the largest formal Japanese garden this side of Tokyo. The 30-acre park, named for Hawaii's last monarch, Queen Liliuokalani, is as pretty as a postcard and was created to honor the Japanese immigrants, with bonsai, carp ponds, pagodas, and a moon-gate bridge. ⏱ 20-30 min. Admission free; open 24 hr.

Retrace your route back to Hwy. 19 and turn right. At the stoplight at Waianuenue Ave. (Hwy. 200) turn left, and park in the first block. Walk up Waianuenue Ave. to Keawe St. On the corner is:

11 ★ kids **Bears' Coffee.** Try to grab a table outside so you can people-watch as you sip on the Bears' strong coffee and nibble on a just-baked pastry. 106 Keawe St. ☎ 808/935-0708. No credit cards. $.

If you are here on a Saturday, turn around and head back to Hilo Bay on Waianuenue Ave., and turn right on Kamehameha Ave. Go about 3 blocks, and start looking for parking. The farmers market is held on the corner of Kamehameha Ave. and Mamo St.

12 ★★★ **Hilo Farmers Market.** The state's best farmers market, with a staggering variety of local flowers and produce. ⏱ 30min-1hr. See p 265.

Continue on Kamehameha Ave. On the left is:

13 ★ kids **Mokupapapa Discovery Center.** This 4,000-square-foot center is perfect for kids, who can explore the northwest Hawaiian Islands coral reef ecosystem. Through interactive displays, engaging three-dimensional models, and an immersion theater, the kids can learn natural science, culture, and history while having a great time. A 2,500-gallon saltwater aquarium provides a habitat for a collection of fish from the northwest Hawaiian Islands reefs. Lots of fun at a terrific price: free! ⏱ 30 min.-1 hr. 308 Kamehameha Ave., Suite 203. ☎ 808/933-8180. www.hawaiireef.noaa.gov. Free admission. Tues-Sat 9am-4pm.

Continue on Kamehameha Ave. and turn right on Ponahawai St. Turn left on Komohana St., left on Nowelo St., and left on Imiloa Place.

14 ★★★ kids **Imiloa Astronomy Center of Hawaii.** Do not miss this incredible planetarium/museum. It will be the highlight of Hilo. Perched high on a hill, overlooking Hilo Bay, titanium cones representing the volcanoes of the Big Island rise majestically. Even the landscaping of the 9-acre property is spectacular, featuring the largest and most diverse collections of native and Hawaiian "canoe" plants (plants the Polynesians brought with them on their canoes). The landscaping mimics the vegetation of the different elevations as you travel from the ocean to the top of Mauna Kea. Inside the 12,000-square-foot gallery, some 300 interactive

> *The Imiloa Astronomy Center of Hawaii is a top-flight planetarium and museum on nine incredibly landscaped acres.*

exhibits weave the science of astromony with the Hawaiian culture and describe the story of human exploration of the skies and the ocean (*imiloa* means "explorer" or "seeker of the truth"). Make sure you schedule your trip to correspond to one of the shows at the planetarium, which has a state-of-the-art digital projection and sound system. Your kids will want to stay here for hours; allow at least a half-day to really explore and play with all the exhibits. There's a cafe on-site so you can plan to eat lunch here. ⏱ 3–4 hr. 600 Imiloa Place, Hilo. ☎ 808/969-9700. www.imiloahawaii.org. Admission adults $17.50, children 4–12 $9.50, children under 4 free. Tues–Sun 9am–4pm.

15 ☕ kids **Imiloa Sky Garden Restaurant.** Take a break at the Imiloa and wander over to their light-filled cafe. Order an espresso and try something from the dessert menu, like the Hilo homemade ice cream or the lilikoi cheesecake. Let the *keiki* (kids) order from the kid's menu. 600 Imiloa Place. ☎ 808/969-9700. $.

> *Babbling creeks, Japanese bridges, and pagodas combine with lush landscaping to make Liliuokalani Gardens a serene experience.*

The Big Island with Kids

If you are traveling with *keiki* (children) in tow, you might want to take the following suggested itinerary, which emphasizes more things for the kids. I've set out a very limited, relaxed itinerary so the kids don't get overtired and cranky. Highlights are playing on the beach and seeing a real live volcano. This tour will take you from Kailua-Kona to the volcano to Hilo, and then back to Kona.

> *Kids love the calm waters, tranquil lagoons, and turquoise pools at Kahaluu Beach Park.*

START & FINISH Kailua-Kona. **TRIP LENGTH** 4 days and 135 miles.

Day 1

❶ **Ellison S. Onizuka Space Center.** You've finally arrived on the Big Island after a very long trip. The kids are antsy. If you have a spare adult in the group, have one person wait for the luggage and the other take the kids over to this center, located at the Kona Airport. Kids can check out a real moon rock and launch their very own miniature space shuttles until your bags turn up. See p 54, ㉞.

From the airport turn right on Hwy. 19, and head to your accommodation in Kailua-Kona. After the intersection of Palani Rd. in Kailua-Kona, Hwy. 19 becomes Hwy. 11. Check into your hotel, then get back on Hwy. 11, heading south. Just after MM 118, look for the sign to Kamehameha III Rd. Turn right (toward the ocean) at the sign. About 1½ miles down the road, turn right onto Alii Dr. Just after MM 5, pull into the parking lot on the left for the Kahaluu Beach Park.

❷ ★★ **Kahaluu Beach Park.** This is the most popular beach on the Kona Coast and perfect for kids because the outlying reef-protected lagoons knock down most waves and make the inshore waters very calm. Coconut trees line a narrow salt-and-pepper-sand shore that gently slopes to turquoise pools. The schools of brilliantly colored tropical fish that weave in and out of the reef make this a great place to snorkel. In summer, it's also an ideal spot for children and beginning snorkelers; the water is so shallow that you can

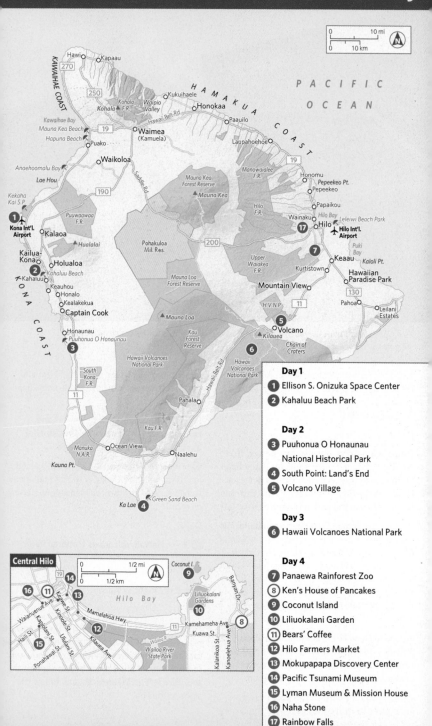

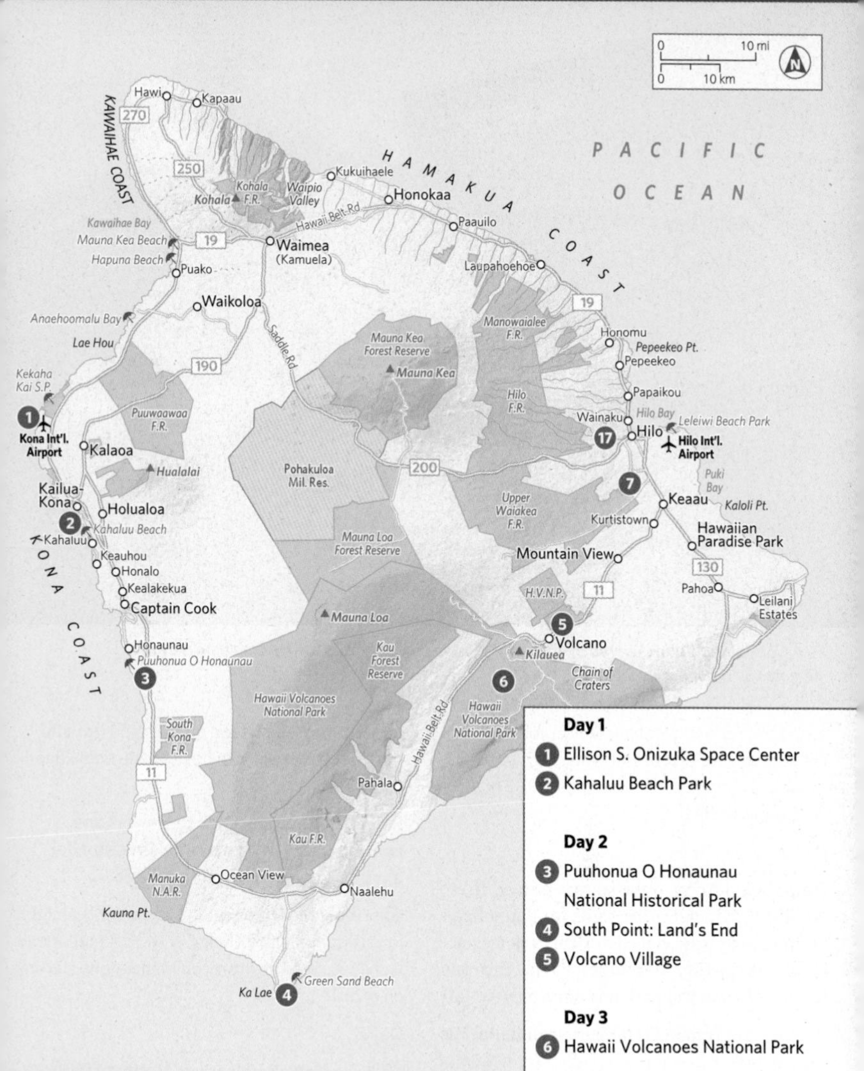

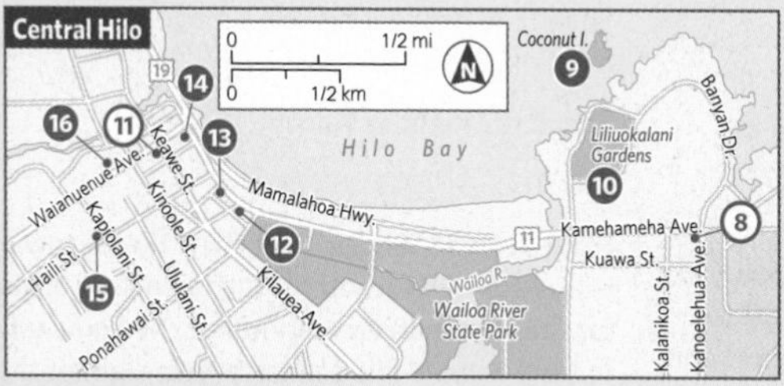

Day 1

1. Ellison S. Onizuka Space Center
2. Kahaluu Beach Park

Day 2

3. Puuhonua O Honaunau National Historical Park
4. South Point: Land's End
5. Volcano Village

Day 3

6. Hawaii Volcanoes National Park

Day 4

7. Panaewa Rainforest Zoo
8. Ken's House of Pancakes
9. Coconut Island
10. Liliuokalani Garden
11. Bears' Coffee
12. Hilo Farmers Market
13. Mokupapapa Discovery Center
14. Pacific Tsunami Museum
15. Lyman Museum & Mission House
16. Naha Stone
17. Rainbow Falls

> *The lack of vegetation caused by the sulfur dioxide emission from the Halema'uma'u Crater creates an otherworldly look.*

just stand up if you feel uncomfortable. But in winter, there's a rip current when high surf rolls in; look for the lifeguard warnings. ⏱ 1–2 hr. Alii Dr., just past MM 5.

Day 2

From Kailua-Kona, drive south on Hwy. 11. At MM 104, look for the signs for Puuhonua O Honaunau National Historical Park (also known as the City of Refuge). Follow the road to the ocean to the park entrance on your left.

❸ ★★★ **Puuhonua O Honaunau National Historical Park.** Kids will love this ancient "City of Refuge," with its fierce, haunting idols, displays of ancient Hawaii, and a great rock wall—1,000 feet long, 10 feet high, and 17 feet thick. If they get bored, there's a great beach behind the display with tide pools they can play in. See p 210, ❸.

Return to Hwy. 11 and continue south for about 34 miles. Just past MM 70 is the turnoff to Land's End. Turn right (toward the ocean) and continue 11 miles to the end of the road.

❹ ★★★ **South Point: Land's End.** Here's a great place to let the kids get out of the car and stretch their legs. Keep an eye on them and don't let them get too close to the edge. See p 210, ❹.

Retrace your steps back to Hwy. 11 and continue, now in an easterly direction, for about 42 miles to Volcano Village.

❺ ★ **Volcano Village.** Plan to spend the night in this quaint artsy village at 4,000 feet above sea level. See lodging recommendations starting on p 280.

Day 3

❻ ★★★ **Hawaii Volcanoes National Park.** Spend the day touring Pele's magnificent creation. See p 228.

Spend the night in Volcano Village.

Day 4

From Volcano Village, take Hwy. 11 east toward Hilo. After the turnoff for the town Keaau, look for the sign that says STAINBACK HWY./KALANI 19. Just beyond it is a small brown sign for the zoo. Turn left on Mamaki St., and follow the signs to the zoo.

7 ★ **Panaewa Rainforest Zoo.** This 12-acre oo, nestled in the heart of the Panaewa Forest eserve south of Hilo, is the only outdoor ainforest zoo in the United States. Some 50 pecies of animals from rainforests around the lobe call Panaewa home—including several ndangered Hawaiian birds. All of them are xhibited in a natural setting. This is one of he few zoos where you can observe Sumatran igers, Brazilian tapirs, and the rare pygmy ippopotamus, an endangered "minihippo" ound in western Africa. 1–2 hr. 800 Stainback wy. (off Hwy. 11), Hilo. ☎ 808/959-7224. www. ilozoo.com. Free admission. Daily 9am–4pm.

etrace your route back to Hwy. 11 and turn eft toward Hilo. At the intersection of Hwy. 11 nd Hwy. 19 turn left onto Hwy. 19, and then urn immediately left into the parking lot of:

8 **Ken's House of Pancakes.** For a quick break after the zoo, stop by Hilo's favorite family restaurant and the only 24-hour coffee shop on the Big Island. The waitresses will treat your little ones like their favorite nieces or nephews. 1730 Kamehameha Ave. ☎ 808/935-8711. $.

From the parking lot, turn right on Hwy. 11 and get in the left-turn lane. Make a left at the light onto Banyan Dr. Drive past the Hilo Hawaiian Hotel, and park close to the bridge to Coconut Island.

9 **Coconut Island.** The kids will love exploring this tiny island while you enjoy one of the best views of Mauna Kea. This island, which the Hawaiians called Mokuola, is the site of an ancient legend. The famous demigod, Maui, lived in Hilo and was quite the fisherman. His secret was a magical canoe and magical fishhook. One day, Maui thought about all the time he spent going to the other islands to fish. If he could join all the Hawaiian Islands into one big island, he could really save time fishing. So Maui gathered all the Hawaiian chiefs and told them about his plan. They all agreed to help.

Maui cautioned the chiefs that when they were helping him pull the islands together, no matter what, they absolutely could not look back until the islands were completely joined. The chiefs all agreed, and that night they set out to join the Big Island to its neighbor, Maui. Maui the demigod fastened his magical fishhook onto Maui the island, and the chiefs

> *The Panaewa Rainforest Zoo is a favorite destination for families, with 50 species represented in a beautiful, natural setting.*

pulled with all their might. They began to feel the island moving, but one chief just had to peek and see how close the islands were. The spell was broken and the island of Maui disappeared. All that remained was a small piece of the island where the demigod's fishhook remained. And that is how a piece of Maui, now called Mokuola, is in Hilo Bay. ⏱ 20–30 min.

Cross Banyan Dr. to the large park.

⑩ ★★ **Liliuokalani Garden.** A great place for kids to run and play. They may also enjoy the bonsai plants, carp ponds, pagodas, and moongate bridge. See p 212, ⑩.

Retrace your route back to Hwy. 19 and turn right. At the stoplight at Waianuenue Ave. (Hwy. 200), turn left and park in the first block. Walk up Waianuenue Ave. to Keawe St. On the corner is:

---

⑪ ☕ ★ **Bears' Coffee.** A great place to grab a quick snack if you need one. See p 212, ⑪.

If you are here on a Saturday, turn around and head back to Hilo Bay on Waianuenue Ave. and turn right on Kamehameha Ave. Go about 3 blocks and start looking for parking. The farmers market is held on the corner of Kamehameha Ave. and Mamo St.

⑫ **Hilo Farmers Market.** Shopping can be an adventure for your gang, especially when they can check out exotic fruit like mangosteen, lychee, liliquoi, and dragon fruit. See p 265.

Continue on Kamehameha Ave. On the left is:

⑬ ★ **Mokupapapa Discovery Center.** See p 212, ⑬.

Continue on Kamehameha Ave. for a couple of blocks to Kalakaua St. On the left is:

⑭ **Pacific Tsunami Museum.** Even more interesting than the exhibits here are the volunteers who survived Hawaii's most deadly "walls of water" in 1946 and 1960, both of which reshaped the town of Hilo. Visitors can listen to their stories of terror and view a range

> *The 4,000-square-foot Mokupapapa Discovery Center gives visitors a fascinating look at Hawaii's colorful coral reef system.*

> *Merchants from all over Hawaii bring a cornucopia of delicious indigenous fruits and vegetables to Hilo Farmers Market.*

of exhibits, from interactive computers to a children's section to a display on what happens when a local earthquake triggers a seismic wave, as it did in 1975 during the Big Island's last tsunami. ⏱ 1 hr. 130 Kamehameha Ave. ☎ 808/935-0926. www.tsunami.org. Admission $7 adults, $6 seniors, $2 children (6–17), 5 and under free. Mon–Sat 9am–4pm.

From Kamehameha Ave., turn left on Kalakaua St., then left on Kinoole St., and then right on Haili St. About ½ block past Kapiolani St., look for:

⑮ ★ **Lyman Museum & Mission House.** The oldest wood-frame house on the island was built in 1839 by David and Sarah Lyman, a missionary couple who arrived from New England in 1832. The structure combines New England and Hawaiian architectural styles, and is built of hand-hewn koa planks and native timbers. Here the Lymans received such guests as Mark Twain and Hawaii's monarchs. The well-preserved house is the best example of missionary life and times in Hawaii. You'll find lots of artifacts from the 19th-century, including furniture and clothing from the Lymans. The Mission House is shown by guided tour.

The Lyman Museum houses two major exhibit galleries. The **Earth Heritage Gallery** focuses on the natural history of the islands, with geology and volcanology exhibits, a mineral rock collection that's rated one of the best in the country, and a section on local flora and fauna. The **Island Heritage Gallery** features displays on Hawaiian culture, including a replica of a grass *hale* (house), as well as on other cultures transplanted to Hawaii's shores. ⏱ 1–2 hr. 276 Haili St. (at Kapiolani St.). ☎ 808/935-5021. www.lymanmuseum.org. Admission $10 adults, $8 seniors over 60, $3 children (6–17), $21 per family. Mon–Sat 9:30am–4:30pm. Tours 11am, 1pm, and 3pm.

Turn left on to Haili St., then left again at Keawe St. and left on Waianuenue Ave. The stone is in front of the Hilo Library.

⑯ **Naha Stone.** This 2½-ton stone was used as a test of royal strength: Ancient legend said that whoever could move the stone would conquer and unite the islands. As a 14-year-old boy, King Kamehameha the Great moved the stone—and later fulfilled his destiny. The Pinao Stone, next to it, once guarded an ancient temple. ⏱ 10 min. In front of Hilo Public Library, 300 Waianuenue Ave.

Continue driving west on Waianuenue Ave. for about 1 mile. Just past Kaumana Dr., look for Rainbow Dr. on the right.

⑰ ★ **Rainbow Falls.** See p 211, ⑦.

Northern Big Island: Kohala & Waimea

The northern tip of the Big Island is loaded with history and culture, and in 3 days you can get a good feel for how this region has gone from ancient Hawaii to cattle ranching to modern times. The 3-day tour begins in Kailua-Kona. You'll explore South Kohala, North Kohala, and the center of the Big Island: Waimea, Honokaa, and Waipio.

> *Take a guided shuttle tour to see the Waipio Valley, a lush tropical paradise with beautiful secluded coves and black-sand beaches.*

START Kailua-Kona. FINISH Waipio. TRIP LENGTH 3 days and 54 miles.

Day 1

From Kailua-Kona drive north on Hwy. 19. Look for the sign for the Mauna Lani Resort, which will be just before MM 73. Turn left (toward the ocean) into the resort on Mauna Lani Dr. At the roundabout turn right. Just before you reach the Fairmont Orchid, look for a sign on your left directing you to:

❶ ★ kids **Puako Petroglyph Archaeological District.** Here's a chance to see a part of Hawaii's history that few visitors see: the strange drawings on lava rocks. Go early in the morning for the best viewing; once the sun gets too high, some of the etchings are hard to see. See p 48, ㉓.

Retrace your steps back to Hwy. 19 and turn left, retracing your route. At the intersection of Hwy. 19 and Hwy. 270, turn left (toward the ocean) onto Hwy. 270. Look on the left for the entry sign to:

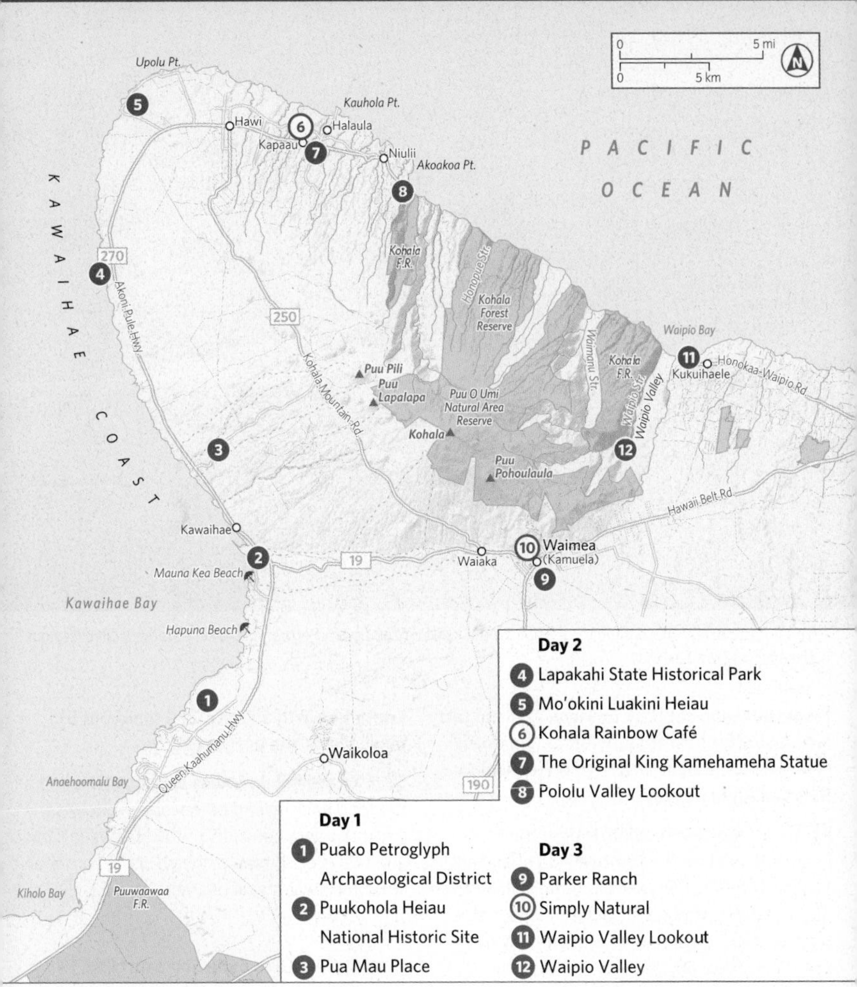

❷ ★★★ kids **Puukohola *Heiau* National Historic Site.** You'll be swept up in the fascinating history of Hawaii at this historic temple. See p 49, ㉔.

Return to Hwy. 270 and turn left. Just past MM 6 look on your right for the entry for Kohala Estates, and turn right on Ala Kahua Dr. Go ½ mile up the hill to the gate at a lava rock wall.

❸ kids **Pua Mau Place.** This terrific botanical garden has wonderful whimsical sculpture scattered throughout its 45 acres. See p 49, ㉕.

Day 2

Drive north on Hwy. 270. Continue about 7½ miles to just after MM 13, and look on your left (ocean side) for the sign for:

❹ ★ kids **Lapakahi State Historical Park.** If you've wondered what ancient Hawaii looked like, this 14th-century fishing village offers a glimpse into the lifestyle. See p 50, ㉖.

If you have called ahead and it is a "working" Saturday, then proceed to the next stop, the Mo'okini *Heiau*. If not, skip this next stop. IT IS NOT OPEN TO THE PUBLIC unless it is a working Saturday and you have made a reservation.

> *You'll find ancient hieroglyphic carvings on the rocks of the Puako Petroglyph Archaeological District near the Mauna Lani Resort.*

From Lapakahi, get back on Hwy. 270 and turn left. Just after MM 18, turn left at Old Coast Guard Rd., and then turn right on the Old Railroad Right of Way.

5 ★★ kids **Mo'okini Luakini *Heiau.*** Here's a chance to explore the spiritual side of ancient Hawaii at this 1,500-year-old temple (Hawaii's oldest, largest, and most sacred religious site), once used by kings to pray and offer human sacrifices. See p 50, 27.

Back on Hwy. 270 turn left and drive about 5 miles. Pass through the town of Hawi, and into Kapaau. Just after MM 23, look on your left. Across the street from the King Kamehameha Statue and the Civic Center is:

6 kids **Kohala Rainbow Café.** See p 52, 28.

7 ★★ kids **The Original King Kamehameha Statue.** There's a copy in Honolulu, but this one's the real deal. See p 52, 29.

Trip Tip

Spend the night on the Kohala Coast. My lodging recommendations start on p 280.

Continue north on Hwy. 270 for about 5½ miles to the end of the road.

8 ★★★ kids **Pololu Valley Lookout.** The end of the road and the end of this day overlooks the vertical jade green cliffs of the Hamakua Coast and two islets offshore, which you've probably seen in Hawaii travel posters. See p 52, 30.

Day 3

From Kailua-Kona drive north on Hwy. 19 about 33 miles to the intersection of Hwy. 19 and Hwy. 270. Turn right and continue on Hwy. 19, now headed east toward Waimea. At the stoplight at Hwy. 190, turn left and immediately get in the right lane to enter:

9 ★ kids **Parker Ranch.** The *paniolo* (cowboy) tradition began here in 1809, when John Parker, a 19-year-old New England sailor, jumped ship and rounded up wild cows for King Kamehameha. See p 48, 22.

Continue driving east toward Honokaa on Hwy. 19. Just before MM 42, turn left (toward the ocean) onto Hwy. 240, which goes through the town of Honokaa (where Hwy. 240 is called Marmane St.).

How to Get into Waipio Valley

Do not attempt to drive your rental car into Waipio Valley; cars frequently get stuck down there. A better option is the **Waipio Valley Shuttle** (☎ 808/775-7121), a 90- to 120-minute guided tour (Mon–Sat 9am–4pm). Get your tickets ($45 adults, $20 children 11 and under) at Waipio Valley Art Works, on Hwy. 240, 2 miles from the lookout (☎ 808/775-0958). You can also explore the valley on a narrated 90-minute **Waipio Valley Wagon Tour** (☎ 808/775-9518; www.waipiovalleywagontours.com), a historical ride by mule-drawn surrey. Tours are offered Monday through Saturday at 10:30am, 12:30pm, and 2:30pm ($55 adults, $50 seniors, $25 children 4–12). Call for reservations.

(10) ★ kids **Simply Natural.** Stop for picnic supplies or an ice cream cone. See p 47, (19).

Continue west on Marmane St. (Hwy. 240) another 7 miles to the end. Park in the parking lot. Do NOT attempt to drive into the valley without a four-wheel-drive vehicle.

(11) ★★★ kids **Waipio Valley Lookout.** A grassy park on the edge of Waipio Valley's sheer cliffs, with splendid views of the wild oasis below, is a great place for a picnic; you can sit at old redwood picnic tables and watch the white combers race along the black-sand beach at the mouth of the valley. From the lookout, you can hike down into the valley. ***Warning:*** Do not attempt to drive your rental car down into the valley (even if you see someone else doing it). The problem is not so much going down as coming back up. Every day, rental cars have to be "rescued" and towed back up to the top, at great expense to the driver. **20 min. End of Hwy. 240.**

(12) ★★ kids **Waipio Valley.** Long ago, this lush, tropical place was the valley of kings, who called it the valley of "curving water" (which is what *Waipio* means). From the black-sand bay at its mouth, Waipio sweeps 6 miles between sheer, cathedral-like walls that reach almost a mile high. Once 40,000 Hawaiians lived here, amid taro, red banana, and wild guava in an area etched by streams and waterfalls. Only about 50 Hawaiians live in the valley today, tending taro, fishing, and soaking up the ambience of this old Hawaiian place. The sacred valley is steeped in myth and legend. Many of the ancient royals are buried here; some believe they rise up to become Marchers of the Night, whose chants reverberate through the valley. The caskets of Hawaiian chiefs Liloa and Lono Ika Makahiki, stolen from the Bishop Museum, are believed to have been brought here by Hawaiians. Do not take your rental car here; see the box at left for options to get into Waipio Valley. **1–3 hr.**

> *The majestic 8-foot, 6-inch King Kamehameha Statue still commands visitors' attention on the Kohala Coast.*

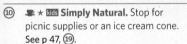

Kona

Most visitors to the Big Island see the town of Kailua-Kona, but few realize its rich cultural history, its culinary aspects, and the wonderful opportunities in surrounding communities. Below is a 3-day itinerary highlighting Kona's Hawaiian past, its vibrant present, and hints of things to come in the future. The 3-day trip starts each day in Kailua-Kona, so I recommend you find lodging here (lodging suggestions begin on p 280).

> *Puuhonua O Honaunau National Historical Park features a spectacular array of fierce idols.*

START Kailua-Kona. **FINISH** Kealakekua. **TRIP LENGTH** 3 days and 88 miles.

Day 1

From Kailua-Kona take Hwy. 19 north to MM 93, and turn left (toward the ocean) at the sign for the Kona Airport. At the stop sign turn right and park in the airport lot. Ellison S. Onizuka Space Center is across the street from the parking lot, by the airport terminals.

❶ kids **Ellison S. Onizuka Space Center.** This small museum honors Big Island–born astronaut Ellison Onizuka, who died in the 1986 *Challenger* space shuttle disaster. See p 54, ㉞.

From the airport return to Hwy. 19 and turn right. Just past MM 94, turn right and drive nearly to the end of the road.

❷ **Natural Energy Laboratory of Hawaii Authority (NELHA).** Visit the Big Island of the future at this experimental technology lab. See p 55, ㉟.

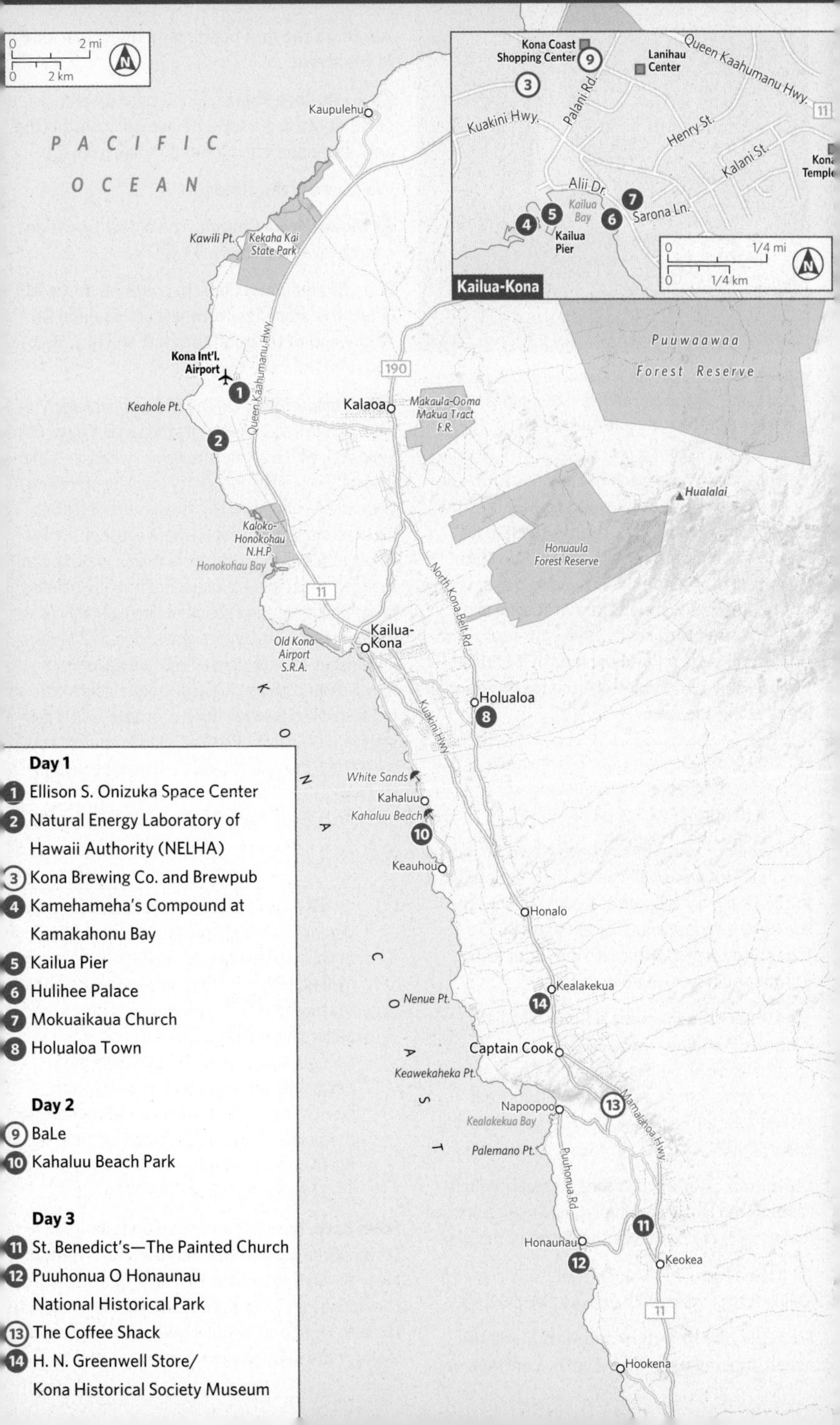
0 2 mi
0 2 km
N
PACIFIC OCEAN
Kaupulehu
Kawili Pt.
Kekaha Kai State Park
Kona Int'l. Airport
Keahole Pt.
Queen Kaahumanu Hwy.
190
Kalaoa
Makaula-Ooma Makua Tract F.R.
Puuwaawaa Forest Reserve
Hualalai
Honuaula Forest Reserve
Kaloko-Honokohau N.H.P.
Honokohau Bay
11
North Kona Belt Rd.
Kailua-Kona
Old Kona Airport S.R.A.
Holualoa
Kuakini Hwy.
KONA COAST
White Sands
Kahaluu
Kahaluu Beach
Keauhou
Honalo
Kealakekua
Nenue Pt.
Captain Cook
Keawekaheka Pt.
Napoopoo
Kealakekua Bay
Mamalahoa Hwy.
Palemano Pt.
Puuhonua Rd.
Honaunau
Keokea
Hookena
Kona Coast Shopping Center
Lanihau Center
Queen Kaahumanu Hwy.
Palani Rd.
Kuakini Hwy.
Henry St.
Kalani St.
Kona Temple
Alii Dr.
Kailua Bay
Sarona Ln.
Kailua Pier
0 1/4 mi
0 1/4 km
Kailua-Kona
Day 1
1 Ellison S. Onizuka Space Center
2 Natural Energy Laboratory of Hawaii Authority (NELHA)
3 Kona Brewing Co. and Brewpub
4 Kamehameha's Compound at Kamakahonu Bay
5 Kailua Pier
6 Hulihee Palace
7 Mokuaikaua Church
8 Holualoa Town
Day 2
9 BaLe
10 Kahaluu Beach Park
Day 3
11 St. Benedict's—The Painted Church
12 Puuhonua O Honaunau National Historical Park
13 The Coffee Shack
14 H. N. Greenwell Store/ Kona Historical Society Museum

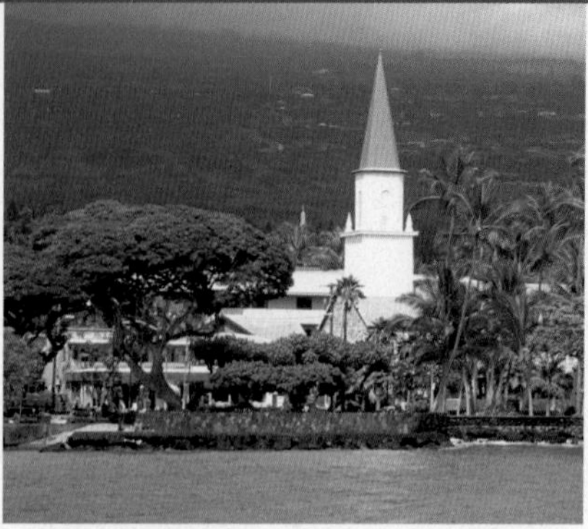

> *The Mokuaikaua Church is Hawaii's oldest Christian house of worship, and its 112-foot-steeple is still the tallest structure in Kailua-Kona.*

Retrace your route back to Hwy. 19, turn right, and drive about 7 miles to Kailua-Kona. Turn right (toward the ocean) at Palani Rd. At the second stoplight on Palani Rd., turn right (north) on Kuakini Hwy. and drive approximately ½ mile to the first stop sign, Kaiwi St., and turn right. Take your first right on Pawai Place, and follow it until it ends at the brewery parking lot. Watch for directional signs along the way.

③ **Kona Brewing Co. & Brewpub.** Take a break at the Big Island's first microbrewery. See p 55, ㊱.

Retrace your route back out to Kaiwi St., and turn left (toward the ocean), then left again at the four-way stop onto Kuakini Hwy. At the light turn left again onto Palani St. Go ½ block and turn into the parking lot at King Kamehameha's Kona Beach Hotel.

❹ ★★ kids **Kamehameha's Compound at Kamakahonu Bay.** Travel to the past to see a spiritual side of the Hawaiian culture at the sacred place King Kamehameha the Great retired to after he united the Hawaiian Islands. See p 55, ㊲.

Leave your car parked in King Kamehameha's Kona Beach Hotel parking lot, and walk from the historical grounds across the street to the pier.

❺ **Kailua Pier.** This historic pier at the center of Kailua town buzzes with activity. See p 56, ㊳.

From the pier turn right and walk along the ocean, making a right on Alii Dr. Continue on Alii Dr. to the first building on the ocean side of the street.

❻ ★★**Hulihee Palace.** Don't pass up an opportunity to see a royal palace on U.S. soil (the only other one is in Honolulu). See p 56, ㊴.

Walk across the street.

❼ **Mokuaikaua Church.** The oldest Christian church in Hawaii. See p 57, ㊵.

From Mokuaikaua Church, continue down Alii Dr. At the stop sign, turn left up Hualalai Rd. At the end of the road turn left on Hwy. 180, and drive into the town.

❽ **Holualoa Town.** On the slope of Hualalai Volcano above Kailua-Kona sits the small village of Holualoa, which attracts travelers weary of super-resorts. This funky upcountry town, centered on two-lane Mamalahoa Highway, is nestled amid a lush, tropical landscape where avocados grow as big as footballs. Little more than a wide spot in the road, Holualoa is a cluster of brightly painted, tin-roofed plantation shacks enjoying a revival as B&Bs, art galleries, and quaint shops. In 2 blocks, it manages to pack in two first-rate galleries, a frame shop, a potter, a glassworks, a goldsmith, an old-fashioned general store, a vintage 1930s gas station, a tiny post office, a Catholic church, and the Kona Hotel, a hot-pink clapboard structure that looks like a Western movie set—you're welcome to peek in, and you should. ⏱ 1 hr. Hwy. 180.

Day 2

⑨ kids **BaLe.** Before you head out for a day at the beach, pick up a picnic lunch at this statewide chain, which specializes in "fast" French-Vietnamese sandwiches, Vietnamese rice and noodle entrees, and bakery items. It's a nondescript place in a local shopping center but with great deals, like sandwiches on homemade French rolls. This family-run restaurant is the perfect place to stop before heading for the beach. Kona Coast Shopping Center, 74-5588 Palani Rd. ☎ 808/327-1212. $.

From BaLe, turn left and head up Palani Rd. (toward the mountain), and then turn right on Hwy. 11. Just after MM 118, turn right (toward the ocean) on King Kamehameha III Rd. At Alii Dr. turn right and about 1 mile down the road, look for the sign on your left to:

10 ★★ kids **Kahaluu Beach Park.** Spend the entire day at the beach. Kona's terrific weather (350 days of sunshine) and calm ocean waters (since it sits in the lee of the massive Mauna Kea Volcano, protecting it from harsh weather most of the time) make this the perfect place. See p 237.

Day 3

From Kailua-Kona take Hwy. 11 south. At MM 104, turn right (toward the ocean) at the sign for the City of Refuge (Keala O Keawe Rd.). Go about 1 mile to the first turnoff to the right (there will be a visitor marker at the turn). Turn right onto Painted Church Rd. Continue along a narrow, winding road about ¼ mile to:

11 ★ kids **St. Benedict's—The Painted Church.** Oh, those Belgian priests—what a talented lot. In the late 1800s, Father John Berchman Velghe borrowed a page from Michelangelo and painted biblical scenes inside St. Benedict's Catholic Church so the illiterate Hawaiians could visualize the white man's version of creation. ⏲ 30 min. 84-5140 Painted Church Rd. www.thepaintedchurch.org. ☎ 808/328-2227.

Continue down Painted Church Rd. When it ends, turn left on Midddle Keei Rd. When that road forks, stay left onto Napoopoo Rd. Follow Napoopoo Rd. down to the ocean. Look for the sign on your left to the entrance to the park.

12 ★★★ kids **Puuhonua O Honaunau National Historical Park.** From a spot sacred to missionaries to a spot sacred to the Hawaiians. See p 210, 3.

Retrace your route back up Napoopoo Rd., and at the hairpin turn in the road, veer right, back onto Middle Keei Rd. Take Middle Keei Rd. back to Hwy. 11 and turn left. A couple of miles up the road, look on the left (ocean side) for:

---

13 ☕ ★★ kids **The Coffee Shack.** See p 208, 2.

Leaving the Coffee Shack, turn left on Hwy. 11. Between MM 11 and MM 12, look on the ocean side (left side) of the street for:

14 ★★ kids **H. N. Greenwell Store/Kona Historical Society Museum.** This well-organized museum is housed in the historic Greenwell Store, built in 1875 by Henry Nicholas Greenwell out of native stone. Antiques, artifacts, and

> *Packed with antiques, historical artifacts, and photos, the Kona Historical Society Museum offers a compelling look into Hawaii's history.*

photos tell the story of this fabled coast. The museum is filled with items that were common to everyday life here when coffee growing and cattle raising were the main industries. Stocked with accurate reproductions of goods that filled the shelves and hung from the ceiling joists, the store offers a glimpse of the past, complete with storekeepers, dressed in period costumes, offering visitors St. Jacobs Oil to cure their arthritis or rheumatism. The Historical Society has another project in the works: the Kona Heritage Ranch, an outdoor museum on the daily life of a rancher in 1890, which will be located next door to the Greenwell Store. As part of the project, the Kona Historical Society has created a replica of an 1890 Portuguese stone oven, the first of several structures and programs planned for the Kona Heritage Ranch. An informal group gathers every Thursday to learn about wood-fired baking techniques. ⏲ 1 hr. Hwy. 11, btw. MM 111 and MM 112, Kealakekua. ☎ 808/323-3222 or 808/323-2006. www.konahistorical.org. Admission $7 adults, $3 children (5–12). Mon–Fri 10am–2pm. Parking on grassy area next to Kona Specialty Meats parking lot.

Hawaii Volcanoes National Park

The erupting volcano was the guiding light that led the Polynesian people to the Hawaiian Islands more than 1,600 years ago. This is the sacred site of numerous legends, and today the volcano goddess, Pele, is still creating additional land. Because the park is so big, I've provided a driving tour below. But the natural beauty of this park and the spirit of this sacred land can be experienced only by getting out of the car and walking around, so do stop at each site and explore on foot. If you have time to do some hiking, even better—pick up some trail maps at park headquarters.

> *Glowing lava from an erupting volcano flows into the ocean, creating new coral rock beneath the water.*

From Kailua-Kona take Hwy. 11 south for 96 miles, about a 2½–3 hour drive.

❶ ★★★ kids **Kilauea Visitor Center.** Don't pass up the visitor center located just beyond the Hawaii Volcanoes National Park's entrance station, not only to get the latest information on the eruption and which areas of the park are open but also to get an overview of this fabulous park and see the 25-minute film "Born of Fire, Born of the Sea," shown every hour on the hour from 9am to 4pm. ⏱ 1 hr. Crater Rim Dr. at the park entrance. ☎ 808/985-6000. Daily 9am–5pm. Free admission.

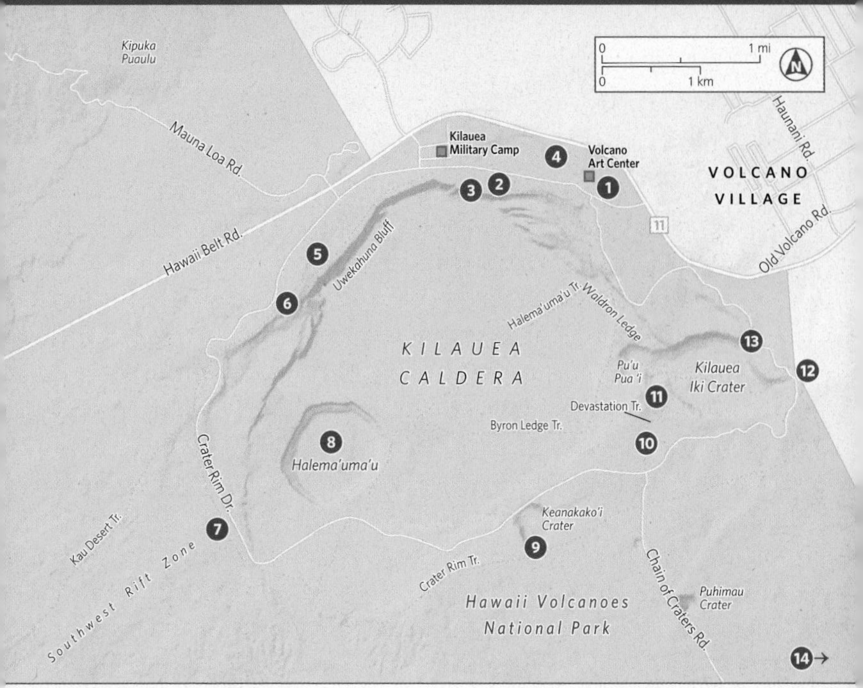

1 Kilauea Visitor Center
2 Steam Vents
3 Steaming Bluff
4 Sulphur Banks (Ha'akkulamanu)
5 Kilauea Overlook
6 Thomas A. Jaggar Museum
7 Southwest Rift Zone
8 Halema'uma'u Crater
9 Keanakako'i
10 Devastation Trail
11 Pu'u Pua 'i Overlook
12 Thurston Lava Tube
13 Kilauea Iki Overlook
14 Seeing the Volcano After Dark

From the visitor center, turn left on Crater Rim Dr. Just under a mile on the left is:

2 ★★ kids **Steam Vents.** Park and walk over to the crater on the left side of the road. You'll see steam pouring from where groundwater has trickled down to the hot volcanic rocks underneath and is rising back up to the surface as steam. You'll notice that there is very little vegetation in the area; this is because the area underground is white-hot—only grasses with a very shallow root system can grow here. ⏱ 10 min.

Take the short walk (look for the sign) from the Steam Vents parking lot to:

3 **Steaming Bluff.** Perched on the edge of the volcano's caldera is this area littered with cracks formed by the fuming volcano underground. On the surface, volcanic steam pours into the atmosphere. ⏱ 15 min.

Retrace your steps back to the parking area. Across the street is the trail head to Sulphur Banks (which is wheelchair accessible, with a paved path and boardwalk). Follow the short trail to:

4 **Sulphur Banks (Ha'akkulamanu).** Here, volcanic gases mingle with groundwater to produce a steam that contains carbon dioxide, sulfur dioxide, and hydrogen sulfide—and a

> The Kilauea Caldera Overlook is a great place to get a glimpse of the lava flow from the erupting Halema'uma'u.

Warning

If you have heart or respiratory problems or if you're pregnant, don't attempt any hike in the park; the fumes will bother you.

distinctive smell (like rotten eggs). Some sulfur gases deposit pure crystals at Sulphur Banks. ***Warning:*** Visitors with heart or respiratory problems (such as asthma), pregnant women, infants, or young children should NOT take this walk. ⏲ 20 min.

Continue on Crater Rim Dr. about ¾ mile from the Steaming Bluff parking lot. Look for the sign pointing to a picnic area for the:

❺ **Kilauea Overlook.** Get your camera out—this is an excellent opportunity to see the vastness of Kilauea Caldera (a very large crater formed by collapse). The caldera is about 2 miles wide and more than 3 miles long. This is also a great place to get a photo of the now erupting Halemaumau, which is the main pit crater within Kilauea Caldera. And, since you are away from the smell of Sulphur Banks, it's a great place for a picnic. ⏲ 10–30 min.

Continue on Crater Rim Dr. The next left after the Kilauea Overlook is:

❻ **Thomas A. Jaggar Museum.** This interesting museum exhibits equipment once used by scientists to study the volcano, including seismographs that record the tremors in the volcano as you watch (very spooky) and displays of the gear the volcanologists wore to get up-close-and-personal to the red-hot lava. The gift shop features volcano-related books, videos, CDs, maps, and other special items. On the way to and from the parking lot, stop and take in the incredible view of the volcano. The museum also has a floor-to-ceiling window with interpretive signs about the volcano

A Volcano Visiting Tip

Thanks to its higher elevation and windward (rainier) location, this neck of the woods is always colder than it is at the beach. If you're coming from the Kona side of the island in summer, expect it to be at least 10° to 20° cooler at the volcano; bring a sweater or light jacket. In the winter months, expect temperatures to be in the 40s or 50s Farenheit (single digits to midteens Celsius), and dress accordingly. Always have rain gear on hand, especially in winter.

(a great place to spend time in bad weather). Next door is the U.S. Geological Survey's Hawaiian Volcano Observatory, but it is not open to the public. 30 min.

Continuing on Crater Rim Dr., look for the sign to the Southwest Rift Zone.

7 **Southwest Rift Zone.** A rift zone is a weakness in a volcano's structure and generally it is where future eruptions originate. This rift zone goes from Kilauea's summit down to the ocean. The large cracks you see here date back to an 1868 earthquake and the colorful "stripes" you see along the cracks are from the ash, cinder, and pumice from the 1790 eruption. According to the National Parks Department, the lack of vegetation here is due to acid rain that forms due to the sulfur dioxide emitted from Halema'uma'u Crater. ***Warning:*** Anyone with breathing or heart problems (or young children or pregnant women) should not stop here, as it is generally downwind from Halema'uma'u Crater. Simply roll up all your car windows and continue driving to Keanakako'i Overlook, p 232, 9. 15 min.

Continue on Crater Rim Dr., and turn in at the sign for Halema'uma'u Crater. Park the car and take the 10-minute walk to the overlook.

8 **Halema'uma'u Crater.** As we went to press, the volcano was currently erupting from this crater, which according to Hawaiian legend, is the home of the volcano goddess, Pele. From the overlook you have a fantastic view of her home about 3,000 feet across and 300 feet deep. In 1924, Halema'uma'u was only 1,500 feet in diameter but was filled by a lake of molten lava. ***Warning:*** Anyone with breathing or heart problems (or young children or pregnant women) should not stop here. Simply roll up all your car windows and continue driving to Keanakako'i Overlook, p 232, 9. 15-20 min.

Continue on Crater Rim Dr. for just over a mile. On the right, you'll see the sign for Keanakako'i. As we went to press, due to the very high level of sulfur dioxide gas and an eruption from a new vent in Halema'uma'u, access to Keanakako'i was closed, but it may be open when you are here.

> *You might catch a glimpse of some of Hawaii's dwindling native bird species on a visit to Hawaii Volcanoes National Park.*

> *The lifeless landscape of Devastation Trail offers a startling look at the powerful impact of a 1959 eruption on the environment.*

9 **Keanakako'i.** When you are about a half-mile from the Halemaumau parking lot, you'll see hardened lava from a September 1982 eruption across the road. The smooth, swirly lava is called *pahoehoe* lava. The other type of lava you'll see is called *a'a,* and it appears as chunks of rocks ranging from the size of golf balls to soccer balls.

Keanakako'i, which means "cave of the adzes," was once the place where ancient Hawaiians gathered stone to make tools. In 1974 the eruption added 20 feet to the original site. At the overlook you can see the still-fuming deep fissures from that 1974 eruption. Bring your camera, as the overlook is one of the best places in the park to get a glimpse of both 13,677-foot Mauna Loa and 13,796-foot Mauna Kea. ⏱ 10 min.

Continue on Crater Rim Rd. for about a mile. Bypass the Chain of Craters (blocked by a 1995 lava flow and closed ever since). Park at the entrance to Devastation Trail on your left.

10 **Devastation Trail.** This half-mile trail offers a startling look at the powers of the 1959 volcanic eruption on the environment. It's paved and accessible to wheelchairs and strollers. The trail ends at Pu'u Pua 'i Overlook, so you can either walk the trail out and back or have the driver of the car drop you off and meet you at the next stop. ⏱ 30 min–1 hr.

Continue on Crater Rim Dr., about ½ mile, to:

11 **Pu'u Pua 'i Overlook.** The translation of this Hawaiian name is "gushing hill," which it was during the 1959 eruption. You have a great view here of how Kilauea Iki's "curtain of fire," as they called the fountaining lava, eventually created this spatter cone. ⏱ 15 min.

Continue on Crater Rim Dr. just over 1¼ miles through increasingly lush vegetation. Look on your right for the:

12 **Thurston Lava Tube.** You'll hike down into a natural bowl in the earth, a forest preserve that the lava didn't touch—full of native birds

> *The Thurston Lava Tube is a near-perfect natural tunnel created by a river of hot molten lava several hundred years ago.*

and giant tree ferns. Then you'll see a black hole in the earth; step in. It's all drippy and cool here, with bare roots hanging down. The lava tube, only a third-mile long, will take you 10 to 20 minutes to walk through. It was discovered in 1913 by Lorrin Thurston, a local newspaper publisher. Today it is cool inside, but a few hundred years ago a river of hot orange lava ran through the tube, just as today, a river of lava travels in underground tubes from the Pu'u O'o to the ocean. ⏱ 10–20 min.

Continue on Crater Rim Dr. about ½ mile to the turnoff for the:

⑬ **Kilauea Iki Overlook.** It may be hard to believe by looking at the serene scene today, but in 1959 this crater had fountains of lava shooting up nearly 2,000 feet high. Today the crater is a mile long and 3,000 feet across, and the floor is 400 feet below the overlook. If you have the time, take the 4-mile loop hike that circles Kilauea Iki. ⏱ 10 min. to take in the view; 2 hr. to hike.

About 1½ hours before sunset, head out of the park and head east down Hwy. 11. Turn right onto Hwy. 130 at Keaau, and go past Pahoa to the end of the road. (The drive takes the better part of an hour.) From here (depending on the flow), it's about a mile walk over sharp-crusted lava. Park rangers will tell you how to get to the best viewing locations, or you can call ahead (☎ 808/985-6000) to check where the current eruption is and how to get there. Be forewarned that the flow changes constantly and, on some days, may be too far from the road to hike.

⑭ **Seeing the Volcano After Dark.** If the volcano is erupting, be sure to see it after dark. Brilliant red lava snakes down the side of the mountain and pours into the sea, creating a vivid display you'll never forget. Be sure to heed the rangers: In the past, a handful of hikers who ignored their directions died en route. New lava can be unstable and break off without warning. Take water, a flashlight, and your camera, and wear sturdy shoes. ⏱ 2 hr., including the drive to get there.

VOLCANOES

The Explosive Origins of the Islands

BY DAN TUCKER

VOLCANOES ARE MORE than a fact of life in Hawaii—they literally are Hawaii. Rising from the ocean floor, these giant mountains of cooled-down molten lava, groomed by wind and water, form the dramatic cliffs, crags, and otherworldly shapes that define the Hawaiian landscape.

Hawaii is home to seven major volcanoes, including two of the nine monitored by the U.S. Geological Survey. Kilauea, on the Big Island, has been erupting continuously since 1983, making it one of the most active in the world. Flowing molten magma, lava tubes, and other evidence of the astonishing geological forces at work are easily and safely observed in Hawaii Volcanoes National Park.

Plates and Hot Spots: An Island Assembly Line

Geologists believe that the Hawaiian Islands formed over millions of years as the Pacific Plate, one of the largest of earth's tectonic plates, passed over a "hot spot" deep in earth's mantle, the layer just below earth's crust. Hot magma from within the hot spot expanded upward through the crust, spewing molten lava onto the ocean floor. In effect, this movement is a slow-motion assembly line. The Pacific Plate is still sliding northwestward at a rate of about 2.75 to 3.50 inches per year.

This theory is supported by the relative age of the volcanoes that form the islands progressively from the Big Island, where volcanoes are still active, to the northwest end, where the volcanoes are about 30 million years old.

Active (and Potentially Active) **Volcanoes in Hawaii**

HALEAKALA
Location: East Maui **Elevation:** 10,023 feet **Latest activity:** 1790 **Good to know:** 97 percent of Haleakala's volume is below sea level.

HUALALAI
Location: Western corner of Big Island **Elevation:** 8,271 feet **Latest activity:** 1800–01 **Good to Know:** 80 percent of Hualalai's surface has been covered by lava flows in the past 5,000 years.

KILAUEA
Location: SE edge of Big Island **Elevation:** 4,190 feet **Latest activity:** Ongoing from 1983 **Good to know:** Originally thought to be an outgrowth of Mauna Kea, Kilauea was discovered in recent decades to be a volcano in its own right.

KOHALA
Location: NW tip of Big Island **Elevation:** 5,480 feet **Latest activity:** 120,000 years ago **Good to know:** Hawaii's oldest volcano; at its greatest extent 250,000–300,000 years ago, was probably twice its present width.

LOIHI
Location: On the seafloor, approximately 19 miles south of Kilauea. **Elevation:** 3,180 feet below sea level **Latest activity:** Unknown **Good to know:** Submarine volcano (seamount); seismically active; and young—thought to be the likely site of the next Hawaiian island.

MAUNA KEA
Location: Big Island **Elevation:** 13,796 feet **Latest activity:** 4,000 years ago **Good to know:** The tallest volcano in Hawaii, Mauna Kea shows clear evidence of glacial activity.

MAUNA LOA
Location: Big Island **Elevation:** 13,680 feet **Latest activity:** 1984 **Good to know:** From underwater base to summit, Mauna Loa is the largest volcano on the planet: 56,000 feet.

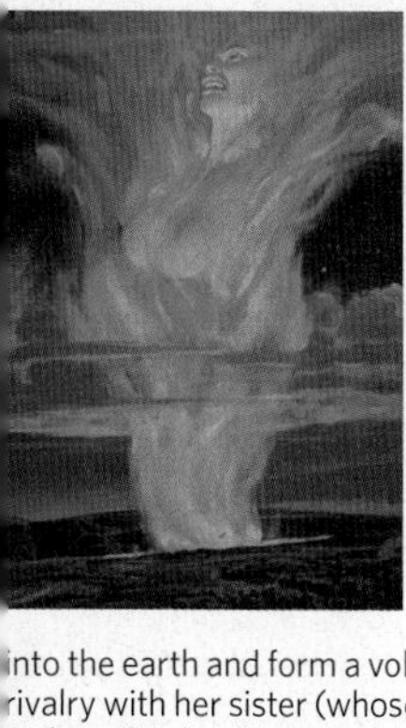

Lore and Legend

According to legend, Kilauea is the home of Pele, the hot-tempered Hawaiian volcano goddess. Pele, born in Tahiti, traveled by canoe first to Kauai, then to Oahu and Maui, in each place using her *paoa* (digging stick) to strike deep into the earth and form a volcano. She had a bitter rivalry with her sister (whose husband she had seduced), who dampened each successive volcano with sea water. After an epic battle, Pele settled on the island of Hawaii, where she made a home in Halema'uma'u Crater, at the summit of Kilauea.

Kilauea is said to be the navel of the world, where the gods created earth. It is the site of the largest collection of petroglyphs in Hawaii, with more than 15,000 carvings.

Big Island Beaches A to Z

★★ kids **Anaehoomalu Bay (A-Bay)** WAIKOLOA The Big Island makes up for its dearth of beaches with a few spectacular ones, like Anaehoomalu, or A-Bay, as the locals call it. This popular gold-sand beach, fringed by a grove of palms and backed by royal fishponds still full of mullet, is one of Hawaii's most beautiful. Swimming, snorkeling, diving, kayaking, and windsurfing are all excellent here (equipment rental and instruction are available at the north end of the beach). Endangered green sea turtles gather at the far end of the bay. Facilities include restrooms, showers, picnic tables, equipment rental, and plenty of parking. Waikoloa Beach Resort, Waikoloa Beach Dr., off Hwy. 11 at MM 76.

★ **Green Sand Beach (Papakolea Beach)** SOUTH POINT Hawaii's famous green-sand beach is located at the base of Puu o Mahana, an old cinder cone spilling into the sea. The sand is crushed olivine, a green semiprecious mineral found in eruptive rocks and meteorites. If the surf's up, check out the beach from the cliff's edge; if the water's calm, it's generally safe to swim. To get to Green Sand Beach from the boat ramp at South Point, follow the trail; even if you have a four-wheel-drive vehicle, you may want to walk because the trail is very, very bad in parts. Make sure you have appropriate closed-toed footwear: tennis shoes or hiking boots. The beginning of the trail is hardened lava. After the first 10 to 15 minutes of walking, the lava disappears, and the trail begins to cross pastureland. After some 30 to 40 minutes more, you'll see an eroded cinder cone by the water; continue to the edge, and there lie the green sands below.

The best way to reach the beach is to go over the edge from the cinder cone. From the cinder cone, go over the overhang of the rock, and you'll see a trail. Going down to the beach is very difficult and treacherous; you'll have to make it over and around big lava boulders, dropping down 4 to 5 feet from boulder to boulder in certain spots. When you get to the beach, watch the waves to be sure they don't break over the entire beach. If you walk on the beach, always keep one eye on the ocean and stick close to the rock wall. There can be strong rip currents here. Allow a minimum of 2 to 3 hours for this entire excursion. End of South Point Rd., off Hwy. 11 btw. MM 70 and MM 69.

> *At the base of Puu o Mahana, the famous Green Sand Beach is comprised of semiprecious minerals found only in volcanic rocks and meteorites.*

Big Island Beaches A to Z

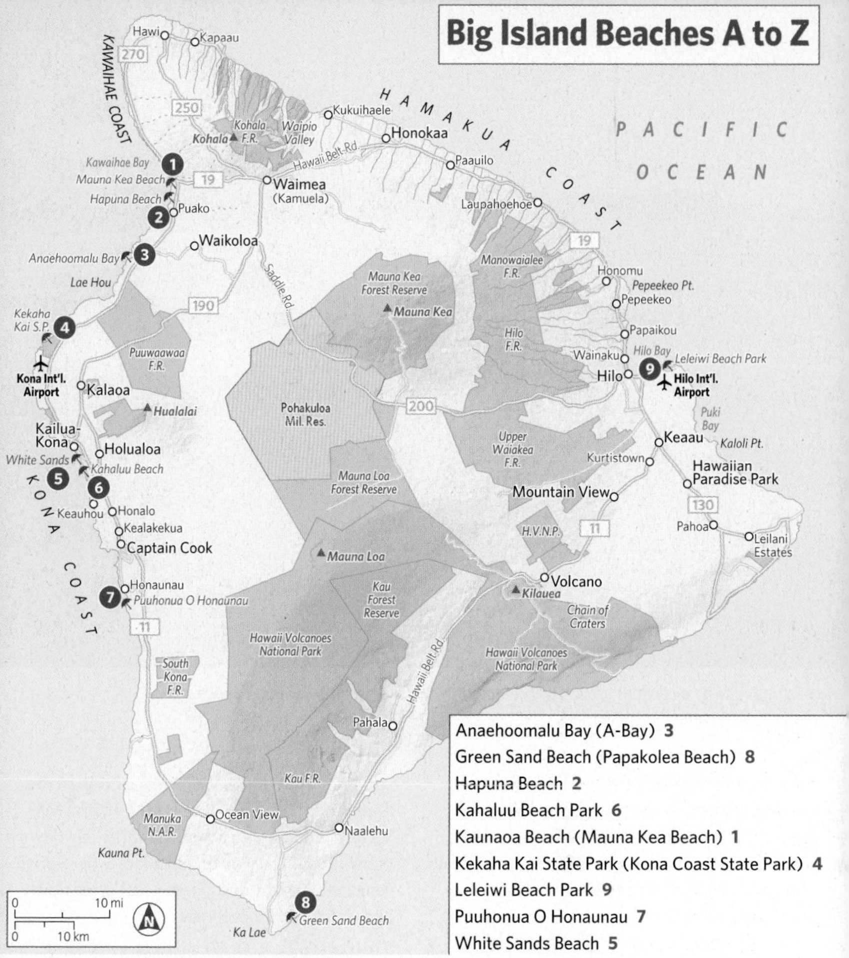

Anaehoomalu Bay (A-Bay) **3**
Green Sand Beach (Papakolea Beach) **8**
Hapuna Beach **2**
Kahaluu Beach Park **6**
Kaunaoa Beach (Mauna Kea Beach) **1**
Kekaha Kai State Park (Kona Coast State Park) **4**
Leleiwi Beach Park **9**
Puuhonua O Honaunau **7**
White Sands Beach **5**

★★★ **Hapuna Beach** KOHALA COAST
Just off Queen Kaahumanu Highway, south of the Hapuna Beach Prince Hotel, lies this big, wide crescent of gold sand. In summer, when the beach is widest, the ocean calmest, and the crowds biggest, this is the island's best beach for swimming, snorkeling, and bodysurfing. But beware of Hapuna in winter, when its thundering waves, strong rip currents, and lack of lifeguards can make it dangerous. Facilities include A-frame cabins for camping, pavilions, restrooms, showers, and plenty of parking. Hapuna Beach Rd., off Hwy. 11 just before MM 69, Kohala Coast.

★★ kids **Kahaluu Beach Park** KEAUHOU
This is the most popular beach on the Kona Coast; these reef-protected lagoons attract 1,000 people a day almost year-round. Kahaluu is the best all-around beach on Alii Drive, with coconut trees lining a narrow sand shore that gently slopes to turquoise pools. The schools of brilliantly colored tropical fish that weave in and out of the reef make this a great place to snorkel. In summer, it's great for kids and beginning snorkelers, but in winter, there's a rip current when high surf rolls in; look for the lifeguard warnings. Facilities include parking, beach-gear rentals, a covered pavilion, restrooms, barbecue pits, and a food concession. It gets crowded, so stake out a spot early. Alii Dr., btw. MM 4.5 and MM 5.5.

> *Surrounded by a coconut grove and protected by two lava points, Kaunaoa Beach offers calm waters for swimmers.*

★★★ **Kaunaoa Beach (Mauna Kea Beach)** KOHALA COAST A coconut grove sweeps around this golden crescent, where the water is calm and protected by two black-lava points. The sandy bottom slopes gently into the bay, which often fills with tropical fish, sea turtles, and manta rays. Swimming is excellent year-round, except in rare winter storms. Snorkelers prefer the rocky points, where fish thrive in the surge. Facilities include restrooms, showers, and ample parking, but there are no lifeguards. Rockefeller Rd., Mauna Kea Beach Hotel, Mauna Kea Resort, off Hwy. 11 just before MM 68.

★ **Kekaha Kai State Park (Kona Coast State Park)** KONA COAST This beach has 5 miles of shoreline with a half-dozen long, curving beaches and a big cove on Mahaiula Bay, as well as archaeological and historical sites. The series of well-protected coves are excellent for swimming, and there's great snorkeling and diving offshore; the big winter waves attract surfers. Facilities include restrooms, picnic tables, and barbecue pits; you'll have to bring your own drinking water. 2 miles north of the Kona Airport on Hwy. 11 btw. MM 90 and MM 91; turn left at a sign pointing improbably down a bumpy road. You won't need a four-wheel-drive vehicle to make it down here—just drive slowly and watch out for potholes.

★ **Leleiwi Beach Park** KEAUKAHA This unusual cove of palm-fringed, black-lava tide pools fed by freshwater springs and rippled by gentle waves is a photographer's delight—one of Hawaii's most beautiful beaches and the perfect place to take a plunge. In winter, big waves can splash these ponds, but the shallow pools are generally free of currents and ideal for kids, especially in the protected inlets at the center of the park. Leleiwi often attracts endangered sea turtles, making this one of Hawaii's most popular snorkeling spots. It's just outside Hilo on Kalanianaole Avenue. Facilities include restrooms, showers, lifeguards, picnic pavilions, and paved walkways. Kalanianaole Ave., 2 miles SE of Hilo Airport.

> *Kaunaoa Beach's calm currents and abundant opportunities to mingle with sea life make it a top destination for kayakers.*

★ **Puuhonua Ō Honaunau** SOUTH KONA
Just past the National Park, this black-and-white sandy beach offers great snorkeling and a shady area for picnics. Facilities include portable restrooms, picnic tables, and barbecue pits; bring your own water. Turn off Hwy. 11 btw. MM 103 and MM 104 and go 3½ miles down Hwy. 160.

★ **White Sands Beach** KONA COAST
This small, white-sand pocket beach about 4 miles south of Kailua-Kona is sometimes called Disappearing Beach because it does just that, especially at high tide or during storms. On calm days, the water is perfect for swimming and snorkeling. Locals teach their children how to surf and boogie board here. In winter the waves swell to expert levels, attracting surfers and spectators. Facilities include restrooms, showers, lifeguards, and a small parking lot. Alii Dr. at MM 4, Kailua-Kona.

> *Leleiwi Beach Park attracts snorklers hoping to encounter endangered sea turtles. Watch out for big waves (and surfers) in winter.*

The Big Island's Best Hiking & Camping

Hawaii Volcanoes National Park

Don't miss this opportunity to see Mother Nature (or as the Hawaiians say, Pele, the volcano goddess) at work. The Hawaii Volcanoes National Park has well defined trails that take you right up to the action and through some otherworldly landscapes you will never see anywhere else.

Hiking.

Devastation Trail. Up on the rim of Kilauea Iki Crater, you can see what an erupting volcano did to a once-flourishing ohia forest. The scorched earth, with its ghostly tree skeletons, lies in sharp contrast to the rest of the lush forest. Everyone can take this .5-mile hike on a paved path across the eerie bed of black cinders. The trail head is on Crater Rim Road at Puu Puai Overlook.

Halemaumau Trail. This moderate 3.5-mile hike starts at the visitor center, goes down 500 feet to the floor of Kilauea Crater, crosses the crater, and ends at Halemaumau Overlook.

> *Hikers check out the devastation wrought by Pele on the Kilauea Iki Trail.*

Kilauea Iki Trail. You'll experience the work of the volcano goddess, Pele, firsthand on this hike. The 4-mile moderate trail begins at the visitor center, descends through a forest of ferns into still-fuming Kilauea Iki Crater, and then crosses the crater floor past the vent where a 1959 lava blast shot a fountain of fire 1,900 feet into the air for 36 days. Allow 2 hours.

Kipuka Puaulu (Bird Park) Trail. This easy, 1.5-mile, hour-long hike lets you see native Hawaiian flora and fauna in a little oasis of living nature in a field of lava. A display at the trail head on Mauna Loa Road describes the plants and birds you'll see on the walk. Go early in the morning or in the evening (or, even better, just after a rain) to see native birds like the apapane (a small bright-red bird with black wings and tail) and the iiwi (larger and orange-vermilion, with a curved orange bill). Native trees along the trail include giant ohia, koa, soapberry, kolea, and mamani.

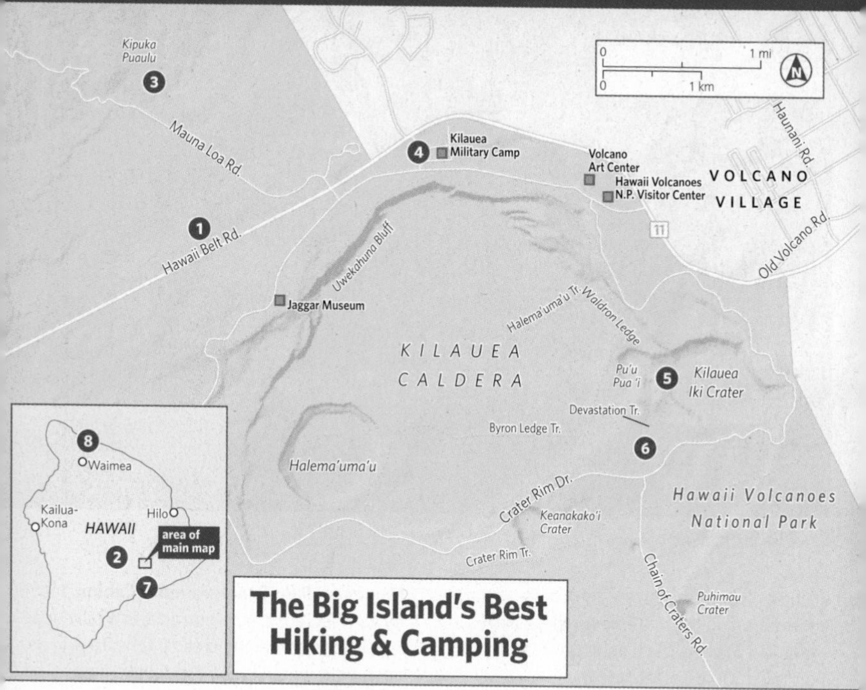

The Big Island's Best Hiking & Camping

Hiking

Devastation Trail **6**

Kilauea Iki Trail **5**

Kipuka Puaulu (Bird Park) Trail **3**

Mauna Loa Trail **2**

Waimanu Valley's Muliwai Trail **8**

Camping

Halape Shelter **7**

Kilauea Military Camp **4**

Namakani Paio **1**

Mauna Loa Trail. Probably the most challenging hike in Hawaii, this trail goes 7.5 miles from the lookout to a cabin at 10,035 feet and then 12 more miles up to the primitive Mauna Loa summit cabin at 13,250 feet, where the climate is subarctic and overnight temperatures are below freezing year-round. This 4-day round-trip requires advance planning, great physical condition, and registration at the visitor center. Call ☎ 808/985-6000 for maps and details. The trail head begins where Mauna Loa Road ends, 14 miles north of Hwy. 11.

Camping.

Halape Shelter. This backcountry site, about 7 miles from the nearest road (you have to hike in), is the place for those who want to get away from it all and enjoy their own private white-sand beach. The small three-sided stone shelter, with a roof but no floor, can accommodate two people comfortably. You can pitch a tent inside, but if the weather is nice, you're better off setting up outside. There's a catchment water tank, but check with rangers on the water situation before

> *Namakani Paio Campground.*

hiking in (sometimes they don't have accurate information on the water level; bring extra water just in case). The only other facility is a pit toilet. Go on weekdays if you're really looking for an escape. It's free to stay here, but you're limited to 3 nights. Permits are available at the Hawaii Volcanoes National Park Visitor Center on a first-come, first-served basis, no earlier than noon on the day before your trip. For more information, call ☎ 808/985-6000.

Kilauea Military Camp. A mile from the visitor center (accessible by car), is a rest-and-recreation camp for active and retired military personnel. Facilities include 75 one- to three-bedroom cabins with fireplaces (some with a Jacuzzi), cafeteria, bowling alley, bar, general store, weight room, and tennis and basketball courts. Rates are based on rank, ranging from $67 to $205 a night. Call ☎ 808/967-8333 on the Big Island or 808/438-6707 on Oahu (www.kmc-volcano.com).

Namakani Paio. Tent camping is free; no reservations are required. Stays are limited to 7 days per year. Backpack camping at hiker shelters and cabins is available on a first-come, shared basis, but you must register at the Hawaii Volcanoes National Park Visitor Center. There is also a pavilion with picnic tables and a fireplace (but no wood is provided). The site is accessible by car.

Namakani Paio Campground & Cabins. Just 5 miles west of the park entrance is a tall eucalyptus forest where you can pitch a tent in an open grassy field (you have to hike here). The trail to Kilauea Crater is just a half-mile away. No permit is needed, but stays are limited to 7 days. Facilities include pavilions with barbecues and a fireplace, picnic tables, outdoor dish-washing areas, restrooms, and drinking water. There are also 10 cabins that accommodate up to four people each. Each cabin has a covered picnic table at the entrance and a fireplace with a grill. Toilets, sinks, and hot showers are available in a separate building. You can get groceries and gas in the town of Volcano, 4 miles away. Make cabin reservations through Volcano House, P.O. Box 53, Hawaii National Park, HI 96718 (☎ 808/967-7321); the cost is $40 per night for two adults (and two children), $48 for three adults, and $56 for four adults.

Waimanu Valley's Muliwai Trail

Hiking & Camping. This difficult 2- to 3-day backpacking adventure—only for the hardy—takes you to a hidden valley some call Eden, with virgin waterfalls and pools and spectacular views. The trail, which goes from sea level to 1,350 feet and down to the sea again, takes more than 9 hours to hike in and more than 10 hours to hike out. Be prepared for clouds of bloodthirsty mosquitoes, and look out for wild pigs. If it's raining, forget it: You'll have 13

> *Get a breathtaking view of the crater left by a 1959 eruption from an overlook at the top of the Kilauea Iki Trail.*

streams to cross before you reach the rim of Waimanu Valley, and rain means flash floods.

You must get permission to camp in Waimanu Valley from the Division of Forestry and Wildlife, 19 East Kawili St., Hilo, HI 96720 (☎ 808/974-4217; www.hawaiitrails.org). Permits to the nine designated campsites are assigned by number. They're free, but you're limited to a 7-day stay. Facilities are limited to two composting pit toilets. The best water in the valley is from the stream on the western wall, a 15-minute walk up a trail from the beach. All water must be treated before drinking. The water from the Waimanu Stream drains from a swamp, so skip it. Be sure to pack out what you take in.

To get to the trail head, take Hwy. 19 to the turnoff for Honokaa; drive 9½ miles to the Waipio Valley Lookout. Unless you have a four-wheel-drive-vehicle, this is where your hike begins. Walk down the road and wade the Wailoa Stream; then cross the beach and go to the northwest wall. The trail starts here and goes up the valley floor, past a swamp, and into a forest before beginning a series of switch-backs that parallel the coastline. These switch-backs go up and down about 14 gulches. At the ninth gulch, about two-thirds of the way along the trail, is a shelter. After the shelter, the trail descends into Waimanu Valley, which looks like a smaller version of Waipio Valley but without a sign of human intrusion.

> *Hiking to Thurston Lava Tube in Hawaii Volcanoes National Park.*

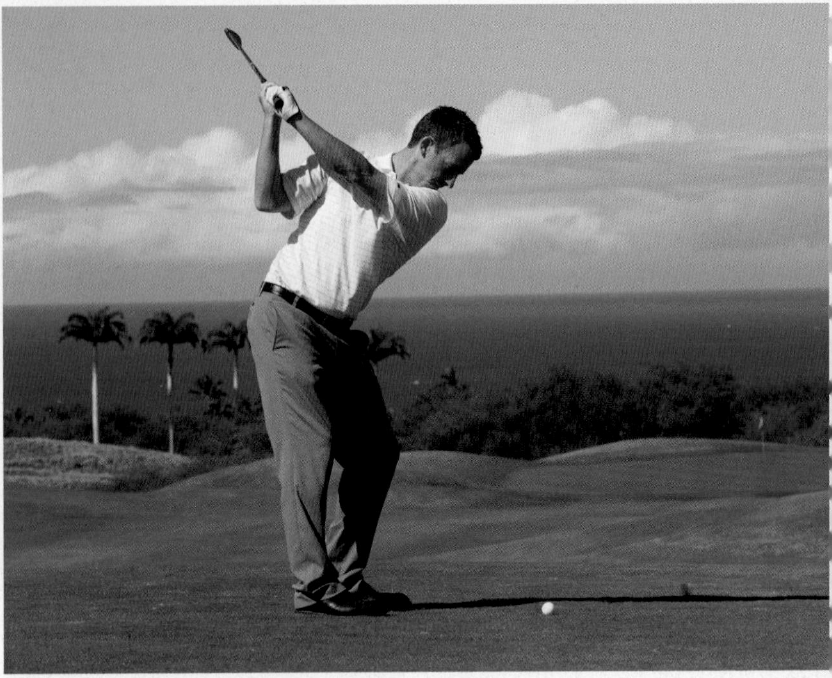

The Big Island's Best Golf Courses

Hamakua Country Club. This funky 9-hole course, built in the 1920s, sits on a steep hill overlooking the ocean. It's a par-33, 2,520-yard course. Architect Frank Anderson managed to squeeze in 9 holes by crisscrossing holes across fairways—you may never see a layout like this again. The course is open to non-members on weekdays only; you don't need a tee time. No carts. On the ocean side of Hwy. 19 (41 miles from Hilo), Honokaa. ☎ 808/775-7244. Greens fees $20 for 18 holes (you play the 9-hole course twice).

★★★ **Hapuna Golf Course.** Designed by Arnold Palmer and Ed Seay, this 6,027-yard, environmentally sensitive links-style course extends from the shoreline to 700 feet above sea level, with views of the pastoral Kohala Mountains and the Kohala coastline. The elevation changes on the course keep it challenging (and windy at the higher elevations). Facilities include putting greens, driving ranges, lockers, showers, a pro shop, and restaurants. Hapuna Beach Prince Hotel, off Hwy. 19 (near MM 69). ☎ 808/880-3000. www.hapunabeachprincehotel.com. Greens fees: $165 ($125 for resort guests) before 1 pm; $145/$105 after 1 pm.

> *Take a swing at the Arnold Palmer–designed, 6,027-yard-long Hapuna Golf Course, which plays from sea level to a 700-foot altitude.*

Hilo Municipal Golf Course. This is a great course for the casual golfer—flat, scenic, and fun. ***Warning:*** Don't go after a heavy rain (especially in winter), when the fairways can get really soggy. Wonderful trees (monkeypod, coconut, eucalyptus, banyan) dot the grounds, and the views—of Mauna Kea on one side and Hilo Bay on the other—are breathtaking. There are four sets of tees, with a par-71 from all; the back tees give you 6,325 yards of play. Week-

days are your best bet for tee times. 340 Haihai St. (btw. Kinoole and Iwalani sts.), Hilo. ☎ 808/959-7711. Greens fees: $29 weekdays; $34 Sat–Sun and holidays. From Hilo, take Hwy. 11 toward Volcano; turn right at Puainako St. (at Prince Kuhio Shopping Center), left on Kinoole, and then right on Haihai St.

★★★ **Mauna Kea Golf Course.** A massive renovation recently replaced all the greens, tees, fairways, and rough with new hybrids of turf that can be groomed for the skill levels of both resort and professional golfers. This breathtakingly beautiful par-72, 7,114-yard championship course, designed by Robert Trent Jones, Jr., is consistently rated one of the top golf courses in the United States. The signature 3rd hole is 175 yards long; the Pacific Ocean and shoreline cliffs stand between the tee and the green, giving every golfer, from beginner to pro, a real challenge. Facilities include putting greens, a driving range, lockers and showers, a pro shop, and a restaurant. Book ahead; the course is very popular. Mauna Kea Beach Resort, Hwy. 19 (near MM 68). ☎ 808/882-5400. www.maunakeabeachhotel.com. Greens fees $210 ($150 for resort guests).

★★★ **Mauna Lani Frances I'i Brown Championship Courses.** The **Mauna Lani South Course,** a 7,029-yard par-72, has an unforgettable ocean hole: the downhill, 221-yard, par-3 7th, which is bordered by the sea, a salt-and-pepper-sand dune, and lush kiawe trees. The **North Course** may not have the drama of the oceanfront

> *The frequently photographed 15th hole at Mauna Lani's South Course.*

> *Bordered by Hilo Bay and local foliage, the relatively flat and easy Hilo Municipal Golf Course is paradise for beginners.*

holes, but because it was built on older lava flows, the more extensive indigenous vegetation gives the course a Scottish feel. The hole that's cursed the most is the 140-yard, par-3 17th, which plays right into the surrounding lava field. Facilities include two driving ranges, a golf shop (with teaching pros), a restaurant, and putting greens. Mauna Lani Dr., off Hwy. 19 (20 miles north of Kona Airport). ☎ 808/885-6655. www.maunalani.com. Greens fees: $260 ($160 for resort guests); twilight rate $100.

Naniloa Country Club. At first glance, this semiprivate, 9-hole course looks pretty flat and short, but once you get beyond the 1st hole—a wide, straightforward 330-yard par-4—things get challenging. The tree-lined fairways require straight drives, and the huge lake on the 2nd and 5th holes is sure to haunt you. Very popular with both locals and visitors. Rental clubs are available. 120 Banyan Dr. (at the intersection of Hwy. 11 and Hwy. 19). ☎ 808/935-3000. Greens fees: $25 ($15 Naniloa Hotel guests) Mon-Fri; $35/$25 Sat-Sun; twilight rates are $10 less.

Volcano Golf and Country Club. Located at an altitude of 4,200 feet, this public course got its start in 1922, when the Blackshear family put in a green using old tomato cans for the holes. The par-72 course is unusually landscaped, making use of the pine and ohia trees scattered throughout. It's considered challenging by locals. ***Some tips from the regulars:*** Because the course is at such a high altitude, the ball travels farther than you're probably used to, so club down. Also, play a pitch-and-run game—the greens are slick. Hwy. 11, on the right side, just after the entrance to Hawaii Volcanoes National Park. ☎ 808/967-7331. www.volcanogolfshop.com. Greens fees $64.

Benefiting from a recent massive renovation, Mauna Kea Golf Course offers both unique challenges and beautiful scenery.

Waikoloa Beach Course. This pristine 18-ole, par-70 course certainly reflects the motto f designer Robert Trent Jones, Jr.: "Hard par, asy bogey." Most golfers remember the par-5, 05-yard 12th hole, a sharp dogleg left with unkers in the corner and an elevated tee sur-ounded by lava. Facilities include a golf shop, estaurant, and driving range. 1020 Keana Place adjacent to the Waikoloa Beach Marriott Resort nd Hilton Waikoloa Village), Waikoloa. ☎ 877/ VAIKOLOA (924-5656) or 808/886-6060. vww.waikoloagolf.com. Greens fees: $195 ($130 or resort guests); twilight rate $75.

Waikoloa Kings' Course. This sister course o the Waikoloa Beach Course is about 500 ards longer. Designed by Tom Weiskopf nd Jay Morrish, the 18-hole links-style tract eatures a double green at the 3rd and 6th oles and several carefully placed bunkers that ften come into play due to the ever-present rade winds. Facilities include a pro shop and showers. 600 Waikoloa Beach Dr. (adjacent to the Waikoloa Beach Marriott Resort and Hilton Waikoloa Village), Waikoloa. ☎ 877/WAIKOLOA (924-5656) or 808/886-7888. www.waikoloabeachresort.com. Greens fees: $175 ($125 for resort guests); twilight rate $75.

Waikoloa Village Golf Club. This semiprivate 18-hole, par-72 course is hidden in the town of Waikoloa and usually overshadowed by the glamour resort courses along the Kohala Coast. But this beautiful Robert Trent Jones, Jr.,–designed course offers great views and some great golfing. I'm particularly fond of the 18th hole: This par-5, 490-yard thriller doglegs to the left, and the last 75 yards up to the green are water, water, water. Enjoy the fabulous views of Mauna Kea and Mauna Loa. Waikoloa Rd., Waikoloa Village, off Hwy. 19 (18 miles north of Kona Airport). ☎ 808/883-9621. www.waikoloa.org. Greens fees $95. Turn left at the Waikoloa sign; it's about 6 miles up, on your left.

Big Island Adventures on Land

Where to Bike on the Big Island

Contact the **Big Island Mountain Bike Association,** P.O. Box 6819, Hilo, HI 96720 (☎ 808/961-4452), for its free brochure, *Big Island Mountain Biking,* which has safety tips as well as information on great off-road trails for both beginner and advanced riders.

Bicycling

★ **Hawaiian Pedals.** They have a huge selection of bikes: cruisers ($20 a day), mountain bikes and hybrids ($35 a day), and racing bikes and front-suspension mountain bikes ($45 a day). A bike rack goes for $5 a day, and you pay only for the days you actually use it (the honor system): If you have the rack for a week but use it for only 2 days, you'll be charged just $10. The folks at the shops are friendly and knowledgeable about cycling routes all over the Big Island. Kona Inn Shopping Village, Alii Dr., Kailua-Kona (☎ 808/329-2294) and Hawaiian Pedals Bike Works, Hale Hana Centre, 74-5583 Luhia St., Kailua-Kona (☎ 808/326-2453). www.hawaiianpedals.com.

> *Horseback may be best way to travel the 6 miles of tropical beauty between the mile-high walls surrounding the Waipio Valley.*

Orchid Isle Bicycling. The half-day (3-4 hr.) and full-day (4-6 hr.) bicycling tours offered here range from a casual ride to intense mountain biking at its best. The locations are diverse, from the rolling hills of a Kona coffee farm to awesome views of the Waipio Valley Lookout. Most tours include round-trip transportation from hotels, van support, tour guide, helmets, gloves, water, snacks, and lunch on the full-day trips. ☎ 877/592-BIKE (592-2453) or 808/327-0087. www.cyclekona.com. Tours start at $100.

Birding

Native Hawaiian birds are few—and dwindling. But Hawaii still offers extraordinary birding for anyone nimble enough to traverse tough, mucky landscape. And the best birding is on the Big Island; birders the world over come here hoping to see three Hawaiian birds, in particular: akiapolaau, a woodpecker wannabe with a war club-like head; nukupuu, an elusive little yellow bird with a curved beak, one of the crown jewels of Hawaiian birding; and alala, the critically endangered Hawaiian crow that's now almost impossible to see in the wild.

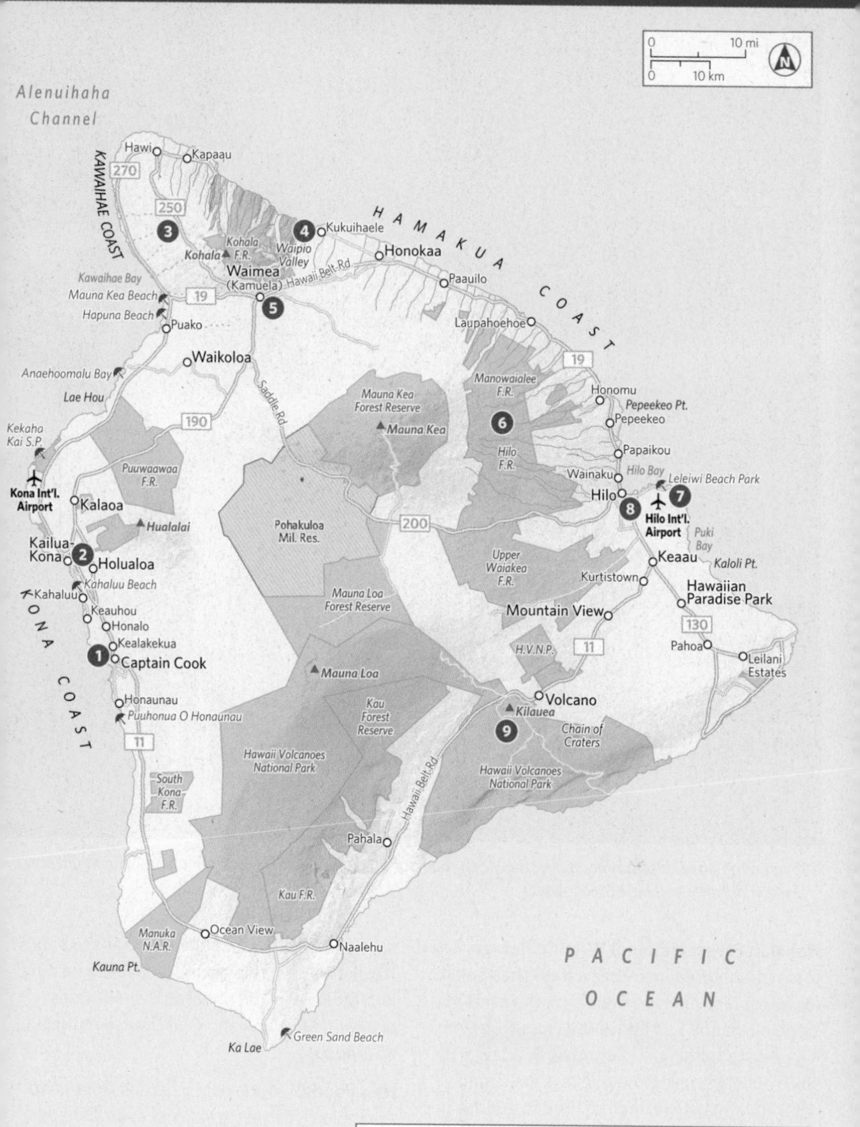

Big Island Adventures on Land

Bicycling

Hawaiian Pedals **2**

Orchid Isle Bicycling **2**

Birding

Hakalau Forest National Wildlife Refuge **6**

Hawaii Volcanoes National Park **9**

Hilo Ponds **7**

Horseback Riding

King's Trail Rides **1**

Kohala Na'alapa **3**

Parker Ranch **5**

Waipio Na'alapa Trail Rides **4**

Tennis

Hoolulu Tennis Stadium, Hilo **8**

> *If you don't have the stamina to bike the steep road out of Waipio Valley (pictured above) you might try a route that takes you past the lookout.*

Hakalau Forest National Wildlife Refuge. The first national wildlife refuge established solely for forest bird management is on the eastern slope of Mauna Kea above the Hamakua Coast. It's open for birding on Saturday, Sunday, and state holidays, using the public access road only. You must call ahead of time to get the gate combinations of the locked gates and to register. Contact Refuge Manager Richard Wass, Hakalau Forest, 154 Waianuenue Ave., Room 219, Hilo, HI 96720 (☎ 808/933-6915; Richard_Wass@mail.fws.gov).

Hawaii Volcanoes National Park. The best places for accomplished birders to go on their own are the ohia forests of this national park, usually at sunrise or sunset, when the little forest birds seem to be most active. You might spot some Hawaiian nene geese at the park's Kipuka Nene Campground, a favorite nesting habitat. Geese and pheasants sometimes appear on the Volcano Golf Course in the afternoon.

Hilo Ponds. Ducks, coots, herons (night and great blue), cattle egrets, and even Canada and snow geese fly into these popular coastal wetlands in Hilo, near the airport. Take Kalanianaole Hwy. about 3 miles east, past the industrial port facilities to Loko Waka Pond and Waiakea Pond.

Horseback Riding

King's Trail Rides. Experienced riders should sign up for a 4-hour trip, which includes 2 hours of riding for a maximum of four people. The trip heads down the mountain along Monument Trail to the Captain Cook Monument in Kealakekua Bay, where you'll stop for lunch and an hour of snorkeling. 81-6420 Hwy. 11 at MM 111, Kealakekua. ☎ 808/323-2388. www.konacowboy.com. $135 weekday, $150 weekend, including lunch and gear.

★ **Kohala Na'alapa.** Take an unforgettable journey into the rolling hills of Kahua and Kohala ranches, past ancient Hawaiian ruins, through lush pastures with grazing sheep and cows, and along mountaintops with panoramic coastal views. The horses and various riding areas are suited to everyone, from first-timers to experienced equestrians. There are two trips a day: a 2½-hour tour at 9am for $89 and a 1½-hour tour at 1:30pm for $68. No riders over 230 pounds, no pregnant riders, and no children under 8 permitted. Kohala Mountain Rd. (Hwy. 250) at MM 11 (ask for directions to the stables at the security-guard station). ☎ 808/889-0022; www.naalapastables.com. Rides from $68.

Parker Ranch. Visitors can explore Parker Ranch and its vast 175,000-acre working cattle ranch. You'll learn firsthand about the ranch, its history, and its variety of plant life, and you may even catch glimpses of pheasants, francolins, or wild pigs. Rides (suitable for beginners) are available three times daily at 8:15am, 12:15pm, and a sunset ride at 4pm. Morning and noon rides are 2 hours, and the sunset ride is 1½ hours. Kids must be at least 7 years old. Riders will feel like Hawaiian *paniolo* (cowboys) as they ride through stone corrals where up to 5,000 Hereford cattle were rounded up after being brought down from the slopes of Mauna Kea. A visit to the racetrack where Parker Ranch thoroughbreds were trained is included in the excursion. The rides all begin at the Blacksmith Shop on Pukalani Rd. ☎ 808/885-7655; www.parkerranch.com/horseback.html. Rides $79.

★ **Waipio Na'alapa Trail Rides.** The 2½-hour tours of Waipio Valley depart Monday through Saturday at 9:30am and 1pm (don't forget your camera). The guides are well-versed in Hawaiian history and provide running commentary as you move through this historic place. Check in at Waipi'o Valley Artworks, Hwy. 240, Kukuihaele. ☎ 808/775-0419; www.naalapastables.com. The cost is $89. No children under 8, pregnant riders, or riders over 230 pounds.

> *Multiple guided-tour options get bird-watchers close to the islands' exotic and endangered species.*

Tennis

You can play for free at any Hawaii County tennis court. The best courts in Hilo are at the **Hoolulu Tennis Stadium,** located next to the Civic Auditorium on Manono Street. Most resorts in the Kona-Kohala area do not allow non-guests to use their tennis facilities. For a detailed list of all courts on the island, contact Hawaii County Department of Parks and Recreation, 25 Aupuni St., Hilo, HI 96720 (☎ 808/961-8720; www.hawaii-county.com/parks/parks.htm).

Guided Bird Tours

If you don't know an apapane from a nukupuu, go with someone who does. Contact **Hawaii Forest & Trail,** 74-5035-B Queen Kaahumanu Hwy. (behind the Chevron Station), Kailua-Kona (☎ 800/464-1993 or 808/331-8505; www.hawaii-forest.com), to sign up for the ★★ **Rainforest and Dry Forest Adventure Tour,** led by naturalist Rob Pacheco. On this tour you'll venture into pristine rainforest to see rare and endangered Hawaiian birds. Immersed in this world of giant ferns and crisp mountain air, you will also learn about Hawaii's unique botany and evolution. This full-day tour costs $179 and includes pick-up, midmorning snack with coffee, lunch, beverages, day pack, binoculars, walking stick, and rain gear.

Big Island Adventures in the Ocean

If you come to Hawaii and don't get out on the water (or under it), you'll miss half the fun. The year-round calm waters along the Kona and Kohala coasts are home to spectacular marine life and offer a multitude of watersports options, from snorkeling to boating—even a submarine dive.

Boating

★★ **Body Glove Cruises.** The *Body Glove,* a 55-foot trimaran that carries up to 100 passengers, runs an adventurous sail-snorkel-dive-cruise ($120 adults, $78 children 6–12) to Pawai Bay, a marine preserve where you can snorkel, scuba dive, swim, or just hang out on the deck for a couple of hours. After a buffet deli lunch spread, you might want to take the plunge off the boat's waterslide or diving board before heading back to Kailua Pier. The boat departs daily from the pier at 9am and returns at 1:30pm. The only thing you need to bring is a towel; snorkeling equipment (and scuba equipment, if you choose to dive) is provided. They also offer whale-watching in season ($78 adults, $58 children) and a Sunset Cocktail Sail ($87 adults, $58 children). **Kailua Pier.** ☎ 800/551-8911 or 808/326-7122. www.bodyglovehawaii.com.

★★★ **Captain Dan McSweeney's Year-Round Whale-Watching Adventures.** Hawaii's most impressive visitors—45-foot humpback whales—return to the waters off Kona every winter. Capt. Dan McSweeney, a whale researcher for more than 25 years, works daily with the whales, so he has no problem finding them. In humpback season—roughly December to April—Dan makes two 3-hour trips daily. From July 1 to December 20, he schedules one morning trip on Tuesday, Thursday, and Saturday to look for pilot, sperm, false killer, melon-headed, pygmy killer, and beaked whales. Captain Dan guarantees a sighting, or he'll take you out again for free. No cruises in

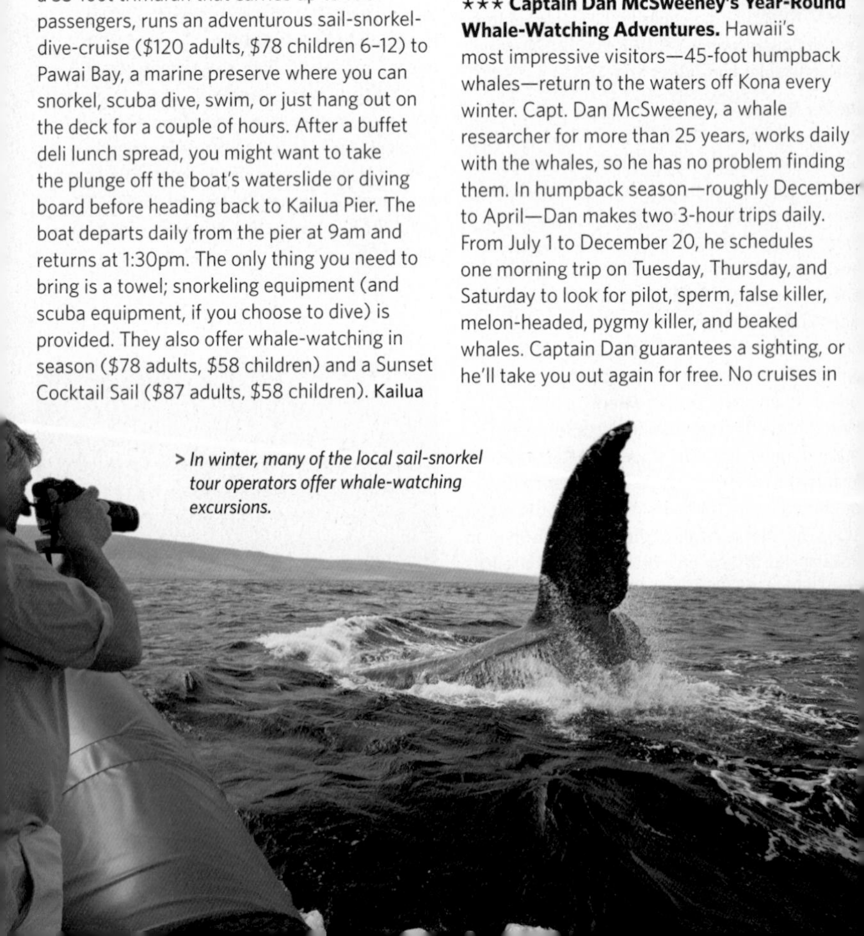

> *In winter, many of the local sail-snorkel tour operators offer whale-watching excursions.*

Big Island Adventures in the Ocean

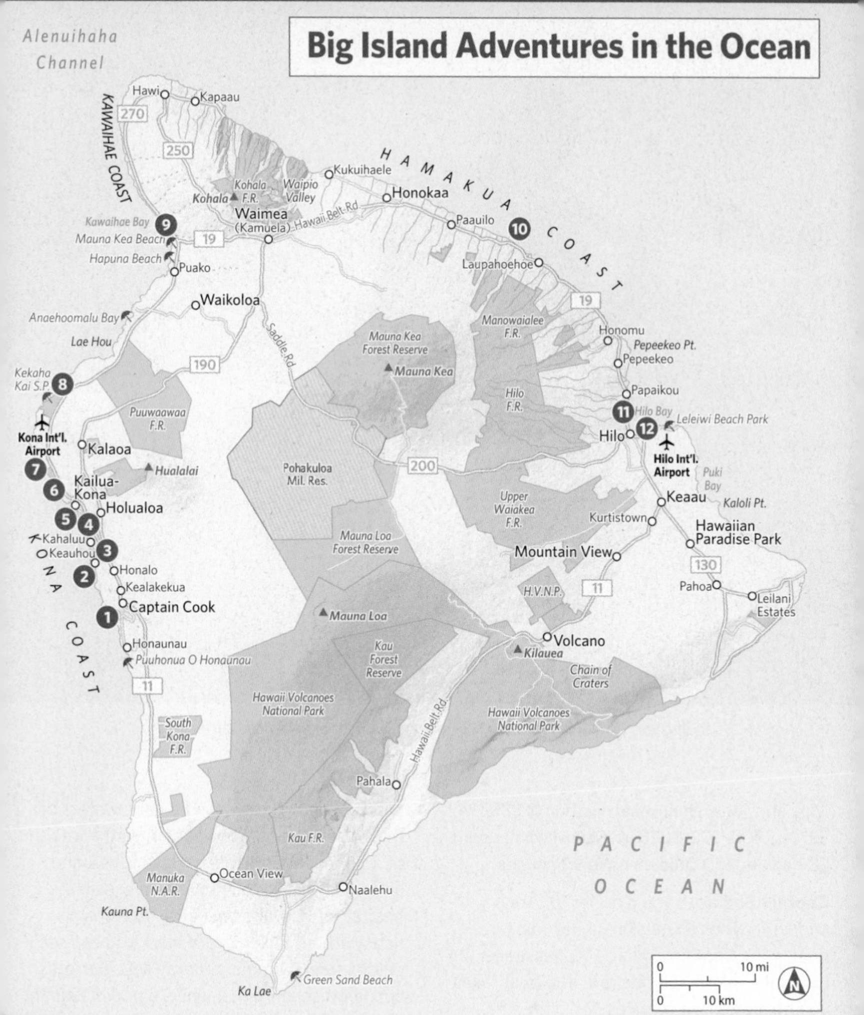

Boating

Body Glove Cruises **5**

Captain Dan McSweeney's Year-Round Whale-Watching Adventures **7**

Captain Zodiac **7**

Fair Wind Snorkeling and Diving Adventures **1**

Kamanu Charters **5**

Kealakekua Bay **1**

Kekaha Kai Beach Park **8**

King Kamehameha's Kona Beach Hotel **5**

Parasailing

UFO Parasail **5**

Scuba Diving

Diving with Manta Rays **2**

Sport Fishing

Honokohau Harbor **7**

Kailua Bay **5**

Kawaihae Harbor **9**

Keauhou Bay **2**

Submarine Dives

Atlantis Submarines **5**

Surfing

Banyan's **3**

Hilo Bay Front Park **12**

Honolii Point **11**

Kahuluu Beach **4**

Keaukaha Beach Park **12**

Lyman's **3**

Pine Trees **6**

Kayaking

Hamakua Coast **10**

Honokohau Harbor **7**

Kailua Bay **5**

> *Riding the pounding surf on the Big Island is a challenge even for experienced surfers.*

May and June. Honokohau Harbor. ☎ 888/942-5376 or 808/322-0028. www.ilovewhales.com. $80 adults, $70 children up to 90 pounds.

Captain Zodiac. If you'd prefer to take a snorkel-cruise to Kealakekua Bay in a small boat, go in Captain Zodiac's 16-passenger, 24-foot inflatable rubber life raft. The boat takes you on a wild ride 14 miles down the Kona Coast to Kealakekua, where you'll spend about an hour snorkeling in the bay and then enjoy snacks and beverages at the picnic site. Trips are twice daily, from 8am to 12:15pm and from 12:45 to 5pm. ***Warning:*** Pregnant women and those with bad backs should avoid this often-bumpy ride. Gentry's Marina, Honokohau Harbor. ☎ 808/329-3199. www.captainzodiac.com. $93 adults, $78 children 4–12 for 4-hour tour; $65 adults, $59 children 4–12 for 3-hour whale-watching (book online for better rates).

★★★ kids **Fair Wind Snorkeling and Diving Adventures.** This tour company offers a snorkel trip to Kealakekua Bay, one of the best snorkel spots in Hawaii. The calm waters of this underwater preserve teem with a wealth of marine life. Coral heads, lava tubes, and underwater caves all provide an excellent habitat for Hawaii's vast array of tropical fish. Without looking very hard, you can see octopi, free-swimming moray eels, parrotfish, and goatfish; once in a while, a pod of spinner dolphins streak across the bay. Tours are on luxury catamarans and include breakfast and/or lunch and snorkel gear; some trips have a scuba diving option as well. 78-7130 Kaleiopapa St., Kailua-Kona. ☎ 800/677-9461 or 808/322-2788. www.fair-wind.com. $75–$155 adults, $45–$75 children (4–12) depending on length of tour.

★★ **Kamanu Charters.** This sleek catamaran, 36 feet long and 22 feet wide, provides a laid-back sail-snorkel cruise from Honokohau Harbor to Pawai Bay. The 3½-hour trip includes a tropical lunch (deli sandwiches, chips, fresh island fruit, and beverages), snorkeling gear, and personalized instruction for first-time snorkelers. The *Kamanu* sails Monday through

> *A kayaker gets a dramatic view of lava pouring into the ocean.*

Saturday (weather permitting) at 9am and 1:30pm. Honokohau Harbor. ☎ 800/348-3091 or 808/329-2021. www.kamanu.com. $80 adults, $50 children 12 and under.

Body Boarding, Boogie Boarding & Bodysurfing

On the Kona side of the island, the best beaches for body boarding and bodysurfing are **Hapuna Beach, White Sands Beach,** and **Kekaha Kai State Park.** On the east side, try **Leleiwi Beach.** See full descriptions of all these beaches starting on p 236.

Kayaking

Imagine sitting at sea level, eye to eye with a turtle, a dolphin, even a whale—it's possible in an oceangoing kayak. Anyone can kayak in calm waters: Just get in, find your balance, and paddle. After a few minutes of instruction and a little practice in a calm area (like the lagoon in front of **King Kamehameha's Kona Beach Hotel**), you'll be ready to explore. Beginners can practice their skills in **Kailua** and **Kealakekua bays;** intermediates might try paddling from **Honokohau Harbor** to **Kekaha Kai Beach Park;** the **Hamakua Coast** is a challenge for experienced kayakers.

You can rent one- and two-person kayaks (and other ocean toys) from ★★★ **Aloha Kayak** (☎ 877/322-1444 or 808/322-2868; www.alohakayak.com) for $25 for a half-day single and $45 double ($35 for a full-day single and $60 double). They also have a unique tour from Keauhou Bay and the Captain Cook Monument, with Hawaiian guides showing you sea caves and snorkeling areas full of fish and turtles. The tours are either 4 hours ($89 adults, $45 children 11 and under) or 2½ hours ($65 adults, $33 children) and include all equipment, beverages, snorkeling gear, and snacks.

Parasailing

Get a bird's-eye view of Hawaii's pristine waters with **UFO Parasail** (☎ 800/FLY-4UFO (359-4836) or 808/325-5836; www.ufoparasail.net). UFO offers parasail rides daily from 8am to 2pm from Kailua Pier. The

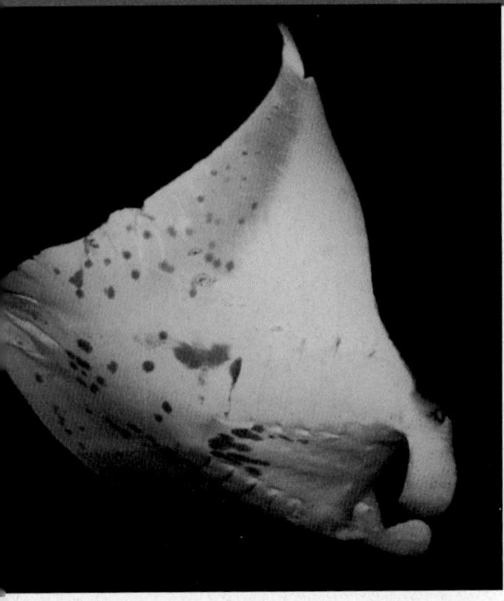

> *Two-tank manta ray night dives are a popular option on the Big Island; book in advance.*

cost is $61 for the standard flight of 7 minutes of air time at 400 feet, and $70 for a deluxe 10-minute ride at 800 feet. You can go up alone or with a friend; no experience is necessary. ***Tip:*** Take the early-bird special (when the light is fantastic and the price is right) at 8am for just $56 (for 400 ft.) or $66 (for 800 ft.).

Scuba Diving

The Big Island's leeward coast offers some of the best diving in the world; the water is calm, warm, and clear. There are nearly two dozen dive operators on the west side of the Big Island, plus a couple in Hilo.

"This is not your mother or father's dive shop," says Jeff Kirschner, of the newly opened **BottomTime,** Outrigger Keauhou Beach Resort, 74-5590 Luhia St. (☎ 866/GO-DIVEN (463-4836) or 808/331-1858; www.bottomtimehawaii.com). "This is a dive shop for today's diver." Kirschner claims what sets BottomTime apart is their willingness to take their 34-foot catamaran (complete with showers, TV, and restrooms) to unusual dive sites, and "not those sites just 2 minutes from the mouth of the harbor." BottomTime also offers introductory dives in enriched air (Nitrox) for $175 and two-tank dives for $130.

One of Kona's oldest dive shops, **Jack's Diving Locker,** 75-5819 Alii Dr. (☎ 800/345-4807 or 808/329-7585; www.jacksdivinglocker.com), has recently purchased another longtime dive shop, Kona Coast Divers, and has combined the two businesses into one. The 8,000-square-foot dive center has a swimming pool (with underwater viewing windows), retail store, classrooms, full-service rentals, and a full-service sports diving and technical diving facility. They offer the classic two-tank dive for $125 and a two-tank manta ray night dive for $145. If Jack's manta ray dive is booked, try **Sandwich Isle Divers,** 75-5729 Alii Dr., in the back of the Kona Market Place (☎ 888/743-3483 or 808/329-9188; www.sandwichisledivers.com). It offers two-tank nighttime manta dives for $125 (including equipment) and $105 if you have your own gear.

If you're looking for an **all-diving vacation,** you might think about spending a week on the 80-foot *Kona Aggressor II* (☎ 800/344-5662 or 808/329-8182; www.aggressor.com), a live-aboard dive boat that promises to provide you with unlimited underwater exploration, including day and night dives, along 85 miles of the Big Island's coastline. You might spot harmless 70-foot whale sharks, plus not-so-harmless tiger and hammerhead sharks, as well as dolphins, whales, monk seals, and sea turtles. Ten divers are accommodated in five staterooms. Rates start at $2,195 for 7 days (without gear), double occupancy, which includes excellent accommodations and all meals. Rental gear is available.

Snorkeling

Much of the Big Island's **best snorkeling** is easily accessible to anyone with fins and a mask. Just relax and float along as you watch multihued tropical fish flit by. The cheapest place to get great rental equipment is **Snorkel Bob's,** in the parking lot of Huggo's Restaurant at 75-5831 Kahakai Rd., at Alii Dr., Kailua-Kona (☎ 808/329-0770; www.snorkelbob.com). For guided sail-snorkel trips, see "Boating," p 252.

Snuba

If you're not quite ready to make the commitment to scuba but you want more time underwater than snorkeling allows, **Big Island Snuba Tours** (☎ 808/326-7446; www.snubabigisland.com) may be the answer. Just like in scuba, the diver wears a regulator and

SNORKEL GUIDE

The Big Island's Best Snorkeling

A Hapuna Beach (p 237) is the island's best beach for swimming, snorkeling, and bodysurfing (at least in summer—winter waters are too rough). The best place at this beach for snorkeling is at the foot of the Hapuna Beach Prince Hotel, in a secluded little cove where you can snorkel with schools of yellow tangs, needlefish, and green sea turtles. **B Kahaluu Beach Park** (p 237) is a great choice for first-time snorkelers; schools of brilliantly colored tropical fish weave in and out of the reef, and in summer the water is so shallow that you can just stand up if you feel uncomfortable. **C Kekaha Kai State Park, or Kona Coast State Park** (p 238), features about 5 miles of shoreline with a half-dozen long curving beaches and a big cove on Mahaiula Bay. The series of well-protected coves are excellent for swimming, and there's great snorkeling and diving offshore. The extensive reef at **D Puako** provides excellent snorkeling (swim a few yards offshore for clear water); I love the outer edge of the curved bay for the best viewing of fish. Turtles are frequently seen here. **E Puuhonua O Honaunau National Park** has great snorkeling around the numerous underwater lava formations. **F White Sands** (p 239), a small white-sand pocket beach about 4½ miles south of Kailua-Kona, is perfect for swimming and snorkeling on calm days.

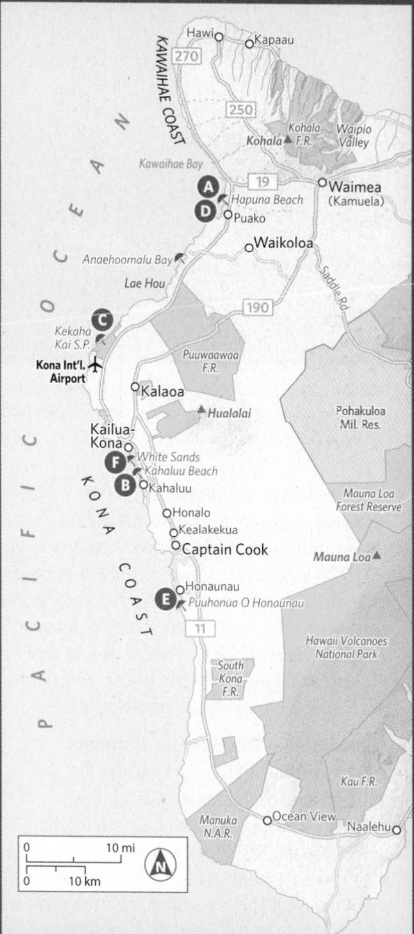

> *Enjoy a 400-foot aerial perspective of the beauty below on one of the many daily parasail rides from Kailua Pier for as little as $56.*

mask; however, the tank floats on the surface on a raft and is connected to the diver's regulator by a hose that allows the diver to go 20 to 25 feet down. You need only 15 minutes of instruction before you're ready to go. Snuba can actually be easier than snorkeling, as the water is calmer beneath the surface. It costs $89 to Snuba dive from the beach, $145 from a boat; children must be at least 8 years old.

Sport Fishing: The Hunt for Granders

If you want to catch fish, it doesn't get any better than the Kona Coast, known internationally as the marlin capital of the world. Big-game fish, including gigantic blue marlin and other Pacific billfish, tuna, mahimahi, sailfish, swordfish, ono (also known as wahoo), and giant trevally (ulua), roam the waters here. When anglers here catch marlin that weigh 1,000 pounds or more, they call them granders; there's even a "wall of fame" on Kailua-Kona's Waterfront Row, honoring 40 anglers who've nailed more than 20 tons of fighting fish.

Nearly 100 charter boats with professional captains and crew offer fishing charters out of **Keauhou, Kawaihae, Honokohau,** and **Kailua Bay harbors.** If you're not an expert angler, the best way to arrange a charter is through a booking agency like the **Charter Desk at Honokohau Marina** (☎ 888/KONA-4-US (566-2487) or 808/329-5735; www.charterdesk.com) or **Charter Services Hawaii** (☎ 800/567-2650 or 808/334-1881; www.konazone.com). Either one will sort through the more than 40 different types of vessels, fishing specialties, and personalities to match you with the right boat. Prices range from $625 to $1,300 or so for a full-day exclusive charter (you and up to five of your friends have the entire boat to yourselves); or for $95 you can share a boat with others and rotate your turn at pulling in the big one. ***Note:*** Many captains now tag and release marlins; other fish caught belong to the boat (not to you)—that's island style. If you want to eat your catch or have your trophy marlin mounted, arrange it with the captain before you go.

Serious sport fishers should call the boats directly. They include ***Kilakila* Sport Fishing** (☎ 808/936-5168; www.kilakilasportfishing.com), **Marlin Magic** (☎ 808/325-7138; www.marlinmagic.com), and **The Charter Desk** (☎ 808/325-1513; www.charterdesk.com/ihunui.html). If you aren't into hooking a 1,000-pound marlin or 200-pound tuna and just want to go out to catch some smaller fish and have fun, I recommend ★★ **Reel Action Light Tackle Sportfishing** (☎ 808/325-6811; www.charternet.com/fishers/hawaii-free.html). All of the above outfitters operate out of Honokohau Harbor.

Submarine Rides

★ **Atlantis Submarines.** Venture 100 feet below the sea in a high-tech, 65-foot submarine. On a 1-hour trip, you'll be able to explore a 25-acre coral reef that's teeming with schools of colorful tropical fish. Look closely and you might catch glimpses of moray eels—or even

> *The Big Island is a huge destination for big-game sport fishermen on the hunt for bluefish, swordfish, and 1,000-pound marlins like this one.*

a shark—in and around the reef. On selected trips, you'll watch as divers swim among these aquatic creatures, luring them to the view ports for face-to-face observation. 75-5656 Kuakini Hwy. (across the street from Kailua Pier), Kailua-Kona. ☎ 800/548-6262. www.atlantisadventures.com. Trips leave daily btw. 10am and 3pm. $80 adults, $41 children under 12.

Surfing

Most surfing off the Big Island is for the experienced only. As a general rule, the beaches on the north and west shores of the island get northern swells in winter, while those on the south and east shores get southern swells in summer. Experienced surfers should check out the waves at **Pine Trees** (north of Kailua-Kona), **Lyman's** (off Alii Dr. in Kailua-Kona), and **Banyan's** (also off Alii Dr.); reliable spots on the east side of the island include **Honolii Point** (outside Hilo), **Hilo Bay Front Park,** and **Keaukaha Beach Park.** But there are a few sites where beginners can catch a wave, too: You might want to try **Kahaluu Beach Park** (p 237), where the waves are manageable most of the year, other surfers are around to give you pointers, and there's a lifeguard on shore. You can rent a board from **Pacific Vibrations,** 75-5702 Likana Lane (just off Alii Dr., across from the pier), Kailua-Kona (☎ 808/329-4140; www.laguerdobros.com/pacvib/pacificv.html). Short boards go for $15 a day, long boards for $20.

If you're interested in **lessons,** I'd suggest calling **Ocean Eco Tours** (☎ 808/324-SURF (324-7873); www.oceanecotours.com), one of the few companies on the Big Island that teaches surfing. Private lessons cost $150 per person (including all equipment) and usually last a minimum of 2 hours; 2- to 3-hour group lessons go for $95 (also including all equipment), with a maximum of four students. Both teachers love this ancient Hawaiian sport, and their enthusiasm is contagious. The minimum age is 8, and you must be a fairly good swimmer.

THE OUTRIGGER CANOE

A Symbol of a Culture

BY MEGAN McFARLAND

HAWAIIANS HAVE BEEN MASTERS of the outrigger canoe since the first Polynesians landed on the islands' shores about 1,500 years ago. Today, outrigger canoeing is the official state sport, and dozens of canoeing clubs throughout the islands cater to a growing interest—and pride—in this oldest of Hawaiian traditions.

SURVIVAL AND SPORT: The Canoe in Early Hawaii

'ar more than a simple mode of transportation, the canoe in ancient Hawaii was inextricably woven into he culture: as an expression of royal power, the basis of its early naval fleet, a favorite sport, an essential ool for fishing and survival, and an art form.

Outrigger canoes have one or more lateral support floats (outriggers) or can be double-hulled, like oday's catamarans. Historically, the one-piece hulls were carved from the hardwood koa tree; the floats ind other parts were lashed together with coconut-fiber cord. Sails were mats woven from pandanus eaves. Finding the proper tree and fashioning the canoe were serious religious matters, since the ca- ioe's performance in Hawaii's rough ocean waters could determine life or death. A priest often oversaw he proceedings, and offerings of fish, pigs, and flowers were made upon completion of a canoe.

Canoe racing was a physically rigorous sport, and races were held primarily for serious gambling ourposes, not for fun. It's estimated that when the Europeans arrived in the 18th-century there were is many as 12,000 canoes in Hawaii, though canoe racing, like surfing, was banned once missionaries irrived about 1820.

The Voyage of the *Hokulea*

n 1973, Ben Finney, an inthropologist and pro- essor at the University of Hawaii, co-founded he Hawaiian Voyaging Society to prove that it vas possible for ancient Polynesians to complete ong-distance, planned oyages between islands n the Pacific. Finney and his team built the *Hokulea*, a 62-foot replica of an incient double-hulled voyaging canoe, the first built in Hawaii in more than 600 ears. The *Hokulea* departed Honolua Bay, Maui, on May 1, 1976, and reached heering crowds in Tahiti—a distance of 2,400 miles—34 days later, on June 4. A Satawelese navigator, Mau Piailug, guided the *Hokulea* and its Hawaiian crew vithout charts or instruments, using the ancient art of wayfinding by celestial oodies and ocean swells. The successful voyage of the *Hokulea* sparked a state- vide resurgence in the popularity of outrigger canoe racing as an expression of Hawaiian pride and culture. The famous vessel has sailed numerous trips hroughout the Pacific since then and serves today as a "floating classroom" in Hawaii. A worldwide voyage of the *Hokulea* is planned for spring 2012.

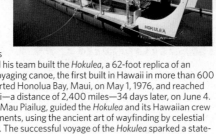

WATCHING A RACE Racing season generally falls between May and September. Courses run from as short as 4.5 nautical miles to upward of 40 nautical miles. See p 584 for details on obtaining an event schedule.

THE GREAT MIGRATION: Polynesia to Hawaii

Centuries before European explorers were plying the world's oceans, the Hawaiians' ancestors, the Polynesians, were using sophisticated long-distance navigation techniques and large, double-hulled outrigger canoes to travel thousands of miles in the vast Pacific.

From their earliest origins in Southeast Asia, these early navigators traveled to the western edge of Polynesia (Micronesia) between 3000 and 1500 B.C. Sometime between A.D. 300 and 700, the Polynesians arrived in New Zealand, the Easter Islands (Rapa Nui), and Hawaii. From there, they steadily moved west and north to colonize eastern Polynesian islands like Samoa and Tonga.

The Polynesians and Hawaiians practiced star map navigation, which uses the rising points of the stars, and observation of the sun, moon, ocean swells, and flight patterns of birds, as a natural compass to steer the course.

Big Island Shopping A to Z

Alohawear

★ Sig Zane Designs HILO

My favorite stop in Hilo, and I'm not alone: Sig Zane Designs evokes such loyalty that people make special trips from the outer islands for this inspired line of authentic Hawaiian-wear. The partnership of Zane and his wife, the revered hula master Nalani Kanaka'ole, is stunningly creative. Everything sold here centers on the Sig Zane fabric designs: bedcovers, cushions, fabrics, clothing, accessories, and custom-ordered upholstery. To add to the delight, Sig and his staff take time to talk story and explain the significance of the images or simply chat about Hilo, hula, and Hawaiian culture. 122 Kamehameha Ave. ☎ 808/935-7077. AE, DISC, MC, V. Map p 236.

Antiques

Antiques & Orchids CAPTAIN COOK

Beverly Napolitan and her husband took over Captain Cook's oldest building (built in 1906) and filled it with an eclectic array of antiques, collectibles, and fresh orchids. There are a few vintage Hawaiian items, lots of teacups, old kimonos, etched glass and crystal lamps, and a red wooden veranda where high tea is served on Saturday (11am–4pm), complete with homemade scones and Devonshire cream. You can't miss this green building with white trim, on the mauka (inland) side of the highway in Captain Cook. Hwy. 11. ☎ 808/323-9851. Map p 263.

Art

Gallery of Great Things WAIMEA

Here's an eye-popping assemblage of local art and Pacific Rim artifacts. Browse under the watchful gaze of an antique Tongan war club (not for sale) and authentic rhinoceros- and deer-horn blowguns from Borneo. You'll find jewelry, glassware, photographs, greeting cards, antique kimonos, vintage clothing, fiber baskets, and hand-turned bowls of beautifully grained woods, along with treasures by local artists (photos, paintings, and more). In Parker Sq., Hwy. 19. ☎ 808/885-7706. AE, DISC, MC, V. Map p 263.

★★ Harbor Gallery KAWAIHAE

This gallery in the industrial harbor area of Kawaihae features works by more than 150 artists, primarily from the Big Island. The range is vast—from jewelry, to basketry, to ceramics,

> Hilo's Sig Zane Designs is a must-stop destination for quality Hawaiian merchandise at reasonable prices.

Big Island Shopping A to Z

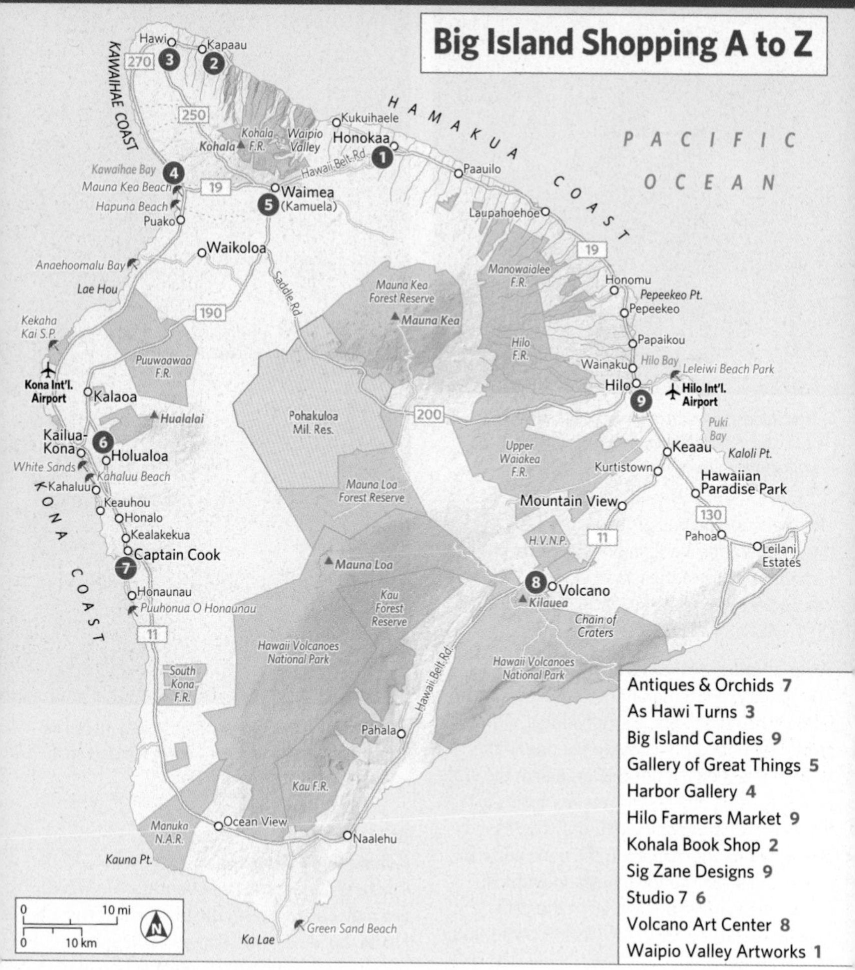

to heirloom-quality koa furniture. In Kawaihae Shopping Center, Hwy. 270, just north of Hwy. 19. ☎ 808/882-1510. AE, DISC, MC, V. Map above.

Studio 7 HOLUALOA
Some of Hawaii's most respected artists, among them gallery owners Setsuko and Hiroki Morinoue, exhibit their works in this serenely beautiful studio. Smooth pebbles, stark woods, and a garden setting provide the backdrop for Hiroki's paintings and prints and Setsuko's pottery, paper collages, and wall pieces. This is the hub of the Holualoa art community; activities include workshops, classes, and special events by visiting artists. Mamalahoa Hwy. ☎ 808/324-1335. MC, V. Map above.

Volcano Art Center HAWAII VOLCANOES NATIONAL PARK The Volcano Island's frontier spirit and raw, primal energy have spawned a close-knit community of artists, and the Volcano Art Center (VAC) is the hub of the island's arts activity. Housed in the original 1877 Volcano House, VAC is a not-for-profit art-education center that offers exhibits and shows that change monthly, as well as workshops and retail space. Of the 300 artists represented, 90% come from the Big Island. The fine crafts include baskets, jewelry, mixed-media pieces, stone- and wood-carvings,

> *Ths Islands' top artists showcase their work at Studio 7 in Holualoa, which also offers workshops, classes, and events.*

and the wood diaries of Jesus Sanchez, a third-generation Vatican bookbinder who has turned his skills to the island woods. In Hawaii Volcanoes National Park. ☎ 808/967-8222. AE, DISC, MC, V. Map p 263.

Waipio Valley Artworks KUKUIHAELE
This gallery/boutique offers treasures for the home. The focus here is strictly local, with a strong emphasis on woodwork—one of the largest selections, if not the largest, in the state. Bowls, rocking chairs, and jewelry boxes exhibit flawless craftsmanship and richly burnished grains. More affordable are the pens and hair accessories. Deli sandwiches and Tropical Dreams ice cream are served in the cafe. Kukuihaele Rd., off Hwy. 240. ☎ 808/775-0958. MC, V. Map p 263.

co-KEY, co-KEY: What Is That Noise?

That loud noise you hear after dark, especially on the eastern side of the Big Island, is the cry of the male coqui frog looking for a mate. A native of Puerto Rico, where the frogs are kept in check by snakes, the coqui frog came to Hawaii in plant material, found no natural enemies, and spread across the Big Island (and Maui). A chorus of several hundred coqui frogs is deafening (up to 163 decibels, or the noise level of a jet engine from 100 ft.). In some places, like Akaka Falls, there are so many frogs that they now are chirping during daylight hours.

> *Top local crafts from carvings to jewelry can be found at the Volcano Art Center, which is located in the historic 1877 Volcano House.*

Bookstores

Kohala Book Shop KAPAAU
The largest new and used bookstore in Hawaii is a major attraction in the town's historic Hotel Nanbu building. You'll find everything from out-of-print first editions to popular fiction to titles on Hawaii and Oceania. Hwy. 270 (Akoni Pule Hwy.), a block from the Kamehameha Statue. ☎ 808/889-6732. http://kohalabooks.big808.com. Map p 263.

Edibles

Big Island Candies HILO
Abandon all restraint: The chocolate-dipped shortbread and macadamia nuts, not to mention the free samples, will make it very hard to be sensible. The Hawaiian Da-Kine line is irrepressibly local: mochi crunch, fortune cookies, animal crackers, and other morsels—all dipped in chocolate. By far the best are the shortbread cookies, dipped in chocolate, peanut butter, and white chocolate. 585 Hinano St. ☎ 800/935-5510 or 808/935-8890. www.bigislandcandies.com. Map p 263.

Hilo Farmers Market HILO

This farmers market embodies what I love most about Hawaii: local color, good soil and weather, the mixing of cultures, and new adventures in taste. More than 200 vendors from around the island bring their flowers, produce, and baked goods to this teeming corner of Hilo every Saturday from sunrise to 4pm. (Go early for the best selection.) Expect to find a stunning assortment: fresh homegrown oyster mushrooms from Kona; the creamy, sweet Indonesian fruit called mangosteen; warm breads; an array of flowers; fresh aquacultured seaweed; corn from Pahoa; Waimea strawberries; taro and taro products; foot-long miso-flavored and traditional Hawaiian laulau; made-from-scratch tamales; and fabulous ethnic vegetables. Although it's also open on Wednesday, Saturday is the day when all the vendors are there. Kamehameha Ave. at Mamo St. ☎ 808/933-1000. Map p 263.

Fashion

As Hawi Turns HAWI

You never know what you'll find in this whimsical, delightful shop of women's clothing and accessories. The windows might be filled with painted paper lanterns in the shapes of stars, or retro-painted switch plates, or kicky straw hats paired with bias-cut silk dresses and quirky jewelry. Hwy. 270 (Akoni Pule Hwy.). ☎ 808/889-5023.

Bet You Can't Eat Just One

Hawaii Island Gourmet Products, which, under the brand Atebara Chips, has been making potato and taro- and shrimp-flavored chips in Hilo for 70 years, recently added a couple of new products that you just cannot miss: purple sweet potato chips and delicious chocolate-covered sweet potato, taro, and regular potato chips (the first-place winner at the Taste of Hilo). You can find them at most stores on the Big Island (or at the major resorts on the Big Island), or contact them directly (☎ 808/969-9600; www.hawaiichips.com). ***Warning:*** As we say in Hawaii, these chips are so *ono* (delicious) that you will be mail-ordering more when you get home.

> *Browse for new and used titles at Kohala Book Shop.*

Big Island Restaurant Best Bets

Best on the Beach
Brown's Beach House $$$ Fairmont at Mauna Lani, Kohala Coast (p 270).

Best Breakfast
The Coffee Shack $ Hwy. 11, Captain Cook (p 272).

Best Burger
Jackie Rey's Ohana Grill $$ 75-5995 Kuakini Hwy., Kailua-Kona (p 273).

Best for Families
Aloha Angel Café $$ Hwy. 11, Kainaliu (p 268).

Best Fast Mexican
Habanero's $ Keauhou Shopping Center, Keauhou (p 272).

Best Filipino
Tex Drive In & Restaurant $ Hwy. 19, Honokaa (p 279).

Best Fish
Quinn's Almost by the Sea $$ 75-5655A Palani Rd., Kailua-Kona (p 277).

Best French
La Bourgogne $$$ Hwy. 11, Kailua-Kona (p 275).

Best Hawaii Regional Cuisine
Merriman's $$$ In Opelu Plaza, Hwy. 19, Waimea (p 275).

Best Italian
Pescatore $$ 235 Keawe St., Hilo (p 277).

Best Japanese
Kenichi Pacific $$$ Keauhou Shopping Center, Keauhou (p 274).

Best Meals under $10
BaLe $ Kona Coast Shopping Center, 74-5588 Palani Rd., Kailua-Kona (p 268).

Best Pasta
Cafe Pesto $$ Multiple locations (p 271).

Best Pizza
Boston Basil's $ 75-5707 Alii Dr., Kailua-Kona (p 270).

Most Romantic
Pahu i'a $$$$ In the Four Seasons Resort, Queen Kaahumanu Hwy., Kailua-Kona (p 277).

Best Splurge
Roy's Waikoloa Bar & Grill $$$$ Kings' Shops, Waikoloa Beach Resort, 250 Waikoloa Beach Dr. (p 278).

Best Sushi
Sansei Seafood Restaurant & Sushi Bar $$$ Queen's Market Place, Waikoloa Beach Resort (p 278).

Most Trendy
Hilo Bay Café $$ Waiakea Center, 315 Makaala St., Hilo (p 272).

Best View
★ **Huggo's $$$** 75-5828 Kahakai Rd., Kailua-Kona (p 272).

> *Trendy Hilo Bay Café offers inventive Pacific Rim cuisine in an elegant setting.*

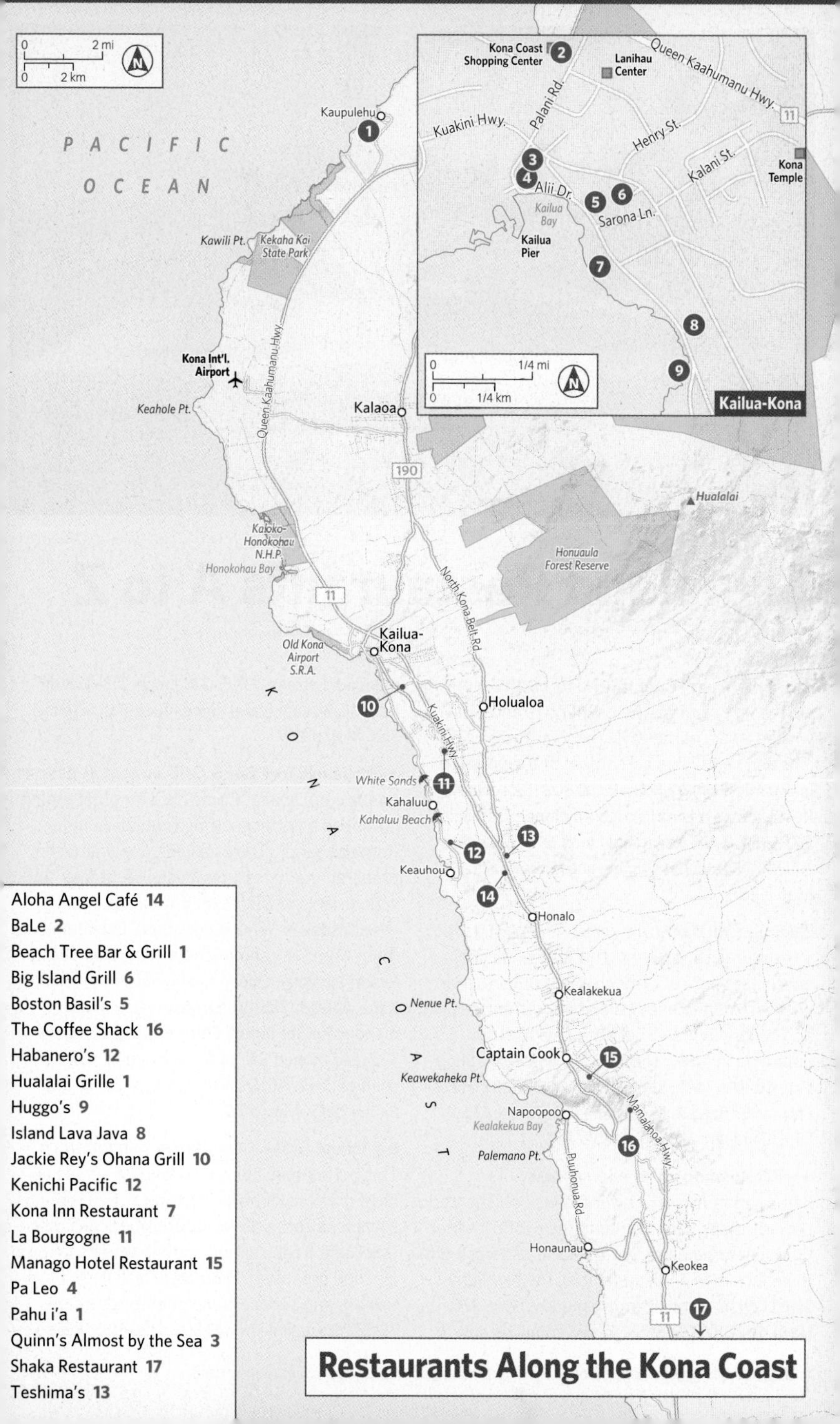

Aloha Angel Café 14
BaLe 2
Beach Tree Bar & Grill 1
Big Island Grill 6
Boston Basil's 5
The Coffee Shack 16
Habanero's 12
Hualalai Grille 1
Huggo's 9
Island Lava Java 8
Jackie Rey's Ohana Grill 10
Kenichi Pacific 12
Kona Inn Restaurant 7
La Bourgogne 11
Manago Hotel Restaurant 15
Pa Leo 4
Pahu i'a 1
Quinn's Almost by the Sea 3
Shaka Restaurant 17
Teshima's 13

Restaurants Along the Kona Coast

Big Island Restaurants A to Z

kids **Aloha Angel Café** KAINALIU *ISLAND CUISINE* Large servings, heroic burgers and sandwiches, and a home-style menu attract vegetarians and carnivores alike. Most of the produce is organic. Hwy. 11, Kainaliu. ☎ 808/322-3383. Reservations recommended for dinner. Entrees: $6.95–$9.95 breakfast and lunch, $13–$22 dinner. AE, MC, V. Breakfast, lunch, and dinner daily. Map p 267.

kids **BaLe** KAILUA-KONA *FRENCH-VIETNAMESE SANDWICHES & BAKERY* This statewide chain specializes in "fast" French-Vietnamese sandwiches, Vietnamese rice and noodle entrees, and bakery items. A perfect place to stop before heading for the beach. Kona Coast Shopping Center, 74-5588 Palani Rd. ☎ 808/327-1212. Entrees $7.50–$11; sandwiches $3.50–$6. MC, V. Lunch and dinner daily. Map p 267.

★★ kids **Bamboo** HAWI *PACIFIC RIM* Bamboo's fare, island favorites in sophisticated presentations, complements the exotic interior. Produce from nearby gardens and fish fresh off the chef's own hook are among the highlights. Live Hawaiian music on weekends. Hwy. 270, Hawi. ☎ 808/889-5555. Reservations recommended. Entrees: $7.95–$18 lunch, $13–$38 dinner. MC, V. Lunch and dinner Tues–Sat, brunch Sun. Map p 269.

★ kids **Beach Tree Bar & Grill** HUALALAI RESORT *CASUAL GOURMET* Come here for outstanding cuisine in a perfect setting (outside, just feet from the sand). The excellent, imaginatively prepared menu features fresh fish, steaks, and vegetarian specialties. Buffet on Saturday; Wednesday is "Viva Italia" night. Entertainment from 5 to 8pm nightly. In the Four Seasons Resort Hualalai, Queen Kaahumanu Hwy., Kailua-Kona. ☎ 808/325-8000. Reservations recommended for Sat buffet. Entrees: $17–$22 lunch, $22–$47 dinner; Sat buffet $78 adults, $37 children 5–12. AE, DC, DISC, MC, V. Lunch and dinner daily. Map p 267.

Big Island Grill KAILUA-KONA *AMERICAN* This perpetually busy local favorite serves up huge portions of home cooking at 1970s prices. Loyal fans come for localized American cuisine (excellent fresh salmon and the world's tastiest mashed potatoes). ***Warning:*** You'll likely have to wait, and service can sometimes be slow. 75-5702 Kuakini Hwy. ☎ 808/326-1153. Reserva-

> *The food at Brown's Beach House lives up to the spectacular tropical lagoon setting.*

Northern Big Island Hotels & Restaurants

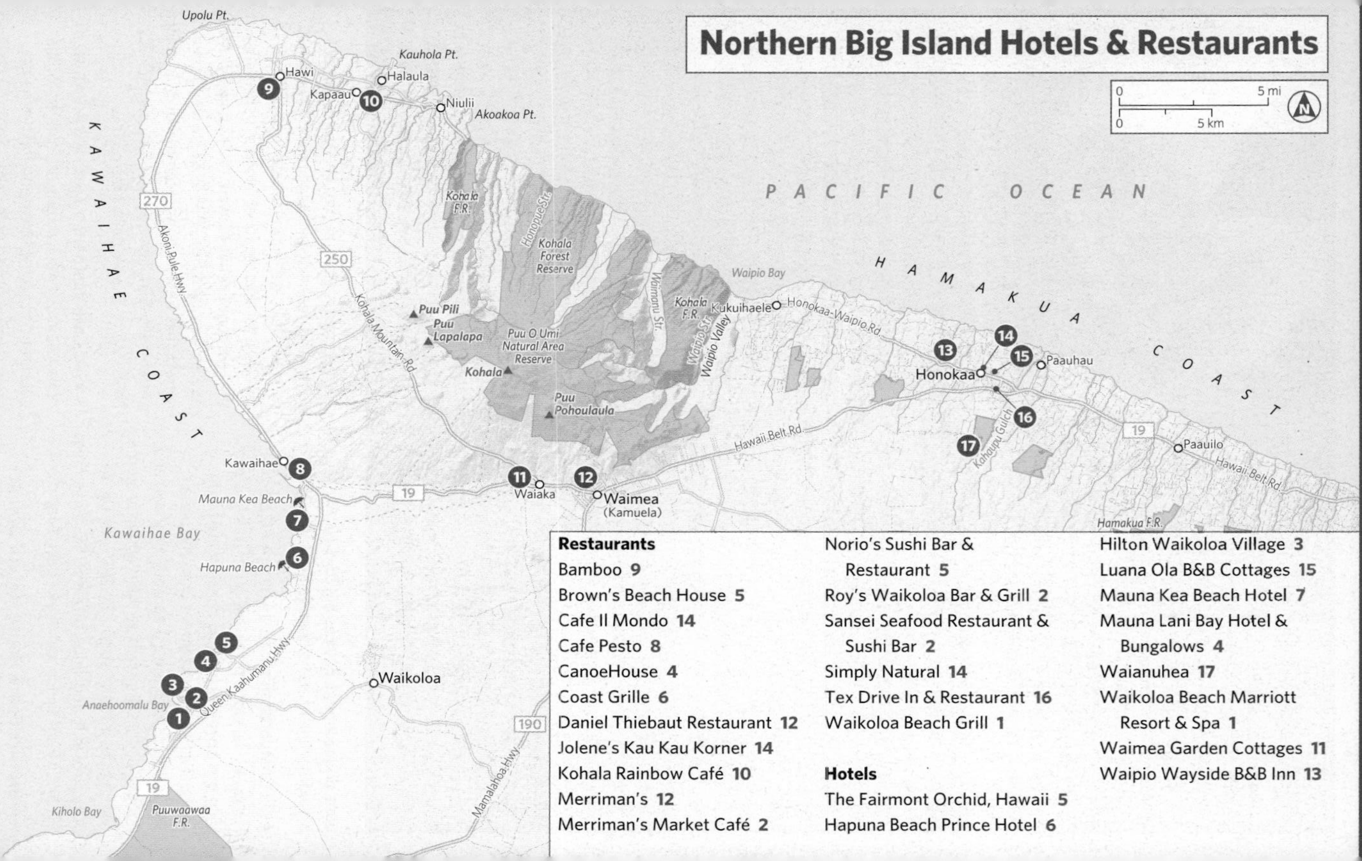

Restaurants

- Bamboo **9**
- Brown's Beach House **5**
- Cafe Il Mondo **14**
- Cafe Pesto **8**
- CanoeHouse **4**
- Coast Grille **6**
- Daniel Thiebaut Restaurant **12**
- Jolene's Kau Kau Korner **14**
- Kohala Rainbow Café **10**
- Merriman's **12**
- Merriman's Market Café **2**
- Norio's Sushi Bar & Restaurant **5**
- Roy's Waikoloa Bar & Grill **2**
- Sansei Seafood Restaurant & Sushi Bar **2**
- Simply Natural **14**
- Tex Drive In & Restaurant **16**
- Waikoloa Beach Grill **1**

Hotels

- The Fairmont Orchid, Hawaii **5**
- Hapuna Beach Prince Hotel **6**
- Hilton Waikoloa Village **3**
- Luana Ola B&B Cottages **15**
- Mauna Kea Beach Hotel **7**
- Mauna Lani Bay Hotel & Bungalows **4**
- Waianuhea **17**
- Waikoloa Beach Marriott Resort & Spa **1**
- Waimea Garden Cottages **11**
- Waipio Wayside B&B Inn **13**

Kona Coffee Craze!

The Big Island is the home of Kona coffee. Most of the farms are concentrated in the North and South Kona districts, where coffee remains a viable industry. Following are the best places to learn more about coffee growing and enjoy some of the delicious brew.

Kona Blue Sky Coffee Company, in Holualoa (☎ 877/322-1700 or 808/322-1700; www.konablueskycoffee.com), which handles its own beans exclusively, from picking to grinding. You can buy coffee on the farm itself and see the operation from field to final product.

Also in Holualoa, 10 minutes from Kailua-Kona, **Holualoa Kona Coffee Company** (☎ 800/334-0348 or 808/322-9937; www.konalea.com) purveys organic Kona from its own farm and other growers. Not only can you buy premium, unadulterated Kona coffee here, but you can also witness the hulling, sorting, roasting, and packaging of beans on a farm tour Monday through Friday from 8am to 3pm. Also in this upcountry village, the **Holuakoa Cafe,** Hwy. 180 (☎ 808/322-2233), is famous for high-octane espresso, ground from fresh-roasted Kona Blue Sky beans.

In Kealakekua, **Kona Joe Coffee Farm and Chocolate Company** (79-7346 Mamalahoa Hwy., btw. MM 113 and MM 114; ☎ 808/322-2100; www.konajoe.com), home of the world's first trellised coffee farm, offers free guided tours daily from 8:30am to 5pm. You'll see the unique plants on their patented trellis system as well as live demonstrations on roasting, sorting, brewing, and panning.

Some other coffees to watch for: **Bong Brothers** (☎ 808/328-9289; www.bongbrothers.com) thrives with its coffees, roadside fruit stand, and natural-foods deli that sells smoothies and healthful foods. Aficionados know that **Langenstein Farms** (☎ 808/328-8356; www.kona-coffee.com/konastore) distributes excellent Kona coffee and distinctively tasty macadamia nuts in the town of Honaunau. They also have great tours of the farm; just give them a call and they'll set something up. **Rooster Farms,** also in Honaunau (☎ 808/328-9173; www.roosterfarms.com), enjoys an excellent reputation for the quality of its organic coffee beans. The **Bad Ass Coffee Company** (www.badasscoffee.com) has franchises in Kainaliu, Kawaihae, Honokaa, Keauhou, and Kailua-Kona (and even a number of branches on the mainland), all selling its 100% Kona as well as coffees from Molokai, Kauai, and other tropical regions. A good bet in Hilo is **Bears' Coffee,** 106 Keawe St. (☎ 808/935-0708), the quintessential sidewalk coffeehouse and a Hilo stalwart.

tions not accepted. Entrees $6.25–$20. AE, MC, V. Breakfast, lunch, and dinner daily. Map p 267.

★ kids **Boston Basil's** KAILUA-KONA *PIZZA/ITALIAN* Delicious pizza and other Italian dishes for great prices, especially considering the location, just across the street from the ocean. Very popular with the 20-something crowd and hungry visitors drawn in by the wonderful aroma wafting out into the street. 75-5707 Alii Dr. ☎ 808/326-7836. Individual pizzas $9.95–$12; entrees $9–$15. MC, V. Lunch and dinner daily. Map p 267.

★★ **Brown's Beach House** MAUNA LANI RESORT *BIG ISLAND CUISINE* The spectacular setting (candlelit seating by a nearby lagoon) complements a menu that keeps getting better by the year. My picks include kiawe-grilled fresh island catch with tomato fondue or sizzling ahi tataki with local exotic mushrooms. At the Fairmont Orchid, Hawaii, 1 N. Kaniku Dr., Mauna Lani Resort. ☎ 808/885-2000. www.fairmont.com/orchid. Reservations recommended for dinner. Entrees: $19–$24 lunch, $30–$68 dinner. AE, DC, DISC, MC, V. Dinner daily. Map p 269.

★★ kids **Cafe Pesto** HILO AND KAWAIHAE *MEDITERRANEAN/ITALIAN* Fans drive miles for the gourmet pizzas, calzones, and fresh organic greens. Honey-miso crab cakes, Santa Fe chicken pasta, and sweet roasted peppers are other fa-

Hotels & Restaurants in Hilo

Restaurants
- Cafe Pesto 8
- Hilo Bay Café 20
- Ken's House of Pancakes 18
- Kuhio Grille 20
- Miyo's 13
- Naung Mai 10
- Nihon Restaurant & Cultural Center 14
- Nori's Saimin & Snacks 11
- Ocean Sushi Deli 7
- Pescatore 6
- Queen's Court Restaurant 15
- Restaurant Miwa 12
- Royal Siam Thai Restaurant 9
- Seaside Restaurant 19

Hotels
- The Bay House 4
- Dolphin Bay Hotel 3
- Hale Kai Hawaii 5
- Hilo Seaside Hotel 17
- The Inn at Kulaniapia 1
- The Palms Cliff House Inn 5
- Shipman House Bed & Breakfast 2
- Uncle Billy's Hilo Bay Hotel 16

vorites. In Kawaihae Shopping Center, at Kawaihae Harbor, Pule Hwy. and Kawaihae Rd. ☎ 808/882-1071; also at S. Hata Building, 308 Kamehameha Ave. ☎ 808/969-6640. Entrees: $9–$20 lunch, $15–$32 dinner; pizzas $9–$18. AE, DC, DISC, MC, V. Lunch and dinner daily. Maps p 269 and p 271.

★ kids **Cafe Il Mondo** HONOKAA *PIZZA/ESPRESSO BAR* A classical and flamenco guitarist, owner Sergio Ramirez occasionally plays solo guitar in his restaurant while contented diners tuck into the stone oven-baked pizzas. Sandwiches in freshly baked buns, soup, and roasted chicken round out the menu; all greens are fresh, local, and organic. Mamane St., Honokaa. ☎ 808/775-7711. Pizzas $10–$19; sandwiches $6.50; pasta $12. No credit cards. Lunch and dinner Tues–Sat. Map p 269.

★★ **CanoeHouse** MAUNA LANI RESORT *HAWAII REGIONAL CUISINE* Enjoy legendary sunset views as you feast in the open-air dining room. ***Tip:*** Ask for a table outside and go at sunset. The menu includes great fish items (sweet-and-sour chili prawns), meats (Mongolian BBQ rack of lamb), and even vegetarian items. At Mauna Lani Bay Hotel and Bungalows, 68-1400 Mauna Lani Dr. ☎ 808/881-7911. Reservations recommended. Entrees $29–$48. AE, DC, DISC, MC, V. Dinner daily. Map p 269.

> *The Aloha Angel Café offers a home-style menu and reasonable prices.*

★★ **Coast Grille** MAUNA KEA RESORT *STEAK/SEAFOOD/HAWAII REGIONAL CUISINE* Open-air seating, a famous oyster bar, and an extensive seafood selection served in multicultural preparations draw diners to this resort restaurant. Hapuna Beach Prince Hotel, 62-100 Kaunaoa Dr. ☎ 808/880-1111. www.hapunabeachprincehotel.com. Reservations recommended. Entrees $28-$55. AE, DISC, MC, V. Dinner daily. Map p 269.

★★ kids **The Coffee Shack** CAPTAIN COOK *COFFEEHOUSE/DELI* Great food, crisp air, and a sweeping ocean view make the Coffee Shack one of South Kona's great finds. At lunch you can enjoy an imported beer, with excellent sandwiches on home-baked breads and salads made with organic lettuces. Hwy. 11, 1 mile south of Captain Cook. ☎ 808/328-9555. Most items less than $10; pizzas $9-$13. DISC, MC, V. Breakfast and lunch daily 7:30am-3pm. Map p 267.

★★ **Daniel Thiebaut Restaurant** WAIMEA *FRENCH-ASIAN* This restaurant features Big Island products (Kamuela Pride beef, Kahua Ranch lettuces) as interpreted by the French-trained Thiebaut. Highlights include a Hunan-style rack of lamb, wok-fried scallops, and crispy avocado spring rolls with a smoked tomato coulis. Quality varies: If Chef Daniel is in, you will most likely get an excellent meal. 65-1259 Kawaihae Rd. (the Historic Yellow Building). ☎ 808/887-2200. www.danielthiebaut.com. Reservations recommended. Entrees $20-$33; Sun brunch buffet $23. AE, DISC, MC, V. Dinner daily, brunch Sun. Map p 269.

Habanero's KEAUHOU *MEXICAN* Come here for great, fast Mexican food at budget prices. Tasty egg dishes star at breakfast, followed by burritos (the fish with black beans is my favorite), soft and hard tacos, nachos, tostadas, quesadillas, and enchiladas for lunch and dinner. Bring cash. Keauhou Shopping Center, Keauhou. ☎ 808/324-HOTT (324-4688). All items under $9. No credit cards. Lunch and dinner Mon-Sat. Map p 267.

★★ **Hilo Bay Café** HILO *PACIFIC RIM* This upscale eatery features a creative menu ranging from house-made ravioli (stuffed with artichoke hearts, roasted garlic, and cream cheese) to potato-crusted fresh catch. Mellow jazz wafts from speakers, and plush chairs at low tables fill out the room. Don't miss eating here. Waiakea Center, 315 Makaala St. ☎ 808/935-4939. Reservations recommended for dinner. Entrees: $8-$15 lunch, $9-$26 dinner. AE, DISC, MC, V. Lunch Mon-Sat, dinner daily. Map p 271.

★★ **Hualalai Grille** HUALALAI RESORT *CONTEMPORARY PACIFIC* Chef Alan Wong, one of the founders of Hawaii Regional Cuisine, has taken the helm at this popular golf club restaurant with an ocean view. Lunch features soups, sandwiches, and daily specials; dinner entrees include steamed moi (raised on property at Hualalai Resort) and mac nut-crusted lamb chops. Service needs improvement. In the Hualalai Resort, Queen Kaahumanu Hwy. ☎ 808/325-8525. www.hualalairesort.com. Entrees: $12-$21 lunch, $37-$54 dinner. Reservations recommended. AE, DC, MC, V. Lunch and dinner daily. Map p 267.

★ **Huggo's** KAILUA-KONA *PACIFIC RIM/SEAFOOD* The main Huggo's dining room still hums with diners murmuring dreamily about the view (the tables are so close to the water you can see the entire curve of Kailua Bay), but ★ **Huggo's on the Rocks,** a mound of thatch, rock, and grassy-sandy ground right next to Huggo's, is a sunset-lover's nirvana. At sundown it's packed with people sipping mai tais and noshing on poke, sandwiches, plate lunches, and sashimi. From 6:30 to 11am, this same location turns into ★★ **Java on the Rocks**—sip Kona coffee, enjoy your eggs, and watch the waves roll onto the shore. At the senior Huggo's, fresh seafood remains the signature dish. 75-5828 Kahakai Rd. ☎ 808/329-1493. www.huggos.com. Reservations recommended. Entrees: $11-$21 lunch, $23-$54 dinner. AE, DC, DISC, MC, V. Lunch and dinner daily. Map p 267.

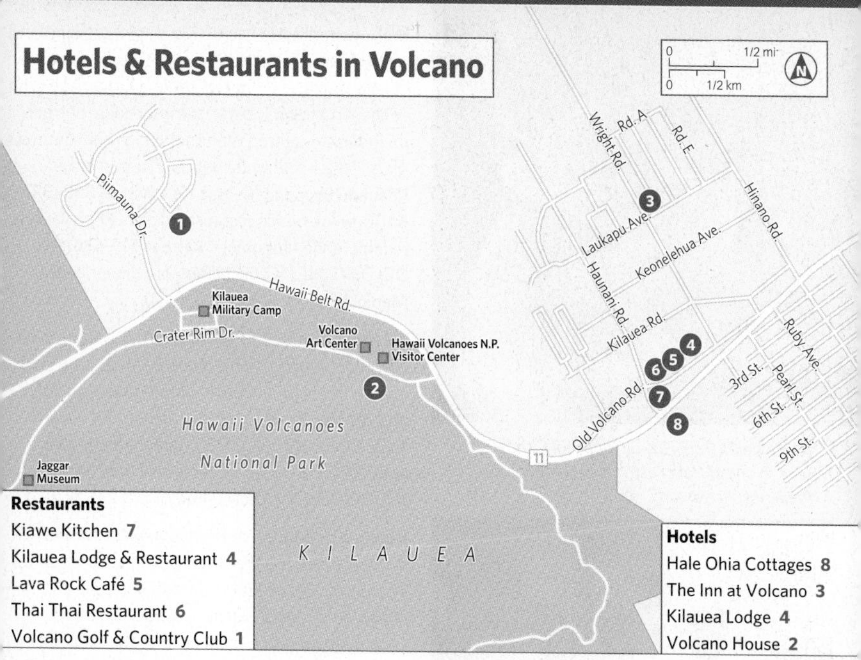

★ **Island Lava Java** KAILUA-KONA *AMERICAN* Sip espresso drinks, chow down on good food, and enjoy the unimpaired view of Kailua Bay. The breakfast menu features pancakes and eggs; lunch brings sandwiches and burgers; and dinner ranges from sandwiches to steak to fresh fish. The price and the view make up for the inconsistent service. 75-5799 Alii Dr., Kailua-Kona. ☎ 808/327-2161. Entrees: $3.75-$13 breakfast, $6.25-$15 lunch, $6.95-$17 dinner. AE, DISC, MC, V. Breakfast, lunch, and dinner daily. Map p 267.

★★ **Jackie Rey's Ohana Grill** KAILUA-KONA *ECLECTIC* This off-the-beaten-path eatery is hard to categorize, but you can count on great food at wallet-pleasing prices. Locals pile in at lunch for burgers and sandwiches. On weekdays, a happy-hour crowd downs a few brews and *pupu* (appetizers). Starting at 5pm, families with kids in tow show up for the delicious curry-crusted ahi and beef short ribs. Weekends bring music and dancing starting at 8:30pm. 75-5995 Kuakini Hwy., Kailua-Kona. ☎ 808/327-0209. Reservations recommended for dinner. Entrees: $7-$12 lunch, $11-$24 dinner. MC, V. Lunch Mon-Fri, dinner Mon-Sat. Map p 267.

> *Café Il Mondo offers organic, fresh food and flamenco music. Try the oven-baked pizzas and sandwiches on fresh-baked buns.*

> *Need a break from Hawaii Regional Cuisine? Head to one of Cafe Pesto's two locations for a superior slice of Italy.*

> *You'll delight in the tasteful atmosphere at the moody, jazz-themed, plush Hilo Bay Café... and the food's pretty appetizing too!*

Jolene's Kau Kau Korner HONOKAA *AMERICAN/LOCAL* Choose from saimin, stir-fried tempeh with vegetables, sandwiches, plate lunches, and familiar selections of local food at this homey place. At Mamane St. and Lehua, Honokaa. ☎ 808/775-9498. Entrees: $7–$9.50 lunch, $8.95–$19 dinner. No credit cards. Lunch Mon–Fri, dinner Mon, Wed, and Fri. Map p 269.

★★★ **Kenichi Pacific** KEAUHOU *PACIFIC RIM FUSION/SUSHI BAR* This gem of a restaurant features fantastic Pacific Rim fusion cuisine and a sushi bar. The tempting appetizer menu includes ginger-marinated squid, Dungeness crab cakes, and fresh lobster summer rolls. Entrees include pan-seared mahimahi in a miso beurre blanc sauce and macadamia-crusted lamb. Keauhou Shopping Center, Keauhou. ☎ 808/322-6400. www.kenichirestaurants.com. Reservations recommended for dinner. Entrees $19–$36. AE, DC, DISC, MC, V. Lunch Tues–Fri, dinner daily. Map p 267.

kids **Ken's House of Pancakes** HILO *AMERICAN/LOCAL* The only 24-hour coffee shop on the Big Island, Ken's fulfills basic dining needs simply and efficiently, with a good dose of local color. Very local, very Hilo. 1730 Kamehameha Ave. ☎ 808/935-8711. Most items less than $8. AE, DC, DISC, MC, V. Daily 24 hr. Map p 271.

Kiawe Kitchen VOLCANO *PIZZA/MEDITERRANEAN* A great place to stop after viewing the volcano. The pizza is excellent (all fresh ingredients). Enjoy lamb, pasta dishes, salads, and soup as you sip on some local beer or Kona coffee. 19-4005 Haunani Rd., Volcano. ☎ 808/967-7711. Entrees: $10–$13 lunch, $16–$25 dinner. MC, V. Lunch and dinner daily. Map p 273.

★ **Kilauea Lodge & Restaurant** VOLCANO *CONTINENTAL* Diners travel long distances to escape from the crisp upland air into the warmth of this high-ceilinged lodge. The European cooking is a fine culinary act. Favorites include the fresh catch, hasenpfeffer, potato-leek soup (all flavor and no cream), and Alsatian soup. Hwy. 11 (Volcano Village exit). ☎ 808/967-7366. Reservations recommended. Entrees $20–$40. AE, MC, V. Dinner daily. Map p 273.

Kohala Rainbow Café KAPAAU *GOURMET DELI* This place is known for its healthful fare and made-with-care wraps, such as the Kamehameha Wrap with kalua pork, two different cheeses, and a Maui onion dressing. Soups, sandwiches, burgers, and salads are also available. Hwy. 270, Kapaau, in front of the King Kamehameha Statue. ☎ 808/889-0099. Entrees under $10. MC, V. Lunch Mon–Fri. Map p 269.

★ **Kona Inn Restaurant** KAILUA-KONA *AMERICAN/SEAFOOD* Enjoy the open-air oceanfront setting and sunset views along with a huge menu that includes everything from nachos to fresh fish served Cajun style

> *Come for the sunsets at Kohala's open-air CanoeHouse. Stay for the delicious fish, barbecue, and veggie delicacies.*

or broiled and basted in lemon butter. Watch for the daily specials on the less expensive Cafe Grill menu. **In Kona Inn Shopping Village, 75-5744 Alii Dr. ☎ 808/329-4455. Reservations recommended for dinner. Entrees $16–$36; Cafe Grill $7–$13. AE, MC, V. Lunch and dinner daily. Map p 267.**

Kuhio Grille HILO *AMERICAN/HAWAIIAN* This coffee/saimin shop is a popular local hang-out. Specialties include saimin, taro-corned-beef hash, chicken yakitori, burgers, fried rice, and a 1-pound laulau with kalua pork dubbed the "Kanak Atak." Breakfast is served all day at the counter. **In Prince Kuhio Plaza. ☎ 808/959-2336. Entrees $7–$20. AE, DISC, MC, V. Breakfast, lunch, and dinner daily. Map p 271.**

★★ **La Bourgogne** KAILUA-KONA *CLASSIC FRENCH* This intimate restaurant serves classic French fare with skillful elegance. The roast duck breast with raspberries and pine nuts is exactly the kind of dish that characterizes La Bourgogne—presented attractively, with an unbeatable match of flavors and textures. **Hwy. 11, 3 miles south of Kailua-Kona. ☎ 808/329-6711. Reservations recommended. Entrees $28–$36. AE, DC, DISC, MC, V. Dinner Tues–Sat. Map p 267.**

★ kids **Lava Rock Café** VOLCANO *ECLECTIC/ LOCAL* The cross-cultural menu at this cheerful, airy oasis includes omelets and pancakes, teriyaki beef and chicken, serious desserts (like mango cheesecake), fresh catch, steak-and-shrimp combos, and "seismic sandwiches" (which the cafe will pack for hikers). **Hwy. 11 (Volcano Village exit, next to Kilauea Kreations). ☎ 808/967-8526. Entrees: $4.50–$9 lunch, $7–$18 dinner. MC, V. Breakfast and lunch daily, dinner Mon–Sat. Map p 273.**

Manago Hotel Restaurant CAPTAIN COOK *AMERICAN* The dining room of the decades-old Manago Hotel is a local legend, greatly loved for its unpretentious, tasty food at bargain prices. When the akule or opelu are running, count on a rush by the regular customers. **In the Manago Hotel, Hwy. 11, Captain Cook. ☎ 808/323-2642. Reservations recommended for dinner. Entrees $8–$14. DISC, MC, V. Breakfast, lunch, and dinner Tues–Sun. Map p 267.**

★★ **Merriman's** WAIMEA *HAWAII REGIONAL CUISINE* Merriman's is peerless. Among my many favorites are the Caesar salad with sashimi, Pahoa corn and shrimp fritters, and the sautéed, sesame-crusted fresh catch with

> ABOVE *The Coffee Shack also serves delicious seafood.* BELOW *Huggo's offers entertainment chasers with its magnificent mai tais.*

spicy lilikoi sauce. Still the best, and busiest, dining spot in Waimea. In Opelu Plaza, Hwy. 19. ☎ 808/885-6822. Reservations recommended. Entrees: $12–$24 lunch, $23–$45 dinner. AE, MC, V. Lunch Mon–Fri, dinner daily. Map p 269.

★ kids **Merriman's Market Cafe** WAIKOLOA BEACH RESORT *MEDITERRANEAN/DELI*
Peter Merriman, of Merriman's restaurant in Waimea (above), has opened this tiny, casual "market cafe" featuring cuisines of the Mediterranean made with fresh local produce, house-made sausages, artisan-style breads, and great cheeses and wines. Kings' Shops, Waikoloa Beach Resort, 250 Waikoloa Beach Dr., Waikoloa. ☎ 808/886-1700. Entrees: $9–$17 lunch, $17–$30 dinner. AE, MC, V. Lunch and dinner daily. Map p 269.

Miyo's HILO *JAPANESE*
Miyo's offers home-cooked, healthy food (no MSG) served in an open-air room on Wailoa Pond, where curving footpaths and greenery fill the horizon. The sesame chicken (deep-fried and boneless with a spine-tingling sesame sauce) is a bestseller. In Waiakea Villas, 400 Hualani St. ☎ 808/935-2273. Entrees $6–$15. MC, V. Lunch and dinner Mon–Sat. Map p 271.

Naung Mai HILO *THAI*
This quintessential hole in the wall fills up quickly. The flavors are assertive, the produce comes straight from the Hilo Farmers Market, and the prices are good. Best choices here are any of the curries (green, red, yellow, and Mussaman), spring rolls, and a Tom Yum spicy soup that is legendary. 86 Kilauea Ave. ☎ 808/934-7540. Reservations recommended. Entrees $10–$14. MC, V. Lunch Mon–Fri, dinner Mon–Sat. Map p 271.

★ **Nihon Restaurant & Cultural Center** HILO *JAPANESE* This restaurant offers a beautiful view of Hilo Bay on one side and the soothing green sprawl of Liliuokalani Gardens on the other. The menu features steak-and-seafood combination dinners and selections from the sushi bar. Not cheap, but good value. 123 Lihiwai St. ☎ 808/969-1133. Reservations recommended. Entrees $9–$20. AE, DC, DISC, MC, V. Lunch and dinner Mon–Sat. Map p 271.

★ **Norio's Sushi Bar & Restaurant** MAUNA LANI RESORT *JAPANESE* This upscale sushi bar serves traditional Japanese delicacies plus a few signature items such as *kushi katsu* (a panko-fried pork loin and onion skewer served with sesame katsu sauce). Sit at the 15-seat sushi bar to watch master sushi chef Norio Yamamoto at work. Fairmont Orchid. ☎ 808/885-2000. www.fairmont.com/orchid. Reservations recommended. Entrees $32–$50. AE, DC, DISC, MC, V. Dinner daily. Map p 269.

★ **Nori's Saimin & Snacks** HILO *SAIMIN/NOODLE SHOP* Unmarked and not visible from the street, Nori's is located across from the Hilo Lanes bowling alley, down a short driveway into an obscure parking lot. Look for the neon sign of chopsticks and a bowl. The menu includes 16 varieties of noodle soups and the best saimin on the island, plus plate lunches and legendary desserts. 688 Kinoole St. ☎ 808/935-9133. Most items less than $8.50; "big plate" dinner for 2 $19. AE, DC, MC, V. Lunch daily, dinner Tues–Sun. Map p 271.

★ **Ocean Sushi Deli** HILO *SUSHI*
Hilo's nexus of affordable sushi. Local-style specials stretch purist boundaries but are so

much fun: lomi salmon, oyster nigiri, ahi poke roll, and special new rolls that use thin sheets of tofu skins and cooked egg. Traditionalists have plenty to choose from as well. **239 Keawe St. ☎ 808/961-6625. Sushi boxes $4.75–$50; sushi family platters $20–$50. MC, V. Lunch and dinner Mon–Sat. Map p 271.**

★★★ **Pahu i'a** HUALALAI RESORT *CONTEMPORARY PACIFIC CUISINE* You can't find a better oceanfront location on the Big Island—Pahu i'a sits just feet from the lapping waves. The food features fresh produce and seafood from the island—and even from the resort's own aquaculture ponds, which teem with shrimp and moi (threadfin). Top-drawer. **In the Four Seasons Resort, Queen Kaahumanu Hwy., Kailua-Kona. ☎ 808/325-8000. Reservations recommended. Breakfast buffet $28; dinner entrees $30–$60. AE, DC, DISC, MC, V. Breakfast and dinner daily. Map p 267.**

Pa Leo KAILUA-KONA *PACIFIC RIM* Pa Leo dishes up very good fresh fish (crusted with taro and drizzled with lehua honey-lime tartar sauce), chicken (in a pineapple-ginger-apple sauce), and meats (rack of lamb with ginger cream). It overlooks the pier and Ahuena Heiau (King Kamehameha's temple). Service is friendly but can be slow. **Alii Dr., Kailua-Kona. ☎ 808/329-5550. Reservations a must. Entrees $12–$32. AE, MC, V. Lunch and dinner daily Map p 267.**

★ **Pescatore** HILO *SOUTHERN ITALIAN* An ornate interior (vintage velvet chairs, koa walls) and superb food make this the best special-occasion restaurant in Hilo. Try the fresh catch, offered in several preparations, or the paper-thin ahi carpaccio. Breakfast is terrific, too. **235 Keawe St. ☎ 808/969-9090. Reservations recommended for dinner. Entrees: $5–$8 breakfast, $5–$12 lunch, $16–$29 dinner. AE, DC, DISC, MC, V. Breakfast, lunch, and dinner daily. Map p 271.**

Queen's Court Restaurant HILO *AMERICAN/BUFFET* Generous and well-rounded offerings at budget-friendly prices. You can eat a la carte Monday through Thursday, but it's the buffets (a Hawaiian lunch buffet Fri, seafood Fri–Sun, and Dungeness crab/prime rib Mon–Thurs) throughout the week that draw throngs of local families. **In the Hilo Hawaiian Hotel, 71 Banyan Dr. ☎ 808/935-9361. Reservations recommended. Hawaiian lunch buffet $16; prime rib/crab buffet $27; seafood buffet $30. AE, DC, DISC, MC, V. Breakfast, lunch, and dinner Mon–Sat, brunch and dinner Sun. Map p 271.**

> *The Pahu i'a's view is the best item on the menu.*

★ kids **Quinn's Almost by the Sea** KAILUA-KONA *STEAK/SEAFOOD* Quinn's has a nautical/sports-bar atmosphere and offers casual alfresco dining on a garden lanai. The menu is surf-and-turf basic: burgers, sandwiches (including fresh ahi or ono when available), and a limited dinner menu of dependably good fresh fish and steaks. **75-5655A Palani Rd. ☎ 808/329-3822. Entrees $7.95–$24. MC, V. Lunch and dinner daily. Map p 267.**

★ **Restaurant Miwa** HILO *JAPANESE* This quintessential neighborhood sushi bar offers shabu-shabu (you cook your own ingredients in a heavy pot), tempura, fresh catch, and a full sushi selection. Don't miss the haupia (coconut pudding) cream-cheese pie if it's available. **In the Hilo Shopping Center, 1261 Kilauea Ave. ☎ 808/961-4454. Reservations recommended. Entrees $9–$37 (most $10–$15). AE, DC, DISC, MC, V. Lunch Mon–Sat, dinner daily. Map p 271.**

★ **Royal Siam Thai Restaurant** HILO *THAI* This popular neighborhood restaurant serves consistently good Thai curries in a simple

> *If you're in Waimea, don't miss sampling the delicious Hawaii Regional Cuisine served at Merriman's.*

A Lunch for All Five Senses

Hidden in the tall eucalyptus trees outside the old plantation community of Paauilo is the **Hawaiian Vanilla Company,** on Paauilo Mauka Road, (☎ 808/776-1771; www.hawaiianvanilla.com). The company hosts one of the truly sensuous experiences on the Big Island. Owner Jim Reddekopp gives a presentation on how vanilla is grown, how it's used in the meal you will be eating, and just about everything else you ever wanted to know about this magical orchid and bean. The four-course, 2-hour Hawaiian Vanilla Luncheon is available on Friday (12:30–2:30pm; reservations required). Cost is $49 and worth every penny. Also available are vanilla tastings, which include a 45-minute presentation and samples from the kitchen for $15 (Mon, Tues, and Fri at 10am). Check out the retail store for vanilla products ranging from beans to extracts, teas to lotions.

room just off the sidewalk. Fresh herbs and vegetables from the owner's gardens add an extra zip to the platters of noodles, soups, curries, and specialties. 70 Mamo St. ☎ 808/961-6100. Entrees $9–$13. AE, DC, DISC, MC, V. Lunch Mon–Sat, dinner daily. Map p 271.

★★★ **Roy's Waikoloa Bar & Grill** WAIKOLOA BEACH RESORT *PACIFIC RIM/EURO-ASIAN* Roy's offers a golf course view and the East-West cuisine and upbeat service that are Roy Yamaguchi signatures. Favorites include Szechuan baby back ribs, blackened island ahi, and other fresh fish topped with exotic sauces such as gingered lime-chile butter. Kings' Shops, Waikoloa Beach Resort, 250 Waikoloa Beach Dr. ☎ 808/886-4321. www.roysrestaurant.com. Reservations recommended. Entrees $26–$33. AE, DC, DISC, MC, V. Dinner daily. Map p 269.

★★★ **Sansei Seafood Restaurant & Sushi Bar** WAIKOLOA BEACH RESORT *SUSHI BAR/CONTEMPORARY JAPANESE* Sansei's tirelessly creative menu of Japanese and East-West delicacies includes panko-crusted ahi sashimi, sashimi trio, ahi carpaccio, and Asian shrimp cakes. There's karaoke on Friday nights. Queen's Market Place, Waikoloa Beach Resort. ☎ 808/886-6286. www.sanseihawaii.com. Reservations recommended. Entrees $19–23, sushi $3.50–$17. AE, DISC, MC, V. Dinner daily. Map p 269.

★★ **Seaside Restaurant** HILO *STEAK/SEAFOOD* This is a casual local favorite—a Hilo signature with a character all its own. You can even get mullet and *aholehole* (a silvery mountain bass) that are fished out of the restaurant's own pond shortly before you arrive (but you must call ahead). They also serve very fresh sushi Wednesday through Sunday. The outdoor tables are fabulous at dusk when the light reflects on the ponds with an otherworldly glow. 1790 Ka-

Tropical Dreams Ice Cream

You'll find Tropical Dreams ice creams served all over the island, but the company got its start in North Kohala. **Kohala Coffee Mill and Tropical Dreams Ice Cream,** Hwy. 270, Hawaii (☎ 808/889-5577), serves upscale ice creams, along with sandwiches, pastries, and a selection of island coffees. The Tahitian vanilla and lychee ice creams are local legends, but I also love the macadamia nut torte and lilikoi bars, made by a local pastry chef. Jams, jellies, herb vinegars, Hawaiian honey, herbal salts, and macadamia nut oils are among the gift items for sale. It's open Monday to Friday from 6am to 6pm, and Saturday and Sunday from 7am to 5:30pm.

lanianaole Ave. ☎ 808/935-8825. Reservations recommended. Entrees $15–$30. AE, DC, MC, V. Dinner Tues–Sun. Map p 271.

kids **Shaka Restaurant** NAALEHU *AMERICAN/LOCAL* Shaka serves up huge servings of plate lunches and American fare at budget-friendly prices in a casual atmosphere. Locals come here for the plate lunches, honey-dipped fried chicken, and the fresh catch. Bring the kids; they'll love the pizza. Hwy. 11. Naalehu. ☎ 808/929-7404. Entrees $4.50–$8.95 lunch, $4.50–$22 dinner. MC, V. Lunch and dinner daily. Map p 267.

★ kids **Simply Natural** HONOKAA *HEALTH FOOD/SANDWICH SHOP* This charming deli offers friendly service, wholesome food, and a vintage interior. The menu features sautéed mushroom-onion sandwiches, tempeh burgers, and breakfast delights that include taro-banana pancakes. Mamane St., Honokaa. ☎ 808/775-0119. Deli items $3.50–$7.95. No credit cards. Lunch Mon–Sat. Map p 269.

★ kids **Teshima's** HANALO *JAPANESE/AMERICAN* This is local style all the way. Shrimp tempura, sukiyaki, and such combinations as steak and shrimp tempura or the deep-sea trio of shrimp tempura, fried fish, and sashimi are favorites. Hwy. 11, Honalo. ☎ 808/322-9140. Reservations recommended. Complete dinners $19 and under. No credit cards. Breakfast, lunch, and dinner daily. Map p 267.

Tex Drive In & Restaurant HONOKAA *AMERICAN/LOCAL ETHNIC* Residents have been gathering here for decades over early morning coffee and breakfast. Try the popular Portuguese malassadas (a cakelike doughnut without a hole). The menu has a local flavor and features ethnic specialties: Korean chicken, teriyaki meat, and kalua pork. Hwy. 19, Honokaa. ☎ 808/775-0598. Entrees $7.95–$12. DC, DISC, MC, V. Breakfast, lunch, and dinner daily. Map p 269.

Thai Thai Restaurant VOLCANO *THAI* My favorite dish here is the green papaya salad made with tomatoes, crunchy green beans, green onions, and a heap of raw and roasted peanuts—a symphony of color, aroma, texture, and flavor. You'll also find curries, satays, noodles, and stir-fries on the menu. 19-4084 Old Volcano Rd. ☎ 808/967-7969. Entrees $9–$15. Dinner daily 5–9pm. Map p 273.

Volcano Golf & Country Club VOLCANO *AMERICAN/LOCAL* This golf course clubhouse has a reputation as a low-key purveyor of local favorites. Choose from chicken or fish sandwiches, hamburgers, pastas, saimin, stir-fry, and Hawaiian stew with rice. Hwy. 11 (at MM 30). ☎ 808/967-8228. Reservations recommended for large groups. Breakfast items under $9; lunch items under $9.75. AE, DC, DISC, MC, V. Lunch and dinner daily. Map p 273.

Waikoloa Beach Grill WAIKOLOA BEACH RESORT *ECLECTIC* The eclectic menu at this golf course clubhouse restaurant ranges from local fish to a traditional tomato curry with marinated chicken and naan bread. Save room for the delectable desserts. 69-1022 Keana Pl., Waikoloa Beach Resort. ☎ 808/886-6131. Dinner reservations recommended. Entrees: $8.95–$19 lunch, $23–$39 dinner. AE, DC, DISC, MC, V. Lunch and dinner daily. Map p 269.

★ **What's Shakin'** PEPEEKEO *HEALTH FOOD* Dishes include blue-corn tamales with homemade salsa, teriyaki-ginger tempeh burgers, wraps, and several lunch specials daily. The owners' 20-acre farm supplies bananas and papayas for fresh-fruit smoothies. Sit outside to enjoy the staggering ocean view. 27-999 Old Mamalahoa Hwy. (on the 4-mile scenic drive), Pepeekeo. ☎ 808/964-3080. Most items less than $8.50; smoothies all $5.75. MC, V. Lunch and dinner daily.

Big Island Hotel Best Bets

Most Romantic
Horizon Guest House $$$ Hwy. 11, Honaunau (p 284).

Most Historic
Hale Ohia Cottages $$ Hale Ohia Rd., off Hwy. 11), Volcano (p 284).

Most Luxurious Hotel
Four Seasons Resort Hualalai at Historic Kaupulehu $$$$$ 72-100 Ka'upulehu Dr., Kailua-Kona (p 283).

Most Luxurious Condo
Kanaloa at Kona $$$ 78-261 Manukai St., Keauhou (p 285).

Best Moderately Priced Hotel
Dolphin Bay Hotel $$ 333 Iliahi St., Hilo (p 282).

Best Budget Hotel
Kona Tiki Hotel $ 75-5968 Alii Dr., Kailua-Kona (p 287).

Best for Kids
Kona Village Resort $$$$$ Kona Village Rd., off Hwy. 19, north of the Kona International Airport, by MM 89, Kailua-Kona (p 287).

Best Value
Waipio Wayside B&B Inn $$ Hwy. 240 (btw. MM 3 and MM 4), Honokaa (p 291).

Most Charming B&B
Holualoa Inn $$$ 76-5932 Mamalahoa Hwy., Holualoa (p 284).

> *Kailua-Kona's Four Seasons Resort Hualalai.*

Best View
Hapuna Beach Prince Hotel $$$$ At Mauna Kea Resort, 62-100 Kaunaoa Dr., Kohala Coast (p 284).

Best Club-Level Amenities
The Fairmont Orchid, Hawaii $$$$$ 1 N. Kaniku Dr., Mauna Lani Resort, Kohala Coast (p 283).

Best Service
Four Seasons Resort Hualalai at Historic Kaupulehu $$$$$ 72-100 Ka'upulehu Dr., Kailua-Kona (p 283).

Best Spa
Mauna Lani Bay Hotel & Bungalows $$$$$ 68-1400 Mauna Lani Dr., Mauna Lani Resort, Kohala Coast (p 289).

Most Hawaiian Resort
Kona Village Resort $$$$$ Kona Village Rd., off Hwy. 19, north of the Kona International Airport, by MM 89, Kailua-Kona (p 287).

Best Fantasy Resort
Hilton Waikoloa Village $$$$ 69-425 Waikoloa Beach Dr., Waikoloa Beach Resort (p 284).

Best Off the Beaten Path
The Palms Cliff House Inn $$$$ Hwy. 19 (close to MM 13), Honomu (p 289).

Most Serene
South Point Banyan Tree House $$ At Hwy. 11 and Pinao St., Waiohinu (p 290).

Best Family Condo
Kona Seaspray $$ 78-6671 Alii Dr., Keauhou (p 287).

Hotels Along the Kona Coast

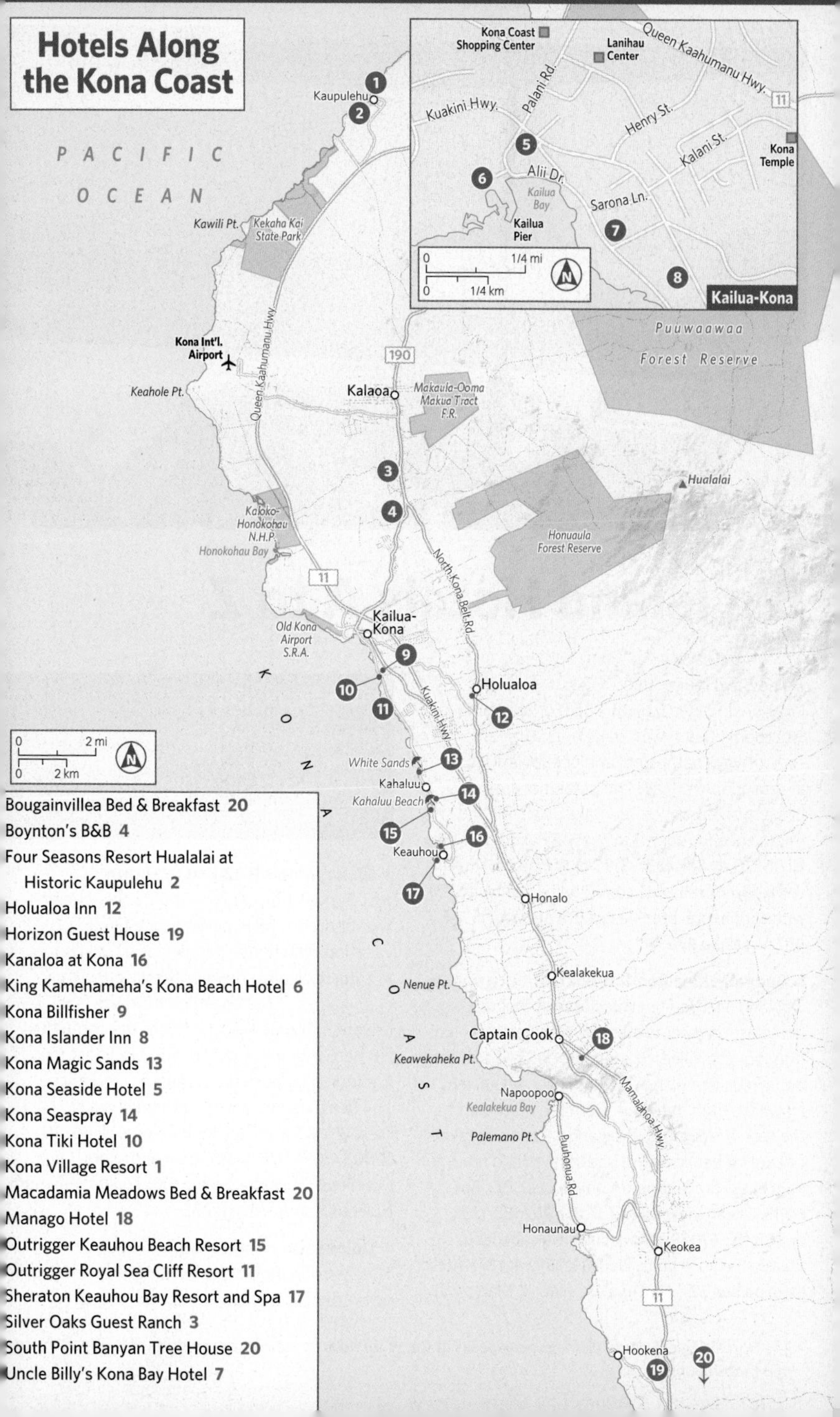

Bougainvillea Bed & Breakfast **20**
Boynton's B&B **4**
Four Seasons Resort Hualalai at Historic Kaupulehu **2**
Holualoa Inn **12**
Horizon Guest House **19**
Kanaloa at Kona **16**
King Kamehameha's Kona Beach Hotel **6**
Kona Billfisher **9**
Kona Islander Inn **8**
Kona Magic Sands **13**
Kona Seaside Hotel **5**
Kona Seaspray **14**
Kona Tiki Hotel **10**
Kona Village Resort **1**
Macadamia Meadows Bed & Breakfast **20**
Manago Hotel **18**
Outrigger Keauhou Beach Resort **15**
Outrigger Royal Sea Cliff Resort **11**
Sheraton Keauhou Bay Resort and Spa **17**
Silver Oaks Guest Ranch **3**
South Point Banyan Tree House **20**
Uncle Billy's Kona Bay Hotel **7**

Big Island Hotels A to Z

★ **The Bay House** HILO
Overlooking Hilo Bay, this B&B offers immaculate rooms (each with oak floors, king-size bed, sofa, private bathroom, and oceanview lanai) at reasonable prices. The breakfast area also has a refrigerator, coffeemaker, toaster, and microwave for common use. 42 Pukihae St., Hilo, HI 96720. ☎ 888/235-8195 or ☎ 808/961-6311. www.bayhousehawaii.com. 3 units. Doubles $150 with continental breakfast; extra person $15. AE, MC, V. Map p 271.

★ **Bougainvillea Bed & Breakfast** OCEAN VIEW
Don and Martie Jean Nitsche built their bed-and-breakfast on 3 acres bursting with gardens—colorful bougainvillea, a pineapple patch, and a fishpond, plus a pool, hot tub, and even an ancient Hawaiian path that went from the mountain to the sea. The lovely setting and Martie's breakfast (including her secret-recipe banana and mac-nut pancakes) draw people from all over. P.O. Box 6045, Ocean View, HI 96737. ☎ 800/688-1763 or 808/929-7089. www.bougainvilleabedandbreakfast.com. 4 units. Doubles $89 with breakfast; extra person $15. AE, DC, DISC, MC, V. Map p 281.

More Hotel Maps

See also "Northern Big Island Hotels & Restaurants" (p 269), "Hotels & Restaurants in Hilo" (p 271), and "Hotels & Restaurants in Volcano" (p 273).

★ kids **Boynton's B&B** KAILUA-KONA
Just 3 miles from Kailua-Kona is this quaint two-bedroom B&B, perfect for a family vacation. The house perches at 1,000 feet in a quiet country neighborhood; guests can enjoy views of the coastline from the lanai. A private entrance leads you into the complete kitchen, which is stocked with breakfast fixings (including eggs, cereals, muffins, and juice). The beach is just a 5-minute drive away. 74-4920-A Palani Rd., Kailua-Kona, HI 96740. ☎ 808/329-4178. www.konabandb.com. 1 unit. Doubles $120; extra person $15; 3-night minimum. No credit cards. Map p 281.

★ **Dolphin Bay Hotel** HILO
This 2-story, motel-like building, 4 blocks from downtown, is a clean, family-run property

> *The Horizon Guest House provides peak peeks at the south Kona coastline from 40 acres of luxury at the top of a 1,100-foot bluff.*

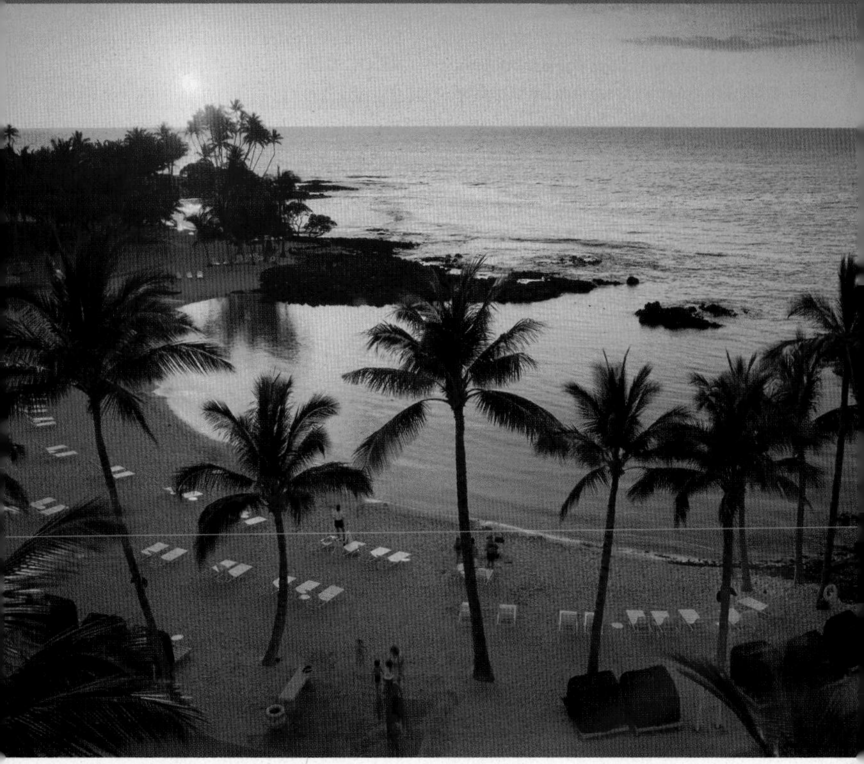

> *Sports programs, entertainment, and awesome ocean views are the signature of Kohala's fabulous Fairmont Orchid.*

that offers good value in a quiet garden setting. Ceiling fans help cool the rooms, which are brightly painted and outfitted with rattan furniture. 333 Iliahi St., Hilo, HI 96720. ☎ 808/935-1466. www.dolphinbayhilo.com. 18 units. Doubles: $99–$119 studio, $139 1-bedroom apt, $149 2-bedroom apt; extra person $10. MC, V. Map p 271.

★★★ kids **The Fairmont Orchid, Hawaii** MAUNA LANI RESORT This elegant beach resort takes full advantage of the spectacular ocean views and historical sites on its 32-acre grounds. The sports facilities here are extensive, and there's an excellent Hawaiiana program covering everything from paddling a Hawaiian canoe to strumming a ukulele. 1 N. Kaniku Dr., Kohala Coast, HI 96743. ☎ 866/540-4474 or 808/885-2000. www.fairmont.com/orchid. 540 units. Doubles $399–$4,499; extra person $75. AE, DC, DISC, MC, V. Map p 269.

★★★ kids **Four Seasons Resort Hualalai at Historic Kaupulehu** KAILUA-KONA This is a great place to relax in the lap of luxury. The Four Seasons has no concrete corridors and no massive central building—it looks like a 2-story town house project, clustered around three seaside swimming pools and a snorkeling pond. 72-100 Ka'upulehu Dr., Kailua-Kona, HI 96740. ☎ 888/340-5662 or 808/325-8000. www.fourseasons.com/hualalai. 243 units. Doubles $725–$1,115; extra person $170. AE, DC, DISC, MC, V. Map p 281.

★ **Hale Kai Hawaii** HILO An eye-popping view of the ocean runs the entire length of this house; you can sit on the wide deck and watch the surfers slide down the waves. All rooms have that fabulous ocean view through sliding-glass doors. Guests have access to a pool and hot tub. Breakfast is a treat, with entrees like homemade mac-nut waffles or double cheese soufflé. 111 Honolii Pali, Hilo, HI 96720. ☎ 808/935-6330. www.halekaihawaii.com. 4 units. Doubles $140–$160 with gourmet breakfast; extra person $20; 2-night minimum. MC, V. Map p 271.

★ **Hale Ohia Cottages** VOLCANO
Just a mile from Hawaii Volcanoes National Park, Hale Ohia offers a choice of suites and four guest cottages—one with an unusual bedroom made from a 1930s redwood water tank. The surrounding botanical gardens contribute to the overall tranquil ambience of the estate. P.O. Box 758 (Hale Ohia Rd., off Hwy. 11), Volcano, HI 96785. ☎ 800/455-3803 or 808/967-7986. www.haleohia.com. 8 units. Doubles $105–$299 with continental breakfast; extra person $25. MC, V. Map p 273.

★★ **Hapuna Beach Prince Hotel** MAUNA KEA RESORT This hotel enjoys one of the best locations on the Kohala Coast, adjacent to the magnificent white sands of Hapuna Beach. Hotel guests, many from Japan, tend to dress up here. The rooms are comfortable and take advantage of the fabulous ocean view and sea breezes, but they're small for a luxury hotel. Service is friendly and caring. At Mauna Kea Resort, 62-100 Kaunaoa Dr., Kohala Coast, HI 96743. ☎ 888/9-PRINCE (977-4623) or 808/880-1111. www.princeresortshawaii.com. 350 units. Doubles $395–$690; extra person $60. AE, DC, MC, V. Map p 269.

Hilo Seaside Hotel HILO
Lush tropical gardens surround this family-operated hotel, across Hilo Bay on historic Banyan Drive. It's not fancy, but it's budget-friendly and makes a great home base for exploring East Hawaii. 126 Banyan Dr. (off Hwy. 19), Hilo, HI 96720. ☎ 800/560-5557 or 808/935-0821. www.hiloseasidehotel.com. 135 units. Doubles $138–$150; extra person $20. AE, DC, MC, V. Map p 271.

★ kids **Hilton Waikoloa Village** WAIKOLOA BEACH RESORT This hotel is a fantasy world all its own. Its high-rise towers are connected by silver-bullet trams and boats; the kids will love it, but Mom and Dad may get a little weary waiting for the tram or boat to take them to breakfast. The contemporary guest rooms are spacious and luxurious, with built-in platform beds, lanais, and loads of amenities. 69-425 Waikoloa Beach Dr., Waikoloa, HI 96738. ☎ 800/HILTONS (445-8667) or 808/886-1234. www.hiltonwaikoloavillage.com. 1,240 units. Doubles $229–$649; extra person $45; daily resort fee $15. AE, DC, DISC, MC, V. Map p 269.

★★ **Holualoa Inn** HOLUALOA
The quiet, secluded setting of this B&B, 1,350 feet above Kailua-Kona, provides stunning panoramic views of the entire coast. This contemporary home has six private suites and window-walls that roll back to embrace the gardens and views. The 30-acre estate includes 3,000 coffee trees, which are the source of the morning brew. It's a 15-minute drive to Kailua-Kona and about 20 minutes to the beach, but the pool has a stunning view of the sparkling Pacific below. P.O. Box 222 (76-5932 Mamalahoa Hwy.), Holualoa, HI 96725. ☎ 800/392-1812 or 808/324-1121. www.holualoainn.com. 6 units. Doubles $260–$375 with breakfast; 2-night minimum. AE, DC, DISC, MC, V. Map p 281.

★★ **Horizon Guest House** HONAUNAU
This is the Hawaiian hideaway of your dreams. Its 40 acres of pastureland are located at an altitude of 1,100 feet. Each unit features Hawaiian furnishings and private lanais with coastline views. The property features barbecue facilities, gardens, an outdoor shower, and beach toys. P.O. Box 268, Honaunau, HI 96726. ☎ 888/328-8301 or 808/328-2540. www.horizonguesthouse.com. 4 units. Doubles $250 with gourmet breakfast; 2-night minimum. MC, V. Map p 281.

★ **The Inn at Kulaniapia** HILO
The view from this off-the-beaten-track inn is worth the price alone: the 120-foot Kulaniapia Waterfall in one direction and the entire town of Hilo sprawled out 850 feet below in another direction. This is *the* place for a romantic getaway. Breakfast includes fresh fruit grown on the 22-acre property and just-baked breads. The rooms are well appointed, with balconies. P.O. Box 646, Hilo, HI 96721. ☎ 866/935-6789 or 808/935-6789. www.waterfall.net. 4 units. Doubles $119–$129 with breakfast; extra person $20. AE, MC, V. Map p 271.

The Inn at Volcano VOLCANO
This B&B has a storybook, enchanting quality to it. Rooms are individually decorated; one with memorabilia from the owners' extensive travels to Africa, another with Victorian decor. They're exquisitely done but not always practical for things like storing toiletries. There's a separate cabin located next door to the Inn. P.O. Box 998,

> *Want to really get away? Kona's Holualoa Inn has six private suites on 30 lush elevated acres with panoramic vistas of the Pacific.*

Volcano, HI 96785. ☎ 800/937-7786 or 808/967-7786. www.volcano-hawaii.com. 5 units. Doubles $159–$289 with gourmet breakfast. AE, DC, DISC, MC, V. Map p 273.

★★ kids **Kanaloa at Kona** KEAUHOU
These big, comfortable, well-managed, and spacious vacation condos, on 16 landscaped acres, border the rocky coast beside Keauhou Bay, 6 miles south of Kailua-Kona. They're exceptional units, ideal for families, with comforts such as huge bathrooms with whirlpool bathtubs and spacious lanais. 78-261 Manukai St., Kailua-Kona, HI 96740. ☎ 800/959-5662 or 808/322-9625. www.outrigger.com. 76 units. Doubles: $249–$365 1-bedroom apt, $279–$499 2-bedroom apt. AE, DC, DISC, MC, V. Map p 281.

★ **Kilauea Lodge** VOLCANO
This popular roadside lodge sits on 10 wooded and landscaped acres. Its rooms offer heating systems and hot-towel warmers, beautiful art, fresh flowers, and, in some, fireplaces. There's also a 1929 two-bedroom cottage with a fireplace and a full kitchen. P.O. Box 116 (1 block off Hwy. 11 on Old Volcano Rd.), Volcano, HI 96785. ☎ 808/967-7366. www.kilauealodge.com. 17 units. Doubles: $160–$215 rooms, $190–$280 cottages; with breakfast; extra person $20. AE, MC, V. Map p 273.

King Kamehameha's Kona Beach Hotel
KAILUA-KONA The location is terrific, right on the ocean, but this 30-plus-year-old hotel looks tired. Though they're showing their age, rooms are clean and can have views of an ancient banyan tree, the Kailua Pier, or sparkling Kailua Bay. The hotel's own small gold-sand beach is right out the front door. 75-5660 Palani Rd., Kailua-Kona, HI 96740. ☎ 800/367-2111 or 808/329-2911. www.konabeachhotel.com. 460 units. Doubles $118–$179; extra person $35. AE, DC, DISC, MC, V. Map p 281.

kids **Kona Billfisher** KAILUA-KONA
This well-maintained property is within walking distance of downtown Kailua-Kona. The ocean is just across the street, but the nearest swimming

> *Delightful decor and romantic seclusion are the draws of the Horizon Guest House, located on beautiful pastureland with ocean views.*

beach is a mile away (there is a pool on-site as well). Each unit comes with a full kitchen and a balcony and features new furnishings and king-size beds. Alii Dr. (across from the Royal Kona Resort), c/o Hawaii Resort Management, P.O. Box 39, Kailua-Kona, HI 96745. ☎ 800/622-5348 or 808/329-3333. www.konahawaii.com. 60 units. Doubles: $115–$150 1-bedroom, $135–$165 2-bedroom; $35 booking fee, $35–$45 cleaning fee, and $5–$6 a day for using the A/C; 3-night minimum. DC, DISC, MC, V. Map p 281.

Kona Islander Inn KAILUA-KONA
This is the most affordable place to stay in Kailua-Kona. The lush gardens surrounding these small, plantation-style buildings make it hard to believe you're smack-dab in the middle of downtown. The central location—across the street from the historic Kona Inn Shops—is convenient but can be noisy. Built in 1962, the complex is showing some signs of age, but units are well-maintained. 75-5776 Kuakini Hwy. (south of Hualalai Rd.), Kailua-Kona. c/o Hawaii Resort Management, P.O. Box 39, Kailua-Kona, HI 96745. ☎ 800/622-5348 or 808/329-3333. www.konahawaii.com. 80 units. Doubles $80–$110. DC, DISC, MC, V. Map p 281.

★ **Kona Magic Sands** KAILUA-KONA
This is one of the best oceanfront deals you'll find on a Kona condo, and the only one with a beach for swimming and snorkeling right next door. These studio units aren't large or luxurious, but every one has a lanai that steps out over the ocean and sunset views that you'll dream about long after you return home. 77-6452 Alii Dr. (next to Magic Sands Beach Park). c/o Hawaii Resort Management, P.O. Box 39, Kailua-Kona, HI 96745. ☎ 800/622-5348 or 808/329-3333. Fax 808/326-4137. www.konahawaii.com. 37 units. Doubles $115–$170; $85 cleaning fee; 3-night minimum. DC, DISC, MC, V. Map p 281.

Kona Seaside Hotel KAILUA-KONA
Located in the heart of Kailua-Kona, the Kona Seaside is just steps away from Kailua Bay and Kailua-Kona's shopping, restaurants, and historic sites. The rooms are large and comfy (even if they don't have fancy soaps and extra amenities), but they can be noisy (ask for one away from the road). 75-5646 Palani Rd. (at Kuakini Hwy.), Kailua-Kona, HI 96740. ☎ 800/560-5558 or 808/329-2455. www.sand-seaside.com. 225 units. Doubles $138–$150; extra person $20. AE, DC, MC, V. Map p 281.

★ **Kona Seaspray** KEAUHOU
Kona Seaspray is just across from the Kahaluu Beach Park, possibly the best snorkeling area in Kona. The rates are a great deal when you consider that the one-bedroom apartments easily sleep four and the two-bedroom unit can sleep six. All apartments have a full kitchen, and there's also a barbecue area. Every unit has a lanai and fabulous ocean view. 78-6671 Alii Dr. (reservations c/o Johnson Resort Properties, 78-6665 Alii Dr.), Kailua-Kona, HI 96740. ☎ 808/322-2403. www.konaseaspray.com. 12 units. Doubles: $140–$175 1-bedroom, $155–$190 2-bedroom/2-bathroom; extra person $20; $55–$75 cleaning fee; 3-night minimum. AE, DISC, MC, V. Map p 281.

★★ **Kona Tiki Hotel** KAILUA-KONA
This is one of the best budget deals in Hawaii. All of the rooms are tastefully decorated and feature queen-size beds, ceiling fans, mini-fridges, and private lanais overlooking the ocean. Although it's called a hotel, this small, family-run operation is more like a large B&B, with lots of aloha and plenty of friendly conversation at the morning breakfast buffet around the pool. 75-5968 Alii Dr. (about a mile from downtown Kailua-Kona), Kailua-Kona, HI 96740. ☎ 808/329-1425. www.konatiki.com. 15 units. Double $69–$92 with continental breakfast; extra person $9; children 2–12 $6; 3-night minimum. No credit cards. Map p 281.

★ kids **Kona Village Resort** KAILUA-KONA
This exclusive, one-of-a-kind haven by the sea features a wonderful dark-sand beach and individual thatched-roof, island-style bungalows. The resort resembles an eclectic Polynesian village, with historic sites and beaches. The room rate includes all meals—the Friday-night luau here is fabulous—plus all snorkeling equipment and other beach toys are complimentary. P.O. Box 1299, Kailua-Kona, HI 96745. ☎ 800/367-5290 or 808/325-5555. www.konavillage.com. 125 units. Doubles $660–$1,475; extra person $245 adults (13 and older), $180 children 10–12, $135 children 5–9. AE, DC, MC, V. Map p 281.

★ **Luana Ola B&B Cottages** HONOKAA
These off-the-beaten-path, plantation-style, open-room cottages hearken back to the romantic 1940s. Furnished in rattan and wicker, each

> *African and Victorian decor combine with a tropical setting to give the Inn at Volcano a unique fairy tale feeling.*

> *Kona Village Resort's 82 spa-like oceanfront acres provide a perfect respite for weary souls.*

features a kitchenette and sleeps up to four. One unit has a spectacular ocean view; the ocean view from the other unit isn't as panoramic. The cottages are within walking distance to Honokaa town yet far enough away to feel the peace and quiet of this bucolic area. P.O. Box 1967, Honokaa, HI 96727. ☎ 800/357-7727 or 808/775-1150. www.island-hawaii.com. 2 units. Doubles $100–$125 with continental breakfast; extra person $15; 2-night minimum. MC, V. Map p 269.

★ kids **Macadamia Meadows Bed & Breakfast** WAIOHINU You'll find one of the Big Island's most welcoming B&Bs on an 8-acre working macadamia nut farm, in a great place for star-gazing, just 45 minutes from Volcanoes National Park. This is an excellent place for children; because the owner has children herself, the entire property is very kid-friendly. In addition to exploring the groves of mac-nut trees, kids can swim in the pool or play tennis. 94-6263 Kamaoa Rd., Waiohinu. Reservations: P.O. Box 756, Naalehu, HI 96772. ☎ 888/929-8118 or 808/929-8097. Fax 808/929-8097. www.macadamiameadows.com. 5 units. Doubles $119–$149 with continental breakfast; extra person $15 adult, $10 children under 18. AE, DISC, MC, V. Map p 281.

Manago Hotel CAPTAIN COOK This living relic is still operated by the third generation of the same friendly Japanese family that opened it in 1917. It offers clean accommodations and generous helpings of aloha at budget prices. The ultraspartan older rooms (with community bathrooms) are strictly for desperate budget travelers. The rooms with private bathrooms are still pretty sparse (no TV), but they're spotlessly clean and surrounded by Japanese gardens with a koi pond. The Japanese rooms have tatami mats to sleep on and *furo* (deep hot tubs) in each room. P.O. Box 145, Captain Cook, HI 96704. ☎ 808/323-2642. www.managohotel.com. 63 units. Doubles $33–$75; extra person $3. DISC, MC, V. Map p 281.

★★ **Mauna Kea Beach Hotel** MAUNA KEA RESORT The beach out front is divine, the landscaped grounds have a maturity seen nowhere else on this coast, and its loyal old-money guests keep returning to savor the relaxed clubby ambience, remote setting, world-class golf course, and old Hawaii ways. Recently renovated rooms are large and luxurious. This is the place to go to be pampered. 62-100 Mauna Kea Beach Dr., Kohala Coast, HI 96743. ☎ 866/977-4589 or 808/882-7222. www.maunakearesort.com. 310 units. Doubles $450–$1,000. AE, DC, MC, V. Map p 269.

★★ kids **Mauna Lani Bay Hotel & Bungalows** MAUNA LANI RESORT Come here to enjoy sandy beaches, lava tide pools, and gracious hospitality. Plush guest rooms, arranged to capture maximum ocean views, are outfitted with teak accents, and each has a lanai. Interior atrium gardens have pools in which endangered baby sea turtles are raised. A shoreline trail leads across the whole 3,200-acre resort. 68-1400 Mauna Lani Dr., Kohala Coast, HI 96743. ☎ 800/367-2323 or 808/885-6622. www.maunalani.com. 342 units. Doubles $445–$935. AE, DC, DISC, MC, V. Map p 269.

★ **Outrigger Keauhou Beach Resort** KEAUHOU Located on 10 acres, this resort has the perfect setting, on a large reef system (where sea turtles come ashore for a brief nap), and next door to one of Kona's best white-sand beaches, Kahuluu. The rooms are small (a family of four should get two rooms); the oceanview rooms are well worth the extra money. 78-6740 Alii Dr., Kailua-Kona, HI 96740. ☎ 800/OUTRIGGER (688-7444) or 808/322-3441. www.outrigger.com. 309 units. Doubles $249–$409; extra person $50. AE, DC, DISC, MC, V. Map p 281.

kids **Outrigger Royal Sea Cliff Resort** KAILUA-KONA Families will love these luxuriously appointed apartments and their affordable rates. The architecturally striking 5-story white buildings that make up this resort/condo complex, 2 miles from Kailua-Kona, are stepped back from the ocean for maximum views and privacy. There's no ocean swimming here, but there's a decent swimming beach about a mile away. 75-6040 Alii Dr., Kailua-Kona, HI 96740. ☎ 800/688-7444 or 808/329-8021. www.outrigger.com. 148 units. Doubles: $219–$259 studio, $249–$419 1-bedroom, $289–$549 2-bedroom. AE, DC, DISC, MC, V. Map p 281.

★★ **The Palms Cliff House Inn** HONOMU Perched on the side of a cliff a 15-minute drive from Hilo, this grand old Victorian-style inn is surrounded by manicured lawns and fuit and macadamia nut trees. Eight oversize suites, filled with antiques and equipped with DVD players, fireplaces, and private lanais, all overlook the ocean. Enjoy a gourmet breakfast on the wraparound lanai overlooking the rolling surf. P.O. Box 189, Honomu, 96728. ☎ 866/963-6076 or 808/963-6076. www.palmscliffhouse.com. 8 units. Doubles $250–$440 with gourmet breakfast. AE, DC, DISC, MC, V. Map p 271.

★ kids **Sheraton Keauhou Bay Resort and Spa** KEAUHOU The lobby and main dining room of this resort have incredible views of Keauhou Bay. Tucked in around the tropical gardens and splashing waterfalls, the mammoth freshwater pool includes its own small man-made beach, the island's largest water slide, bubbling whirlpool spas, and a children's play area. 78-128 Ehukai St., Kailua-Kona, HI 96740. ☎ 866/716-8109 or 808/930-4900. www.sheratonkeauhou.com. 522 units. Doubles $350–$460; extra person $60. AE, DC, DISC, MC, V. Map p 281.

★★ **Shipman House Bed & Breakfast** HILO Built in 1900, this home (on both the state and national registers of historic places) features plenty of old-world charm with 21st-century conveniences, including full bathrooms with all the amenities. All five guest bedrooms are large, with 10- to 12-foot ceilings and touches like heirloom furnishings and hand-woven lauhala mats. 131 Kaiulani St., Hilo, HI 96720. ☎ 800/627-8447 or 808/934-8002. www.hilo-hawaii.com. 5 units. Doubles $219–$250 with continental breakfast; extra person $25. AE, MC, V. Map p 271.

★★ **Silver Oaks Guest Ranch** KAILUA-KONA This guest ranch consists of two cottages spread over a 10-acre working ranch complete with friendly horses (no riding, just petting), the cutest Nigerian dwarf goats, chickens, and wild turkeys. The ranch sits at 1,300 feet, where the temperatures are mild year-round. The views are spectacular, some 40 miles of coastline from the ocean to Mauna Loa. Reservations: 75-1027 Henry St., Suite 310, Kailua-Kona, HI 96740. ☎ 877/325-2300 or 808/325-2000. www.silveroaksranch.com. 2 units. Doubles $200; extra person $15; 5-night minimum. MC, V. Map p 281.

★ **South Point Banyan Tree House** WAIOHINU Couples looking for an exotic place to nest should try this treehouse nestled inside a huge Chinese banyan tree. The cottage comes complete with see-through roof that lets the outside in, plus a comfy, just-for-two hot tub on the wraparound deck. Inside there's a queen-size bed and a kitchen with microwave and two-burner stove. At Hwy. 11 and Pinao St., Waiohinu. ☎ 715/302-8180. www.southpointbth.com. 1 unit. Doubles $185; 2-night minimum. No credit cards. Map p 281.

Uncle Billy's Hilo Bay Hotel HILO Uncle Billy's is one of the least expensive places to stay along Banyan Drive. The guest rooms are simple: bed, TV, phone, closet, and bathroom—that's about it. The walls seem paper thin, and it can get very noisy at night (you may want to bring ear plugs), but at these rates, you're still getting your money's worth. 87 Banyan Dr. (off Hwy. 19), Hilo, HI 96720. ☎ 800/367-5102 or 808/961-5818. www.unclebilly.com. 144 units. Doubles $104–$119; extra person $14. AE, DC, DISC, MC, V. Map p 271.

Uncle Billy's Kona Bay Hotel KAILUA-KONA An institution in Kona, Uncle Billy's is where visitors from the other islands stay. The rooms are old but comfortable and come with large lanais; most also have minifridges (request one at booking), and 16 are condo-style units with kitchenettes. This budget hotel is a good place to sleep, but don't expect new furniture or fancy soap in the bathroom. 75-5739 Alii Dr., Kailua-Kona, HI 96740. ☎ 800/367-5102 or 808/961-5818. www.unclebilly.com. 139 units. Doubles $119–$144; extra person $14. AE, DC, DISC, MC, V. Map p 281.

Volcano House VOLCANO This mountain lodge, which evolved out of a grass lean-to in 1865, is Hawaii's oldest visitor accommodation. It stands on the edge of Halemaumau's bubbling crater, and although the view of the crater is still an awesome sight, don't expect the Ritz here—rooms are very plain. The location is about all this place has going for it; stay elsewhere if you can't get a room facing the volcano. P.O. Box 53, Hawaii Volcanoes National Park, HI 96718. ☎ 808/967-7321. www.volcanohousehotel.com. 42 units. Doubles $100–$230; extra person $20. AE, DC, DISC, MC, V. Map p 273.

★★ **Waianuhea** HONOKAA This oasis of luxury and relaxation (on 7 beautifully landscaped acres) features five posh rooms with soaking tubs, gas or wood stoves, phones, and flatscreen LCD satellite TV. The sumptuous main room has highly polished wood floors, a rock fireplace, and custom Italian sofas. Nightly wine tastings with gourmet hors d'oeuvres, an outdoor hot tub, and a guest minikitchen stocked with a range of goodies add to the appeal. 45-3503 Kahana Dr. (P.O. Box 185), Honokaa, HI 96727. ☎ 888/775-2577 or 808/775-1118. www.waianuhea.com. 5 units. Doubles $195–$400 with gourmet breakfast. AE, MC, V. Map p 269.

★ **Waikoloa Beach Marriott Resort & Spa** WAIKOLOA BEACH RESORT This resort has always had one outstanding attribute: an excellent location on Anaehoomalu Bay. The gentle sloping beach has everything: swimming, snorkeling, diving, kayaking, windsurfing, and even

> *One of the Fairmont Orchid's elegant guest rooms.*

old royal fishponds. The property still isn't as posh as other luxury hotels along the Kohala Coast, but it also isn't nearly as expensive. Another plus: the 5,000-square-foot Mandara Spa. 69-275 Waikoloa Beach Dr., Waikoloa, HI 96738. ☎ 800/886-6789 or 808/886-6789. www.marriotthawaii.com. 555 units. Doubles $425–$600; extra person $40; daily resort fee $16. AE, DC, DISC, MC, V. Map p 269.

★★ **Waimea Garden Cottages** WAIMEA
These cozy Hawaiian cottages sit among rolling hills on pastoral ranch land, with a babbling stream and mountain views. One unit has the feel of an old English country cottage, with oak floors, a fireplace, and French doors opening onto a spacious brick patio. The other is a remodeled century-old Hawaiian wash house filled with antiques, with eucalyptus-wood floors and a full kitchen. Off Mamalahoa Hwy., 2 miles west of Waimea town center. Reservations c/o Hawaii's Best Bed & Breakfasts, P.O. Box 758, Volcano, HI 96785. ☎ 800/262-9912 or 808/263-3100. Fax 808/962-6360. www.bestbnb.com. 2 units. Doubles $170 with continental breakfast; extra person $20; 3-night minimum. No credit cards. Map p 269.

★★ **Waipio Wayside B&B Inn** HONOKAA
This restored Hamakua Sugar supervisor's home, built in 1938, sits nestled among fruit trees and tropical flowers. The comfortable house, done in old Hawaii style, features a sunny lanai with hammocks overlooking a yard lush with fruit trees. There are five vintage rooms to choose from: My favorite is the "Bird's-Eye" Room, with double doors that open onto the deck; I also love the Library Room, which has an ocean view, hundreds of books, and a skylight in the shower. P.O. Box 840, Honokaa, HI 96727. ☎ 800/833-8849 or 808/775-0275. www.waipiowayside.com. 5 units. Doubles $99–$190 with continental breakfast; extra person $25. MC, V. Map p 269.

Big Island Nightlife & Entertainment A to Z

Bars & Cocktail Lounges

Atrium Bar MAUNA LANI RESORT
Immensely talented in hula and song, members of the Lim family perform in the intimate setting of this bar. Mauna Lani Bay Hotel, 68-1400 Mauna Lani Dr. ☎ 808/885-6622. Map p 293.

Honu Bar MAUNA LANI RESORT
This popular nightspot at the Mauna Lani Bay Hotel is a chic place for live light jazz with dancing, fine wines, light suppers, and after-dinner drinks. Mauna Lani Bay Hotel, 68-1400 Mauna Lani Dr., ☎ 808/885-6622. Map p 293.

Hawaii Calls Restaurant & Lounge WAIKOLOA BEACH RESORT A bright new venue for local musicians, with live music nightly from 8:30 to 11:30pm. Waikoloa Beach Marriott 69-275 Waikoloa Beach Dr. ☎ 808/886-6789. Map p 293.

Luana Lounge MAUNA LANI RESORT
Enjoy a leisurely afternoon or evening here with your favorite tropical drink overlooking the ocean. The perfect place for a drink and nibble at sunset. Fairmont Orchid Hawaii, 1 N. Kaniku Dr. ☎ 808/885-2000. Map p 293.

Malolo Lounge WAIKOLOA BEACH RESORT
Sip a libation in this comfy lounge as you enjoy nightly live entertainment: Hawaiian music (5-8pm) and jazz (9pm-midnight). Hilton Waikoloa Beach, 69-425 Waikoloa Beach Dr. ☎ 808/886-1234. Map p 293.

Reef Lounge MAUNA KEA RESORT
This relaxing open-air lounge features live Hawaiian music and a hula dancer nightly. Hapuna Beach Prince Hotel, 62-100 Kaunaoa Dr. ☎ 808/880-1111. Map p 293.

Dancing & Live Music

Blue Dolphin Restaurant KAWAIHAE
This place is off the beaten path for visitors but well-known locally. Come for an eclectic mix of music (jazz, rock, swing, Hawaiian, even big-band) Wednesday through Saturday. 61-3616 Kawaihae Rd., Kawaihae. ☎ 808/882-7771. Map p 293.

> *The Friday night luau at Kona Village Resort offers great food and raucous entertainment.*

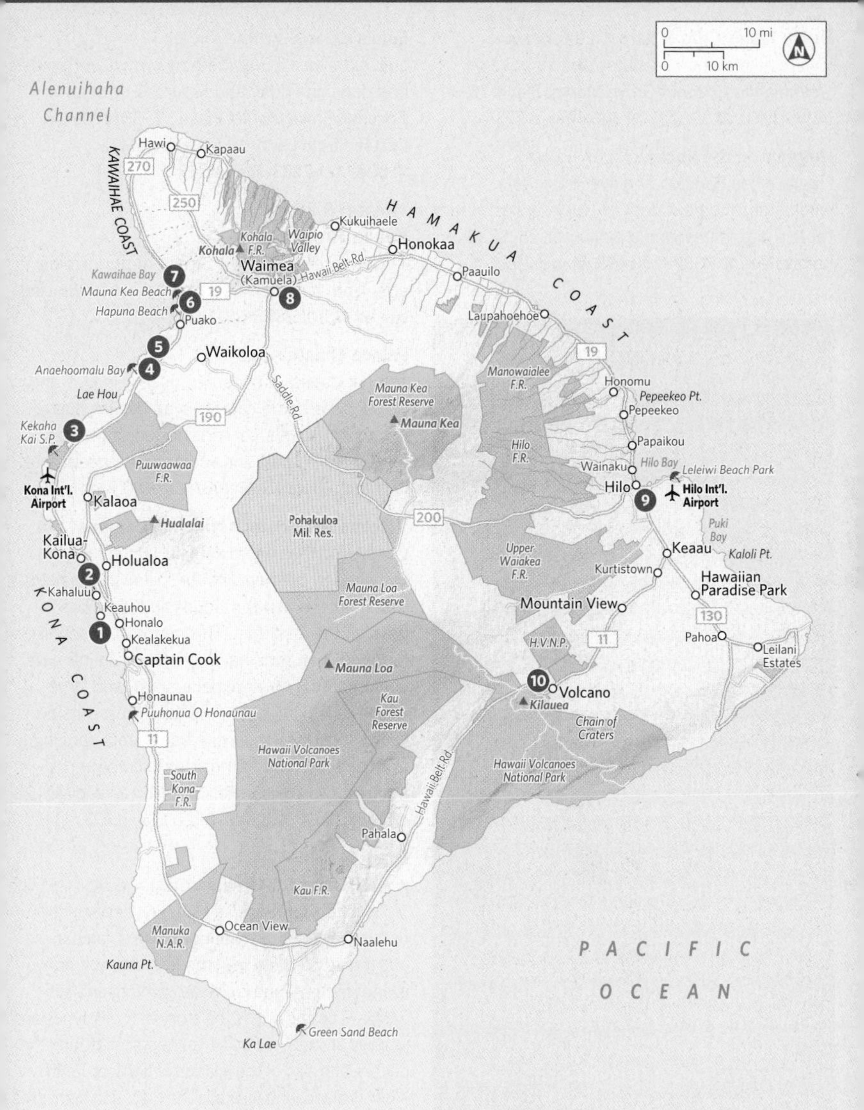

Big Island Nightlife & Entertainment

Atrium Bar **5**
Blue Dolphin Restaurant **7**
Durty Jake's Café & Bar **2**
Fairmont Orchid **5**
Hawaii Calls Restaurant & Lounge **6**
Honu Bar **5**
Huggo's on the Rocks **2**
Kahilu Theatre **8**
Kona Village Luau **3**
Luana Lounge **5**
Lulu's **2**
Malolo Lounge **4**
Palace Theater **9**
Reef Lounge **6**
Sheraton Keauhou Bay Resort & Spa **1**
Volcano Art Center's Niaulani Campus **10**

Durty Jake's Café & Bar KAILUA-KONA
Live rock 'n' roll on Saturday and karaoke on weeknights. Coconut Grove Market Place, 75-5819 Alii Dr. ☎ 808/329-7366. Map p 293.

Huggo's on the Rocks KAILUA-KONA
Huggo's has dancing and live music on weekends, and next door at Huggo's Restaurant there's jazz, blues, and a piano bar. 75-5828 Kahakai Rd. ☎ 808/329-1493. Map p 293.

Old-Style Hawaiian Entertainment

The plaintive drone of the conch shell pierces the air, calling all to assemble. A sizzling orange sun sinks slowly toward the cobalt waters of the Pacific. In the distance, the majestic mountain, Mauna Kea, reflects the waning sun's light with a fiery red that fades to a hazy purple and finally to an inky black as a voluptuous full moon dramatically rises over her shoulder.

It's **Twilight at Kalahuipua'a,** a monthly Hawaiian cultural celebration that includes storytelling, singing, and dancing on the oceanside, grassy lawn at **Mauna Lani Bay Resort** (☎ 808/885-6622). These full-moon events, created by Daniel Akaka, Jr., who is Mauna Lani Resort's director of cultural affairs, hark back to another time in Hawaii, when family and neighbors would gather to sing, dance, and "talk story."

Each month guests, ranging from the ultra-well-known in the world of Hawaiian entertainment to the virtually unknown local *kupuna* (elders), gather to perpetuate the traditional folk art of storytelling, with plenty of music and dance thrown in.

Twilight at Kalahuipua'a, always set on a Saturday closest to the full moon, really gets underway at least an hour before the 5:30pm start, when people from across the island and guests staying at the hotel begin arriving. They carry picnic baskets, mats, coolers, babies, and cameras. A sort of oceanside, premusic tailgate party takes place with *kamaaina* (native-born) families sharing their plate lunches, sushi, and beverages with visitors, who have catered lunches, packaged sandwiches, and taro chips, in a truly old-fashioned demonstration of aloha.

Lulu's KAILUA-KONA
Lulu's draws a 20-something crowd, with music and dancing Friday and Saturday until 1am. Coconut Grove Market Place, 75-5819 Alii Dr., upstairs from Durty Jake's (see p 292). ☎ 808/321-2633. Map p 293.

Theater & Shows

Kahilu Theatre WAIMEA
This theater features a variety of performing arts, from hula to music to drama. 67-1186 Lindsey Rd. ☎ 808/885-6017. Map p 293.

Palace Theater HILO
This neoclassical wonder first opened in 1925 and has reopened for film festivals, art movies, hula, community events, concerts (including the Slack Key Guitar Festival), and all manner of special entertainment. 38 Haili St. ☎ 808/934-7010. Map p 293.

Volcano Art Center's Niaulani Campus VOLCANO The name Niaulani, which means "brushed by the heavens" or "billowing heavens," describes the way the clouds and fog move through the rainforest. This new 4,400-square-foot administration building houses an intimate Great Room with a fireplace, sofas, and large windows looking out to the fern forest outside. Check local listings for the free events, ranging from cultural talks to music and dance performances. Old Volcano Rd. (btw. MM 27 and MM 28 off Hwy. 11). ☎ 908/967-8222. Map p 293.

Luau

★★ kids **Fairmont Orchid** KOHALA COAST
"A Gathering of Kings," a luau/Polynesian show, features a series of traditional Polynesian dance and music, blended with modern choreography, island rhythms, and high-tech lighting and set design. The show tells the story of the Polynesians' journey across the Pacific to Hawaii, featuring the culture and arts of the islands of Samoa, Tahiti, New Zealand, and Hawaii. The luau also highlights the cuisine of these Pacific islands. Shows are Tuesday and Saturday at 5pm. Fairmont Orchid, 1 North Kohala Dr., Kohala Coast. ☎ 808/329-8111. www.islandbreezeluau.com. AE, MC, V. Tickets $99 adults, $65 children 6–12, children 5 and under free. Map p 293.

★★★ kids **Kona Village Luau** KONA
The longest continuously running luau on the island is still the best—a combination of an authentic Polynesian venue with impressive entertainment and the spirit of old Hawaii. The feast begins with

a ceremony in a sandy kiawe grove, where the pig is unearthed from its rock-heated underground oven. In the open-air dining room, next to prehistoric lagoons and tropical gardens, you'll sample a Polynesian buffet: the shredded kalua pork, *poisson cru,* poi, laulau (butterfish, seasoned pork, and taro leaves cooked in ti leaves), lomi salmon, ahi poke, coconut pudding, taro chips, steamed breadfruit, and more. The Polynesian revue, a fast-moving, mesmerizing tour of South Pacific cultures, manages—miraculously—to avoid being clichéd or corny. The luau takes place Wednesday and Friday at 5pm. **In Kona Village Resort. ☎ 808/325-5555. www.konavillage.com. AE, DC, MC, V. Reservations required. Tickets $98 adults, $67 children 6–12, $40 children 2–5. Map p 293.**

Sheraton Keauhou Bay Resort & Spa KONA
The luau and entertainment show, "Firenesia," is oceanside each Monday evening overlooking Keauhou Bay. The show weaves dances, music, and chants into a story about a young Polynesian looking for the gift of fire. Dinner at Firenesia features Hawaiian lu'au favorites such as kalua pork, poi, and lomi salmon coupled with green salads, fresh fruit, teriyaki New York strip loin, mahimahi, and desserts. Performed on Monday, Wednesday, and Friday at 6pm. **Sheraton Keauhou Bay Resort, 78-128 Ehukai St. ☎ 808/930-4828. www.sheratonkeauhou.com. AE, MC, V. Tickets $80–$95 adults, $50–$60 children 6–12, children 5 and under free. Map p 293.**

> *Hilo's classic art-deco Palace Theater was built in 1925 and is now home to festivals, concerts, and special events.*

An Evening Under the Stars

This is one of those unique experiences that you will remember long after your tan has faded. Perched on the vantage point of 3,200 feet on the slopes of the Kohala Mountains, **"An Evening at Kahua Ranch"** is a night under the stars, with wonderful food, great entertainment, fun activities, and storytelling around a traditional campfire.

The evening begins when you are picked up at your hotel. As you relax in the air-conditioned van, enjoying the scenic coastline, your guide spins stories about this historic area. Arriving at the 8,500-acre working cattle ranch, you are personally greeted by the ranch owner, John Richards. When the sun starts to sink into the Pacific, beer, wine, and soft drinks are served as John talks about how cattle ranching came to Hawaii and how they manage the ranch in the 21st-century.

A traditional ranch-style barbecue of sirloin steak, chicken, locally grown potatoes, Waimea corn on the cob, baked beans, Big Island green salad, Kona coffee, and dessert is served shortly after sunset.

After dinner the fun and games begin: Local entertainers pull out guitars, line dancing gets going on the dance floor, and several *paniolo* (cowboy) activities take place. You can choose from learning how to rope, playing a game of horseshoes, or trying your hand at branding (a cedar shingle—yours to take home as a souvenir).

When the stars come out, there's an 8-inch telescope for gazing into the moon or searching for distant planets. A campfire gets started, and the ranch's cowboys come over and start telling stories as you toast marshmallows for old-fashioned s'mores over a crackling campfire.

The entire experience from transportation to dinner and entertainment is only $125 per person. For more information call ☎ 808/987-2108 (www.evening-at-kahua.com).

SIMMER

6 Maui

My 14 Favorite Maui Moments

To experience the true magic of Maui, just step outside and let the spirit of the Valley Isle whisper her secrets to you in the glow of a sunrise, the reflection of the moon on the inky ocean, the perfume of flowers dancing in the air, or the murmur of a tropical breeze through a bamboo forest. You'll be enchanted forever.

> PREVIOUS PAGE *Windsurfers love the powerful winter breezes and smooth surf at Hookipa Beach.* THIS PAGE *Watching the sun rise atop Haleakala.*

❶ **Watching windsurfers ride the waves at Hookipa.** This windsurfing mecca draws daredevils from around the globe to ride, sail, pirouette, and flip over the waves. It's the best free show in town. See p 356.

❷ **Smelling the sweet scent of ginger waft through the air on the windy road to Hana.** At every twist in the road you are greeted by exotic tropical blossoms, thundering waterfalls, breathtaking vistas, and a glimpse at what Maui looked like before it was "discovered." See p 342.

❸ **Walking the shoreline trail at Waianapanapa.** Wander back in time: past lava cliffs, a tropical forest, an ancient *heiau* (temple), mysterious caves, an exploding blowhole, native Hawaiian plants, and the ever-changing sea. See p 359.

❹ **Taking a dip in the Seven Sacred Pools.** There's really more than seven of these fern-shrouded waterfall pools, which spill seaward at Oheo Gulch, on the rain-shrouded eastern flanks of Haleakala. See p 349, ❿.

❺ **Greeting the rising sun from atop Haleakala.** Bundle up and drive up the 37 miles from sea level to 10,000 feet to witness the birth of yet another day. Breathing in the rarefied air and

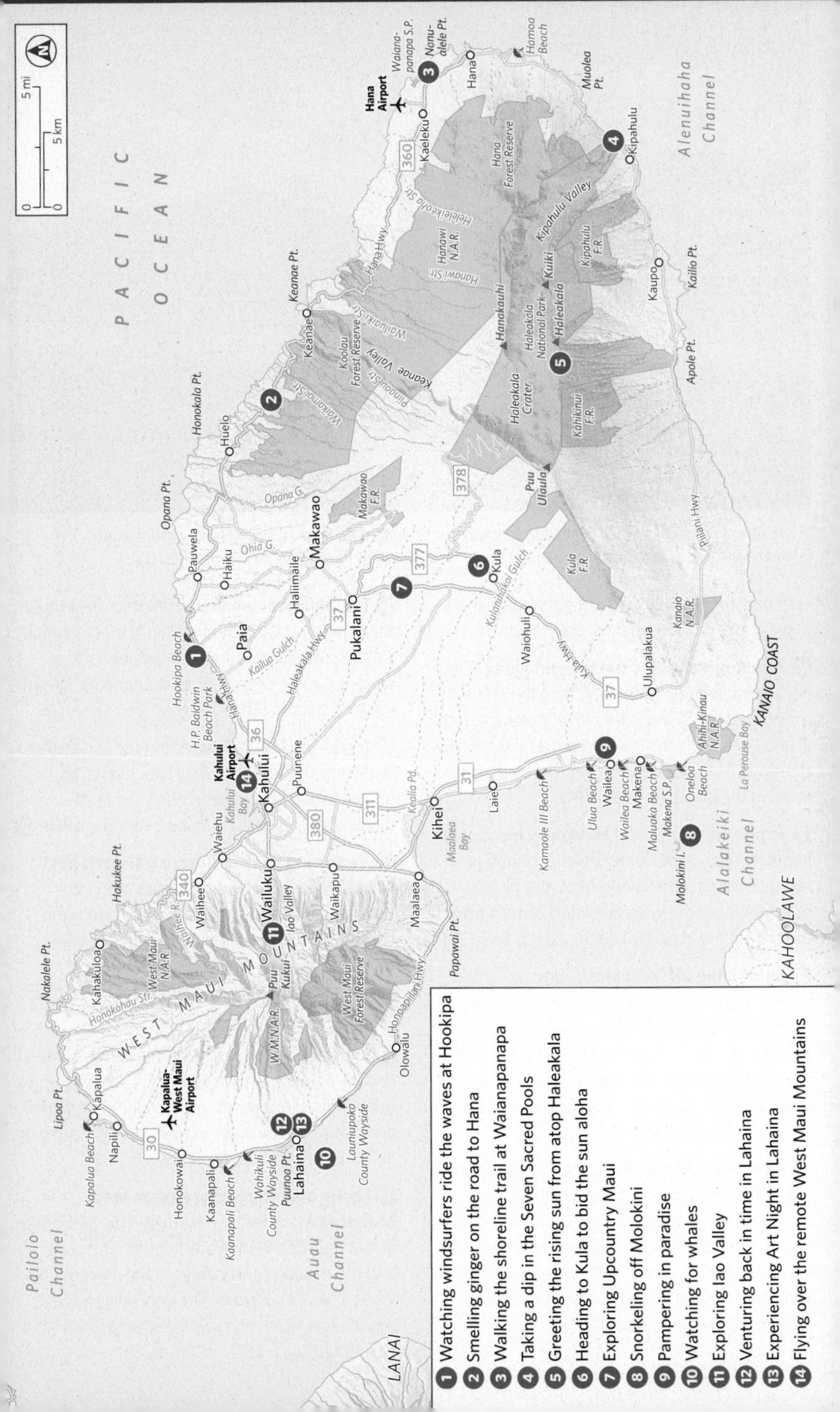

1. Watching windsurfers ride the waves at Hookipa
2. Smelling ginger on the road to Hana
3. Walking the shoreline trail at Waianapanapa
4. Taking a dip in the Seven Sacred Pools
5. Greeting the rising sun from atop Haleakala
6. Heading to Kula to bid the sun aloha
7. Exploring Upcountry Maui
8. Snorkeling off Molokini
9. Pampering in paradise
10. Watching for whales
11. Exploring Iao Valley
12. Venturing back in time in Lahaina
13. Experiencing Art Night in Lahaina
14. Flying over the remote West Maui Mountains

> THIS PAGE *From December to March, you may spot humpbacks breaching and fluking from shore.*
> OPPOSITE PAGE *Take advantage of the opportunity to swim the sacred waters of Oheo Gulch.*

watching the first rays of light streak across the sky is a mystical experience. See p 352.

❻ **Heading to Kula to bid the sun aloha.** The perfect vantage point for watching the sun set over the entire island is this town perched on the side of Haleakala, with vistas across the isthmus, the West Maui Mountains, and Molokai and Lanai in the distance. See p 340.

❼ **Exploring a different Hawaii—Upcountry Maui.** On the slopes of Haleakala, cowboys, farmers, ranchers, and other country people make their homes in serene, neighborly worlds away from the bustling beach resorts. See p 340.

❽ **Snorkeling off Molokini.** Calm, protected waters in the islet's crater, plus an abundance of marine life, make Molokini one of Hawaii's best places to swim with the fishes. Don a mask and snorkel and paddle with turtles, watch clouds of butterflyfish flitter past, and search for tiny damselfish in the coral. See p 374.

❾ **Pampering in paradise.** Maui's spas have raised the art of relaxation and healing to a new level, where you can hear the sound of the ocean, smell the salt air, and feel the caress of the warm breeze, which will soothe out the kinks and send you straight to heaven. See "Relax, Breathe Deep & Say Spaaah," p 325.

❿ **Watching for whales.** From mid-December through the end of March, Maui's most famous visitors, the 50-plus-foot-long humpback whales, can be seen from shore jumping, breaching, and slapping their pectoral fins. See p 376.

⓫ **Exploring Iao Valley.** When the sun strikes Iao Valley in the West Maui Mountains, an almost ethereal light sends rays out in all directions. This really may be Eden. See p 336, ❷.

⓬ **Venturing back in time in a historic port town.** In the 1800s, whalers swarmed into Lahaina, and missionaries fought to stem the spread of their sinful influence. It was a wild time, and this tiny town was an exciting place. Rediscover those wild whaling days for yourself. See p 328.

⓭ **Experiencing Art Night in Lahaina.** Under a canopy of stars, every Friday the town's galleries open their doors, serve pupu and refreshments, and hope you'll wander in to see what's going on in Maui's creative community. See p 328.

⓮ **Flying over the remote West Maui Mountains.** Glide low over razor-thin cliffs, then flutter past sparkling waterfalls and descend into the canyons and valleys of the inaccessible West Maui Mountains. The only way to see this inaccessible and prehistoric area is via helicopter. See p 367.

The Best of Maui in 3 days

Maui may be an island, but it's a big one (48 miles by 26 miles), the second largest of the Hawaiian Islands. If you have only 3 days, see the best Maui has to offer: a beach, the scenic Hana Highway, and the view from the top of the 10,000-foot dormant volcano, Haleakala. Try to base yourself in conveniently located Lahaina-Kaanapali (for hotel recommendations see p 399), which will allow you to hit the island's highlights with a minimum of driving.

START Lahaina/Kaanapali. **FINISH** Paia. **TRIP LENGTH** 3 days and 146 miles.

Day 1

To get to Kapalua Beach from Lahaina/ Kaanapali, take Hwy. 30 north to Kapalua. Go left at the Kapalua Resort sign on Office Rd., and follow the road to the end. Turn left on Honoapiilai Rd. and right (toward the ocean) at the beach access sign next door to the Napili Kai condominium.

❶ ★★★ **Kapalua Beach.** Check in to your hotel, then head for **Kapalua Beach** (p 358). Don't overdo the sun on your first day. Bring plenty of water, sunscreen, and a hat. The adventurous might want to rent snorkel equipment; the lazy might want a flotation device to just relax in the warm water.

Retrace your route back to Hwy. 30 and turn right, continuing into Lahaina town.

② **Honolua Store.** For a quick sandwich or a cold drink, I love this old-fashioned country general store, with surprisingly low prices. 502 Office Rd. just after the entrance to the Ritz Carlton Kapalua. ☎ 808/669-6128. $.

❸ ★★★ **Lahaina.** After an hour or two at the beach, spend a couple of hours walking the historic old town, which at one time was the

> *Kapalua Beach's calm surf and pristine sand make it a perfect destination for families with kids and swimmers of all abilities.*

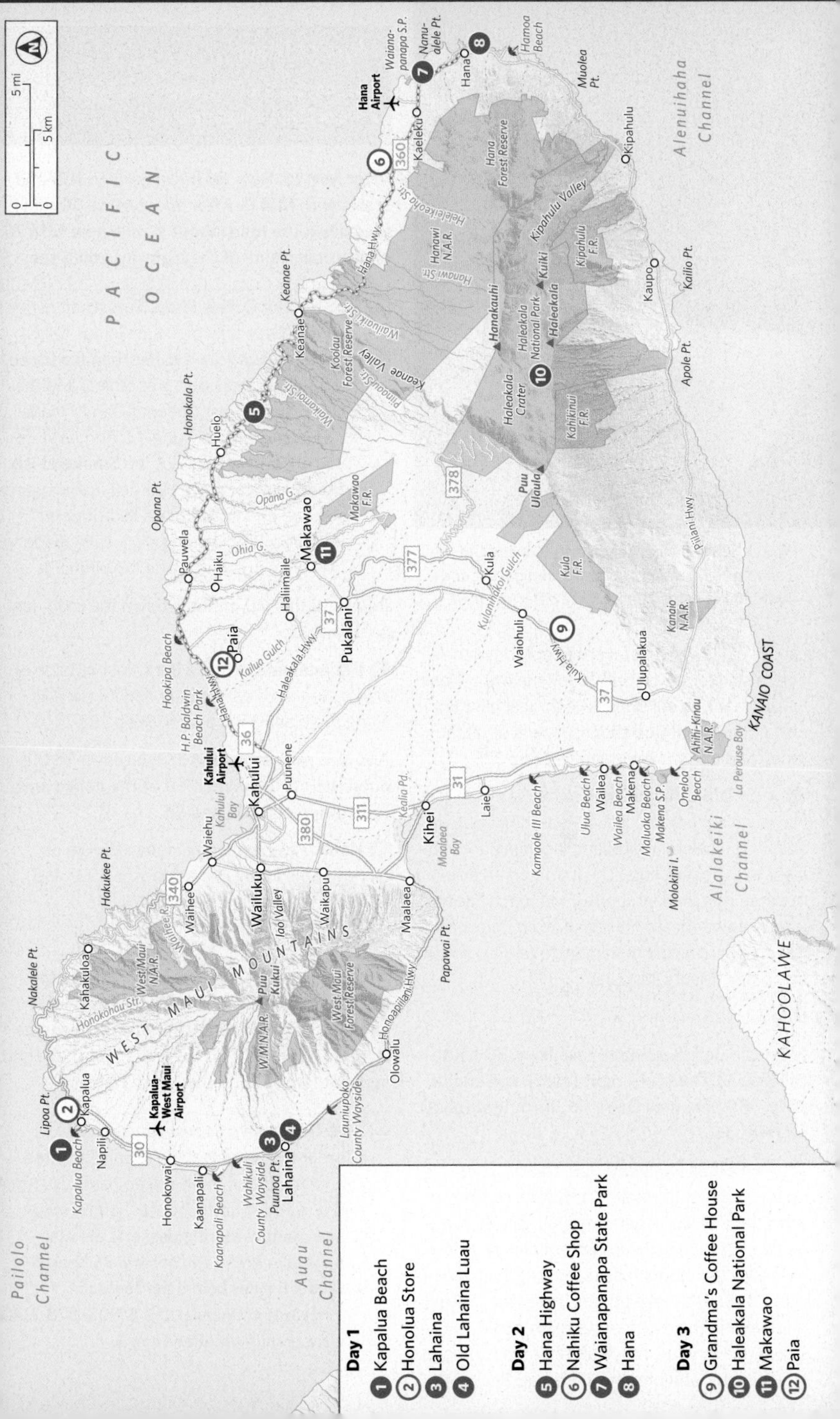
Day 1
1 Kapalua Beach
2 Honolua Store
3 Lahaina
4 Old Lahaina Luau
Day 2
5 Hana Highway
6 Nahiku Coffee Shop
7 Waianapanapa State Park
8 Hana
Day 3
9 Grandma's Coffee House
10 Haleakala National Park
11 Makawao
12 Paia
P A C I F I C
O C E A N
0 5 mi
0 5 km
Pailolo Channel
Auau Channel
Alalakeiki Channel
Alenuihaha Channel
KAHOOLAWE
KANAIO COAST
WEST MAUI MOUNTAINS
Nakalele Pt.
Lipoa Pt.
Kapalua Beach
Kapalua
Napili
Honokowai
Kaanapali
Kaanapali Beach
Wahikuli County Wayside
Puamoa Pt.
Lahaina
Launiupoko County Wayside
Olowalu
Honoapiilani Hwy.
Kapalua-West Maui Airport
Kahakuloa
Honokohau Str.
West Maui N.A.R.
W.M.N.A.R.
Puu Kukui
West Maui Forest Reserve
Papawai Pt.
Maalaea
Waikapu
Iao Valley
Wailuku
Waihee
Waihee R.
Hakukee Pt.
Waiehu
Kahului Bay
Kahului
Kahului Airport
Puunene
Kihei
Maalaea Bay
Kealia Pd.
Laie
Kamaole III Beach
Ulua Beach
Wailea
Wailea Beach
Makena
Maluaka Beach
Makena S.P.
Molokini I.
Oneloa Beach
La Perouse Bay
Ahihi-Kinau N.A.R.
H.P. Baldwin Beach Park
Hookipa Beach
Paia
Kailua Gulch
Hana Hwy.
Haleakala Hwy.
Pukalani
Haliimaile
Makawao
Makawao F.R.
Haiku
Pauwela
Ohia G.
Opana Pt.
Opana G.
Huelo
Honokala Pt.
Waikamoi Str.
Keanae Valley
Koolau Forest Reserve
Piinaau Str.
Keanae
Keanae Pt.
Wailuaiki Str.
Hanawi Str.
Hanawi N.A.R.
Heleleikeoha Str.
Hana Forest Reserve
Kaeleku
Hana Airport
Waianapanapa S.P.
Nanualele Pt.
Hana
Hamoa Beach
Muolea Pt.
Kipahulu
Kipahulu Valley
Kipahulu F.R.
Kuiki
Haleakala
Hanakauhi
Haleakala National Park
Haleakala Crater
Kahikinui F.R.
Puu Ulaula
Kaupo
Kailio Pt.
Apole Pt.
Piilani Hwy.
Kula
Kula F.R.
Kulaniihakoi Gulch
Waiohuli
Kula Hwy.
Ulupalakua
Kanaio N.A.R.
30
340
380
311
31
36
37
377
378
360

> *Kick it Hawaiian and Tahitian style at the Old Lahaina Luau, which offers a roast pig feast and ancient and modern hula dance entertainment.*

capital of Hawaii, the favorite spot for whalers and missionaries as well. Today the oceanfront village features not only its historical past but also unique boutique shops, dozens of restaurants, and options for nightlife. See p 328.

4 ★★★ **Old Lahaina Luau.** Immerse yourself in Hawaiian culture at this luau featuring Tahitian and Hawaiian entertainment, including both ancient and modern hula. The food, served from an open-air thatched structure, is as much Pacific Rim as authentically Hawaiian, from imu-roasted Kalua pork to baked mahimahi to teriyaki sirloin steak. See "Maui's Best Luau," p 397.

Day 2

From Lahaina/Kaanapali take Hwy. 30 south to Hwy. 380 and turn right (east). In Kahului, Hwy. 380 becomes Dairy Rd. Turn right (east) on Hwy. 36.

5 ★★★ **Hana Highway.** You'll likely wake up early on your first day in Hawaii, so take advantage of it and get out as quickly as you can and onto the scenic Hana Highway. Allow at least 3 to 5 hours for the journey. Pull over often, get out to take photos, smell the flowers, and jump in the mountain-stream pools. Wave to everyone, move off the road for those speeding by, and breathe in Hawaii. See p 342.

More of Maui

See chapter 3 for my suggested 1- and 2-week Maui itineraries.

After MM 16, Hwy. 36 becmes Hwy. 360 and starts with MM 0. After about 60 to 90 minutes down the road, about ½ mile past MM 28 on the ocean side of the highway, you'll see:

6 **Nahiku Coffee Shop.** This small coffee shop sells locally made, delicious baked goods, Maui-grown coffee, banana bread, organic tropical-fruit smoothies, and the Original and Best Coconut Candy made by Hana character Jungle Johnny. While you are here, check out the **Smoked Fish Stand,** a great place to stock up on superb smoked and grilled fish. Next door is the **Ti Gallery,** which sells locally made Hawaiian arts and crafts. No phone. $.

Allow another 20 minutes down the road, just past MM 32:

7 **Waianapanapa State Park.** Just outside of Hana, stop at this state park and take a hike along the black-sand beach. See p 363.

About ½ mile after MM 33, you come to the outskirts of Hana. Veer left at the police and fire station onto Ua Kea Rd.

8 **Hana.** After exploring Hana, splurge on dinner at the Hotel Hana-Maui (p 392) and spend the night here. See p 346.

Day 3

Allow at least 2 hours to get from Hana to the top of Haleakala. From Hana head west on Hwy. 31, which after Ulupalakua becomes Hwy. 37. Turn right on Hwy. 377 and then right again at Hwy. 378 to the top of Haleakala.

9 **Grandma's Coffee House.** I always order the homegrown Haleakala coffee and one of the fresh-baked pastries at this tiny wooden coffeehouse. Sandwiches and mouthwatering desserts are also available. At the end of Hwy. 37, Keokea (about 6 miles before the Tedeschi Vineyards in Ulupalakua). ☎ 808/878-2140 www.grandmascoffee.com. $.

> *Scale a 10,000-foot dormant volcano and peek into the crater at Haleakala National Park.*

From Grandma's Coffee House, continue on Hwy. 37. Turn right on Hwy. 377 and then right again on Hwy. 378 to the top of Haleakala.

10 ★★★ **Haleakala National Park.** Leave Hana early and drive around the Kaupo side of Haleakala and then up the 10,000-foot (dormant) volcano. Athough you won't have time on this trip to hike in the crater, spend an hour wandering around. See p 352.

Retrace back down Hwy. 378, then turn right to Hwy. 377 and right again on Hwy. 37. At the light turn right on Makawao Ave., and drive into the town of Makawao. To get to Paia from Makawao, head downhill on Baldwin Ave., which ends in Paia.

11 **Makawao.** Spend some time touring this old cowboy town. See p 318, 11.

12 **Paia.** Plan a sunset dinner here before heading back to the airport and vowing to return and stay longer next time. My top dining picks start on p 388.

From Hwy. 36 in Paia, drive to Kahului, turning right on Dairy Rd. and continuing on to Keolani Place and the airport.

What's in a Name? A Number!

Hawaii residents know the highways by their Hawaiian names; very few know the highway numbers. We've included both the highway name and the highway number on our maps, but to save space in this chapter we refer to the number when giving you directions. Below is a quick reference to the names and numbers of Maui's highways:

Hwy. 30 Honoapiilani Highway

Hwy. 31 Piilani Highway

Hwy. 36 Hana Highway

Hwy. 37 Haleakala & the Kula Highway

Hwy. 311 Mokulele Highway

Hwy. 360 Hana Highway

Hwy. 377 Haleakala Highway

Hwy. 378 Haleakala Highway

Hwy. 380 Kuihelani Highway

Maui with Kids

The number-one rule of touring Maui with kids: *Don't plan too much,* especially with young children, who will be fighting jet lag and trying to get adjusted to a new bed, and might be excited to the point of exhaustion. The 7-day itinerary below is a guide to the various family-friendly activities available on Maui. I'd suggest staying in South Maui (Kihei or Wailea) for the first 2 nights, then move to West Maui (Lahaina or Kaanapali) for the next 2 nights, and then Hana for your last 2 nights.

> *Meet some Maui locals—the green sea turtles, that is—at Maui Ocean Center's popular turtle lagoon.*

START Kihei/Wailea. **FINISH** Iao Valley.
TRIP LENGTH 7 days and 295 miles.

Day 1

1 Kihei/Wailea. Enjoy a lazy day at the beach at **Wailea** (p 359), fronting the Four Seasons and the Grand Wailea resorts, or at the swimming pool at your hotel. Plan an early dinner. My pick of family-friendly eateries in Kihei is either **Shaka Sandwich and Pizza** (p 396) or **Stella Blues Cafe** (p 396). Get to bed early.

Day 2

Allow 1½ to 2 hours from South Maui to the summit. North on Hwy. 31 to Hwy. 311, right on Hwy. 36, and right on Hwy. 37 to Hwy. 377, to Hwy. 378.

2 ★★★ Haleakala. Because of the time difference, your family will likely be up early, so take advantage of it and head up to the 10,000-foot (dormant) volcano **Haleakala.** Depending on the age of your children, you can either **hike in the crater** (p 360), **speed down the mountain on a bicycle** (p 366), or just wander about the park. See p 352.

3 **Kula Lodge.** Have breakfast here on the way either to or from Haleakala. See p 394.

From the summit, retrace Hwy. 378 to Hwy. 377, to Hwy. 37, then turn left (downhill) onto Omaopio Rd. Look for the sign on the left about 2 miles down.

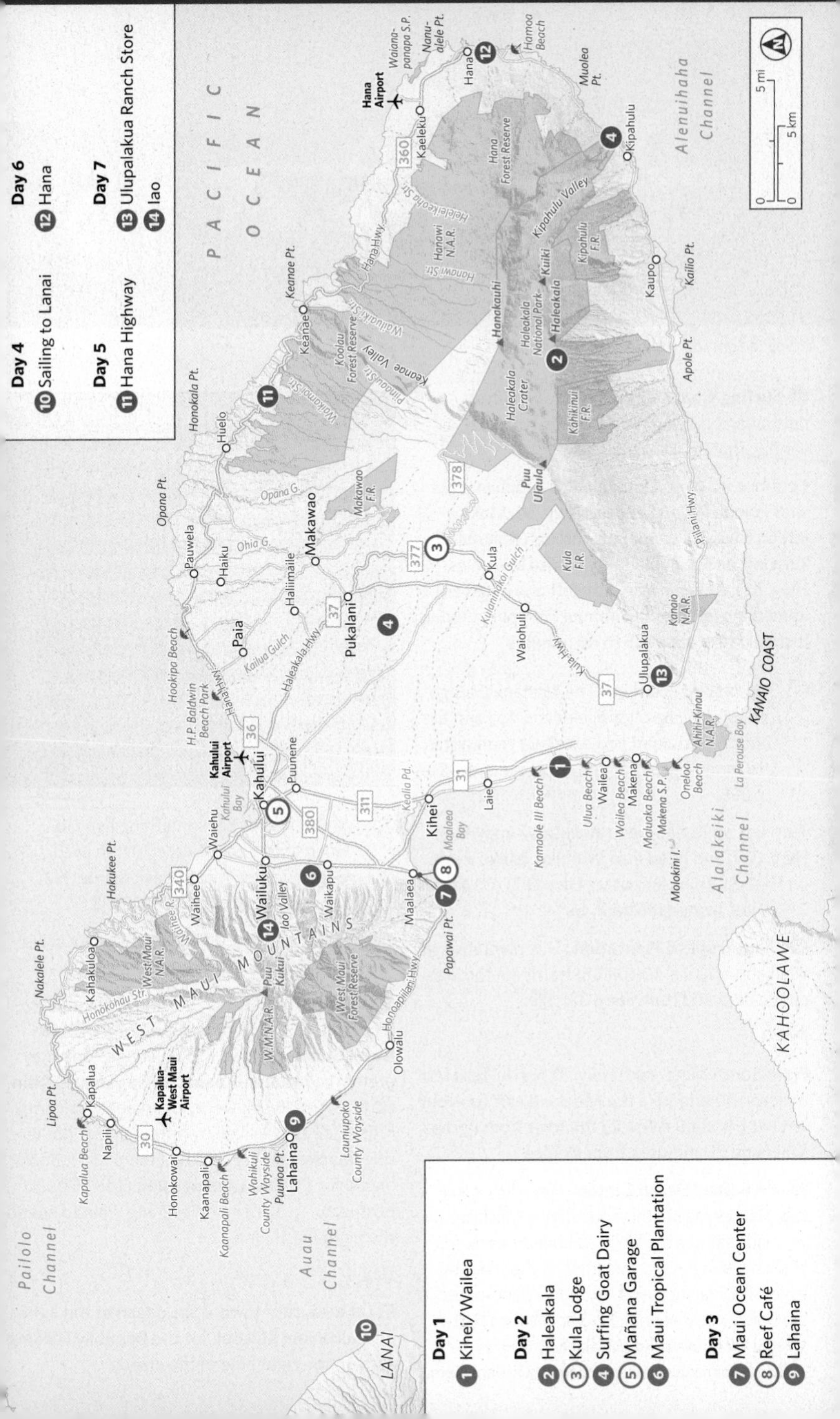
Day 1
1 Kihei/Wailea
Day 2
2 Haleakala
3 Kula Lodge
4 Surfing Goat Dairy
5 Mañana Garage
6 Maui Tropical Plantation
Day 3
7 Maui Ocean Center
8 Reef Café
9 Lahaina
Day 4
10 Sailing to Lanai
Day 5
11 Hana Highway
Day 6
12 Hana
Day 7
13 Ulupalakua Ranch Store
14 Iao
PACIFIC OCEAN
Pailolo Channel
Auau Channel
Alalakeiki Channel
Alenuihaha Channel
LANAI
KAHOOLAWE
WEST MAUI MOUNTAINS
KANAIO COAST
Kahului Airport
Kapalua-West Maui Airport
Hana Airport
Lahaina
Kahului
Wailuku
Kihei
Paia
Pukalani
Makawao
Kula
Hana
Haleakala National Park
Haleakala Crater
Keanae
Kaupo
Kipahulu
Maalaea
Wailea
Makena
Ulupalakua
Kapalua
Napili
Kaanapali
Honokowai
Olowalu
5 mi
5 km

> Sail to Lanai for a snorkeling or hiking tour.

❹ **Surfing Goat Dairy.** The kids will love petting and playing with the kids (the goat variety, that is). See p 323, ❸.

Continue down on Omaopio Rd., which merges with Pulehu Rd. and ends at Hwy. 36. Make a left on Hwy. 36, continuing through Kahului. Turn left on Kaahumanu Ave. (also known as Hwy. 32). At Lono Ave., turn left and make an immediate left into the Kahuui Shopping Center. It should take about 35 to 45 minutes.

⑤ **Mañana Garage.** The Mañana Garage, in Kahului, has "garage decor" to keep the kids entertained and excellent margaritas to remind you that you're on vacation. See p 395.

Turn left on Kaahumanu Ave. (also known as Hwy. 32), and head into Wailuku. Make a left on High St. (also known as Hwy. 30). Go about 2½ miles, just past MM 2, to:

❻ **Maui Tropical Plantation.** This plantation in Waikapu offers a 40-minute tram ride through exotic flora and fruit. See p 322, ❷.

Day 3

From South Maui, take Hwy. 31 north. Turn left on Hwy. 30 and take the Maalaea exit (on your left) at the sign. Allow 15 minutes from north Kihei and 30 minutes from Wailea.

❼ ★★★ **Maui Ocean Center.** After a lazy breakfast, wander over to this aquarium in Maalaea so your kids can see the fabulous underwater world of sharks, stingrays, and starfish, without having to get wet. Plan to spend the morning immersed in the 5-acre oceanarium. ⏱ 2–3 hr. Maalaea Harbor Village, 192 Maalaea Rd., Maalaea. ☎ 808/270-7000. www.mauioceancenter.com. Daily 9am–5pm.

A Great Way to Spend a Rainy Day

If the weather doesn't cooperate with your vacation plans, take the kids to the **Art School at Kapalua** (☎ 808/665-0007; www.kapaluamaui.com), located in a charming 1920s plantation building that was part of an old cannery operation. Local and visiting instructors lead people of all ages and skill levels in creative endeavors of all forms, including photography, figure drawing, ceramics, landscape painting, painting on silk, and the performing arts (ballet, yoga, creative movement, Pilates). Classes are inexpensive. Call the school to see what's scheduled.

⑧ **Reef Café.** Eat something fishy for lunch at this cafe located in the Maui Ocean Center. Maui Ocean Center, 192 Maalaea Rd. ☎ 808/270-7000. $.

Head north on Hwy. 30 to Lahaina. The drive takes about 20 to 30 minutes.

❾ **Lahaina.** Next stop: Take the kids underwater in a Jules Verne–type submarine with **Atlantis Submarines** (p 375). Younger kids may prefer the **Lahaina-Kaanapali Sugarcane Train** (☎ 808/667-6851, www.sugarcanetrain.com). Kids of all ages will enjoy hitting one of the terrific **beaches** on West Maui (see p 356). Book ahead for the **Old Lahaina Luau** (see "Maui's Best Luau," p 397) in the evening. Plan to spend the night in Lahaina.

Day 4

In Lahaina, turn toward the ocean at the light on Dickenson St. Look for the Republic Parking sign on the right side of the street.

10 ★★★ **Sailing to Lanai. Trilogy** (p 372) is the best sailing/snorkeling trip in Hawaii, so don't miss it. In the afternoon, wander around Lahaina (p 328). In the evening, kids can search the skies with a computer-driven telescope with the **Star Searches** program at the Hyatt Regency Maui Kaanapali (☎ 800/233-1234 or 808/661-1234; www.maui.hyatt.com).

Day 5

Go south on Hwy. 30, then right on Hwy. 380, and right again on Hwy. 36 to Hana.

11 ★★★ **Hana Highway.** Pack a lunch and spend the entire day driving the unforgettable Hana Highway. Spend 2 nights in Hana. See p 342.

Day 6

12 ★★★ **Hana.** You'll have no trouble filling up a whole day in Hana. In particular I recommend an early-morning hike along the black sands of **Waianapanapa State Park** (p 346, 2) and a picnic lunch at **Oheo Gulch** (p 349, 10). Splurge on dinner and eat in the dining room at the **Hotel Hana-Maui** (p 392). See p 346.

Continue past Hana on Hwy. 31 to Ulupalakua; allow 45 to 60 minutes driving time.

Day 7

13 **Ulupalakua Ranch Store.** Let the kids stretch their legs and grab lunch at the small deli inside this eclectic general store. See p 341, 4.

Go north on Hwy. 37 and left on Hwy. 36 through Kahului and Wailuku. Continue straight at light at Main St./Hwy. 30, and follow Iao Valley Rd. to the end. The drive will take 45 to 60 minutes.

14 **Iao.** If you have some time, I'd recommend spending the afternoon at the **Hawaii Nature Center** (875 Iao Valley Rd. ☎ 808/244-6500; www.hawaiinaturecenter.org), which has some 30 interactive exhibits (adults $6; children 12 and under $4). Don't miss the guided Rainforest Walk through **Iao Valley State Park** (p 336, 2), ($30 adult, $20 kids 12 and under).

Family-Friendly Events

Your trip may be a little more enjoyable with the added attraction of attending a celebration, festival, or party on Maui. Check out the following events:

Chinese New Year, Lahaina. Lahaina rolls out the red carpet with a traditional lion dance, accompanied by fireworks, food booths, and a host of activities. January or February. Information: ☎ 888/310-1117.

Whale Day Celebration, Kalama Park, Kihei. In early to mid-February, this daylong celebration features a parade of whales, entertainment, a crafts fair, games, and food. Information: ☎ 808/249-8811; www.visitmaui.com.

Ocean Arts Festival, Lahaina. Kids will love this mid-March event with marine-related activities, games, and a touch-pool exhibit for children. Information: ☎ 888/310-1117; www.visitlahaina.com.

East Maui Taro Festival, Hana. At the end of March or in early April, this festival lets you taste taro in many different forms, from poi to chips. Information: ☎ 808/248-8972; www.calendarmaui.com.

Annual Lei Day Celebration, islandwide. May Day is Lei Day in Hawaii, celebrated with lei-making contests, pageantry, arts and crafts, and concerts. Information: ☎ 808/875-4100; www.visitmaui.com.

King Kamehameha Celebration, islandwide. June 10 is a state holiday with a massive floral parade, *hoolaulea* (party), and much more. Information: ☎ 888/310-1117; www.visitlahaina.com.

Fourth of July. Lahaina holds an old-fashioned Independence Day celebration with fireworks. Information: ☎ 888/310-1117; www.visitlahaina.com. Kaanapali puts on a grand old celebration with live music, children's activities, and fireworks. Information: ☎ 808/661-3271.

Maui County Fair, War Memorial Complex, Wailuku. Late September. This traditional county fair features a parade, amusement rides, live entertainment, and exhibits. Information: ☎ 800/525-MAUI (525-6284); www.calendarmaui.com.

Halloween in Lahaina. There's Carnival in Rio, Mardi Gras in New Orleans, and Halloween in Lahaina. Come to this giant costume party (some 20,000 people show up) on the streets of Lahaina. Information: ☎ 888/310-1117; www.visitlahaina.com.

Romantic Maui

Maui's sensual side makes it the perfect place to fall in love. The smell of flowers in the air, the sound of the waves rolling in, and the exotic beauty beckon lovers. I suggest spending the first 3 nights in Lahaina, then on to Hana for a couple of nights, with your last night in the Upcountry area.

> *Stirring sunsets, pristine beaches, moody lounges, and luaus all combine to make Maui one of earth's finest destinations for couples.*

START Lahaina. **FINISH** Paia.
TRIP LENGTH 7 days and 333 miles.

Day 1

❶ ★ **Lahaina.** Don't leave Kahului Airport without giving your sweetie a sweet-smelling flower lei (and a kiss). Plan to spend the first 3 nights in Lahaina (p 328). Book my favorite Hawaii experience, the **Old Lahaina Luau** (see "Maui's Best Luau," p 397), where the two of you can watch the sunset as you sip a tropical drink. See p 328.

Day 2

Allow 2 hours to get to the summit. Head south on Hwy. 30, then go right on Hwy. 380, right on Hwy. 36, and right again on Hwy. 37. Go left on Hwy. 377 to Hwy. 378, which takes you to the summit.

❷ ★★★ **Haleakala.** Since you'll still be on mainland time, plan to make the most of it and get up early and drive up 10,000 feet to the dormant volcano, Haleakala National Park, in time for the sunrise. The two of you cuddled up in a blanket (it's cold at 10,000 ft.), watching the stars slowly fade and the dim rays of dawn appear, will be one of your fondest memories. See p 352.

From the summit of Haleakala to the Kula Lodge: Retrace your steps back down the summit Hwy. 378 to Hwy. 377. Kula Lodge is after MM 5 on your left.

③ **Kula Lodge.** Enjoy a big breakfast as you look over the isthmus of Maui. Get a takeout picnic lunch before you leave. See p 394.

Continue down the mountain on Hwy. 377, and turn left on Waipoli Rd. (just before MM 14). Drive to the end of the road.

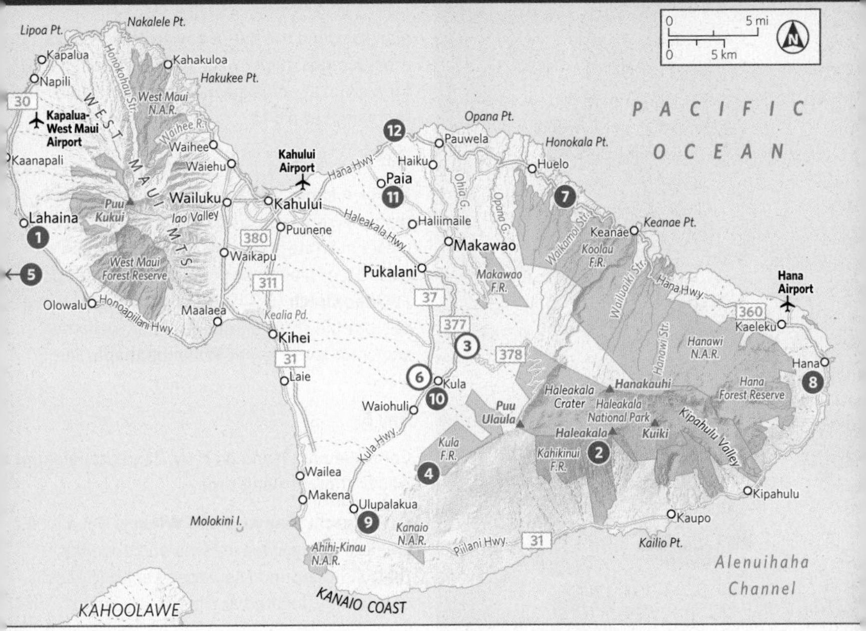

Day 1

1 Lahaina

Day 2

2 Haleakala

3 Kula Lodge

4 Polipoli State Park

Day 3

5 Sailing to Lanai

6 Harold W. Rice Memorial Park

Day 4

7 Hana Highway

Day 5

8 Hana

Day 6

9 Tedeschi Vineyard and Winery

10 Alii Kula Lavender Farm

Day 7

11 Paia

12 Hookipa Beach Park

4 **Polipoli State Park.** Walk in total silence (except for the sounds of the native birds) among the pine, redwood, and eucalyptus trees. You probably won't see another soul in the 21,000-acre forest reserve at 5,300 feet. Have a picnic, take a nap, and return to Lahaina for another sunset dinner in Lahaina at Lahaina Store Grille and Oyster Bar (p 395). **See p 362.**

To return to Lahaina, backtrack to Hwy. 377, turn left, then turn right on Hwy. 37, and retrace your steps to Lahaina.

Day 3

To get from Lahaina to Lanai via ferry, drive toward the ocean at the light on Dickenson St. in Lahaina and look for the Republic Parking sign on the right side of the street.

5 ★★★ **Sailing to Lanai.** Nothing is more romantic than the wind kissing your face and the sun warming your body as the two of you sail offshore to Lanai with my favorite sailing company, **Trilogy** (p 372). They hand you hot cinnamon rolls and coffee as soon as you step on, and after sailing the 9 miles to Lanai, they'll take you on an excursion on the island and serve you a barbecue lunch.

> *Picking out a sensuous, fragrant lei sets the mood for a perfect romantic getaway.*

From Lahaina, go to Paia to get fixings for a romantic sunset picnic. Drive south on Hwy. 30, go right on Hwy. 380 and right again on Hwy. 36, into Paia. Turn left on Baldwin Ave. From Paia to Harold Rice Park, continue up Baldwin Ave. to Makawao, turn left on Makawao Ave. and left again on Kula Hwy. (Hwy. 37) for about 6½ miles, where the park is just before MM 14.

⑥ **Harold W. Rice Memorial Park.** Gather up the ingredients for a picnic dinner (I like **Moana Bakery & Cafe,** p 396) and drive to this park in Kula to see the sunset. For a truly magical evening, linger over a bottle of wine or dessert until the stars come out.

Day 4

From Lahaina, south on Hwy. 30, right on Hwy. 380, right on Hwy. 36 to Hana.

⑦ ★★★ **Hana Highway.** Bring your swimsuit, put the top down and turn the radio up, and plan to spend the entire day cruising Maui's most famous curvy road. Stop at waterfalls, go for a swim in pools, pack a picnic, and enjoy the moment. See p 342.

Day 5

⑧ ★★★ **Hana.** Luscious Hana is the perfect place for romance. Choose from a perfect crescent white-sand bay at **Hamoa Beach** (p 356), or plan to soak in the freshwater pools at **Oheo Gulch** (p 349, ⑩), watching the waves roll into the shore. Around sunset, walk the ancient Hawaii trail at **Waianapanapa**. See p 363.

Day 6

Continue past Hana on Hwy. 31 to Ulupalakua. Allow 1 hour driving time.

⑨ **Tedeschi Vineyard and Winery.** Get a picnic lunch before you leave Hana and drive the "backside" around Maui past Kaupo to Maui's only winery, located at Ulupalakua Ranch. After sampling a few of Maui's wines, select a bottle and have your picnic lunch on the grounds of the old estate. See p 341, ④.

Head north on Hwy. 37 and go right on Hwy. 377, about ¼ mile, rounding a bend, then take a quick right up Waipoli Rd.

⑩ **Alii Kula Lavender Farm.** Pick up lavender bubble bath and a lavender candle. Plan to spend your final night soaking in a romantic hot lavender bath in Maui's Upcountry. 1100 Waipoli Rd., Kula. ☎ 808/878-3004. www.aliikulalavender.com.

Day 7

Retrace your steps to Hwy. 37, take a right at the light on Makawao Rd., and then at the stop sign in Makawao town, go left down Baldwin Ave.

⑪ **Paia.** On your last day, drive to Paia and have breakfast at **Moana Bakery & Cafe** (p 396). Then wander in the shops of this tiny town (see my shopping picks starting on p 378).

Turn right on Hwy. 36.

⑫ **Hookipa Beach Park.** Watch the surfers and windsurfers as you feel the warm wind caress your face. Be sure to get a photo of the two of you with the ocean in the background. See p 356.

Pampering in Paradise

Hawaii's spas have raised the art of relaxation and healing to a new level. The traditional Greco-Roman–style spas, with lots of marble and big tubs in closed rooms, have evolved into airy, open facilities that embrace the tropics. Spa-goers in Hawaii are looking for a sense of place, steeped in the culture. They want to hear the sound of the ocean, smell the salt air, and feel the caress of the warm breeze. They want to experience Hawaiian products and traditional treatments they can get only in the islands.

The spas of Hawaii, once nearly exclusively patronized by women, are now attracting more male clients. There are special massages for children and pregnant women, and some spas have created programs to nurture and relax brides on their big day.

Today's spas offer a wide diversity of treatments. Massage styles include Hawaiian lomilomi, Swedish, aromatherapy (with sweet-smelling oils), craniosacral (massage of the head), shiatsu (no oil—just deep thumb pressure on acupuncture points), Thai (another oil-less massage involving stretching), and hot stone (with heated, and sometimes cold, rocks). There are even side-by-side massages for couples. The truly decadent might even try a duo massage—not one, but *two* massage therapists working on you at the same time.

Massages are just the beginning. Body treatments, for the entire body or for just the face, involve a variety of herbal wraps, masks, or scrubs using a range of ingredients, from seaweed to salt to mud, with or without accompanying aromatherapy, lights, and music.

After you have been rubbed and scrubbed, most spas offer an array of water treatments—a sort of hydromassage in a tub with jets and an assortment of colored crystals, oils, and scents.

Those are just the traditional treatments. Most spas also offer a range of alternative healthcare, such as acupuncture, chiropractic, and other exotic treatments like ayurvedic and *siddha* from India or *reiki* from Japan. Many places offer specialized, cutting-edge treatments, like the Grand Wailea Resort's full-spectrum color-light therapy pod (based on NASA's work with astronauts).

Once your body has been pampered, spas also offer a range of fitness facilities (weight-training equipment, racquetball, tennis, golf) and classes (yoga, aerobics, step, spinning, stretch, tai chi, kickboxing, aquacize). Several even offer adventure fitness packages (from bicycling to snorkeling). For the nonadventurous, most spas have salons dedicated to hair and nail care and makeup.

If all this sounds a bit overwhelming, not to worry: All the spas in Hawaii have individual consultants who will help you design an appropriate treatment program to fit your individual needs.

Of course, all this pampering doesn't come cheap. Massages are generally $175 to $250 for 50 minutes and $250 to $295 for 80 minutes; body treatments are in the $150 to $250 range; and alternative healthcare treatments can be as high as $200 to $300. But you may think it's worth the expense to banish your tension and stress.

Maui History & Culture

It is possible to walk back in history on Maui, to the ancient Hawaiians who first came to the island, to the missionaries and whalers who arrived in the 1800s, to the plantation workers and cowboys of the 1900s—there are even vestiges of the hippies of the 1960s and 1970s. Plan to spend your first night in West Maui, the second night in Wailuku, and the third night in Hana.

> *Haiwana's Bailey House Museum was home to a missionary and is filled with his period paintings and native arts and crafts.*

START Lahaina. **FINISH** Paia. **TRIP LENGTH** 4 days and 190 miles.

Day 1

1 Lahaina. On the day of your arrival, head for this old town, which has archeological evidence dating back to A.D. 700. Plan your first cultural experience at the ★★★ **Old Lahaina Luau** (see "Maui's Best Luau," p 397). ⏱ 1-3 hrs. See p 328.

Day 2

Take Hwy. 30 north to Kaanapali, a 5-minute drive.

2 Whalers Village Museum. This museum celebrates the "Golden Era of Whaling" (1825-1860), where harpoons and scrimshaw are on display; the museum has even re-created the cramped quarters of a whaler's seagoing vessel. ⏱ 30 min. Whalers Village, 2435 Kaanapali Pkwy., Lahaina. ☎ 808/661-5992. www.whalersvillage.com. Daily 9:30am–10 pm. Free admission.

Continue north on Hwy. 30 to Kapalua, a 10- to 15-minute drive.

3 Kapalua. To go back even farther in time, drive out to Kapaluua ("two borders"), where on the hill, oceanside of the Ritz-Carlton Kapalua, the burial sites of hundreds of ancient Hawaiians were discovered in the sand during construction of the hotel. The hotel was moved inland to avoid disrupting the graves. A historic plaque details the site's history. ⏱ 15 min.

**Continue north, past Kapalua, on Hwy. 30 (which becomes Hwy. 340 then Hwy. 330,

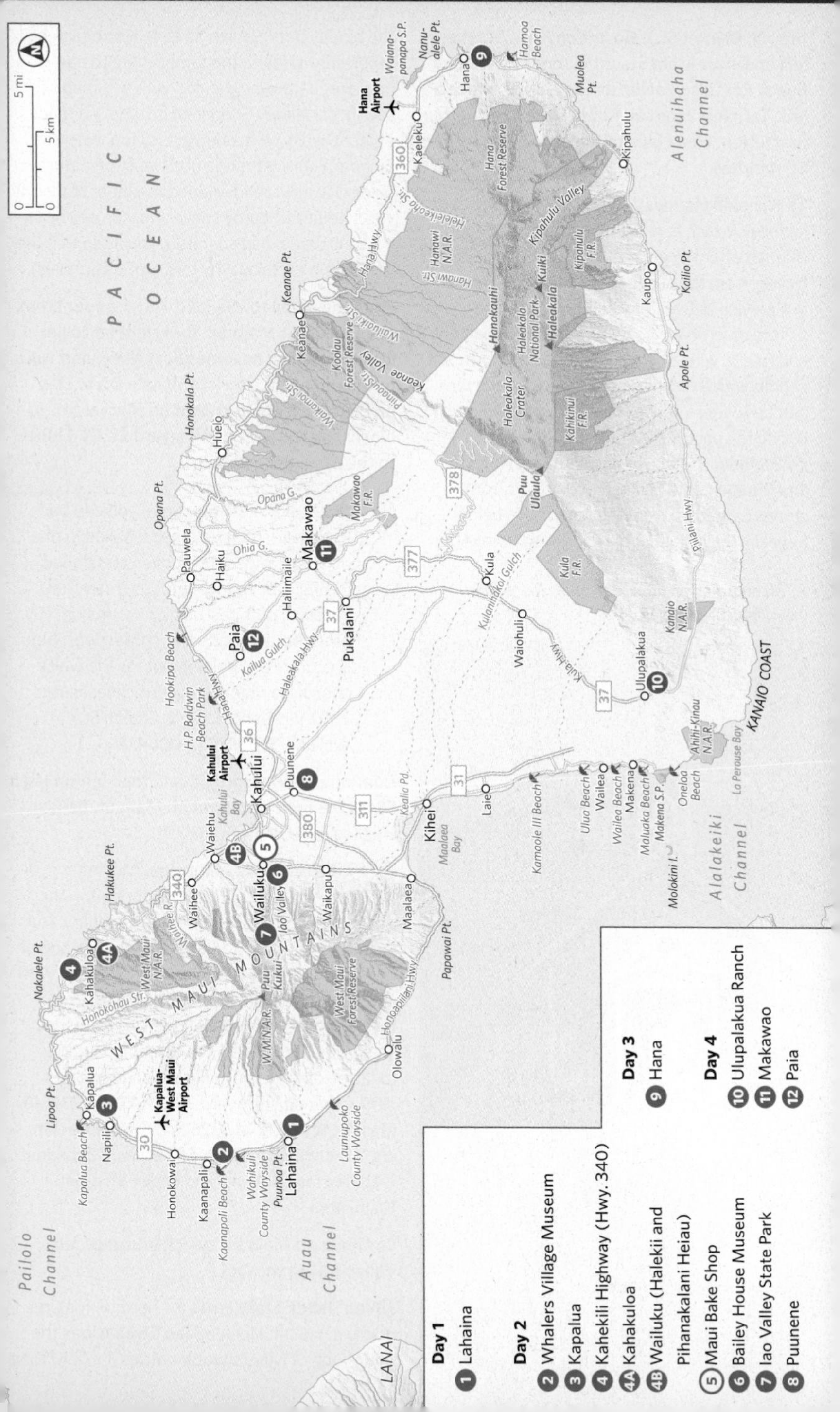
Day 1
1 Lahaina
Day 2
2 Whalers Village Museum
3 Kapalua
4 Kahekili Highway (Hwy. 340)
4A Kahakuloa
4B Wailuku (Halekii and Pihanakalani Heiau)
5 Maui Bake Shop
6 Bailey House Museum
7 Iao Valley State Park
8 Puunene
Day 3
9 Hana
Day 4
10 Ulupalakua Ranch
11 Makawao
12 Paia
PACIFIC OCEAN
Pailolo Channel
Auau Channel
Alalakeiki Channel
Alenuihaha Channel
LANAI
WEST MAUI MOUNTAINS
KANAIO COAST
Lahaina
Kaanapali
Honokowai
Napili
Kapalua
Kapalua-West Maui Airport
Kahakuloa
Waihee
Waiehu
Wailuku
Kahului
Kahului Airport
Paia
Haiku
Pauwela
Makawao
Pukalani
Haliimaile
Puunene
Kihei
Maalaea
Olowalu
Kula
Waiohuli
Ulupalakua
Keanae
Huelo
Kaeleku
Hana
Hana Airport
Kipahulu
Kaupo
Wailea
Makena
Laie
Haleakala National Park
Haleakala Crater
Hana Forest Reserve
Koolau Forest Reserve
West Maui Forest Reserve
Makawao F.R.
Kula F.R.
Kahikinui F.R.
Kipahulu F.R.
Kanaio N.A.R.
Ahihi-Kinau N.A.R.
Hanawi N.A.R.
West Maui N.A.R.
W.M.N.A.R.
Puu Kukui
Puu Ulaula
Hanakauhi
Kuiki
Haleakala
Molokini I.
Nakalele Pt.
Lipoa Pt.
Hakukee Pt.
Papawai Pt.
Opana Pt.
Honokala Pt.
Keanae Pt.
Nanu-alele Pt.
Muolea Pt.
Kailio Pt.
Apole Pt.
Puunoa Pt.
Kealia Pd.
Maalaea Bay
Kahului Bay
La Perouse Bay
Hookipa Beach
H.P. Baldwin Beach Park
Kapalua Beach
Kaanapali Beach
Wahikuli County Wayside
Launiupoko County Wayside
Kamaole III Beach
Ulua Beach
Wailea Beach
Maluaka Beach
Makena S.P.
Oneloa Beach
Hamoa Beach
Waianapanapa S.P.
Iao Valley
Keanae Valley
Kipahulu Valley
Hana Hwy.
Haleakala Hwy.
Kula Hwy.
Piilani Hwy.
Honoapiilani Hwy.
30
31
36
37
311
340
360
377
378
380
0 5 mi
0 5 km

then N. Market St.). Go left on Mills St., then left on Lower Main St. until it ends at Waiehu Beach Rd. (also known as Hwy. 340); make a left. Turn left again on Kuhio St., and make the first left on Hea Place to the end. Allow 45 to 60 minutes.

4 Kahekili Highway (Hwy. 340). Along this highway, which is really more a two-lane road (named after the great chief Kahekili, who built houses from the skulls of his enemies), nestled in a crevice between two steep hills, is the picturesque village of **A Kahakuloa** ("the tall hau tree"), with a dozen weatherworn houses, a church with a red-tile roof and vivid green taro patches, where life here has not changed much during the past few decades. Continue into **B Wailuku** to see two ancient sites: **Halekii and Pihanakalani *Heiau*,** built in 1240 from stones carried up from the Iao Stream below. Kahekili, the last chief of Maui, lived here. After the bloody battle at Iao Stream, Kamehameha I reportedly came to the temple here to pay homage to the war god, Ku, with a human sacrifice. Halekii ("House of Images") is made of stone walls with a flat, grassy top, whereas Pihanakalani (gathering place of supernatural beings) is a pyramid-shaped mount of stones. If you sit quietly nearby (never walk on any *heiau*—it's considered disrespectful), you'll see that the view alone explains why this spot was chosen.

> This church in picturesque Kahakuloa Village is a popular photo op.

From the *heiau* to Wailuku, retrace your steps back to Lower Main St. Turn right on Lower Main St., which becomes East Main, and veer to the right at the fork to Waiale Dr. to stay on East Main St. Turn right on Market St., go 1 block, and turn left on Vineyard St. Go 1 block to the Maui Bake Shop.

5 **Maui Bake Shop.** Sure, you can buy the great-smelling breads, baked in one of Maui's oldest brick ovens (installed in 1935), or the sumptuous fresh-fruit gâteaux, puff pastries, or dozens of other baked goods and confections, but I recommend holding out for the white-chocolate macadamia nut cheesecake. 2092 Vineyard St. (at N. Church St.), Wailuku. ☎ 808/242-0064. $.

Continue up Vineyard St. and then left on High St. At the light turn right on Main St. Bailey House Museum is on the left.

6 ★★ Bailey House Museum. Moving forward—both literally and historically—the next stop is the 1833 home of missionary and sugar planter Edward Bailey, containing one of my favorite treasure-troves of Hawaiiana, with everything from scary temple images, dog-tooth necklaces, a rare lei made of tree-snail shells, and Bailey's own landscape paintings to latter-day relics like Duke Kahanamoku's 1919 redwood surfboard. ⏱ 30–45 min. 2375-A Main St. ☎ 808/244-3326. www.mauimuseum.org. Admission $7 adults, $5 seniors, $2 children 7-12, free for children 6 and under. Mon-Sat 10am-4pm.

Continue up Main St., which becomes Iao Valley Rd., to the end.

7 Iao Valley State Park. It's hard to imagine that the peaceful looking **Iao Stream** was the site of one of Maui's worst battles. In 1790 King

> *Hawaii's* heiau *(temples) were sacred places of worship and sacrifice. Native Hawaiians still consider these places sacred, so if you visit, please don't walk on the* heiau *or climb on the rocks.*

Kamehameha the Great and his men engaged in the bloody battle of Iao Valley to gain control of Maui. When the battle ended, so many bodies blocked Iao Stream that the battle site was named Kepaniwai, or "damming of the waters." The park and stream get their name from the **Iao Needle,** a phallic rock that juts an impressive 2,250 feet above sea level. *Iao* means "supreme light." See p 336, ❷.

Retrace your steps to Main St. and continue straight through Wailuku and Kahului. Turn right at the light onto S. Puunene Ave., continue to Hansen Rd. in Puunene, and turn left. The museum is on the corner.

❽ **Puunene.** In the middle of the central Maui plains, the town of Puunene ("goose hill") has almost disappeared. Once a thriving sugar plantation town with hundreds of homes, a school, a shopping area, and a community center, today Puunene is little more than the sugar mill, a post office, and the **Alexander & Baldwin Sugar Museum,** Puunene Ave./Hwy. 350 and Hansen Road (☎ 808/871-8058; www.sugarmuseum.com). This former sugar mill superintendent's home has been converted into a museum that tells the story of sugar in Hawaii, from how sugar is grown, to how it is harvested and milled. It also recounts how Samuel Alexander and Henry Baldwin managed to acquire huge chunks of land from the Kingdom of Hawaii, then ruthlessly fought to gain access to water on the other side of the island, making sugarcane an economically viable crop. Spend the night in the historic **Old Wailuku Inn at Ulupono** (p 402), a 1924 former plantation manager's home that's been lovingly restored. ⏱ **30 min. to see the museum.**

Day 3

From Wailuku to Hana, take Kaahumanu Ave. (Hwy. 32), turn right on Hana Hwy. (Hwy. 36, then Hwy. 360) to Hana. Allow 2 to 3 hours from Wailuku to Hana.

> THIS PAGE *A former sugar mill town, Paia was once the North Shore's industrial center. Today it's a windsurfing mecca and counterculture enclave.* OPPOSITE PAGE *Iao Valley State Park offers many spectacular vistas of the park's namesake Iao Needle—don't forget your camera.*

❾ ★★★ **Hana.** The Hana coast is rich in Hawaiian history and the scene of many turning points in Hawaiian culture. The ancient chants tell of rulers like the 15th-century Piilani, who united the island of Maui and built fishponds, irrigation fields, and paved roads and constructed the massive **Piilanihale *Heiau*** (temple), which still stands today (p 346, ❶). It was Piilani's sons and grandson who finished the *heiau* and built the first road to Hana from West Maui, not only along the coast, but also up the Kaupo Gap and through the Haleakala Crater. The next stop is **Hana Cultural Center and Museum** (p 347, ❸), with the **Kauhala O Hana,** composed of four traditional Hawaiian *hale* (houses) for living, meeting, cooking, and canoe-building or canoe storage. In Hana Bay lies a 386-foot, red-faced cinder cone, **Kauiki Hill** (p 347, ❺), the scene of numerous fierce battles in ancient Hawaii and the birthplace of Queen Kaahumanu in 1768. ⏱ **2-3 hrs. Also see p 346.**

From Hana to Ulupalakua Ranch, continue on Hwy. 360 (which is renamed Hwy. 31 past Kaupo) past Hana all the way into Ulupalakua. Allow 1 hour driving time.

Day 4

❿ **Ulupalakua Ranch.** High on the slopes of Haleakala, Ulupalakua ("breadfruit ripening") tells Maui's agricultural history and is home to Maui's only winery. **See p 341, ❹.**

To get from Ulupalakua to Makawao, continue north on the same Hwy. (now named Hwy. 37) for about 14 to 15 miles. Turn right at the light on Makawao Ave. (Hwy. 365). Allow about 30 minutes driving time.

⓫ **Makawao.** This cowboy town dates back to 1888 when the Haleakala Ranch was founded to control the cattle introduced in Hawaii in 1793. Seventeen years later the *pipi'ahiu* (wild cattle) were being hunted upcountry since their numbers grew well above expectations. The horse didn't show up on Maui until Richard Cleveland offered horses as a gift to King Kamehameha the Great in 1803. Today cowboys still ride their horses into Makawao ("forest beginning") and tie up at the hitching posts along Baldwin Ave. ⏱ **1 hr.**

Drive down Baldwin Ave. to the end. Allow 15 to 20 minutes driving time.

⓬ **Paia.** This former plantation village was once a thriving sugar mill town. Paia ("noisy") became the most important community along Maui's North Shore during the 1880s when the Alexander and Baldwin Company built the first sugar mill on the island just outside of town. The mill is still here, but the population shifted to Kahului in the 1950s when subdivisions opened there, leaving Paia to shrivel up and die. But the town has proved remarkably adaptable, becoming a popular hippie hangout in the 1960s and 1970s (some of the shops still have a bit of residual counterculture from those days) and developing an international reputation as a windsurfing mecca in the 1980s. ⏱ **1 hr.**

THE LEI

Hawaii's Sensuous Adornment

BY JEANETTE FOSTER

THERE'S NOTHING like a lei. The stunning tropical beauty of the delicate garland, the deliciously sweet fragrance of the blossoms, the gentle way the flowers curl softly around your neck. There's no doubt about it: Getting lei'd in Hawaii is a sensuous experience. Leis are one of the nicest ways to say hello, good-bye, congratulations, I salute you, my sympathies are with you, or I love you. The custom of giving leis can be traced back to Hawaii's very roots; according to chants, the first lei was given by Hiiaka, the sister of the volcano goddess Pele; she presented Pele with a lei of lehua blossoms on a beach in Puna. The presentation of a kiss with a lei didn't come about until World War II; it's generally attributed to an entertainer who kissed an American officer on a dare and then quickly presented him with her lei, saying it was an old Hawaiian custom. Leis are the perfect symbol for the islands: They're given in the moment and their fragrance and beauty are enjoyed in the moment, but even after they fade, their spirit of aloha lives on.

The Lei of the Land

Lei-making is a tropical art form. All leis are fashioned by hand in a variety of traditional patterns; some are sewn with hundreds of tiny blooms or shells, or bits of ferns and leaves. Some are twisted, some braided, some strung; all are presented with love. Every island has its own special lei flower, pictured below.

ILIMA On Oahu the choice is the ilima, a small orange flower.

MOKIHANA Kauai uses this fragrant, green vine and berry.

LEHUA Big Islanders prefer the lehua, a large, delicate red puff.

KUKUI Molokai uses the kukui, which blooms on candlenut trees.

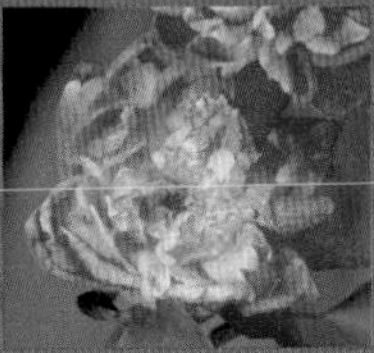

LOKELANI The lei of choice on Maui is the lokelani, a small rose.

KAUNAOA On Lanai, it's the kaunaoa, a bright yellow moss.

KAHELELANI
Residents of Niihau use the island's abundant seashells to make leis that were once prized by royalty and are now worth a small fortune.

Maui's Farmlands

When people think of Maui, flowers or a lei come to mind, but Maui is a breadbasket to the world, its lush fields producing everything from tropical fruit and exotic flowers to breadfruit and lavender—even goat cheese and wine. This 3-day itinerary explores Maui's bounty.

> *The Maui Tropical Plantation tour gives you an up-close look at how everything from macadamia nuts to bananas are grown and harvested.*

START Kapalua. **FINISH** Kahanu Garden. **TRIP LENGTH** 3 days and 116 miles.

Day 1

Start at the Kapalua Villas Reception Center, across from the Honolua Store.

1 kids **Maui Gold Pineapple Tour.** Start with Hawaii's king of fruits. This 2-hour tour, led by experienced plantation workers, takes you through a pineapple field in the midst of a harvest. The colorful commentary weaves the pineapple's history into facts about its growing and harvesting cycles. ⏲ 1½–2 hr. Office Rd./Village Rd., Kapalua. ☎ 808/665-4386. www.kapalua.com/adventures. $40 adults, $32 children 2–11.

Go south on Hwy. 30 for 27 miles. Allow 40 to 45 minutes driving time.

2 kids **Maui Tropical Plantation Tour.** The Maui Tropical Plantation tour takes you by tram through a 60-acre working plantation of tropical fruits and flowers (papaya, guava, mango, macadamia nuts, coffee, avocado, banana, sugarcane, star fruit, and more). The narrated tour takes about an hour. Kids will love

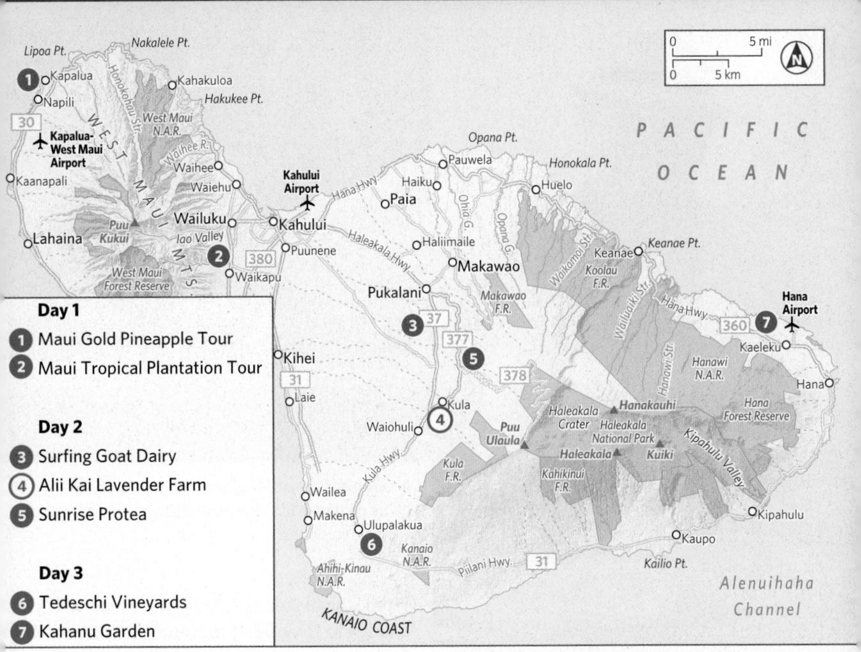

it—and don't forget to stop by the store and pick up your favorite fruit. ⏱ 1–1½ hr. Btw. MM 2 and MM 3, on Hwy. 30, Waikapu. ☎ 800/451-6805. www.mauitropicalplantation.com. Daily 9am–5 pm. $14 adults, $5 children 3–12.

Day 2

From Waikapu to the Surfing Goat Dairy, head north on Hwy. 30, turn right at the light on Main St., and continue through Wailuku and Kahului. At the intersection of Kaahumanu Ave. and Hwy. 36 turn right. After the light at the intersection of Dairy Rd. (Hwy. 380), get in the right lane and veer to the right on Pulehu Rd. About 5 miles up the road, veer left at the fork onto Omaopio Rd. Look for the sign on the right, about a mile up the road. Allow 30 to 40 minutes driving time.

3 kids **Surfing Goat Dairy.** In Kula, just beyond the sugarcane fields on the slopes of Haleakala, some 140 dairy goats blissfully graze 42 acres and contribute milk for the 24 different cheeses made here every day. Make reservations for the 2-hour **Grand Dairy Tour** (offered every other Sat.), where you can learn how to milk a goat, make cheese, and sample the different varieties; or drop by for the 20-minute Casual Dairy Tour. ⏱ 1–2 hr. 3651 Omaopio Rd., Kula. ☎ 808/878-2870. www.surfinggoatdairy.com. Casual Tour $7, Grand Tour $25. Mon, Wed, Fri 10am–4pm; Tues, Thurs, Sat 10am–3:15pm; Sun 10am–1pm.

From the Surfing Goat Dairy to the Alii Kula Lavendar Farm, continue up Omaopio Rd. to Hwy. 37 and turn right. Take the second left after Rice Park on Hwy. 377 (Kekaulike Ave.), drive about ¼ mile, and after rounding the bend, take a quick right up Waipoli Rd. Allow 20 to 30 minutes driving time.

④ **Alii Kula Lavender Farm.** Stop here for lunch and a tour to see the varieties that bloom year-round. In addition to checking out all the products made from lavender, be sure to book the 50-minute **walking tour,** which explores the grounds and includes lunch. 1100 Waipoli Rd., Kula ☎ 808/878-3004, www.aliikulalavender.com. Walking tour with lunch $37.

From the lavender farm to the protea farm, turn right on Kekaulike Ave. (Hwy. 377) and then right again on Haleakala Hwy. (Hwy. 378). Allow 15 minutes driving time.

> *Check out the Alii Kula Lavender Farm and stay for a luscious lunch made with the farm's lavender products.*

> *Get a gander at Maui's most unusual flower: the protea, which grows exclusively on the island's volcanic slopes.*

5 **Sunrise Protea.** After lunch you should have plenty of time to see the otherworldly protea, Maui's most unusual flower (actually native to South Africa). On Haleakala's rich volcanic slopes, Sunrise Protea offers a walk-through garden tour, a gift shop, friendly service, and a larger-than-usual selection of these exotic flowers. If you can arrange it, go on a Tuesday or a Friday, when the just-cut flowers come in from the fields. 30 min.–1 hr. Haleakala Hwy., Kula. ☎ 800/222-2797. www.sunriseprotea.com.

Day 3

From Kula take Hwy. 378 to Hwy. 377 to a left turn on Hwy. 37. The winery is another 12 miles down the road. Allow 30 to 45 minutes driving time.

6 **Tedeschi Vineyards.** Plan to arrive in time for the free 10:30am tour (the other tours are at 1:30 and 3pm) of the grounds and wine producing operation at Maui's only winery, on Ulupalakua Ranch. See p 341, 4.

From Ulupalakua take Hwy. 31 (which will change to Hwy. 360) to Hana. Just before MM 31, turn down Ulaino Rd. to the ocean. Allow about an hour's driving time.

7 kids **Kahanu Garden.** The world's largest collection of breadfruit trees, a staple crop for Pacific Islanders, can be found here. The garden has some 130 distinct varieties gathered from 20 tropical island groups. Also here is the **Canoe Garden,** which assembles all the useful plants that the early Polynesian settlers brought to Hawaii: sugarcane, banana, sweet potato, taro, turmeric, and paper mulberry (used to make kapa cloth). 🕒 1½ hr. Ulaino Rd. (turn toward the ocean at MM 31, off the Hana Hwy.). ☎ 808/248-8912; www.ntbg.org/gardens/kahanu.php. Mon–Fri 10am–2pm. $10 adults, children 12 and under free.

Maui Farmers Markets

If you want the freshest Maui fruits, flowers, and produce (at budget prices), show up at one of Maui's several outdoor farmers markets: At the **Queen Ka'ahumanu Center** Tuesday, Wednesday, and Friday 8am–2pm; at the **Maui Mall Shopping Center** Tuesday, Wednesday, and Friday 8am–5pm; and Upcountry at the **Eddie Tam Community Center** in Makawao on Saturday from 6am–noon.

Relax, Breathe Deep & Say Spaaah

Hawaii's spas are airy, open facilities that embrace the tropics. Here are your best options on Maui:

Spa Grande at the Grand Wailea Resort (☎ 800/SPA-1933 (772-1933) or 808/875-1234; www.grandwailea.com): This is Hawaii's biggest spa, at 50,000 square feet and with 40 treatment rooms. The spa incorporates the best of the Old World (romantic ceiling murals, larger-than-life Roman-style sculptures, mammoth Greek columns, huge European tubs), the finest Eastern traditions (a full Japanese-style traditional bath and various exotic treatments from India), and the lure of the islands (tropical foliage, ancient Hawaiian treatments, and island products). This spa has everything from a top fitness center to a menu of classes and is constantly on the cutting edge of the latest trends.

Spa Kea Lani at the Fairmont Kea Lani Maui (☎ 866/540-4456 or 808/875-4100; www.fairmont.com/kealani/Recreation/SPA, pictured): This intimate, Art Deco boutique spa (just a little over 5,000 sq. ft., with nine treatment rooms), which opened in 1999, is the place for personal and private attention. The fitness center next door is open 24 hours (a rarity in Hawaiian resorts) with a personal trainer on duty some 14 hours a day.

Spa Moana at the Hyatt Regency Maui Resort & Spa (☎ 808/661-1234; www.maui.hyatt.com/hyatt/pure/spas): The island's first oceanfront spa, this $3.5-million, 9,000-square-foot facility offers an open-air exercise lanai, wet-treatment rooms, massage rooms, a relaxation lounge, sauna and steam rooms, a Roman pool illuminated by overhead skylights, and a duet treatment suite for couples.

Spa at the Ritz-Carlton Kapalua (☎ 800/262-8440 or 808/669-6200; www.ritzcarlton.com): Book a massage on the beach. The spa itself is welcoming and wonderful, but there is nothing like smelling the salt in the air and feeling the gentle caress of the wind in your hair while experiencing a true Hawaiian massage.

Spa at the Four Seasons Resort Maui at Wailea (☎ 800/334-6284 or 808/874-8000; www.fourseasons.com/maui/spa): Imagine the sounds of the waves rolling on Wailea Beach as you enjoy a soothing massage in the privacy of your cabana, tucked into the beachside foliage. This is the place to come to be absolutely spoiled. Yes, there's an excellent workout area and tons of great classes, but this spa's specialty is hedonistic indulgence.

West Maui

This is the fabled Maui you see on postcards: jagged peaks, green valleys, crystal-clear water, and sandy beaches: the epitome of paradise. This stretch of coastline along Maui's "forehead," from Kapalua to the historic port of Lahaina, is the island's most bustling resort area (with South Maui close behind). Expect a few mainland-style traffic jams.

> *Luxury hotels and championship golf courses line the calm and pristine 3-mile shoreline of Kaanapali Beach.*

START Olowalu. FINISH Kapalua.
TRIP LENGTH 1 day and 17 miles.

❶ kids **Olowalu.** Most visitors drive right past this tiny hamlet, 5 miles south of Lahaina. If you blink you'll miss the general store and Chez Paul restaurant (p 390). Olowalu ("many hills") was the scene of a 1790 massacre: The Hawaiians stole a skiff from the USS *Eleanora,* and the captain of the ship retaliated by mowing them down with his cannons, killing 100 people and wounding many others. Stop at **mile marker (MM) 14,** for snorkeling over a turtle-cleaning station (where turtles line up to have cleaner wrasses pick off small parasites) about 150 to 225 feet out from shore. ⏱ 2 hrs. if snorkeling.

Take Hwy. 30 north for 7 miles (15 min.).

❷ ★★★ **Lahaina.** Plan a minimum of a half day in Lahaina. See p 328.

Take Hwy. 30 for 3 miles north of Lahaina (5 to 10 min.).

❸ **Kaanapali.** Hawaii's first master-planned resort consists of pricey midrise hotels lining nearly 3 miles of gold-sand beach. Golf greens wrap around the slope between beachfront and hillside properties. Inside Kaanapali Resort, turn toward the ocean from Hwy. 30 onto Kaanapali Pkwy. to reach Whalers Village, a seaside mall in Kaanapali that has adopted the whale as its mascot. You can't miss it: A huge, almost life-size metal sculpture of a mother whale and two nursing calves greets you. The reason to

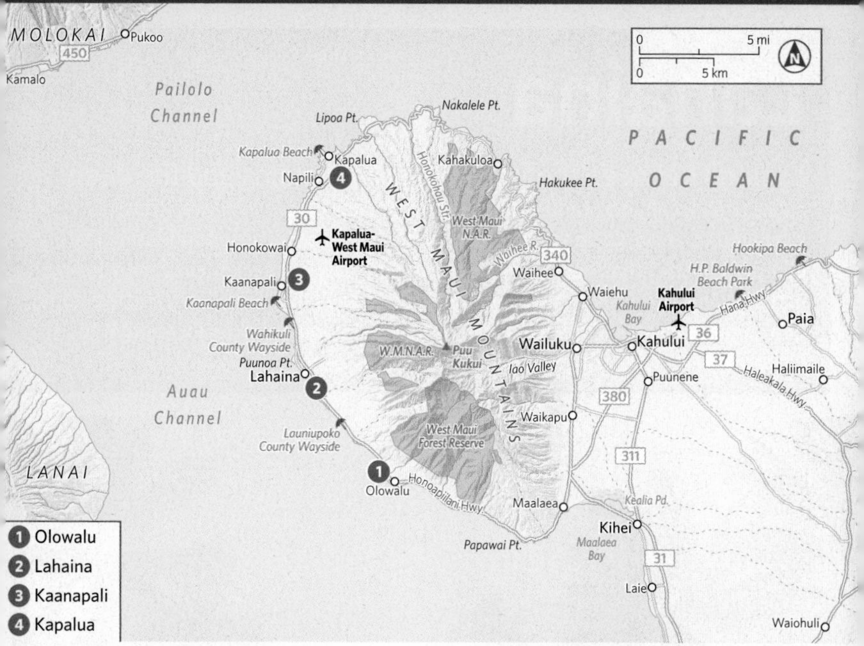

stop here is the kids **Whalers Village Museum** (p 314, ❷). This tiny museum celebrates the "Golden Era of Whaling" (1825–1860) with such displays as harpoons, scrimshaw, and a re-creation of the cramped quarters of a whaler's seagoing vessel. Self-guided audio tours and short videos are available throughout the day. ⏱ 30 min. Whalers Village, 2435 Kaanapali Pkwy., Lahaina. ☎ 808/661-5992. www.whalersvillage.com. Daily 9am–10pm. Free admission.

Continue north on Hwy. 30 for 7 miles (10 to 15 min.).

❹ ★ **Kapalua.** As you continue up Hwy. 30, the vista opens up to fields of silver-green pineapple and manicured golf fairways. Turn down the country lane of Pacific pines toward the sea to the exclusive domain of the luxurious Ritz-Carlton Kapalua (p 403), located next to two bays that are marine-life preserves (with fabulous surfing in winter). The resort has an art school, a golf school, three golf courses (p 364), historic features, a collection of swanky condos and homes, and wide-open spaces that include a rainforest preserve—all open to the general public. Pack a picnic lunch and plan to spend the rest of the day here.

> *Just 5 miles south of Lahaina you'll find some of the island's best snorkeling in the calm, clear waters off Olowalu.*

Lahaina

Located between the West Maui Mountains and the deep azure ocean, Lahaina stands out as one of the few places in Hawaii that has managed to preserve its 19th-century heritage while still accommodating 21st-century guests. It has been the royal capital of Hawaii, the center of the whaling industry, the place where missionaries tried to save the Hawaiians, and the home of a sugar plantation. Today it's one of the most popular towns for visitors to explore.

> *A former whaling town, Lahaina combines a 19th-century look and feel with luxurious 21st-century amenities.*

START Baldwin Home Museum on Front St.
FINISH Lahaina Jodo Mission on Ala Moana St.
TRIP LENGTH 3–4 hours and 2 miles.

❶ **Baldwin Home Museum.** The oldest house in Lahaina, this coral-and-rock structure was built in 1834 by the Rev. Dwight Baldwin, a doctor with the American missionaries. Next door is the **Masters' Reading Room,** Maui's oldest building. ⏱ 30 min. 120 Dickenson St. (at Front St.). ☎ 808/661-3262. www.lahainarestoration.org. Admission $3 adults, $5 families. Daily 10am–4pm.

Cross Front St. at Hotel St., and walk toward the water to Wharf St.

❷ **Pioneer Inn.** Wander into Lahaina's first hotel, which looks pretty much the way it did when it was built in 1901. If the walls of this old building could talk, they would be singing about some pretty wild parties at the turn of the 20th-century. George Freeland, of the Royal Canadian

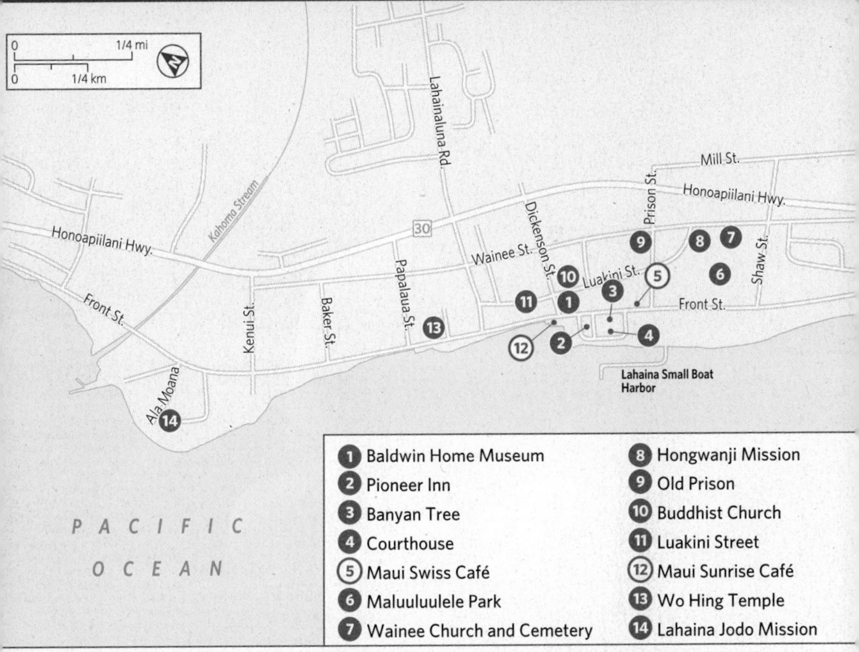

Mounted Police, tracked a criminal to Lahaina and then fell in love with the town. He built the hotel in 1901 but soon discovered that Lahaina wasn't the tourist mecca it is today. You can still stay here (p 399), or just stop for a cold drink at the old bar on the south side of the hotel and watch the goings-on at the harbor. **⏱ 30 min. if you stop for a drink. 658 Wharf St. ☎ 808/661-3636. www.pioneerinnmaui.com.**

Cross Hotel St. to the park.

3 kids **Banyan Tree.** Of all the banyan trees in Hawaii, this is the greatest of all—so big that you can't get the whole thing in your camera's viewfinder. It was only 8 feet tall when it was planted in 1873 by Maui sheriff William O. Smith to mark the 50th anniversary of Lahaina's first Christian mission. Now it's more than 50 feet tall, has 12 major trunks, and shades two-thirds of an acre in Courthouse Square. **⏱ 15 min. At the Courthouse Bldg., 649 Wharf St.**

Continue along Wharf St.

4 Courthouse. This building has served as customhouse, post office, tax collector's office, and government offices as well as a courthouse. Upstairs on the second floor is the Lahaina Heritage Museum, with exhibits on the history and culture of Lahaina. **⏱ 20 min. 648 Wharf St., Lahaina. ☎ 808/661-1959. www.visitlahaina.com. Free admission. Daily 9am–5pm.**

Continue down Front St.

> *Reminders of Lahaina's thriving whaling history are found all over the streets of this anachronistic harbor town.*

> *The massive Buddha at the Jodo Mission was erected on the 100th anniversary of Japanese workers' arrival on Lahaina plantations.*

⑤ **Maui Swiss Café.** Stop here for tropical smoothies, great espresso, and affordable snacks. Sit in the somewhat funky garden area, or (my preference) get your drink to go and wander over to the seawall to watch the surfers. 640 Front St. ☎ 808/661-6776. www.swisscafe.net. $.

Continue down Front St. to Shaw St.

❻ **Maluuluulele Park.** This sacred spot to Hawaiians is now the site of a park and ball field. This used to be a village, Mokuhinia, with a sacred pond that was the home of a *moo* (a spirit in the form of a lizard), which the royal family honored as their personal guardian spirit. 5-10 min. Front and Shaw sts.

Turn left on Shaw St., and left on Wainee St.

❼ **Wainee Church and Cemetery.** This was the first stone church built in Hawaii (1828–1832). The current church has been standing since 1953. Be sure to walk around to the back of the church, where you'll see some of the oldest palm trees in Lahaina. Next door, the first Christian cemetery in Hawaii, the Wainee Cemetery (established in 1823), tells a fascinating story of old Hawaii, with graves of Hawaiian chiefs, commoners, missionaries, and sailors. 10–15 min. Wainee and Shaw sts.

Continue on Wainee St.

❽ **Hongwanji Mission.** The original temple was built in 1910 by members of Lahaina's Buddhist sect. The current building, housing a temple and language school, was constructed in 1927. The public is welcome to attend the New Year's Eve celebration, Buddha's birthday in April, and O Bon Memorial Services in August. 5 min. Wainee and Luakini sts.

Continue on Wainee St. to Prison St.

❾ **Old Prison.** The Hawaiians called the prison Hale Paahao ("stuck in irons house"). Sailors who refused to return to their boats at sunset were sent here. 5 min. Wainee and Prison sts.

Continue on Wainee St., turn left on Hale St., and right on Luakini St.

⓾ **Buddhist Church.** This green wooden Shingon Buddhist temple is typical of myriad Buddhist churches that sprang up all over the island when the Japanese laborers were brought to work in the sugarcane fields. ⏱ 2 min. Luakini and Hale sts.

Continue on Luakini St.

⓫ **Luakini Street.** "Luakini" translates as a *heiau* (temple) where the ruling chiefs prayed and where human sacrifices were made. This street received its unforgettable name after serving as the route for the funeral procession of Princess Harriet Nahienaena, sister of Kings Kamehameha II and III. A convert to Protestantism, she had fallen in love with her brother at an early age. Just 20 years earlier, their relationship would have been nurtured in order to preserve the purity of the royal bloodlines. The missionaries, however, frowned on brothers and sisters marrying. In August 1836 the couple had a son, who lived a few short hours. Nahienaena never recovered and died in December of that same year (the king was said to mourn her death for years, frequently visiting her grave at the Wainee Cemetery). The route of her funeral procession through the breadfruit and koa trees to the cemetery became known as "Luakini," in reference to the gods "sacrificing" the beloved princess. Luakini St.

Retrace back to Dickenson St., and turn right. Cross Front St. to the ocean side.

⓬ **Maui Sunrise Café.** Take a break at this teeny-tiny cafe located on Front Street, next door to the library. Grab a cup of java and one of their delicious baked goods and relax in the patio garden out back. 693A Front St., Lahaina. ☎ 808/661-8558. $.

Turn left on Front St. when leaving the cafe.

⓭ **Wo Hing Temple.** The Chinese were among the various immigrants brought to Hawaii to work in the sugarcane fields. In 1909 several Chinese workers formed the Wo Hing society, a chapter of the Chee Kun Tong society, which dates from the 17th-century. In 1912 they built this social hall for the Chinese community. Completely restored, the Wo Hing Temple contains displays and artifacts on the history of the Chinese in Lahaina. Next door in the old cookhouse is a theater with movies of Hawaii taken by Thomas Edison in 1898 and 1903. ⏱ 20 min. Front St. (btw. Wahie Lane and Papalaua St.). ☎ 808/661-3262. Admission by donation. Daily 10am–4pm.

> *Built as a social hall by early 20th-century Chinese immigrants, the Wo Hing Temple offers fascinating films and artifacts of that period.*

Continue down Front St., and turn left toward the ocean on Ala Moana St.

⓮ **Lahaina Jodo Mission.** This site has long been held sacred. The Hawaiians called it Puunoa Point, which means "the hill freed from taboo." Once a small village named Mala ("garden"), this peaceful place was a haven for Japanese immigrants, who came to Hawaii in 1868 as laborers for the sugarcane plantations. In 1968, on the 100th anniversary of Japanese presence in Hawaii, a Great Buddha statue (some 12 ft. high and weighing 3½ tons) was brought here from Japan. ⏱ 10–15 min. 12 Ala Moana St. (off Front St., near the Mala Wharf). ☎ 808/661-4304. Free admission. Daily during daylight hours.

South Maui

This is the hottest, sunniest, driest coastline on Maui—

Arizona by the sea. Rain rarely falls, and temperatures stick around 85°F (30°C) year-round. On former scrubland from Maalaea to Makena, where cacti once grew wild and cows grazed, are now four distinct areas—Maalaea, Kihei, Wailea, and Makena—and a surprising amount of traffic.

> *Ahihi-Kinau's water is as clear and smooth as glass. The beach is also the starting point for a hike on the King's Highway Trail.*

START Ahihi-Kinau Natural Area and Preserve. FINISH Maalaea. TRIP LENGTH 20 miles, but allow a full day to truly experience Maui's southern shore.

Drive south on Makena Rd., past Puu Olai to Ahihi Bay, where the road turns to gravel. Go another 2 miles along the coast to La Pérouse Bay.

❶ ★ **Ahihi-Kinau. La Pérouse Monument** is a pyramid of lava rocks that marks the spot where the first Westerner to "discover" the island, French explorer Admiral Comte de La Pérouse, set foot on Maui in 1786. Park here and if you're up for it, start your hike. Bring plenty of water and sun protection, and wear hiking boots that can withstand walking on lava. From La Pérouse Bay, you can pick up the old **King's Highway Trail,** which once circled the island. Walk along the sandy beach at La Pérouse; if the water is calm, take a swim, but if it's rough, just enjoy the view. Look for the trail indentation in the lava at the end of the sandy beach, which leads down to the lighthouse at the tip of Cape Hanamanioa, about a mile round-trip. Give yourself an hour or two to enjoy the peace and quiet.

Retrace your route back to Makeana Rd. Go left on Makena Alanui Rd., which becomes Wailea Alanui Rd. at the Shops at Wailea.

② **Longhi's.** I love to sit in the open air, sip a latte, and munch on Longhi's huge fresh baked cinnamon rolls. Big eaters may want to try the eggs Benedict or Florentine with a light, but flavorful, hollandaise and perfect baguette. See p 395.

Retrace your route back to Makeana Rd. and head toward Makena Landing Beach Park, a distance of 2 miles.

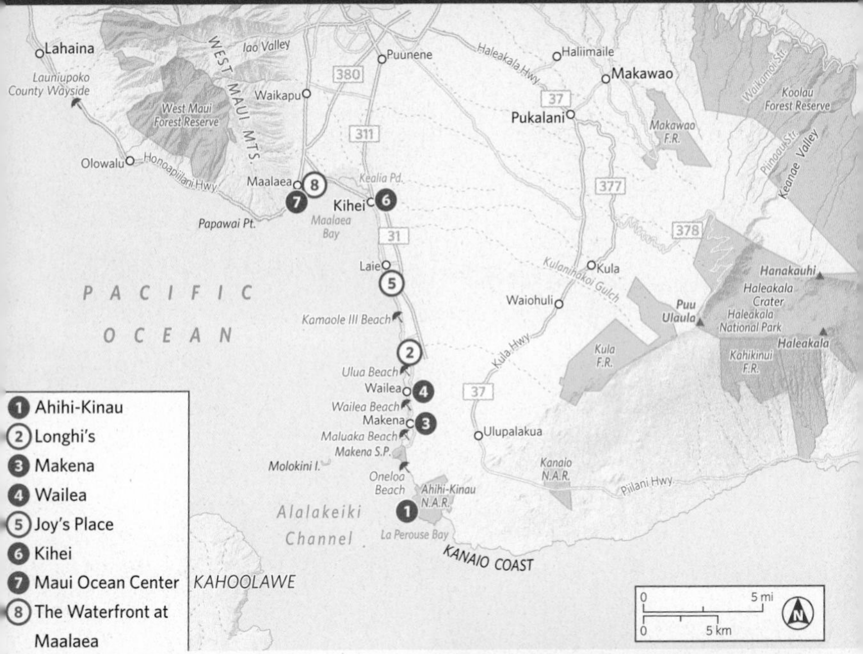

3 ★ **Makena.** After passing through well-groomed (some say overmanicured) Wailea, suddenly the road enters raw wilderness. This beach park has generally calm waters teeming with colorful tropical fish. It's the perfect place for beginner kayakers and snorkelers. Dino Ventura of **Makena Kayak Tours** (p 370) specializes in teaching first-time kayakers. For one of the more history-rich spots in this area, go south on Makena Road from the landing; on the right is **Keawali Congregational Church** (☎ 808/879-5557), built in 1855 with walls 3 feet thick. Surrounded by ti leaves, which by Hawaiian custom provides protection, and built of lava rock with coral used as mortar, this Protestant church sits on its own cove with a gold-sand beach. It always attracts a Sunday crowd for its 9:30am Hawaiian-language service. Take some time to wander through the cemetery; you'll see some tombstones with a ceramic picture of the deceased on them, which is an old custom. ⏲ **About 3½ hr. if you take the kayak tour, 1 hr. if you don't.**

Retrace your route back to Makena Rd. Go left on Makena Alanui Rd., which becomes Wailea Alanui Rd. Look for the blue sign noting public beach access, a couple of miles down the road.

Trip Tip

Before you start this tour, pack a swimsuit, towels, good hiking shoes, sunscreen, a hat, and plenty of water, and (depending on what you want to do) rent snorkel gear and/or a kayak (see p 370 for equipment rental information). Be sure to get up early to avoid the hot sun; you'll want to start off before 7am in the winter and 6am in the summer for the most comfortable temperatures.

4 ★ **Wailea.** A manicured oasis of multimillion-dollar resort hotels line 2 miles of palm-fringed gold coast. It's like Beverly Hills by the sea, except California never had it so good: warm, clear water full of tropical fish; year-round sunshine and clear blue skies; and hedonistic pleasure palaces on 1,500 acres of black-lava shore. This is the playground of the private jet set. The planned resort development—practically a well-heeled town—has an upscale shopping village, three prized golf courses of its own and three more in close range, and a tennis complex. For an up-close look, park in the public beach access lot and walk the ocean-front coastal trail, a 3-mile round-trip path with

> *Makena Kayak Tours specialize in teaching first-timers and take you off the coastline of Wailea in waters brimming with tropical fish.*

pleasing views everywhere you look—out to sea and to the neighboring islands, or inland to the broad lawns and gardens of the hotels. The trail's south end borders an extensive garden of native coastal plants, as well as ancient lava-rock house ruins juxtaposed with elegant oceanfront condos. But the chief attractions, of course, are those five outstanding beaches (the best is Wailea, p 359). ⏱ 1 hr.

Go left on Wailea Alanui Rd. and left again at the stop sign to Okolani Dr., which becomes Kihei Rd. It's about 3½ miles.

---

⑤ kids **Joy's Place.** Stop for lunch at this tiny hole in the wall. I recommend getting your food to go and taking it to the beach, just across the street. **See p 394.**

Continue north on Kihei Rd. for 2½ miles.

❻ Kihei. Kihei is a nearly continuous series of condos and minimalls lining South Kihei Road. This is Maui's best vacation bargain: Budget travelers flock to the eight sandy beaches along this scalloped, condo-packed, 7-mile stretch of coast. Kihei is neither charming nor quaint, but it does offer sunshine, affordability, and convenience, plus a couple of terrific places that showcase island wildlife. To get some background on the whales that visit Hawaii from December to April, stop by the **Hawaii Humpback Whale Sanctuary Center,** 726 Kihei Rd. (☎ 808/879-2818; www.hawaiihumpbackwhale.noaa.gov). This small educational center has dozens of exhibits, artifacts, and displays on whales, turtles, and other ocean life. Allow about 30 minutes here, then continue on Kihei Road north to **Kealia Pond National Wildlife Preserve** (☎ 808/875-1582), a 700-acre U.S. Fish and Wildlife wetland preserve where endangered Hawaiian stilts, coots, and ducks hang out and splash. These ponds work two ways: as bird preserves and as sedimentation basins that keep the coral reefs from silting from runoff. You can take a

>*The rich and famous flock to Wailea for the luxury hotels that line its two miles of perfect white-sand beaches.*

self-guided tour along a boardwalk dotted with interpretive signs and shade shelters, through sand dunes, and around ponds to Maalaea Harbor. The boardwalk starts at the outlet of Kealia Pond on the ocean side of North Kihei Road (near MM 2 on Hwy. 31). Among the Hawaiian water birds seen here are the black-crowned night heron, Hawaiian coot, Hawaiian duck, and Hawaiian stilt. There are also shorebirds like sanderling, Pacific golden plover, ruddy turnstone, and wandering tattler. From July to December the hawksbill turtle comes ashore here to lay her eggs. Allow at least an hour, longer if the turtles are around.

Continue north on Hwy. 31, then go left on Hwy. 30 to the Maalaea turnoff. It's about 3 miles.

7 ★★★ kids **Maui Ocean Center.** The windy oceanfront village of Maalaea centers on a small boat harbor (with a general store, a couple of restaurants, and a huge new mall) and the Maui Ocean Center, an aquarium/ocean complex. This 5-acre facility houses the largest aquarium in Hawaii and features one of Hawaii's largest predators: the tiger shark. Exhibits are geared toward the residents of Hawaii's ocean waters. As you walk past the three dozen or so tanks and numerous exhibits, you'll slowly descend from the "beach" to the deepest part of the ocean, without ever getting wet. Start at the surge pool, where you'll see shallow-water marine life like spiny urchins and cauliflower coral, then move on to the reef tanks, turtle pool, touch pool (with starfish and urchins), and eagle ray pool before reaching the star of the show: the 100-foot-long, 600,000-gallon main tank featuring tiger, gray, and white-tip sharks, as well as tuna, surgeonfish, triggerfish, and numerous other tropicals. A walkway goes right through the tank, so you'll be surrounded on three sides by marine creatures. If you're a certified scuba diver, you can participate in the **Shark Dive Maui Program,** which allows you (for $199) to plunge into the aquarium with sharks, stingrays, and tropical fish. ***Tip:*** Buy your tickets online to avoid the long admission lines. ⏱ 2 hr. or more. Maalaea Harbor Village, 192 Maalaea Rd. (the triangle btw. Honoapiilani Hwy. and Maalaea Rd.). ☎ 808/270-7000. www.mauioceancenter.com. Admission $25 adults, $22 seniors, $18 children 3-12. Daily 9am-5pm (until 6pm July-Aug).

---

(8) kids **The Waterfront at Maalaea.** Stop for dinner at this family-owned restaurant, known for its fresh seafood. See p 397.

Central Maui

This flat, often windy corridor between Maui's two volcanoes is where you'll most likely arrive—it's the site of the main airport. It's also home to the majority of the island's population, the heart of the business community, and the local government (courts, cops, and county/state government agencies). You'll find good shopping and dining bargains as well.

START Wailuku. **FINISH** Puunene.
TRIP LENGTH 1 day and 11 miles.

SITE GUIDE PAGE 338

1 Wailuku. With its faded wooden storefronts, old plantation homes, and shops straight out of the 1940s, Wailuku is like a time capsule. This quaint little town is worth a brief visit for its history and architecture. Wailuku has played a significant role in Maui's history over the past 225 years. One of Hawaii's bloodiest battles took place here in 1790, when Kamehameha the Great fought the Maui chiefs in his bid to unite the Hawaiian Islands. The town of Wailuku (which means "bloody waters") took its name from that battle in which the carnage was so intense that the 4-mile Iao Stream actually turned red from the slaughter. Wailuku was also where the missionaries landed in the mid-1800s to "save" the natives and convert them to Christianity. You can see still the New England architectural influences they brought with them in this quaint community. Plan to spend a couple of hours here.

Continue up Main St. west, which will be renamed Io Valley Rd., for about 3½ miles

2 ★★ kids **Iao Valley.** A 2,250-foot needle pricks gray clouds scudding across the blue sky. The air is moist and cool and the shade a welcome comfort. This is Iao ("Supreme Light") Valley, the eroded volcanic caldera of the West Maui Mountains and a 6-acre state park. The head of Iao Valley is a broad circular amphitheater where four major streams converge into Iao Stream. At the back of the amphitheater is rain-drenched **Puu Kukui,** the West Maui Mountains' highest point. No other Hawaiian valley lets you go from seacoast to rainforest so easily. This peaceful valley, full of tropical plants, rainbows, waterfalls, swimming holes, and hiking trails, is a place of solitude, reflection, and escape. Pack a picnic and take your swimsuit. ⏱ 1–2 hr. Iao Valley State Park, Iao Valley Rd., Wailuku. ☎ 808/984-8109. Daily 10am–4pm.

Retrace your route to the light at Main and High sts. (Hwy. 30), turn left, and drive 3 miles south.

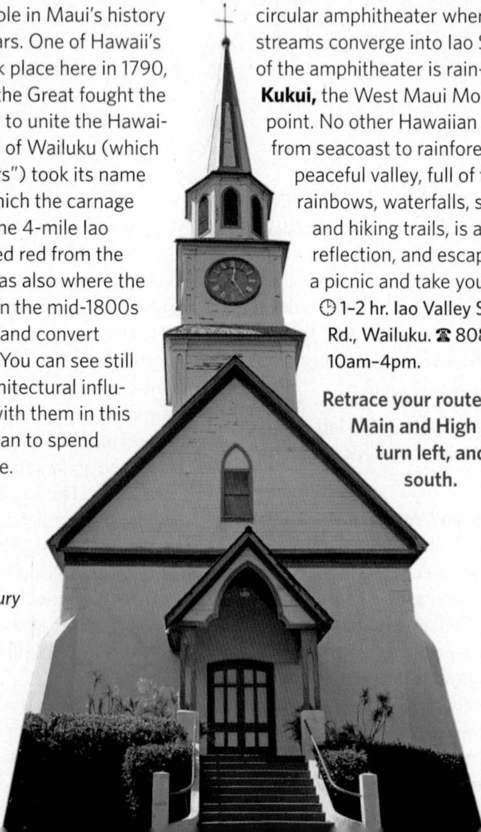

> *Missionaries came to Maui in the 18th-century to "save" the native population. Their influence is still apparent in the architecture.*

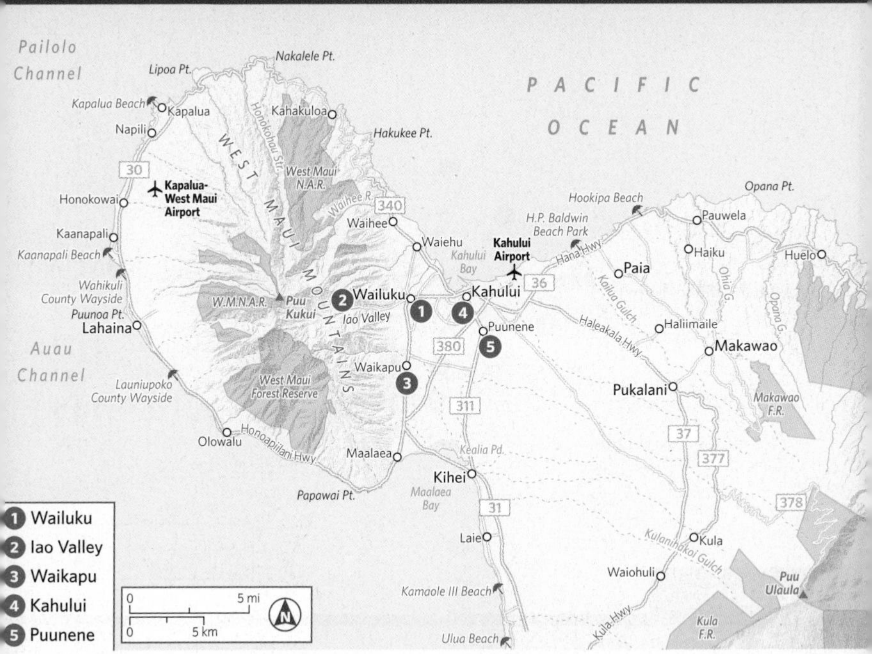

3 kids **Waikapu.** The tiny, one-street village of Waikapu has at least one attraction that's worth checking out: The 40-minute narrated tram ride around fields of pineapple, sugarcane, and papaya trees at **Maui Tropical Plantation** (p 322, 2) lets you relive Maui's agricultural past. ⏱ 1 hr.

Turn left on Hwy. 30 out of Maui Tropical Plantation, turn right on Waiko Rd., and go left on Hwy. 380 to Kahului, where the road is also called Dairy Rd. Turn left at Hwy. 36. Park across the street from Cutter Automotive, where hwys. 37 and 36 intersect. It's about 4 miles.

4 **Kahului.** As you drive through Maui's most populated town, look out on the miles of subdivisions: This is "Dream City," home to thousands of former sugarcane workers who dreamed of owning their own homes away from the plantations. Despite some shopping opportunities (p 378), this is not a place to spend your vacation. However, one attraction that is worth visiting—incongruously located under the airport flight path, next to Maui's busiest intersection and across from Costco in Kahului's new business park—is **Kanaha**

Where the Locals Eat

Located in the northern section of Wailuku, **Takamiya Market,** 359 N. Market St. (☎ 808/244-3404), is much loved by locals as the place to stock up on picnic fare and mouthwatering ethnic foods for sunset gatherings. Unpretentious home-cooked foods from East and West are prepared daily and served on plastic-foam plates. From the chilled-fish counter come fresh sashimi and poke (raw fish with seaweed and onions) and an assortment of prepared foods like shoyu chicken, tender fried squid, roast pork, Kalua pork, laulau, Chinese noodles, fiddlehead ferns, and Western comfort foods, such as corn bread and potato salad. Fresh produce and paper products are also available, but it's the prepared foods and fresh-fish counter that have made Takamiya's a household name in central Maui.

Wildlife Sanctuary (Haleakala Hwy. Ext. & Hana Hwy.; ☎ 808/984-8100). A 150-foot trail meanders along the shore to a shade shelter

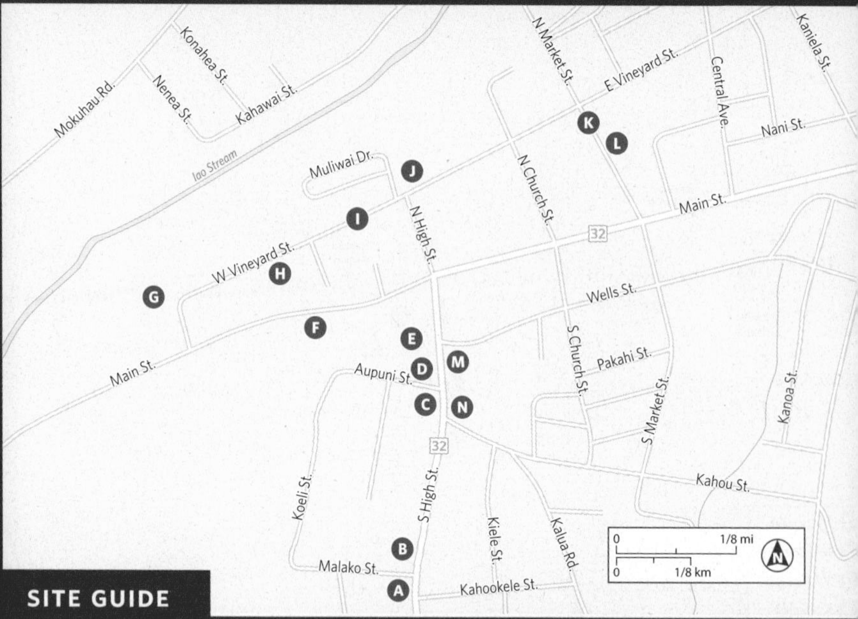

SITE GUIDE

1 Wailuku

The A **Wailuku Elementary School** (355 S. High St.) has housed Maui schoolchildren since 1904. It was designed by prolific architect C. W. Dickey. Next door is the B **Wailuku Union Church** (327 S. High St.), built in 1911. The C **Wailuku Public Library** (251 S. High St.), another Dickey building, was built in 1928. Yet another Dickey design, the D **Territorial Building** (151 S. High St.), built in 1930, is a great example of Dickey's trademark wide, overhanging eaves. Next door is the E **Kaahumanu Church** (103 High St.), named after Queen Kaahumanu, the monarch whose conversion to Christianity prompted thousands to follow her lead. The Queen attended services in a grass-hut structure here; the current church was built in 1876. The small cemetery contains the graves of the first missionaries. The F **Bailey House Museum** (p 316, 6) building was used as Hawaii's first boarding school for girls (plan for about half an hour at the museum). The many ethnic groups who flocked to Maui during the sugar boom years are represented at the Wailuku G **Cemetery** (Ilima and Vineyard sts.). Built in 1895, the H **Iao Congregational Church** (2371 Vineyard St.) continues to be very active in the community. On eclectic I **Vineyard Street,** you'll see beautifully restored buildings next to dilapidated shacks. Stop for a snack at the J **Maui Bake Shop** (2092 Vineyard St., p 316, 5). Local residents call K **Market Street** Antique Row for the collectibles and antiques shops that line the street. Opened in 1928 and built in Spanish Mission style, L **Iao Theater** (68 N. Market St., pictured here, p 406) was once the main entertainment venue of Wailuku, featuring both movies and live stage acts with such stars as Frank Sinatra. It's now home to Maui OnStage (www.mauionstage.com), which produces and hosts live theater and other events. Built in 1907, the M **Old State Court House** (190 S. High St.) was hearing trials up until a few years ago. Built in 1925, the N **Old County Building** (210 S. High St.) still holds a few county offices.

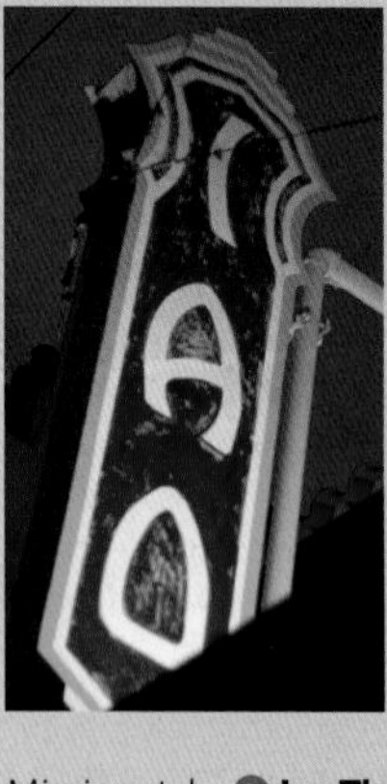

and lookout to the permanent home of the endangered Hawaiian black-necked stilt, whose population is now down to about 1,000. It's also a good place to see endangered Hawaiian Koloa ducks, stilts, coots, and other migrating shorebirds. Plan a quick 10-minute drive through Kahului and another 15-minute walk wandering the wildlife sanctuary.

Take Hwy. 36 to the intersection at Dairy Rd. and turn right. Make a left on Puunene Ave. and another left on Hansen Rd.

5 **Puunene.** To soak up a little more of Maui's colorful history, drive out to this town in the middle of the central Maui plains. Once a thriving sugar plantation town with hundreds of homes, a school, a shopping area, and a community center, Puunene today has little more than the sugar mill, a post office, and the **Alexander & Baldwin Sugar Museum** (p 317, 8). You can tour the museum in 15 minutes, then step outside, breathe in the smells of the nearby sugar mill, and watch what is left of the green sugarcane blowing in the wind. This part of Maui is quickly disappearing.

> ABOVE *The charming and historic Iao Theater in Wailuku plays host to Maui's rich community theater tradition.* BELOW *The natural beauty of the Iao Valley.*

Upcountry Maui

After a few days at the beach, you'll probably take notice of the 10,000-foot mountain in the middle of Maui. The slopes of Haleakala ("House of the Sun") are home to cowboys, farmers, and other country people who wave back as you drive by. Crisp air, emerald pastures, eucalyptus, flower farms, and even a misty California redwood grove are the highlights of this tropical Olympus.

> *Makawao's Hui No'eau Visual Arts Center is Maui's premier arts collective. It's also proof that this is no longer a sleepy cowboy town.*

START Makawao. FINISH Ulupalakua.
TRIP LENGTH 24 miles, but plan on a full day.

1 ★ **Makawao.** Until recently, this small, two-street upcountry town consisted of little more than a post office, gas station, feed store, bakery, and restaurant/bar serving the cowboys and farmers living in the surrounding community; the hitching posts outside storefronts were really used to tie up horses. As the population of Maui started expanding in the 1970s, a health-food store popped up, followed by boutiques and a host of health-conscious restaurants. The result is an eclectic amalgam of old *paniolo* (cowboy) Hawaii and the baby boomer trends of transplanted mainlanders. **Hui No'eau Visual Arts Center** (p 380). Hawaii's premier arts collective, is definitely worth a stop. ⏱ 1-2 hrs.

Take Makawao Ave. to the light at Hwy. 37, turn left, and head up the mountain. Go left on Hwy. 377. Allow 25 minutes.

2 **Kula Lodge.** Take a lunch break here not only for the food but also for the million-dollar vista that pans the flanks of Haleakala, central Maui, the ocean, and the West Maui Mountains. See p 394.

3 ★ **Kula.** A feeling of pastoral remoteness prevails in this upcountry community of old flower farms, humble cottages, and new suburban ranch houses with million-dollar views that take in the ocean, isthmus, West Maui Mountains, Lanai, and Kahoolawe off in the distance. At night the lights run along the gold coast like a string of pearls, from Maalaea

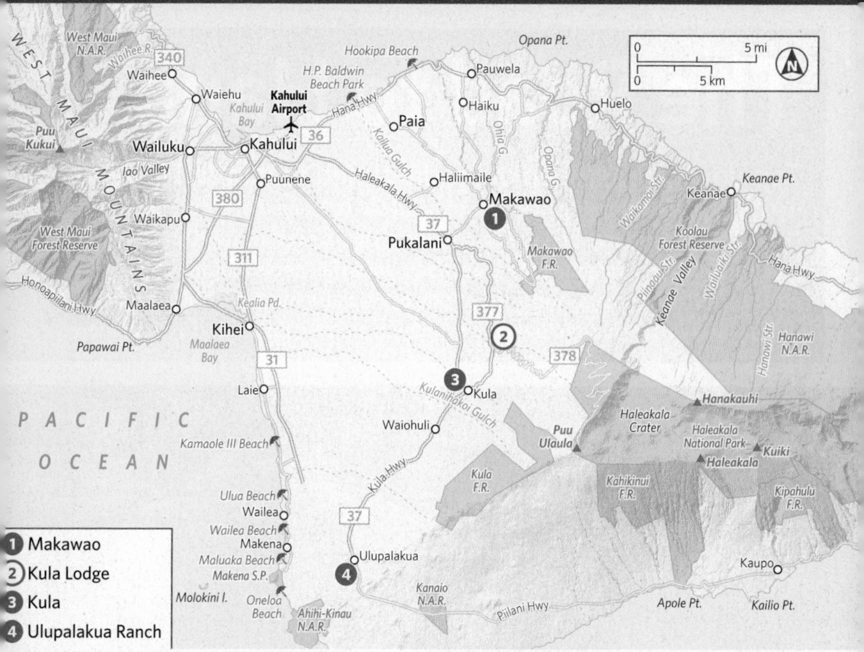

o Puu Olai. Kula sits at a cool 3,000 feet, just ›elow the cloud line, and from here a winding oad snakes its way up to Haleakala National 'ark. Everyone here grows something—Maui ›nions, carnations, orchids, and proteas, those trange-looking blossoms that look like *Star 'rek* props. Must stops are: **Alii Kula Lavender 'arm** (p 323, ④ and **Surfing Goat Dairy** p 323, ❸).

:ontinue on Hwy. 37 for 14 miles.

❹ **Ulupalakua Ranch.** On the southern houlder of Haleakala, this 20,000-acre spread ›as once owned by legendary sea captain ames Makee, celebrated in the Hawaiian ong and dance *Hula O Makee.* Wounded in Honolulu waterfront brawl in 1843, Makee noved to Maui and bought Ulupalakua. He enamed it Rose Ranch, planted sugar as a cash rop, and grew rich. He also added 1,600 head f livestock to the ranch. King David Kalakaua, ne Merrie Monarch, visited the ranch so often cottage was built for him on the property, 'hich still exists today as the site of the **'edeschi Vineyard**'s tasting room. This is the nly winery on Maui, and it was established in 974 by Napa vintner Emil Tedeschi, who began growing Californian and European grapes here. Across from the winery are the remains of the three smokestacks of the **Makee Sugar Mill,** built in 1878. This is home to Maui artist Reems Mitchell, who carved the mannequins on the front porch of the Ulupalakua Ranch Store: a Filipino with his fighting cock, a cowboy, a farmhand, and a sea captain, all representing the people of Maui's history. Tedeschi Vineyards, Off Hwy. 37 (Kula Hwy.). ☎ 808/878-6058. www.mauiwine.com. Daily 10am–5pm. Free tastings; tours given 10:30am, 1:30pm, and 3pm.

Polo, Parades, and Rodeos

Maui's Upcountry events center around polo, parades, and rodeos. In April the **Maui Polo Season** begins (☎ 808/877-7744 for information). In July, two Makawao events take place: the **Fourth of July Makawao Parade,** one of Maui's oldest parades (☎ 808/572-9565), followed by the **Fourth of July Makawao Rodeo,** where the top rodeo riders from across the state compete (☎ 808/572-8102).

The Road to Hana

Top down, sunscreen on, radio tuned to a little Hawaiian music on a Maui morning: It's time to head out to Hana along the Hana Highway (Hwy. 36). This wiggle of a road runs along Maui's northeastern shore, winding past taro patches, magnificent seascapes, waterfall pools, botanical gardens, and verdant rainforests, and ends at one of Hawaii's most beautiful tropical places. Bring a few beach towels, a swimsuit, a picnic lunch, and your camera.

> *The 54 bridges and natural beauty along the road to Hana makes the drive an arresting holiday activity.*

START Kahului. **FINISH** Nahiku. **TRIP LENGTH** 50 miles. **The drive takes at least 3 hours, but to really enjoy the trip, plan to spend all day.**

❶ **Fueling up in Kahului.** Before you even start out, fill up your gas tank. Don't wait to get gas in Paia, the last place for gas until you get to Hana (even by Maui standards the gas in Paia is unbelievably expensive). Plan to leave early—Hana is some 54 bridges and 600 hairpin turns down the road.

From Kahului take Hwy. 36 to Paia.

② **Charley's.** Pull into quaint Paia for a big hearty breakfast at a reasonable price. 142 Hana Hwy. ☎ 808/579-9453. $-$$.

Continue on Hwy. 36, stopping just before MM 9.

❸ ★ **Hookipa Beach Park.** Hookipa ("hospitality") is where the top-ranked windsurfers come to test themselves against the forces of nature: thunderous surf and forceful wind. See p 356.

Make a small detour off the Hana Hwy. turnin left at Hahana Rd., between MM 13 and 14.

❹ ★★ kids **Jaws.** If it's winter and surf's up, here's your chance to watch expert tow-in surfers battle the mammoth waves (60 ft. or so) off Pauwela Point. The area is known as Jaws because the waves will chew you up.

Just before MM 15.

⑤ **Maui Grown Market and Deli.** This is my pick for the best "bang for your buck" picnic lunch. A mere $9 gets you a sandwich (I love the avo-veggie, but they also have pastrami, roast beef, turkey, an tuna) with two cookies, a mac-nut candy bar, chips or fruit, and soda or water. Han Hwy. ☎ 808/572-1693. $.

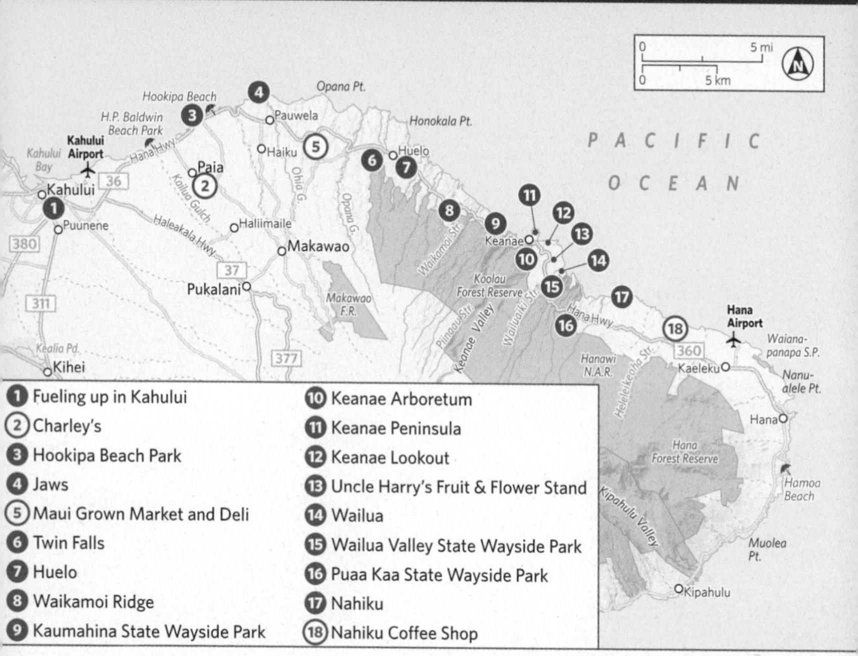

After MM 16, the road is still called the Hana Hwy., but the number changes from Hwy. 36 to Hwy. 360, and the mile markers go back to 0. Drive to MM 2.

6 **Twin Falls.** Pull over on the mountainside and park, then walk about 3 to 5 minutes to the waterfall and pool. The mountain stream is chilly when you first get in, but it's good for swimming. If it's crowded, keep going—plenty of other swimming holes and another waterfall are coming up.

Just before MM 4 on a blind curve, look for a double row of mailboxes on the left.

7 **Huelo.** This is a great side trip to see some of Maui's history. Down the road lies a hidden Hawaii of an earlier time, where an indescribable sense of serenity prevails. Hemmed in by Waipo and Hoalua bays is the remote community of Huelo, which means "tail end" or "last." This fertile area once supported a population of 75,000; today only a few hundred live in the scattered homes here. Stop in at the historic 1853 **Kaulanapueo Church.**

Continue to MM 9.

8 kids **Waikamoi Ridge.** This small state wayside area with restrooms, picnic tables, and a barbecue area has an easy .75-mile loop trail hike. It starts just behind the QUIET: TREES AT WORK sign.

Just past MM 12:

9 kids **Kaumahina State Wayside Park.** This is a good pit stop (with restrooms) and a lovely place for a picnic. It also offers wonderful views and a great photo op of the rugged coastline all the way down to the jutting Keanae Peninsula.

Between MM 16 and MM 17.

Travel Tip

Forget your mainland road manners. Practice aloha: Give way at the one-lane bridges, wave at oncoming motorists, and let the big guys in 4WDs with pig-hunting dogs in the back have the right of way—it's just common sense, brah. If the guy behind you blinks his lights, let him pass. And don't honk your horn—in Hawaii it's considered rude.

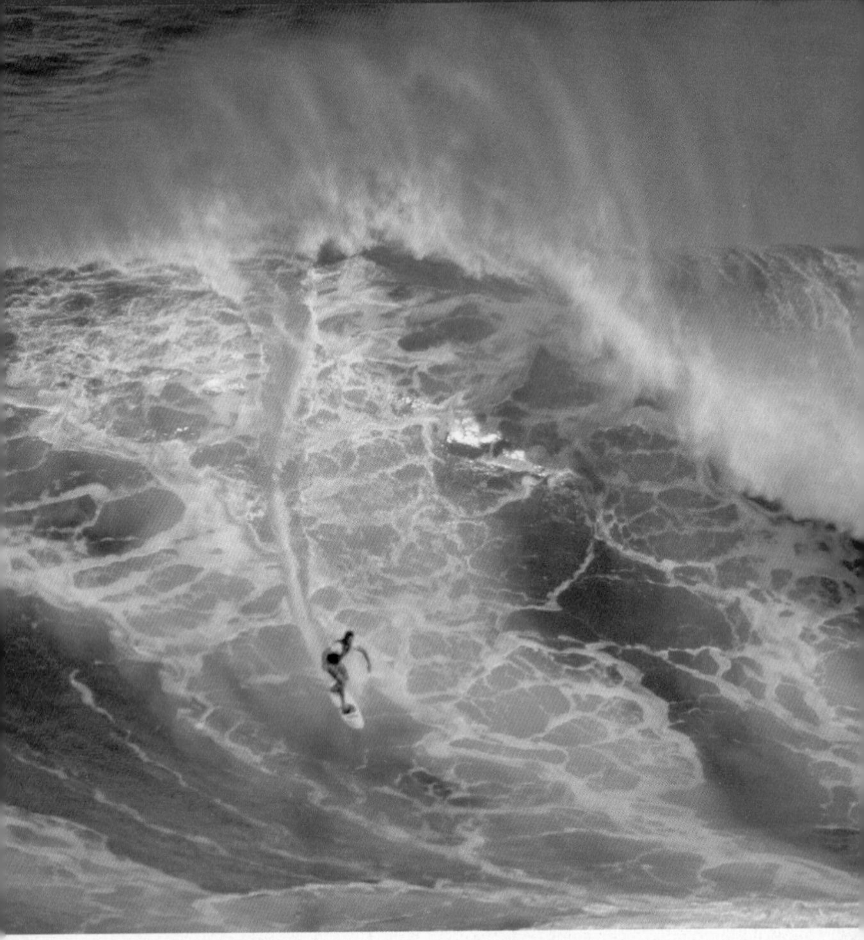

> *Each winter surfers are chewed up by 60-foot swells at "Jaws" off Pauwela Point.*

10 ★★ kids **Keanae Arboretum.** Here the region's botany is divided into three parts: native forest; introduced forest; and traditional Hawaiian plants, food, and medicine. You can swim in the pools of Piinaau Stream or press on along a mile-long trail into Keanae Valley, and a tropical rainforest.

11 ★★★ kids **Keanae Peninsula.** The old Hawaiian village of **Keanae** ("the mullet") stands out against the Pacific like a place time forgot. It's one of the last coastal enclaves of native Hawaiians, who still grow taro in patches and pound it into poi, pluck *opihi* (limpet) from tide pools along the jagged coast, and cast throw-nets at schools of fish. Be sure to see the **Keanae Congregational Church,** built in 1860 of lava rocks and coral mortar.

Just past MM 17.

12 kids **Keanae Lookout.** Get out your camera: From this spot you can see the entire Keanae Peninsula's checkerboard pattern of green taro fields and its ocean boundary etched in black lava. The peninsula was created when an eruption of Haleakala flowed through the Koolau Gap and down Keanae Valley, adding this geological punctuation to the rugged coastline.

Around MM 18.

⑬ **Uncle Harry's Fruit & Flower Stand.** You'll start to see numerous small stands selling fruit or flowers. Many of these stands work on the honor system: You leave your money in the basket and select your purchase. My favorite is Uncle Harry's; his family sells a variety of fruits and juices here Monday through Saturday.

Just after Uncle Harry's, look for the Wailua Rd. off to the left.

⑭ **Wailua.** This road will take you through the hamlet of homes and churches of Wailua. Behind the pink **St. Gabriel's Church** is the smaller, blue and white **Coral Miracle Church,** home of **Our Lady of Fatima Shrine.** According to legend, in 1860 the men of this village were building a church with stone made from offshore coral. But the coral was in deep water, and the men could only dive for a few pieces at a time, making the construction of the church an arduous project. A freak storm hit the area and deposited the coral from the deep onto a nearby beach. The Hawaiians gathered what they needed and completed the church. Afterward, another freak storm hit the area and swept the remaining coral back out to sea.

Just before MM 19.

⑮ ★ **Wailua Valley State Wayside Park.** Climb up the stairs for a view of the Keanae Valley, waterfalls, and Wailua Peninsula. On a really clear day, you can see up the mountain to the Koolau Gap.

Halfway between MM 22 and MM 23.

⑯ **Puaa Kaa State Wayside Park.** The sound of waterfalls (Puaa Kaa means "open laughter") provides the background music for this small park area with restrooms, a phone, and a picnic area. A well-marked path takes you to the falls and a swimming hole. There are ginger plants everywhere: Pick some flowers and enjoy their sweet smell as you travel.

Just after MM 25 is a narrow 3-mile road leading from the highway, at about 1,000-ft. elevation, down to sea level.

⑰ **Nahiku.** At one time this was a thriving village of thousands; today the population has dwindled to fewer than a hundred—a few Hawaiian families, but mostly extremely wealthy mainland residents who jet in for a few weeks at a time to their luxurious vacation homes. At the end of the road, you can see the remains of an old wharf from the town's rubber plantation days (and there are still some rubber trees along the road). There's a small picnic area off to the side, from which you may spot dolphins in the bay.

> *The peninsula that hosts the spectacular Keanae Lookout was created by volcanic lava flows that shaped its craggy coastline.*

Go ½ mile past MM 28. On the ocean side of the road is:

⑱ **Nahiku Coffee Shop.** Stop in for some Maui-grown coffee and locally baked treats. See p 304, ⑥.

Hana

Green, tropical Hana is the type of small coastal village most people dream of when they decide to visit Maui. Here you'll find a rainforest dotted with cascading waterfalls and sparkling blue pools, red- and black-sand beaches, and lush tropical scenery. Most visitors will zip through Hana, perhaps taking a quick look at a few sights before buzzing on down the road. They might think they've seen Hana, but they definitely haven't experienced its true beauty and serenity.

> *Hana's rainforests are filled with lush tropical beauty, isolated beaches, and waterfalls that pour into sparkling pools, such as the ones at Oheo Gulch, pictured here.*

START Hana. **FINISH** Kaupo.
TRIP LENGTH 2 days and 12 miles.

Day 1

From Hwy. 360 turn toward the ocean on Ulaino Rd., by MM 31. The drive takes about 5 minutes.

❶ kids ★★ **Kahanu Garden.** This 472-acre garden contains plant collections from the Pacific Islands, including the largest-known collection of breadfruit. The real draw here is the **Piilanihale *Heiau.*** Believed to be the largest in the state, it measures 340 feet by 415 feet, and it was built in a unique terrace design not seen anywhere else in Hawaii. The walls are some 50 feet tall and 8 to 10 feet thick. Historians believe that Piilani's two sons and his grandson built the mammoth temple, which was dedicated to war, sometime in the 1500s. ⏱ 30 min. Ulaino Rd. ☎ 808/248-8912. www.ntbg.org. Admission $10. Mon–Fri 10am–2pm.

At MM 32:

❷ ★★★ kids **Waianapanapa State Park.** On the outskirts of Hana, shiny black-sand Waianapanapa Beach appears like a vivid dream, with bright green jungle foliage on three sides and cobalt-blue water lapping at its shore. Swimming isn't the best here, but you can hike a trail (p 363) along the flow that passes by sea cliffs, lava tube, arches, and the beach. See p 359.

Follow Hwy. 360. The road splits about ½ mile past MM 33, at the police station. Both roads go through Hana, but the lower road, Uakea Rd., is more scenic.

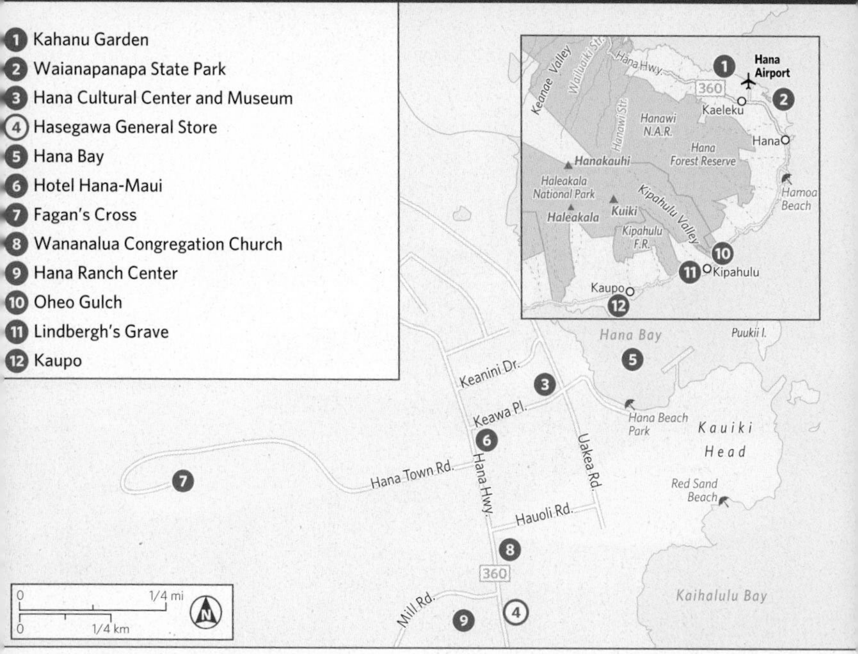

3 ★ **Hana Cultural Center and Museum.** This small building has an excellent collection of Hawaiian quilts, artifacts, books, and photos. Also on the grounds is **Kauhala O Hana,** composed of four *hale* (houses) for living, meeting, cooking, and canoe-building or canoe storage. ⏱ 30 min. 4974 Uakea Rd. ☎ 808/248-8622. www.hookele.com/hccm. Daily 10am–4pm.

Turn toward the mountains at Keawa Place, then go left on Hwy. 360 for ½ mile.

4 **Hasegawa General Store.** For lunch, I usually head for this legendary general store, established in 1919. The aisles are choked with merchandise: organic dried fruit, every type of soda and juice you can imagine, a variety of breads and lunchmeats, baby food, and napkins and other necessities. Stock up, then head to Hana Bay for a picnic. Hwy. 360, Hana. ☎ 808/248-8231.

Trace your route back to Uakea Rd., and turn right to the bay. It's less than ½ mile.

5 ★ kids **Hana Bay.** You'll find restrooms, showers, picnic tables, barbecue areas, and even a snack bar (which I would pass on—it's overpriced). Enjoy watching the activities in the bay—fishermen, surfers, swimmers, and beachcombers—as you eat your lunch. Then take a short 5- to 10-minute hike to the 386-foot red-faced cinder cone beside the bay. This is **Kauiki Hill,** the scene of numerous fierce battles of ancient Hawaii and the birthplace of Queen Kaahumanu in 1768. Look for the trail along the hill on the wharf side, and follow the path through the ironwood trees; the lighthouse on the point will come into view, and you'll see pocket beaches of red cinder below. Honeymooners might want to picnic in this romantic, secluded spot. ⏱ 1–2 hr.

Cross Uakea Rd. and drive up Keawa Place. Turn left on Hwy. 360. It's less than ½ mile.

Travel Tip

See Hana's attractions, especially the pools, ponds, waterfalls, and hikes, early in the day. You'll have them all to yourself. The day-tourists arrive in Hana around 11am and stay until about 4pm; that's when the area is overrun with hundreds and hundreds of people in a hurry and wanting to see everything in just a few hours.

> ABOVE *The Hotel Hana-Maui, one of Hawaii's best resorts.* BELOW *The 30-foot Fagan's Cross, made of lava stone, greets hikers on the Hana coast.*

❻ **Hotel Hana-Maui.** If you can afford it, spend the night at the best hotel in Hana (and one of the state's top resorts). Even if you don't stay here, plan on taking a look around this charming resort, and consider staying for a drink or a meal. See p 400.

On the green hills across the street from Hotel Hana-Maui.

❼ kids **Fagan's Cross.** If you have a carload of kids and don't think they'd settle down long enough to tour the Hotel Hana-Maui, then take them for a hike up this hill to the 30-foot-high white cross, made of lava rock and erected in memory of Paul Fagan, who founded the Hana Ranch as well as the Hotel Hana-Maui. The 3-mile round-trip hike provides a gorgeous view of the Hana coast, especially at sunset, when Fagan himself liked to climb this hill. Watch your step as you ascend this steep hill, and enter the pastures at your own risk; they're often occupied by glaring bulls and cows with new calves. ⏱ 1–2 hr. Hana Hwy., across from the Hotel Hana-Maui.

Day 2

Turn right on Hwy. 360, and go just past Hauoli Rd.

❽ **Wananalua Congregation Church.** Stop in and see this historic coral-stone church, completed in 1842 during the missionary rush to convert the natives. Hawaiians believe it was built atop an old Hawaiian *heiau* (temple), considered very bad luck. ⏱ 15 min. Hwy. 30, just past Hauoli Rd.

Just past the church, on the right side of Hwy. 360.

❾ **Hana Ranch Center.** This small cluster of one-story buildings is the commercial center for Hana, with a post office, bank, general store, the Hana Ranch Stables, and a restaurant and snack bar. Hwy. 360.

Continue past Hana on Hwy. 360 for 8 miles.

❿ ★★★ kids **Oheo Gulch.** This is the Kipahulu end of Haleakala National Park. For years people called this series of step waterfalls and pools "Seven Sacred Pools," a misnomer created back in the 1940s (there are way more than seven pools, and *all* water in Hawaii is considered sacred). You can also reach the magnificent 400-foot **Waimoku Falls** via an often-muddy, but rewarding, hour-long uphill hike. The Kipahulu rangers offer safety information, exhibits, books, and a variety of walks and hikes year-round; check at the station for current activities. Expect showers on the Kipahulu coast. ☎ 808/248-7375. www.nps.gov/hale. $5 per person or $10 per car.

A mile past Oheo Gulch on the ocean side of the road.

⓫ **Lindbergh's Grave.** First to fly across the Atlantic Ocean, Charles A. Lindbergh (1902–1974) found peace in the Pacific; he settled in Hana, where he died of cancer in 1974. The famous aviator is buried under river stones behind the 1857 **Palapala Hoomau Congregational Church;** his tombstone is engraved with his favorite words, from the 139th Psalm: "If I take the wings of the morning and dwell in the uttermost parts of the sea . . . ." ⏱ 15 min.

About 5 miles farther down Hwy. 360:

> *Oheo Gulch, a dazzling series of pools and cataracts cascading to the sea, is so popular it has its own roadside parking lot.*

⓬ **Kaupo.** If you still have daylight, you can continue on to the highlights of remote, rural Kupo. These include the restored **Huialoha Congregationalist "Circuit" Church,** originally constructed in 1859, and the **Kaupo Store,** an eclectic old country store that carries a range of bizarre goods and doesn't keep any of its posted hours. It's a fun place to "talk story" with the staff. ☎ 808/248-8054. Mon–Fri 7:30am–4:30pm, or whenever they feel like opening.

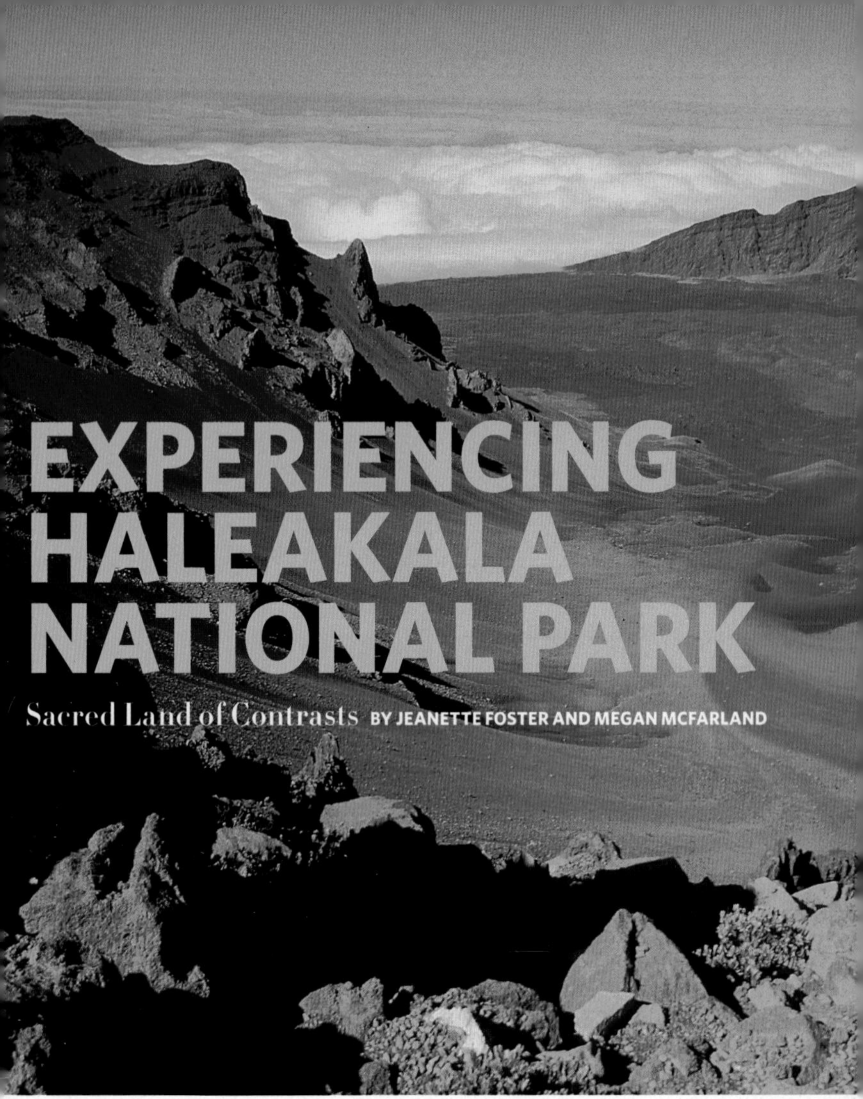

EXPERIENCING HALEAKALA NATIONAL PARK

Sacred Land of Contrasts

BY JEANETTE FOSTER AND MEGAN MCFARLAND

DOMINATING THE EAST SIDE OF MAUI IS is the 10,000-foot summit of Mount Haleakala, long recognized by Hawaiians as a sacred site. The volcano and its surrounding wilderness, extending down the volcano's southeastern flank to Maui's eastern coast, offer spectacular treats for the senses. There are two separate and distinct destinations within the park: Haleakala Summit and the Kipahulu coast, home to Oheo Gulch.

At the summit, you'll encounter dry alpine air, multihued volcanic landscapes, dramatic mists and clouds, and views of three other islands on a clear day; near the sea, the lush green of a subtropical rainforest takes over. You'll find freshwater pools, towering ohia and koa trees, ginger and ti plants, kukui, mango, guava, and bamboo.

Ancient chants tell of Pele, the volcano goddess, and one of her siblings doing battle on the crater floor where Kawilinau (Bottomless Pit) now stands. The only people allowed into this sacred area were the *kahuna* (masters), who took their apprentices to live for periods of time in this intensely spiritual place. Today, New Agers revere Haleakala as one of earth's most powerful energy points.

The Lay of the Land

Scientists believe that the Haleakala volcano began its growth on the ocean floor about 2 million years ago, as magma from below the Pacific Ocean floor erupted through cracks in the Pacific Plate (see "Volcanoes," p 234). The volcano has erupted numerous times over the past 10,000 years. Though the most recent eruption is thought to have occurred about 1790, Haleakala is still considered an active volcano.

You'll pass through as many ecological zones on a 2-hour drive from the humid coast to the harsh summit of the mountain as you would on a journey from Mexico to Canada, and the temperature can vary 30 degrees from sea level to summit.

Haleakala is home to more endangered species than any other national park in the U.S., and the park was designated an International Biosphere Reserve in 1980. Among the rare birds you may see here:

Nene

HAWAIIAN GOOSE

BRANTA SANDWICHENSIS

A relative of the Canada goose, the nene is Hawaii's state bird, standing about 2 feet tall with a black head and yellow cheeks. The wild nene on Haleakala number fewer than 250, and the species remains endangered.

Uau

HAWAIIAN PETREL

PTERODROMA SANDWICHENSIS

These large, dark gray-brown and white birds travel as far as Alaska and Japan on two-week feeding trips. Their status is listed as vulnerable; it's estimated that fewer than 1,000 birds are nesting on the Haleakala Crater.

Kike Koa

MAUI PARROTBILL

PSEUDONESTOR XANTHOPHRYS

One of Hawaii's rarest birds, it has an olive green body and yellow chest. Its strong, hooked, parrot-like bill is used to pry chunks of koa bark as it searches for food.

Akohekohe

CRESTED HONEYCREEPER

PALMERIA DOLEI

Listed as a critically endangered species, this bird is native only to a 22-mile-square area on the northeastern slope of Haleakala. It has primarily black plumage, with bright-orange surrounding the eyes and nape, and a furl of white feathers sprouting over the beak.

The "House of the Sun"

According to ancient legend, Haleakala got its name from a clever trick that the demigod Maui pulled on the sun. Maui's mother, the goddess Hina, complained one day that the sun sped across the sky so quickly that her tapa cloth couldn't dry.

Maui, known as a trickster, devised a plan. The next morning he went to the top of the great mountain and waited for the sun to poke its head above the horizon. Quickly, Maui lassoed the sun, bringing its path across the sky to an abrupt halt. The sun begged Maui to let go, and Maui said he would on one condition: that the sun slow its trip across the sky to give the island more sunlight. The sun assented. In honor of this agreement, the Hawaiians call the mountain Haleakala, or "House of the Sun."

To this day, the top of Haleakala has about 15 minutes more sunlight than the communities on the coastline below.

Haleakala National Park

At once forbidding and compelling, Haleakala National Park is Maui's main natural attraction. More than 1.3 million people a year ascend the 10,023-foot-high mountain to peer down into the crater of the world's largest dormant volcano. But there's more to do here than simply stare into a big black hole: Just going up the mountain is an experience in itself. Where else on the planet can you climb from sea level to 10,000 feet in just 37 miles, or a 2-hour drive? The snaky road passes through big puffy cumulus clouds to offer magnificent views of the isthmus of Maui, the West Maui Mountains, and the Pacific Ocean.

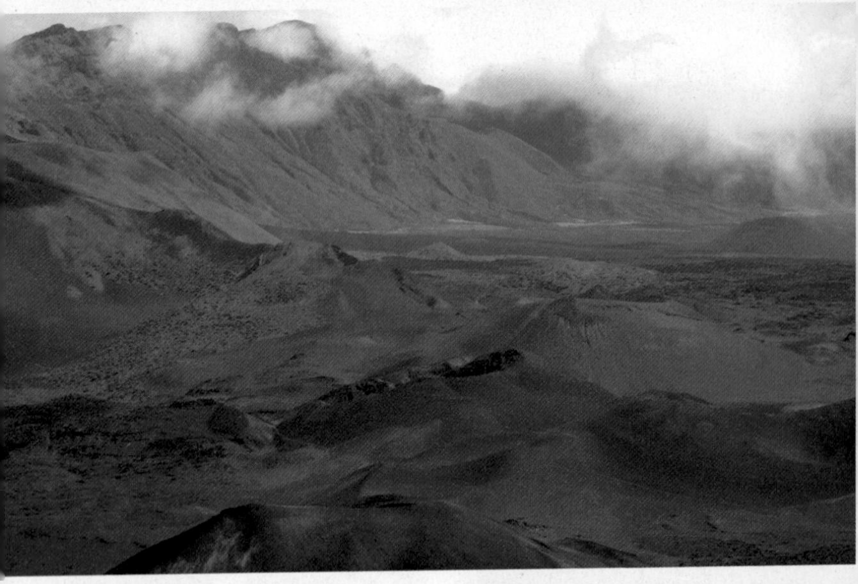

> *Descend the treacherous Haleakala Crater Road along at least 33 switchbacks and through multiple climate changes into the belly of the volcano.*

START Kahului. FINISH Puu Ulaula Overlook. TRIP LENGTH 37 miles, about a 2-hour drive.

From Kahului, take Hwy. 37 to Hwy. 377 to Hwy. 378.

1 ★★★ **Haleakala Crater Road.** If you look on a Maui map, almost in the middle of the part that resembles a torso, there's a black wiggly

Seeing Stars

From May to September, the rangers at Haleakala National Park host the Kilo Hoku Star Program. For about an hour, rangers tell ancient Hawaiian stories, point out the major constellations, and reveal the secrets of Polynesian navigation. In Hosmer Grove, just outside the park entrance (☎ 808/572-4400; www.nps.gov/hale).

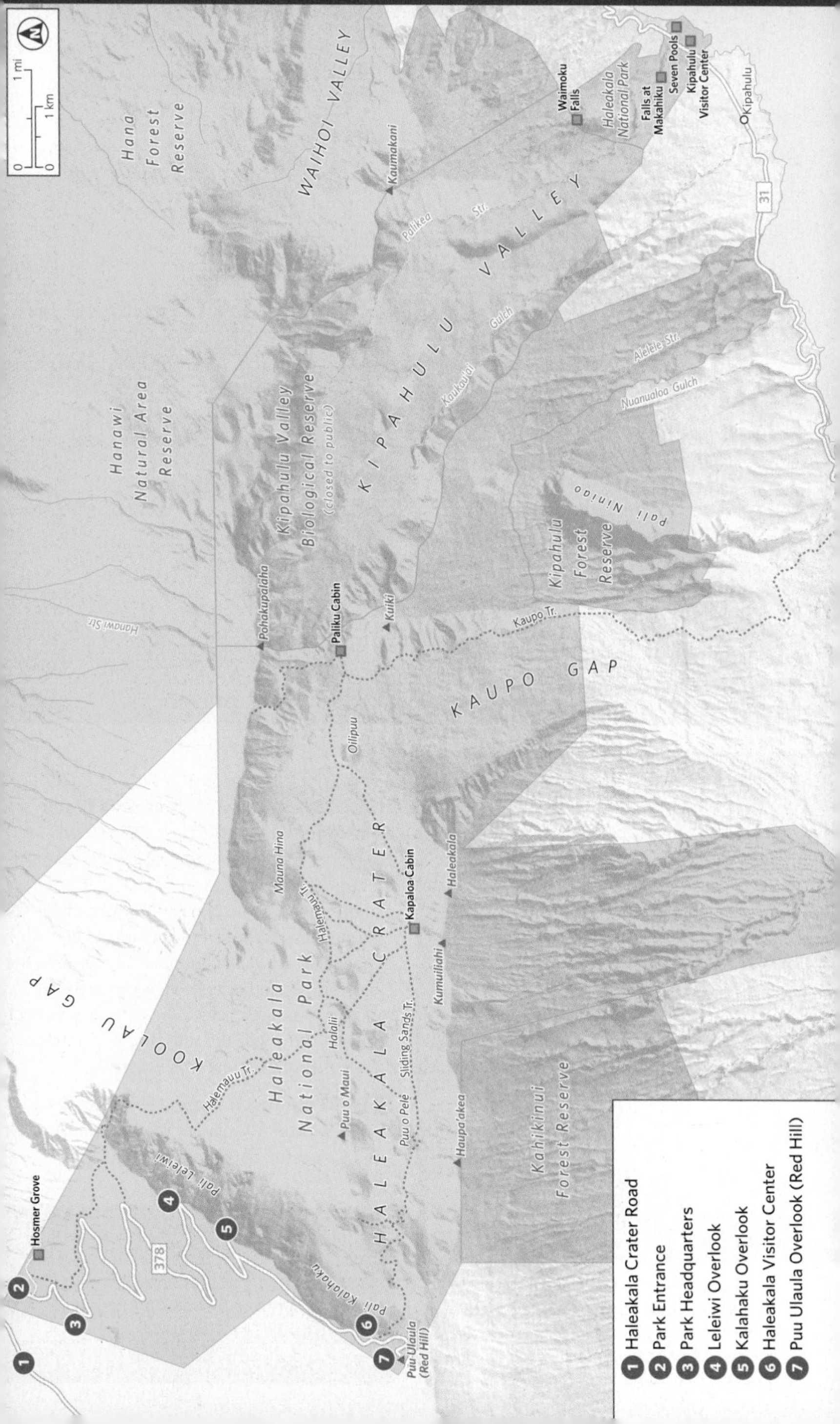

Hana Forest Reserve
Hanawi Natural Area Reserve
Kipahulu Valley Biological Reserve (closed to public)
WAIHOI VALLEY
KIPAHULU VALLEY
Kaumakani
Palikea Str.
Kaukaui'ai Gulch
Alelele Str.
Nuanualoa Gulch
Pali Ninião
Kipahulu Forest Reserve
Waimoku Falls
Haleakala National Park
Falls at Makahiku
Seven Pools
Kipahulu Visitor Center
Kipahulu
31
Hanawi Str.
Pohakupalaha
Paliku Cabin
Kuiki
Kaupo Tr.
KAUPO GAP
Oilipuu
Mauna Hina
Halemauu Tr.
HALEAKALA CRATER
Kapaloa Cabin
Haleakala
Kumuiliahi
Haleakala National Park
Halalii
Sliding Sands Tr.
Puu o Maui
Puu o Pele
Haupa'akea
Kahikinui Forest Reserve
KOOLAU GAP
Hosmer Grove
378
Pali Leleiwi
Pali Kalahaku
Puu Ulaula (Red Hill)
0 1 mi
0 1 km
1 Haleakala Crater Road
2 Park Entrance
3 Park Headquarters
4 Leleiwi Overlook
5 Kalahaku Overlook
6 Haleakala Visitor Center
7 Puu Ulaula Overlook (Red Hill)

> ABOVE *Catch an out-of-this-world perspective into a volcano's crater from the Leleiwi Overlook.* BELOW *At the Kalahaku Overlook you'll see the rare Hawaiian silversword plant, which can take up to 50 years to bloom.*

line that looks like this: WWWWW. That's **Hwy. 378,** also known as **Haleakala Crater Road**—one of the fastest-ascending roads in the world. This grand corniche has at least 33 switchbacks; passes through numerous climate zones; goes under, in, and out of clouds; takes you past rare silversword plants and endangered Hawaiian geese sailing through the clear, thin air; and offers a view that extends for more than 100 miles. Along the way, expect fog, rain, and wind. You may also encounter stray cattle and downhill bicyclists.

❷ **Park Entrance.** A ranger will collect the entrance fee of $10 per car (or $2 for a bicycle), good for a week of unlimited entry.

Trip Tip

On your way back down the mountain, put your car in low gear; that way, you won't destroy your brakes by riding them the whole way down.

Before You Go

At the 10,023-foot summit, weather changes fast. With wind chill, temperatures can be below freezing any time of year. Summer can be dry and warm, winters wet, windy, and cold. Before you go, get current weather conditions from the park (☎ 808/572-4400) or the **National Weather Service** (☎ 808/871-5054). Bring water and a jacket or a blanket, especially if you go up for sunrise. If you're not a morning person, don't worry—sunset is also spectacular.

From sunrise to noon, the light is weak, but the view is usually free of clouds. The best time for photos is in the afternoon, when the sun lights the crater and clouds are few. Go on full-moon nights for spectacular viewing. However, even when the forecast is promising, the weather at Haleakala can change in an instant—be prepared.

This is a high-altitude area; due to the lack of oxygen, you might suffer lightheadedness, shortness of breath, or nausea. People with asthma, pregnant women, heavy smokers, and those with heart conditions should be especially careful in the rarefied air.

> *Haleakala is one of the last places on earth you can see nene geese.*

3 **Park Headquarters.** Stop and get used to the altitude at 7,000 feet. You can pick up information on park programs and activities or get camping permits; restrooms, a pay phone, and drinking water are also available. ☎ 808/572-4400. www.nps.gov/hale. Daily 8am–4pm.

4 ★ **Leleiwi Overlook.** Just beyond mile marker 17, pull into the parking area. A short trail leads you to a panoramic view of the lunarlike crater. When the clouds are low and the sun is in the right place, usually around sunset, you can experience a phenomenon known as the "Specter of the Brocken"—you can see a reflection of your shadow, ringed by a rainbow, in the clouds below. It's an optical illusion caused by a rare combination of sun, shadow, and fog that occurs in only three places on the planet: Hawaii, Scotland, and Germany.

5 ★ **Kalahaku Overlook.** This is the best place to see a rare **silversword.** These botanical wonders take from 4 to 50 years to bloom, and then, usually between May and October, send up a 1- to 6-foot stalk with a purple bouquet of sunflower-like blooms.

6 ★ **Haleakala Visitor Center.** Not quite at the summit, this small building offers a panoramic view of the volcanic landscape, with photos identifying the various features, and exhibits that explain its history, ecology, geology, and volcanology. Park staff are often handy to answer questions. The only facilities are restrooms and water. Rangers offer excellent, informative, and free **naturalist talks** at 9:30, 10:30, and 11:30am daily in the summit building, and lead guided hikes from here (p 360). Near the summit, 11 miles from park entrance. ☎ 808/572-4400. www.nps.gov/hale. Daily 6:30am–3:30pm.

7 ★ **Puu Ulaula Overlook (Red Hill).** This is the volcano's highest point—you'll feel as if you're at the edge of the earth. You'll also notice a mysterious cluster of buildings officially known as Haleakala Observatories, but unofficially called **Science City.** If you do go up for the daily miracle of sunrise, when the sun seems to rise out of the vast crater, the building at Puu Ulaula Overlook, a triangle of glass that serves as a windbreak, is the best viewing spot. From here you can see all the way across Alenuihaha Channel to the often snowcapped summit of Mauna Kea on the Big Island.

Maui Beaches A to Z

★★ kids D. T. Fleming Beach Park WEST MAUI
This quiet, out-of-the-way beach cove, named after the man who started the commercial growing of pineapples on Maui, is a great place to take the family. Ironwood trees provide shade and the waters are generally good for swimming and snorkeling. Facilities include restrooms, showers, picnic tables, barbecue grills, and parking. Past MM 30, Honoapiilani Hwy. (Hwy. 30), Kapalua.

★★ Hamoa Beach EAST MAUI
This half-moon-shaped, gray-sand beach (a mix of coral and lava) in a truly tropical setting is a favorite among sunbathers seeking rest and refuge. The 100-foot-wide beach is three football fields long and sits below 30-foot black-lava sea cliffs. Hamoa is often swept by powerful rip currents. Surf breaks offshore and rolls ashore, making this a popular surfing and bodysurfing area. The calm left side is best for snorkeling in summer. The nearby Hotel Hana-Maui has numerous facilities for guests; there's an outdoor shower and restrooms for nonguests. Parking is limited. Haneoo Rd., off Hana Hwy. (Hwy. 360), Hana.

★ Hookipa Beach Park UPCOUNTRY
Due to its constant winds and endless waves, Hookipa attracts top windsurfers and wave jumpers from around the globe. Surfers and fishermen also enjoy this small gold-sand beach at the foot of a grassy cliff, which provides a natural amphitheater for spectators. Weekday afternoons are the best time to watch the daredevils fly over the waves. When the water is flat, snorkelers and divers explore the reef. Facilities include restrooms, showers, pavilions, picnic tables, barbecue grills, and a parking lot. 2 miles past Paia, MM 9, Hana Hwy. (Hwy. 36), Paia.

H. P. Baldwin Park UPCOUNTRY
This beach park draws lots of Maui residents. The surf breaks along the entire length of the white-sand beach, creating perfect conditions for body boarding. On occasion the waves get big enough for surfing. A couple of swimming areas are safe enough for children: one in the lee of the beach rocks near the large pavilion, and another at the opposite end of the beach, where beach rocks protect a small

> *Sunbathers can either challenge or simply admire Hookipa Beach's pounding surf, which is perfect for watersports.*

Maui's Beaches A to Z

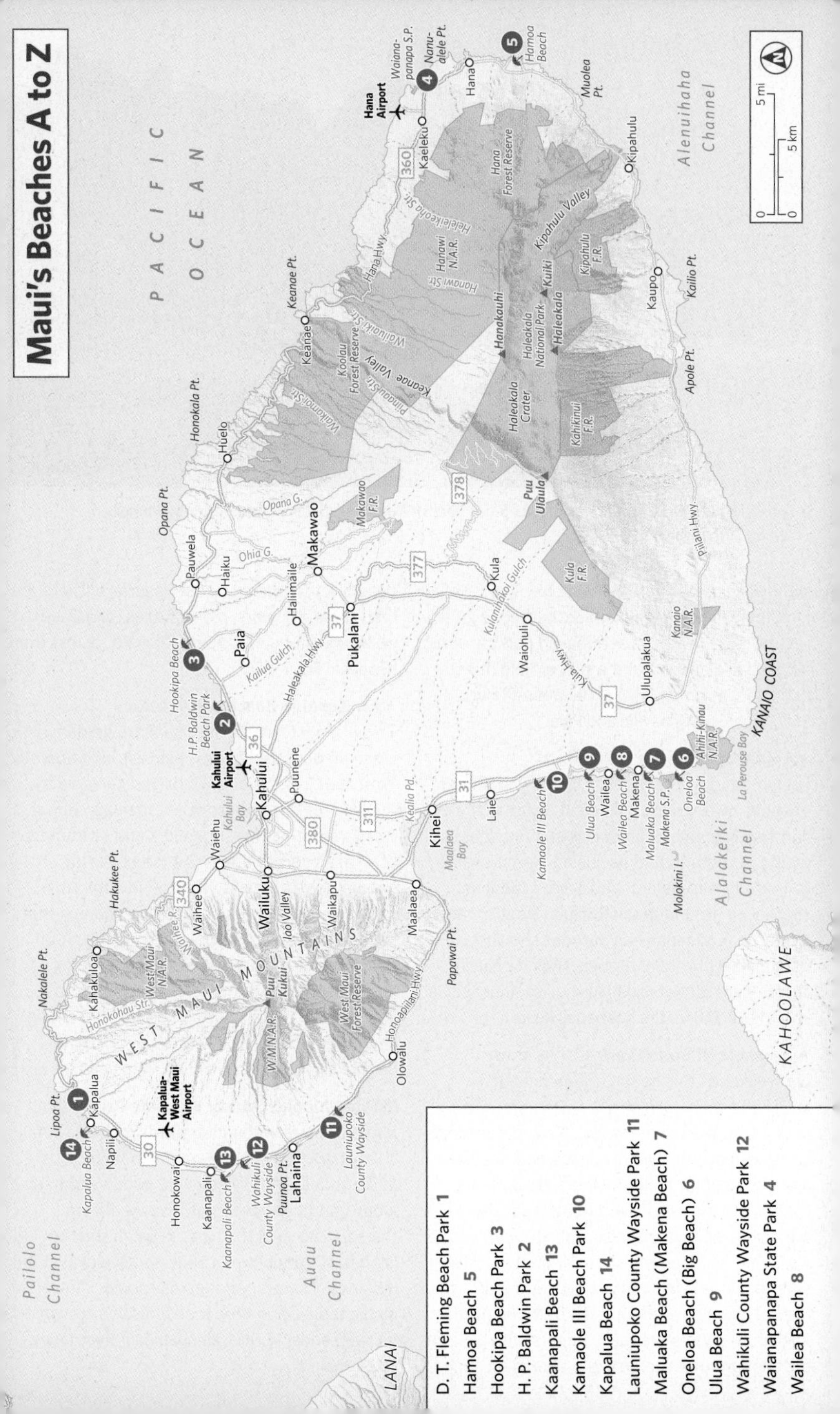

- D. T. Fleming Beach Park 1
- Hamoa Beach 5
- Hookipa Beach Park 3
- H. P. Baldwin Park 2
- Kaanapali Beach 13
- Kamaole III Beach Park 10
- Kapalua Beach 14
- Launiupoko County Wayside Park 11
- Maluaka Beach (Makena Beach) 7
- Oneloa Beach (Big Beach) 6
- Ulua Beach 9
- Wahikuli County Wayside Park 12
- Waianapanapa State Park 4
- Wailea Beach 8

> *Snorkeling is superb around the jagged Black Rock at Kaanapali Beach. More daring swimmers can try cliff diving.*

swimming area. There's a large pavilion with kitchen facilities, picnic tables, barbecue grills, restrooms, showers, a semipaved parking area, a baseball diamond, and a soccer field. It gets busy on weekends. MM 6, Hana Hwy. (Hwy. 360), btw. Sprecklesville and Paia.

★★ **Kaanapali Beach** WEST MAUI
Four-mile-long Kaanapali is one of Maui's best beaches, with grainy gold sand as far as the eye can see. Because Kaanapali is so long, there's plenty of room to find seclusion. Summertime swimming is excellent, and there's fabulous snorkeling around **Black Rock,** in front of the Sheraton. Kaanapali has outdoor showers. Parking is a problem, though. Look for beach access signs off Kaanapali Pkwy. (off Honoapiilani Hwy., Hwy. 30), in the Kaanapali Resort.

★ **Kamaole III Beach Park** SOUTH MAUI
On weekends this beach is jampacked with fishermen, picnickers, swimmers, and snorkelers. During the week, "Kam-3," as locals call it, can be empty. This beach park features a playground for children and a grassy lawn that meets the sand. Swimming is safe here, but scattered lava rocks are toe stubbers at the waterline, and parents should watch to make sure that kids don't venture too far out, because the bottom slopes off quickly. Both the north and south shores are rocky fingers with a surge big enough to attract fish and snorkelers, and the winter waves attract bodysurfers. There are restrooms, showers, picnic tables, barbecue grills, and lifeguards. South Kihei Rd., across from Keonekai Rd., Kihei.

★★★ **Kapalua Beach** WEST MAUI
This is a postcard-perfect beach: a golden crescent bordered by two palm-studded points. Protected from strong winds and currents by the lava rock promontories, Kapalua's calm waters are great for snorkelers and swimmers of all ages and abilities, and the bay is big enough to paddle a kayak around without getting into the more challenging channel that separates Maui from Molokai. Fish hang out by the rocks, making it great for snorkeling. You'll also find outdoor showers, restrooms, lifeguards, a rental shack, and plenty of shade. Parking is limited. Past MM 30, by Napili Kai Beach Resort, Honoapiilani Rd., Kapalua.

kids **Launiupoko County Wayside Park** WEST MAUI Families with children will love this small shady park with a large wading pool for kids and a small sandy beach with good swimming when conditions are right. The view from the park is one of the best: You can see the islands of Kahoolawe, Lanai, and Molokai in the distance. There's parking, restrooms, showers, picnic tables, and barbecue grills. It's crowded on weekends. 18 MM, Honoapiilani Hwy. (Hwy. 30), Lahaina.

★★ **Maluaka Beach (Makena Beach)** SOUTH MAUI This is the place for views: Molokini Crater and Kahoolawe are both visible in the distance. Maluaka itself is a short, wide, palm-fringed crescent of golden, grainy sand set between two black lava points and bounded by big sand dunes topped by a grassy knoll. Swimming and kayaking in the mostly calm bay are first-rate. Facilities include restrooms, showers, a landscaped park, lifeguards, and roadside parking. Along Makena Alanui Rd., look for the shoreline access sign near the Makena Prince Hotel, turn right, and head down to the shore on Makena Rd., Makena.

★★ **Oneloa Beach (Big Beach)** SOUTH MAUI Oneloa lives up to its name ("long sand"), with a beach that stretches 3,300 feet long and more than 100 feet wide. Mauians come here to swim, fish, snorkel, sunbathe, surf, and enjoy the view of Kahoolawe and Lanai. During storms, however, big waves lash the shore and a strong rip current sweeps the sharp drop-off, posing a danger for inexperienced open-ocean swimmers. On the other side of Puu Olai is **Little Beach,** a small pocket beach where nudists work on their allover tans, to the chagrin of authorities (be warned: you can get a lewd-conduct ticket if you join in). Parking is available, as are portable toilets. S. Makena Rd., Makena.

★ **Ulua Beach** SOUTH MAUI One of the most popular beaches in Wailea, Ulua is a long, wide, crescent-shaped gold-sand beach between two rocky points. When the ocean is calm, Ulua offers Wailea's best snorkeling; when it's rough, the waves are excellent for bodysurfers. Crowded conditions make it perfect for meeting people. Ulua has showers and restrooms. Look for the blue shoreline access sign, on Wailea Alanui Dr., Wailea.

Wahikuli County Wayside Park WEST MAUI This small stretch of beach is one of Lahaina's most popular beach parks. It's packed on weekends, but during the week it's a great place for swimming, snorkeling, sun-bathing, and picnics. There's parking here, plus restrooms, showers, and small covered pavilions with picnic tables and barbecue grills. MM 23, Honoapiilani Hwy. (Hwy. 30), btw. Lahaina and Kaanapali.

★ **Waianapanapa State Park** EAST MAUI This 120-acre beach park has 12 cabins (p 363), picnic tables, barbecue grills, restrooms, showers, a parking lot, a shoreline hiking trail (p 363), and a black-sand beach. This is a wonderful area for hiking (but bring insect repellent) and picnicking. Swimming is generally unsafe due to powerful rip currents and strong waves breaking offshore, which roll into the beach unchecked. Waianapanapa is crowded on weekends; weekdays are generally a better bet. 4 miles before Hana, MM 32, Hana Hwy. (Hwy. 360), Hana.

The Legend of Waianapanapa

Waianapanapa Park gets its name from the legend of Waianapanapa Cave. Chief Kaakea, a jealous and cruel man, suspected his wife, Popoalaea, of having an affair. Popoalaea left her husband and hid herself in a chamber of a cave. A few days later, when Kaakea was passing by the cave, the shadow of a servant gave away Popoalaea's hiding place, and Kaakea killed her. During certain times of the year, the water in the tide pool turns red as a tribute to Popoalaea, commemorating her death. (Scientists claim, however, that the change in color is due to the presence of small red shrimp.)

★★ **Wailea Beach** SOUTH MAUI From the beach, the view out to sea is magnificent, framed by neighboring Kahoolawe and Lanai and the tiny crescent of Molokini. Grab your sweetie at sunset and watch the clear waters tumble to shore. It's as romantic as you can get. Facilities include restrooms, outdoor showers, and limited free parking. Look for the blue shoreline access sign, on Wailea Alanui Dr., Wailea.

Maui's Best Hiking & Camping

In the past 3 decades, Maui has grown from a rural island to a fast-paced resort destination, but its natural beauty largely remains, and there are still many places that can be explored only on foot. Bring your own gear—there are no places to rent camping equipment on Maui.

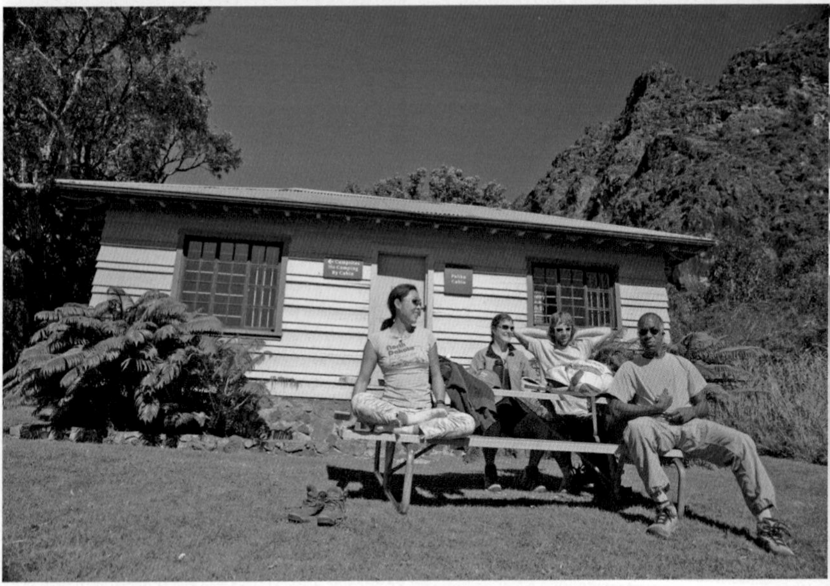

> *Book way in advance if you want to camp at one of Haleakala's cabins.*

★★★ Haleakala National Park

Hiking. The best way to see Maui's dormant volcano is on foot. The terrain inside the wilderness area of the volcano, which ranges from burnt-red cinder cones to ebony-black lava flows, is simply spectacular. Inside the crater there are some 27 miles of hiking trails, two camping sites, and three cabins. The best route takes in two trails: into the crater along **Sliding Sands Trail,** which begins on the rim at 9,800 feet and descends into the belly of the beast, to the valley floor at 6,600 feet; and back out along **Halemauu Trail.** The 11-mile, one-way descent takes 9 hours. The return ascent is about the same, so it's a 2-day hike for most people; see "Cabin Camping" for overnight options. For more on visiting Haleakala, see p 352.

Camping. Hosmer Grove, located at 6,800 feet, is a small open grassy area surrounded by a forest near the entrance to Haleakala National Park. This is the best place to spend the night in a tent if you want to see the Haleakala sunrise. No permits are needed at Hosmer Grove, and there's no charge, but you can stay

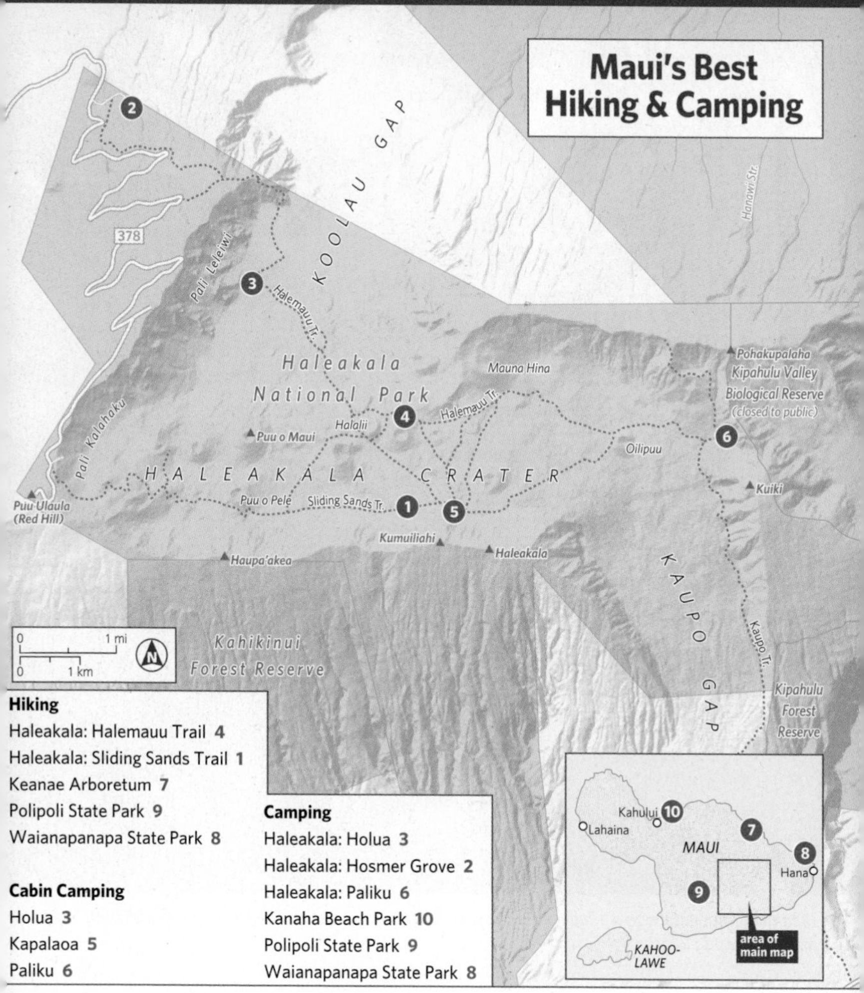

for only 3 nights in a 30-day period. The two tent-camping areas inside the volcano are **Holua,** just off Halemauu at 6,920 feet; and **Paliku,** just before the Kaupo Gap at the eastern end of the valley, at 6,380 feet. Facilities at both campgrounds are limited to pit toilets and nonpotable catchment water. Camping is free but limited to 2 consecutive nights and no more than 3 nights a month inside the volcano. Permits are issued daily at park headquarters on a first-come, first-served basis.

Cabin Camping. The three cabins inside the crater are spaced so that each one is an easy walk from the other: **Holua** cabin is on the Halemauu Trail, **Kapalaoa** cabin on Sliding Sands Trail, and **Paliku** cabin on the eastern end by the Kaupo Gap. Each has 12 padded bunks (but no bedding; bring your own), a table, chairs, cooking utensils, a two-burner propane stove, and a wood-burning stove with firewood (you might also have a few cockroaches). The rates are $55 a night for groups of one to six. The cabins are so popular that the National Park Service has a lottery system for reservations. Requests for cabins must be made 3 months in advance. You're limited to no more than 2 nights in one cabin and no more than 3 nights within the wilderness per month.

> *Commune with nature on a 2-mile hike through the Keanae Arboretum, which is packed with both native and introduced plants.*

Kanaha Beach Park

Camping. Located next to the Kahului Airport, this county park has two separate areas for camping: 7 tent sites on the beach and an additional 10 tent sites inland. This well-used park is a favorite of windsurfers, who take advantage of the strong winds that roar across this end of the island. Facilities include a paved parking lot, portable toilets, outdoor showers, barbecue grills, and picnic tables. Camping is limited to 3 consecutive days; the permit fee is $3 per adult and 50¢ for children, per night, and can be obtained from the Maui County Parks and Recreation Department (see "Getting a Camping Permit," p 363). On Alahao St. in Kahului, just west of the Kahului Airport.

Keanae Arboretum

Hiking. About 47 miles from Kahului, along the Hana Highway, is an easy 2-mile, family walk through the Keanae Arboretum that passes through a forest with both native and introduced plants. Allow 1 to 2 hours, longer if you take time out to swim in the pools of Piinaau Stream. Take rain gear and mosquito repellent. 47 miles from Kahului, along the Hana Hwy.

★ Polipoli State Park

Hiking & Camping. Polipoli, located at 5,300–6,200 feet within the 21,000-acre Kula and Kahikinui Forest Reserve on the slope of Haleakala, doesn't seem like the "typical" picture of Hawaii. But there's great hiking on the Polipoli

Getting a Camping Permit

All campers on Maui must have a permit (with the exception of campers at Hosmer Grove). The requirements vary, but it will take time and effort to get a permit. For camping in Haleakala contact **Haleakala National Park,** P.O. Box 369, Makawao, HI 96768 (☎ 808/572-4400; www.nps.gov/hale); for state parks contact **Hawaii State Department of Land and Natural Resources,** State Parks Division, P.O. Box 621, Honolulu, HI 96809 (☎ 808/587-0300; www.hawaiistateparks.org/camping); and for county parks contact **Maui County Parks and Recreation,** 700 Halia Nakoa St., Wailuku, HI 96793 (☎ 808/270-7230; www.mauicounty.gov).

Loop, an easy, 5-mile hike that takes about 3 hours and branches out to a variety of longer trails. You'll meander through groves of eucalyptus, swamp mahogany, and hybrid cypress. Dress warmly. Camping is allowed in the park with a $5-per-night permit from the Division of State Parks (see "Getting a Camping Permit," above). Take Hwy. 37 to Keokea and turn right on Hwy. 337; after less than ½ mile turn on Waipoli Rd. and continue for 10 miles to the park.

★★★ **Waianapanapa State Park Hiking & Camping.** Tucked in a tropical jungle, on the outskirts of the little coastal town of Hana, is Waianapanapa State Park, a black-sand beach set in an emerald forest, with camping and hiking. The **coastal trail** is an easy 6-mile hike that parallels the sea, along lava cliffs and a forest of lauhala trees. Allow 4 hours for the hike; the best time of day is either the early morning or the late evening, when the light on the lava and surf makes for great photos. The park has 12 cabins and a tent campground. (Go for the cabins; torrential rain sometimes turns the campground into something resembling a mud-wrestling arena.) The cabins are the best lodging deal on Maui, and everyone knows it, so reserve way in advance. For just $45 you get a kitchen, living room, bedroom, bathroom, and basic furnishings (sheets, towels, dishes, etc.). It's rustic—this is a step above camping—but you can't beat the setting. Tent-camping is $5 per night but limited to 5 nights in a 30-day period. For cabin reservations or camping permits, contact the State Parks Division (see "Getting a Camping Permit," above). Just after MM 32, turn off the Hana Hwy. (Hwy. 360) at the Waianapanapa State Park sign. Continue down Waianapanapa Rd. to the end.

> *Waianapanapa State Park's stunning and remote black-sand beach is just a 6-mile hike from the town of Hana.*

Maui's Best Golf Courses

In some circles, Maui is synonymous with golf. The island's world-famous golf courses start at its very northern tip, roll around to Kaanapali, and continue down to Kihei and Wailea in the south. Golfers new to Maui should know that it's windy here, especially between 10am and 2pm.

> *The sun sets on Kapalua Resort's Plantation Course. Most courses on Hawaii offer twilight rates—reduced greens fees for late afternoon tee times.*

Elleair Maui Golf Club. Sitting in the foothills of Haleakala, this course offers spectacular ocean vistas from every hole. ***Warning:*** In the afternoon the winds bluster down Haleakala with great gusto. Facilities include a clubhouse, driving range, putting green, pro shop, and lessons. 1345 Piilani Hwy. (near Lipoa St. turnoff), Kihei. ☎ 808/874-0777. www.elleairmauigolfclub.com. Greens fees: $120; twilight rate $95.

★ **Kaanapali Courses.** Both courses at Kaanapali offer a challenge to all golfers, from high handicappers to near-pros. The par-71, nearly 6,700-yard **Royal Kaanapali Course** is a true Robert Trent Jones, Sr., design, with the largest, most contoured greens on Maui. The par-70, 6,400-yard **Kaanapali Kai** is an Arthur Jack Snyder design, with narrow, hilly fairways. Facilities include a driving range, putting course, and clubhouse with dining. Off Hwy. 30, Kaanapali. ☎ 808/661-3691. www.kaanapali-golf.com. Greens fees for Royal Kaanapali Course: $235, $190 guests; $120 twilight. Greens fees for Kaanapali Kai: $195, $150 guests; twilight rate $95.

★★★ **Kapalua Resort Courses.** The views from these championship courses are worth the greens fees alone. The par-72, 6,761-yard **Bay Course** (☎ 808/669-8820) was designed by Arnold Palmer and Ed Seay. The greens are difficult to read. The **Plantation Course** (☎ 808/669-8877) is a Ben Crenshaw/Bill Coore design. This 6,547-yard, par-73 course is excellent for developing your low shots and precise chipping. Facilities include locker rooms, a driving range, and an excellent restaurant. Off Hwy. 30, Kapalua. ☎ 877/KAPALUA (527-2582). www.kapaluamaui.com. Greens fees for Bay Course: $220, guests $183; twilight rate $138; Plantation Course: $298, guests $218; twilight rate $158.

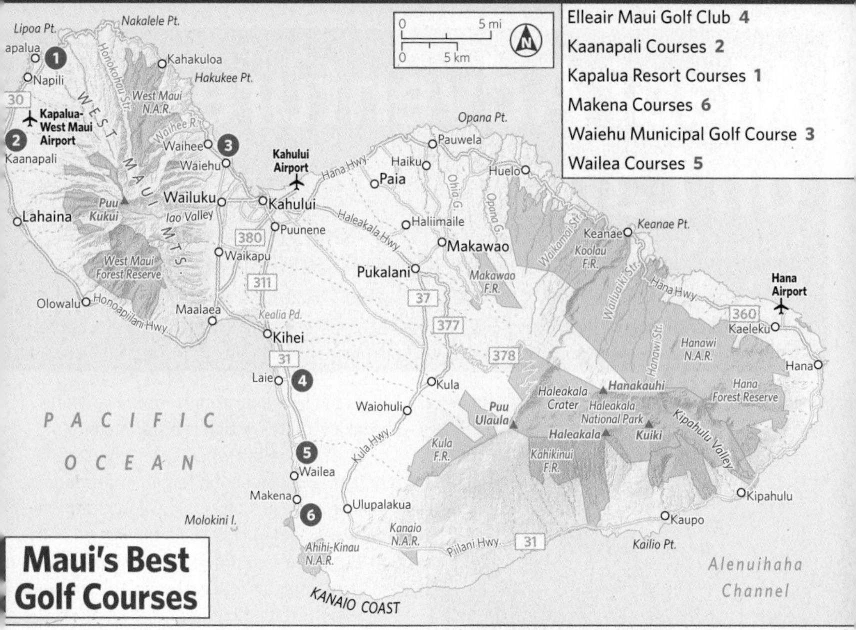

Maui's Best Golf Courses

★★ **Makena Courses.** Here you'll find 36 holes of "Mr. Hawaii Golf"—Robert Trent Jones, Jr.—at his best. Add to that spectacular views: Molokini islet looms in the background, and humpback whales gambol offshore in winter. The par-72, 6,876-yard **South Course** has a couple of holes you'll never forget. The par-72, 6,823-yard **North Course** is more difficult and more spectacular. Facilities include a clubhouse, a driving range, two putting greens, a pro shop, lockers, and lessons. 5415 Makena Alanui Dr., just past the Maui Prince Hotel. ☎ 808/879-3344. www.maui.net/~makena. Greens fees (the higher rates are charged in winter): $155–$200, guests $125–$130; twilight rate $135, guests $110.

Waiehu Municipal Golf Course. This public, oceanside, par-72 golf course is like playing two different courses: The first 9 holes, built in 1930, are set along the dramatic coastline, while the back 9 holes, added in 1966, head toward the mountains. It's a fun course that probably won't challenge your handicap. Facilities include a snack bar, driving range, practice greens, golf-club rental, and clubhouse. 200 Halewaiu Rd. at Lower Waiehu Beach Rd., Wailuku, HI 96793. ☎ 808/270-7402. hi-mauicounty.civicplus.com/facilities.asp. Greens fees: $69 Mon–Fri, $74 Sat–Sun and holidays.

Travel Tip

Golf Club Rentals (☎ 808/665-0800; www.mauiclubrentals.com) has custom-built clubs for men, women, and juniors (both right- and left-handed), which can be delivered island-wide; the rates are $25 to $30 a day.

★★ **Wailea Courses.** There are three courses to choose from at Wailea. The **Blue Course,** a par-72, 6,758-yard course designed by Arthur Jack Snyder, is for duffers and pros alike. A little more difficult is the par-72, 7,078-yard championship **Gold Course,** with the classic Robert Trent Jones, Jr., challenges, including natural hazards like lava rock walls. The **Emerald Course,** also designed by Robert Trent Jones, Jr., has tropical landscaping and a player-friendly design. Facilities include two pro shops, restaurants, locker rooms, and a complete golf training facility. Wailea Alanui Dr. (off Wailea Iki Dr.), Wailea. ☎ 888/328-MAUI (328-6284) or 808/875-7450. www.waileagolf.com. Greens fees: $225, guests $180–$190; twilight rate $135.

Maui Adventures on Land

Maui is known for its crystal-clear waters, but there are plenty of land-based adventures you can enjoy here. Haleakala is perfect for bicycling and horseback riding. The warm, sunny days means great conditions for tennis. And the real daredevils can try a zip-line.

> *Fly past 1,000-foot cliffs and cascading waterfalls while learning fascinating Hawaiian history on a Blue Hawaiian helicopter tour.*

Bicycling

Biking Down a Volcano. It's not even close to dawn, but here you are, rubbing your eyes awake, riding in a van up the long dark road to the top of Maui's sleeping volcano. It's colder than you ever thought possible for a tropical island. The air is thin. You stomp your chilly feet while you wait, sipping hot coffee. Then comes the sun, exploding over the yawning Haleakala Crater, which is big enough to swallow Manhattan whole—it's a mystical moment you won't soon forget, imprinted on a palette of dawn colors. Now you know why Hawaiians named Haleakala the House of the Sun. But there's no time to linger: Decked out in your screaming yellow parka, you mount your steed and test its most important feature, the brakes—because you're about to coast down a 10,000-foot volcano. All rates include hotel pickup, transport to the top, bicycle, safety equipment, and meals. Wear layers of warm clothing—there may be a 30°F (-1°C) change in temperature from the top of the mountain to the ocean. Generally, the tour groups will not take riders under 12, but younger children can ride along in the van that accompanies the groups. Pregnant women should also ride in the van. My first pick for cruising down Haleakala is Maui's oldest downhill company, **Maui Downhill.** 199 Dairy Rd., Kahului ☎ 800/535-BIKE (535-2453) or 808/871-2155. www.mauidownhill.com. Book online for $120.

Biking on Your Own. If you want to avoid the crowd and go down the mountain at your own pace, call **Haleakala Bike Company** (☎ 888/922-2453; www.bikemaui.com). They will outfit you with the latest gear and take you up Haleakala. Trips start at $100; they also have bicycle rentals for touring other parts of Maui on your own (from $35 a day).

If you just want to rent a bike, **Maui Sunriders Bike Company,** 71 Baldwin Ave., Paia (☎ 866/500-BIKE 500-2453; www.mauibikeride.com) rents bikes from $30 a day. For information on bikeways and maps, get a copy of the *Maui County Bicycle Map,* which has

Maui Adventures on Land

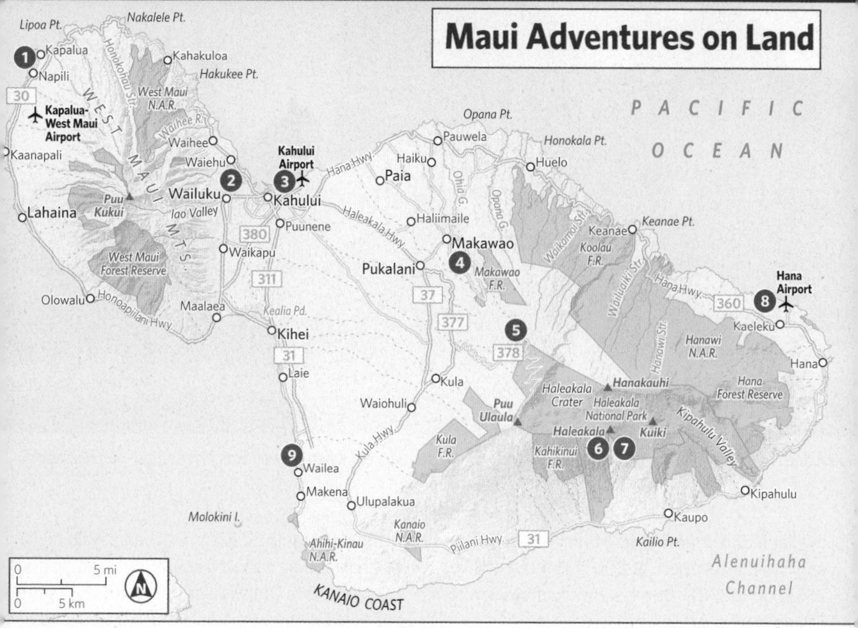

Bicycling

Biking Down A Volcano **6**

Helicopter Tours

Blue Hawaiian **3**

Horseback Riding

Haleakala **7**

Makawao **4**

Wailuku **2**

Spelunking

Maui Cave Adventures **8**

Tennis

Kapalua Tennis Garden and Village Tennis Center **1**

Wailea Tennis Club **9**

Ziplining

Skyline Eco-Adventures' Zipline Haleakala Tour **5**

nformation on road suitability, climate, trade winds, mileage, elevation changes, bike shops, safety tips, and various bicycling routes. The nap is available at bike shops all over the sland. A great book for mountain bikers who want to venture out on their own is John Alford's *Mountain Biking the Hawaiian Islands,* published by Ohana Publishing (www. bikehawaii.com).

Helicopter Tours

Blue Hawaiian. Only a helicopter can bring you face to face with remote sites like Maui's little-known Wall of Tears, near the summit of Puu Kukui in the West Maui Mountains. You'll glide through canyons etched with 1,000-foot waterfalls and over dense rainforests; you'll climb to 10,000 feet, high enough to glimpse the summit of Haleakala, and fly by the dramatic vistas at Molokai. My favorite helicopter tour is **Blue Hawaiian,** which not only takes you on the ride of your life but has the best pilots: part Hawaiian historian, part DJ, part tour guide, and part amusement-ride operator. As you soar through the clouds, you'll learn about the island's flora, fauna, history, and culture. One of the reason I always choose Blue Hawaiian is because they are the only helicopter company in the state to have the latest high-tech, environmentally friendly (and quiet) Eco-Star helicopter, specially designed for air-tour operators. Flights vary from 30 to 100 minutes. A keepsake DVD of your flight is

> *See Haleakala, Makawao, and Wailuku the way Westerners did when Hawaii was first settled—on horseback.*

available (so your friends at home can ooh and aah). Kahului Airport. ☎ 800/745-BLUE (745-2583) or 808/871-8844; www.bluehawaiian.com. Flights start at $160.

Horseback Riding

Haleakala on Horseback. If you'd like to ride down into Haleakala Crater, contact **Pony Express Tours,** which offers a variety of rides down to the crater floor and back up, and shorter 1- and 2-hour rides at Haleakala Ranch. Hwy. 378, Kula. ☎ 808/667-2200 or 808/878-6698. www.ponyexpresstours.com. Crater rides from $182.

Makawao. Maui offers spectacular adventure rides through rugged ranch lands, into tropical forests, and to remote swimming holes. My favorite is **Piiholo Ranch,** in Makawao. A working cattle ranch, owned by the *kamaaina* (longtime resident) Baldwin family, Piiholo Ranch offers a horseback riding adventure with a variety of different rides to suit your ability, from the morning picnic ride (a 3½-hour ride on the ranch with a picnic lunch), to private rides. Waiahiwi Rd., Makawao. ☎ 866/572-5544 or 808/357-5544. www.piiholo.com. Rides start at $120.

Wailuku. For an "out west" type of adventure, I recommend riding with **Mendes Ranch & Trail Rides.** The 300-acre Mendes Ranch is a real-life working cowboy ranch that has the essential elements of an earthly paradise—rainbows, waterfalls, palm trees, coral-sand beaches, lagoons, tide pools, a rainforest, and its own volcanic peak (more than a mile high). Allan Mendes, a third-generation wrangler, will take you from the edge of the rainforest out to the sea. On the way, you'll cross tree-studded meadows where Texas longhorns sit in the shade and pass a dusty corral where Allan's father, Ernest, a champion roper, may be breaking a wild horse. Allan keeps close watch, turning often in his saddle to make sure everyone is happy. He points out flora and fauna and fields questions, but generally just lets you soak up Maui's natural splendor in golden silence. My favorite is the morning ride, which lasts 2 hours and ends with a barbecue back at the corral. 3530 Kahekili Hwy., 5 miles past Wailuku. ☎ 808/244-7320; www.mendesranch.com. $110.

Spelunking

★ **Maui Cave Adventures.** Don't miss the opportunity to see how the Hawaiian Islands were made by exploring a million-year-old underground lava tube/cave. Guide Chuck Thorne offers a look at this unique geological feature. After more than 10 years of leading scuba tours through underwater caves around Hawaii, Chuck discovered some caves on land that he wanted to show visitors. When the land surrounding the largest cave on Maui went on the market in 1996, Chuck snapped it up and started his own tour company. Ulaino Rd. (off the Hana Hwy. just south of MM 1). ☎ 808/248-7308; www.mauicave.com. Self-guided tours only; $12. Mon–Sat 10:30am–3:30pm.

Tennis

★★★ **Kapalua Tennis Garden and Village Tennis Center.** Opened in 1979, the tennis garden has ten plexipave courts paired in tiered clusters, with four lit for night play and surrounded by lush tropical foliage. Each set of courts is secluded in landscaped privacy with its own viewing lanai. Also available: private lessons, stroke-of-the-day clinics, drop-in clinics, and tournaments. The staff will match you up with a partner if you need one. Kapalua Resort. ☎ 808/665-9112. www.kapalua.com/recreation/tennis. Court fees: $16 per player, $14 guests.

Maui County Parks & Recreation. Maui has excellent public tennis courts; all are free and available from daylight to sunset (a few are even lit for night play until 10pm). The courts are available on a first-come, first-served basis; when someone's waiting, limit your play to 45 minutes. Most public courts are not conveniently located near the major resort areas. The exceptions to that rule are in Kihei (in Kalama Park on S. Kihei Rd. and in Waipualani Park on W. Waipualani Rd. behind the Maui Sunset Condo), in Lahaina (in Malu'uou o lele Park, at Front and Shaw sts.), and in Hana (in Hana Park, on the Hana Hwy.). For a complete list of courts, call the county at ☎ 808/243-7230.

★★ **Wailea Tennis Club.** Ranked for more than a decade as one of the country's 50 best resorts. Facilities include 11 plexipave courts (3 lit for night play), backboard or wall, pro shop, 6 USPTA pros available for lessons, and 3 doubles clinics per week. 131 Wailea Iki Pl., Wailea. ☎ 808/879-1958. www.waileatennis.com. Court fees: $16 per player, $15 guests.

Zip-Lining

Skyline Eco-Adventures' Zip-line Haleakala Tour. This adventure blends a short hike through a eucalyptus forest with four "zip-line" crossings. During the zip-line crossing, you'll be outfitted with a seat harness and connected to a cable, then launched from a 70-foot-high platform to "zip" along the cable suspended over the slopes of Haleakala. From this viewpoint, you fly over treetops, valleys, gulches, and waterfalls at 10 to 35 mph. These bird's-eye tours operate daily and take riders from ages 12 and up, weighing between 80 and 300 pounds. P.O. Box 880518, Pukalani, HI 96788. ☎ 808/878-8400. www.skylinehawaii.com. $90 ($80 if you book online).

> *Tear through Haleakala's treetops at 10 to 35 miles per hour on a zip-line tour with Skyline Eco-Adventures.*

Maui Adventures in the Ocean

To really appreciate Maui, you need to get off the land and get on the sea. Trade winds off the Lahaina Coast and the strong wind that rips through Maui's isthmus make sailing around the island exciting. Or you can go sport fishing and challenge yourself to a battle with a 1,000-pound marlin; slowly glide over the water in a kayak; or plunge beneath the waves to really see the Neptunian world. Whatever adventure thrills you, you will find it on Maui.

> *Professional guides will take you 2½ miles around Makena Landing to get a close-up view of beautiful, secluded coves and coral.*

Bodysurfing

Riding the waves without a board and becoming one with the rolling water is a way of life in Hawaii. Some bodysurfers just rely on their hands to ride the waves; others use a hand board, boogie board, or body board. Both bodysurfing and body boarding require a pair of open-heeled swim fins to help propel you through the water. **H. P. Baldwin Park** (p 356), just outside of Paia, has great bodysurfing waves nearly year-round. In winter Maui's best bodysurfing spot is **Mokuleia Beach,** known locally as Slaughterhouse because of the cattle slaughterhouse that once stood here, not because of the waves—although they are definitely for expert bodysurfers only. Storms from the south bring fair bodysurfing conditions and great boogie boarding to the lee side of Maui: **Oneloa** (p 359) in Makena, **Ulua** (p 359) in Wailea, **Kamaole III** (p 358) in Kihei, and **Kapalua** (p 358) are all good choices.

Ocean Kayaking

Makena Kayak Tours. This is my favorite kayak-tour operator for the uninitiated. Professional guide Dino Ventura leads a 2½-hour trip from Makena Landing and loves taking first-timers over the secluded coral reefs and into remote coves. His wonderful tour will be a highlight of your vacation. ☎ 877/879-8426 or 808/879-8426. www.makenakayaks.com. Tours start at $55, including refreshments and equipment.

Maui Adventures in the Ocean

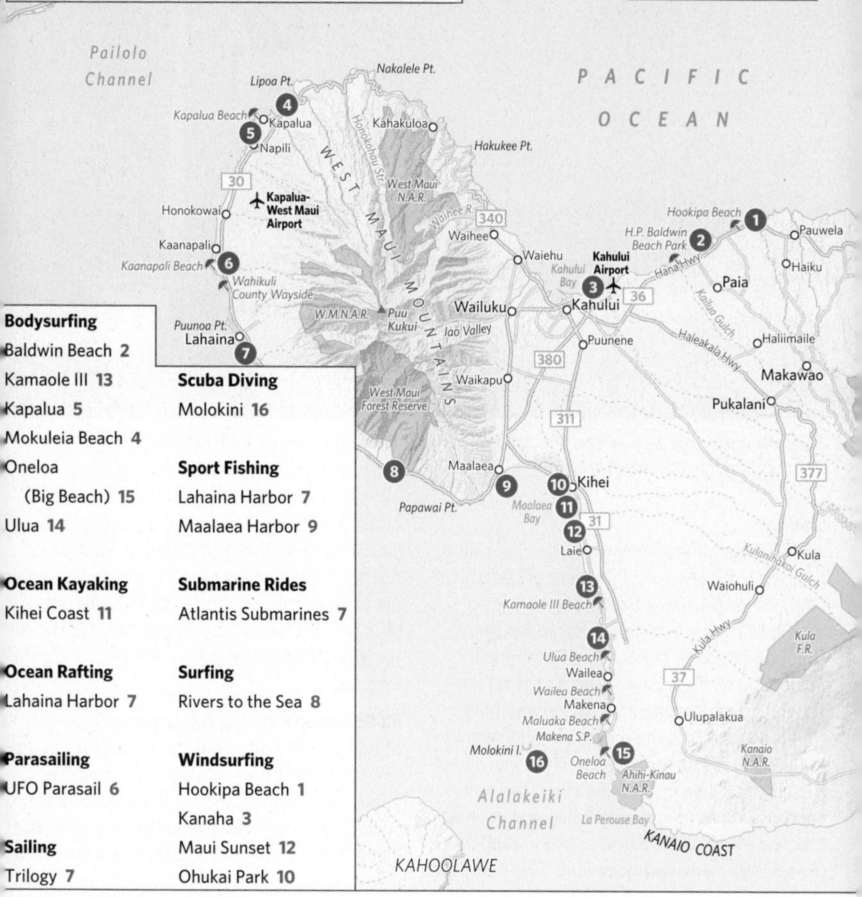

Ocean Rafting

Hawaiian Ocean Raft. If you're semi-adventurous and looking for a more intimate experience with the sea, try ocean rafting. The inflatable rafts hold 6 to 24 passengers. Hawaiian Ocean Raft is one of the best (and most reasonable) outfitters on the island. Their 5-hour tour takes in 3 snorkeling stops, and includes searching for dolphins, continental breakfast, and midmorning snacks. Lahaina Harbor, ☎ 888/677-RAFT (677-7238) or 808/667-2191. www.hawaiioceanrafting.com. From $74 adults, $53 kids 5–12.

Parasailing

UFO Parasail. This ocean adventure sport involves sailing through the air, suspended under a large parachute attached by a towline to a speedboat. I recommend the early-bird special at 8am (when the light is fantastic). They'll pick you up at Kaanapali Beach. Parasailing tours don't run during whale season, which is roughly December through May. ☎ 800/FLY-4-UFO (359-4836) or 808/661-7-UFO (661-7836). www.ufoparasail.net. $65 standard (400 ft.) or $75 deluxe (800 ft.).

> *Sample the islands' best snorkel and sailing experience on a 9-mile voyage from Lahaina Harbor to beautiful Hulopoe Beach in Lanai.*

Sailing

★★★ **Trilogy** offers my favorite snorkel-sail trips. Hop aboard one of the fleet of custom-built, 54- to 64-foot-long catamarans for a 9-mile sail from Lahaina Harbor to Lanai's Hulopoe Beach (p 454), a terrific marine preserve. You'll get a fun-filled day of sailing, snorkeling, swimming, and whale-watching (in season). This is the only cruise with rights to take you to Hulopoe Beach. They also have trips to Molokini and Honolua Bay. The crews are fun and knowledgeable. Lahaina Harbor. ☎ 888/225-MAUI (225-6284) or 808/TRILOGY (874-5649). www.sailtrilogy.com. Trips from $64.

Scuba Diving

You can see a great variety of tropical marine life (more than 100 endemic species found nowhere else on the planet), explore sea caves, and swim with sea turtles and monk seals in the clear tropical waters off Maui. Trade winds often rough up the seas in the afternoon, so most dive operators schedule early-morning dives. Everyone dives **Molokini,** a marine-life park and one of Hawaii's top dive spots. This crescent-shaped crater has three tiers of diving: a 35-foot plateau inside the crater basin, a wall sloping to 70 feet just beyond the inside plateau, and a sheer wall on the outside and back-side of the crater that plunges 350 feet. This underwater park is very popular thanks to calm, clear, protected waters and an abundance of marine life, from manta rays to clouds of yellow butterflyfish. Even novices can try diving—most operators offer no-experience-necessary dives, ranging from $100 for one tank to $150 for two tanks. You can learn from this glimpse into the sea world whether diving is for you.

Ed Robinson's Diving Adventures is the only Maui company rated one of Scuba Diver magazine's five-best dive operators. Ed, a widely published underwater photographer, offers specialized charters for small groups. Kihei Boat Ramp. ☎ 800/635-1273 or 808/879-3584. www.mauiscuba.com. Two-tank dive starting at $130.

Snorkeling

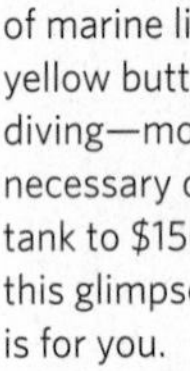

Snorkeling is a major attraction in Maui—and almost anyone can do it. All you need are a mask, a snorkel, fins, and some basic swimming skills. Floating over underwater worlds through colorful clouds of tropical fish is like a dream. In many places all you have to do is wade into the water and look down. If you've never snorkeled before, most resorts and excursion boats offer instruction, but it's plenty easy to figure it out for yourself.

Snorkel Bob's (www.snorkelbob.com) has snorkel gear, boogie boards, and other ocean toys at four locations: Dickenson Square,

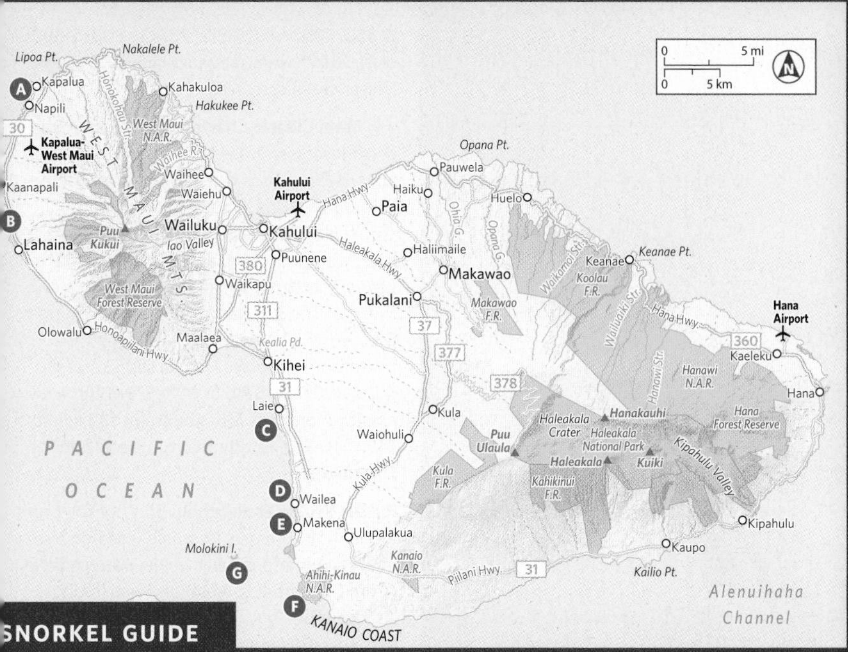

SNORKEL GUIDE

Maui's Best Snorkeling

The water at A **Kapalua Beach** (p 358) s so clear that you can spot the colorful :ropical fish from the sand. The lava rock promontories protect the area from strong winds and currents, making the water calm, and Kapalua's two jutting rock points at either end of the beach attract lots of fish. Located in the Kaanapali Beach Resort (p 358), in front of the Sheraton Hotel, B **Black Rock** not only has clear, calm water, but is also populated with clouds of tropical fish. You might even spot a turtle or two. At C **Kamaole III Beach Park** (p 358), head straight to the rocky fingers extending out at the north and south shores; they're fish magnets. Snorkel at D **Ulua Beach** (p 359) in the morning when the waters are calm; local winds kick up around noon. E **Makena Landing** (look for the shoreline access sign near the Makena Prince and turn right on Makena Rd.) is popular with local residents on weekends, so plan to go on a weekday and you could have the entire bay to yourself. My favorite snorkel tour is to follow the rocky shoreline looking for fish. Fishing is strictly *kapu* (forbidden) at F **Ahihi-Kinau Natural Preserve** (pictured; see also p 332, 1), and the fish know it—they're everywhere. This 2,000-acre state natural area reserve in the lee of Cape Kinau, on Maui's rugged south coast, offers a series of rocky coves and black-lava tide pools. See p. 374 for information on snorkel-sail cruises to G **Molokini.**

> *Kids love the small waves, clear water and superb snorkeling at Black Rock near Lahilahi Point at Makaha Beach in Maui.*

Dickenson and Wainee streets, Lahaina (☎ 808/662-0104); Napili Village, 5425-C Lower Honoapiilani Hwy., Napili (☎ 808/669-9603); in North Kihei at Azeka Place II, 1279 S. Kihei Rd. #310 (☎ 808/875-6188); and in South Kihei/Wailea at the Kamaole Beach Center, 2411 S. Kihei Rd., Kihei (☎ 808/879-7449). All locations are open daily from 8am to 5pm.

Snorkel-Sail Cruises to Molokini

Like a crescent moon fallen from the sky, the crater of **Molokini** sits almost midway between Maui and the uninhabited island of Kahoolawe. Its concave side serves as a natural sanctuary for tropical fish and snorkelers, who commute daily in a fleet of dive boats to this marine-life preserve. Note that in high season, Molokini can be very crowded.

★★★ **Trilogy.** Trilogy tops the list of my favorite snorkel-sail trips. Hop aboard one of the fleet of custom-built 54- to 64-foot catamarans. This half-day trip leaves from Maalaea Harbor and includes breakfast and a barbecue lunch. ☎ 888/225-MAUI (225-6284) or 808/TRILOGY (874-5649). www.sailtrilogy.com. $118 adults, half-price children 3–12.

★★ **Maui Classic Charters.** Take a morning or afternoon smorkel-sail cruise to Molokini aboard *Four Winds II,* a 55-foot, glass bottom catamaran. Trips include a continental breakfast; a barbecue lunch; complimentary beer, wine, and soda; complimentary snorkeling gear and instruction; and sport fishing along the way. The company also offers a "Dolphin Discovery" trip and whale-watching trips (in season). Maalaea Harbor, slip 55 and slip 80. ☎ 800/736-5740 or 808/879-8188. www.mauicharters.com. Morning cruise $89 adults, $59 children 3–12; afternoon cruise $42 adults, $30 children.

Pacific Whale Foundation. This not-for-profit foundation supports its whale research by offering numerous daily whale-watch cruises (from December to May) and year-round snorkel tours, out of both Lahaina and Maalaea harbors. 300 Maalaea Rd., Suite. 211, Wailuku. ☎ 800/942-5311 or 808/879-8811. www.pacificwhale.org. Snorkeling cruises from $80 adults, $35 children 7–12.

Pride of Maui. For a high-speed, action-packed snorkel-sail experience, consider a cruise aboard the *Pride of Maui.* These 5½-hour snorkel cruises take in not only Molokini, but also Turtle Bay and Makena. Continental breakfast, barbecue lunch, gear, and instruction are included. Maalaea Harbor. ☎ 877/TO-PRIDE (867-7433) or 808/242-0955. www.prideofmaui.com. Snorkeling cruises $90 adults, $56 children 3–12. Rates lower for shorter afternoon cruises.

Sport Fishing

Marlin (as big as 1,200 lb.), tuna, ono, and mahimahi await the baited hook in Maui's coastal and channel waters. No license is required; just book a sport fishing vessel out of **Lahaina** or **Maalaea** harbors. Most charter boats that troll for big-game fish carry a maximum of six passengers. You can walk the docks, talking to captains and crews, or book through **Sportfish Hawaii** (☎ 877/388-1376 or 808/396-2607; www.sportfishhawaii.com). Prices vary widely, but a shared boat for a half-day of fishing starts at $139; a shared full day of fishing starts at around $199. A half-day

> Wonder at Hawaii's beauty from beneath the sea on an Atlantis Submarine tour.

exclusive (you get the entire boat) starts at $599; a full-day exclusive starts at $999. Also, many boat captains tag and release marlin or keep the fish for themselves (sorry, that's Hawaii style). If you want to eat your mahimahi for dinner or have your marlin mounted, tell the captain before you go.

Submarine Rides

Atlantis Submarines. Plunge 100 feet under the sea in a state-of-the-art, high-tech submarine and meet swarms of vibrant tropical fish up close and personal as they flutter through the deep blue waters off Lahaina. Trips leave from Lahaina Harbor every hour on the hour from 9am to 2pm. Allow 2 hours for this underwater adventure. 658 Front St., Lahaina. ☎ 800/548-6262 or 808/667-7816. www.atlantisadventures.com. $81 adults, $41 children under 12 (children must be at least 3 ft. tall). Book online and save 10%. Trips every hour on the hour 9am–2pm.

Surfing

Rivers to the Sea. Tide and Kiva Rivers, two local brothers (actually twins) who have been surfing since they could walk, are the best surf instructors I've seen. The lessons are 2 hours long and include equipment and instruction.

Day Cruises to Molokai & Lanai

You can travel across the seas by ferry from Maui to Molokai on the ***Molokai Princess*** (☎ 800/275-6969 or 808/667-6165). Ferries leave from Lahaina Harbor; the round-trip cost for the 90-minute ride is $138 adults, $70 kids 3–12. **Expeditions Lahaina/Lanai Passenger Ferry** (800/695-2624 or 808/661-3756; www.go-lanai.com) makes the 9-mile channel crossing from Lahaina Harbor five times a day. Baggage is limited to two checked bags and one carry-on. The trip takes 45 to 60 minutes and costs $50 adults, $40 kids 2–11.

> *If you've always wanted to learn how to shred the waves, you'll be in good hands with the instructors at Rivers to the Sea.*

Tide, who has been surfing for 25 years, says they decide where the lesson will take place based on the client's ability and where the surf is on that day. He says he has beginners standing up during their first lesson. Rivers to the Sea. ☎ 808/280-8795 or 808/280-6236. www.riverstothesea.com. $75 group instruction.

Whale-Watching

Every winter pods of Pacific humpback whales make the 3,000-mile swim from the chilly waters of Alaska to bask in Maui's summery shallows, fluking, spy-hopping, spouting, and having an all-around swell time. Whale-watching season usually begins in December or January and lasts until April or sometimes May. You don't have to take a boat to see these magnificent leviathans; you can just look out to sea. There's no best time of day for whale-watching, but the whales seem to appear when the sea is glassy and the wind calm. Once you see one, keep watching in the same vicinity—they might stay down as long as 20 minutes. Bring binoculars, if you can.

Some good whale-watching points on Maui are: **Olowalu Reef,** along the straight part of Honoapiilani Hwy., between McGregor Point and Olowalu; on the way to Lahaina at **McGregor Point,** at mile marker 9 (just before you get to the Lahaina Tunnel); and at **Wailea Marriott Resort,** where you can look for whales

Not So Close! They Hardly Know You

In your excitement at seeing a whale or a school of dolphins, don't get too close—both are protected under the Marine Mammals Protection Act. Swimmers, snorkelers, divers, kayakers, and windsurfers must stay at least 300 feet away from all whales, dolphins, and other marine mammals. And yes, visitors have been prosecuted for swimming with dolphins! If you have any questions, call the **National Marine Fisheries Service** (☎ 808/541-2727) or the **Hawaiian Islands Humpback Whale National Marine Sanctuary** (☎ 800/831-4888).

:hrough the telescope installed by the Hawaiian slands Humpback Whale National Marine Sanctuary. But the best whale-watching spot on the island is from the top of **Puu Olai,** near the Maui Prince Hotel. On this 360-foot cinder cone overlooking Makena Beach, you'll be at the right elevation to see Pacific humpbacks as they dodge Molokini and cruise up Alalakeiki Channel between Maui and Kahoolawe. If you don't see one, you'll at least have a whale of a view.

For a closer look at these giants, take **a whale-watching cruise.** The **Pacific Whale Foundation,** 101 N. Kihei Rd., Kihei (☎ 800/942-5311 or 808/249-8811; www.pacificwhale.org), is a nonprofit foundation in Kihei that supports its whale research by offering cruises and snorkel tours, some to Molokini and Lanai. They have numerous daily trips to choose from (snorkeling cruises from $80 adults, $35 children 7-12). Cruises are offered from December through May, out of both Lahaina and Maalaea harbors. In season, many snorkel-sail companies offer whale-watching cruises as well (see "Sailing," p 372, and "Snorkel-Sail Cruises to Molokini," p 374).

Windsurfing

Maui has Hawaii's best windsurfing beaches. In winter, windsurfers from around the world flock to the town of Paia to ride the waves. **Hookipa Beach Park** (p 356), known all over the globe for its brisk winds and excellent waves, is the site of several world-championship contests. **Kanaha,** west of Kahului Airport, also has dependable winds. When the winds turn northerly, the northern end of Kihei is the spot to be: **Ohukai Park,** the first beach as you enter South Kihei Road from the northern end, has not only good winds but parking and good access to the water. Experienced windsurfers here are found in front of the Maui Sunset Condo, 1032 S. Kihei Rd., near Waipuilani Street (a block north of McDonald's), which has great windsurfing conditions but a very shallow reef (not good for beginners). For lessons (from $79), contact **Hawaiian Island Surf and Sport,** 415 Dairy Rd., Kahului (☎ 800/231-6958 or 808/871-4981; www.hawaiianisland.com).

> *You'll float on air (and water) when you learn to windsurf at the best beaches for the sport in the world.*

Maui Shopping Best Bets

Best Alohawear
Moonbow Tropics, 36 Baldwin Ave. (p 379)

Best Asian Antiques
Brown-Kobayashi, 160-A N. Market St. (p 379)

Best Hawaiian Antiques
Bird of Paradise Unique Antiques, 56 N. Market St. (p 379)

Best Place to Browse
Bailey House Gift Shop, 2375-A Main St. (p 385)

Best Edible Souvenir
Broke Da Mouth Cookies, 190 Alamaha St. (p 381)

Best Gifts
Maui Crafts Guild, 69 Hana Hwy. (p 384)

Best Gifts for the Kids
Maui Ocean Center, Maalaea Harbor Village, 192 Maalaea Rd. (p 385)

Best Hawaiian CDs
Totally Hawaiian Gift Gallery, Lahaina Cannery Mall, 1221 Honoapiilani Hwy. (p 384)

Best Hand-Blown Glass
Ki'i Gallery, in the Grand Wailea Resort and The Shops at Wailea (p 380)

Best High Fashion
Maggie Coulombe, 505 Front St. (p 381)

Best Leis
K-Mart, 424 Dairy Rd. (p 382)

Best Shoes
Sandal Tree, Whalers Village, 2435 Kaanapali Pkwy. (p 385)

Best Shopping Mall
Queen Kaahumanu Center, 275 Kaahumanu Ave. (p 386)

Best Sinfully Delicious Bakery
T. Komoda Store and Bakery, 3674 Baldwin Ave (p 381)

Best Souvenir to Ship Home
Sunrise Protea, Haleakala Hwy. (p 384)

Best Swimwear
Lightning Bolt Maui Inc., 55 Kaahumanu Ave. (p 379)

Best T-shirt Selection
Crazy Shirts, multiple locations (p 387)

> *Bird of Paradise Unique Antiques features everything from vintage furniture to classic clothing to oldies on vinyl and cassette.*

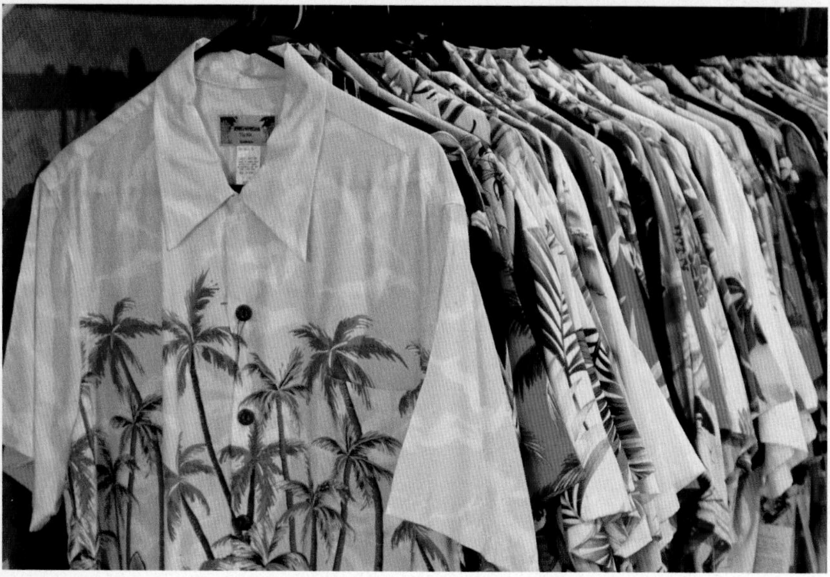

Maui Shopping A to Z

Alohawear

kids **Lightning Bolt Maui Inc.** KAHULUI
I love the excellent selection of women's board shorts, aloha shirts, swimwear, sandals and shoes, and all the necessary accoutrements for fun in the sun. 55 Kaahumanu Ave. ☎ 808/877-3484. AE, DC, MC, V. Map p 383.

★★ **Moonbow Tropics** PAIA
I've found some top-label aloha shirts here. 36 Baldwin Ave. ☎ 808/579-8592. AE, DISC, MC, V. Map p 380.

Tropo MAKAWAO
A good stop for stylish men's alohawear. 3643 Baldwin Ave. ☎ 808/573-0356. AE, MC, V. Map p 387.

Antiques & Collectibles

★★ **Bird of Paradise Unique Antiques** WAILUKU Great Hawaiiana nostalgia items, ranging from 1940s rattan furniture to vintage aloha shirts, and even classic Hawaiian music on cassettes. 56 N. Market St. ☎ 808/242-7699. AE, MC, V. Map p 383.

★ **Brown-Kobayashi** WAILUKU
The focus here is gracious living with Asian antiques, Japanese kimonos and obi, exotic Chinese woods, and more. 160-A N. Market St. ☎ 808/242-0804. AE, MC, V. Map p 383.

Duck Soup PUUNENE
I've found terrific deals on jewelry, handbags, and artwork at this virtually unknown warehouse full of Asian and Indonesian treasures. The location is way off the beaten path; call first for directions. Off Hwy. 311, about a mile from Puunene, near the Maui Animal Shelter and the Central Maui Baseyard. ☎ 808/871-7875. MC, V. Map p 380.

Art

★ **'Ano 'Ano Gallery and Gifts** KAHULUI
A real find for affordable art, with some 50 different Maui artists represented. You'll find everything from oil paintings to gold jewelry to carved wood art. Maui Mall, 70 E. Kaahumlanu Ave. ☎ 808/873-0233. AE, DC, DISC, MC, V. Map p 383.

> *Moonbow Tropics offers an impressive array of authentic aloha shirts.*

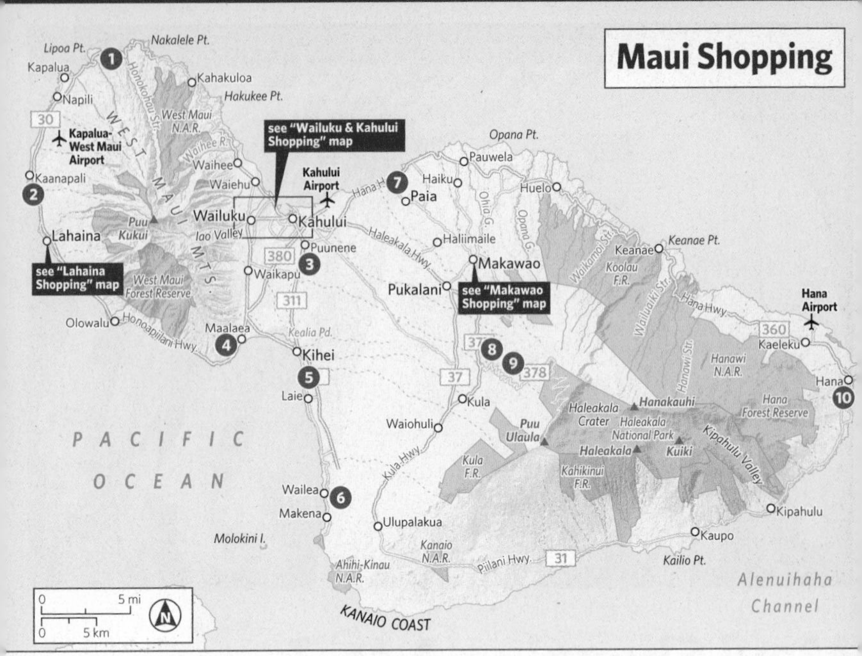

Crazy Shirts **2, 5, 6**
CY Maui **6**
Duck Soup **3**
Hana Coast Gallery **10**
Hasegawa General Store **10**
Hemp House **7**
Honolua Store **1**
Ki'i Gallery **6**
Maui Crafts Guild **7**
Maui Hands **2, 7**
Maui Ocean Center **4**
Moonbow Tropics **7**
Nell **6**
Paul Ropp **2**
Proteas of Hawaii **9**
Sandal Tree **2, 6**
The Shops at Wailea **6**
Sunrise Protea **8**

★★★ **Hana Coast Gallery** HANA
If you go to only one gallery, make it this one. Tucked away in a posh hideaway hotel, this award-winning gallery is devoted entirely to Hawaii's top art: sculptures, paintings, prints, feather work, stonework, and carvings. Maui's best selection under one roof. In the Hotel Hana-Maui. ☎ 808/248-8636. AE, MC, V. Map above.

★★ **Hui No'eau Visual Arts Center** MAKAWAO
I can spend hours wandering the gift shop, which features many one-of-a-kind works by local artists and artisans. 2841 Baldwin Ave. ☎ 808/572-6560. www.huinoeau.com. AE, DISC, MC, V. Map p 387.

Ki'i Gallery WAILEA
I can't pass by this shop (featuring glass in all forms, from handblown vessels to jewelry) without stopping in to browse. Multiple locations: The Grand Wailea Resort, ☎ 808/874-3059; and The Shops at Wailea. ☎ 808/874-1181. www.kiigallery.com. AE, DC, DISC, MC, V. Map above.

★ **Lahaina Arts Society Galleries** LAHAINA
Changing monthly exhibits showcase the Maui artist-members, with pieces ranging from paintings to fiber art, ceramics, sculpture, prints, jewelry, and more. "Art in the Park" fairs are offered every second and fourth weekend of the month. 648 Wharf St. ☎ 808/661-3228. MC, V. Map p 381.

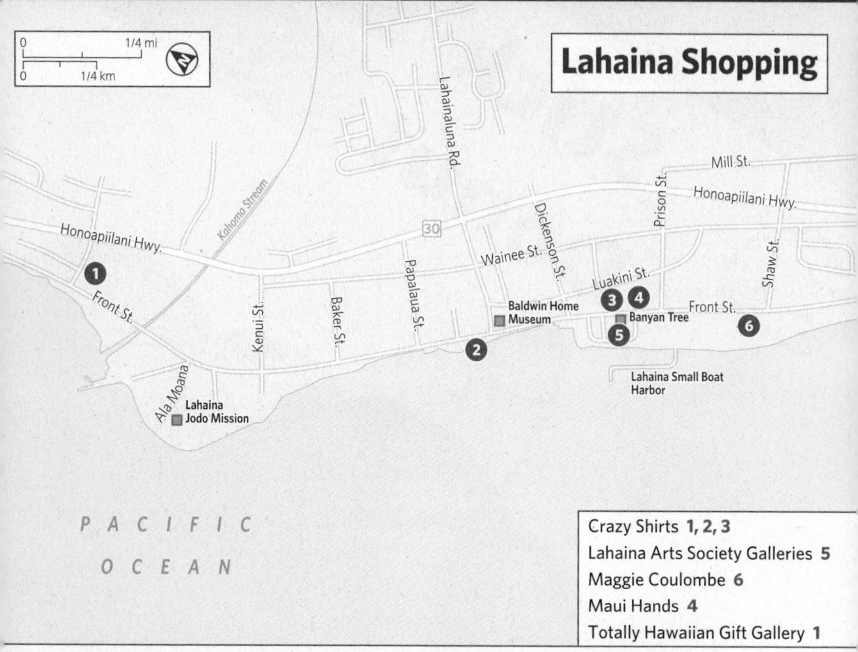

Crazy Shirts	**1, 2, 3**
Lahaina Arts Society Galleries	**5**
Maggie Coulombe	**6**
Maui Hands	**4**
Totally Hawaiian Gift Gallery	**1**

★ **Sherri Reeve Gallery and Gifts** MAKAWAO
I tell friends: If you want to take a little bit of the vibrant color and feel of the islands home with you, stop by this upcountry gallery, featuring everything from inexpensive cards, hand-painted tiles, and T-shirts to original works and limited editions. 3669 Baldwin Ave. ☎ 808/572-8931. www.sreeve.com. AE, DISC, MC, V. Map p 387.

Edibles

★★★ kids **Broke da Mouth Cookies** KAHULUI
This store is my weakness: terrific cookies ranging from chocolate mac-nut, oatmeal raisin, and shortbread to almond, peanut butter, and coconut crunch. ***Warning:*** These cookies are so good, don't plan to buy them for take-home gifts—you'll eat them long before you get home. 190 Alamaha St. ☎ 808/873-9255. No credit cards. Map p 383.

★ kids **T. Komoda Store and Bakery** MAKAWAO
The smell alone draws me into this old-fashioned bakery and store. I recommend getting here early before their famous cream puffs are sold out. Also check out the sinfully delicious cinnamon rolls, doughnuts, pies, and chocolate cake. 3674 Baldwin Ave. ☎ 808/572-7261. No credit cards. Map p 387.

Fashion

CY Maui WAILEA
Women looking for washable, flowing clothing in silks, rayons, and natural fibers will love this shop. In The Shops at Wailea, 3750 Wailea Alanui Dr. ☎ 808/891-0782. AE, MC, V. Map p 380.

★ **Collections** MAKAWAO
One of my favorites, this eclectic shop is filled with spirited clothing reflecting the ease and color of island living. 3677 Baldwin Ave. ☎ 808/572-0781. MC, V. Map p 387.

Hemp House PAIA
Here you'll find a surprisingly great selection of clothing and accessories made of hemp (jeans, linenlike pants, dresses, shirts, etc.), a sturdy, eco-friendly, and sensible fiber. 16 Baldwin Ave. ☎ 808/579-8880. AE, DISC, MC, V. Map p 380.

★ **Holiday & Co.** MAKAWAO
I love to wander around this tiny store checking out the collection of surprisingly attractive natural fiber women's clothing, ranging from easygoing dresses to shawls and even a few aloha shirts. 3681 Baldwin Ave. ☎ 808/572-1470. AE, DC, DISC, MC, V. Map p 387.

★★ **Maggie Coulombe** LAHAINA
I cannot resist this high-fashion store with

> *The declicious inventory of the T. Komoda Store and Bakery in Makawao.*

the unique designs of Maggie Coulombe. The latest couture, jersey, linen, pareo, and shoes, plus accessories, jewelry, purses, and a few surprises. 505 Front St. ☎ 808/662-0696. www.maggiecoulombe.com. AE, DC, DISC, MC, V. Map p 381.

★ **Nell** WAILEA
Top labels and elegant clothing are the stars here. Fairmont Kea Lani Maui hotel. ☎ 808/875-4100, ext. 390. AE, MC, V. Map p 380.

Paul Ropp KAANAPALI
The Bali fashion designer's only store outside of Indonesia features his lively, colorful, and eccentric style of clothing, which is perfect for Maui's tropical climate. In Whalers Village, 2435 Kaanapali Pkwy. ☎ 808/661-8000. AE, DISC, MC, V. Map p 380.

Flowers & Leis

K-Mart KAHULUI
I've scoured the island and, surprisingly, this chain store has some of the most unusual and outstanding leis on Maui and at very moderate prices. 424 Dairy Rd. ☎ 808/871-8553. AE, DISC, MC, V. Map p 383.

Proteas of Hawaii KULA
In addition to flowers, Proteas of Hawaii offers regular walking tours of the University of Hawaii Extension Service gardens across the street. 417 Mauna Place. ☎ 808/878-2533. www.proteasofhawaii.com. MC, V. Map p 380.

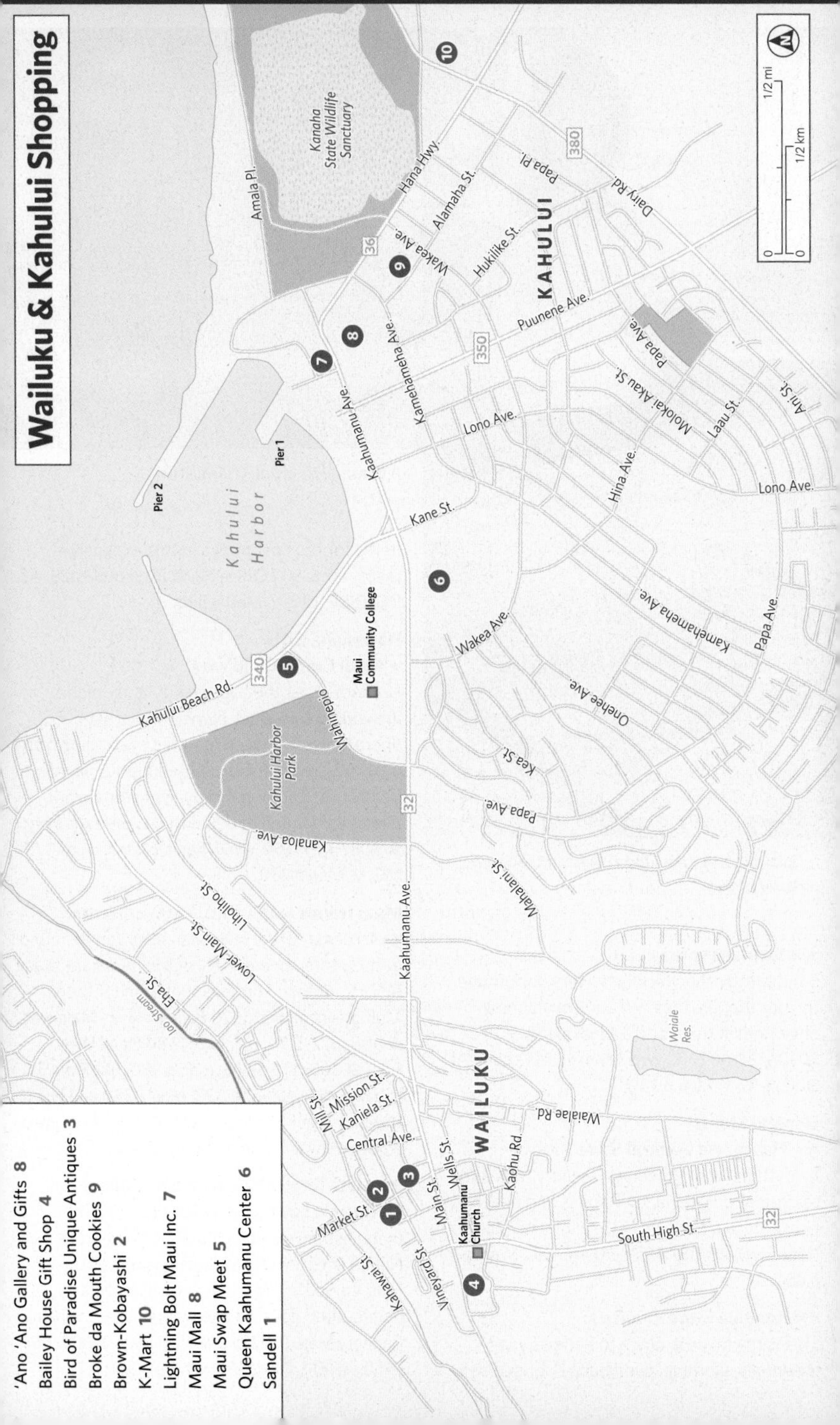
Wailuku & Kahului Shopping
'Ano 'Ano Gallery and Gifts 8
Bailey House Gift Shop 4
Bird of Paradise Unique Antiques 3
Broke da Mouth Cookies 9
Brown-Kobayashi 2
K-Mart 10
Lightning Bolt Maui Inc. 7
Maui Mall 8
Maui Swap Meet 5
Queen Kaahumanu Center 6
Sandell 1
Kahului Harbor
Pier 1
Pier 2
Amala Pl.
Kanaha State Wildlife Sanctuary
Hana Hwy.
36
Alamaha St.
Papa Pl.
380
Dairy Rd.
Wakea Ave.
Hukilike St.
KAHULUI
Puunene Ave.
350
Kamehameha Ave.
Kahumanu Ave.
Lono Ave.
Molokai Akau St.
Papa Ave.
Laau St.
Ani St.
Hina Ave.
Kane St.
Kamehameha Ave.
Papa Ave.
Maui Community College
Wakea Ave.
Onehee Ave.
Kahului Beach Rd.
340
Wahinepio
Kahului Harbor Park
Kea St.
Papa Ave.
Kanaloa Ave.
32
Kaahumanu Ave.
Mahalani St.
Liholiho St.
Lower Main St.
Eha St.
Iao Stream
Waiale Res.
WAILUKU
Mill St.
Mission St.
Kaniela St.
Central Ave.
Waiale Rd.
Market St.
Main St.
Wells St.
Kaohu Rd.
Vineyard St.
Kaahumanu Church
Kahawai St.
South High St.
32
0 1/2 mi
0 1/2 km
N

> *Colorful cards, tiles, and T-shirts at the Sherri Reeve Gallery.*

> *Blown glass art at Ki'i Gallery.*

★★ Sunrise Protea KULA
Send these otherworldly flowers back home to your friends; they will survive shipping anywhere in the world. Haleakala Hwy. ☎ 808/876-0200. www.sunriseprotea.com. AE, DISC, MC, V. Map p 380.

General Stores

★★ Hasegawa General Store HANA
Everything from groceries to every tape and CD that mentions Hana, to T-shirts and beach toys choke the aisles of this old-fashioned store. Hana Hwy. ☎ 808/248-8231. AE, MC, V. Map p 380.

★★ Honolua Store KAPALUA
This is my favorite place to get everyday essentials, clothing, even budget-priced deli items for the best prices in this expensive resort area. 502 Office Rd. ☎ 808/669-6128. AE, DC, DISC, MC, V. Map p 380.

Hawaiiana Gifts

★ Maui Crafts Guild PAIA
I cannot resist the high quality and unique artwork at this artist-owned and artist-operated guild, which features everything from pit-fired raku to hand-painted fabrics, jewelry, beadwork, traditional Hawaiian stone work, and even banana bark paintings. 69 Hana Hwy. ☎ 808/579-9697. www.mauicraftsguild.com. AE, MC, V. Map p 380.

Maui Hands MAKAWAO, PAIA, LAHAINA, KAANAPALI Great Hawaiian gifts can be found at this store, where 90% of the items are made by Maui artists at prices that aren't inflated. Multiple locations: 3620 Baldwin Ave., Makawao, ☎ 808/572-5194, map p 387; 84 Hana Hwy., Paia, ☎ 808/579-9245, map p 380; 612 Front St., Lahaina, ☎ 808/667-9898, map p 381; and Hyatt Regency Maui, Kaanapali, ☎ 808/667-7997, map p 380. www.mauihands.com. AE, MC, V.

★★★ kids Totally Hawaiian Gift Gallery LAHAINA I have spent hours browsing this unique store, checking out everything from Niihau shell jewelry to excellent Hawaiian CDs, carved wood bowls, Hawaiian quilts, handcrafted dolls, and koa works of art. Lahaina Cannery Mall, 1221 Honoapiilani Hwy. ☎ 808/667-2558. AE, DC, DISC, MC, V. Map p 381.

> *Hui No'eau Visual Arts Center features the work of local artists.*

Museum Stores

★★★ **Bailey House Gift Shop** WAILUKU

For made-in-Hawaii items, Bailey House is a must-stop. Plan to spend some time browsing. This small shop packs a wallop with its selection of remarkable gift items. Hawaiian music, exquisite woods, traditional Hawaiian games, pareus and books, lauhala hats hanging in midair, hand-sewn pheasant hatbands, jams and jellies, Maui cookbooks, and an occasional Hawaiian quilt are some of the treasures to be found here. Bailey House Museum Shop, 2375-A Main St. ☎ 808/244-3326. MC, V. Map p 383.

★★ kids **Maui Ocean Center** MAALAEA

This huge (6,000-sq.-ft.) store sells plush stuffed marine animals; nature books; an array of fine artwork, jewelry, and Hawaiiana created by some of the island's most prominent artists; and T-shirts. Maalaea Harbor Village, 192 Maalaea Rd. (the triangle btw. Honoapiilani Hwy. and Maalaea Rd.). ☎ 808/270-7000. AE, DISC, MC, V. Map p 380.

Shoes

★★★ **Sandal Tree** KAANAPALI, WAILEA

My favorite store for sandals, Sandal Tree sells even more: rubber thongs, Top-Siders, dressy pumps, athletic shoes, designer footwear, and even hats. Sandal Tree carries Mephisto and Arche comfort sandals, Donald Pliner, Anne Klein, Charles Jourdan, and beachwear and casual footwear for all tastes. Prices are realistic too. Multiple locations: Whalers Village, 2435 Kaanapali Pkwy. ☎ 808/667-5330, map p 380; Grand Wailea Resort, 3850 Wailea Alanui Dr., Wailea ☎ 808/874-9006, map p 380; Hyatt Regency Maui, 200 Nohea Kai Dr. ☎ 808/661-3495, map p 380. AE, MC, V.

> *You'll find a tropical cornucopia of thousands of unique local products at the Maui Ocean Center.*

> *Sunrise Protea will ship its unique and beautiful flowers to friends and family back home.*

Shopping Centers

Maui Mall KAHULUI
My first stop on Maui always is this mall. I head straight for **Long's Drugs** and **Star Market** for items liked bottled water and a snack or two to take on the road. The mall houses lots of boutique shops and eateries. You have to stop by **Tasaka Guri Guri,** the decades-old purveyor of inimitable icy treats that are neither ice cream nor shave ice, but something in between. 70 E. Kaahumanu Ave. ☎ 808/877-7559. Map p 383.

★ kids **Queen Kaahumanu Center** KAHULUI
Just 10 minutes from the Kahului Airport on Hwy. 32, Kaahumanu's 100-plus shops, restaurants, and theaters cover all the bases, from Arts and Crafts to a **Foodland Supermarket** and everything in between: a thriving food court; the island's best beauty supply, **Lisa's Beauty Supply & Salon** (☎ 808/877-6463), and its sister store for cosmetics, **Madison Avenue Day Spa and Boutique** (☎ 808/873-0880); mall standards like **Sunglass Hut, Radio Shack,** and **Local Motion** (surf and beach wear); and standard department stores like **Macy's** and **Sears.** 275 Kaahumanu Ave. ☎ 808/877-3369. www.queenkaahumanucenter.com. Map p 383.

★ **The Shops at Wailea** WAILEA
Although the chains rule **(The Gap, Louis**

Maui Swap Meet

Looking for a deal? Head to the **swap meet,** Saturday from 7am to 1 pm, where you can find everything from Maui produce, to vintage John Kelly prints and 1930s collectibles, to stuff that should have gone directly to the dump. Admission is 50¢, and it's worth the price for the entertainment factor alone. This large and popular event takes place on the Maui Community College campus, in Kahului, on 4½ acres (enough for 300 vendors and plenty of parking). The colorful Maui specialties include vegetables from Kula and Keanae, fresh taro, plants, proteas, crafts, household items, homemade ethnic foods, and baked goods, including some fabulous fruit breads. Students sell art work and ceramics, and the culinary arts program has prepared food for sale. Kahului Beach Road and Wahine Pio Ave. (access via Wahine Pio Ave). Call ☎ 808/877-3100 for more info.

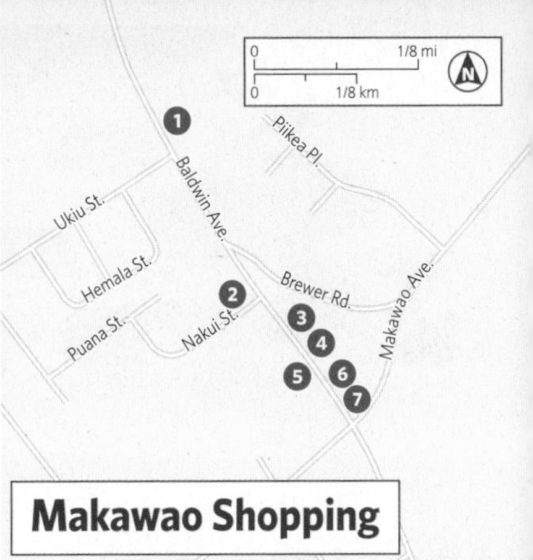

Collections 6
Holiday & Co. 7
Hui No'eau Visual Arts Center 1
Maui Hands 2
Sherri Reeve Gallery and Gifts 4
T. Komoda Store and Bakery 5
Tropo 3

Vuitton, Banana Republic, Tiffany, Crazy Shirts, Honolua Surf Co.) at this glamorous high-end shopping center, I still love it for small boutique "finds" amongst the nearly 60 shops in the complex (like **Martin & MacArthur** furniture and gift gallery, a great place to window-shop). 3750 Wailea Alanui Dr. ☎ 808/891-6770. Map p 380.

T-Shirts

★★ **Crazy Shirts** KAANAPALI, LAHAINA, KIHEI, WAILEA Confession: A huge portion of my wardrobe consists of Crazy Shirts T-shirts. From the "Gone to Maui" to the "Aloha Hula," these 100% cotton T-shirts not only last for years, they are the perfect souvenir and gift to take home. Multiple locations: Whalers Village, ☎ 808/661-0117, map p 381; 865 Front St., ☎ 808/661-4775, map p 381; Wharf Cinema, ☎ 808/661-4712, map p 381; Piilani Village Shopping Center, ☎ 808/875-6440, map p 380; Lahaina Cannery Mall, ☎ 808/661-4788, map p 380; and Shops at Wailea, ☎ 808/875-6435, map p 380. www.crazyshirts.com AE, DISC, MC, V.

> *Options at the Shops at Wailea run the gamut from high-end international chains to quirky, local shops.*

Sandell WAILUKU
If you want the "inside-scoop" on Maui politics and social commentary, stop by and chat with artist/illustrator/cartoonist David Sandell, who has been commenting on Maui since the early 1970s through his artwork. Check out his budget-priced T-shirts. 133 Market St. ☎ 808/249-0234. No credit cards. Map p 383.

Maui Restaurant Best Bets

Best on the Beach
Hula Grill $$$ Whalers Village, Kaanapali (p 392)

Best Breakfast
Charley's Restaurant $$ 142 Hana Hwy., Paia (p 390)

Best Budget Deli
CJ's Deli and Diner $ Kaanapali Fairway Shops (p 390)

Best Burger
Cheeseburger in Paradise $ 811 Front St., Lahaina (p 390)

Best Crepes
Cafe des Amis $$ 42 Baldwin, Paia (p 390)

Best Family Restaurant
Stella Blues Cafe $$ Azeka II Shopping Center, Kihei (p 396)

Best French
Gerard's $$$$ 174 Lahainaluna Rd., Lahaina (p 392)

Best Fresh Fish
Pineapple Grill Kapalua $$$ 200 Kapalua Dr. (p 396)

Best Italian
Vino Italian Tapas & Wine Bar $$$ Kapalua Village Course Golf Club House (p 396)

Best Luau
Old Lahaina Luau $$$$$ 1251 Front St., Lahaina (p 397)

Best Meal under $10
Joy's Place $ 1993 S. Kihei Rd., Kihei (p 394)

Best Fast Mexican
Maui Tacos $ Napili, Lahaina, Kihei, Kahului, (p 395)

Best Pasta
Longhi's $$$ Lahaina Wailea (p 395)

Best People-Watching
Milagros Food Company $$ Hana Hwy., Paia (p 395)

Best Pizza
Shaka Sandwich & Pizza $$ 1770 S. Kihei Rd., Kihei (p 396)

Most Romantic
Lahaina Store Grille and Oyster Bar $$ 744 Front St., Lahaina (p 395)

Best Splurge
Mama's Fish House $$$$ 799 Poho Place, Kuau (p 395)

Best Sushi
Sansei Seafood Restaurant and Sushi Bar $$$ Office Rd., Kapalua (p 396)

Best Trendy Scene
Lahaina Grill $$$$ 127 Lahainaluna Rd., Lahaina (p 394)

Best View
Kula Lodge $$$ 15200 Haleakala Hwy., Kula (p 394)

> *A panko-crusted ahi roll at Sansei Seafood Restaurant and Sushi Bar.*

Maui Hotels and Restaurants

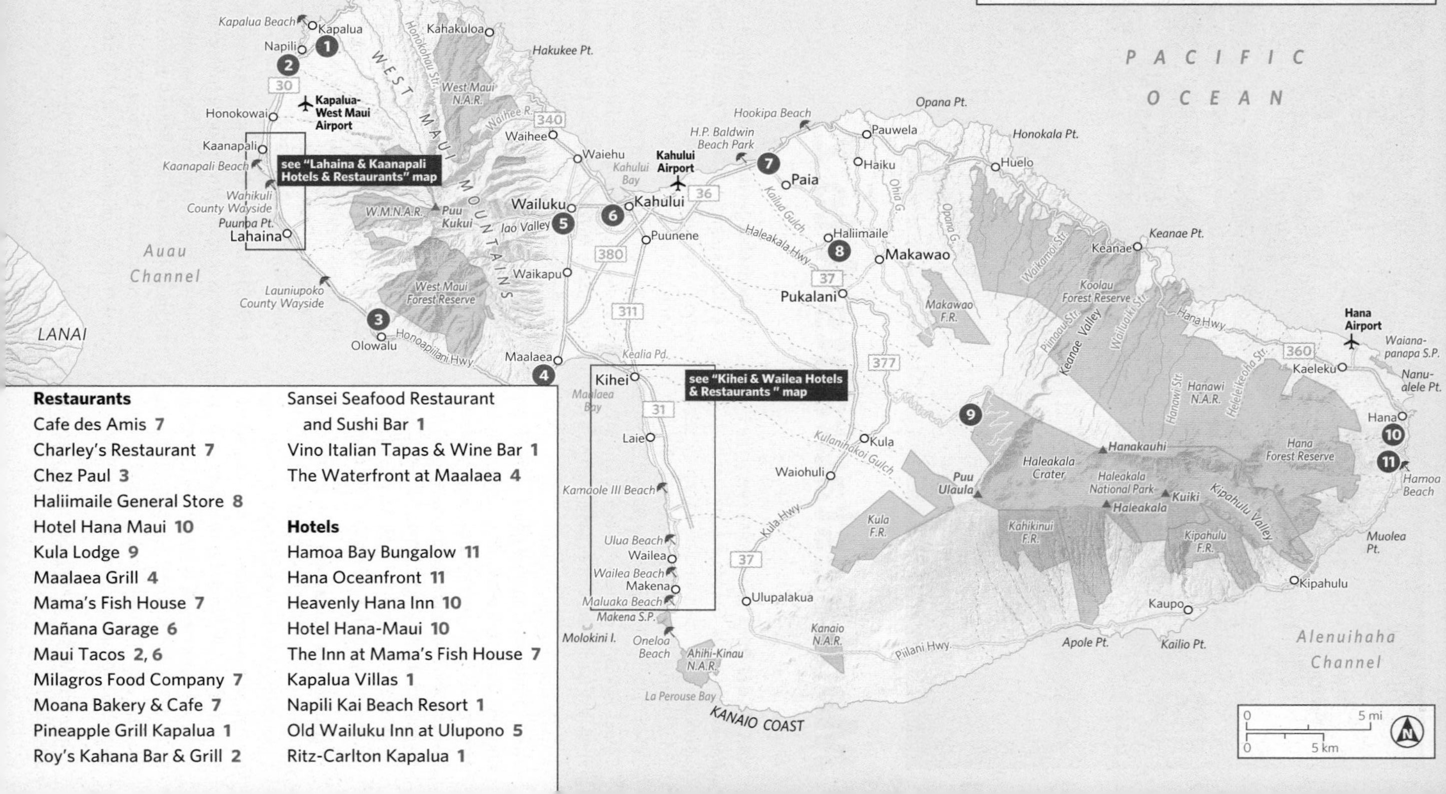

Restaurants
Cafe des Amis 7
Charley's Restaurant 7
Chez Paul 3
Haliimaile General Store 8
Hotel Hana Maui 10
Kula Lodge 9
Maalaea Grill 4
Mama's Fish House 7
Mañana Garage 6
Maui Tacos 2, 6
Milagros Food Company 7
Moana Bakery & Cafe 7
Pineapple Grill Kapalua 1
Roy's Kahana Bar & Grill 2
Sansei Seafood Restaurant and Sushi Bar 1
Vino Italian Tapas & Wine Bar 1
The Waterfront at Maalaea 4

Hotels
Hamoa Bay Bungalow 11
Hana Oceanfront 11
Heavenly Hana Inn 10
Hotel Hana-Maui 10
The Inn at Mama's Fish House 7
Kapalua Villas 1
Napili Kai Beach Resort 1
Old Wailuku Inn at Ulupono 5
Ritz-Carlton Kapalua 1

Maui Restaurants A to Z

★★ **Cafe des Amis** PAIA *CREPES/MEDITERRANEAN/INDIAN* Crepes are the star here, just edging out the incredibly cheap authentic Indian curries. Finish your meal with the best coffee in Paia. 42 Baldwin Ave. ☎ 808/579-6323. Crepes $7.25–$9, dinner entrees $11–$15. MC, V. Breakfast, lunch, and dinner daily. Map p 389.

★ **Caffé Ciao** WAILEA *ITALIAN* This charming trattoria not only has an elegant and reasonably priced outdoor restaurant, but also an everything-you-could-possibly-want takeout deli. Fairmont Kea Lani Hotel, 4100 Wailea Alanui. ☎ 808/875-4100. Entrees: $13–$20 lunch, $17–$36 dinner; pizzas $17–$19. AE, DC, DISC, MC, V. Lunch (seasonally) and dinner daily. Map p 393.

★ kids **Charley's Restaurant** PAIA *AMERICAN/MEXICAN* One of the best breakfasts on Maui, this landmark is a cross between a 1960s hippie hangout, a windsurfers' power-breakfast spot, and a honky-tonk bar that gets going after dark. 142 Hana Hwy. ☎ 808/579-9453. Entrees: $3.75–$12 breakfast and lunch, $10–$22 dinner. AE, DISC, MC, V. Breakfast, lunch, and dinner daily (bar food until 12:30am). Map p 389.

kids **Cheeseburger in Paradise** LAHAINA & WAILEA *AMERICAN* Always crowded and always noisy (with live music every night), this shrine to the American classic has good value, great grinds, and a killer ocean view. Multiple locations; the restaurant is called Cheeseburger Island Style in Wailea. 811 Front St., Lahaina ☎ 808/661-4855; and 3750 Wailea Nui Dr., Wailea, ☎ 808/874-8990. www.cheeseburgerland.com. Burgers $7–$10. AE, DISC, MC, V. Breakfast, lunch, and dinner daily. Map p 391.

★★ **Chez Paul** OLOWALU *FRENCH* Located in the middle of nowhere, this classic French restaurant offers elegant food in a casual setting. It's pricey but worth every penny. MM 15, Honoapiilani Hwy. ☎ 808/661-3843. www.chezpaul.net. Entrees $29–$39. DISC, MC, V. Daily 6–8:30pm. Map p 389.

★ kids **CJ's Deli and Diner** KAANAPALI *AMERICAN/DELI* It's worth the drive to sample the "comfort food" at this hip, happening deli, with prices so low you won't believe you're still on Maui. Kaanapali Fairway Shops, 2580 Keka'a Dr. (just off Honoapiilani Hwy.). ☎ 808/667-0968.

> *Return to the '50s at Peggy Sue's soda shop, which serves juicy burgers, shakes, and affordable kids' meals.*

Lahaina & Kaanapali Hotels & Restaurants

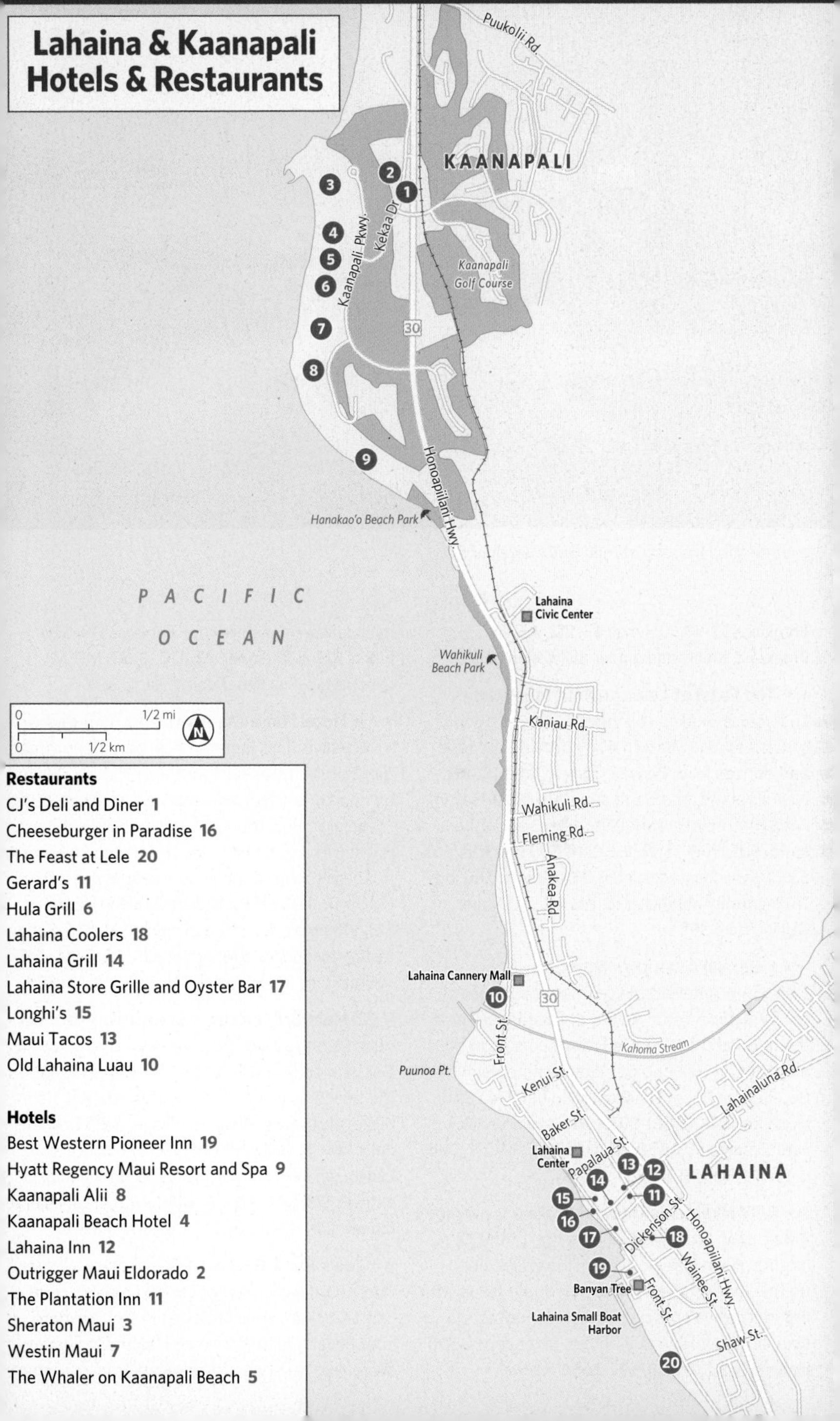

Restaurants

CJ's Deli and Diner **1**
Cheeseburger in Paradise **16**
The Feast at Lele **20**
Gerard's **11**
Hula Grill **6**
Lahaina Coolers **18**
Lahaina Grill **14**
Lahaina Store Grille and Oyster Bar **17**
Longhi's **15**
Maui Tacos **13**
Old Lahaina Luau **10**

Hotels

Best Western Pioneer Inn **19**
Hyatt Regency Maui Resort and Spa **9**
Kaanapali Alii **8**
Kaanapali Beach Hotel **4**
Lahaina Inn **12**
Outrigger Maui Eldorado **2**
The Plantation Inn **11**
Sheraton Maui **3**
Westin Maui **7**
The Whaler on Kaanapali Beach **5**

> *Eat right on the sand at Hula Grill's Barefoot Bar.*

Breakfast $3–$9.50; lunch $7–$12. AE, MC, V. Breakfast, lunch, and dinner daily. Map p 391.

★★ **The Feast at Lele** LAHAINA *POLYNESIAN* Luau cuisine taken to a new level: The owners of Old Lahaina Luau (p 407) provide the food and dances from Hawaii, Tonga, Tahiti, Cook, New Zealand, and Samoa in an outdoor setting with white-cloth, candlelit tables set on the sand. 505 Front St. ☎ 886/244-5353 or 808/667-5353. www.feastatlele.com. $110 adults, $80 kids 2–12; gratuity not included. AE, MC, V. Dinner daily. Map p 391.

★★★ **Gerard's** LAHAINA *FRENCH* Chef Gerard Reversade (a frequent winner of the Wine Spectator Award of Excellence) is at the helm of this creative French cuisine in the elegant setting of an old Victorian home, with excellent service. The Plantation Inn, 174 Lahainaluna Rd. ☎ 808/661-8939. www.gerardsmaui.com. Entrees $33–$50. AE, DC, DISC, MC, V. Daily 6–9pm. Map p 391.

★★★ kids **Haliimaile General Store** HALIIMAILE *AMERICAN* Chef Bev Gannon, one of the 12 original Hawaii Regional Cuisine chefs, heads up this foodie haven in the pineapple fields with her innovative spin on good ol' American cuisine, bridging Hawaii with her Texas roots. 900 Haliimaile Rd. ☎ 808/572-2666. www.haliimailegeneralstore.com. Entrees: $10–$20 lunch, $22–$39 dinner. AE, DC, DISC, MC, V. Lunch Mon–Fri, dinner daily. Map p 389.

★★★ **Hotel Hana-Maui** HANA *HAWAII REGIONAL CUISINE* This ingredient-driven menu (fresh fish caught by local fishermen, produce grown by nearby farmers, and seasonal fruit) is served in the graceful setting of the open-air dining room with large windows. Not cheap, but worth it. There's a buffet and show every Friday (6–8:30pm). Hana Hwy. ☎ 808/248-8211. Entrees: $13–$18 breakfast, $10–$21 lunch, $31–$36 dinner; tasting menu $55–$75; buffet $50. AE, DISC, MC, V. Breakfast, lunch, and dinner daily. Map p 389.

★ kids **Hula Grill** KAANAPALI *HAWAII REGIONAL CUISINE/SEAFOOD* Skip the main dining room. Dig your toes in the sand at the Barefoot Bar on the beach as you chow down on burgers, fish, pizza, and salad. Whalers Village, 2435 Kaanapali Pkwy. ☎ 808/667-6636. www.hulagrill.com. Lunch and Barefoot Bar menus $9–$18; dinner entrees $18–$34. AE, DC, DISC, MC, V. Lunch and dinner daily. Map p 391.

★★ **Joe's Bar & Grill** WAILEA *AMERICAN GRILL* The 270-degree view of the golf course, tennis courts, ocean, and Haleakala is secondary to chef Beverly Gannon's (see Haliimaile General Store, above) style of American home cooking,

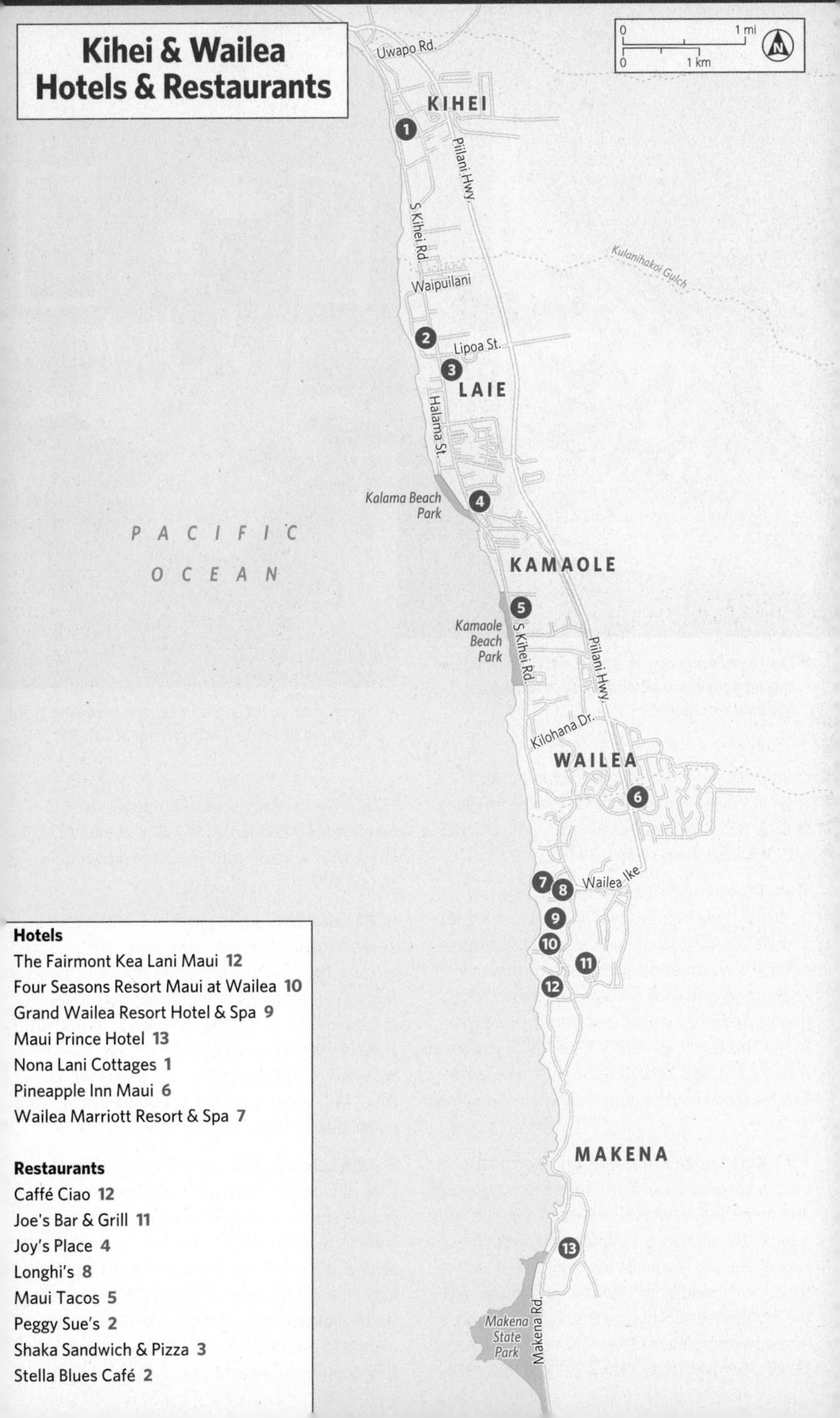
Kihei & Wailea
Hotels & Restaurants
0
1 mi
0
1 km
N
Uwapo Rd.
KIHEI
Piilani Hwy.
S. Kihei Rd.
Kulanihakoi Gulch
Waipuilani
Lipoa St.
LAIE
Halama St.
Kalama Beach Park
PACIFIC
OCEAN
KAMAOLE
Kamaole Beach Park
S. Kihei Rd.
Piilani Hwy.
Kilohana Dr.
WAILEA
Wailea Ike
MAKENA
Makena State Park
Makena Rd.
1
2
3
4
5
6
7
8
9
10
11
12
13
Hotels
The Fairmont Kea Lani Maui 12
Four Seasons Resort Maui at Wailea 10
Grand Wailea Resort Hotel & Spa 9
Maui Prince Hotel 13
Nona Lani Cottages 1
Pineapple Inn Maui 6
Wailea Marriott Resort & Spa 7
Restaurants
Caffé Ciao 12
Joe's Bar & Grill 11
Joy's Place 4
Longhi's 8
Maui Tacos 5
Peggy Sue's 2
Shaka Sandwich & Pizza 3
Stella Blues Café 2

> *The island's priciest (and most delicious) seafood is served fresh in a beautiful beach setting at Mama's Fish House.*

> *Tequila shrimp, firecracker rice, and smashing sushi are among the tasty treats offered at Lahaina Gril.*

from meatloaf to roasted portobello mushrooms. Wailea Tennis Club, 131 Wailea Ike Place. ☎ 808/875-7767. Entrees $20–$32. AE, DC, DISC, MC, V. Dinner daily. Map p 393.

Joy's Place KIHEI *HEALTHFUL DELI/SANDWICHES* If you are in Kihei and are looking for a healthful, delicious lunch at a rock-bottom price, it's worth hunting around for this tiny hole in the wall with humongous sandwiches, fresh salads, hot soups, and yummy desserts. Island Surf Building, 1993 S. Kihei Rd. (entrance on Auhana St.). ☎ 808/879-9258. All items under $12. No credit cards. Lunch daily 10am–5pm. Map p 393.

★ kids **Kula Lodge** KULA *HAWAII REGIONAL CUISINE/AMERICAN* With huge breakfasts and awe-inspiring views, this upcountry lodge is a must-stop for visitors going up (or down) Haleakala. My favorites are the Kula onion soup (with Maui's famous sweet onions) and the clubhouse sandwich (smoked turkey on a homemade bun with spicy orange BBQ sauce). 15200 Haleakala Hwy. (Hwy. 377). ☎ 808/878-1535. www.kulalodge.com. Entrees: $7.50–$16 breakfast, $11–$18 lunch, $14–$28 dinner. AE, DC, DISC, MC, V. Breakfast, lunch, and dinner daily. Map p 389.

★ kids **Lahaina Coolers** LAHAINA *AMERICAN/INTERNATIONAL* Kauwabunga dude: Hungry surfers on a tight budget who want the most bang for their bucks hang out at this ultracasual indoor/outdoor restaurant. 180 Dickensen St. ☎ 808/661-7082. www.lahainacoolers.com. Entrees: $8–$10 breakfast, $9–$13 lunch, $10–$25 dinner. AE, DC, DISC, MC, V. Breakfast, lunch, and dinner daily (full menu until midnight). Map p 391.

★★ kids **Lahaina Grill** LAHAINA *NEW AMERICAN* Chic diners flock to this Lahaina hot spot for the tequila shrimp with firecracker rice, Kona coffee-roasted rack of lamb, Maui onion-crusted seared ahi, and Kalua duck quesadilla. Special kids' menu. 127 Lahainaluna Rd. ☎ 808/667-5117. www.lahainagrill.com. Entrees $26–$62; tasting menu $74. AE, DC, DISC, MC, V. Dinner daily (bar open until midnight). Map p 391.

★★ Lahaina Store Grille and Oyster Bar

LAHAINA *MAUI ISLAND CUISINE/OYSTER BAR*
Get a reservation for sunset on the rooftop of this historic 1916 building and be prepared to eat some of the best food on Maui. *Foodies take note:* Consider asking for a reservation at the table *inside* the exhibition kitchen, where Chef Klink will show off his culinary talents. 744 Front St. ☎ 808/661-9090. Entrees: $6–$19 lunch, $10–$19 dinner. MC, V. Lunch and dinner daily (raw oyster bar open until midnight). Map p 391.

★★ Longhi's LAHAINA & WAILEA *ITALIAN*
The open-air room, black-and-white-checkered floor, and yummy Italian cuisine (plus terrific breakfasts) make this a must try. Multiple locations: The Shops at Wailea, 3750 Wailea Alanui Dr., ☎ 808/891-8883; and 888 Front St., Lahaina, ☎ 808/667-2288. www.longhi-maui.com. Entrees: $10–$19 breakfast, $12–$25 lunch, $17–$42 dinner. AE, DC, MC, V. Breakfast, lunch, and dinner daily. Map p 391, 393.

★ Maalaea Grill MAALAEA *AMERICAN/LOCAL*
In the windy Maalaea Harbor, this elegant restaurant (wood floors, high ceilings, and ocean view), run by culinary duo Michael and Dana Pastul (of Maui's Café O'Lei restaurants), offers a relaxing location for a range of culinary opportunities from coconut fried shrimp to seared fresh fish. 300 Maalaea Rd. ☎ 808/243-2206. Entrees $14–$33. MC. V. Lunch and dinner daily. Map p 389.

★★ Mama's Fish House KUAU *SEAFOOD*
This South Seas fantasy worthy of Gauguin, located on the beach in an old home, serves the most expensive fresh fish on Maui. It's worth every penny. 799 Poho Place, just off the Hana Hwy. ☎ 808/579-8488. www.mamasfishhouse. om. Entrees: $29–$36 lunch, $35–$55 dinner. AE, DC, DISC, MC, V. Lunch and dinner daily. Map p 389.

★★ kids Mañana Garage KAHULUI *LATIN AMERICAN* The clever industrial motif (table bases like hubcaps, a vertical garage door as a divider for private parties, gleaming chrome and cobalt walls) complements the brilliantly conceived and executed cuisine (from fried green tomatoes to barbecued ribs). 33 Lono Ave. ☎ 808/873-0220. Entrees: $7–$13 lunch, $16–$29 dinner. AE, DISC, MC, V. Lunch and dinner Mon and Wed–Sat; dinner Sun. Map p 389.

Roselani: Maui's Best Ice Cream

Aloha, ice cream aficionados: For the culinary experience of your trip, try **Roselani Ice Cream,** Maui's only made-from-scratch, old-fashioned ice cream. The more than 40 flavors range from traditional vanilla to haupia (made from coconut and macadamia nut), the popular chocolate macadamia nut, Kona mud pie, mango and cream, coconut pineapple, and my favorite, luau fudge pie. For a list of hotels, restaurants, parlors, and grocery stores carrying Roselani, either ☎ 808/244-7951 or check online at www.roselani.com.

kids Maui Tacos NAPALI, LAHAINA, KIHEI & KAHULUI *MEXICAN* Hungry surfers, discerning diners, burrito buffs, and Hollywood glitterati flock to this fast, healthy, and cheap taco chain, where gourmet Mexican is served on paper plates. Multiple locations: Napili Plaza, 5095 Napili Hau St., ☎ 808/665-0222; Lahaina Square, 840 Wainee St., Lahaina, ☎ 808/661-8883; Kamaole Beach Center, 2411 S. Kihei Rd., Kihei, ☎ 808/879-5005; and Queen Kaahumanu Center, 275 Kaahumanu Ave., Kahului, ☎ 808/871-7726. www.mauitacos.com. Entrees $4–$7.50. AE, DC, DISC, MC, V. Breakfast, lunch, and dinner daily. Map p 389, 391, 393.

★ Milagros Food Company PAIA *SOUTHWESTERN/ SEAFOOD* Sit outdoors and watch the parade of people, from tie-dyed hippies to ultra-chic Euro-trash, as you tuck into the blend of Southwestern and Pacific Rim cuisine at this casual eatery. Hana Hwy. and Baldwin Ave.

> *Crusted Big Island kampachi at Pineapple Grill.*

☎ 808/579-8755. Entrees: $6–$9 breakfast, $7–$12 lunch, $14–$25 dinner. DC, MC, V. Breakfast, lunch, and dinner daily. Map p 389.

★★ kids **Moana Bakery & Cafe** PAIA *LOCAL/EUROPEAN* Paia's most creative cuisine (with Asian and European influences) highlights the menu at this quasi-stylish cafe. Entertainment 3 nights a week ranges from jazz to Hawaiian to Latin. 71 Baldwin Ave. ☎ 808/579-9999. Entrees: $6–$13 breakfast and lunch, $7–$29 dinner. MC, V. Breakfast and lunch daily; dinner Tues–Sun. Map p 389.

kids **Peggy Sue's** KIHEI *AMERICAN* This 1950s-style diner has oodles of charm (old-fashioned soda-shop stools and jukeboxes on every Formica table). You'll find sodas, shakes, floats, egg creams, and milkshakes, along with burgers, fries, and kids' meals for just $3.95. Azeka Place II, 1279 S. Kihei Rd. ☎ 808/875-8944. Entrees $6–$12. AE, DISC, MC, V. Lunch and dinner daily. Map p 393.

★★★ **Pineapple Grill Kapalua** KAPALUA *PACIFIC ISLAND* If you only have one night to eat on the island of Maui, this is the place. Executive Chef Joey Macadangdang (a protégé of Roy Yamaguchi of Roy's Kahana Bar & Grill, below) brilliantly combines Asian/Filipino ingredients into culinary masterpieces. The dining room overlooks the rolling hills of the Kapalua Golf Course. 200 Kapalua Dr. ☎ 808/669-9600. www.pineapplekapalua.com. Entrees: $7–$17 lunch, $17–$39 dinner. AE, MC, V. Breakfast, lunch and dinner daily. Map p 389.

★★ **Roy's Kahana Bar & Grill** KAHANA *EURO-ASIAN* Roy's has no dramatic view and is located upstairs in a shopping mall. It's packed every night for one reason—fabulous food. Kahana Gateway Shopping Center, 4405 Honoapiilani Hwy. ☎ 808/669-6999. www.roysrestaurant.com. Entrees $14–$31. AE, DC, DISC, MC, V. Dinner daily. Map p 389.

★★ **Sansei Seafood Restaurant & Sushi Bar** KAPALUA *PACIFIC RIM* Perpetual award-winner Sansei offers an extensive menu of Japanese and East-West delicacies that are part fusion, part Hawaii Regional Cuisine. Multiple locations Office Rd., Kapalua, ☎ 808/669-6286; Kihei Tow Center, Kihei, ☎ 808/879-0004. www.sanseihawaii.com. Entrees $16–$43. AE, DISC, MC, V. Dinner daily. Map p 389.

kids **Shaka Sandwich & Pizza** KIHEI *PIZZA* Award-winning pizzas, New York–style heroes, Philly cheese steaks, calzones, salads, just-baked garlic bread, and homemade meatball sandwiches. Everything's made with fresh Mau produce. 1770 S. Kihei Rd. ☎ 808/874-0331. Sandwiches $4.35–$11; pizzas $13–$26. No credit cards. Lunch and dinner daily. Map p 393.

★ kids **Stella Blues Cafe** KIHEI *AMERICAN* Stella's has something for everyone—vegetarians, kids, pasta and sandwich lovers, and hefty steak eaters. Grateful Dead posters line the walls of this loud, lively, irreverent, and unpretentious eatery, and a covey of gleaming motorcycles is invariably parked outside. Azeka II Shopping Center, 1279 S. Kihei Rd. ☎ 808/874-3779. Entrees $8–$23. AE, DC, DISC, MC, V. Breakfast, lunch, and dinner daily. Map p 393.

★★ **Vino Italian Tapas & Wine Bar** KAPALUA *ITALIAN* Overlooking the rolling hills of the

Maui's Best Luau

★★★ kids **Old Lahaina Luau** (1251 Front St., Lahaina; ☎ 800/248-5828 or 808/667-1998; www.oldlahainaluau.com, map p 391), located on a 1-acre oceanfront site, has great food and entertainment in a peerless setting. Local craftspeople display their wares only a few feet from the ocean. Seating is provided on lauhala mats for those who wish to dine as the traditional Hawaiians did, but there are tables for everyone else. This luau offers a healthy balance of entertainment, showmanship, authentic high-quality food, educational value, and sheer romantic beauty. The luau begins at sunset and features Tahitian and Hawaiian entertainment, including ancient hula, hula from the missionary era, modern hula, and an intelligent narrative on the dance's rocky course of survival into modern times. The entertainment is riveting, even for jaded locals. The food, served from an open-air thatched structure, is as much Pacific Rim as authentically Hawaiian: imu-roasted Kalua pork, baked mahimahi in Maui-onion cream sauce, guava chicken, teriyaki sirloin steak, lomi salmon, poi, dried fish, poke, Hawaiian sweet potato, sautéed vegetables, seafood salad, and the ultimate taste treat, taro leaves with coconut milk. It costs $96 for adults, $65 for kids 12 and under.

:apalua Golf Course, this well-designed restauant features tapas (small plates) of exquisite talian dishes that will inspire you to sing an ıria. Kapalua Village Course Golf Club House,)ffice Rd. ☎ 808/661-VINO (661-8466). Reservaions recommended. Tapas $6–$18; large plates 19–$38. AE, DISC, MC, V. Lunch and dinner daily. Map p 389.

★★ kids **The Waterfront at Maalaea** MAALAEA *SEAFOOD* The family-owned Waterfront has won many prestigious awards for service, view, and most of all, just-caught seafood. Try to come around sunset, when the harbor views are stunning. 50 Hauoli St. ☎ 808/244-9028. www.waterfrontrestaurant.net. Entrees $19–$38. AE, DC, DISC, MC, V. Dinner daily. Map p 389.

Maui Hotel Best Bets

Most Romantic
Hamoa Bay Bungalow $$$ Hana Hwy., Hana (p 400)

Most Historic
Old Wailuku Inn at Ulupono $$ 2199 Kahookele St., Wailuku (p 402)

Most Luxurious Hotel
The Fairmont Kea Lani Maui $$$$$ 4100 Wailea Alanui Dr., Wailea (p 399)

Most Luxurious Condo
Kaanapali Alii $$$$ 50 Nohea Kai Dr., Kaanapali (p 400)

Best Moderate Hotel
Lahaina Inn $$ 127 Lahainaluna Rd., Lahaina (p 401)

Best Budget Hotel
Nona Lani Cottages $$ 455 S. Kihei Rd., Kihei (p 402)

Best for Kids
Four Seasons Resort Maui at Wailea $$$$$ 3900 Wailea Alanui Dr., Wailea (p 399)

Best Value
Pineapple Inn Maui $$ 3170 Akala Dr., Kihei (p 402)

Best View
Napili Kai Beach Resort $$$ 5900 Honoapiilani Rd., Napali (p 401)

> *Nearly all the guest rooms at Four Seasons Resort Maui at Wailea have ocean views.*

Best Club-Level Amenities
Ritz-Carlton Kapalua $$$$ 1 Ritz-Carlton Dr., Kapalua (p 403)

Best Service
Four Seasons Resort Maui at Wailea $$$$$ 3900 Wailea Alanui Dr., Wailea (p 399)

Best Spa
Grand Wailea Resort Hotel & Spa $$$$$ 3850 Wailea Alanui Dr., Wailea (p 399)

Most Hawaiian Resort
Hotel Hana-Maui $$$$$ Hana Hwy., Hana (p 400
Kaanapali Beach Hotel $$ 2525 Kaanapali Pkwy., Kaanapali (p 401)

Best Fantasy Resort
Hyatt Regency Maui Resort and Spa $$$$ 20(Nohea Kai Dr., Kaanapali (p 400)

Best Off the Beaten Path
The Inn at Mama's Fish House $$$ 799 Poho Place, Kuau (p 400)

Best Environmentally Correct
Westin Maui $$$$$ 2365 Kaanapali Pkwy., Kaanapali (p 403)

Best Family Condo
Outrigger Maui Eldorado $$$$ 2661 Kekaa Dr., Kaanapali (p 402)

Maui Hotels A to Z

ds **Best Western Pioneer Inn** WEST MAUI
his turn-of-the-century, two-story, plantation-tyle hotel overlooking the Lahaina harbor, has ·een remodeled with vintage bathrooms. 658 Vharf St. (in front of Lahaina Pier), Lahaina, HI ·6761. ☎ 800/457-5457 or 808/661-3636. www. ·ioneerinnmaui.com. 34 units. Doubles $160-·190. AE, DC, DISC, MC, V. Map p 391.

★★ **The Fairmont Kea Lani Maui** WAILEA
'ou get your money's worth at this luxurious esort: an entire suite including a kitchenette, en-ertainment center, sofa bed, spacious bedroom, ·nd large lanai. 4100 Wailea Alanui Dr., Wailea, ·II 96753. ☎ 866/540-4456 or 808/875-4100. ·www.fairmont.com/kealani. 450 units. Doubles 395–$895. AE, DC, DISC, MC, V. Map p 393

★★ kids **Four Seasons Resort Maui at Wailea** VAILEA Attentive, but not cloying, service and ·he most kid-friendly hotel on Maui, with cook-·es and milk on arrival, children's menus, and ·omplimentary baby gear (from cribs to stroll-·rs). You can even prepurchase necessities like diapers and baby food; the hotel will have them waiting for you when you arrive. Spacious rooms feature furnished lanais and grand bathrooms. Prepare to be spoiled. 3900 Wailea Alanui Dr., Wailea, HI 96753. ☎ 800/334-MAUI (334-6284) or 808/874-8000. www.fourseasons.com/maui. 380 units. Doubles $495–$1,025. AE, DC, MC, V. Map p 393.

More Hotel Maps

See the maps on p 389, 391, and 393 for hotel locations.

★★★ kids **Grand Wailea Resort Hotel & Spa** WAILEA Hawaii's largest (50,000 sq. ft.) and most elaborate spa, with every kind of body treatment you can imagine, plus the use of the numerous baths, hot tubs, mineral pools, saunas, steam rooms, and other relaxation amenities in the his-and-her spa area. 3850 Wailea Alanui Dr., Wailea, HI 96753. ☎ 800/888-6100 or 808/875-1234. www.grandwailea.com.

· *If pampering's what you're after, the Grand Wailea has an array of body treatments, hot tubs, saunas, and more.*

> *Sitting on 66 seaside acres, the Hotel Hana-Maui offers old-world elegance and modern comforts in a unparalleled setting.*

780 units. Doubles $495–$905. AE, DC, DISC, MC, V. Map p 393.

★ **Hamoa Bay Bungalow** HANA
Romance blooms in this 600-square-foot Balinese-style tree-top studio, with hot tub and beckoning bamboo bed, close to Hamoa Beach. P.O. Box 773, Hana, HI 96713. ☎ 808/248-7884. www.hamoabay.com. 2 units. Doubles $225. MC, V. Map p 389.

★★ **Hana Oceanfront** HANA
Serenity reigns at these two comfy, plantation-style cottages (polished bamboo flooring and fully appointed gourmet kitchens), located just across the street from Hamoa Bay. P.O. Box 843, Hana, HI 96713. ☎ 808/248-7558. www.myoceancottage.com. 2 units. Doubles $225–$250. MC, V. Map p 389.

★★ **Heavenly Hana Inn** HANA
Each suite in this Japanese-style inn has a sitting room, polished hardwood floors, separate bedroom with a raised platform bed, and black-marble soaking tub. P.O. Box 790, Hana, HI 96713. ☎ 808/248-8442. www.heavenlyhanainn.com. 3 units. Doubles $190–$260. AE, DISC, MC, V. Map p 389.

★★★ kids **Hotel Hana-Maui** HANA
The atmosphere, the landscape, and the culture of old Hawaii set in 21st-century accommodations. The hotel sits on 66 rolling seaside acres, with an excellent spa and access to one of the best beaches in Hana. P.O. Box 9, Hana, HI 96713. ☎ 800/321-HANA (321-4262) or 808/248-8211. www.hotelhanamaui.com. 66 units. Doubles $425–$895, suites from $1,125. AE, DC, DISC, MC, V. Map p 389.

★★ kids **Hyatt Regency Maui Resort and Spa** KAANAPALI This fantasy resort features a half-acre outdoor pool with a 150-foot lava tube slide, a cocktail bar under the falls, a "honeymooner's cave," and nine waterfalls; plus a collection of exotic birds in the lobby (pink flamingos, penguins, and macaws) and an eclectic Asian and Pacific art collection. 200 Nohea Kai Dr., Kaanapali, HI 96761. ☎ 800/233-1234 or 808/661-1234. www.maui.hyatt.com. 806 units. Doubles $365–$765. AE, DC, DISC, MC, V. Map p 391.

★★ **The Inn at Mama's Fish House** KUAU
Located off the beaten path, nestled in a coconut grove on secluded Kuau Beach, these expertly decorated duplexes sit next door to Mama's Fish House (p. 395; guests get a discount on meals). 799 Poho Place (off the Hana Hwy. in Kuau), Paia, HI 96779. ☎ 800/860-HULA (860-4852) or 808/579-9764. www.mamasfishhouse.com. 6 units. Doubles $175–$575. AE, DISC, MC, V. Map p 389.

★★ kids **Kaanapali Alii** KAANAPALI
The height of luxury, these oceanfront condominium units sit on 8 landscaped acres right on Kaanapali Beach and combine all the amenities of a luxury hotel (including a 24-hr. front desk) with the convenience of a condominium. There's even a yoga class on Monday, Wednesday, and Friday on the lawn. 50 Nohea Kai Dr., Kaanapali, HI 96761. ☎ 866/664-6410 or 808/667-1400. www.kaanapali-alii.com. 264 units. Doubles $330–$685. AE, DC, DISC, MC, V. Map p 391.

Sunsets on Maui

Nightlife in Maui begins at sunset, when all eyes turn westward to see how the day will end. And what better way to take it all in than over cocktails? With views of Molokai to the northwest and Lanai to the west, Kaanapali and West Maui boast panoramic vistas unique to this island. In South Maui's resort areas of Wailea and Makena, tiny Kahoolawe and the crescent-shaped Molokini islet are visible on the horizon, and the West Maui Mountains look like an entirely separate island. No matter what your vantage point, you are likely to be treated to an astonishing view.

In Kaanapali, park in Whalers Village and head for **Leilani's** or **Hula Grill** (p 404), next to each other on the beach. Both have busy, upbeat bars and tables bordering the sand. These are happy places for great people-watching; gazing at the lump of Lanai, which looks to be a stone's throw away; and enjoying end-of-day rituals like mai tais and margaritas.

Lahaina is a sunset-lover's nirvana, lined with restaurants that have elevated mai tais to an art form. If you love loud rock, head for **Cheeseburger in Paradise** (p 404). At the southern end of Lahaina, in the 505 Front St. complex, **Pacific'o** is a solid hit, with a raised bar, seating on the ocean, and a backdrop of Lanai across the channel. A few steps away sister restaurant **I'o** shares the same vista, with an appetizer menu and a techno-curved bar that will wow you as much as the drop-dead-gorgeous view.

In Wailea head for the oceanside beach walk trail, or stop at any of the beach coves and watch the sun sink into the ocean. The restaurants at the new Shops at Wailea, including the highly successful **Tommy Bahama** (☎ 808/875-9983) and **Longhi's** (☎ 808/891-8883), are a noteworthy addition to the sunset scene.

Farther south, in Makena, you can't beat the Maui Prince's **Molokini Lounge** (see Maui Prince Hotel below), with its casual elegance and unequaled view of Molokini islet on the ocean side and, on the mauka (inland) side, a graceful, serene courtyard with ponds, rock gardens, and lush foliage.

Don't forget the upcountry view—a perfect way to end the day if you don't mind the drive. ★★**Kula Lodge** (☎ 808/878-2517) has a phenomenal view that takes in central Maui, the West Maui Mountains (looking like Shangri-La in the distance), and the coastline.

★ kids **Kaanapali Beach Hotel** KAANAPALI
Old Hawaii values and customs reign here, from the Hawaiian hula and music in the open courtyard every night to the extensive Hawaiiana program (learn to cut pineapple, weave lauhala, even dance the *real* hula). 2525 Kaanapali Pkwy., Kaanapali, HI 96761. ☎ 800/262-8450 or 808/661-0011. www.kbhmaui.com. 430 units. Doubles $199–$355 with breakfast. AE, DC, DISC, MC, V. Map p 391.

★★ kids **Kapalua Villas** KAPALUA
The palatial condo units dotting the oceanfront cliffs and fairways of this idyllic coast are a (relative) bargain, especially for big families. 500 Office Rd., Kapalua, HI 96721. ☎ 800/545-0018 or 808/665-5400; www.kapaluavillas.com. Doubles: $259–$279 1-bedroom, $359–$379 2-bedroom, $479–$499 3-bedroom. AE, DC, DISC, MC, V. Map p 389.

★ **Lahaina Inn** LAHAINA
Victorian antiques-stuffed rooms at terrific prices located in the heart of Lahaina, with an excellent restaurant and bar downstairs (Lahaina Grill, p 394). The caveat: the rooms are on the small side. 127 Lahainaluna Rd. (near Front St.), Lahaina, HI 96761. ☎ 800/669-3444 or 808/661-0577. www.lahainainn.com. 12 units. Doubles $150–$205. AE, MC, V. Map p 391.

★★ **Maui Prince Hotel** MAKENA
Tranquility reigns at this end-of-the-road resort with a golden-sand beach, a koi-filled waterfall stream, and an ocean view from every clutter-free room. 5400 Makena Alanui, Makena, HI 96753. ☎ 800/321-6284 or 808/874-1111. www.mauiprincehotel.com. 310 units. Doubles $355–$525. AE, DC, MC, V. Map p 393.

★★ kids **Napili Kai Beach Resort** NAPILI
Ocean views of Molokai and Lanai,

> *Local charm is abundant at the Inn at Mama's Fish House, which offers one- and two-bedroom efficiencies on the ocean.*

Hawaii-style architecture, a secluded gold-sand beach, and choice of hotel rooms or condos make this resort very popular. 5900 Honoapiilani Rd. (at the extreme north end of Napili, next to Kapalua Resort), Napili, HI 96761. ☎ 800/367-5030 or 808/669-6271. www.napilikai.com. 162 units. Doubles: $235–$335 hotel room, $335–$430 studio, $475–$650 1-bedroom, $845–$965 2-bedroom. AE, DISC, MC, V. Map p 389.

★ **Nona Lani Cottages** KIHEI
The best bargain on Maui. These self-contained cottages sit among palm, fruit, and sweet-smelling flowering trees, right across the street from a white-sand beach. 455 S. Kihei Rd. (just south of Hwy. 31), P.O. Box 655, Kihei, HI 96753. ☎ 800/733-2688 or 808/879-2497. www.nonalanicottages.com. 11 units. Doubles $120–$150. No credit cards. Map p 393.

★★ **Old Wailuku Inn at Ulupono** WAILUKU
This 1924 former plantation manager's home, lovingly restored, offers a genuine old-Hawaii experience with a gourmet breakfast to boot. 2199 Kahookele St. (at High St., across from the Wailuku School), Wailuku, HI 96732. ☎ 800/305-4899 or 808/244-5897. www.mauiinn.com. 10 units. Doubles $165–$195 with breakfast. MC, V. Map p 389.

B&B Etiquette

In Hawaii, it is traditional and customary to remove your shoes before entering anyone's home. The same is true for most bed-and-breakfast facilities. Most hosts post signs or will politely ask you to remove your shoes before entering the B&B. Not only does this keep the B&B clean, but you'll be amazed how relaxed you feel walking around barefoot. If this custom is unpleasant to you, a B&B may not be for you. Consider a condo or hotel, where no one will be particular about your shoes.

If you have never stayed at a B&B, here are a few other hints: Generally the hosts live on property, and their part of the house is off-limits to guests (you do not have the "run of the house"). Most likely there will be a common area that you can use. Don't expect daily maid service. Your host may "tidy up" but will not provide complete maid service. Also, don't expect amenities like little bottles of shampoo and conditioner; this is a B&B, not a resort. Remember you are sharing your accommodations with other guests, so be considerate (in other words, quiet) when you come in late at night.

Some hotels, resorts, condos, and vacation rentals may allow smoking in the guest rooms (most also have no-smoking rooms available), but the majority of bed-and-breakfasts forbid smoking in the rooms. If this matters to you, be sure to check the policy of your accommodation before you book.

★ kids **Outrigger Maui Eldorado**
KAANAPALI My pick of condos for families features spacious units, grassy play areas outside, safe swimming, beach cabanas, and a barbecue area. 2661 Kekaa Dr., Kaanapali, HI 96761. ☎ 888/339-8585 or 808/661-0021. www.outrigger.com. 204 units. Doubles: $279–$329 studio, $335–$389 1-bedroom, $475–$599 2-bedroom. AE, DC, DISC, MC, V. Map p 391.

★★ **Pineapple Inn Maui** KIHEI
This charming inn offers impeccably decorated, soundproof rooms; a giant saltwater pool and Jacuzzi overlooking the ocean; and wallet-pleasing prices, making it a terrific vacation value. 3170 Akala Dr., Kihei, HI 96753. ☎ 877/212-MAUI

> *Kaanapali Beach Hotel has an irresistible local style and a real Hawaiian warmth that's missing from many other Maui properties.*

(6284) or 808/298-4403. www.pineappleinnmaui.com. Doubles $119–$149; cottage $195–$215 for four. No credit cards. Map p 393.

★★ **The Plantation Inn** LAHAINA
This romantic, Victorian-style inn features period furniture and four-poster canopy beds. Guests get a discount at the excellent French restaurant Gerard's (p 392), next door. 174 Lahainaluna Rd. (btw. Wainee and Luakini sts., 1 block from Hwy. 30), Lahaina, HI 96761. ☎ 800/433-6815 or 808/667-9225. www.theplantationinn.com. 19 units. Doubles $169–$255 with breakfast. AE, DC, DISC, MC, V. Map p 391.

★★★ kids **Ritz-Carlton Kapalua** KAPALUA
If you can afford it, stay on the Club Floor—it offers the best amenities in the state, including French-roast coffee in the morning, a buffet at lunch, cookies in the afternoon, and pupus and drinks at sunset. 1 Ritz-Carlton Dr., Kapalua, HI 96761. ☎ 800/262-8440 or 808/669-6200. www.ritzcarlton.com. 548 units. Doubles $365–$675; Club Floor from $900. AE, DC, DISC, MC, V. Map p 389.

★★ kids **Sheraton Maui** KAANAPALI
"Family suites" are great for those traveling with kids—they include three beds, a sitting room with full-size couch, and two TVs, both equipped with Nintendo. Fun activities for kids range from Hawaiian games to visits to nearby attractions. 2605 Kaanapali Pkwy., Kaanapali, HI 96761. ☎ 888/488-3535 or 808/661-0031. www.sheraton-maui.com. 510 units. Doubles $405–$695. AE, DC, DISC, MC, V. Map p 391.

★★ **Wailea Marriott Resort & Spa** WAILEA
This classic, open-air, 1970s-style hotel in a tropical garden by the sea gives you a sense of what Maui was like before the big resort boom. 3700 Wailea Alanui Dr., Wailea, HI 96753. ☎ 800/367-2960 or 808/879-1922. www.marriotthawaii.com. 545 units. Doubles $475–$800. AE, DC, DISC, MC, V. Map p 393.

★ kids **Westin Maui** KAANAPALI
This resort emphasizes a healthful environment (smoking is no longer allowed in guest rooms although it is allowed in some public areas). Kids will love the "aquatic playground." 2365 Kaanapali Pkwy., Kaanapali, HI 96761. ☎ 888/625-4949 or 808/667-2525. Fax 808/661-5764. www.westinmaui.com. 758 units. Doubles $440–$710. AE, DC, DISC, MC, V. Map p 391.

★★ **The Whaler on Kaanapali Beach** KAANAPALI This elegant, private, luxurious condo complex is an oasis in the heart of Kaanapali, right on the world-famous beach. 2481 Kaanapali Pkwy. (next to Whalers Village), Kaanapali, HI 96761. ☎ 866/77-HAWAII (774-2924) or 808/661-4861. www.resortquesthawaii.com. 360 units. Doubles: $176–$224 studio, $198–$296 1-bedroom, $260–$520 2-bedroom. AE, DC, DISC, MC, V. Map p 391.

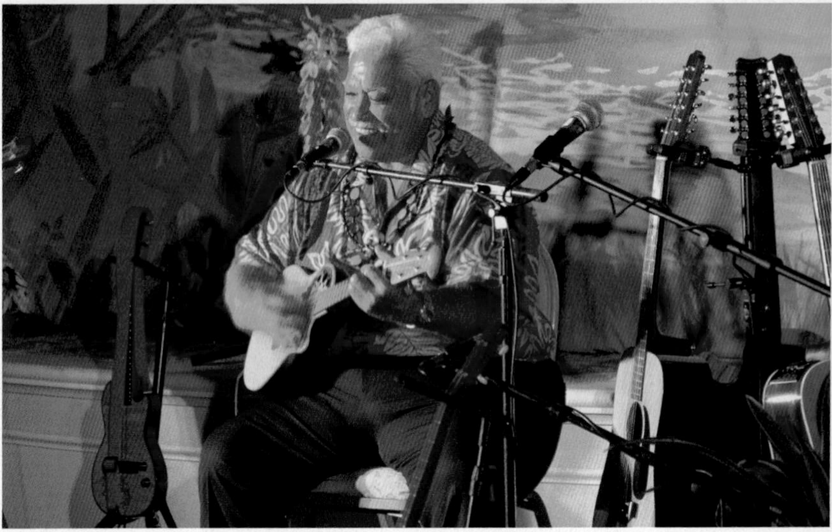

Maui Nightlife & Entertainment A to Z

Bars & Cocktail Lounges

★★ Casanova MAKAWAO
If a big-name mainland band is resting up on Maui following a sold-out concert on Oahu, you may find its members setting up for an impromptu night here. After the diners depart, at 9:45pm, the DJs take over on Wednesday (ladies' night) and, on Thursday, Friday, and Saturday, live entertainment draws fun-lovers from even the most remote reaches of the island. Expect good blues, rock 'n' roll, reggae, jazz, Hawaiian, and the top names in local and visiting entertainment. I love the live jazz Sunday afternoons from 3 to 6 pm. 1188 Makawao Ave. ☎ 808/572-0220. Map p 405.

Cheeseburger in Paradise LAHAINA
Loud, live, tropical rock blasts into the streets and out to sea nightly from 4:30 to 11pm. Front/Lahainaluna sts. ☎ 808/661-4855. Map p 405.

★★ Hapa's Night Club KIHEI
When I'm hungry for the sweet sounds of local music, I give Hapa's a call to make sure Hawaiian's on tap for the night. 41 E. Lipoa St. ☎ 808/879-9001. Map p 405.

Hard Rock Café LAHAINA
Quickly becoming the "scene" for 20-somethings, with occasional live music, but mainly DJs, and very loud speakers. 900 Front St. ☎ 808/667-7400. Map p 406.

★ Kahului Ale House KAHULUI
Local residents gather here to sing karaoke on Sunday, Monday, and Wednesday from 10pm to 2am. There's live music Thursday and Friday and a DJ on Saturday from 10pm. 355 E. Kamehameha Ave. ☎ 808/877-9001. Map p 405.

★ Leilani's/Hula Grill KAANAPALI
Both oceanfront restaurants have busy, upbeat bars and tables bordering the sand. Hula Grill's Barefoot Bar appetizer menu is a cut above. Leilani's has live music daily from 3:30 to 6pm, while at Hula Grill the happy hour starts at 3pm, with live music at 6pm. Whalers Village. Leilani's ☎ 808/661-4495). Hula Grill ☎ 808/667-6636. Map p 405.

> *Local legends perform Tuesday nights at the Ritz-Carlton as part of the Masters of Hawaiian Slack Key Guitar Series.*

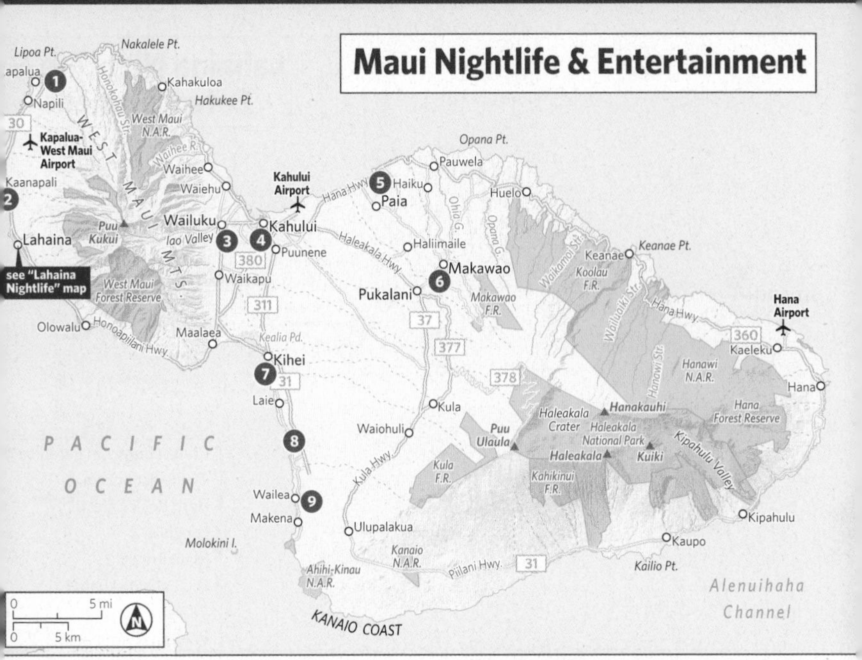

Casanova 6
Hapa's Night Club 7
Iao Theater 3
Kahului Ale House 4
Kupanaha 2
Leilani's/Hula Grill 2
Lobby Lounge at Four Seasons 9
Mañana Garage 4
Masters of Hawaiian Slack Key Guitar Series 1
Maui Arts & Cultural Center 4
Moana Bakery & Café 5
Sports Page Bar 8

The Hawaiian Mai Tai

Some insist on viewing the sunset with a homemade mai tai. The entire day can be built around this ritual—shopping for the mai tai ingredients, checking the angle of the sun, and swimming with the knowledge that your big salty thirst will soon be quenched with a tall homemade mai tai on one of the world's best beaches. When the sun is low, mix lime juice, lemon juice, orange juice, passion-orange-guava juice, and grapefruit juice (fresh, if possible). Pour this concoction over ice in tall frosty glasses, and then add Meyer's rum, in which Tahitian vanilla beans have been soaking for days. (Add cinnamon if desired, or soak a cinnamon stick with the rum and vanilla beans.) A dash of angostura bitters, a few drops of Southern Comfort as a float, a sprig of mint, a garnish of fresh lime, and voilà!—you have a homemade mai tai, a cross between a planter's punch and the classic Trader Vic's mai tai. As the sun sets, lift your glass, and savor the moment, the setting, and the first sip—not a bad way to end the day.

In Hawaii, the mai tai is more than a libation. It's a festive, happy ritual that signals holiday, vacation, or a time of play, not work. Computers and mai tais don't mix. Hammocks and mai tais do. Sunsets and mai tais go hand in hand.

★ **The Lobby Lounge at Four Seasons** WAILEA
For a quiet evening, I recommend sinking into the plush furniture, ordering an exotic drink (you know—the kind that comes with a lot of fruit), and enjoying the gentle jazz or soft Hawaiian music. Nightly live music from 8:30 to 11:30pm. Four Seasons Wailea. ☎ 808/874-8000. Map p 405.

Longhi's LAHAINA
Live salsa or jazz spills out into the streets from 9:30pm on weekends. I love people-watching here—it's a real mix, from Midwestern tourists to the occasional rock star. 888 Front St. ☎ 808/667-2288. Map above.

★★ kids **Mañana Garage** KAHULUI
This eclectic family restaurant attracts a 30- to 40-year-old crowd. Live music Wednesday through Saturday nights, from 6:30pm. 33 Lono Ave. ☎ 808/873-0220. Map p 405.

Maui Brews LAHAINA
A young, hip crowd comes to this late-night restaurant-turned-nightclub. Every night there's swing, salsa, reggae, and jams, either live or with a DJ. 900 Front St. ☎ 808/667-7794. Map above.

★★ kids **Moana Bakery & Café** PAIA
This retro restaurant is my favorite place to relax with live music, and you can bring the entire family. Vintage Hawaiian 6:30 to 9pm on Wednesday; smooth jazz and hot blues 6:30 to 9pm on Friday; and flamenco guitar and gypsy violin 6 to 9pm on Sunday. 71 Baldwin Ave. ☎ 808/579-9999. Map p 405.

Sports Page Bar KIHEI
Stuffed with visitors, this typical sports bar features live music Monday through Saturday from 9pm. 2411 S. Kihei Rd. ☎ 808/879-0602. Map p 405.

Dance, Theater, and Shows

Iao Theater WAILUKU
It's not Broadway, but Maui does have live community theater, ranging from locally written productions to well-known plays to musicals. 68 N. Market St. ☎ 808/244-8680 or 808/242-6969 for the box office and program information. www.mauionstage.com. Map p 405.

★★★ kids **Kupanaha** KAANAPALI
This dinner show features magic, illusions, and the story of the Hawaii fire goddess, Pele, presented through hula and chant performed by children. It gets my vote for a great family outing. The shows are Tuesday through Saturday from 5 to 8pm. Kaanapali Beach Hotel. ☎ 808/661-0011. www.kbhmaui.com. Dinner &

show $89–$99 adults, $58 teens (ages 13–20), and $41 children ages 6–12 (free for children 5 and under). Map p 405.

★★★ **Maui Arts and Cultural Center** KAHULUI This is the island's most prestigious entertainment venue, a first-class center for the visual and performing arts. Bonnie Raitt has performed here, as have Hiroshima, Pearl Jam, Ziggy Marley, Tony Bennett, the American Indian Dance Theatre, the Maui Symphony Orchestra, and Jonny Lang, not to mention the finest in Hawaiian talent. The center is as precious to Maui as the Met is to New York, with a visual-arts gallery, an outdoor amphitheater, offices, rehearsal space, a 300-seat theater for experimental performances, and a 1,200-seat main theater. The center's activities are well publicized locally, so check the local newspaper, the *Maui News*, or ask your hotel concierge what's going on during your visit. 1 Cameron Way. ☎ 808/242-7469. www.mauiarts.org. Ticket prices vary. Map p 405.

★★★ kids **'Ulalena** LAHAINA Don't miss this! Everyone in your family, from grandma to the kindergartener, will be riveted during this incredible show, which weaves Hawaiian mythology with drama, dance, and state-of-the-art multimedia capabilities in a brand-new, multimillion-dollar theater. A local and international cast performs Polynesian dance, original music, acrobatics, and chant to create an experience that often leaves the audience speechless. It's interactive, with dancers coming down the aisles, drummers and musicians in surprising corners, and mind-boggling stage and lighting effects that draw the audience in. Performances are Tuesday through Saturday at 6:30pm. Maui Myth and Magic Theatre, 878 Front St. ☎ 877/688-4800 or 808/661-9913. www.ulalena.com. $60–$130 adults, $40–$85 kids 12 and under. Map p 406.

★ **Warren & Annabelle's** LAHAINA This unusual magic/comedy cocktail show stars illusionist Warren Gibson and "Annabelle," a ghost from the 1800s who plays the grand piano as Warren dazzles you with his sleight-of-hand magic. 900 Front St. ☎ 808/667-6244. www.warrenandannabelles.com. $56–$95. Map p 406.

Hawaiian Music

★★★ kids **Masters of Hawaiian Slack Key Guitar Series** KAPALUA For a chance to experience a side of Hawaii that few visitors are privileged to see, plan to experience this weekly, Tuesday night production in the comfort of the Ritz-Carlton's amphitheater. Host George Kahumoku, Jr., introduces a new slack-key master every week. Not only is there incredible Hawaiian music and singing, but George and his guest "talk story" about old Hawaii, music, and Hawaiian culture. Napili Kai Beach Resort, Napili. ☎ 808/669-3858. www.slackkey.com. $45. Map p 405.

Luaus

★★★ kids **Old Lahaina Luau** LAHAINA Accept no substitutes: This is the best luau on Maui (perhaps in the entire state). See "Maui's Best Luau," p 397, and The Feast at Lele, p 392.

The Best Place in the World to See a Movie

If you're headed to Maui in June, pick your dates around the **Maui Film Festival** ☎ 808/579-9244; www.mauifilmfestival.com (which always starts the Wednesday before Father's Day); this is an event you won't want to miss. The 5-day festival premiers nightly films in the Celestial Cinema, an under-the-stars, open-air "outdoor theater" on the Wailea Golf Course, which features a 50-ft.-wide screen in Dolby Digital Surround Sound. Festival organizer and film producer Barry Rivers said his criteria for selecting the films, many of which have become box office hits, is that they be "life-affirming."

In addition to the 5 days and nights of films, film workshops, and filmmaker panels, there is also terrific food: A Taste of Wailea, an event that features the culinary masterpieces of Maui's top chefs, is held at sunset, at the top of the Wailea Golf Course, where the view of the ocean, Kahoolawe, and Lanai is almost as delicious as the food.

For the family, there's a Father's Day Concert of contemporary Hawaiian music, a sand sculpture contest, and picnics.

For those interested in Hawaiian culture, the festival presents TheStarShow, where live images of celestial objects are projected onto the screen as experts in Polynesian astronomy and cultural history take the audience on a tour of the night sky and Polynesian navigation lore.

7 Molokai

My 12 Favorite Molokai Moments

Born of volcanic eruptions 1.5 million years ago, Molokai remains a time capsule on the dawn of the 21st-century. It has no deluxe resorts, no stoplights, and no buildings taller than a coconut tree. Molokai is the least developed, most "Hawaiian" of all the islands, making it especially attractive to adventure travelers and peace seekers. Here are just a few of my favorite experiences on Molokai.

> PREVIOUS PAGE *Helicopter tours offer breathtaking views of golf courses that hug Papohaku Beach on Molokai's magnificent western coast.* THIS PAGE *Three miles of smooth sand on the pristine Pacific shore make Papohaku Beach a perfect location for a stroll.*

❶ **Riding a mule into a leper colony.** Don't pass up the opportunity to see the hauntingly beautiful Kalaupapa peninsula. Buzzy Sproat's mules go up and down a 3-mile trail to Molokai's famous leper colony. The views are breathtaking: You'll see the world's highest sea cliffs (over 300 stories tall) and waterfalls plunging thousands of feet into the ocean. If you're afraid of heights, catch the views from the Kalaupapa lookout, in Palaau State Park. See p 419, ❼.

❷ **Celebrating the ancient hula.** Celebrate the birth of the hula at the weekend-long **Ka Hula Piko Festival.** You'll get to see the real hula, plus enjoy music, food, and crafts. See "A Weekend of Hula," p 423.

❸ **Strolling the sands at Papohaku.** Go early, when the tropical sun isn't so fierce, and stroll this 3-mile stretch of unspoiled golden sand on Molokai's West End. See p 425.

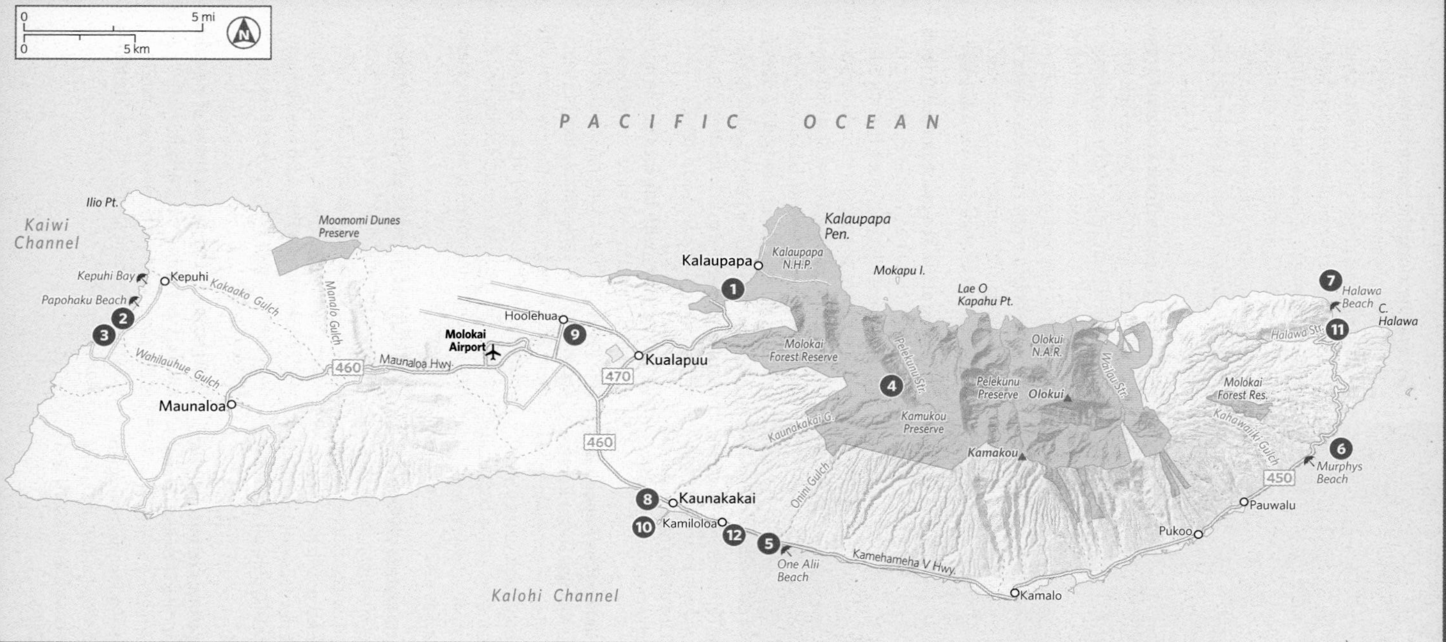

1. Riding a mule into a leper colony
2. Celebrating the ancient hula
3. Strolling the sands at Papohaku
4. Traveling back in time on the Pepeopae Trail
5. Soaking in the warm waters off One Alii Beach Park
6. Snorkeling among clouds of butterfly fish
7. Kayaking along the north shore
8. Watching a sunset from a coconut grove
9. Tasting aloha at a macadamia nut farm
10. Talking story with the locals
11. Hiking into paradise at Halawa Valley
12. Relaxing to the gentle tunes of Hawaiian music

> *THIS PAGE The Molokai Forest Reserve Pepeopae Trail features up close and personal contact with the island's spectacular indigenous foliage. OPPOSITE PAGE Sunset at Kapuaiwa Coconut Grove.*

4 Traveling back in time on the Pepeopae Trail. Hike through the Molokai Forest Reserve and back a few million years in time. Along the misty trail (actually a boardwalk across the bog), expect close encounters of the botanical kind: mosses, sedges, violets, lichens, and knee-high ancient ohia. See p 427.

5 Soaking in the warm waters off One Alii Beach Park. Spend the afternoon in the sun at this thin strip of sand, once reserved for the *alii* (chiefs) and the oldest public beach park on Molokai. It's often crowded with families on weekends, but it can be all yours on weekdays. See p 425.

6 Snorkeling among clouds of butterflyfish. The calm waters off Murphy (Kumimi) Beach, on the east end, are perfect for snorkelers. Just don your gear and head to the reef, where you'll find lots of exotic tropical fish, including long-nosed butterflyfish, saddle wrasses, and convict tangs. See p 424.

7 Kayaking along the north shore. This is the Hawaii of your dreams: waterfalls thundering down sheer cliffs, remote sand beaches, miles of tropical vegetation, and the wind whispering in your ear. The best times to go are late March and early April, or in summer, especially August to September, when the normally galloping ocean lies down flat. See p 430.

8 Watching a sunset from a coconut grove. Kapuaiwa Coconut Grove/Kiowea Park, off Maunaloa Highway (Hwy. 460), is a perfect place to watch the sunset. The sky behind the coconut trees fills with a kaleidoscope of colors as the sun sinks into the Pacific. Be careful where you sit, though: Falling coconuts could have you seeing stars well before dusk. See p 422, 1.

9 Tasting aloha at a macadamia nut farm. It could be the owner, Tuddie Purdy, and his friendly disposition that make the macadamia nuts here taste so good. Or it could be his years of practice in growing, harvesting, and shelling them on his 1½-acre farm. Either way, Purdy produces a perfect crop. See how he does it on a short, free tour of Purdy's All-Natural Macadamia Nut Farm in Hoolehua, just a nut's throw from the airport. See p 421, 13.

10 Talking story with the locals. The number one favorite pastime of most islanders is "talking story," or exchanging experiences and knowledge. You can probably find residents more than willing to share their wisdom with you while fishing from the wharf at Kaunakakai (p 423, 2), hanging out at Molokai Fish & Dive (p 431), or having coffee at any of the island's restaurants.

11 Hiking into paradise at Halawa Valley. Of the five great valleys of Molokai, only Halawa is easily accessible. A guided hike includes lessons on history, culture, and flora, and ends at 250-foot Moaula Falls with a refreshing swim. See "Halawa Valley: A Hike Back in History," p 419.

12 Relaxing to the gentle tunes of Hawaiian music. Every Friday from 4–6pm Hotel Molokai is the place to be for home-grown music, when local residents perform. See "Nightlife on Molokai," p 443.

HAWAII'S MOST DANGEROUS INVADERS

A Who's Who of Invasive Species

BY JEANETTE FOSTER

THERE'S TROUBLE in Paradise—serious trouble. Invasive species not native to Hawaii have destroyed native forests, killed the majority of the native birds, obliterated decades-old indigenous trees, and wiped out endemic fish found nowhere else on the planet.

The flora and fauna in Hawaii, the most isolated chain in the world, never developed defensive properties to warn off predators because there were no predators. Today, there are more endangered species per square mile in Hawaii than any other place on the planet.

RATS

Rats came to Hawaii either on outrigger canoes steered by the Polynesians or on the whaling ships that showed up in the 1800s (or possibly both). Either way, the result was that rats ate birds' eggs and destroyed their habitat in the native forests.

MONGOOSES

The small Indian mongoose was brought to Hawaii by sugar planters in 1883 as a solution to the rat problem. Unfortunately, no one considered that rats are nocturnal and the mongoose is not. Instead of killing rats, mongooses quickly started feasting on the eggs and chicks of native birds.

ERYTHRINA GALL WASP

This tiny wasp came to Hawaii in recent years. It lays its eggs in the leaves and stems of wiliwili trees, creating an outbreak of tumors (galls) on the leaves. The

infected tree dies, and the wind carries diseased leaves off to infect more wiliwili trees.

TILAPIA
Blame the scientists for this one, too. This fish was introduced to Hawaii as an aquaculture crop. The problem is that tilapia can survive in both salt and fresh water, and feed on almost anything from algae to insects. In particular, tilapia have had damaging effects on Hawaii's native shrimp and gobies.

GORILLA SEAWEED
In the 1970s, scientists introduced this edible seaweed to Hawaiian waters thinking it would make a good aquaculture crop. Since then this quickly growing seaweed has taken over several reefs, forming large, thick mats that overgrow and kill coral and other seaweeds, essentially smothering the reefs.

PIGS
Feral pigs (brought by early Polynesians) have had an impact on nearly every native plant community in Hawaii. They eat native plants, allowing invasive plants to become established. The holes they leave behind fill with water, allowing mosquitoes carrying avian malaria to breed. With destruction of native vegetation comes the destruction of native bird and insect populations as well.

MAN
The species that has done the most damage to Hawaii's endemic flaura and fauna is man. From clear-cutting land (destroying Hawaii's native forests and all the plant, bird, and insect species found there) to polluting the pristine waters with agricultural and other chemicals, to filling in sand at beaches, to creating harbors, to channeling streams, man's impact on the islands is unequaled.

The Best of Molokai in 3 Days

Only 38 miles from end to end and just 10 miles wide, Molokai stands like a big green wedge in the blue Pacific. This long narrow island is like yin and yang: on the West End of the island is a flat, austere, arid desert; on the East End is a lush, green, tropical Eden. This itinerary starts and ends each day in Kaunakakai.

> *The Molokai Mule Ride to the Kalaupapa Peninsula brings you to unparalleled vistas of the Island's rocky coastline cliffs.*

START & FINISH Kaunakakai.
TRIP LENGTH 3 days and 112 miles.

Day 1

1 ★ **Kaunakakai.** Start off your trip by exploring Molokai's biggest town. ⏲ 2 hr. See p 422.

---

(2) ☕ ★ **Outpost Natural Foods.** Before you leave town, get a picnic lunch from the island's only health food restaurant. See p 439.

From Kaunakakai, head east on Hwy. 450 (Kamehameha V Hwy.) to MM (mile marker) 6.

3 **Kalokoeli Pond.** No visit to Molokai is complete without at least a passing glance at the island's **ancient fishponds,** a singular achievement in Pacific aquaculture. Hawaiians

More of Molokai

See chapter 3 for my suggested 1-week Molokai itinerary.

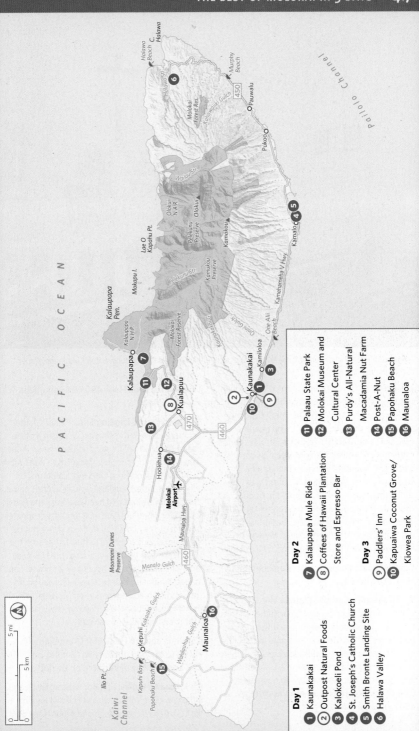

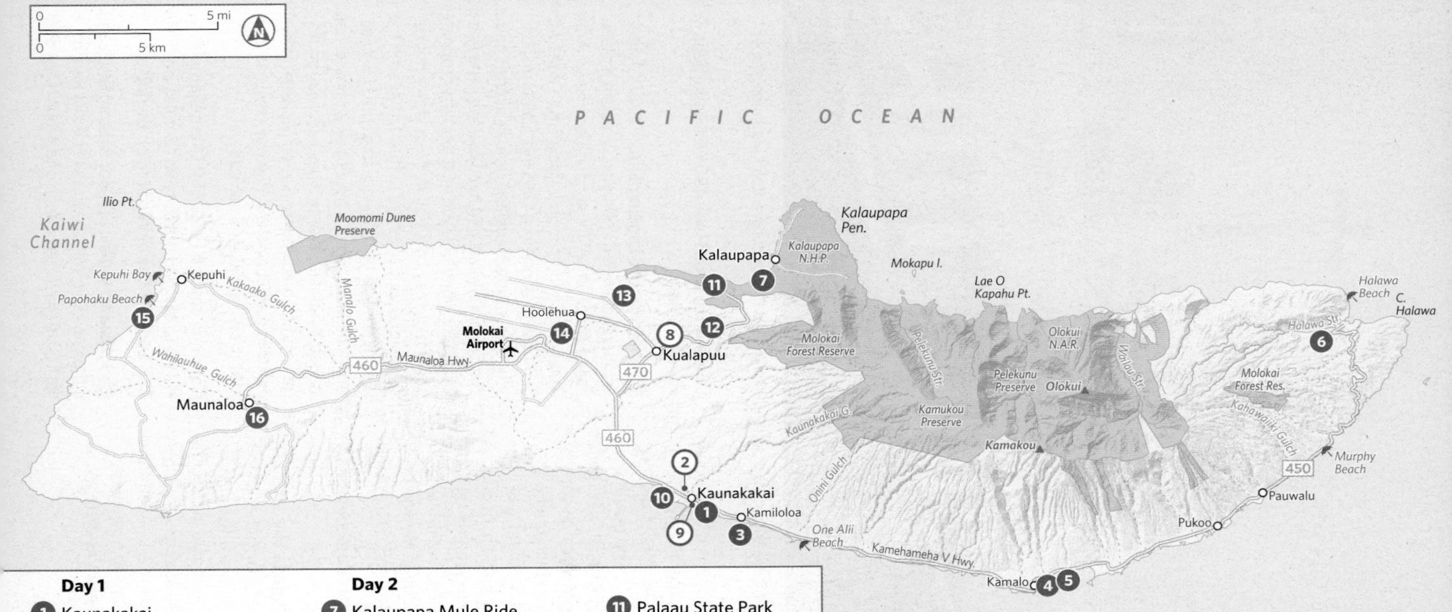

Day 1

1. Kaunakakai
2. Outpost Natural Foods
3. Kalokoeli Pond
4. St. Joseph's Catholic Church
5. Smith Bronte Landing Site
6. Halawa Valley

Day 2

7. Kalaupapa Mule Ride
8. Coffees of Hawaii Plantation Store and Espresso Bar
11. Palaau State Park
12. Molokai Museum and Cultural Center
13. Purdy's All-Natural Macadamia Nut Farm
14. Post-A-Nut
15. Papohaku Beach
16. Maunaloa

Day 3

9. Paddlers' Inn
10. Kapuaiwa Coconut Grove/ Kiowea Park

> *St. Joseph's Catholic Church, built in 1876, was where local legend Fr. Damien treated Kalaupapa's leper community.*

perfected aquaculture in A.D. 1400. They built gated, U-shaped stone and coral walls on the shore to catch fish on the incoming tide, then would raise them in captivity. The result: a constant, ready supply of fresh fish. The ponds stretch for 20 miles along Molokai's south shore and are visible from Kamehameha V Highway (Hwy. 450). It took something like a thousand people to tend a single fishpond, and more than 60 ponds once existed on this coast. Some are silted in by red-dirt runoff from south coast gulches; others have been revived by folks who raise fish and seaweed. ⏱ **10–15 min.**

Continue east on Hwy. 450 (Kamehameha V Hwy.) to MM 10.

4 St. Joseph's Catholic Church. This little 1876 wood-frame church is one of four Father Damien, the priest who treated the lepers at Kalaupapa, built "topside" on Molokai. Restored in 1971, the church stands beside a seaside cemetery, where feral cats play under the gaze of a Damien statue amid gravestones decorated with flower leis. ⏱ **10–15 min. King Kamehameha V Hwy. (Hwy. 450), just after MM 10.**

Continue east on Hwy. 450 (Kamehameha V Hwy.) to MM 11.

5 Smith Bronte Landing Site. In 1927 Charles Lindbergh soloed the Atlantic Ocean in a plane called *The Spirit of St. Louis* and became an American hero. That same year, Ernie Smith and Emory B. Bronte took off from Oakland, California, on July 14, in a single-engine Travelair aircraft named *The City of Oakland,* and headed across the Pacific Ocean for Honolulu. The next day, after running out of fuel, they crash-landed in a kiawe thicket on Molokai, but emerged unhurt to become the first civilians to fly to Hawaii from the U.S. Mainland. The flight took 25 hours and 2 minutes and landed Smith and Bronte a place in aviation history—and a roadside marker on Molokai. ⏱ **10–15 min. King Kamehameha V Highway (Hwy. 450), at MM 11, on the makai (ocean) side.**

Continue east on Hwy. 450 (Kamehameha V Hwy.) to the end of the road (2 miles past MM 25). Look for the picnic area on the left.

6 ★ Halawa Valley. Stop for a picnic lunch and, if the waves permit, a swim at Halawa Beach Park (p. 424). A pavilion and restrooms are on the left side of the road, just before it ends. Of the five great valleys of Molokai, only Halawa, with its two waterfalls, golden beach, sleepy lagoon, great surf, and offshore island, is easily accessible. Unfortunately, the trail through fertile Halawa Valley, which was inhabited for centuries, and on to the 250-foot Moaula Falls, has been closed for some time. There is one operator who conducts hikes to the falls (see box at right). You can spend a day at the county beach park, but do not venture into the valley on your own; the land in the valley is privately owned, and you could be prosecuted for trespassing. ⏱ 1–3 hr. End of Hwy. 450, past MM 25.

Day 2

From Kaunakakai take Hwy. 460 west. Just after MM 4, turn right on Hwy. 470. The mule stables are just after MM 4 on your left.

❼ ★★★ **Ride a Mule to Kalaupapa.** Get up early for the Molokai Mule Ride down into the Kalaupapa Peninsula. This is an all-day experience that you will remember the rest of your life. Starting at the top of the nearly perpendicular ridge (1,600 ft. high), Buzzy Sproat's surefooted mules step down the narrow, muddy 3-mile trail daily, rain or shine, pausing often on the 26 switchbacks to calculate their next move—and always, it seems to me, veering a little too close to the edge. Each switchback is numbered; by the time you get to number four, you'll catch your breath, put the mule on cruise control, and begin to enjoy Hawaii's most awesome trail ride. ⏱ 6–8 hr. 100 Kalae Hwy. Suite 104, on Hwy. 470, 5 miles north of Hwy. 460. ☎ 800/567-7550; www.muleride.com. Tours daily at 8am. $165 per person. Riders must be at least 16 years old and physically fit.

From the mule stables, retrace your route on Hwy. 470, turn left at Farrington Ave. (Hwy. 480) and then right again into Coffees of Hawaii.

⑧ **Coffees of Hawaii Plantation Store and Espresso Bar.** You'll be hungry after the mule ride, so head straight for this coffee bar for espresso drinks, sandwiches, salads, and desserts. The Malulani Estate and Muleskinner coffees sold here are grown on the 500-acre plantation surrounding the shop. Hwy. 480 (near the junction of Hwy. 470), Kualapuu. ☎ 808/567-9490. $.

Halawa Valley: A Hike Back in History

"There are things on Molokai, sacred things, that you may not be able to see or may not hear, but they are there," says Pilipo Solotario, who was born and raised in Halawa Valley and survived the 1946 tsunami that barreled into the ancient valley. "As Hawaiians, we respect these things."

"I see my role, and I'm nearly 70 years old, as educating people, outsiders, on our culture, our history," he said at the beginning of his cultural hike into his family property in Halawa Valley. "To really appreciate Molokai, you need to understand and know things so that you are *pono*, you are right with the land and don't disrespect the culture. Then, then you see the real Molokai."

Solotario and his family, who own the land in the valley, are the only people allowed to lead hikes into Halawa. They lead daily tours, which begin at the County Park pavilion, with a history of the valley, a discussion of the Hawaiian culture, and a display of the fruits, trees, and other flora you will be seeing in the valley. Along the hike, Solotario stops to point out historical and cultural aspects, including a sacred *heiau*. At the waterfalls visitors can swim in the brisk pool water. The cost for the 4-hour tour is $75. Contact **Molokai Fish & Dive** (☎ 808/553-5926; www.molokaifishanddive.com) for reservations. Bring insect repellent, water, a snack, and a swimsuit.

Retrace your route back to Hwy. 470, turn left on Hwy. 460, and follow it into Kaunakakai.

Day 3

⑨ **Paddlers' Inn.** Before you leave town stop here for breakfast and a picnic lunch to eat on the beach. 10 Mohala St. See p 440.

Leave Kaunakakai heading west on Hwy. 460. Just about a mile outside of town is:

❿ kids **Kapuaiwa Coconut Grove/Kiowea Park.** See p 422, ❶.

From the park continue on Hwy. 460, and turn right on Hwy. 470. Go to the end of the road (about 5 miles) to:

> *The mule tours and hikes down the Kalaupapa cliffs from the forest to the coast offer the best experience of Molokai's beauty.*

⑪ ★★ **Palaau State Park.** This 234-acre piney-woods park, 8 miles out of Kaunakakai, doesn't look like much until you get out of the car and take a hike, which literally puts you between a rock and a hard place. Go right, and you end up on the edge of Molokai's magnificent sea cliffs, with a panoramic view of Kalaupapa; go left, and you come face to face with a stone phallus. Six feet high and pointed at an angle that means business, Molokai's famous **Phallic Rock** is a fertility tool: According to Hawaiian legend, a woman who wishes to become pregnant need only spend the night near the rock and, *voilà!* Supposedly, it belonged to Nanahoa, a demigod who quarreled with his wife, Kawahuna, over a pretty girl. In the tussle, Kawahuna was thrown over the cliff, and both husband and wife were turned to stone. Phallic Rock is at the end of a well-worn uphill path. Of all the phallic rocks in Hawaii and the Pacific, this is the one to see. It's featured on a postcard with a tiny, awestruck Japanese woman standing next to it. ⏱ 30 min–1 hr. At the end of Hwy. 470, Kalae.

Head back on Hwy. 470. Two miles down the road on the right is:

⑫ **Molokai Museum and Cultural Center.** En route to the California Gold Rush in 1849, Rudolph W. Meyer (a German professor) came to Molokai, married the high chieftess Kalama, and began to operate a small sugar plantation near his home. Now on the National Register of Historic Places, this restored 1878 sugar mill, with its century-old steam engine, mule-driven cane crusher, copper clarifiers, and redwood evaporating pan, is the last of its kind in Hawaii. The mill also houses a museum that traces the history of sugar growing on Molokai and has special events, such as wine tastings, an annual music festival, and occasional classes in ukulele making and loom weaving. Call for a schedule. ⏱ 1 hr. Hwy. 470 (just after the turnoff for the Ironwood Hills Golf Course and 2 miles below Kalaupapa Overlook), Kalae. ☎ 808/567-6436. Admission $3.50 adults, $2 students. Mon–Sat 10am–2pm.

Continue down Hwy. 470, and turn right on Farrington Ave. (Hwy. 480). Turn right on Lihi Pali Ave. and look for the sign to:

> *The hiking trail to the 250-foot Moaula Falls in the Halawa Valley is closed to individuals, but challenging tours offer a magnificent payoff.*

> *The Big Wind Kite Factory offers a colorful and unique array of locally made kites and offers flying lessons for kids.*

⑬ ★ kids **Purdy's All-Natural Macadamia Nut Farm (Na Hua O'Ka Aina).** The Purdys have turned macadamia-nut buying into entertainment, offering tours of the homestead and giving lively demonstrations of nutshell-cracking in the shade of their towering trees. The tour of the 70-year-old nut farm explains the growth, bearing, harvesting, and shelling processes. 🕒 1 hr. Lihi Pali Ave. (behind Molokai High School), Hoolehua. ☎ 808/567-6601. www.molokai-aloha.com/macnuts. Free admission. Mon–Fri 9:30am–3:30pm; Sat 10am–2pm. Closed holidays.

Retrace your route back to Farrington Ave. (Hwy. 480), turn right, and then turn left on Puu Peelua Ave. (Hwy. 481). On the corner is:

⑭ ★ kids **Post-A-Nut.** Postmaster Margaret Keahi-Leary will help you say "Aloha" with a Molokai coconut. Just write a message on the coconut with a felt-tip pen, and she'll send it via U.S. mail. Coconuts are free but postage averages $7.50–$11 to the mainland. 🕒 10–15 min. Hoolehua Post Office, Puu Peelua Ave. (Hwy. 481), near Maunaloa Hwy. (Hwy. 480). ☎ 808/567-6144. Mon–Fri 7:30–11:30am and 12:30–4:30pm.

Continue down Hwy. 481 (Puu Peelua Ave.). When it ends, turn left on Hwy. 460, drive 9 miles, and turn right down Kaluakoi Rd. (also known as Kepuhi Rd.) just before MM 15. Follow this road about 5 miles to:

⑮ ★★ **Papohaku Beach.** Nearly 3 miles long and 300 feet wide, gold-sand Papohaku Beach is one of the biggest in Hawaii. Enjoy a picnic lunch here. 🕒 2–3 hr. See p 425.

Retrace your route back up to Hwy. 460 and turn left, which takes you to:

⑯ **Maunaloa.** This old hilltop plantation town is now a ghost town after expensive Molokai Ranch closed in 2008. Cowboys used to ride the range on **Molokai Ranch,** a 65,000-acre spread surrounding Maunaloa, but that shut down, too. The reason to go here now is to see the best store on the island: the **Big Wind Kite Factory & the Plantation Gallery** (see p 436). 🕒 1–2 hr. End of Hwy. 460. Maunaloa.

To get back to Kaunakakai, retrace your route back up to Hwy. 460, which will take you back.

Kaunakakai

On the red-dirt southern plain, where most of the island's 7,000 residents live, this rustic village looks like the set of an old Hollywood western, with sun-faded clapboard houses and horses tethered on the side of the road. Mile marker 0, in the center of town, divides the island into east and west. Eastbound, along the coastal highway named for King Kamehameha V, are Gauguin-like, palm-shaded cottages set on small coves or near fishponds; spectacular vistas that take in Maui, Lanai, and Kahoolawe; and a fringing coral reef visible through the crystal-clear waves.

> *Kapuaiwa Coconut Grove harbors 1,000 majestic palm trees stretching along 10 acres.*

START Kapuaiwa Coconut Grove. **FINISH** One Alii Beach Park. **TRIP LENGTH** 1 day and 5 miles.

Just about a mile outside of Kaunakakai, on the west side of town, on Hwy. 460 is:

1 ★ kids **Kapuaiwa Coconut Grove/Kiowea Park.** This royal grove—1,000 coconut trees on 10 acres planted in 1863 by the island's high chief Kapua'iwa (later, King Kamehameha V)—is a major roadside attraction. The shoreline park is a favorite subject of sunset

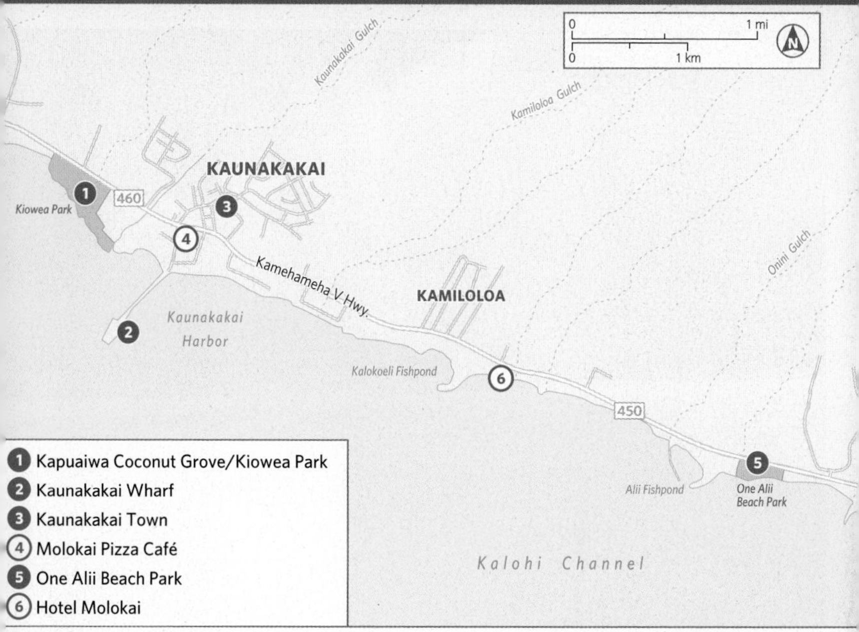

photographers and visitors who delight in a hand-lettered sign that warns: DANGER: FALLING COCONUTS. In its backyard, across the highway, stands Church Row: seven churches, each a different denomination—clear evidence of the missionary impact on Hawaii. ⏱ 10–15 min. Hwy. 460, near MM 1.

Head back east to Kaunakakai. At the intersection of Hwy. 460 and Kaunakakai Place, turn right toward the ocean and drive out on the wharf.

2 **Kaunakakai Wharf.** The half-mile-long wharf is Molokai's lifeline. The *Molokai Princess* ferry drops off and picks up passengers every day here, and barges bring in nearly everything that isn't grown or made on the island. Walk the wharf checking out the fishing and sailing boats. ⏱ 20–30 min. Kaunakakai Wharf.

Head down the wharf back to Kaunakakai.

3 **Kaunakakai Town.** Take an hour and walk this tiny town, stopping to check out the shops (see p 434). ⏱ 1–2 hr.

4 **Molokai Pizza Cafe.** Stop to enjoy the excellent pizza and sandwiches served at this popular gathering place. See p 439.

Take Hwy. 450 east. Just after MM 3 look for the park on the right.

5 ★ kids **One Alii Beach Park.** Spend the afternoon in the sun at the oldest public beach park on Molokai. ⏱ 2–3 hr. See p 425.

Retrace your steps back to Kaunakakai via Hwy. 460. The Hotel Molokai is a mile down the road, just after MM 2 on the ocean side of the street.

6 **Hotel Molokai.** After a day at the beach, stop by this oceanfront hotel for a quick snack or dinner. See p 438.

A Weekend of Hula

Hula is the heartbeat of Hawaiian culture, and Molokai is its birthplace. Although most visitors to Hawaii never get to see the real thing, it's possible to see it here—once a year, on the third Saturday in May, when Molokai celebrates the birth of the hula at its **Ka Hula Piko Festival.** The weekend-long affair includes dance, music, food, and crafts. For details, contact the Molokai Visitor Association (☎ 800/800-6367 or 808/553-3876; www.molokai-hawaii.com).

Molokai Beaches A to Z

★ Halawa Beach Park HALAWA
At the foot of scenic Halawa Valley is this beautiful black-sand beach with a palm-fringed lagoon, a wave-lashed island offshore, and a distant view of the West Maui Mountains across the Pailolo Channel. The swimming is safe in the shallows close to shore, but where the waterfall stream meets the sea, the ocean is often murky and unnerving. In winter, winter swells on the north side of the bay attract surfers. Facilities are minimal; bring your own water. Past MM 25, King Kamehameha V Hwy. (Hwy. 450) east to the end.

Kawaaloa Bay NORTH SHORE
Located on the northwest shore of Molokai, adjacent to the Moomomi Dunes, this beach's turbulent offshore waters are often dangerous, and there is no lifeguard, so it's best to stay on land and walk the golden-sand. Because of its remote location, generally the beach is empty—it's a great place to have all to yourself. End of Moomomi Rd.

Kepuhi Beach MAUNALOA
Golfers see this picturesque golden strand in front of the Kaluakoi Resort and Golf Course as just another sand trap, but sunbathers like the semiprivate grassy dunes; they're seldom, if ever, crowded. Beachcombers often find what they're looking for here, but swimmers have to dodge lava rocks and risk riptides. And look out for errant golf balls. There are no facilities or lifeguards, but cold drinks and restrooms are handy at the resort. Kaluakoi Rd., Kaluakoi Resort.

Murphy Beach Park (Kumimi Beach Park)
WAIALUA This small park (sometimes called Jaycees Park) is shaded by ironwood trees that line a white-sand beach. It's generally a very safe swimming area. On calm days snorkeling and diving are great outside the reef. Fishermen

> *The golden sand at huge, beautiful Papohaku Beach stretches out for 3 miles.*

Molokai's Beaches A to Z

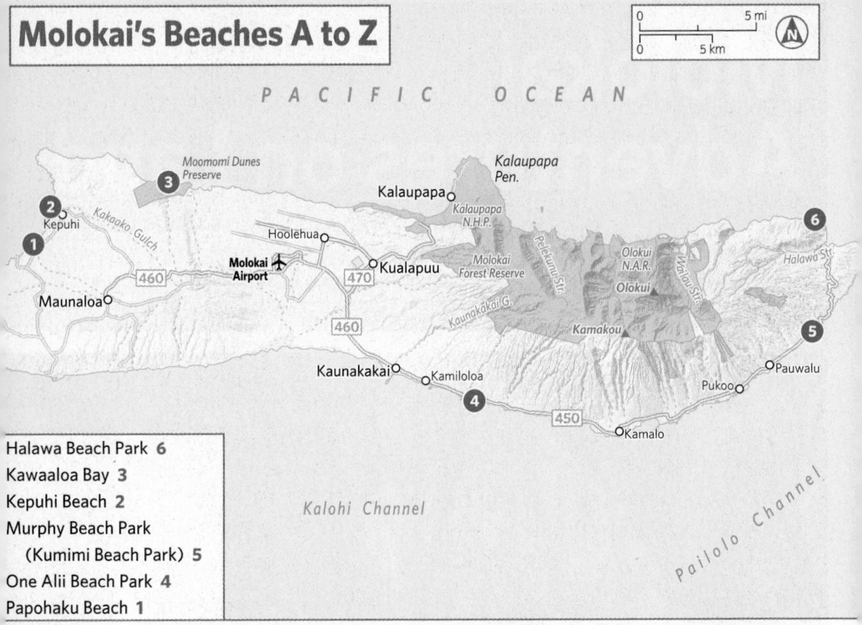

also frequently come here to look for papio and other island fish. Facilities include pavilions, picnic tables, and barbecue grills. **Hwy. 450, btw. MM 20 and MM 21.**

One Alii Beach Park KAUNAKAKAI
This thin strip of sand, once reserved for the *alii* (chiefs), is the oldest public beach park on Molokai. You'll find One Alii Beach Park (*One* is pronounced *o*-nay, not *won*) by a coconut grove on the outskirts of Kaunakakai. Safe for swimmers of all ages and abilities, it's often crowded with families on weekends, but it can be all yours on weekdays. Facilities include outdoor showers, restrooms, and free parking. **Hwy. 450, just after MM 3.**

★★ **Papohaku Beach Park** MAUNALOA
Nearly 3 miles long and 300 feet wide, gold-sand Papohaku Beach is one of the biggest in Hawaii (17-mile-long Polihale Beach on Kauai is the biggest). It's great for walking, beachcombing, picnics, and sunset watching year-round. The big surf and riptides make swimming risky except in summer, when the waters are calmer. Go early in the day when the winds are calm. Facilities include outdoor showers, restrooms, picnic grounds, and free parking. **Kaluakoi Rd., Kaluakoi Resort.**

> *Kepuhi is a popular place for beachcombers.*

Molokai Adventures on Land

Molokai, with its rural atmosphere and dramatic terrain, is made for hiking. My favorite trails are below, along with advice on camping, bike riding, golfing, and tennis.

> *The lush vegetation is a spectacular highlight of any hike in Molokai's remote Halawa Valley.*

Camping

Camping on Molokai takes some perseverance, as getting a permit can be time-consuming. Be sure to bring all your own camping gear, as there is no place to rent camping gear on the island.

⋆ **Papohaku Beach Park.** This drive-up seaside site on the island's West End makes a great getaway. Facilities include restrooms, drinking water, outdoor showers, barbecue grills, and picnic tables. Groceries and gas are available in Maunaloa, 6 miles away. Kaluakoi Resort is a mile away. **Get camping permits by contacting Maui County Parks Department, P.O. Box 526, Kaunakakai, HI 96748. ☎ 808/553-3204.** www.mauicounty.gov. **Camping is limited to 3 days. $5–$8 per non-resident adult per night.**

⋆⋆ **Palaau State Park.** At the end of Hwy. 470 is this 234-acre park of piney woods, home to the Kalaupapa Lookout (the best vantage point

Molokai Adventures on Land

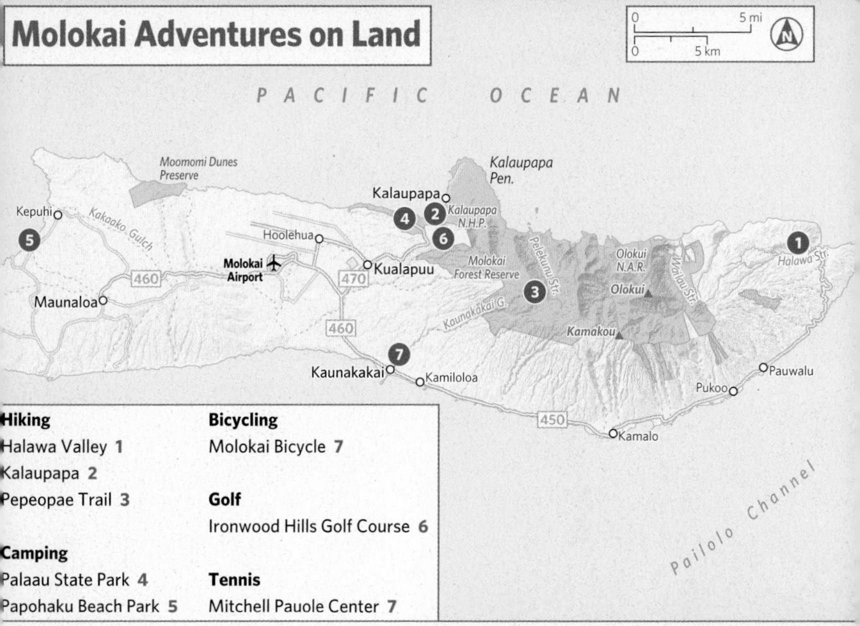

or seeing the historic leper colony if you're not iiking or riding a mule in). It's airy and cool in he park's ironwood forest, where many love o camp at the designated state campground. Camping fees for Hawaii state parks are $5 per ampsite per night, and you'll need a permit from he State Division of Parks. ☎ 808/567-6618. www.hawaiistateparks.org/camping/maui.cfm. ee p 420, ⓫.

Hiking

★★ **Halawa Valley.** Much of Halawa Valley is rivate property, so you'll have to arrange for guided tour to hike in. See "Halawa Valley: A Hike Back in History," p 419.

★★ **Kalaupapa.** This hike to the site of Molokai's famous leper colony is like going down a switchback staircase with what seems ke a million steps. You don't always see the reathtaking view because you're too busy watching your step. It's easier going down than p (surprise!)—in about an hour, you'll go 2½ niles, from 2,000 feet to sea level. The trip up ometimes takes twice as long. **The trail head tarts on the mauka (inland) side of Hwy. 470, ust past the mule barn. Check in at 7:30am, get permit, and go before the mule train departs. ou must be 16 or older (it's an old state law that kept kids out of the leper colony) and should be in good shape. Wear good hiking boots or sneakers.**

> *The trail to the Kalaupapa Lookout will bring you to a magnificent vantage point of the peninsula.*

★★ **Pepeopae Trail.** This awesome hike takes you back a few million years. On the cloud-draped trail (actually a boardwalk across the bog), you'll see mosses, sedges, native violets, knee-high ancient ohia, and lichens that evolved in total isolation over eons. Eerie, intermittent mists blowing in and out will give you an idea of this island at its creation. The narrow

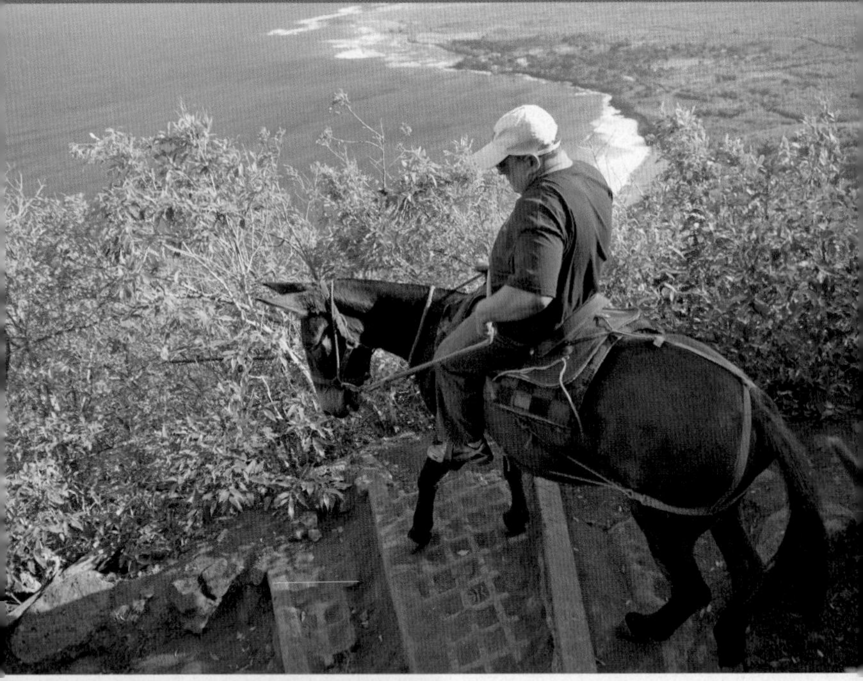

> *The spectacular cliffs at Kalaupapa National Park are taller than 3 Empire State Buildings.*

> *Some of the impressive landmarks you'll find along the natural Pepeopae Trail in Molokai Forest Reserve are man-made by native artists.*

boardwalk, built by volunteers, protects the bog and keeps you out of the primal ooze. Don't venture off it; you could damage this fragile environment or get lost. You can go it alone or sign up for a guided hike with the Nature Conservancy of Hawaii, which guards this unusual ecosystem. For information, write to the Nature Conservancy (www.nature.org) at 1116 Smith St., Suite 201, Honolulu, HI 96817 The 3-mile round-trip takes about 1½ hr. to hike—but first you have to drive about 20 miles from Kaunakakai, deep into the Molokai Forest Reserve on a four-wheel-drive road. Plan a full day for this outing. Call ☎ 808/537-4508 or 808/553-5236 to check on the condition of the ungraded, four-wheel-drive-only, red-dirt road that leads to the trail head and to let people know that you'll be up there.

Golf

Golf is one of Molokai's best-kept secrets: It's challenging and fun, tee times are open, and the rates are lower than your score will be.

Ironwood Hills Golf Course. Built in 1929 by Del Monte Plantation for its executives, this

Tips on Safe Hiking & Camping

Water might be everywhere in Hawaii, but it more than likely isn't safe to drink. Most stream water must be treated because cattle, pigs, and goats have probably contaminated the water upstream. The department of health continually warns campers about the bacterium *Leptospira,* which is found in freshwater streams throughout the state and enters the body through breaks in the skin or through the mucous membranes. It produces flulike symptoms and can be fatal. Firewood isn't always available, so it's a good idea to carry a small, light backpacking stove, which you can use both to boil water and to cook meals. Make sure that your drinking water is safe by vigorously boiling it. If boiling is not an option, use tablets with hydroperiodide; portable water filters will not screen out *Leptospira.* Remember, the island is not crime-free: Never leave your valuables (wallet, airline ticket, and so on) unprotected. Carry a day pack if you have a campsite, and never camp alone. Some more do's and don'ts: Do bury personal waste away from streams, don't eat unknown fruit, do carry your trash out, and don't forget there is very little twilight in Hawaii when the sun sets—it gets dark quickly.

nusual course is one of the oldest in the state. t sits in the cool air at 1,200 feet, with its rich oliage, open fairways, and spectacular views of he rest of the island. **Off Kalae Hwy., just before he mule barn on the road to the lookout. ☎ 808/567-6000. Greens fees $31.**

icycling

⁄lolokai is a great place to see by bicycle. The oads are not very busy and there are great laces to pull off the road and take a quick dip. **Aolokai Bicycle,** 80 Mohala St., Kaunakakai ☎ 808/553-3931; www.bikehawaii.com/ nolokaibicycle) offers bike rentals for $15 a lay, or $70 a week, including a complimentary elmet and lock.

ennis

he only two tennis courts on Molokai are ocated at the **Mitchell Pauole Center,** in aunakakai (☎ 808/553-5141). Both are lit or night play and are available free on a first-come, first-served basis, with a 45-minute time limit if someone is waiting. You can also rent tennis rackets ($5 a day, $24 a week) and balls ($3 a day, $12 a week) from **Molokai Outdoors Activities** (☎ 877/553-4477 or 808/553-4477; www.molokai-outdoors.com).

> *The majestic Halawa Falls cascade 250 feet down into the remote valley, which can only be reached by guided tour.*

Molokai Adventures in the Ocean

Molokai offers some of the best kayaking in Hawaii and some prime fishing opportunities. Here's my advice on the best places for these and other ocean adventures, such as snorkeling, body boarding, and surfing.

> *Molokai's rugged shoreline and dramatic cliffs provide some of Hawaii's most scenic kayaking.*

Body Boarding, Boogie Boarding & Bodysurfing

Molokai has only three beaches that offer good waves for body boarding and bodysurfing: Papohaku, Kepuhi, and Halawa (p 424). Even these beaches are only for experienced bodysurfers, due to the strength of the rip currents and undertows. You can rent boogie boards with fins for just $5 a day or $20 a week at **Molokai Outdoors Activities** (☎ 877/553-4477 or 808/553-4477; www.molokai-outdoors.com).

Kayaking

During the summer months, when the waters or the north shore are calm, Molokai offers some o the most spectacular kayaking in Hawaii. However, most of Molokai is for the experienced kayaker only. You must be adept in paddling through open ocean swells and rough waves.

Molokai Outdoors Activities (☎ 877/553-4477 or 808/553-4477; www.molokai-outdoors.com) has a "downwinder" tour: 6 miles of Molokai's reef as you paddle down-

Molokai Adventures in the Ocean

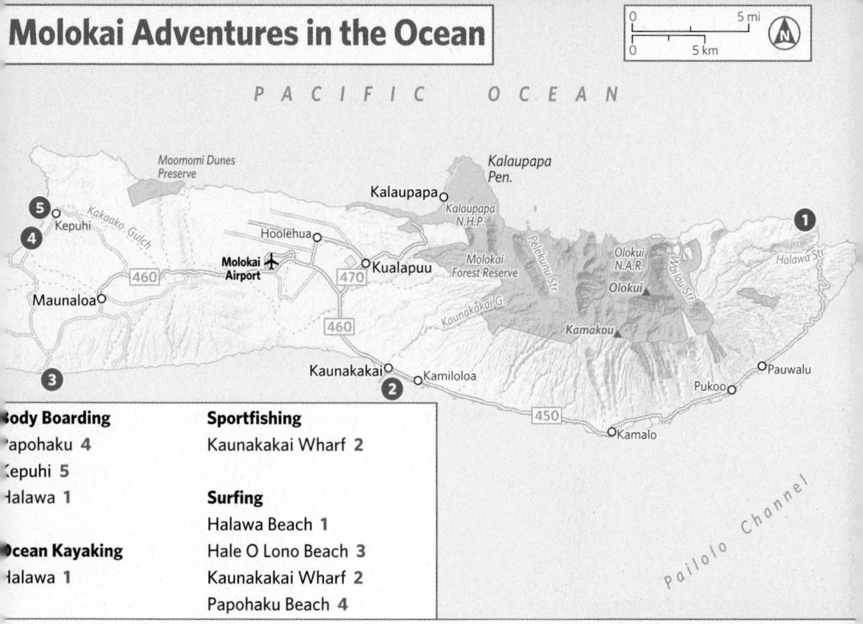

wind ($89, plus $10 for lunch per person). They also rent kayaks; rates start at $26 a day. For serious kayakers, they can help arrange your north shore excursion by renting ocean kayaks with rudders and arranging transportation to and from Halawa Valley with a boat pickup from one of the valleys on the back-side.

Scuba Diving

Want to see turtles or manta rays up close? How about sharks? Molokai resident Bill Kapuni has been diving the waters around the island his entire life; he'll be happy to show you whatever you're brave enough to encounter. You can book him through **Molokai Fish & Dive** (☎ 808/553-5926; www.molokaifishanddive.com), which offers scuba diving trips from $135 (two-tank dive) to $275 (three-tank dive).

Snorkeling

When the waters are calm, Molokai offers excellent snorkeling; you'll see a wide range of butterflyfish, tangs, and angelfish. Good snorkeling can be found—when conditions are right—at many of Molokai's beaches. **Molokai Outdoors Activities** (☎ 877/553-4477 or 808/553-4477; www.molokai-outdoors.com) has the best prices on snorkeling rentals ($6 a day, or $24 a week, for fins, mask, and snorkel). Molokai Outdoors also offers snorkel/kayak tours for $69 per person. Other options for snorkel gear rental include **Molokai Fish & Dive,** in the lobby of Hotel Molokai, just outside Kaunakakai with another location in Kaunakakai (☎ 808/553-5926; www.molokaifishanddive.com).

For snorkeling tours on a boat, Walter Naki of **Molokai Action Adventures** (☎ 808/558-8184) offers leisurely snorkeling, diving, and swimming trips in his 21-foot Boston Whaler for $50 per person for a 4- to 6-hour custom tour.

Sport Fishing

Fun Hogs Hawaii. Deep-sea fishing on a 27-foot, fully equipped sport-fishing vessel. Prices are $400 for six passengers for 4 hours, $417 for 6 hours, and $521 for 8 hours. Book through Molokai Outdoors Activities, p. 433.

Hallelujah Hou Fishing. This is our top pick for fishing trips. Captain Clay, who is also a minister and the nicest guy you may ever meet, leads light-tackle guided fishing trips on his 24-foot power catamaran. The price is $395 to $495 for up to four adults for a half-day. He provides all tackle and bottled water; you bring the sunscreen. If you catch something, he'll

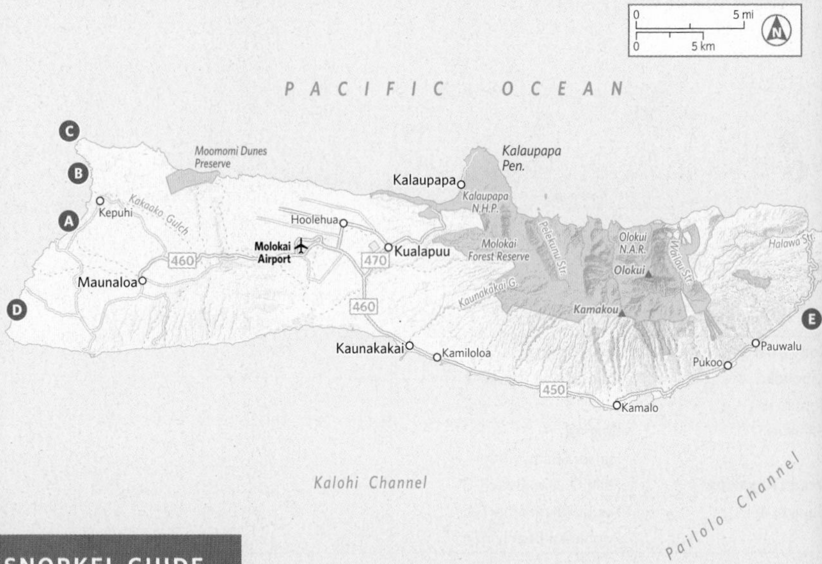

SNORKEL GUIDE

Molokai's Best Snorkeling

Ⓐ **Kawaikiunui,** Ⓑ **Ilio Point,** and Ⓒ **Pohaku Moiliili,** on the West End, are all special places seldom seen even by those who live on Molokai. You can reach Kawaikiunui and Pohaku Moiliili on foot after a long, hot, dusty ride in a four-wheel-drive vehicle, but it's much easier and quicker to go by sea. See above for places to rent a kayak and get advice. It's about 2 miles as the crow flies from Pohaku Moiliili to Ilio Point. Ⓓ **Kapukahehu (Dixie Maru) Beach** is a gold-sand, well-protected family beach with a close and shallow reef. The name Dixie Maru comes from a 1920s Japanese fishing boat stranded off the rocky shore. One of the Molokai Ranch cowboys hung the wrecked boat's nameplate on a gate by Kapukahehu Beach, and the name stuck. To get here, take Kaluakoi Road to the end of the pavement, and then follow the footpath 300 feet to the beach. Ⓔ **Murphy (Kumimi) Beach Park** (p 424) is located between mile markers 20 and 21, off Kamehameha V Highway. The reef here is easily reachable, and the waters are calm year-round.

Surfing is one Molokai's primary attractions, and lessons and equipment are readily available at almost any beach.

even filet your fish for dinner. ***Note:*** There's no "head" (toilet) on the boat. ☎ 808/336-1870; www.hallelujahhoufishing.com.

Molokai Action Adventures. For fly-fishing or light-tackle reef-fish trolling, contact Walter Naki at Molokai Action Adventures. A full-day trip in his 21-foot Boston Whaler, for up to four people, is $400. ☎ 808/558-8184.

Molokai Fish & Dive. Fishing tours for $400 for a half-day, and $600 for a full day. ☎ 808/553-5926. www.molokaifishanddive.com.

Molokai Outdoors Activities. If you just want to try your luck casting along the shoreline, here's where you'll find the least expensive fishing rods for rent ($5 a day or $24 for the week) plus advice on where they're biting. ☎ 877/553-4477 or 808/553-4477. www.molokai-outdoors.com.

Surfing

Depending on the time of year and the wave conditions, Molokai can offer some great surfing for the beginner, as well as the expert. **Molokai Outdoors Activities** (☎ 877/553-4477 or 808/553-4477; www.molokai-outdoors.com) not only will know where the waves are, but they also rent gear: soft surfboards for $13 a day. Good surfing spots include Kaunakakai Wharf in town (p 423, ❷), Hale O Lono Beach and Papohaku Beach on the West End (p 425), and Halawa Beach on the East End (p 424).

Molokai Shopping A to Z

Alohawear

Imamura Store KAUNAKAKAI
Wilfred Imamura, whose mother founded this store, recalls the old railroad track that stretched from the pier to a spot across the street: "We brought our household things from the pier on a hand-pumped vehicle." His store, appropriately, is a leap into the past, a marvelous amalgam of precious old-fashioned things. Rubber boots, Hawaiian-print tablecloths, Japanese tea plates, ukulele cases, plastic slippers, and even coconut bikini tops line the shelves. But it's not all nostalgia: The Molokai T-shirts, jeans, and palaka shorts are of good quality and inexpensive, and the pareu fabrics are a find. ☎ 808/553-5615. MC, V.

★ **A Touch of Molokai** KALUAKOI
Even though the Kaluakoi Hotel is closed, this fabulous shop remains open. It is well worth the drive. The surf shorts and aloha shirts sold here are better than the norm, with attractive, up-to-date choices by Jams, Quiksilver, and other name brands. Tencel dresses, South Pacific shell necklaces (up to $400), and a magnificent, hand-turned milo bowl also caught my attention. Most impressive are the wiliwili, kamani, and soapberry leis and a handsome array of lauhala bags, all made on Molokai. At Kaluakoi Hotel & Golf Club. ☎ 808/552-0133. MC, V.

Coffee

★ **Coffees of Hawaii Plantation Store and Espresso Bar** KUALAPUU This is a fairly slick—for Molokai—combination coffee bar, store, and gallery for more than 30 artists and craftspeople from Hawaii. The 500-acre plantation surrounding the shop provides the coffees sold here. The gift items are worth a look: pikake and plumeria soaps from Kauai, perfumes and pure beeswax candles from Maui, koa bookmarks and hair sticks, pottery, woods, and baskets. Hwy. 480 (near the junction of Hwy. 470). ☎ 800/709-BEAN (709-2326) or 808/567-9023, MC, V.

Drugstore

Molokai Drugs KAUNAKAKAI
David Mikami, whose father-in-law founded this pharmacy in 1935, has made this more than a

> *Rich with treasures from Hawaii's past and quality products from the present, the Imamura Store is a can't-miss shopping spot.*

Molokai's Best Shopping

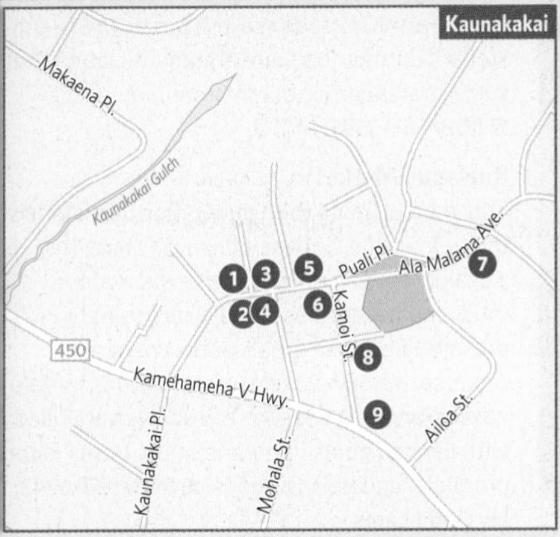

Bamboo Pantry **7**
Big Wind Kite Factory & the Plantation Gallery **11**
Coffees of Hawaii Plantation Store and Espresso Bar **13**
Friendly Market Center **6**
Imamura Store **5**
Kualapuu Market **12**
Mana'e Goods and Grindz **15**
Misaki's Grocery and Dry Goods **4**
Molokai Drugs **8**
Molokai Fish & Dive **1**
Molokai Museum Gift Shop **14**
Molokai Surf **9**
Molokai Wines & Spirits **3**
Take's Variety Store **2**
A Touch of Molokai **10**

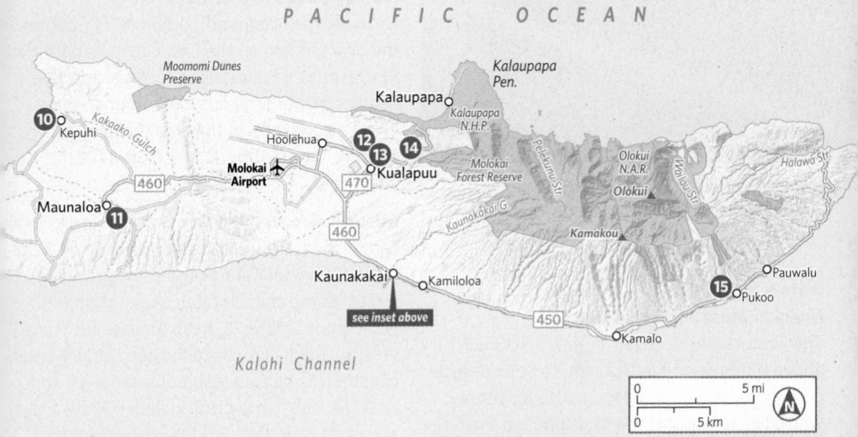

drugstore. It's a gleaming, friendly stop full of life's basic necessities. Here you'll find the best selection of guidebooks, books about Molokai, and maps, as well as greeting cards, paperbacks, cassette players, flip-flops, and every imaginable essential. The Mikamis are a household name on the island, not only because of their pharmacy but also because the family has shown exceptional kindness to the often economically strapped Molokaians. Kamoi Professional Center. ☎ 808/553-5790. MC, V.

General Store

Take's Variety Store KAUNAKAKAI
If you need luggage tags, buzz saws, toys, candy, cloth dolls, canned goods, canteens, camping equipment, hardware, batteries, candles, pipe fittings, fishing supplies—whew!—and other products for work and play, this 54-year-old variety store is the answer. You may suffer from claustrophobia in the crowded, dusty aisles, but Take's carries everything. ☎ 808/553-5442. MC, V.

> **Shopping on Molokai**
>
> Most of the retail shops in Kaunakakai sell T-shirts, muumuu, surf-wear, and informal apparel. There are also several good options for food shopping. Other than that, serious shoppers will be disappointed, unless they love kites or native wood vessels.

> *Stop at Coffees of Hawaii at the end of your Molokai Mule Ride for java, sandwiches, and desserts.*

Gifts & Souvenirs

Molokai Museum Gift Shop KALAE
This restored 1878 sugar mill sits 1,500 feet above the town of Kualapuu. It's a considerable drive from town, but a good cause for those who'd like to support the museum and the handful of local artisans who sell their crafts, fabrics, cookbooks, quilt sets, and other gift items in the tiny shop. There's also a modest selection of cards, T-shirts, coloring books, and, at Christmas, handmade ornaments made of lauhala and koa. Meyer Sugar Mill, Hwy. 470 (just after the turnoff for the Ironwood Hills Golf Course, and 2 miles below Kalaupapa Overlook). ☎ 808/567-6436. No credit cards.

Grocery Stores

Friendly Market Center KAUNAKAKAI
You can't miss this salmon-colored wooden storefront on the main drag of "downtown" Kaunakakai, where you'll find people of all generations talking story. Friendly has everything from local poi to Glenlivet, with an especially good selection of produce and healthy foods—blue-corn tortilla chips, soy milk, organic brown rice, pasta sauces, and Kumu Farms macadamia-nut pesto, the island's stellar gourmet food, are among the items that surpass standard grocery-store fare. ☎ 808/553-5595. MC, V.

Kualapuu Market KUALAPUU
This market, in its third generation, is a stone's throw from the Coffees of Hawaii store. It's a scaled-down, one-stop shop with wine, food, and necessities—and a surprisingly presentable, albeit small, assortment of produce, from Molokai sweet potatoes to Ka'u navel oranges in season. The shelves are filled with canned goods, propane, rope, hoses, paper products, and baking goods. ☎ 808/567-6243. No credit cards.

Mana'e Goods and Grindz PUKOO
Formerly the Neighborhood Store 'N Counter, the only grocery on the East End sells batteries, film, aspirin, cookies, beer, Molokai produce, candies, paper products, and other sundries. There's good food at the breakfast and lunch counter, too (p 438). ☎ 808/558-8498. No credit cards.

Misaki's Grocery and Dry Goods KAUNAKAKAI
Established in 1922, this third-generation local legend is one of Kaunakakai's two grocery stores. Some of its notable items: chopped garlic from California, fresh luau leaves (taro greens), fresh okra, Boca Burgers, large Korean chestnuts in season, gorgeous bananas, and an ATM. The fish section includes akule and ahi, fresh and dried, but the stock consists mostly of meats, produce, baking products, and a humongous array of soft drinks. Liquor, stationery, candies, and paper products round out the selection at this full-service grocery. ☎ 808/553-5505. MC, V.

Hawaiian Books & CDs

★★ kids **Big Wind Kite Factory & the Plantation Gallery** MAUNALOA Jonathan and Daphne Socher, kite designers and inveterate Bali-philes, have combined their interests in a kite factory/import shop that dominates the commercial landscape of Maunaloa, the reconstituted plantation town. Maunaloa's naturally windy conditions make it ideal for kite-flying classes, which are offered free when conditions are right. The adjoining Plantation Gallery features local handicrafts uch as milo-wood bowls, locally made T-shirts, lawaii-themed sandblasted glassware, baskets f lauhala and other fibers, and Hawaiian-music Ds. There are also many Balinese handicrafts, om jewelry to clothing and fabrics. ☎ 808/552-364. MC, V.

itchen

Bamboo Pantry KAUNAKAKAI
's hard to believe this creative kitchenware, utlery, and specialty foods store is located in ne heart of Kaunakakai. "Gifts for the home" nclude everything from dishes, woven baskets, lassware, and high-end pots and pans to ourmet food. 107 Ala Malama St. ☎ 808/553-300 MC, V.

urf-Wear

Molokai Surf KAUNAKAKAI
kateboards, surf shorts, sweatshirts, unglasses, T-shirts, footwear, boogie boards, ackpacks, and a broad range of clothing and ccessories for life in the surf and sun. 130 amehameha V Hwy. ☎ 808/553-5093 MC, V.

-Shirts & Souvenirs

Molokai Fish & Dive KAUNAKAKAI
Here you'll find the island's largest selection f T-shirts and souvenirs, crammed in among shing, snorkeling, and outdoor gear that you an rent or buy. Find your way among the shnets, boogie boards, diving equipment, amboo rakes, beach towels, postcards, juices nd soft drinks, disposable cameras, and taggering miscellany of this store. One entire vall is lined with T-shirts, and the selection of Molokai books and souvenirs is extensive. The taff is happy to point out the best snorkeling pots of the day. In the lobby of the Hotel Molokai with another location in Kaunakakai. ☎ 808/553-5926 MC, V.

Vine

Molokai Wines & Spirits KAUNAKAKAI
his is your best bet on the island for a decent ottle of wine. The shop offers 200 labels, ncluding Caymus, Silver Oak, Joseph Phelps, Heitz, Bonny Doon, and a carefully culled uropean selection. Snack options include mported gourmet cheeses, salami, and Carr's iscuits. ☎ 808/553-5009. MC, V.

> *Maunaloa's gusty winds make it a natural home for one of the islands' most popular stores: The Big Wind Kite Factory.*

The Perfect Molokai Souvenir

It's small, it's easy to pack and take back home, and it's made only on Molokai. It's Molokai salt. The Hawaii Kai Corporation (www.hawaiikaico.com) has two product lines featuring Molokai salt: the gourmet **Soul of the Sea** ($18 for 12 oz.) and the **Palm Island Gourmet** ($6 for 8 oz.). Soul of the Sea salt is hand-harvested from some of the cleanest ocean water in the state, hand-processed, and hand-packed on Molokai. It comes in three varietals: Papohaku White, Kilauea Black, and Haleakala Red. While making Soul of the Sea salt, Hawaii Kai Corporation gets a byproduct they call Ocean Essence, which they blend with Molokai salt to restore trace minerals lost in the heating process. The result is Palm Island Gourmet, which comes in White Silver, Red Gold, or Black Lava.

Molokai Restaurants A to Z

★ kids **Hotel Molokai** KAUNAKAKAI *AMERICAN/HAWAII REGIONAL CUISINE* The Hotel Molokai's oceanfront dining room evokes the romance of a South Seas fantasy; its atmosphere is unequaled on the island. Try the fresh catch, kalbi ribs, barbecued pork ribs, New York steak, or the lip-smacking coconut shrimp. Hwy. 450, near MM 2. ☎ 808/553-5347. Reservations recommended for dinner. Entrees: $8–$15 lunch, $15–$25 dinner. AE, DC, MC, V. Breakfast, lunch, and dinner daily.

kids **Kamoi Snack-N-Go** KAUNAKAKAI *ICE CREAM/SNACKS* Ice cream made by Dave's on Oahu comes in flavors such as green tea, litchi sherbet, haupia, mango, and many others. If the ice cream doesn't tempt you, maybe something in the aisles full of candies will. In Kamoi Professional Center. ☎ 808/553-3742. Ice cream $2.25–$4.15; sundaes $3.60–$6.40. MC, V. Open daily until 9pm.

★ kids **Kanemitsu's Bakery & Restaurant** KAUNAKAKAI *BAKERY/DELI* Molokai bread—from traditional white and wheat to apricot-pineapple or coconut—is the Kanemitsu signature. Those in the know line up at the bakery's back door beginning at 10pm, when the bread is whisked hot out of the oven and into waiting hands. The cream-cheese-and-jell bread makes a fine substitute for dessert. In the adjoining coffee shop/deli, the hamburgers and egg-salad sandwiches are popular and cheap. 79 Ala Malama St. ☎ 808/553-5855. Most items less than $5.50. AE, MC, V. Restauran Wed–Mon 5:30am–noon; bakery Wed–Mon 5:30am–6:30pm.

★ kids **Mana'e Goods and Grindz** PUKOO *AMERICAN* This quick-stop market/lunch counter is nothing fancy, and that's what I love about it. Favorites include the mahimahi plate lunch, the chicken katsu, burgers (including a killer veggie burger), saimin, and legendary desserts. Brunch is also very popular. Made-on-Maui Roselani ice cream is a featured attraction. A Molokai treasure, this is the only grocery store on the East End. Hwy. 450, near MM 16. ☎ 808/558-8498. Most items less than $10. MC, V. Breakfast and lunch (until 5pm) daily.

> *A large selection of breads, including local fruit varieties, keep customers lining up at Kanemitsu's.*

Molokai's Best Hotels, Restaurants & Nightlife

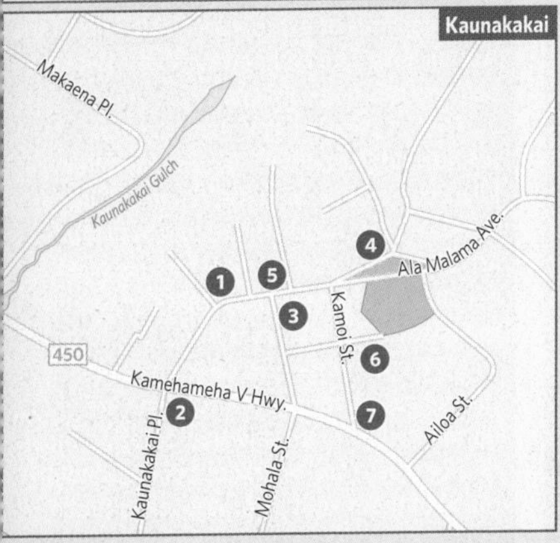

Restaurants
Hotel Molokai **10**
Kamoi Snack-N-Go **6**
Kanemitsu's Bakery & Restaurant **5**
Mana'e Goods and Grindz **13**
Molokai Drive-Inn **7**
Molokai Pizza Café **2**
Outpost Natural Foods **1**
Paddlers' Inn **3**
Sundown Deli **4**

Hotels
A'ahi Place **9**
Aloha Beach House **14**
Country Cottage at Pu'u O Hoku Ranch **15**
Dunbar Beachfront Cottages **12**
Hotel Molokai **10**
Ke Nani Kai Resort **8**
Molokai Shores Suites **11**
Paniolo Hale **8**

Nightlife
Hotel Molokai **10**
Paddlers' Inn **3**

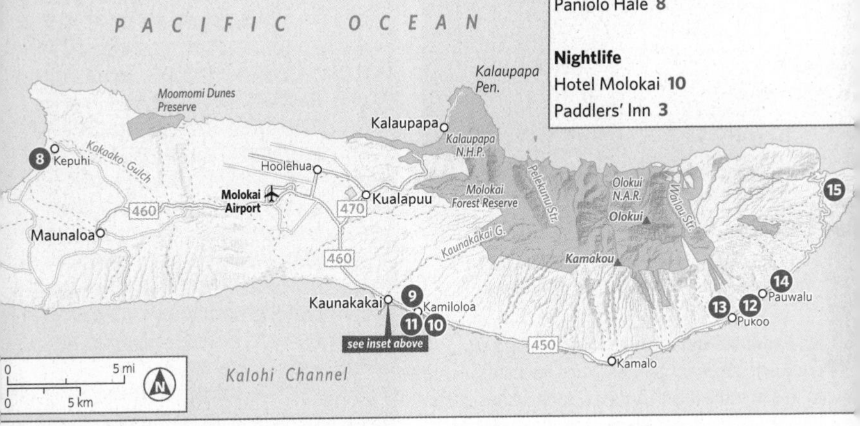

kids **Molokai Drive-Inn** KAUNAKAKAI *AMERICAN/TAKEOUT* It's a greasy spoon, but you can get fresh akule (mackerel) and ahi (when available), plus fried saimin at budget-friendly prices. The honey-dipped fried chicken and shakes are local favorites. This is a fast-food takeout counter, and it doesn't pretend to be otherwise. ☎ 808/553-5655. Most items less than $10. No credit cards. Breakfast, lunch, and dinner daily.

★ kids **Molokai Pizza Cafe** KAUNAKAKAI *PIZZA* The excellent pizzas and sandwiches have made this place a Kaunakakai staple as well as one of my favorite eateries on the island. Pasta, ribs, fresh-fish dinners, and the new addition of "gourmet" hamburgers on homemade buns round out the menu. In Kahua Center, on the old Wharf Rd. ☎ 808/553-3288. Large pizzas $18–$23. No credit cards. Lunch and dinner daily.

★ kids **Outpost Natural Foods** KAUNAKAKAI *VEGETARIAN* The salads, burritos, tempeh sandwiches, and tofu-spinach lasagna served at this tiny health food store are testament to the fact that vegetarian food need not be boring. It's also a great place to pick up local produce. 70 Makaena Place. ☎ 808/553-3377. Entrees $12–$15. AE, DISC, MC, V, Lunch Sun–Fri (closed Sat).

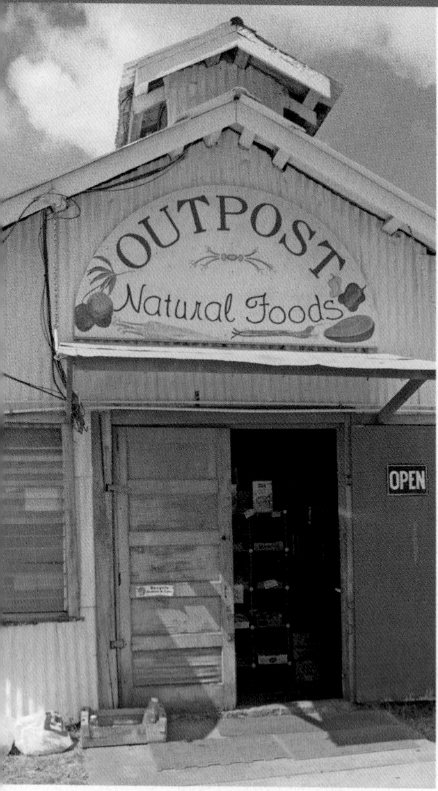

> *The popular Outpost Natural Foods is Molokai's only destination for health food aficionados.*

Dining on Molokai

The good news is that on Molokai, you won't find long lines at overbooked, self-important restaurants. The bad news is that Molokai's culinary offerings are spare.

A lot of people like it that way and acknowledge that the island's character is unchangeably rugged and natural. But a few years ago, when the renovated Hotel Molokai unveiled a tropical fantasy of an oceanfront dining room, it quickly became the island's busiest restaurant.

Even with these new developments, the culinary offerings of the island are dominated by mom-and-pop eateries, most of them fast-food or takeout places and many of them with a home-cooked touch. Personally, I like the unpretentiousness of the island; it's an oasis in a state where plastic aloha abounds. But sybarites, foodies, and pampered oenophiles had best lower their expectations upon arrival.

You'll even find a certain defiant stance against the trappings of modernity. Although some of the best produce in Hawaii is grown on this island, you're not likely to find much of it served in its restaurants, other than in the takeout items at Outpost Natural Foods, or at the Molokai Pizza Cafe and the Hotel Molokai. The rest of the time, content yourself with ethnic or diner fare—or by cooking for yourself. The many visitors who stay in condos find that it doesn't take long to sniff out the best sources of produce, groceries, and fresh fish to fire up at home when the island's other dining options are exhausted. The "Grocery Store" sections in "Shopping" (p 436) will point you in the right direction.

Molokai's restaurants are inexpensive or moderately priced, and several of them do not accept credit cards. Regardless of where you eat, you certainly won't have to dress up. In most cases, we've listed just the town rather than the street address because, as you'll see, street addresses are as meaningless on this island as fancy cars and sequins.

kids **Paddlers' Inn** KAUNAKAKAI *AMERICAN/LOCAL* If you want to meet local residents, come to this friendly place. Burgers, sandwiches, plate lunches, a few vegetarian items, and breakfast specials fill the menu. There's entertainment in the evenings (p 443). 10 Mohala St. ☎ 808/553-5256. www.paddlersinnhawaii.com. Entrees $5–$12 breakfast; $6–$22 lunch; $10–$30 dinner. AE, DC, DISC, MC, V. Breakfast, lunch, and dinner daily.

★ **Sundown Deli** KAUNAKAKAI *DELI* From "gourmet saimin" to sandwiches to spinach pie, Sundown's offerings are home-cooked and healthful, and include vegetarian specials. Vitamins, T-shirts, and snacks are sold in this tiny cafe, but most of the business is takeout. 145 Puali St. (across the street from Veteran's Memorial Park). ☎ 808/553-3713. Entrees $3.95–$7.50. AE, MC, V. Breakfast and lunch Mon–Fri.

Molokai Hotels A to Z

Molokai Hotel Map

See "Molokai's Best Hotels, Restaurants & Nightlife" (p 439) for a map of the lodging and nightlife options in this section.

'ahi Place KAUNAKAKAI
ust outside of Kaunakakai lies this dream acation cottage, complete with a wicker-filled itting area, a kitchen, and two lanais. The ntire property is surrounded by tropical plants, owers, and fruit trees. For those who seek a uiet vacation with no phone or TV to distract ou, this is the place. P.O. Box 2006, Kaunakakai, I 96748. ☎ 808/553-8033. www.molokai.com/ ahi. 1 unit. Doubles $75–$85; with continental reakfast $10 extra; extra person $20; 3-night inimum. No credit cards.

★ kids **Aloha Beach House** PUKOO
his impeccably decorated, two-bedroom, 600-square-foot beach house, right on the hite-sand beach of Waialua, has a huge open living/dining/kitchen area that opens out to an old-fashioned porch. It's fully equipped, from the complete kitchen to a VCR to all the beach toys you can think of. Located just after MM 19, Hwy. 450. Reservations c/o The Rietows, P.O. Box 79, Kilauea, HI 96754. ☎ 888/828-1008 or 808/828-1100. www.molokaivacation.com. 1 unit. Doubles: $290 plus $175 cleaning fee for 2 people; extra person $20 plus additional cleaning fee; 3-night minimum. No credit cards.

★ kids **Country Cottage at Pu'u O Hoku Ranch** HALAWA Pu'u o Hoku ("Star Hill") Ranch spreads across 14,000 acres of pasture and forests about an hour's drive from Kaunakakai. The ranch's rustic cottage sits on 2 tropically landscaped acres, with breathtaking views of rolling hills and the Pacific Ocean. The comfortable wooden cottage features a full kitchen, two bedrooms, two bathrooms, and an enclosed lanai. TVs and VCRs are available on request. There's also a four-bedroom, three-bathroom house on the property. Hwy. 450, at MM 25. Reservations: P.O. Box 1889, Kaunakakai,

Paniolo Hale offers spacious, airy condo units and Old Hawaii style.

> *THIS PAGE & OPPOSITE PAGE The Hotel Molokai's A-Frame Polynesian-style units face a sandy beach in a tropical setting.*

HI 96748. ☎ 808/558-8109. www.puuohoku.com. 2 units. Doubles $140 plus $75 cleaning fee; extra person $20; 2-night minimum. No credit cards.

Staying on Molokai

Molokai is Hawaii's most affordable island, especially in regard to hotels. And most hotel rooms and condo units come with kitchens, which can save you a bundle on dining costs.

The downside is that there aren't too many accommodations options on Molokai—mostly B&Bs, condos, a few quaint oceanfront vacation rentals, and a motel-like hotel. For camping on Molokai, hardy souls can pitch their own tent at the beach or in the cool upland forest (see "Camping," p. 426). We've listed our top picks here; for additional options, contact **Molokai Vacation Properties,** P.O. Box 237, Kaunakakai, HI 96748 (☎ 800/367-2984 or 808/553-8334; fax 808/553-8332; www.molokai-vacation-rental.com).

★★ kids **Dunbar Beachfront Cottages** PUKOO

Each of these two green-and-white plantation-style cottages sits on its own secluded beach (good for swimming)—you'll feel like you're on your own private island. Each cottage sleeps up to four (great for a family), and comes with a full kitchen, VCR, ceiling fans, tropical furniture, a large furnished deck, and views of Maui, Lanai, and Kahoolawe across the channel. Hwy 450, past MM 18. Reservations c/o Matt and Genesis Dunbar, HC01 Box 738, Kaunakakai, HI 96748. ☎ 800/673-0520 or 808/558-8153. www.molokai-beachfront-cottages.com. 2 units. $170 cottage (sleeps up to 4) plus 1-time $75 cleaning charge; 3-night minimum. No credit cards.

★ kids **Hotel Molokai** KAUNAKAKAI

Since the 2008 closing of the Lodge at Molokai Ranch, this nostalgic Hawaiian motel-like complex is the only hotel on the island. The modest hotel is composed of a series of modified A-frame units along a gray-sand beach (not good for swimming). This is a modest budget hotel—the rooms have all the necessities but aren't fancy. Ask for a room with a ceiling fan; most rooms have a lanai. Some units have kitchenettes. Hwy. 450. (P.O. Box 1020), Kaunakakai, HI 96748. ☎ 877/553-5347 on the mainland, or 808/553-5347. www.hotelmolokai.com. 54 units. Doubles $159–$229; suites from $249; extra bed/crib $20. AE, DC, DISC, MC, V.

★ kids **Ke Nani Kai Resort** KALUAKOI RESORT Families will appreciate the space in these large apartments, which have kitchens, washer/dryers, VCRs, attractive furnishings, and breezy lanais. There's a huge pool, a volleyball court, tennis courts, and golf on the neighboring Kaluakoi course, and it's a short walk to the beach. The downside: Maid service is only every third day. In the Kaluakoi Resort development, Kaluakoi Rd., off Hwy. 460 (P.O. Box 289), Maunaloa, HI 96770. Reservations c/o Molokai Vacation Rentals, HC01 Box 237, Kaunakakai, HI 96748. ☎ 800/367-2984 or 808/553-8334. www.molokai-vacation-rental.com. 100 units. $95–$135 1-bedroom apt. (sleeps up to 4); $115–$195 2-bedroom apt. (up to 6); 3-night minimum. AE, DC, DISC, MC, V.

kids **Molokai Shores Suites** KAUNAKAKAI Basic but spacious units with kitchens and large lanais face a small gold-sand beach (not good for swimming) in this quiet complex of three-story Polynesian-style buildings, less than a mile from Kaunakakai. The swimming pool and barbecue area come with an ocean view. No maid service. Units are individually owned, so quality varies. Hwy. 450 (P.O. Box 1037), Kaunakakai, HI 96748. ☎ 800/367-5005 or 808/553-5954. www.castleresorts.com. 102 units. $190–$210 1-bedroom apt. (sleeps up to 4); $250 2-bedroom apt. (up to 6). AE, DC, MC, V.

★ **Paniolo Hale** KALUAKOI RESORT Tucked into a verdant garden on the dry West End, this condo complex has the advantage of being next door to a white-sand beach (not good for swimming). The two-story, old Hawaii ranch-house design is airy and homey, with oak floors and walls of folding-glass doors that open to huge screened verandas. All are spacious and well equipped, with full kitchens and washer/dryers. A pool, paddle tennis, and barbecue facilities are on the property. Ask for a recently renovated unit; they are individually owned, so quality varies. Lio Place (next door to Kaluakoi Resort), Kaluakoi, HI 96770. Reservations c/o Molokai Vacation Rentals, P.O. Box 1979, Kaunakakai, HI 96748. ☎ 800/367-2984 or 808/553-8334. www.molokai-vacation-rental.com. 77 units. $105–$145 double studio; $130–$195 1-bedroom apt. (sleeps up to 4); $225–$275 2-bedroom apt. (up to 6); 3-night minimum (1-week minimum Dec 20–Jan 5). AE, MC, V.

Nightlife on Molokai

Nightlife options on this small, sleepy island are limited. **Hotel Molokai** (p 438), in Kaunakakai, offers live entertainment by local musicians poolside and in the dining room every night. Friday from 4 to 6pm is Aloha Fridays Night, with music and hula from Molokai performers. With its South Seas ambience and poolside setting, it has become the island's premier venue for local and visiting entertainers.

The Paddlers' Inn (p 440), also in Kaunakakai, has become a hotspot for live Hawaiian music, comedy acts, and other entertainment, such as karaoke. Check www.paddlersinnmolokai.com for the current schedule.

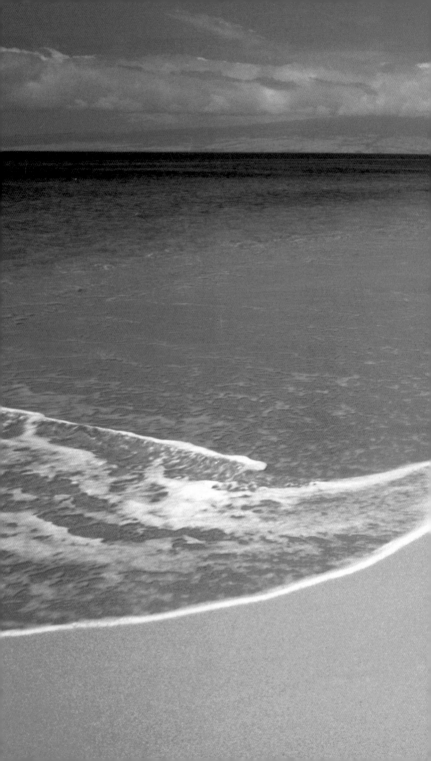

8
Lanai

My 12 Favorite Lanai Moments

Lanai is a place where people come looking for dramatic beauty, quiet, solitude, and an experience with nature. The real Lanai is a multifaceted place that's so much more than a luxury resort—and it's the traveler who comes to discover the island's natural wonders, local lifestyle, and other inherent joys who's bound to have the most genuine island experience. Here are my favorite Lanai experiences.

> PREVIOUS PAGE *Water washes up on the white sands of Lanai's Polihua Beach, where you might find yourself sharing a blanket with a sea turtle.* THIS PAGE *Shipwreck Beach offers Lanai's best beachcombing.*

❶ **Watching the dolphins** leap out of the water as the sun rises over Hulopoe Beach. See p 454.

❷ **Plunging beneath the waves** and snorkeling through a rainbowed sea of tropical fish. See p 459.

❸ **Climbing to the top of the Munro Trail** to see the islands of Maui and Molokai and, in the distance, the peaks of the Big Island. See p 458.

❹ **Sitting on the white sands of Polihua Beach** and watching the endangered sea turtles slowly haul themselves out of the ocean and make a nest for their eggs in the sand. See p 454.

❺ **Standing in awe** of Mother Nature's display at the Garden of the Gods, where mysterious lava formations painted in a brilliant mix of reds, oranges, ochers, and yellows lie scattered over the sunbaked ground. See p 449, ❷.

❻ **Four-wheeling it down to Shipwreck Beach,** then beachcombing the area for the treasures the ocean has brought in. See p 455.

❼ **Talking story** with the local Lanai residents during the weekly Saturday Lanai Marketplace and getting the real "scoop" on Lanai. See p 461.

❽ **Sipping a just-brewed cafe latte** on the sunny deck of Coffee Works and watching the tiny village of Lanai City come to life as the day begins. See p 462.

❾ **Sitting on the steps of the Hotel Lanai** and

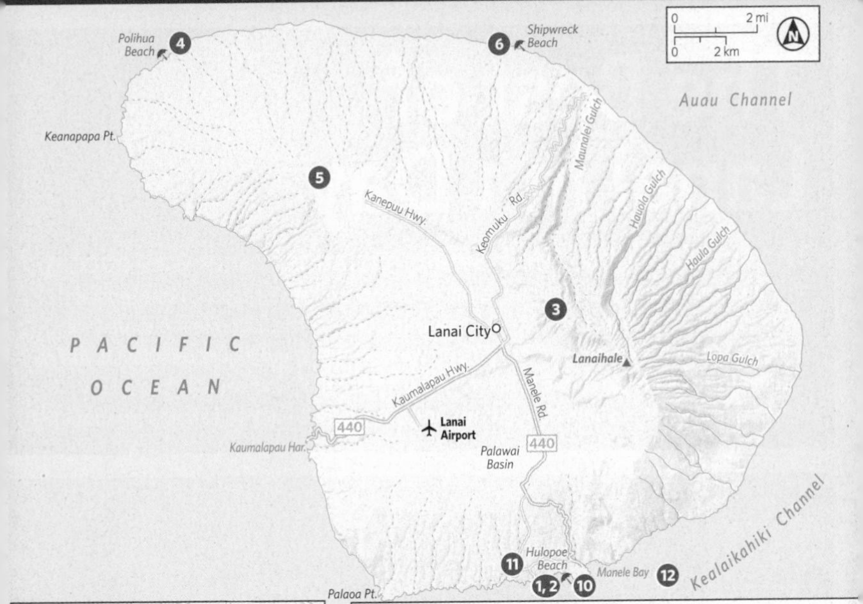

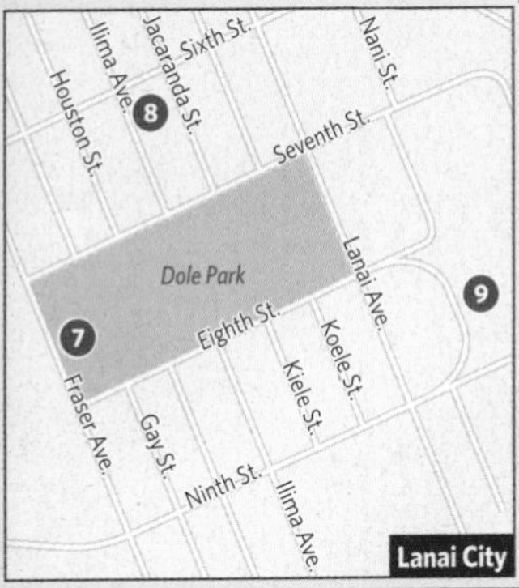

1. Watching the dolphins at Hulopoe Beach
2. Snorkeling at Hulopoe Beach
3. Climbing to the top of Munro Trail
4. Watching turtles at Polihua Beach
5. Garden of the Gods
6. Four-wheeling down to Shipwreck Beach
7. Talking story at the Farmers Market
8. Sipping a just-brewed cafe latte at Coffee Works
9. Sitting on the steps of the Hotel Lanai
10. Exploring the tide pools at Hulepoe Bay
11. Admiring the views from Challenge at Manele Golf Course
12. Diving at Cathedrals

gazing at the zillions of bright stars overhead, as the gentle strumming of a Hawaii ukulele wafts out from inside. See p 465.

10 Exploring the strange creatures in the miniature sea world in the tide pools at Hulopoe Bay, like asteroids (sea stars) and holothurians (sea cucumbers), plus spaghetti worms, barber pole shrimp, and a favorite Hawaiian delicacy, the opihi (a very tasty limpet). See p 454.

11 Pausing during a golf game to admire yet another stunning ocean view on the Challenge at Manele Golf Course. See p 456.

12 Staring up from 35 feet underwater at the incredible way the sunlight pierces through the water at the Cathedrals dive site. See p 459.

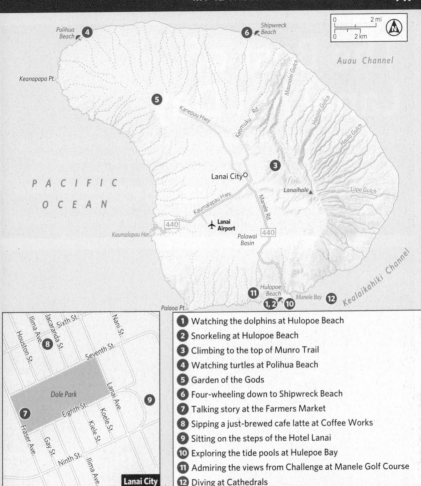

> *The dramatic rock structures of Garden of the Gods at sunset.*

The Best of Lanai in 1 Day

The smallest of all the Hawaiian Islands, Lanai was once a big pineapple plantation and now is home to two exclusive resorts, hundreds of years of history, and just one small town with some of the friendliest people you will ever meet. It's possible to get an overview of this island in just one day. If you're coming from Maui, catch the first ferry, at 6:45am; that way you can see all my favorite spots, get in some beach time, and still make it back to Lahaina for dinner.

> *Daring divers leap off the craggy rocks at Hulopoe Bay, where crystal clear water also attracts snorkelers and swimmers.*

START & FINISH Manele Bay Harbor.
TRIP LENGTH 1 day and 68 miles.

1 Manele Bay Harbor. The morning, with the sunlight glistening on the ocean, is my favorite time of the day. If you're coming by ferry, you'll dock at picturesque Manele Bay Harbor, a small harbor with a handful of boats ranging from old fishing vessels to luxury high-tech yachts. Plan ahead and arrange a four-wheel-drive rental

More of Lanai

See chapter 3 for my suggested 3-day Lanai itinerary.

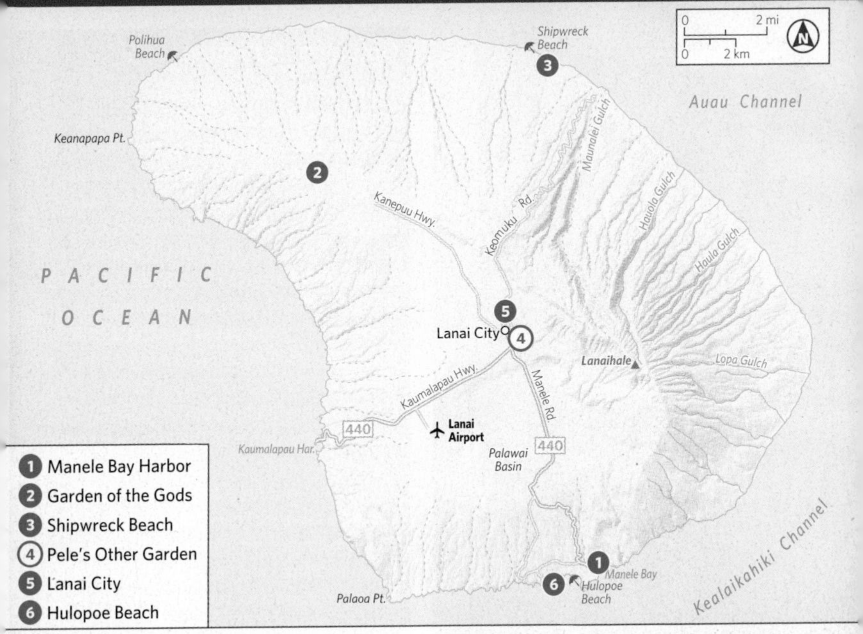

through Expeditions Lahaina (see "Getting to & Around Lanai," p 450); they will pick you up at the harbor and take you to your car.

The car rental van will take you from the harbor up Manele Rd. (Hwy. 440) to the car rental in Lanai City (about 30-40 min.). It's another 14 miles from the car rental on Lanai Ave. to the Garden of the Gods. Turn right onto Lanai Ave., then right (north) again to Hwy. 430 (Keomuku Hwy.). Turn left on Poliha Rd., just behind the stables and before the tennis courts (look for the rock sign). Allow about 25 minutes driving time.

2 ★★ kids **Garden of the Gods.** Head out on the dirt road that leads out of Lanai City, through the now uncultivated pineapple fields, to the Garden of the Gods, on Lanai's north shore. This rugged, barren, beautiful place is full of rocks strewn by volcanic forces and shaped by the elements into a variety of shapes and colors—brilliant reds, oranges, ochers, and yellows. Ancient Hawaiians considered this desolate, windswept place an entirely supernatural phenomenon. Scientists, however, have other, less colorful explanations. Some call the area an "ongoing posterosional event"; others say it's just "plain and simple badlands." Take a four-wheel-drive ride out here and

> *The Garden of the Gods is a natural and astonishing landscape of rock formations of various shapes, sizes, and colors.*

> *Creative classes are offered at the art gallery in beautiful and culturally rich Lanai City.*

decide for yourself. Go early in the morning when the light casts eerie shadows on the mysterious lava formations. 20 min.

Retrace your steps to Hwy. 430 (Keomuku Hwy.) and turn left. Continue down the steep switchback to the ocean. Turn left and drive to the end of the road. Allow 60 minutes to reach the next stop, about 20 miles away on winding dirt roads.

3 ★ kids **Shipwreck Beach.** This 8-mile-long windswept strand on Lanai's northeastern shore is a beachcomber's dream. 1 hr. See p 455.

It will take about 45 minutes to retrace your route back down Hwy. 430 into Lanai City, 12 miles away. Continue down Lanai Ave., then turn right on Eighth St., just after Dole Square. Park next to the square on Eighth across from Houston St.

Getting to & Around Lanai

There are no direct flights from the mainland to Lanai. You'll have to make a connection in Honolulu or Kahului (on Maui), where you catch a plane for the 25-minute flight to Lanai's airport. Twin-engine planes are the only air service to Lanai. Airlines with flights to Lanai include **PW Express** (☎ 888/866-5022 or 808/873-0877; www.pacificwings.com/pwexpress); **go!Express** airline (☎ 888/IFLYGO2 (435-9462); www.iflygo.com); and **Island Air** (☎ 800/652-6541 or 808/565-6744; www.islandair.com). I must tell you that I have gotten less than sterling service from Island Air.

Another option is **Expeditions Lahaina/Lanai Passenger Ferry** (☎ 808/661-3756; www.go-lanai.com), which takes you between Maui and Lanai for $52 for adults round-trip and $42 for children. The ferry runs five times daily. The 9-mile channel crossing takes 45 minutes to an hour, depending on sea conditions. Reservations are strongly recommended (or book online). Baggage is limited to two checked bags and one carry-on.

4 ★★ kids **Pele's Other Garden.** Stop for lunch at this deli and bistro. I love to sit outside under one of the umbrellas and watch the goings-on in the town square. See p 464.

5 ★★ kids **Lanai City.** Perched at 1,645 feet above sea level, in just about the middle of the island, sits this old-fashioned town around Dole Square. Built in 1924, this plantation village is a tidy grid of quaint tin-roofed cottages in bright pastels, with tropical gardens of banana, lilikoi, and papaya. Spend some time exploring the town and checking out the shops. The charming village square is lined with towering Norfolk Island and Cook pines and plantation buildings which house a couple of general stores with basic necessities, a smattering of

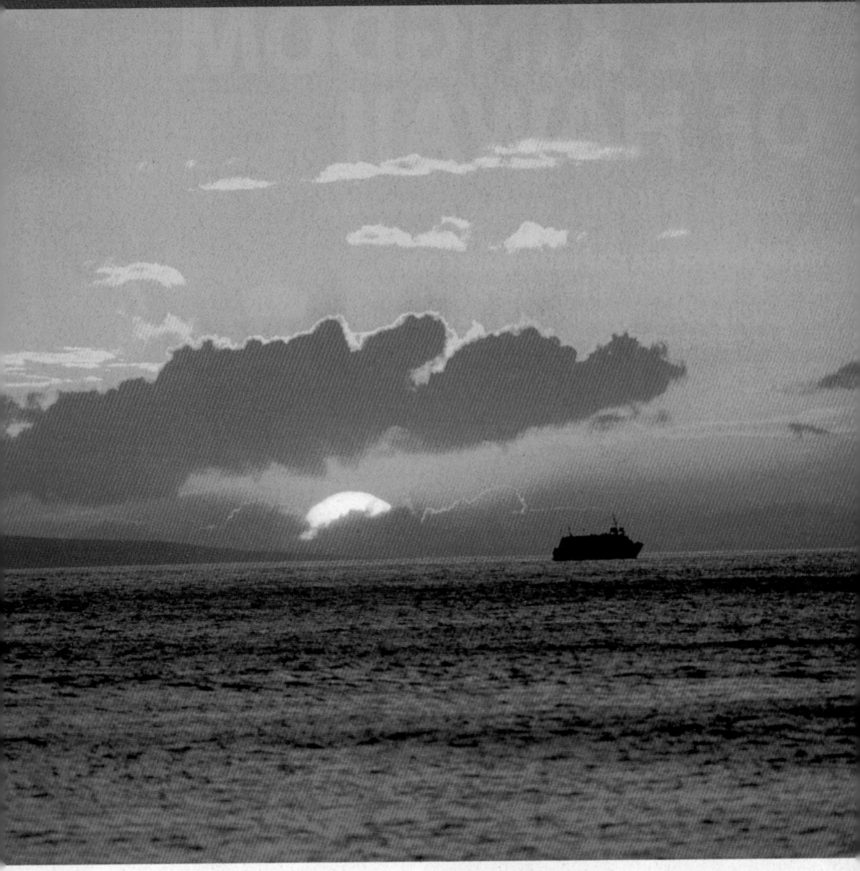

> *The Lahaina/Lanai passenger ferry is the most convenient way to travel between Maui and Lanai.*

restaurants, an art gallery, a whimsical shop, and a few blocks over a post office and a coffee shop that outshines any Starbucks. If you have time, check out the **Lanai Culture and Heritage Center,** room 126 in the Old Dole Building, Lanai Avenue (free admission; ☎ 808/565-7177). The museum's terrific historical photos and artifacts help you explore the history of the island starting from ancient times, when Hawaiian legends speak of the island being populated by *akua* (ghosts); to settlement by native Hawaiians; to the plantation era and up to today. ⏱ 1–2 hr.

Continue down Eighth St. to Fraser Ave. and turn left. Go right at Hwy. 440 (Kaumalapau Hwy.). Turn left at Manele Rd., where Hwy. 440 continues. Continue to the end of the road. Allow 30–35 minutes for the 11-mile trip.

Travel Tip

Lanai has only 30 miles of paved roads and hundreds of miles of unpaved four-wheel-drive roads. When renting a vehicle, always rent a four-wheel-drive so you have the option to really explore this island.

6 ★★★ kids **Hulopoe Beach.** This wide beach is one of my favorites in the entire state. Snorkeling is terrific, especially along the rocks to your left as you face the ocean. Boats cannot anchor in the bay, so you have the entire ocean to yourself. See p 454.

Take the 5-minute walk from Hulopoe Beach to Manele Bay to catch the last ferry back to Lahaina at 6:45pm.

THE KINGDOM OF HAWAII

Centuries of Royal Lineage BY MIKE SPRING

WHEN BRITISH SEA CAPTAIN JAMES COOK arrived in Hawaii in 1778, he was surprised to find a highly organized Hawaiian culture ruled by royal families. Here are some of Hawaii's most notable monarchs, along with some unusual royal traditions.

King Kamehameha I

"THE GREAT" 1810–1819

He conquered the Hawaiian Islands and formally established the Kingdom of Hawaii in 1810. He is represented on the commemorative quarter, minted in 2008 (he beat out portraits of Diamond Head, a hula dancer, and a surfer).

King Kamehameha II

"LIHOLIHO" 1819–1824

Assuming the throne at age 21, he eliminated many ancient Hawaiian rituals—that commoners had to prostrate themselves when a chief approached and that men ate separately from women, among others. Old ways began to dissipate.

King Kamehameha IV

"ALEXANDER LIHOLIHO" 1855–1863

Alexander was fun-loving and lenient, and his reign is often referred to as the "golden age." He tried to limit the influence of missionaries and stopped a U.S. plan to annex the islands, but he was powerless against epidemics—the flu, measles, the common cold—brought by visitors from the U.S. and Europe.

King Kalakaua

"DAVID KALAKAUA" 1874–1891

King Kalakaua loved the good life (he lifted prohibitions on the hula) and helped to revive old traditions, so he was known as the "Merrie Monarch." In 1887, foreign interests forced him to accept the "Bayonet Constitution," which made him a powerless figurehead and disqualified Asians from voting. On a visit to San Francisco he caught a cold and died in the royal suite of the Sheraton Palace.

Queen Liliuokalani

"LYDIA LILIUOKALANI" 1891–1893

This queen tried to implement a new constitution that would restore her right to rule. The U.S. responded by overthrowing the Hawaiian monarchy on January 17, 1893. The queen, held prisoner in Iolani Palace, was found guilty of treason and forced to abdicate in late 1896. Many *kanaka maoli* (native people) today are demanding restoration of rights taken away from them when the U.S. overthrew the monarchy. In 1993, Bill Clinton signed a formal apology for the incident.

Incest

Early visitors to Hawaii noted the tradition of incest among members of the royal families. What particularly struck them was that it was not considered a sin or even unusual by the inhabitants, although the taboo against incest is almost universal. It was imperative that the first wife of the head chief *(alii)* come from the highest rank, for it secured a proper offspring for the succession. The most honored union was that of a brother and sister. The highest-ranking chiefs also married their sisters as a political strategy, to guard them from potential rivals for the throne.

Under foreign influence, the system of royal incest was abandoned in 1819, before the arrival of the first missionaries. There is no word for "incest" in the Hawaiian language.

Kukaniloko Birthing Stones

It was here at this outcrop of lava rocks in Oahu that royal women were brought to give birth—a tradition dating back to the 12th-century. Dozens of chiefs pounded on drums to announce the arrival of newborns and reduce the pain of childbirth. It's believed that some of the stones were also used to map the stars and seasonal changes.

Lanai Beaches A to Z

★★★ Hulopoe Beach MANELE BAY

In 1997, Dr. Stephen Leatherman of the University of Maryland (a professional beach surveyor who's also known as "Dr. Beach") ranked Hulopoe the best beach in the United States. It's easy to see why. This palm-fringed, gold-sand beach is bordered by black-lava fingers that protect swimmers from ocean currents. In summer, Hulopoe is perfect for swimming, snorkeling, or just lolling about; the water temperature is usually in the mid-70s (mid-20s Celsius). Swimming is usually safe, except when swells kick up in winter. The bay at the foot of the Four Seasons Resort Lanai at Manele Bay is a protected marine preserve, with schools of colorful fish and spinner dolphins. Humpback whales cruise by here in winter. Hulopoe is also Lanai's premier beach park, with a grassy lawn, picnic tables, barbecue grills, restrooms, showers, and ample parking. You can camp here, too. Don't miss the Hulopoe tide pools: some of the best lava rock tide pools in Hawaii are found along the south shore of Hulopoe Bay. These miniature sea worlds are full of strange creatures such as asteroids (sea stars) and holothurians (sea cucumbers), not to mention spaghetti worms, barber pole shrimp, and Hawaii's favorite local delicacy, the opihi, a tasty morsel also known as the limpet. Youngsters enjoy swimming in the enlarged tide pool at the eastern edge of the bay. When you explore tide pools, do so at low tide. Never turn your back on the waves. Wear tennis shoes or reef walkers, as wet rocks are slippery. Collecting specimens in this marine preserve is forbidden, so don't take any souvenirs home. **At the end of Hwy. 440 (Manele Bay Rd.), turn right and follow the road to the parking lot at end of street.**

★ Polihua Beach NORTH SHORE

So many sea turtles once hauled themselves out of the water to lay their eggs in the sunbaked sand on Lanai's northwestern shore that Hawaiians named the beach here *Polihua,* or "egg nest." Although the endangered green sea turtles are making a comeback, they're seldom seen here now. You're more likely to spot an offshore whale (in season) or the perennial litter that washes up

> *Calm, beautiful Hulopoe Bay offers great swimming and snorkeling. Kids love splashing in and exploring the tide pools.*

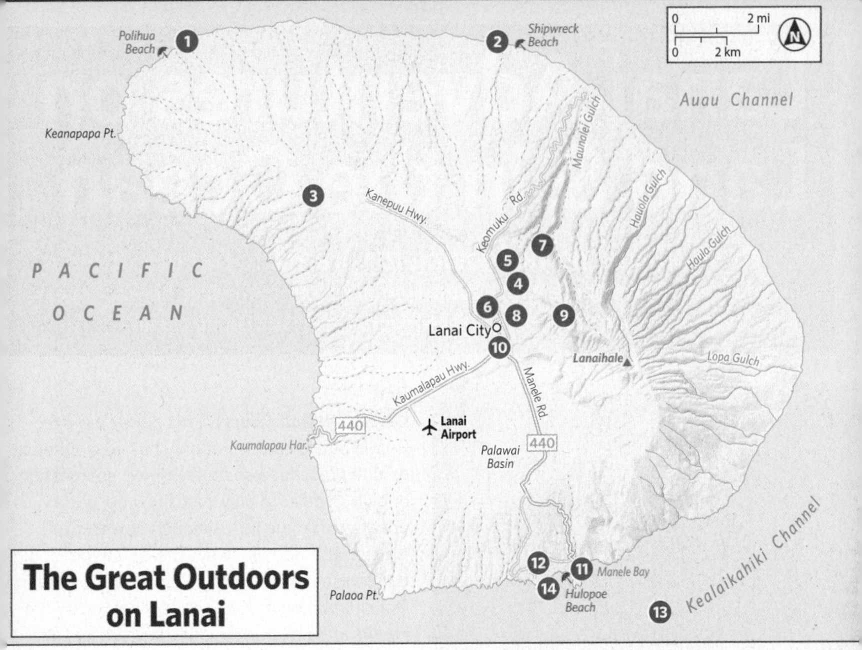

The Great Outdoors on Lanai

Beaches
Hulopoe Beach **14**
Polihua Beach **1**
Shipwreck Beach **2**

Hiking
Kanepuu Preserve **3**
Koele Nature Hike **7**
Munro Trail **9**

Horseback Riding
Four Seasons Lanai Resort's Stables at Koele **6**

Golf
Cavendish Golf Course **5**
The Challenge at Manele **12**
The Experience at Koele **8**

Scuba Diving
Cathedrals I & II **13**

Tennis
Four Seasons Resort Lanai at Koele **4**
Four Seasons Resort Lanai at Manele Bay **11**
Lanai City **10**

onto this deserted beach at the end of Polihua Road, a 4-mile jeep trail. There are no facilities except fishermen's huts and driftwood shelters. Bring water and sunscreen. Beware of the strong currents, which make the water unsafe for swimming. This strand is ideal for beachcombing (those little green-glass Japanese fishing-net floats often show up here), fishing, or just being alone. **From Lanai City take Hwy. 430 out of town, then turn left on Polihua Rd. (follow the signs to the Garden of the Gods). When the highway ends (at the Garden of the Gods), continue on the Polihua Trail (unpaved road), which ends at Polihua Beach.**

★ **Shipwreck Beach** NORTH SHORE

This 8-mile-long windswept strand on Lanai's northeastern shore—named for the rusty ship *Liberty* stuck on the coral reef—is a sailor's nightmare and a beachcomber's dream. The strong currents yield all sorts of flotsam, from Japanese handblown-glass fishing net floats and rare pelagic paper nautilus shells to lots of junk. This is also a great place to spot whales from December to April, when the Pacific humpbacks cruise in from Alaska. The road to the beach is paved most of the way, but you really need a four-wheel-drive vehicle to get down here. **From Lanai City take Hwy. 430 out of town and toward the ocean. The highway ends at an unpaved dirt road; turn left and follow it for 2 miles (you can see the shipwreck out in the ocean). Park in front of the shipwreck.**

Lanai Adventures on Land & in the Ocean

Visitors to Lanai come looking for dramatic beauty, quiet, solitude, and an experience with nature. From hiking to snorkeling, here are some of my favorite ways to enjoy the great outdoors while I'm visiting Lanai.

> *The 3-hour Koele Nature Hike brings you to Koloiki Ridge, where you'll find an unsurpassed view of the Maunalei Valley.*

Golf

Cavendish Golf Course. This quirky par-36, 9-hole public course not only has no clubhouse or club pros, but also no tee times, scorecards, or club rentals. To play, just show up, put a donation into the little wooden box next to the first tee, and hit away. The 3,071-yard E. B. Cavendish–designed course was built by the Dole plantation in 1947 for its employees. The greens are a bit bumpy, but the views of Lanai are great. Next to The Lodge at Koele in Lanai City. No phone. No greens fees but a $5–$10 donation suggested.

★★★ **The Challenge at Manele.** This target-style, desert-links course, designed by Jack Nicklaus, is one of the most challenging in the state. The unique course is routed among lava outcroppings, archaeological sites, kiawe groves, and ilima trees. Facilities include a clubhouse, a pro shop, rentals, a practice area, lockers, and showers. Next to the Four Seasons Resort Lanai at Manele Bay in Hulopoe Bay. ☎ 800/321-4666. Greens fees: $225, $210 for resort guests.

★★ **The Experience at Koele.** This is a traditional par-72 course designed by Greg Norman. Mother Nature reigns throughout: You'll see Cook and Norfolk Island pines, indigenous plants, and lots of water—seven lakes, flowing streams, cascading waterfalls, and one green (the 17th) completely surrounded by a lake. Facilities include a clubhouse, a pro shop, rentals, a practice area, lockers, and showers. Four Seasons Reosrt Lanai, The Lodge at Koele in Lanai City. ☎ 800/321-4666. Greens fees: $225, $210 for resort guests.

> *You'll find the island's best scuba diving off the south shore of Lanai in what the locals call underwater "Cathedrals."*

Hiking

Four Seasons Resorts Hikes. The Four Seasons offers a couple of guided hikes: **The Lodge at Koele** (☎ 808/565-4000; www.fourseasons.com/lanai) has a 2½-hour Koloiki Ridge nature hike through 5 miles of the upland forests of Koele at 11am daily. The fee is $15. The hike is considered "moderate" with both uphill and downhill sections. The trail is unmarked so you must go on the guided hike; meet at the hotel. The **Four Seasons Resort Lanai at Manele Bay** (☎ 808/565-2000; www.fourseasons.com/lanai) has a 1½-hour fitness hike along an old fisherman's trail at 9am Tuesday and Friday, led by Joe West, wildlife and outdoor photographer extraordinaire. Bring your camera and ask Joe for photography tips. Along the way you'll see Lanai's natural beauty and breathtaking coastline. The hike is free. Again, it's a guided hike only, so meet at the hotel.

Kanepuu Preserve Nature Trail. Kanepuu is one of the last remaining examples of the type of forest that once covered the dry lowlands throughout the state. There are some 49 plant species here that are found only in Hawaii. The **Nature Conservancy** (☎ 808/565-7430) conducts guided hikes every month; call for details. To reach the trail take Hwy. 430 from Lanai City and turn left on Polihua Rd. (look for the signs to the Garden of the Gods). Just before the Garden of the Gods, there will be a sign for the Kanepuu Preserve. Park there and follow the signs to the trail head for this brief (1-mile) hike.

Koele Nature Hike. This 3-hour self-guided hike starts by the reflecting pool in the backyard of The Lodge at Koele and takes you on a 5-mile loop through Norfolk Island pines, into Hulopoe Valley, past wild ginger, and up to Koloiki Ridge, with its panoramic view of Maunalei Valley and of Molokai and Maui in the distance. You're welcome to take the hike even if you're not a guest at The Lodge. The path isn't clearly marked—ask the concierge for a free map. I suggest doing this hike in the morning; by afternoon the clouds usually roll in, marring visibility at the top and increasing your chance of being caught in a downpour. The Lodge at Koele reflecting pool.

Special Events

During the annual **Pineapple Festival,** generally the first weekend in July, some of Hawaii's best musicians travel to Lanai for the biggest event on the island. Other special events include the **Aloha Festival** (www.alohafestivals.com), which takes place either the end of September or the first week in October, and the **Christmas Festival,** the first Saturday in December (☎ 808/565-6043).

> *Horseback riding brings you to the places you might miss on foot.*

★★★ **Munro Trail.** If it hasn't been raining and the ground is dry, do a little exploring. The adventurous will spend the day climbing to the top of Lanai at Lanaihale on the Munro Trail. This tough, 11-mile round-trip, uphill climb through the groves of Norfolk Island pines is a lung-buster, but if you reach the top, you'll be rewarded with a breathtaking view of Molokai, Maui, Kahoolawe, the peaks of the Big Island, and—on a really clear day—Oahu in the distance. Figure on 7 hours hiking. The trail follows Lanai's ancient caldera rim, ending up at the island's highest point, Lanaihale. Go in the morning for the best visibility. After 4 miles, you'll get a view of Lanai City. The weary retrace their steps from here, while the more determined go the last 1.25 miles to the top. Diehards head down Lanai's steep south-crater rim to join the highway to Manele Bay. The not-so-adventurous will take a four-wheel-drive vehicle. Pencil in a soak in a hot tub on your return. From Lanai City take Hwy. 430. About 2 miles out of town look for Laniola St. on your right. Turn there and follow it to where the road ends and the trail begins. Follow the trail until it ends, then continue downhill on an unpaved pineapple road which winds its way back to Manele Rd. (Hwy. 440). From here it is 11 miles uphill along the road to Lanai City or 2 miles along the road downhill to Hulopoe Bay.

Horseback Riding

Four Seasons Resort Lanai's Stables at Koele. Horses can take you to many places in Lanai's unique landscape that are otherwise unreachable. This stable offers various daily rides (9am and 1:30pm), including slow, gentle, group rides starting at $95 for a 1½-hour **Paniolo Trail Ride,** which takes you into the hills surrounding Koele. You'll meander through guava groves and ironwood trees; catch glimpses of axis deer, quail, wild turkeys, and Santa Gertrudis cattle; and end with panoramic views of Maui and Lanai. Private rides can be arranged for $160 per person for 2 hours. Kids will love the 15-minute pony rides ($10 per person). Sunset rides (1½ hours) are available for $190 per person. Long pants and closed-toe shoes (like running shoes) are required, and safety helmets are provided. Bring a jacket—the weather is chilly and rain is frequent. Children must be at least 9 years old and 4 feet tall, and riders cannot weigh more than 225 pounds. Four Seasons Resort Lanai, The Lodge at Koele. ☎ 808/565-4424.

Kayaking

Trilogy's 6-hour kayak tour will teach you how to maneuver your boat and take you to remote locations to see Lanai from a very different perspective. The tours, which include lunch and all equipment, are $159 for adults and $80 for children ages 3–15.

Scuba Diving

Trilogy offers two-tank boat dives for $199, which includes all equipment, snacks, and beverages; one-tank beach dives are $95 (including all equipment). Nearby, also on the south shore, two of Hawaii's best-known dive spots are found in Lanai's clear waters: **Cathedrals I** and **II,** so named because the sun lights up an underwater grotto like a magnificent church.

Snorkeling & Sailing

Trilogy has built a well-deserved reputation as the leader in sailing-snorkeling cruises in Hawaii. Their 4-hour **snorkel-sailing trip** aboard its luxury custom catamarans or its 32-foot jet-drive rigid aluminum-inflatable vessel costs $169 for adults ($85 kids 3–15), including lunch, all snorkel equipment, and instruction. The 1½-hour **Marine Mammal Search,** along Lanai's protected coastline, includes sailing past hundreds of spinner dolphins, and during the winter months, searching for humpback whales. It costs $75 for adults ($38 kids) and includes lunch, sodas, snorkel gear, and instruction. If you'd rather go it alone, snorkeling is terrific at Hulopoe Beach (p 454).

Sunset Sail

Trilogy's 2-hour sunset sail is the perfect way to end a day on the island. Gentle breezes fill the sails as you see the island from out at sea and watch the colors come out in the sky as the sun sizzles into the Pacific. Cost is $99 for adults ($50 kids 3–15) and includes both hot and cold appetizers and non-alcoholic beverages (you are welcome to bring your own libation).

Surfing

If you've ever wanted to learn how to surf, let instructor Nick Palumbo, a surfing champion, take you on a four-wheel-drive surfing safari to a secluded surf spot. He'll have you up and riding the waves in no time. His **Lanai Surf School & Surf Safari** (☎ 808/565-7258; www.lanaisurfsafari.com) offers a package that includes a 2½-hour lesson with surfboard, four-wheel-drive transportation, refreshments, and "a really good time" for $185 per person.

Tennis

If you're not a Four Seasons guest, you can play at the public courts, lit for night play, in **Lanai City** (no charge; call ☎ 808/565-6979 for reservations). The **Four Seasons Resort Lodge at Koele** offers three new Premiere Cushion outdoor hard courts. The tennis courts offer complimentary use of Wilson racquets, balls, and bottled ice water for guests. The tennis center at the **Four Seasons Resort Lanai at Manele Bay** offers a full pro shop, use of a ball machine, and weekly tennis mixers and tournaments. Courts are $20 per person for hotel guests (not open to nonguests). For information, call ☎ 808/565-2072.

> *The challenging Munro Trail takes you on an 11-mile trek to Lanai's highest point, where you'll be rewarded with an incredible view.*

Trilogy

The best outfitter on Lanai (and perhaps in the entire state) is **Trilogy Lanai Ocean Sports** (☎ 888/MAUI-800 628-4800; www.visitlanai.com). This is the outfitter for the excellent ocean adventures in this section.

Lanai Shopping A to Z

★ **Central Bakery** LANAI CITY
This is the mother lode of the island's baked delights. The bakery supplies all breads, breakfast pastries, and banquet desserts on the island, as well as specialty ice creams, sorbets, and restaurant desserts. Although it's not your standard retail outlet, you can call in advance, place your order, and pick it up. They prefer as much notice as possible (preferably 48 hr.). Breads (most $4.50) range from walnut-onion to roasted-potato-bacon to olive-onion. They also have cookies, brownies, muffins, croissants (including chocolate croissants), Danishes, and scones, plus an assortment of breakfast pastries. 1311 Fraser Ave. ☎ 808/565-3920.

★★ **Dis 'N Dat** LANAI CITY
This eclectic store must be seen to be believed. You'll find exotic-wood sculptures and carvings; mobiles and wind chimes; handmade jewelry; stained glass; unique garden ornaments and home decor; a large collection of Hawaii slipper necklaces, earrings, anklets, and bracelets; T-shirts; hula lamps; woven baskets; and more. Look for the vivid green shop with hanging chimes and mobiles leading the way to the front door. 418 Eighth St. (at Kilele St.). ☎ 866/DISNDAT (347-6328) or 808/565-9170.

★ **Gifts with Aloha** LANAI CITY
Phoenix and Kimberly Dupree's store of treasures includes fabulously stylish hats, locally made clothing, T-shirts, swimwear, quilts, Jams World dresses, children's clothes, toys, Hawaii-themed CDs, pareu, aloha shirts, handbags, ceramics, and art by local artists (including some of the most beautiful jewelry in the islands). The made-on-Maui soaps and bath products make great gifts. Dole Park, 363 Seventh St. (at Ilima St.) ☎ 808/565-6589.

High Lights LANAI CITY
This full-service salon offers cuts, styling, highlighting, manicures, pedicures, waxing, and so on, plus a wide selection of beauty products for hair and skin, and cosmetics. Walk-ins welcome. 617 Ilima Ave. ☎ 808/565-7207.

International Food & Clothing LANAI CITY
This store sells the basics: groceries, housewares, T-shirts, hunting and fishing supplies, over-the-counter drugs, wine and liquor, paper goods, hardware, and a surprisingly extensive

> *From hula girl lamps to garden ornaments, Dis 'N Dat features an eclectic inventory of local wares.*

Lanai Shopping A to Z

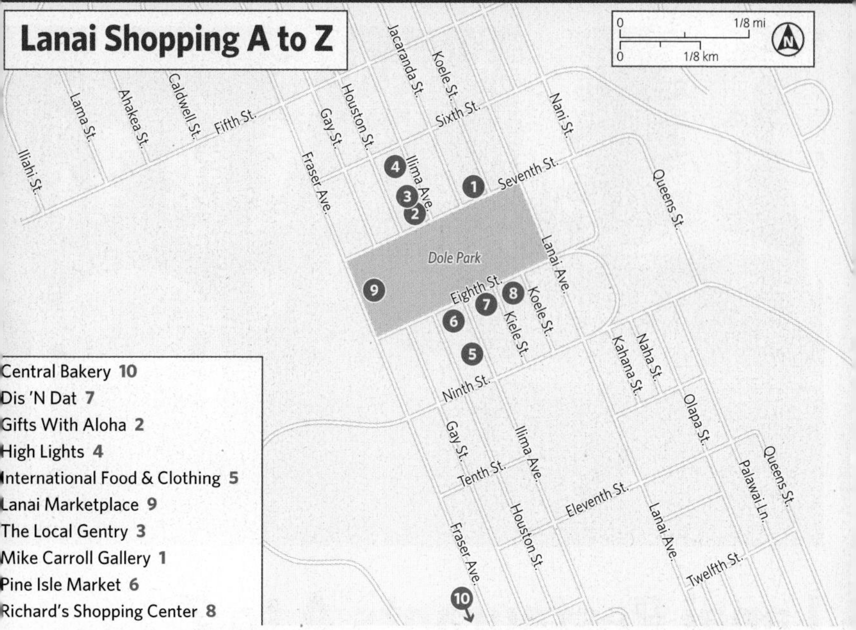

selection of yuppie soft drinks (Sobe, Snapple, and others). It even offers a takeout lunch counter. **833 Ilima Ave. ☎ 808/565-6433.**

Lanai Marketplace LANAI CITY
Everyone on Lanai, it seems, is a backyard farmer. From 7 to 11am or noon on Saturday, they all head to this shady square to sell their dewy fresh produce, home-baked breads, plate lunches, and handicrafts. This is Lanai's version of the green market: petite in scale (like the island) but charming, and growing. Dolores Fabrao's jams and jellies, under the **Fabrao House** label (☎ 808/565-6134 for special orders), are a big seller at the market and at resort gift shops. **Dole Square.**

★★ **The Local Gentry** LANAI CITY
Visiting and local women alike flock to this store for fabulous silk aloha shirts by Tiki, mahogany wood lamps, mermaids and hula girls, inexpensive sarongs, children's clothes, sandals, and other clothing and accessories that are not the standard resort-shop fare. **363 Seventh St. (behind Gifts of Aloha, facing Ilima St.). ☎ 808/565-9130.**

Mike Carroll Gallery LANAI CITY
If he is on the island, you'll find Mike Carroll at work here on his original oil paintings. You'll find an extensive selection of his original work, some limited editions, prints and notecards, plus a dozen or so of Maui and Lanai's top artists and even some locally made, one-of-a-kind jewelry. **443 Seventh St. ☎ 808/565-7122. www.mikecarrollgallery.com.**

Pine Isle Market LANAI CITY
A local landmark for two generations, Pine Isle specializes in locally caught fresh fish, but you can also find fresh herbs and spices, canned goods, electronic games, ice cream, toys, diapers, and other basic essentials of work and play. The fishing section is outstanding, with every lure imaginable. **356 Eighth St. ☎ 808/565-6488.**

Richard's Shopping Center LANAI CITY
The Tamashiros' family business has been on the square since 1946; not much has changed over the years. This general store has a grocery section, paper products, ethnic foods, meats (mostly frozen), liquor, toys, film, cosmetics, fishing gear, sunscreens, clothing, kitchen utensils, T-shirts, aloha shirts, and other miscellany. Half a wall is lined with an extraordinary selection of fishhooks and anglers' needs. **434 Eighth St. ☎ 808/565-6047.**

Lanai Restaurants A to Z

Blue Ginger Cafe LANAI CITY *COFFEE SHOP* A very local, very casual, inexpensive alternative to Lanai's fancy hotel restaurants. The offerings are solid, no-nonsense, everyday fare: The hamburgers on homemade buns are popular. 409 Seventh St. (at Ilima St.), Lanai City. ☎ 808/565-6363. Entrees under $15. No credit cards. Breakfast, lunch, and dinner daily.

Café 565 LANAI CITY *PIZZA/SUBS* Diners at this colorful pizzeria (named after Lanai's phone prefix, 565) spill out of the old house and into the umbrella tables in the front yard. The pizzas here are the real thing, baked in pizza ovens. Hot or cold sub sandwiches (in fresh-baked rolls), daily plate lunch specials, and great salads complete the menu. 408 Eighth St. (at Ilima St.), Lanai City. ☎ 808/565-6622. Sub sandwiches $5-$10; pizza $14-$20; most entrees under $9. No credit cards. Lunch and dinner Mon-Fri, lunch only Sat.

Canoes Lanai LANAI CITY *LOCAL* This hole in the wall is a local institution, with a reputation for serving local-style breakfasts. The fare—fried rice, omelets, short stacks, and simple ham and eggs—is more greasy spoon than gourmet, but it's budget-friendly. 419 Seventh St., Lanai City. ☎ 808/565-6537. Reservations not accepted. Breakfast less than $8.50; lunch sandwiches $2.50-$8.50; burgers $2-$5. No credit cards. Breakfast and lunch Thurs-Tues.

★ **The Challenge at Manele Clubhouse** MANELE *PACIFIC RIM* The view from the alfresco tables here may be the best on the island, encompassing Kahoolawe, Haleakala (on Maui), and, on an especially clear day, the peaks of Mauna Kea and Mauna Loa on the Big Island. You can lunch on salads and sandwiches (Asian tuna salad with grilled ahi, turkey club sandwiches, burgers) or on more substantial entrees, ranging from fish and chips to Kalbi barbecue beef. The clubhouse is casual, the view of the ocean is awe-inspiring, and it's a great gathering place. ☎ 808/565-2230. Reservations recommended. Entrees $28-$39. AE, DC, MC, V. Lunch daily.

★ **Coffee Works** LANAI CITY *COFFEEHOUSE* Oahu's popular Ward Warehouse coffeehouse has opened a branch in Lanai City with a menu of espresso coffees and drinks, ice cream

> *Soups, sandwiches, and pizzas are just some of the tasty choices at the popular Pele's Other Garden.*

Lanai Hotels & Restaurants

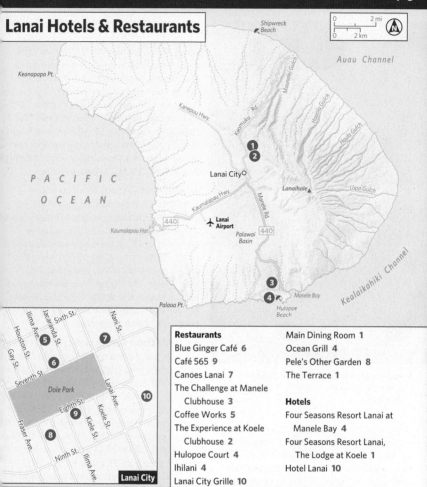

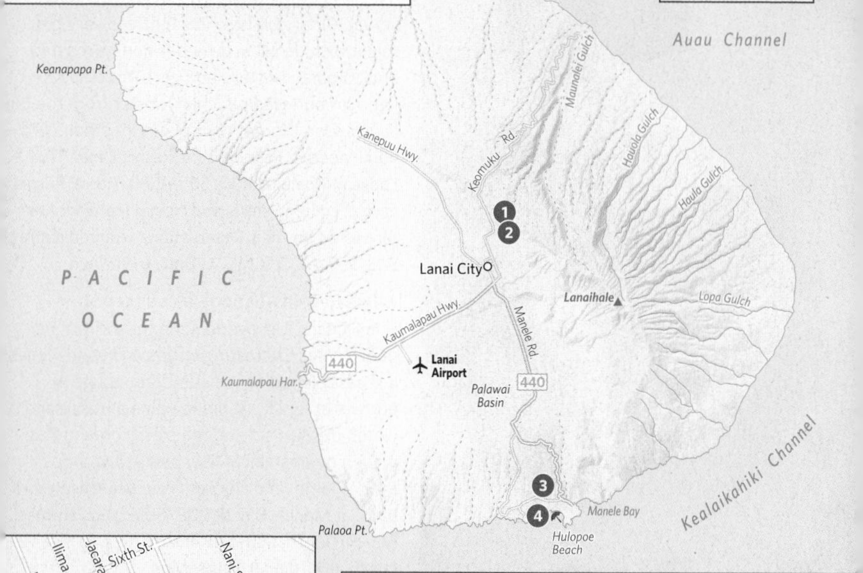

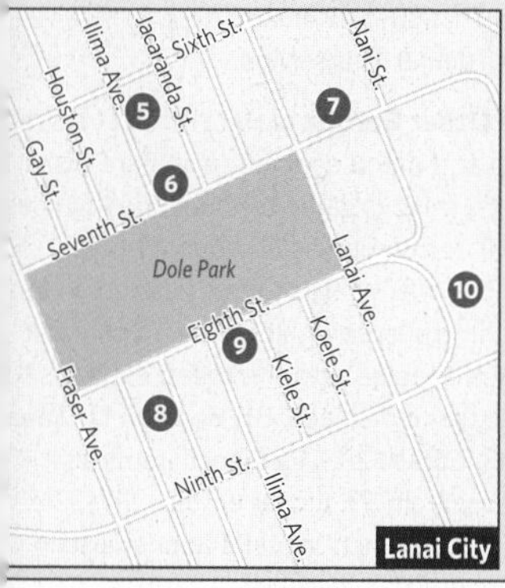

Restaurants
Blue Ginger Café 6
Café 565 9
Canoes Lanai 7
The Challenge at Manele Clubhouse 3
Coffee Works 5
The Experience at Koele Clubhouse 2
Hulopoe Court 4
Ihilani 4
Lanai City Grille 10
Main Dining Room 1
Ocean Grill 4
Pele's Other Garden 8
The Terrace 1

Hotels
Four Seasons Resort Lanai at Manele Bay 4
Four Seasons Resort Lanai, The Lodge at Koele 1
Hotel Lanai 10

including local brands), and a small selection f pastries and sandwiches. It's Lanai City's athering place, a tiny cafe with tables and enches on a pleasing wooden deck just a tone's throw from Dole Park. There are some ice gift items available, including T-shirts, tea nfusers, Chai, teapots, cookies, and gourmet offees. 604 Ilima St., Lanai City (across from he post office). ☎ 808/565-6962. Coffee drinks 3-$6; bagels $3-$8; sandwiches $7-$8. AE, DC, ISC, MC, V. Mon-Tues and Thurs-Sat 6am-4pm closed Wed); Sun 6am-noon.

he Experience at Koele Clubhouse LANAI ITY *AMERICAN* This tiny diner overlooks the erdant, rolling hills of the Experience at Koele olf Course. Oversize sandwiches range from a delicious portobello mushroom on toasted focaccia bread to open-faced chicken salad (with a yummy mango-avocado salsa), smoked turkey club, or a charbroiled cheddar burger. The Experience at Koele Golf Course. ☎ 808/565-4605. Lunch $11-$19. AE, DC, MC, V. Lunch daily.

★★ **Hulopoe Court** HULOPOE BAY *HAWAII REGIONAL CUISINE* This informal dining room serves breakfast and dinner, with a range of items to please most pallets. Four Seasons Resort Lanai at Manele Bay. ☎ 808/565-2290. Entrees $13-$27 breakfast; $19-$35 dinner. AE, DC, MC, V. Breakfast and dinner daily.

★★★ **Ihilani** HULOPOE BAY *ITALIAN* Overlooking the resort and the ocean beyond,

> *An adorable setting and Chef Bev Gannon's delectable dishes are highlights of the Lanai City Grille.*

this classy traditional Italian restaurant serves a range of well-prepared dishes, from inspiring risottos (Puna goat cheese with pine nuts and baby vegetables) to fresh fish (ahi caponata with eggplant), veal, chicken, and beef. **Four Seasons Resort Lanai at Manele Bay. ☎ 808/565-2296. Entrees $29–$50. AE, DC, MC, V. Tues–Sat 6–9:30pm.**

★★ kids **Lanai City Grille** LANAI CITY *COUNTRY CUISINE* Celebrated Maui chef Bev Gannon (Hailiimaile General Store, Joe's Restaurant) redesigned the menu in this cute eatery, and her famous dishes (from meatloaf with a citrus BBQ sauce to pan-seared venison over a mushroom risotto) are served with the freshest ingredients available. Live music on Friday and Saturday from 6:30pm. **In Hotel Lanai, 828 Lanai Ave., Lanai City. ☎ 808/565-7211. www.hotellanai.com. Main courses $19–$33. MC, V. Wed–Sun 6–9pm.**

★★★ **Main Dining Room** LANAI CITY *NEW AMERICAN* This relaxing restaurant, with a roaring fire, bountiful sprays of orchids, and a team of waitstaff serving in hushed voices, serves American favorites. Entrees vary but might include Maui lavender honey-roasted duck breast, mustard and herb-roasted rack of lamb, or buttered poached lobster from the Big Island. Don't forget your platinum credit card—you'll need it. **Four Seasons Resort Lanai, The Lodge at Koele. ☎ 808/565-4580. Attire: Resort casual, collared shirts and closed footwear are requested for men. Reservations required. Entrees $43–$59. AE, DC, MC, V. Daily 6–9:30pm.**

★ **Ocean Grill** HULOPOE BAY *SEAFOOD* The Ocean Grill, overlooking the swimming pool, serves interesting wraps and sandwiches, a great selection of salads, and a range of entrees at lunch. At dinner, dine alfresco and watch the sun set and the stars come out as you enjoy fresh local fish, beef, pork chops, rack of lamb, and chicken. **Four Seasons Resort Lanai at Manele Bay. ☎ 808/565-2092. Entrees: $15–$18 lunch; $30–$44 dinner. AE, DC, MC, V. Lunch daily, dinner Thurs–Mon.**

★★ **Pele's Other Garden** LANAI CITY *DELI/BISTRO* Daily soup and menu specials, excellent pizza, sandwiches, fresh organic produce, fresh juices and special items such as top-quality black-bean burritos make Pele's Other Garden a Lanai City must. In the evening you dine on china at cloth-covered tables, and the menu expands to include pastas and salads. **811 Houston St., Lanai City. ☎ 808/565-9628. Most lunch items less than $9; pizza from $9; dinner entrees $17–$24. AE, DISC, MC, V. Lunch Mon–Fri (dinner also in winter), dinner Sat year-round.**

★★ **The Terrace** LANAI CITY *AMERICAN* Looking out over prim English gardens, this wonderful restaurant is the Lodge's "casual" dining room. Hearty breakfasts of waffles and cereals, fresh local pineapple, frittata, and blue crab Benedict are a grand start to the day. Dinner choices include slow-roasted lamb shank, grilled beef fillet, roasted pork chops, fresh fish of the day, and a couple of vegetarian selections. **Four Seasons Resort Lanai, The Lodge at Koele. ☎ 808/565-4580. Reservations recommended. Entrees: $16–$27 breakfast; $14–$25 lunch; $28–$40 dinner. AE, DC, MC, V. Breakfast, lunch, and dinner daily.**

Lanai Hotels A to Z

Lanai Hotel Map

See "Lanai Hotels & Restaurants" (p 463) for a map of the lodging options in this section.

★★ kids **Four Seasons Resort Lanai at Manele 'ay** HULOPOE BAY Located on a sun-washed outhern bluff overlooking Hulopoe Beach, one f Hawaii's best stretches of golden sand, this J-shaped hotel steps down the hillside to the ool and the beach. Most of the spacious airy ooms open to a breathtaking view of the big lue Pacific. This resort is much less formal han The Lodge (see below) and attracts more amilies. Hulopoe Beach. ☎ 800/321-4666. ww.fourseasons.com/lanai. 236 units. Doubles 415–$1,295. AE, DC, MC, V.

★★ **Four Seasons Resort Lanai, The Lodge at oele** LANAI CITY This inn, which resembles grand English country estate, was recently iven a $50-million makeover. Guest rooms eature four-poster beds, sitting areas, and athrooms with oversize tubs. Understand hat this hotel is not located at the beach ut rather in the cool mist of the mountains, here temperatures drop into the 50s (teens elsius) in winter. Lanai City. ☎ 800/321-4666. ww.fourseasons.com/lanai. 102 units. Doubles 345–$645. AE, DC, MC, V.

> *Vintage Hawaiian surroundings with modern amenities make the plantation-era Hotel Lanai a favorite destination.*

★ kids **Hotel Lanai** LANAI CITY If you're looking for the old-fashioned aloha that Lanai City is famous for, this is the place to stay. This clapboard plantation-era relic has retained its quaint character and lives on as a country inn. All rooms have ceiling fans and private, shower-only bathrooms. The small one-bedroom cottage, with a TV and bathtub, is perfect for a small family. 828 Lanai Ave., Lanai City. ☎ 800/795-7211. www.hotellanai.com. 11 units. Doubles $159–$179; cottage $229; with continental breakfast. AE, MC, V.

Lanai Nightlife

Years ago, when I was on Lanai and asked a local resident about nightlife, she blushed and told me "that's personal." That about sums up nightlife on the island. But there are a few activities available.

The **Great Hall** of the Four Seasons Lodge at Koele (above) features live music every evening (usually a pianist). Also at the Lodge, the **Trophy Room** features table games like pool, shuffleboard, and foosball, plus a 46-inch LCD television.

The open-air Hale **Ahe Ahe Lounge,** in the Four Seasons at Manele Bay (above), has a terrific panoramic view of the ocean. The bar features a poolroom, a games room, and a 46-inch LCD television. Hawaiian entertainment is performed nightly.

Every Friday, from 6:30–9:30pm, follow the local residents to the **Lanai City Grille,** at the Hotel Lanai (p 464), for the best of Hawaiian music on the island. No cover charge; full bar available.

The **Lanai Playhouse,** 456 Seventh St., Lanai City (☎ 808/565-7500) is a historic 1920s building that has won awards for its renovations. It usually shows two movies each evening from Friday to Tuesday (and Wed in summer).

9
Kauai

My 12 Favorite Kauai Moments

On any list of the world's most spectacular islands, Kauai ranks right up there with Bora Bora, Huahine, and Rarotonga. All the elements are here: moody rainforests, majestic cliffs, jagged peaks, emerald valleys, palm trees swaying in the breeze, daily rainbows, and some of the most spectacular golden beaches you'll find anywhere. Here are a few of my favorite Kauai experiences.

> *PREVIOUS PAGE Massive waves slam Kauai's shore so hard that they send funneled seawater shooting into the air near Prince Kuhio Park.* THIS PAGE *Beautiful, secluded Kee Beach was featured in* The Thornbirds.

❶ **Snorkeling Kee Beach.** Rent a mask, fins, and snorkel, and enter a magical underwater world. Facedown, you'll watch brilliant fish dart here and there in water clear as day. Faceup, you'll contemplate green-velvet cathedral-like cliffs under a blue sky, where long-tailed tropical birds ride the trade winds. See p 504.

❷ **Hiking Waimea Canyon, the Grand Canyon of the Pacific.** Ansel Adams would have loved this ageless desert canyon, carved by an ancient river. Sunlight plays against its rusty red cliffs, burnt-orange pinnacles, and blue-green valleys. There's nothing else like it in the islands. See p 508.

❸ **Strolling through Hawaiian history.** Old Waimea town stood witness to a great many key events in Hawaii's history. This quaint, unassuming town is the place where Capt. James Cook "discovered" the Hawaiian Islands, where Russians once built a fort, and where New England missionaries arrived in 1820 to "save the heathens." See p 491, ❺.

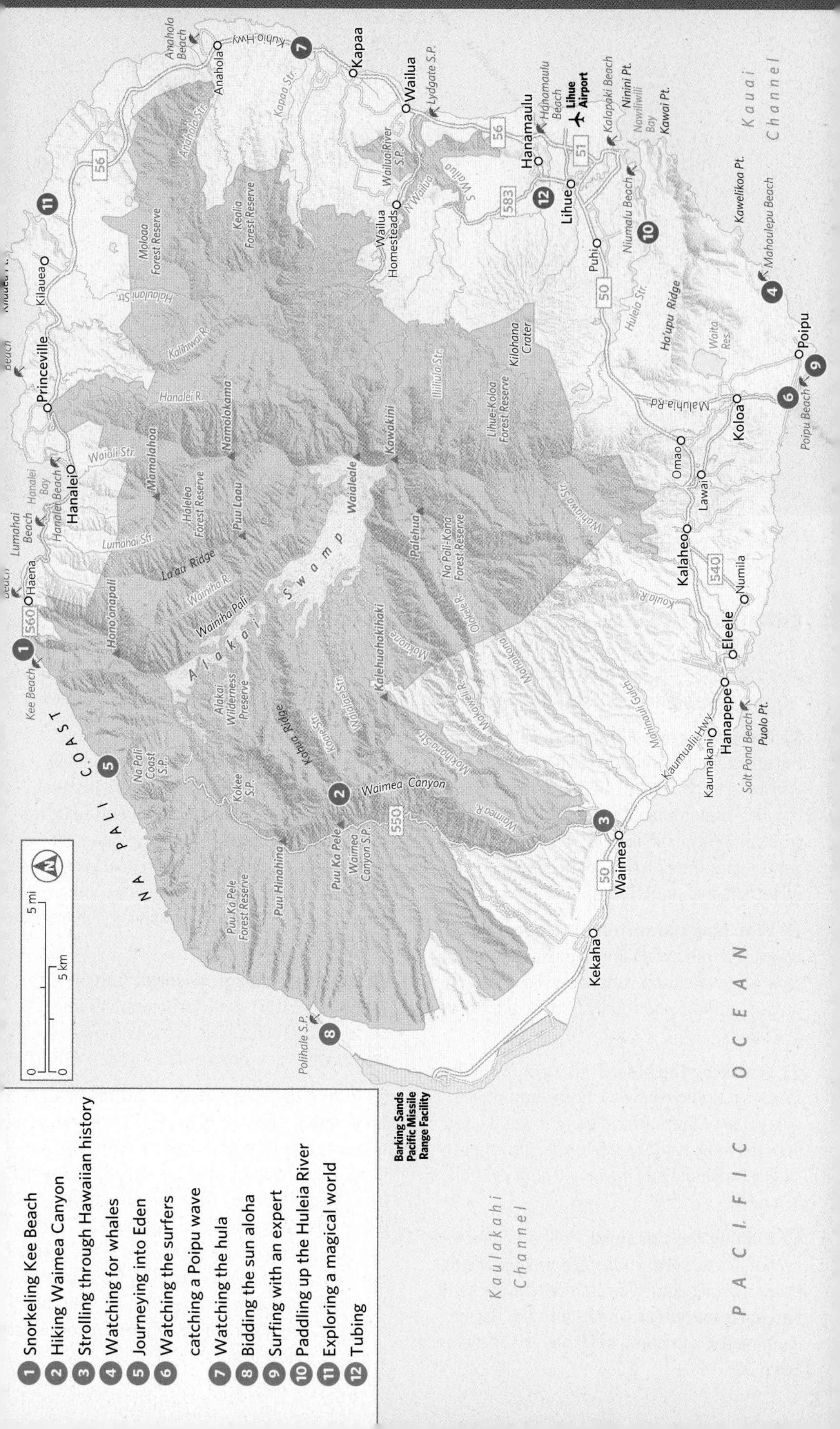
1 Snorkeling Kee Beach
2 Hiking Waimea Canyon
3 Strolling through Hawaiian history
4 Watching for whales
5 Journeying into Eden
6 Watching the surfers catching a Poipu wave
7 Watching the hula
8 Bidding the sun aloha
9 Surfing with an expert
10 Paddling up the Huleia River
11 Exploring a magical world
12 Tubing
0 5 mi
0 5 km
NA PALI COAST
PACIFIC OCEAN
Kaulakahi Channel
Kauai Channel
Barking Sands Pacific Missile Range Facility
Polihale S.P.
Kekaha
Waimea
Waimea Canyon
Waimea Canyon S.P.
Kokee S.P.
Na Pali Coast S.P.
Alakai Wilderness Preserve
Alakai Swamp
Puu Ka Pele Forest Reserve
Kee Beach
Haena
Hanalei
Hanalei Bay
Princeville
Kilauea
Anahola
Kapaa
Wailua
Wailua Homesteads
Lihue
Lihue Airport
Hanamaulu
Puhi
Kilohana Crater
Lihue-Koloa Forest Reserve
Na Pali-Kona Forest Reserve
Halelea Forest Reserve
Moloaa Forest Reserve
Kealia Forest Reserve
Waialeale
Kawaikini
Koloa
Poipu
Poipu Beach
Omao
Lawai
Kalaheo
Numila
Eleele
Hanapepe
Kaumakani
Salt Pond Beach
Ha'upu Ridge
Kawelikoa Pt.
Mahaulepu Beach
Niumalu Beach
Nawiliwili Bay
Kalapaki Beach
Ninini Pt.
Kawai Pt.
Lydgate S.P.
Kaumualii Hwy
Kuhio Hwy
Maluhia Rd

> *THIS PAGE Poipu Beach is a great place for novice surfers. OPPOSITE PAGE A dramatic view of Waimea Canyon.*

❹ **Watching for whales.** Mahaulepu Beach, in the Poipu area, offers excellent land-based viewing conditions for spotting the whales that cruise by December through April. See p 505.

❺ **Journeying into Eden.** For a glimpse of the spectacularly remote Na Pali Coast, all you need to do is hike the first 2 miles along the well-maintained Kalalau Trail into the first tropical valley, Hanakapiai. Hardier hikers can venture another 2 miles to the Hanakapiai waterfalls and pools. See p 515.

❻ **Watching the surfers catching a Poipu wave.** It's free entertainment: Lie back in the sand and watch the surfers on the vividly turquoise, curling, and totally tubular big waves. See p 505.

❼ **Watching the hula.** The Coconut Market-Place, on Kuhio Highway, hosts free shows every day at 5pm. Arrive early to get a good seat for the hour-long performances of both *kahiko* (ancient) and *auwana* (modern) hula. See p 552.

❽ **Bidding the sun aloha.** Polihale State Park, on Kauai's western shore, is a great place to bring a picnic dinner, stretch out on the sand, and toast the sun as it sinks into the Pacific, illuminating the island of Niihau in the distance. See p 505.

❾ **Surfing with an expert.** If seven-time world champ Margo Oberg, a member of the Surfing Hall of Fame, can't get you up on a board riding a wave, nobody can. She promises same-day results even for klutzes. See p 527.

❿ **Paddling up the Huleia River.** Indiana Jones ran for his life up this river to his seaplane in *Raiders of the Lost Ark*. Venture down it yourself in a kayak. The picturesque Huleia winds through tropically lush Huleia National Wildlife Refuge, where endangered species like great blue herons and Hawaiian gallinules take wing. See p 524.

⓫ **Exploring a magical world.** Take the kids to the magical Na Aina Kai Botanical Gardens on some 240 acres sprinkled with life-size (and larger) whimsical bronze statues. See p 498, ❶.

⓬ **Riding the cool waters in a ditch in an inner tube.** Back in the days of the sugar plantations, local kids would grab inner tubes and jump in the irrigation ditches crisscrossing the cane fields for an exciting ride. Today you can enjoy this (formerly illegal) activity by "tubing" the flumes and ditches of the old Lihue Plantation. The gentle gravity-fed flow will carry you through forests, into tunnels, and finally to a mountain swimming hole, where a picnic lunch is served. See p 527.

The Best of Kauai in 3 Days

Kauai, the oldest island of the main Hawaiian chain, lies the farthest north, about 70 miles north of Oahu. It's a small island (33 miles across and 25 miles from the north end to the south) and is easy to tour in 3 days.

> *Seemingly endless trails run throughout the beautiful rainforest and mountains of Kokee State Park.*

START Lihue. **FINISH** Poipu.
TRIP LENGTH 3 days and 150 miles.

Day 1

1 ★★★ See Kauai from a Helicopter. Since you're probably on mainland time and will be wide awake before the break of dawn, plan an early morning **helicopter tour of the island** to get your bearings with a bird's-eye view of the island. See p 520.

From the Heliport at Lihue Airport, follow Hwy. 570 (Ahukini Rd.) to the stoplight, and turn right on Hwy. 51. The name of the highway changes to Hwy. 56 and again, just after the turnoff for Princeville Resort, to Hwy. 560. From here, continue for 10 miles to the end of the road.

2 ★★ Kee Beach. Here you can either hike a couple of miles along the **Na Pali Coast** (see p 515) or cross the highway to the beach for an early morning snorkel. See p 504.

Retrace your route on Hwy. 560 for ⅓ mile. Look on the right side of the road for:

3 ★ Limahuli Garden of the National Tropical Botanical Garden. Out on Kauai's far North Shore, beyond Hanalei and the last wooden bridge, this small garden is tucked into a lush

More of Kauai

See chapter 3 for my 1- and 2-week Kauai itineraries.

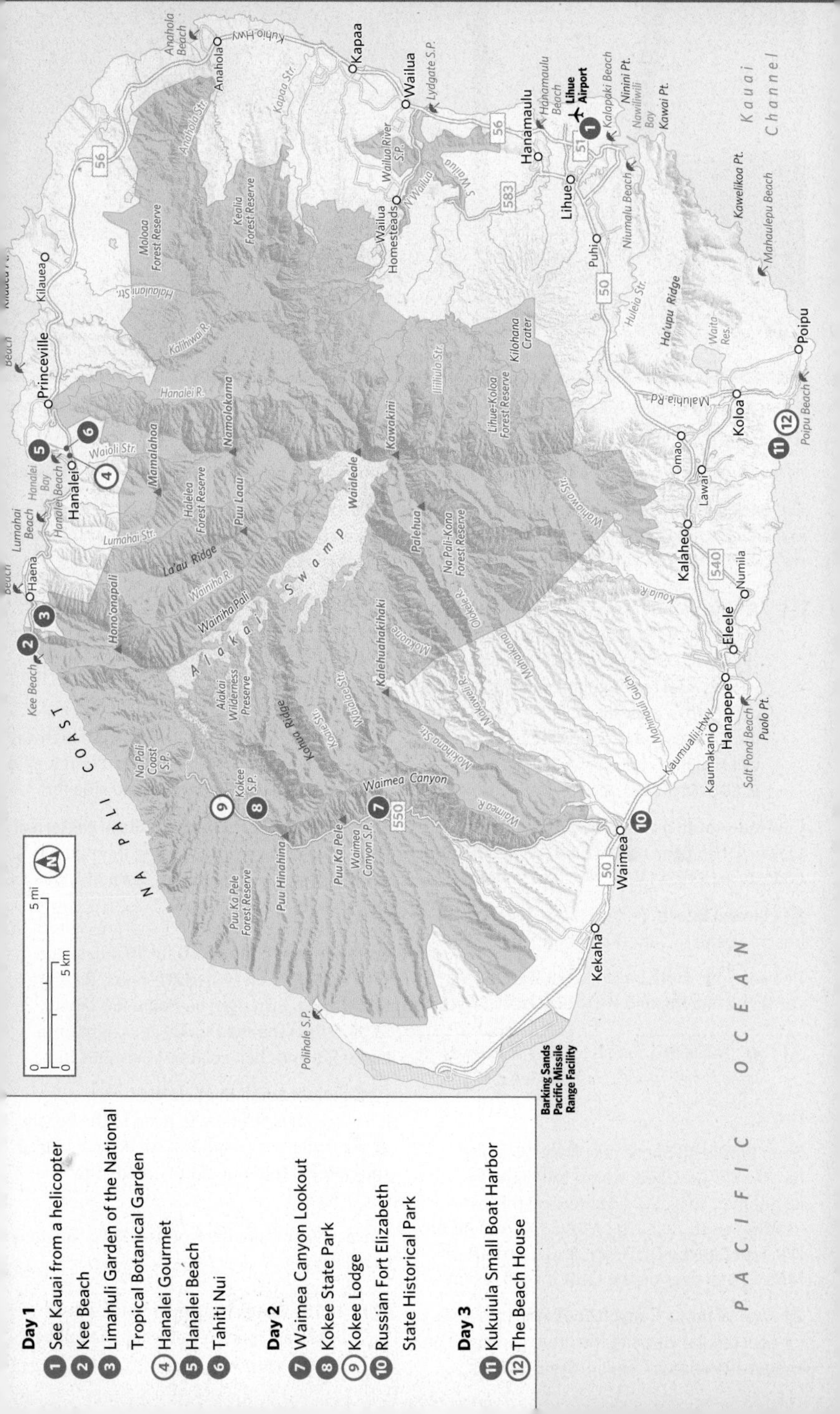
Day 1
1 See Kauai from a helicopter
2 Kee Beach
3 Limahuli Garden of the National Tropical Botanical Garden
4 Hanalei Gourmet
5 Hanalei Beach
6 Tahiti Nui
Day 2
7 Waimea Canyon Lookout
8 Kokee State Park
9 Kokee Lodge
10 Russian Fort Elizabeth State Historical Park
Day 3
11 Kukuiula Small Boat Harbor
12 The Beach House
0 5 mi
0 5 km
NA PALI COAST
PACIFIC OCEAN
Kauai Channel
Princeville
Kilauea
Anahola
Kapaa
Wailua
Hanamaulu
Lihue Airport
Lihue
Puhi
Poipu
Koloa
Omao
Lawai
Kalaheo
Numila
Eleele
Hanapepe
Kaumakani
Waimea
Kekaha
Hanalei
Haena
Kee Beach
Lumahai Beach
Hanalei Bay
Hanalei Beach
Anahola Beach
Lydgate S.P.
Wailua River S.P.
Wailua Homesteads
Kalapaki Beach
Ninini Pt.
Nawiliwili Bay
Kawai Pt.
Niumalu Beach
Kawelikoa Pt.
Mahaulepu Beach
Poipu Beach
Salt Pond Beach
Puolo Pt.
Polihale S.P.
Barking Sands Pacific Missile Range Facility
Moloaa Forest Reserve
Kealia Forest Reserve
Lihue-Koloa Forest Reserve
Kilohana Crater
Halelea Forest Reserve
Na Pali-Kona Forest Reserve
Puu Ka Pele Forest Reserve
Na Pali Coast S.P.
Alakai Wilderness Preserve
Kokee S.P.
Waimea Canyon S.P.
Waimea Canyon
Alakai Swamp
Waialeale
Kawaikini
Namolokama
Mamalahoa
Puu Laau
Hono'onapali
Wainiha Pali
La'au Ridge
Kohua Ridge
Ha'upu Ridge
Puu Hinahina
Puu Ka Pele
Kalehuahakihaki
Palehua
Kaumualii Hwy
Kuhio Hwy
Maluhia Rd
56
50
51
583
540
550

> THIS PAGE *Relaxing at Hanalei Beach.* OPPOSITE PAGE *Exploring the lush tropical beauty of Limahuli Garden.*

valley carved by a waterfall stream. See p 501, ⓮.

Get back on Hwy. 560 heading south to Hanalei, 7½ miles down the road. Look on the right side of the road for the old Hanalei School.

④ **Hanalei Gourmet.** Hanalei hipsters come to this former schoolhouse (built in 1926) to nosh on fresh grilled ahi sandwiches, roasted eggplant sandwiches, and other cross-cultural picks. Pick up a picnic lunch here, and head for the beach. In the Old Hanalei School, 5-5161 Kuhio Hwy. ☎ 808/826-2524. $$.

Continue south on Hwy. 560, and turn left (toward the ocean) on Aku Rd. When the road ends, turn right on Weke Rd. and park at:

❺ **Hanalei Beach.** Enjoy a picnic lunch at the beach. Spend the afternoon here. See p 502.

Retrace your route back to Aku Rd. On the corner of Aku Rd. and Hwy. 560 is:

⑥ **Tahiti Nui.** Finish the day with a *pau hana* (after-work) cocktail. See p 555.

Day 2

From the North Shore take Hwy. 56 south for 27 miles to Lihue, where the highway is renamed Hwy. 50. Continue on this road heading west. Just after MM 23, turn right on Waimea Canyon Dr. (Hwy. 550). Just after MM 10, pull over on the right for the lookout.

❼ ★★★ **Waimea Canyon Lookout.** Stop here for spectacular views of the great gaping gulch known as Waimea Canyon. See p 492, ❾.

Continue on Hwy. 550 another 6 miles to the:

❽ ★★★ kids **Kokee State Park.** Stretch your legs on the hiking trails that meander through this cool rainforest. See p 493, ⓫.

At the entrance to Kokee State Park, off Hwy. 550

⑨ **Kokee Lodge.** Stop for a warm drink and a quick snack at this quaint café in the state park. See p 548.

Take Hwy. 550 to Waimea. When the highway ends, turn left on Hwy. 50 and go about a mile down the road. Look on the ocean side for:

❿ kids **Russian Fort Elizabeth State Historical Park.** Spend some time walking through the ruins of this star-shaped fort. See p 491, ❹.

Day 3

Continue east on Hwy. 50 for 16 miles, and then turn right on Hwy. 530 (Koloa Rd.). At Koloa town, turn right on Poipu Rd. (Hwy. 520). When the road forks, veer right onto Lawai Rd. and then go about 1½ miles to:

⓫ **Kukuiula Small Boat Harbor.** After a day in the mountains, it's time to head to the beach again. If you like sailing and snorkeling, book a **sail-snorkel tour** out of the harbor. See "Sailing," p 522.

Retrace your route back on Lawai Rd. Go about ¾ mile to:

⑫ **The Beach House.** Stop for sunset drinks and pupu, or stay for a fabulous dinner. See p 535.

Kauai with Kids

The number-one rule for seeing Hawaii with kids is don't plan too much—especially with young children, who will be fighting jet lag, trying to get adjusted to a new bed, and possibly excited to the point of exhaustion. The 7-day itinerary below is a guide to various activities. Pick and choose the ones everyone in your family will enjoy.

> *The calm surf and soft sand of Kee Beach make a perfect play spot for the kids.*

START & FINISH Lihue.
TRIP LENGTH 7 days and 259 miles.

Day 1

❶ **Kee Beach State Park.** Take the gang to one of Kauai's most beautiful beaches. Don't forget the beach toys (fins, mask, snorkel) and plenty of sunscreen. See p 504.

Day 2

❷ **Helicopter Ride.** If the kids are old enough (at least 8), plan an early morning **helicopter tour,** so they can see the island from the air. See p 520.

From Lihue, drive north on Hwy. 56 to just beyond the town of Anahola, before MM 14.

③ **Duane's Ono-Char Burger.** Stop at this roadside burger stand for a thick milkshake, I'd recommend the marionberry ice cream shake for an exotic treat. See p 537.

Continue north on Hwy. 56 to just beyond MM 21, and turn right on Wailapa Rd. At the road's end, drive through the iron gates.

❹ ★★★ **Na Aina Kai Botanical Gardens.** Don't miss this magical garden, hidden off the beaten path of the North Shore. It's open

Day 1

1 Kee Beach

Day 2

2 Helicopter Ride
3 Duane's Ono-Char Burger
4 Na Aina Kai Botanical Gardens

Day 3

5 Waimea Canyon
6 Kokee State Park
7 Shrimp Station
8 Russian Fort Elizabeth State Historical Park

Day 4

9 Kukuiula Small Boat Harbor

Day 5

10 Kilauea Point National Wildlife Refuge

Day 6

11 Kauai Museum
12 Kalapaki Beach Hut
13 Kalapaki Beach

Day 7

14 Kilohana
15 Kauai Plantation Railway

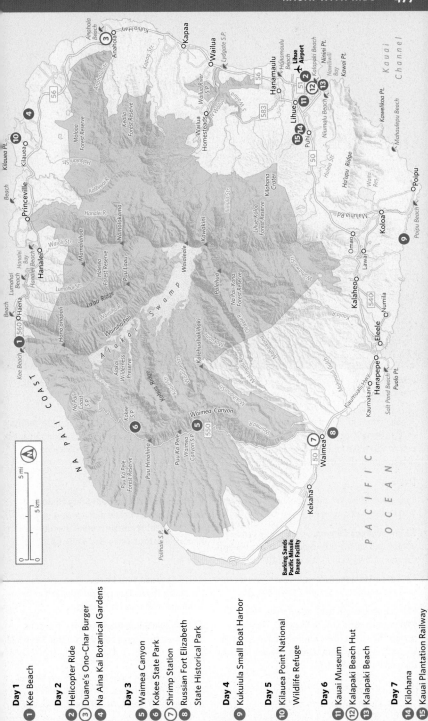

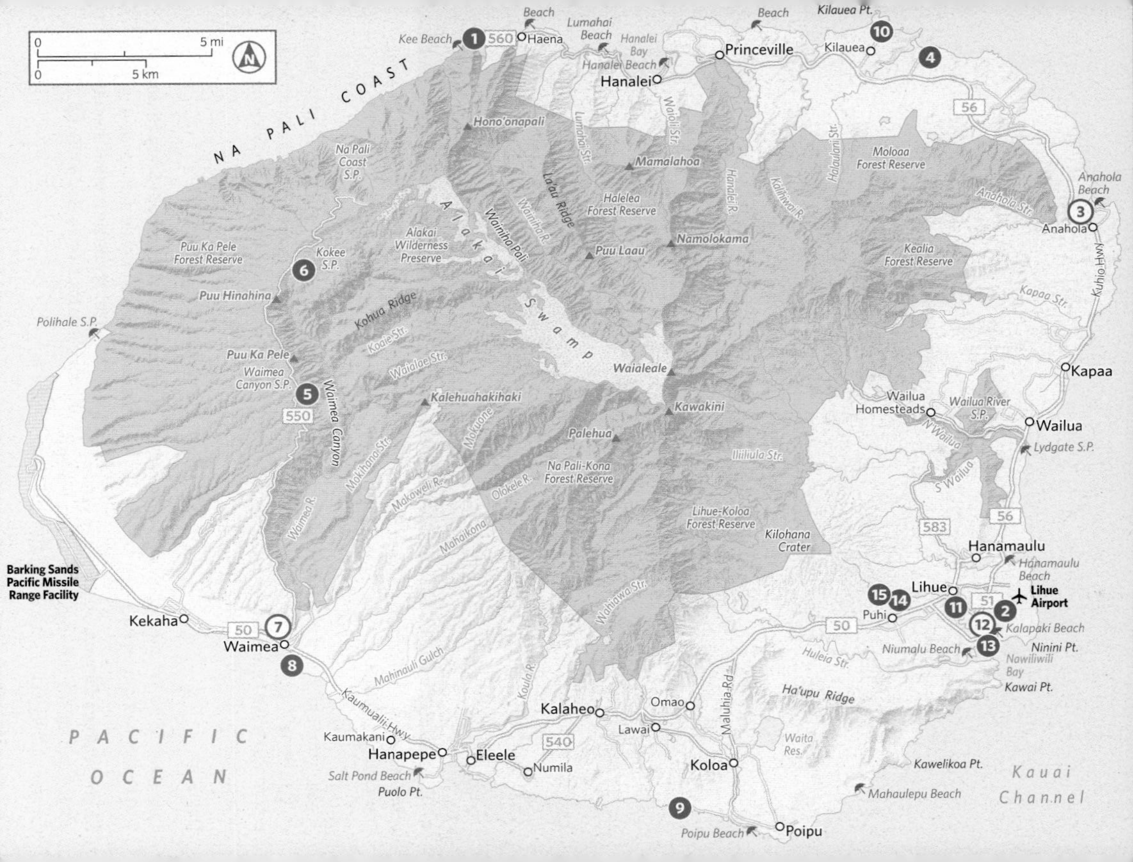

> *Bird-watching is a big draw to Kilauea Point National Wildlife Refuge, which is highlighted by the point's landmark lighthouse.*

Tuesday through Thursday by guided tour only. I strongly recommend reserving a spot before you leave for Hawaii to avoid being disappointed. ⏲ 2–4 hr. See p 498, ❶.

Day 3

Take Hwy. 50 to Waimea, then turn onto Hwy. 550 (Waimea Canyon Rd.).

❺ ★★ **Waimea Canyon.** Spend some time oohing and aahing over the views of the "Grand Canyon of the Pacific." See p 492, ❾.

❻ **Kokee State Park.** Stretch your legs and beat the heat in this cool rainforest. See p 493, ⓫.

Retrace your route back down Hwy. 550 (Waimea Canyon Dr.) to Hwy. 50. Nearly across the street from where Waimea Canyon Dr. ends is the Shrimp Station. Make a left and then an immediate right.

⑦ **Shrimp Station.** This roadside eatery is nothing more than a kitchen with a few picnic tables outside. But the shrimp cooking up inside will make up for the lack of ambience. 9652 Kaumualii Hwy. ☎ 808/338-1242. $$.

Continue east on Hwy. 50.

❽ **Russian Fort Elizabeth State Historical Park.** If a hike at Kokee didn't wear out your kids, let them scramble around the ruins of this historic fort for a while. See p 491, ❹.

Day 4

Kukuiula Small Boat Harbor is near Poipu, on the south shore. From Poipu Rd., turn onto Lawai Rd. and look for the signs.

❾ **Kukuiula Small Boat Harbor.** This is the best place to catch a sail-snorkel trip. See p 522.

Day 5

From Lihue, take Hwy. 50, which is renamed Hwy. 56, for 23 miles. Take the turnoff to Kilauea town, and turn left on Lighthouse Rd.

Follow it to the end of the road.

10 kids **Kilauea Point National Wildlife Refuge.** The 200 acres of ocean cliffs and open grassy slopes of an extinct volcano provide breeding grounds for native Hawaiian seabirds and the nene, the endangered Hawaiian goose. Kilauea Point offers the unique opportunity to view Hawaiian native birds like red-footed boobies, laysan albatrosses, wedge-tailed shearwaters, and other seabirds in their natural habitat. The National Marine Sanctuary waters surrounding the refuge are home to Hawaiian monk seals, green turtles, and, in winter, humpback whales. If your kids are old enough, join a guided hike, or just wander through the fairyland of the wilderness area. 2–3 hr. Kilauea Point Lighthouse, Kilauea ☎ 808/828-1413. www.fws.gov/kilaueapoint.

Retrace your steps down Lighthouse Rd. to Hwy. 56, and turn left to Lihue.

Day 6

11 ★ kids **Kauai Museum.** Get free admission to this museum on "Family Day," the first Saturday of every month. See p 484, 5.

Drive toward the ocean, past Eiwa St. At the intersection with Hwy. 51, continue straight on Hwy. 51 (which is Rice St.). Just after the entrance to the Kauai Marriott Resort & Beach, on the ocean side of the street, look for a large anchor in front of a two-story building.

---

(12) kids **Kalapaki Beach Hut.** Before you head to the beach, get a snack to carry along. This tiny burger hut is tricky to find but worth it for the bargain prices. See p 539.

13 **Kalapaki Beach.** Spend the rest of the day at one of Kauai's best beaches. See p 502.

Day 7

From Lihue, take Hwy. 50 west for 2 miles, past Puhi. On the mountain side of the highway look for:

14 kids ★★ **Kilohana.** While the Depression was raging in the rest of the U.S., sugar was king on Kauai, and sugar plantation owner Gaylord Parke Wilcox was incredibly wealthy. In 1935, Wilcox built a plantation home to show off his prosperity. Designed by British architect Mark Potter, the 16,000-square-foot Tudor-style mansion, costing $200,000 at the time (some $3–$5 million in today's dollars) is still recognized as the most prestigious home on the island. You can tour the incredible home today, free. Housed in the structure are Gaylord's Restaurant, which is in the original dining room, and several small shops featuring art galleries and specialty boutiques. The living room still has furniture from Wilcox's period and the same art on the walls. You can walk the manicured grounds by yourself, take a 20-minute **carriage ride** ($12 adults, $6 children 12 and under), or take a 1-hour historical **horse-drawn sugarcane tour** in an 18-passenger wagon pulled by Clydesdale horses ($29 adults, $15 children 12 and under). 2–4 hr. Hwy. 50, Lihue, HI 96766. ☎ 808/245-5608 for Kilohana, 808/246-9529 for carriage ride and horse-drawn sugarcane tour. www.kilohanakauai.com. Kilohana open Mon–Sat 9:30am–9:30pm, Sunday 9:30am–4:00pm. Carriage ride daily 11am–6pm. Sugarcane tour 11am Mon, Tues, and Thurs.

Next door to the Kilohana complex (on the west side):

15 ★ kids **Kauai Plantation Railway.** The first new railroad to be built in Hawaii in 100 years opened in 2007 after 5 years of work, 6,000 ties, 30,000 hand-driven spikes, and 480,000 pounds of iron rail. The Kauai Plantation Railway is part scenic tour, part cultural tour, part agricultural tour, part educational tour, and 100% fun for the family. The train, consisting of two refurbished diesel engines and four custom passenger cars, travels along a 3-mile figure-eight track through the grounds of Kilohana (see above). The 40-minute tour is narrated by very knowledgeable guides who not only weave in Kauai's history but also point out the more than 50 different crops that have been planted along the train route—everything from sugar, pineapple, and taro to fruit trees, fragrant plants (ginger, gardenia, plumeria), vegetable plants, and even hardwood trees (milo, koa). The train stops briefly at the "animal farm," where some pigs, goats, sheep, chickens, and cows are available for petting. 1 hr. Kilohana, 3-2087 Hwy. 50, Lihue ☎ 808/245-RAIL (245-7245). www.kauaiplantationrailway.com. Admission $18 adults, $14 children 3–12. 10am–2pm.

HAWAII'S POWERFUL PLANTATIONS

The Bittersweet Legacy of Sugar BY LINDA BARTH

COFFEE, PINEAPPLES, AND EVEN MACADAMIA NUTS are all grown on huge farms in Hawaii. But the biggest (and baddest) of them all were the once-dominant sugar plantations. Sugar was Hawaii's claim to fame long before the tourists arrived, with the first plantation opening in 1835. At one time, more than 240,000 acres of sugarcane were under cultivation. But just as quickly as sugar boomed, it went bust, the victim of cheaper labor and cheaper shipping costs elsewhere. In the late 1970s Hawaii produced nearly 1.2 billion tons of sugar; today it produces less than 200 million. Though most of the plantations are long gone, with fields of cane giving way to resorts and golf courses, their impact on Hawaiian culture should not be underestimated.

Plantation Life

Low wages. Abusive overseers. Poor conditions. For plantation workers, these things were all part of the job. The immigrant laborers who built sugar into Hawaii's primary industry were generally treated like indentured servants. They signed binding contracts that required they pay off the cost of their transportation to the islands and their living expenses. Their paltry wages (41¢ per day in 1841) were quickly eaten up by exorbitant rates charged by the company store. A song popular with sugar plantation laborers summed up their lot in life.

SURE A POOR MAN
(PUA MANA NO)
I labored on a sugar plantation
Growing sugarcane
My back ached, my sweat poured,
All for nothing.
I fell in debt at the plantation store.
I fell in debt at the plantation store.
And remained a poor man.

Sugar Shakes Things Up

For all of its geographic isolation, Hawaii's population is a rather astounding ethnic mix. That's thanks almost entirely to the sugar industry, which imported an estimated 337,000 workers from all over the world between the 1840s and the 1940s (native Hawaiian workers were scarce, and demanded higher pay). Smaller groups of workers from Puerto Rico and Germany joined with the masses arriving from China, Japan, and the Philippines (see chart to the right).

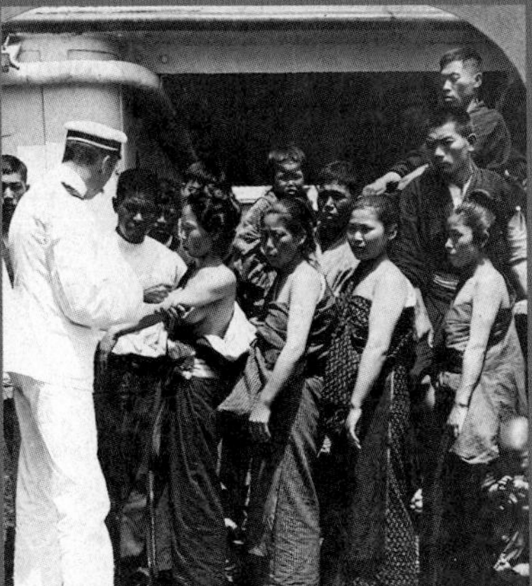

1852–1884	25,250 CHINESE ARRIVE
1878–1884	9,471 PORTUGUESE ARRIVE
1885–1924	200,000 JAPANESE ARRIVE
1903–1905	7,843 KOREANS ARRIVE
1906–1930	112,800 FILIPINOS ARRIVE
1907	2,250 SPANIARDS ARRIVE

Plantations & Politics

Many of Hawaii's first white families were missionaries who "came to do good and stayed to do well." Five prominent families (the Big Five) saw in sugar the potential for major profits, and they wasted no time in making sure their stranglehold on the industry was secure. From the beginning, the U.S. was the predominant beneficiary of all that sweetness. Just one problem: Hawaii was independent,

which meant there were trade tariffs to be paid. No matter—white businessmen simply banded together to push through "reforms" that gave them more and more power. Sanford Dole (pictured above), the son of missionaries, was an advisor to Queen Liliuokalani, but he was also interested in promoting the cause of his family's plantations. He helped lead the 1893 U.S. Marine-backed coup that overthrew the monarchy, then got himself named president of Hawaii from 1894 to 1900, and served as provisional governor after the U.S. annexed the islands.

Lihue & Environs

Most visitors first step foot on Kauai in Lihue, home of the airport. It is also the county (Kauai County is the island of Kauai) seat and was once where sugar planters lived and worked. It is still the major retail area. Spending a day in this small town gives you insight into the history of the island, from the ancient times when a mythological people called menehune once lived, to the days when sugar was king and trains carried the profitable crop across the island, to the modern Kauai today.

> *Housed in a beautiful Greco-Roman building, the Kauai Museum is a former library that displays impressive artifacts of Hawaii's history.*

START Lihue. **FINISH** Wailua. **TRIP LENGTH** 1 day and 10 miles.

From Lihue, take Hwy. 50 for 2 miles, past Puhi, on the mountain side of the highway.

❶ kids **Kilohana.** Tour this former plantation home via carriage ride or horse-drawn wagon around the grounds. See p 479, ⓮.

Next door to the Kilohana complex (on the west side):

❷ ★ kids **Kauai Plantation Railway.** Enjoy a scenic ride as you learn about Kauai's history. See p 479, ⓯.

Take Hwy. 50 east from Puhi toward Lihue. Turn right on Nawiliwili Rd., just past MM 1, before entering the town of Lihue. The Grove Farm Homestead Museum is about ½ mile down the road on the left.

❸ **Grove Farm Homestead Museum.** Be sure to reserve a tour before your visit here. This is Hawaii's best remaining example of a sugar plantation homestead. A visit here lets you experience a day in the life of an 1860s sugar planter and learn how good life was (for some, anyway) when sugar was king. Founded in 1864 by George N. Wilcox, a Hanalei missionary's

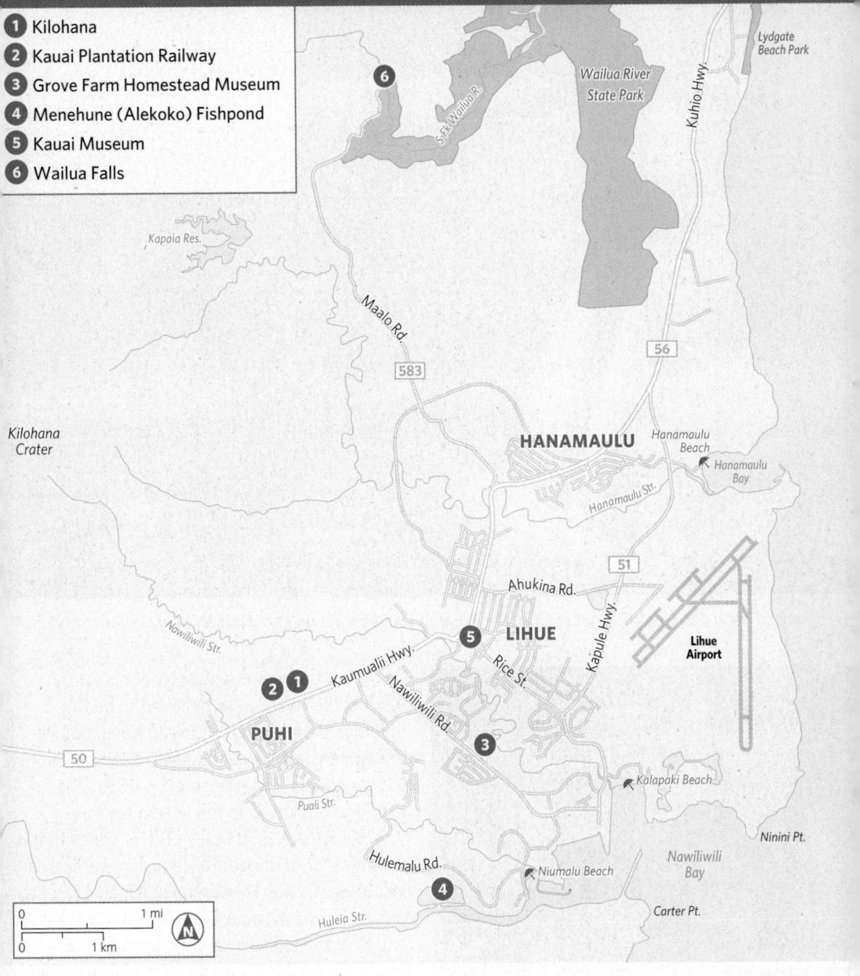

son, Grove Farm was one of the earliest of Hawaii's 86 sugar plantations. A self-made millionaire, Wilcox died a bachelor in 1933, at age 94. His estate looks much like it did when he lived here, complete with period furniture, plantation artifacts, and Hawaiiana. ⏱ 1 hr. **4050 Nawiliwili Rd. (Hwy. 58) at Pikaka St. (2 miles from Waapa Rd.), Lihue. ☎ 808/245-3202. www.hawaiiweb.com/kauai/html/sites/grove_farm_homestead.html. Requested donation $5 adults, $2 children under 12. Tours offered Mon, Wed, and Thurs at 10am and 1pm; reservations required.**

From Grove Farm turn right on Nawiliwili Rd. and right again on Niumalu Rd. When the road forks, veer to the right on to Hulemalu Rd. Up the hill is a lookout where you have a view of the pond, Huleia Stream, and Huleia National Wildlife Reserve.

❹ **Menehune (Alekoko) Fishpond.** Just outside Lihue and Nawiliwili Harbor, on the Huleia River, lies a mystery that still can't be explained. The pond, called Alekoko (rippling blood) and today known as the Menehune Fishpond, was an aquaculture feat built hundreds of years ago. The builders of this

> *You can get a good look at Wailua Falls from a parking lot about 4 miles outside Wailua.*

> *Tour Hawaii's best remaining example of its plantation past at Lihue's Grove Farm Homestead Museum.*

2,700-foot-long stone wall (that cuts off a bend in the river) were believed to be the mythical people who inhabited Kauai before the Polynesians arrived (see "Discovering the Legendary 'Little People,'" p 485). The fishpond is located in the Huleia National Wildlife Refuge, 238 acres of river valley that is a habitat for endangered Hawaiian water birds, including the aeo (Hawaiian stilt), alae Keokeo (Hawaiian coot), alae, ula (Hawaiian gallinule), and Koloa maoli (Hawaiian duck). Although you can see the fishpond and the refuge from the road, the area is not open to the public. Small boats, kayaks, jet skis, windsurfers, and water-skiers use the river. ⏱ **15 min. Halemalu Rd., Niumalu.**

Retrace your route back down Halemalu Rd. Turn right on Nawiliwili Rd. (Hwy. 58), which turns into Hwy. 51. At the intersection, turn left on Rice St. Just over a mile, on the corner of Rice and Eiwa sts., is:

5 ★ kids **Kauai Museum.** The history of Kauai is kept safe in an imposing Greco-Roman building that once served as the town library. This great little museum contains a wealth of historical artifacts and information tracing the island's history, from the beginning of time

Discovering the Legendary "Little People"

According to ancient Hawaiian legend, among Kauai's earliest settlers were the *menehune,* a race of small people who worked at night to accomplish magnificent feats. However, archaeologists say the *menehune* may not be legendary people but in fact non-Polynesian people who once lived on Kauai. These people, believed to be from the Marquesas Islands, arrived in Hawaii between A.D. 0 and 350. When the Polynesians ventured from Tahiti to Hawaii between A.D. 600 and 1100, they fought the *"menehune,"* who were already living in Hawaii. Some scholars claim the Polynesians were more aggressive and warlike than the Marquesans, and in a series of wars, the Tahitians drove the Marquesans north through the island chain to Kauai.

Anthropologists point out that the Tahitian word *manahune,* which means a lower class or a slave, was used to describe the racial hierarchy and not the physical stature of the people already living in Hawaii. In other words, *manahune* (or *menehune*) was used to mean small in the Tahitians' strict caste system, not small in size.

In any case, everyone agrees that these people performed incredible feats, especially the stonework that has stood for centuries. One example by these rock builders, who were able to construct elaborate edifices without using mortar, is the **Menehune Ditch** (Kiki a Ola), along the Waimea River (p 492, ❼). Only a 2-foot-high portion of the wall can be seen today; the rest of the marvelous stonework is buried under the roadbed. To get here from Hwy. 50, go inland on Menehune Road in Waimea; a plaque marks the spot about 1½ miles up.

Another example lies above Nawiliwili Harbor. The **Menehune Fishpond**—which at one time extended 25 miles—is said to have been built in just 1 night, with two rows of thousands of *menehune* passing stones hand to hand. According to legend, the *menehune* were promised that no one would watch them work, but one person did. When the *menehune* discovered the spy, they stopped working immediately, leaving two gaps in the wall. From Nawiliwili Harbor, take Hulemalu Road above Huleia Stream. Look for the Hawaii Convention and Visitors Bureau marker at a turnoff in the road, which leads to the legendary fishpond. Kayakers can paddle up Huleia Stream to see it up close.

through "contact" (when Capt. James Cook "discovered" Kauai in 1778), the monarchy period, the plantation era, and the present. You'll hear tales of the *menehune* (the mythical, elflike people who were said to build massive stoneworks in a single night) and see old poi pounders and idols, relics of sugar planters and *paniolo,* a nice seashell collection, old Hawaiian quilts, feather leis, a replica of a plantation worker's home, and much more—even a model of Cook's ship, the HMS *Resolution,* riding anchor in Waimea Bay. Vintage photographs by W. J. Senda, a Japanese immigrant, show old Kauai, while a contemporary video, shot from a helicopter, captures the island's natural beauty. **🕒 2 hr. 4428 Rice St., Lihue. ☎ 808/245-6931. www.kauaimuseum.org. Admission $10 adults, $8 seniors, $3 students 13–17, $1 children 6–12; free admission the first Sat of every month. Mon–Fri 9am–4pm, Sat 10am–4pm.**

From the Kauai Museum, turn right on Rice St., drive 2 blocks, and turn right on Hwy. 50 (heading north). About a mile down the road, turn left on Maalo Rd. (Hwy. 583). After 4 miles, look for the parking area for Wailua Falls on the right.

❻ Wailua Falls. This is the best place to see cascading waterfalls without a hike into the wilderness. The journey here, about a 4-mile drive outside of town, takes you through rolling hills past former sugarcane fields and across a valley, with majestic mountains in the background. From the Wailua Falls parking lot you can look down at two waterfalls cascading some 80 feet into a large pool. Legend claims that the *alii* (royalty) came to these waterfalls and dived from the cliff into the pool below to show the common people that monarchs were not mere men. Don't try this today. **🕒 20 min. Maalo Rd. (Hwy. 583), Wailua.**

Poipu Resort

No Hawaii resort has a better entrance: On Maluhia Road, eucalyptus trees planted in 1911 as a windbreak for sugarcane fields now form a monumental tree tunnel. The leafy green cool tunnel starts at Kaumualii Highway; you'll emerge at the golden-red beach. Our visit to the Koloa/Poipu/Lawai area takes a day and allows you to see an old plantation town, a natural phenomenon, an incredible botanical garden with a history, and one of Kauai's best beaches.

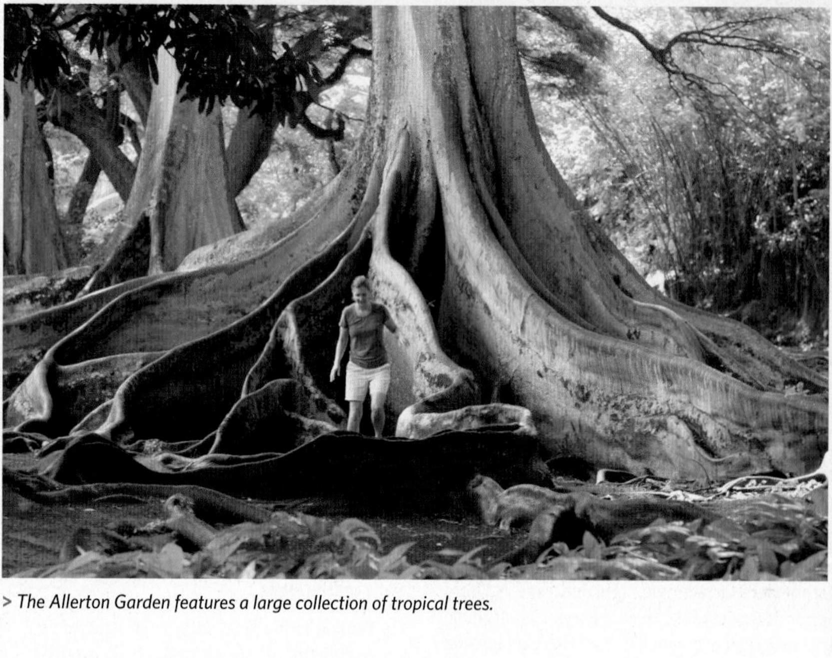

> *The Allerton Garden features a large collection of tropical trees.*

START Koloa. **END** Poipu Beach. **TRIP LENGTH** 1 day and 20 miles.

From Lihue take Hwy. 50 west. Just before MM 7, turn on Maluhia Rd. (Hwy. 520), which ends in Koloa town. Turn left on Koloa Town Rd., and park in the free parking lot.

❶ **Koloa Town.** This tiny old town of gaily painted sugar shacks just inland from Poipu Beach is where the Hawaiian sugar industry was born more than a century and a half ago. The mill is closed, but this showcase plantation town lives on as a tourist attraction, with delightful shops, an old general store, and a vintage Texaco gas station with a 1930s Model A truck in place, just like in the good old days. Walk the shops and check out the eateries. ⌚ 1–2 hr.

From Koloa Town Rd., turn left on Poipu Rd. (Hwy. 520). At the roundabout go about a quarter of the way around and continue on Poipu Rd. About ½ mile down the road on your left, turn into the Poipu Shopping Village.

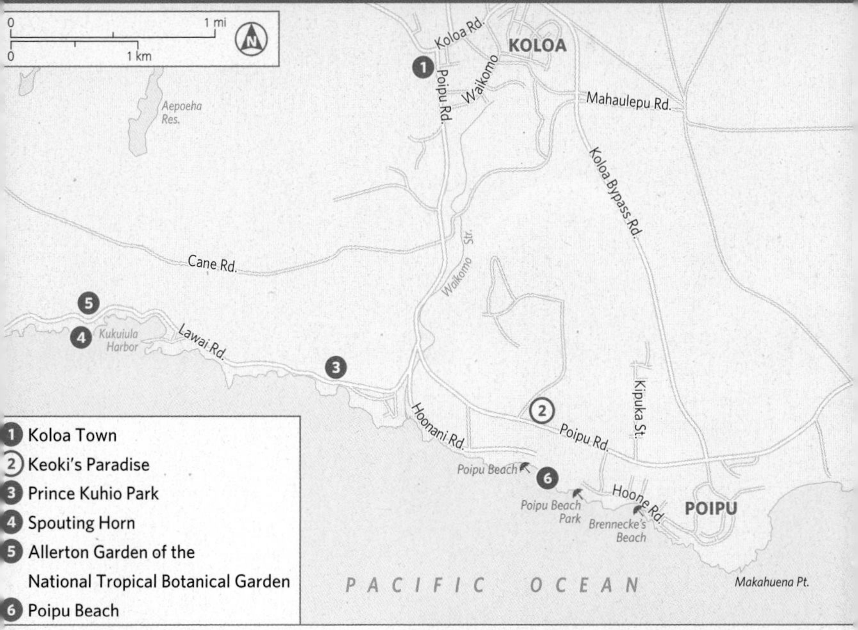

2) **Keoki's Paradise.** Grab a quick snack to either enjoy here in the tropical ambience or to take with you to your next stop at the park to eat outdoors. I recommend the Hula pie. **In Poipu Shopping Village, 2360 Kiahuna Plantation Dr. ☎ 808/742-7534. $$.**

etrace your steps to the roundabout, and go eft onto Lawai Rd. The park is on your right.

3 **Prince Kuhio Park.** This small roadside ark is the birthplace of Prince Jonah Kuhio alanianaole, the "People's Prince," whose Aarch 26th birthday is a holiday in Hawaii. He pened the beaches of Waikiki to the public in 918 and served as Hawaii's second territorial lelegate to the U.S. Congress. What remains ere are the foundations of the family home, royal fishpond, and a shrine where tributes re still paid in flowers. **20–30 min. Lawai Rd., oloa.**

ontinue down Lawai Rd. west to Kukulula ay. Look for the Hawaii Visitors Bureau sign ointing to:

4 ★ kids **Spouting Horn.** This natural henomenon is second only to Yellowstone's ld Faithful. It's quite a sight—big waves hit Kauai's south shore with enough force to send a spout of funneled saltwater 10 feet or more up in the air; in winter, the water can get as high as six stories. Spouting Horn is different from other blowholes in Hawaii in that an additional hole blows air that sounds like a loud moaning. According to Hawaiian legend, this coastline was once guarded by a giant female lizard (Mo'o); she gobbled up any intruders. One day, along came Liko, who wanted to fish in this area. Mo'o rushed out to eat Liko. Quickly, Liko threw a spear right into the giant lizard's mouth. Mo'o then chased Liko into a lava tube. Liko escaped, but legend says Mo'o is still in the tube, and the moaning at Spouting Horn is her cry for help. **30 min. At Kukulula Bay, beyond Prince Kuhio Park.**

Historic Koloa

The **Poipu Beach Resort Association** (☎ 808/742-7444; www.koloaheritagetrail.info) produces a free brochure for the **Koloa Heritage Trail,** which is a 10-mile walk, bike ride, or drive that has some 14 historical stops and markers describing the history and culture of this area.

> *The formal McBryde Garden features beautiful fountains and statues.*

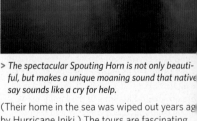

> *The spectacular Spouting Horn is not only beautiful, but makes a unique moaning sound that native say sounds like a cry for help.*

Across the street from Spouting Horn, on the mountain side, is access to the visitor center for:

5 ★ **Allerton Garden of the National Tropical Botanical Garden.** Discover an extraordinary collection of tropical fruit and spice trees, rare Hawaiian plants, and hundreds of varieties of flowers at the 186-acre preserve known as **Lawai Gardens,** said to be the largest collection of rare and endangered plants in the world. Adjacent **McBryde Garden,** a royal home site of Queen Emma in the 1860s, is known for its formal gardens, a delicious kind of colonial decadence. The garden contains fountains, streams, waterfalls, and European statuary. Endangered green sea turtles can be seen here. (Their home in the sea was wiped out years ag by Hurricane Iniki.) The tours are fascinating for green thumbs and novices alike. ⏱ 3–4 hr. Visitor center, Lawai Rd. (across the street from Spouting Horn), Poipu. ☎ 808/742-2623. www.ntbg.org. Allerton Garden admission and tour $4 adults, $20 children 10–12. Guided 2½-hr. tours by reservation only, Mon–Sat at 9am, 10am, 1pm, and 2pm. Self-guided tours of McBryde Garden Mon–Sat 9am–4pm; $20 adults, $10 children

> *Some of the hundreds of types of flowers that make the McBryde Garden such an eye-opening experience.*

5–12 (trams into the valley leave once an hour on the half-hour; last tram 2:30pm). Guided tour of McBryde Garden Sun 9am; $40 adults, $20 children 10–12. Reserve 1 week in advance in peak months of July–Sept.

Retrace your steps back down Lawai Rd. to the roundabout and go three-quarters of the way around to Poipu Rd., heading west (not heading back to Koloa Town). Continue a little over 1 mile to:

6 ★★★ **Poipu Beach.** On Kauai's sun-soaked south shore, this is a pleasant if sleepy resort destination of low-rise hotels set on gold-sand pocket beaches. ⏱ 2 hr. See p 505.

Touring Off the Beaten Path

Get off the beaten path and see the "hidden" Kauai with ★ **Four-Wheel-Drive Backroad Adventure,** 1702 Haleukana St., Lihue, HI 96766 (☎ 800/452-1113 or 808/245-8809; www.alohakauaitours.com). The half-day tour follows a figure-eight path around Kauai, from Kilohana Crater to the Mahaulepu coastline. The tour, done in a four-wheel-drive van, not only stops at Kauai's well-known scenic spots but also travels on sugarcane roads (on private property), taking you to places most people who live on Kauai have never seen. The guides are well versed in everything from native plants to Hawaiian history. Don't forget your camera. The tour costs $70 adults, $50 children 5 to 12. Reservations required.

Western Kauai

This region, west of Poipu, is more remote than its eastern neighbor and lacks its terrific beaches. But it's home to one of Hawaii's most spectacular natural wonders, Waimea Canyon, and one of its best parks, Kokee State Park.

> *The 1-mile wide and 12-mile long Waimea Canyon is a stunning natural formation that's often compared to the Grand Canyon.*

START Hanapepe. **FINISH** Kokee State Park. **TRIP LENGTH** 1 day and 80 miles.

❶ **Hanapepe.** For a quick trip back in time, turn off Hwy. 50 at Hanapepe, once one of Kauai's biggest towns. Founded by Chinese rice farmers, it's so picturesque that it was used as a backdrop for the miniseries *The Thornbirds.* Hanapepe makes a good rest stop on the way to or from Waimea Canyon. It has galleries selling antiques as well as local arts and crafts.

Wander down Hanapepe Rd. At the town's main parking lot look for the sign pointing to the Swinging Bridge.

❷ **Hanapepe Swinging Bridge.** While you're visiting Hanapepe be sure to walk across the suspended old wooden footbridge. Originally built in 1911 and renovated after Hurricane Iniki in 1992, this bridge is a thoroughfare for people living on the other side of the Hanapepe River. The bridge swings, sways, and swoops as you cross from one side to the other. If people are crossing in different directions it becomes a Disneyland-like ride as it bucks and bounces over the swirling muddy water of the river below. ⏱ **20 min. Hanapepe Rd., Hanapepe.**

From Hanapepe Rd., take Hwy. 540 west. Just outside of town after MM 17, turn left toward the ocean on Lolokai Rd. (also known as Salt Pond Rd.).

❸ ★ **Salt Pond Beach Park.** Here you'll find Hawaii's only salt ponds still in production and an excellent place to swim, windsurf, and fish. ⏱ 2 hr. See p 506.

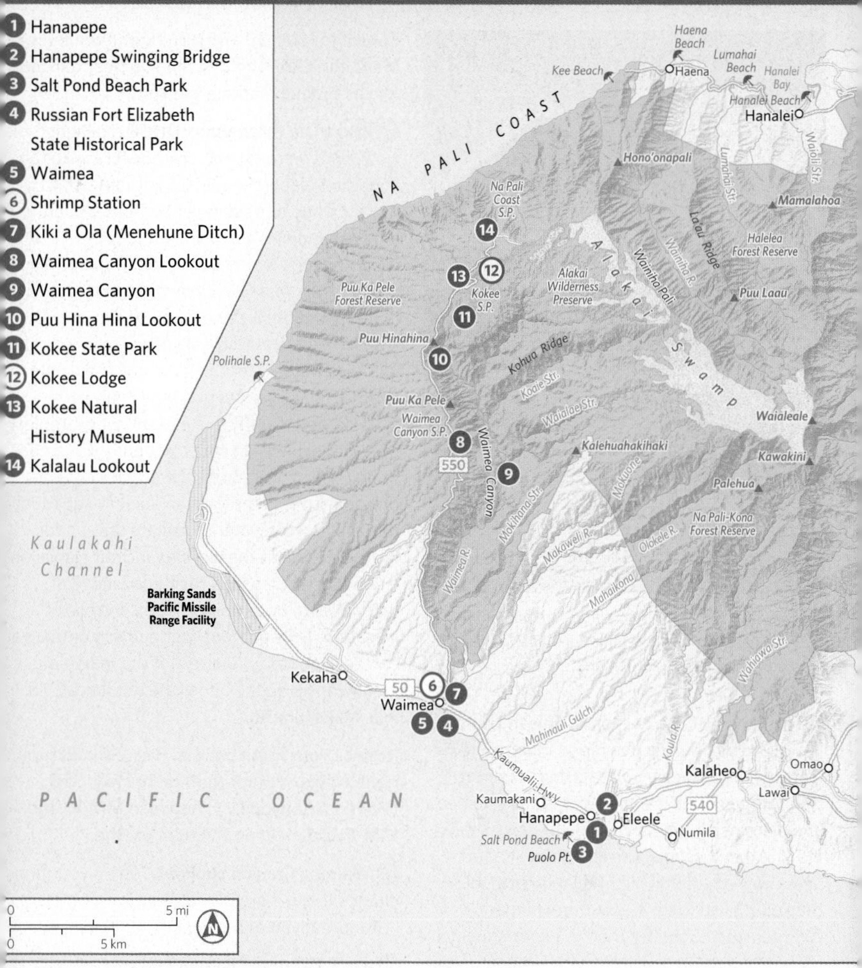

Retrace your route back to Hwy. 540 and turn left. After about 5 miles, just after MM 22 on your left, is:

4 **Russian Fort Elizabeth State Historical Park.** Add the Russians to the list of those who tried to conquer Hawaii. In 1815, a German doctor tried to claim Kauai for Russia. He even supervised the construction of a fort in Waimea, but he and his handful of Russian companions were expelled by Kamehameha I a couple of years later. Now a state historic landmark, the Russian Fort Elizabeth (named for the wife of Russia's Czar Alexander I) is on the eastern headlands overlooking the harbor, across from Lucy Kapahu Aukai Wright Beach Park. The fort, built Hawaiian-style with stacked lava rocks in the shape of a star, once bristled with cannons; it's now mostly in ruins. You can take a free, self-guided tour of the site. It affords a keen view of the west bank of the Waimea River, where Capt. Cook landed, and of the island of Niihau across the channel. ⏱ 30 **min. Hwy. 50 (on the ocean side, just after MM 22), east of Waimea.**

Return to Hwy. 50 and turn left at MM 23. Stop at the library for a map.

5 **Waimea.** Stop at the Waimea Library to get a free map for a self-guided tour of this historic town. This little coastal town, the original capital of Kauai, seems to have quit the march of time. Dogs sleep in the street while

> *The pretty 19th-century architecture and abundance of churches are reminders that Waimea was an early missionary settlement.*

old pickups rust in front yards. The ambience is definitely laid-back. On his search for the Northwest Passage in 1778, British explorer Capt. James Cook dropped anchor at Waimea and discovered a sleepy village of grass shacks. In 1815, the Russians arrived and built a fort here (now a national historic landmark), but they didn't last long: A scoundrel named George Anton Scheffer tried to claim Kauai for Russia, but he was exposed as an impostor and expelled by Kauai's high-ranking *alii,* Kaumualii. Today even Waimea's historic relics are spare and simple: a statue of Cook alongside a bas-relief of his ships, the rubble foundation of the Russian fort, and the remains of an ancient aqueduct unlike any other in the Pacific. Except for an overabundance of churches for a town this size, there's no sign that Waimea was selected as the first landing site of missionaries in 1820. ⏱ 1 hr. Hwy. 50 at MM 23.

From the Library turn right on Hwy. 50. Just a few blocks down the road is:

⑥ **Shrimp Station.** Stop by this roadside cafe and grab some shrimp for a picnic lunch in Waimea Canyon. See p 478, ⑦.

Return to Hwy. 50 and turn right, then left on Menehune Rd. About ½ mile up this road look for the plaque marking the spot.

7 Kiki a Ola (Menehune Ditch). Ancient Hawaiians were expert rock builders, able to construct elaborate edifices without using mortar. They formed long lines and passed stones hand over hand and lifted rocks weighing tons with ropes made from native plants. Their feats gave rise to fantastic tales of *menehune,* elflike people hired by Hawaiian kings to create massive stoneworks in a single night—reputedly for the payment of a single shrimp. (See "Discovering the Legendary 'Little People,'" p 485.) An excellent example of ancient Hawaiian construction is Kiki a Ola, the so-called Menehune Ditch, with cut and dressed stones that form an ancient aqueduct that still directs water to irrigate taro ponds. Historians credit the work to ancient Hawaiian engineers who applied their knowledge of hydraulics to accomplish flood control and irrigation. Only a 2-foot-high portion of the wall can be seen today; the rest of the marvelous stonework is buried under the roadbed. ⏱ 15 min. Menehune Rd.

Retrace your route back to Hwy. 50 and turn right. Make another right on to Hwy. 550 (Waimea Canyon Dr.). Between MM 10 and MM 11, pull over on the right for the:

8 Waimea Canyon Lookout. Here's your first chance to get a great bird's-eye view of the "Grand Canyon of the Pacific." ⏱ 10 min.

9 ★★★ Waimea Canyon. The great gaping gulch known as Waimea Canyon is quite a sight. This valley, known for its reddish lava beds, reminds everyone who sees it of the Grand Canyon. Kauai's version is bursting with ever-changing color, just like its namesake, but it's smaller—only 1 mile wide, 3,567 feet deep, and 12 miles long. A massive earthquake sent a number of streams into the single river that ultimately carved this picturesque canyon. Today the Waimea River—a silver thread of water in the gorge that's sometimes a trickle, often a torrent, but always there—keeps cuttin the canyon deeper and wider, and nobody can say what the result will be 100 million years from now. You can stop by the road and look at the canyon, hike down into it, or swoop throug

The view from Kalalau Lookout at sunset.

t in a helicopter. For more information, see Hiking & Camping," p 508, and "Helicopter Rides," p 520. 1–2 hr. Waimea Canyon Dr. Hwy. 550), Waimea town.

Continue on Waimea Canyon Dr. (Hwy. 550); between MM 13 and MM 14, pull over for:

10 **Puu Hina Hina Lookout.** You are now at 3,336 feet; be sure to pull over and spend a few minutes enjoying more fantastic views of the canyon. The giant white object that looks like a golf ball and defaces the natural landscape is a radar station left over from the Cold War. 10 min.

Continue on Waimea Canyon Dr. (Hwy. 550) for about 3 more miles to the entrance to:

11 ★★★ kids **Kokee State Park.** It's only 16 miles rom Waimea to Kokee, but the 4,345 acres of rainforest here feel like a whole different world. You'll enter a new climate zone, where the breeze has a bite and trees look quite ontinental. You're in a cloud forest on the dge of the Alakai Swamp, the largest swamp n Hawaii, on the summit plateau of Kauai. Days are cool and wet, with intermittent bright unshine, not unlike Seattle on a good day. Bring your sweater and, if you're staying over, be sure you know how to light a fire—overnight ows dip into the 40s (single digits Celsius). The forest is full of native plants, such as mokihana berry, ohia lehua, and iliau (similar o Maui's silversword), as well as imports ke Australia's eucalyptus and California's edwood. Pigs, goats, and black-tailed deer thrive in the forest, but the moa, or Polynesian jungle fowl, is the cock of the walk. 2–3 hr. Hwy. 550.

---

12 **Kokee Lodge.** If you've worked up an appetite, you can stop for a snack here. See p 548.

13 ★ **Kokee Natural History Museum.** This is the best place to learn about the forest and Alakai Swamp before you set off hiking in the wild. The museum shop has great trail information and local books and maps, including the official park trail map. We recommend getting the *Pocket Guide on Native Plants on the Nature Trail for Kokee State Park* and the *Road Guide to Kokee and Waimea Canyon State Park*. Take the **nature walk**—it's the best introduction to this rainforest. It starts behind the museum at the rare Hawaiian koa tree. This easy, self-guided walk of about a quarter mile takes about 20 minutes if you stop and look at all the plants identified along the way. 30 min. Hwy. 550, Kokee. ☎ 808/335-9975; www.kokee.org. Daily 10am–4pm (free admission).

Continue on Hwy. 550 for 2 miles.

14 ★ **Kalalau Lookout.** The spectacular climax of your drive through Waimea Canyon and Kokee is this lookout. When you stand at the lookout, below you is a work in progress that began at least five million years ago. It's hard to stop looking; the view is breathtaking, especially when light and cloud shadows play across the red-and-orange cliffs. 30 min. End of Hwy. 550, Kokee.

The Coconut Coast

The eastern shore of Kauai north of Lihue is a jumble of commerce and condos strung along the coast road named for Prince Kuhio, with several small beaches beyond. Almost anything you need, and a lot of stuff you can live without, can be found along this coast, which is known for its hundreds of coconut trees waving in the breeze. It's popular with budget travelers because of the myriad B&Bs and affordable hotels and condos to choose from, and it offers great restaurants and the island's major shopping areas. It also offers a great look back in history, spectacular waterfalls, a fern grotto, and even a wonderful legend about a giant who fell asleep.

> *A 20-mile river fed by Mount Waialeale flows over the spectacular Opaekaa Falls in Wailua River State Park*

START Wailua. **FINISH** Kapaa.
TRIP LENGTH 1 day and 6 miles.

To get to the Wailua Marina, which is located where the Wailua River dumps into the ocean, take Hwy. 56 into Wailua River State Park, about ¾ mile after MM 5.

1 ★ kids **Fern Grotto.** This is one of Kauai's oldest (since 1946) and most popular tourist attractions. Smith's operates a 157-passenger motorized barge that takes people up- and down-river on a 1 hour and 20 minute cruise, with a hula show on the return trip. At the Fern Grotto landing, you get off the boat and

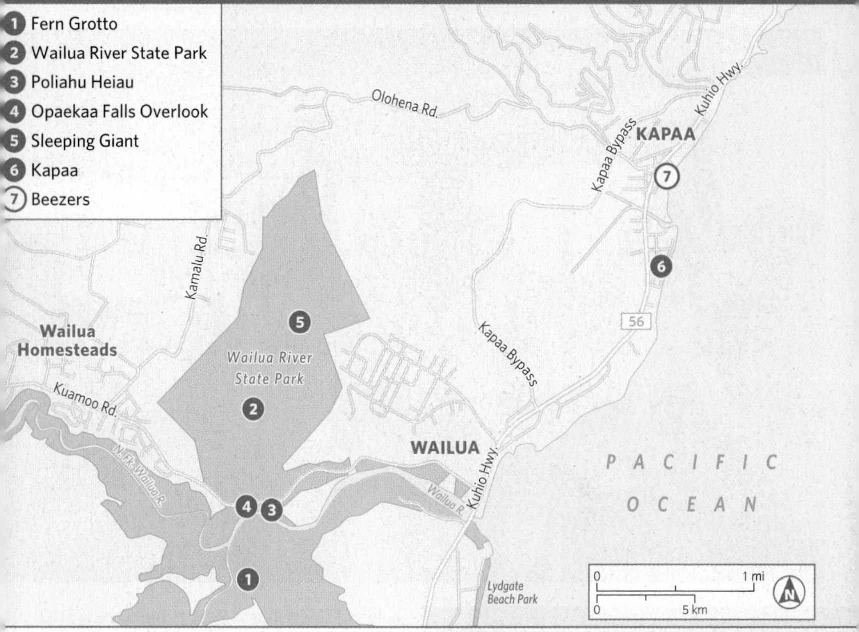

walk through the rainforest to the lush Fern Grotto, the source of many Hawaiian legends and a popular site for weddings. ⏱ 1 hr. **Contact Smith's Motor Boats for tours. ☎ 808/821-6892. www.smithskauai.com. Reservations recommended. Admission $10 adults, $10 children 2-12 (book on their website for a discount). Daily 9am-3:30pm.**

2 ★ kids **Wailua River State Park.** Ancients called the Wailua River "the river of the great sacred spirit." Seven temples once stood along this 20-mile river, which is fed by 5,148-foot Mount Waialeale, the wettest spot on earth. You can go up Hawaii's biggest navigable river by boat or kayak (see p 524), or drive Kuamoo Road (Hwy. 580, sometimes called the King's Highway), which goes inland along the north side of the river from Kuhio Highway (Hwy. 56)—from the northbound lane, turn left at the stoplight just before the ruins of Coco Palms Resort. Kuamoo Road goes past the *heiau* (temple) and historical sites to Opaekaa Falls and Keahua Arboretum, a State Division of Forestry attempt to reforest the watershed with native plants. ⏱ 1–2 hr.

From the Wailua River State Park go back to Hwy. 56 and turn left. From the northbound lane, turn left at the stoplight just before the

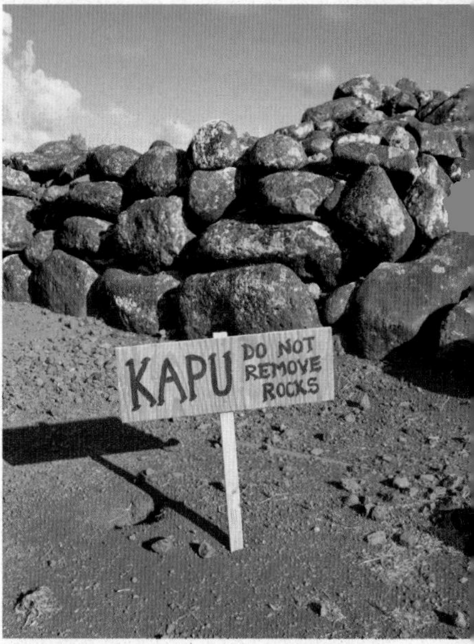

> *Poliahu* Heiau*, the remains of a temple still considered sacred by Hawaiians. Please observe the "KAPU" (forbidden) sign, and don't climb on or take any rocks.*

> ABOVE *Enjoy an entertaining 80-minute cruise upriver to beautiful Fern Grotto, a popular wedding location.* BELOW *A sample of the Grotto's beautiful floral vegatation.*

ruins of Coco Palms Resort onto Hwy. 580 (Kuamoo Rd.), which goes past the *heiau* (temple).

3 **Poliahu *Heiau.*** The large lava rock temple of Kauai's last king, Kaumualii, who died on Oahu in 1824 after being abducted by King Kamehameha II. If you stop here, you'll notice two signs. The first, an official 1928 bronze territorial plaque, says that the royal *heiau* was built by *menehune,* who it explains parenthetically are "Hawaiian dwarves or brownies." A more recent, hand-painted sign warns visitors not to climb on the rocks, which are sacred to the Hawaiian people. ⏱ **15 min.** Hwy. 580 (Kuamoo Rd.).

Continue on Hwy. 580. Within a few hundred feet is the turnoff for:

4 ★★ **Opaekaa Falls Overlook.** Stop and get a good look at this 40-foot waterfall, probably the best-looking drive-up waterfall on Kauai. With the scenic peaks of the Makaleha Mountains in the background and a restored Hawaiian village on the riverbanks, these falls are what the tourist bureau folks call an "eye-popping" photo op. ⏱ **10 min.**

5 **Sleeping Giant.** While you are at the overlook, focus on the mountains in the background. If you squint your eyes just so as you pass the 1,241-foot-high Nounou

Make a Pilgrimage to a Hindu Temple

Believe it or not, a sacred Hindu temple is being carved out of rocks from India on the banks of the Wailua River. The **San Marga Iraivan Temple** is being built to last "a thousand years or more," on the 458-acre site of the Saiva Siddhanta Church monastery. Expected to be completed in 2010, the Chola-style temple is the result of a vision by the late Satguru Sivaya Subramuniyaswami, known to his followers as Gurudeva, the founder of the church and its monastery. He specifically selected this site in 1970, recognizing that the Hawaiians also felt the spiritual power of this place. The Hawaiians called it *pihanakalani,* "where heaven touches the earth."

The granite for the temple is being hand-quarried by some 70 stonemasons in India and then shipped to Kauai for final shaping and fitting on the site. The center of the temple will hold a 700-pound crystal, known as the Sivalingam, now displayed at the monastery's smaller temple on the grounds.

Hindu pilgrims come from around the globe to study and meditate at the monastery. The public is welcome to the monastery temple, open daily from 9am to noon. There also is a weekly guided tour of the grounds that includes the San Marga Iraivan Temple. The weekly tour time varies; for information, call ☎ 808/822-3012, ext. 198, or go to www.himalayanacademy.com.

A few suggestions if you plan to visit: Carry an umbrella (it's very rainy here), and wear modest clothing (no shorts, short dresses, T-shirts, or tank tops). Also, even though this is a monastery, there are lots of people around, so don't leave valuables in your car.

To get there, turn mauka (left, inland) off Kuhio Highway (Hwy. 56) at the lights, just after crossing the bridge, onto Kuamoo Road (btw. Coco Palms Hotel and the Wailua River). Continue up the hill, for just over 4 miles. A quarter mile past the 4-mile marker, turn left on Kaholalele Road and go 1 block to the end of the road. The information center is at 107 Kaholalele. Park on Temple Lane.

The entire district from the river mouth to the summit of Waialeale was once royal land. This sacred, historical site was believed to have been founded by Puna, a Tahitian priest who, according to legend, arrived in one of the first double-hulled voyaging canoes to come to Hawaii, established a beachhead, and declared Kauai his kingdom. All of Kauai's *alii* (royalty) are believed to be descended from Puna. Here, in this royal settlement, are the remains of seven temples, including a sacrificial *heiau,* a planetarium (a simple array of rocks in a celestial pattern), the royal birthing stones, and a stone bell once used to announce a royal birth. (You can still ring the bell.)

.idge, which makes a dramatic backdrop for he coastal villages of Wailua and Waipouli, ou can see the fabled Sleeping Giant, the :gendary giant named Puni who, as the story oes, fell asleep after a great feast. If you don't ee him at first, visualize him this way: His head ; Wailua and his feet are Kapaa. For details n a hike to the top of the Sleeping Giant, see 512.

etrace your route back down Hwy. 580 and urn left onto Hwy. 56 for a couple of miles. ust past MM 8, you enter the town of:

Kapaa. The center of commerce on the ast coast and the capital of the Coconut oast condo-and-hotel district, this restored plantation town looks just like an antique. False-fronted wooden stores line both sides of the highway; it looks as though they've been here forever—until you notice the fresh paint and new roofs and realize that everything has been rebuilt since Hurricane Iniki smacked the town flat in 1992. Kapaa has made an amazing comeback without losing its funky charm. A great place to eat and shop.

In the middle of Kapaa, on Hwy. 56, on the ocean side of the street.

⑦ ★ kids **Beezers.** Stop at this old-fashioned soda fountain for a soda, shake, malt, or banana split. **Kapaa Trade Center, 1380 Kuhio Hwy. ☎ 808/822-4411. $.**

The North Shore

Kauai's North Shore may be the most beautiful place in Hawaii.

Exotic seabirds, a half-moon bay, jagged peaks soaring into the clouds, and a mighty wilderness lie around the bend from the Coconut Coast. The drive along Kuhio Highway (Hwy. 56, which becomes Hwy. 560 after Princeville to the end of the road) displays Kauai's grandeur at its absolute best. Just before Kilauea, the air and the sea change, the light falls in a different way, and the last signs of development are behind you, giving way to roadside fruit stands, a little stone church in Kilauea, two roadside waterfalls, and a long stiltlike bridge over the Kalihiwai Stream and its green river valley.

> *The towering craggy knoll of Ka Ulu O Laka* Heiau, *far above Kee Beach, features a rocky altar dedicated to the goddess of hula.*

START Kailua. **FINISH** Kee Beach.
TRIP LENGTH 1 day and 25 miles.

From Kapaa continue north on Hwy. 56 past MM 21, and turn right on Wailapa Rd. At the road's end, drive through the iron gates.

1 ★★★ kids **Na Aina Kai Botanical Gardens.** Do not miss this magical garden on some 240 acres sprinkled with about 70 life-size (some larger than life-size) whimsical bronze statues. These gardens have everything: waterfalls, pools, arbors, topiaries, colonnades, gazebos, a maze you will never forget, a lagoon with spouting fountains, a Japanese teahouse, and an enchanting path along a bubbling stream to the ocean. A host of different tours is available, from 1½ hours ($25) to 5 hours ($70) long, ranging from casual, guided strolls, to a ride in the covered CarTram, to treks from one end of the gardens to the ocean. A tropical children's

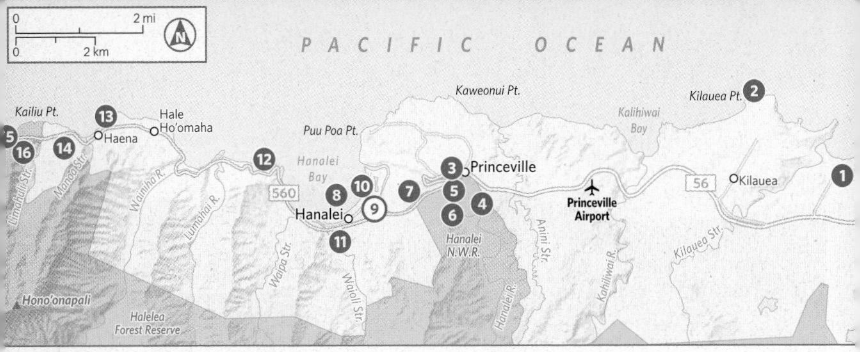

1. Na Ana Kai Botanical Gardens
2. Kilauea Point National Wildlife Refuge
3. Hanalei Valley Lookout
4. Hanalei National Wildlife Refuge
5. Hanalei Bridge
6. Haraguchi Rice Mill
7. Hanalei Buffalo Ranch
8. Hanalei
9. Tropical Taco
10. Hanalei Beach Park
11. Waioli Mission House Museum
12. Lumahai Beach
13. Haena Beach Park
14. Limahuli Garden of the National Tropical Botanical Garden
15. Ka Ulu O Laka Heiau
16. The End of the Road

garden features a gecko hedge maze, a tropical jungle gym, a treehouse in a rubber tree, and a 16-foot-tall Jack and the Bean Stalk Giant. Na Aina Kai is open only 3 days a week; book a tour before you leave for Hawaii to avoid being disappointed. ⏱ 1½ hr. 4101 Wailapa Rd., Kilauea, HI 96754. ☎ 808/828-0525. www.naainakai.com. Open Tues–Thurs 8am–5pm. Tours vary. Advance reservations strongly recommended.

Take Hwy. 56 to the town of Kilauea. Turn left at Kilauea Rd. (also known as Lighthouse Rd.), and follow it to the end.

2 kids **Kilauea Point National Wildlife Refuge.** You'll have a good chance at seeing an endangered nene here, as well as other birds native to Hawaii. See p 478, 10.

Return to Hwy. 56, turn right, and continue north. After Princeville the highway is renamed Hwy. 560. Just past the Princeville Shopping Center is:

3 **Hanalei Valley Lookout.** Peer over the edge into the 917-acre Hanalei River Valley and admire all the shades of green: Green rice, green taro, and green streams lace a patchwork of green ponds that back up to green-velvet Bali Hai cliffs. Don't be put off by the crowds; this is worth a stop. ⏱ 10 min.

4 **Hanalei National Wildlife Refuge.** From the Hanalei Valley Lookout you also see this wildlife refuge, a 917-acre refuge established

> *Waterfalls, Japanese teahouses, statues, and a beautiful path to the ocean make Na Aina Kai Botanical Gardens a can't-miss destination.*

> *Get an utterly emerald view from the Hanalei Valley Lookout: green streams, fields, ponds, and the Bali Hai cliffs.*

in 1972 to provide nesting and feeding habitat for endangered Hawaiian water birds, including the Hawaiian duck (koloa maoli), coot (alae keokeo), moorhen (alae ula), and stilt (aeo). In order to protect the endangered species, most of the Hanalei refuge is closed to the public.

From the overlook go back to Hwy. 560 and turn left to the:

5 **Hanalei Bridge.** This Pratt truss steel bridge, pre-fabbed in New York City, was erected in 1912; it's now on the National Registry of Historic Landmarks. If it ever goes out, the nature of Hanalei will change forever; currently, this rusty, one-lane bridge isn't big enough for a tour bus to cross.

6 **Haraguchi Rice Mill.** On the other side of the bridge is Hawaii's only remaining rice mill. Tucked away on a working wetland taro farm on Kauai's dramatically scenic North Shore, the Haraguchi Rice Mill (which is listed on the National Register of Historic Places) is found within a National Wildlife Refuge. Learn about Hawaii's agricultural and cultural history, view endangered native waterbirds, and explore the cultivation and uses of taro, a traditional Polynesian food source. Then enjoy a complimentary picnic lunch featuring unique items prepared with taro grown on the very farm you visit. Tours are given only on Wednesdays, at 9am. ⏲ 2–3 hr. Because of limited parking, the tours meet at the Haraguchi Rice Mill Kiosk, on Hwy. 560, in Hanalei (in front of Kayak Kauai and next to Hanalei Taro and Juice Co., near the entrance to Hanalei town). Park in the area behind the Rice Mill Kiosk. www.haraguchiricemill.org. Tours $65, including lunch. Tours Wed 9am only. ☎ 808/651-3399.

7 **Hanalei Buffalo Ranch.** If you drive slowly along the Hanalei River you may spot the 200 American bison that roam the riverbanks in the tropical sun. You may even see buffalo grazing in the pastures on your right.

Continue on Hwy. 560 north to the town of Hanalei:

8 ★★★ **Hanalei.** Picture-postcard Hanalei is the laid-back center of North Shore life and an escapist's dream; it's also the gateway to the wild Na Pali Coast. Hanalei is the last great place on Kauai yet to face the developer's blade of progress. On either side of two-lane Kuhio Highway, you'll find just enough shops and restaurants to sustain you for a week's visit.

ut if you're a hiker, surfer, or sailor, Hanalei's atural splendor might just keep you here the est of your life.

---

9) ★ kids **Tropical Taco.** A local institution: Owner Roger Kennedy has been serving up tasty tacos and burritos in Hanalei for more than a quarter of a century. See p 542.

ontinue on Hwy. 560, turn right on Aku Rd. efore Ching Young Village, then take a right n Weke Rd.

0 ★★★ kids **Hanalei Beach Park.** One of lawaii's most gorgeous beaches, where wimming is excellent year-round. See p 502.

ontinue on Hwy. 560 a few blocks to:

1 **Waioli Mission House Museum.** This 50-year-old mission house serves today as a ving museum. Most mission houses are small, ark Boston cottages that violate the tropical ense of place. This 2-story, wood-frame house, uilt in 1836 by Abner and Lucy Wilcox of lew Bedford, Massachusetts, is an excellent xample of hybrid architecture. The house eatures lanais on both stories and a cookhouse 1 a separate building. It has a lava rock himney, ohia wood floors, and Hawaiian koa urniture. Kuhio Hwy. (Hwy. 560), just behind the reen Waioli Huia Church, Hanalei. ☎ 808/245-202. Free admission (donations gratefully ccepted). Tours Tues, Thurs, and Sat 9am–3pm. Reservations required.

ontinue on Hwy. 560 out of Hanalei. After MM 5, look for the scenic overlook on the cean side. The beach is below the overlook.

2 **Lumahai Beach.** A stunning beach but not ood for swimming. If you want to get in the vater, stop here to snap some photos then ontinue on to Haena (the next stop). See 504.

ontinue west on Hwy. 560 to just before MM 9.

3 **Haena Beach Park.** A fabulous place to ick back and enjoy the waves, particularly in ummer. See p 506.

ontinue on Hwy. 560 for about ½ mile. On our left:

14 ★ **Limahuli Garden of the National Tropical Botanical Garden.** Out on Kauai's far North Shore, beyond Hanalei and the last wooden bridge, there's a mighty cleft in the coastal range. Carved by a waterfall stream known as Limahuli, the lush valley sits at the foot of steepled cliffs that Hollywood portrayed as Bali Hai in the film classic *South Pacific*. This small, almost secret garden is ecotourism at its best; botanists here work to save Kauai's endangered native plants. You can take the self-guided tour to view the plants, which are identified in Hawaiian and English, or a 2½-hour guided tour (reserve in advance). From taro to sugarcane, the mostly Polynesian imports tell the story of the people who cultivated the plants for food, medicine, clothing, shelter, and decoration. ⏱ 1–2½ hr. Visitor center ½ mile past MM 9 on Kuhio Hwy. (Hwy. 560), Haena. ☎ 808/826-1053. www.ntbg.org. Admission $15 self-guided, $25 guided; children 12 and under free. Tues–Sat 9:30am–4pm. Advance reservations required for guided tours (book at least 1 week ahead in summer).

Continue on Hwy. 560 for another ½ mile to the end of the road. From the west side of Kee Beach, take the footpath across the big rocks almost to the point; then climb the steep grassy hill.

15 **Ka Ulu O Laka *Heiau.*** On a knoll above the boulders of Kee Beach stands a sacred altar of rocks, often draped with flower leis and ti leaf offerings. The altar is dedicated to Laka, the goddess of hula. In Hawaiian myths, Lohiau, a handsome chief, danced here before the fire goddess, Pele; their passion became *Haena,* which means "the heat." Sometimes, in a revival of the old Hawaiian ways (once banned by missionaries), a mother of a newborn will deposit the umbilical cord of her infant at this sacred shrine. The site is filled with what Hawaiians call *mana,* or power. Dancers of Hawaii's hula *halau* (schools) still climb the cliff, bearing small gifts of flowers. ⏱ 15 min. End of Hwy. 560, Haena.

16 **The end of the road.** The real Hawaii begins where the road stops. This is especially true on Kauai—for at the end of Hwy. 560, the spectacular Na Pali Coast begins. To explore it, you have to set out on foot, by boat, or by helicopter. See p 515.

Kauai Beaches A to Z

kids **Anahola Beach Park** ANAHOLA
This is one of Kauai's safest year-round swimming beaches—great for small children. A shallow offshore reef protects the sandy shoreline from the area's high surf. Surfers are restricted to the north end of the beach. There are no facilities, but there is a part-time lifeguard. Take Kuhio Hwy. to Anahola Rd. (near MM 14), Anahola, North Shore.

★★ **Anini Beach County Park** NORTH SHORE
Anini is one of the safest, most beautiful beaches on Kauai and great for swimming, snorkeling, and diving. It sits on a blue lagoon at the foot of emerald cliffs. Beachcombers love it, too; seashells, cowries, and sometimes even rare Niihau shells can be found here. Anini has a park, a campground, picnic and barbecue facilities, and a boat-launch ramp. Between MM 25 and MM 26. From Kuhio Hwy., take the second or northern Kalihiwai Rd. toward the ocean and turn left on Anini Rd. Anini, North Shore.

★★ **Hanalei Beach** NORTH SHORE
Gentle waves roll across the face of half-moon Hanalei Bay, running up to the wide golden sand; sheer volcanic ridges laced by waterfalls rise to 4,000 feet on the other side. Celebrated in song and hula and featured on travel posters this beach owes its natural beauty to its age—it's an ancient sunken valley with eroded cliffs. Swimming is excellent year-round. It's also popular for body boarding, surfing, fishing, windsurfing, canoe paddling, kayaking, snorkeling, and boating (there's a boat ramp on the west bank of the Hanalei River). Facilities include a lifeguard, a pavilion, restrooms, picnic tables, and parking. Weke Rd., btw. Pilikoa and Aku roads, Hanalei, North Shore.

Hanamaulu Beach Park HANAMAULU
If you are looking for a great picnic beach, this large bay is not only close to Lihue but is protected from the open ocean. However, it is not a great swimming beach due to the dirt entering the bay from Hanamaulu Stream. The waters outside the bay are cleaner and very popular with scuba divers and fishermen. Hanamaulu has no lifeguard but it does have free parking, restrooms showers, and a pavilion. MM 3, Kapule Hwy. (Hwy 51), Hanamaulu.

★ **Kalapaki Beach** LIHUE
The best beach on the eastern coast. Fifty

> *Tunnels Beach, with its gold sand and views of the peaks of Bali Hai, is one of the best-looking beaches in all of Hawaii.*

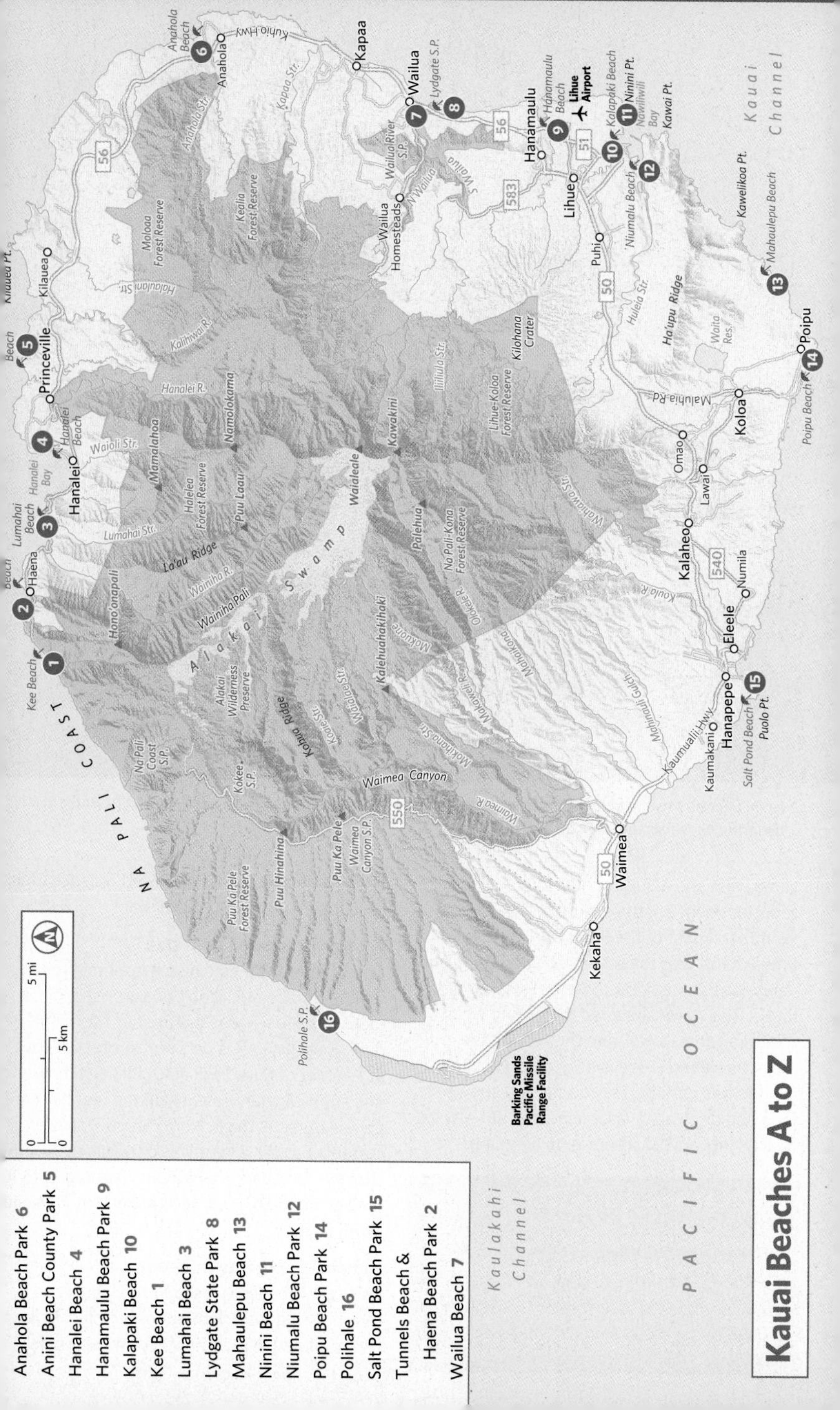
Kauai Beaches A to Z
Anahola Beach Park 6
Anini Beach County Park 5
Hanalei Beach 4
Hanamaulu Beach Park 9
Kalapaki Beach 10
Kee Beach 1
Lumahai Beach 3
Lydgate State Park 8
Mahaulepu Beach 13
Ninini Beach 11
Niumalu Beach Park 12
Poipu Beach Park 14
Polihale 16
Salt Pond Beach Park 15
Tunnels Beach & Haena Beach Park 2
Wailua Beach 7
5 mi
5 km
NA PALI COAST
PACIFIC OCEAN
Kaulakahi Channel
Kauai Channel
Barking Sands Pacific Missile Range Facility
Kee Beach
Haena
Lumahai Beach
Hanalei Bay
Hanalei
Hanalei Beach
Princeville
Kilauea
Anahola Beach
Anahola
Kuhio Hwy
Kapaa
Wailua
Lydgate S.P.
Hanamaulu Beach
Hanamaulu
Lihue Airport
Lihue
Kalapaki Beach
Ninini Pt.
Nawiliwili Bay
Kawai Pt.
Niumalu Beach
Kawelikoa Pt.
Mahaulepu Beach
Poipu
Poipu Beach
Koloa
Maluhia Rd
Omao
Lawai
Kalaheo
Numila
Eleele
Hanapepe
Puolo Pt.
Salt Pond Beach
Kaumakani
Kaumualii Hwy
Waimea
Kekaha
Polihale S.P.
Puhi
Wailua Homesteads
Wailua River S.P.
Moloaa Forest Reserve
Kealia Forest Reserve
Halelea Forest Reserve
Lihue-Koloa Forest Reserve
Na Pali-Kona Forest Reserve
Puu Ka Pele Forest Reserve
Alakai Wilderness Preserve
Alakai Swamp
Waialeale
Kawaikini
Namolokama
Mamalahoa
Puu Laau
Palehua
Kalehuahakihaki
Hono'onapali
Wainiha Pali
La'au Ridge
Kohua Ridge
Ha'upu Ridge
Kilohana Crater
Waimea Canyon
Waimea Canyon S.P.
Puu Ka Pele
Puu Hinahina
Kokee S.P.
Na Pali Coast S.P.
Waita Res.
56
50
51
583
540
550

> *Anini Beach's pristine lagoon combines campgrounds, picnic facilities, perfect sand, and calm water in a beautiful beach experience.*

yards wide and a quarter mile long, Kalapaki is protected by a jetty, making it very safe for swimmers most of the time. During certain times of the year there are strong currents and dangerous shore breaks (watch for warning flags). The waves are good for surfing when there's a winter swell, and the view of the majestic Haupu Ridge is awesome. Facilities include free parking, restrooms, and showers; food and drink are available nearby at Kalapaki Beach Hut (p 539). There is no lifeguard.

Beach Access

Hawaii's beaches belong to the people. All beaches (even those in front of exclusive resorts) are public property and you are welcome to visit them. But look for beach access signs; don't trespass.

Fronting the Kauai Marriott Resort & Beach Club, 3610 Rice St. (Hwy. 51), Nawiliwili.

★★ **Kee Beach** NORTH SHORE
This little reddish gold beach is almost too beautiful to be real. Don't be surprised if it looks familiar—it was featured in *The Thornbirds.* Kee (*kay*-ay) is on a reef-protected cove at the foot of fluted volcanic cliffs. Swimming and snorkeling are safe inside the reef but dangerous outside; those North Shore waves and currents can be killers. This park has restrooms showers, and parking—but no lifeguard. MM 10 (end of the road), Hwy. 560 (Kuhio Hwy.), Haena North Shore.

Lumahai Beach NORTH SHORE
This scenic beach (where Mitzi Gaynor "washed that man right out of her hair" in *South Pacific,* filmed here in 1957) is almost a mile

ɔng and extremely wide. This is ***not*** a good ·wimming beach. When the surf is up there is strong rip current and a powerful backwash, ɫong with a dangerous shore break—high surf as swept people out to sea here. The best ɘason to go to this beach is to picnic under ıe trees and watch the waves roll in. On the astern side (technically Kahalahala Beach), ıe surf is calm enough for swimming only n the few summer days when there are no ·aves—even small ones. Lumahai Beach has o facilities and no lifeguard. **After MM 6, Hwy. 60 (Kuhio Hwy.), Hanalei, North Shore.**

Lydgate State Park COCONUT COAST

his coastal park has a rock-walled fishpond ıat blunts the open ocean waves and provides ne of the few safe swimming beaches on ıe Coconut Coast and the best snorkeling n the eastern shore. This popular park is a reat place for a picnic or for kite flying on the reen. Facilities include a pavilion, restrooms, utdoor showers, picnic tables, barbecue grills, lifeguard, and parking. **Leho Dr., off Hwy. 56 Kuhio Hwy.), just before MM 6.**

★ **Mahaulepu Beach** POIPU

ıahaulepu is the best-looking unspoiled beach Kauai and possibly in the whole state. Its miles of reddish gold grainy sand line the ɔutheastern shore at the foot of 1,500-foot-igh Haupu Ridge. It's ideal for beachcombing nd shell hunting; swimming can be risky, xcept in the reef-sheltered shallows 200 yards est of the sandy parking lot. There are no feguard or facilities—just great natural beauty verywhere you look. **From Grand Hyatt Kauai esort, continue east on Weliweli Rd. Turn right n the unpaved old sugar plantation road heading ward the ocean. Poipu, South Shore.**

inini Beach LIHUE

nis small beach, consisting of two sandy coves ɘparated by lava, is a great place to get away om the crowds. The small northern sandy ɔve has good snorkeling and swimming most f the year. However, high surf can kick up and ɔuthern storms can charge in suddenly. Ninini ɘach has no facilities and no lifeguard. **From e Lihue Airport, take Ahukini Rd. to the old antation dirt road just past the heliport. Take the rt road south about 3 miles to Ninini Point and e beach. Lihue.**

Niumalu Beach Park NAWILIWILI

This is a great place for a picnic. It's located close to Lihue; you can pick up lunch there. Bordered by Nawiliwili Harbor on one end and the small boat ramp on the other, Niumalu sits next to the Menehune Fishpond (p 483, ❹). The beach does not have a lifeguard, but it does have picnic tables, showers, campgrounds, and restrooms. **Niumalu Rd., off Hwy. 58 (Nawiliwili Rd.). Nawiliwili Harbor.**

★ **Poipu Beach Park** POIPU

Big wide Poipu is divided by a sandbar, called a tombolo. On the left, a lava rock jetty protects a sandy-bottomed pool that's perfect for children; on the right, the open bay attracts swimmers, snorkelers, and surfers. And everyone likes to picnic on the grassy lawn graced by coconut trees. It's great for swimming, snorkeling, diving, fishing, surfing, windsurfing, or just exploring the tide pools. And it's very popular. Facilities include a lifeguard, restrooms, showers, picnic areas, and free parking in the red-dirt lot. Brennecke's Beach Broiler (p 535) is nearby. **Hoowili and Poipu Beach roads, Poipu, South Shore.**

★ **Polihale** WESTERN KAUAI

This mini-Sahara on the western end of the island is Hawaii's biggest beach: 17 miles long and as wide as three football fields. The state park includes ancient Hawaiian *heiau* (temple) and burial sites, a view of the "forbidden" island of Niihau, and the famed **Barking Sands Beach,** where footfalls sound like a barking dog. Polihale also takes in the Pacific Missile Range

Hawaiian Monk Seals & Turtles

If you are lucky, you will get to see one of Hawaii's rare Hawaiian monk seals *(Monachus schauinslandi)* or endangered Hawaii green sea turtles *(Chelonia mydas)* when they lumber up on a sunny beach. The Hawaiian monk seal is one of the most endangered species on earth; about 25 of these seals call Kauai home. They are protected by very strict laws, and it is illegal to get closer than 100 feet. When you're taking pictures, stay back, and do not use your flash. The endangered-species laws are strictly enforced on Kauai, and the fines are very steep. For more information, go to www.kauaimonkseal.com.

> THIS PAGE *Kalapaki is great for swimming in summer and surfing when winter swells kick up.* OPPOSITE PAGE *Swim, snorkel, have a picnic, or just relax at Tunnels Beach & Haena Beach Park.*

Facility (a U.S. surveillance center) and Nohili Dune, which is nearly 3 miles long and 100 feet high in some places. Be careful in winter, when high surf and rip currents make swimming dangerous. The safest place to swim is **Queen's Pond,** a small, shallow, sandy-bottomed inlet protected from waves and shore currents. It has facilities for camping, as well as restrooms, showers, picnic tables, and pavilions. There is no lifeguard. End of Kaumualii Hwy. (Hwy. 50); follow the signs through the sugarcane fields. Mana, West Kauai.

Salt Pond Beach Park WESTERN KAUAI
Hawaii's only salt ponds still in production are at Salt Pond Beach, just outside Hanapepe. Generations of locals have come here to swim, fish, and collect salt crystals that are dried in sun beds. The curved reddish gold beach lies between two rocky points and features a protected reef, tide pools, and gentle waves. Swimming here is excellent, even for children; this beach is also good for diving, windsurfing, and fishing. Amenities include a lifeguard, showers, restrooms, a camping area, a picnic area, a pavilion, and a parking lot. End of Lolokai Rd. (Salt Pond Rd.), just outside of Hanapepe, South Shore.

★★ **Tunnels Beach & Haena Beach Park** NORTH SHORE Postcard-perfect, gold-sand Tunnels is one of Hawaii's most beautiful beaches. When the sun sinks into the Pacific along the fabled peaks of Bali Hai, there's no better-looking beach in the islands. Tunnels is excellent for swimming and is safe for snorkeling because it's protected by a fringed coral reef. (However, the waters can get rough in winter.) Around the corner is grainy-gold-sand **Haena Beach Park,** which offers excellent swimming in summer and great snorkeling. But stay out of the water in winter, when the big waves are dangerous. Tunnels has no facilities, but Haena has restrooms, outdoor showers, barbecue grills, picnic tables, a popular grassy park for camping, and free parking (no lifeguard, though). Btw. MM 9 and MM 10, Hwy. 560 (Kuhio Hwy.). Haena, North Shore.

Wailua Beach COCONUT COAST
This popular beach includes Wailua River State Park and Wailua Bay. The draw here is the 100-foot-wide beach that runs for about a half-mile from the Wailua River to a rocky area north. Surfers love this area. However, when the high surf kicks up in winter and into spring, the conditions can become dangerous. At the Wailea River end of the beach you can see boats being launched into the river for water-skiing, jet skiing, kayaking, and outrigger canoeing. At the mouth of the river are a series of Hawaiian *heiau* (temples) and other sacred sites, identified with markers within the state park. There is a part-time lifeguard, but no public facilities. Off Hwy. 56 (Kuhio Hwy.), past MM 6 at Papaloa Rd. Wailua, Coconut Coast.

Kauai's Best Hiking & Camping

Kauai is a hiker's delight. The island's greatest tropical beauty isn't easy to get to—more than 90% of Kauai is inaccessible by road. Trails range from short, easy strolls to several days of trekking. Those interested in seeing the backcountry—complete with virgin waterfalls and quiet meditative settings—should head for Waimea Canyon and Kokee State Park or for the Na Pali Coast and the Kalalau Trail. Most trails are well maintained, but a heavy rainy season can wreak havoc. Always ask about a trail before you go. If you're heading for Kokee, bring rain gear, warm clothes, T-shirts, and shorts—it can be wet, cold, and rainy or hot, dry, and windy (often all on the same day).

> *Campsites along the Na Pali Coast's Kalalau Trail are very popular, so book way in advance.*

★ Mahaulepu Shoreline Trail

Hiking. The shoreline along Kauai's southern coast offers an easy 4-mile round-trip with spectacular scenery, ancient sites, and petroglyphs. The hike begins at Shipwreck's Beach Park at Keoneloa Bay and ends at the remote Mahulepu Beach. Download the free map and guide from the Poipu Beach Resort Association, ☎ 888/744-0888; www.poipubeach.org.

Waimea Canyon Trails

Hiking. The **Canyon Trail** to the east rim gives you a breathtaking view into the 3,567-foot-deep canyon. Park your car at the top of Halemanu Valley Road (btw. MM 14 and MM 15 on Waimea Canyon Rd.). Walk down the not very clearly marked trail on the 3.5-mile round-trip, which takes 2 to 3 hours and leads to Waipoo Falls (as does the next hike) and back.

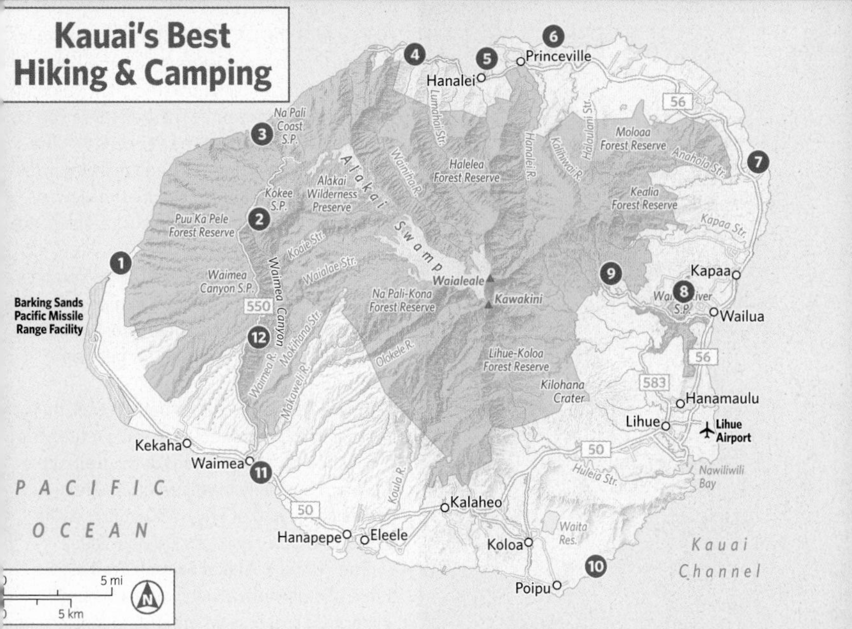

Hiking
Kokee State Park 2
Keahua Arboretum Trail 9
Mahaulepu Shoreline Trail 10
Na Pali Coast State Park 3
The Sleeping Giant Trails 8
Waimea Canyon Trails 12

Camping
Anahola Beach Park 7
Anini Beach County Park 6
Hanalei Beach 5
Kokee State Park 2
Lucy Wright Park 11
Na Pali Coast State Park 3
Polihale State Park 1
YMCA of Kauai–
Camp Naue 4

The 3-hour round-trip hike to ★ **Waipoo Falls** s one of Kauai's best hikes. The two-tiered, 300-foot waterfall that splashes into a natural pool is worth every step it takes to get here. To find the trail, drive up Kokee Road (Hwy. 550) o the Puu Hina Hina Outlook; a quarter-mile past the lookout, near a NASA satellite tracking station on the right, a two-lane dirt road leads o the Waipoo Falls trail head. From here, the trail winds gently through a jungle dotted with wild yellow orchids and flame red torch ginger before it leads you out onto a descending ridge hat juts deep into the canyon. At the end of the promontory, take a left and push on through he jungle to the falls. Reward yourself with a refreshing splash in the pool.

Kokee State Park

Hiking. At the end of Hwy. 550, which leads through Waimea Canyon to its summit, this 4,345-acre state park of high-mountain forest wilderness sits 3,600 ft.–4,000 ft. above sea level. The rainforest, bogs, and breathtaking views of the Na Pali Coast and Waimea Canyon are the draws at Kokee. Among the 45 miles of maintained trails are some of the best hikes in Hawaii. Official trail maps of all the park's trails are for sale for 50¢ at the **Kokee Natural History Museum** (☎ 808/335-9975).

The 3.25-mile **Awaawapuhi Trail** hike (6.5 miles round-trip) takes about 3 hours each way and is considered strenuous by most, but it offers a million-dollar view. Look for the

> *The 3.5 mile round-trip Waimea Canyon Trail hike takes 2 to 3 hours and brings you to the breathtaking Waipoo Falls.*

Getting a Camping Permit

All campers must have a permit. Requirements vary, and you should plan ahead, as it can take a while to get some permits. For permits for **Hawaii State Parks:** Hawaii State Department of Land and Natural Resources, State Parks Division, P.O. Box 621, Honolulu, HI 96809 (☎ 808/589-0300; www.hawaiistateparks.org/camping/kauai.cfm); for **Kauai County** permits, contact: Kauai County Parks and Recreation, 4193 Hardy St., Lihue, HI 96766 (☎ 808/241-6670; www.kauai.gov/Government/Departments/ParksRecreation/CampingInformation/tabid/176/Default.aspx); or the **Kokee Lodge Manager,** P.O. Box 819, Waimea, HI 96796 (☎ 808/335-6061). You can stay at the county parks a maximum of 4 nights, or 12 nights if you are going from one county park to another.

trail head at the left of the parking lot, at mile marker 17, between the museum and Kalalau Lookout. You can pick up a free plant guide for the trail at the museum. The trail takes you to a thin precipice right at the very edge of the Na Pali cliffs for a dramatic and dizzying view. Go early, before clouds obscure the view, or go late in the day; the chiaroscuro sunsets are something to behold.

The **Halemanu-Kokee Trail** takes you on a pleasant, easy-to-moderate 2.5-mile round-trip through a native koa and ohia forest inhabited by native birds. The trail head is near mile marker 15.

Pihea Trail is the park's flattest trail, but it's still a pretty strenuous 7.5-mile round-trip. A new boardwalk on a third of the trail makes it easier, especially in wet weather. The trail begins at the end of Hwy. 550 at Puu o Kila Lookout, which overlooks Kalalau Valley.

The 7-mile ★ **Alakai Swamp Trail** allows a rare glimpse into a wet, cloud-covered wilderness preserve where 460 inches of rain a year is common. A boardwalk protects you from shoe-grabbing mud, but come prepared for rain. The trail head is off Mohihi (Camp 10) Road, just beyond the Forest Reserve entrance sign and the Alakai Shelter picnic area.

Camping. At 4,000 feet, the nights are cold, particularly in winter. Because no open fires are permitted at Kokee, the best deal is the **Kokee Lodge** (p 548), which has 12 cabins for rent at very reasonable rates. The **Kokee Lodge Restaurant** is open daily from 9am to 3:30pm for continental breakfast and lunch. Groceries and gas aren't available in Kokee, so stock up in advance.

The **state campground** at Kokee allows tent camping only. The permits are $5 per night; the time limit is 5 nights in a single 30-day period (see "Getting a Camping Permit," left). Facilities include showers, drinking water, picnic tables, pavilion with tables, restrooms, barbecues, sinks for dishwashing, and electric lights.

The more primitive **backcountry campgrounds** include **Sugi Grove** and **Kawaikoi,** located about 4 miles from park headquarters on the Camp 10 Road, an often muddy and steep four-wheel-drive road. Sugi Grove is located across the Kawaikoi Stream from the Kawaikoi campsite. This is a shady campsite with a single picnic shelter, a pit

A Few Words of Advice

Always check current trail conditions. Up-to-date trail information is available on a bulletin board at the Kokee Natural History Museum. Stay on established trails; it's easy to get lost here. Get off the trail well before dark. Carry water and rain gear—even if it's perfectly sunny when you set out—and wear sunscreen. For complete coverage of the state park, see p 493, 11.

toilet, a stream, and space for several tents. The Kawaikoi site is a 3-acre open grass field, surrounded by Kokee plum trees and forests of koa and ohia. Facilities include two picnic shelters, a composting toilet, and a stream that flows next to the camping area. There is no potable water. Permits are available from the **State Forestry and Wildlife Division,** 3060 Eiwa St., Room 306, Lihue, HI 96766 (☎ 808/274-3444; www.hawaiistateparks.org/camping/kauai.cfm). There's no fee for the permits, but camping is limited to 3 nights. You can also request the *Kauai Recreation Map* (with illustrations of all roads; trails; and picnic, hunting, and camping areas) by mail; contact the Forestry and Wildlife Division at the number above to find out how.

Polihale State Park

Camping. Polihale Beach is spectacular—some 300-feet wide in summer, with rolling sand dunes (some as high as 100 ft.), and the islands of Niihau and Lehua just offshore. Bordered by Na Pali Coast cliffs to the north, razor-sharp ridges and steep valleys to the east, and the blue Pacific to the south and west, this is one of the most dramatic camping areas in the state.

The campgrounds for tent camping are located at the south end of the beach. The camping is on sand, although there are some kiawe trees for shade. (***Warning:*** Kiawe trees drop long thorns, so make sure you have protective footwear.) Facilities include restrooms, showers, picnic tables, barbecues, and a spigot for drinking water. You can purchase supplies about 15 miles away in Waimea. Permits, which are $5 per night, are available through the **State Parks Office,** 3060 Eiwa St., Lihue, HI 96766 (☎ 808/241-3444; www.hawaiistateparks.org/camping/kauai.cfm). You're limited to 5 nights in any 30-day period.

> *Hiking the 4,345-acre rainforest in Kokee State Park introduces you to multiple climates, varied vegetation, and diverse wildlife.*

Lucy Wright Park

Camping. This isn't the best beach park, but it's okay for camping in a pinch, if Polihale is full. The park is named after the first native Hawaiian schoolteacher at Waimea, Lucy Kapahu Aukai Wright (1873–1931). The beach here is full of flotsam and jetsam from the

> *Pitch your tent right on the sand at Polihale State Park.*

river, making it unappealing. Across the river from the park is Russian Fort Elizabeth State Historical Park (p 491, 4). Facilities at Lucy Wright include the camping area, restrooms, a pavilion, picnic tables, and (cold) showers. You need a permit (see "Getting a Camping Permit," p 510). To get to Lucy Wright Park, take Kaumualii Highway (Hwy. 50) to Waimea and turn left on Alawai Road, which leads to the park.

Sleeping Giant Trails

Hiking. The medium-to-difficult **Sleeping Giant Trail (Nounou Mountain Trail East)** takes you up Nounou Mountain, known as Sleeping Giant (it really does look like a giant resting on his back), to a breathtaking panoramic view. The clearly marked trail will gain 1,000 feet in altitude. To get to the trail head, turn mauka (toward the mountain) off Kuhio Highway (Hwy. 56) onto Haleilio Road (btw. Wailua and Kapaa, just past MM 6); follow Haleilio Road for 1½ miles to the parking area, at telephone pole no. 38. From here, signs posted by the State of Hawaii Division of Forestry and Wildlife lead you over the 1.75-mile trail, which ends at a picnic table and shelter.

Nounou Mountain Trail West takes you up Sleeping Giant from the other side of Nounou Mountain and then joins up with the east trail. This trail is shorter than the eastern trail, and you're in forest most of the time. To get to the trail head, take Kuhio Highway (Hwy. 56) to Wailua. Turn left onto Kuamoo Road (Hwy. 580) and continue to Kamalu Road (Hwy. 581), where you turn right. Make a left on Lokelani Street and drive to the end of the road, where there's a parking area and trail head. About a quarter-mile into the hike you will come to a fork with the Kuamoo Trail; veer left. Continue to climb and you will reach the picnic area and shelter.

Keahua Arboretum Trail

Hiking. This easy half-mile loop will take you just a half-hour. To get here, take Kuhio Highway (Hwy. 56) to Wailua. Turn left on Kuamoo Road (Hwy. 580) and continue past the University of Hawaii Agricultural Experimental Station to the Keahua Arboretum The trail head is on the left just past the stream, across the street from the parking lot.

Hiking Safety

Hawaii's search-and-rescue teams are responding to more and more calls about injured, stranded, or missing hikers. The best thing you can do to avoid becoming a statistic is to get Na Ala Hele's (the State of Hawaii's Trail and Access Program) free brochure, *Hiking Safety in Hawaii* (from the State Department of Land and Natural Resources, Division of Forestry & Wildlife, 1151 Punchbowl St., Room 325, Honolulu, HI 96813; ☎ 808/587-0166; or print it off the Web at www.hawaiitrails.org). This free brochure has comprehensive lists of trail safety tips and equipment you'll need; describes what to do in an emergency; and contains other information you should know before you lace up your hiking boots.

If you are not an experienced hiker, consider hiking with a commercial operator, or join a Sierra Club hike. If you have experience hiking, keep these tips in mind when venturing out in Hawaii:

Remember you are a guest in Hawaii and treat the land (especially sacred cultural areas) with respect by following posted signage on the trails. Always start your hikes with clean (well-scrubbed) boots, so you don't unintentionally carry seeds into the island's fragile environment.

Practice courtesy when on a multiple-usage trail. The signs will let you know who to yield to (hikers generally yield to horseback riders, and bikers yield to both hikers and horses).

Plan your hike by informing others where you are going and when you should be back. Learn as much as you can about the hike (the conditions you will encounter and the degree of difficulty) before you set out.

Hike with a partner. Never go alone. Dress in layers to protect yourself from Hawaii's intense tropical sun, carry light rain gear, have a brightly colored jacket (so that if you get lost, people will be able to spot you), and bring a hat, sunglasses, and sunscreen.

Check the weather. Call ☎ 808/245-6001. The bright sunny day can dissolve into wind and rain, and you don't want to be caught in a narrow gully or streambed where flash flooding is possible.

Carry water (2 liters per person per day), a cellphone, and a daypack (holding a whistle, sunscreen, insect repellent, a small flashlight, food, and a basic first-aid kit). Don't drink untreated stream water; *leptospira* (a bacterium that causes a potentially fatal disease in humans) is present in some streams.

Stay on the trail and stay together. Most hikers are injured while wandering off the trail or trying to climb rocks.

Watch the time. Being close to the Equator, Hawaii does not have a very long twilight. Once the sun goes down, it's dark. Be sure to allow enough time to return from your hike, and always carry a flashlight.

If an emergency arises, call 911 and ask for fire/rescue. Tell them what trail you are on and what happened. Make yourself visible with either bright clothing or a flashlight, and use the whistle. Stay calm and stay put. Keep as warm as you can by layering clothing to maintain your body temperature.

Along the trail you'll see kukui trees (which the Hawaiians used as a light source), milo (popular among wood artists), hau, and ohia lehua. As you walk parallel to the stream, be on the lookout for a good swimming area. There are lots of picnic tables and shelters along the trail.

Anahola Beach Park

Camping. Local residents, who love this park and are here almost every day, say that this is the safest year-round swimming beach and great for small children. Facilities include a camping area, a picnic area, barbecue grills, restrooms, and cold showers. A lifeguard is on duty part-time. When you camp here, don't leave your valuables unprotected. You must have a permit (see "Getting a Camping Permit, p 510). To get to Anahola Beach Park, take Kuhio Highway (Hwy. 56) north to Anahola, turn right onto Anahola Road

> *Anini Beach County Park has the island's largest and most popular beach camping site.*

Anini Beach County Park

Camping. This 12-acre park is Kauai's safest beach for swimming and windsurfing. It's also one of the island's most beautiful. One of Kauai's largest beach camping sites, it is very, very popular, especially on summer weekends. Anini has a park, a campground, picnic and barbecue facilities, a pavilion, outdoor showers, public telephones, and a boat-launch ramp. Princeville, with groceries and supplies, is about 4 miles away. You must have a permit (see "Getting a Camping Permit," p 510). Follow Kuhio Highway (Hwy. 56) to Kilauea; take the second exit, called Kalihiwai Road (the first dead-ends at Kalihiwai Beach), and drive a half-mile toward the sea; turn left on Anini Beach Road.

Hanalei Beach

Camping. Camping is allowed at this 2½-acre park on weekends and holidays only. Reserve in advance—it's very popular. Facilities include a lifeguard, a pavilion, restrooms, picnic tables, and parking. You must have a permit (see "Getting a Camping Permit, p 510). To get here, take Kuhio Highway (Hwy. 56), which becomes Hwy. 560 after Princeville. In Hanalei town, make a right on Aku Road just after Tahiti Nui, then turn right again on Weke Road, which dead-ends at the parking lot for the Black Pot section of the beach; the easiest beach access is on your left.

YMCA of Kauai—Camp Naue

Camping. This is the ideal spot to stay before or after conquering the Na Pali trail. This YMCA campsite, located on Kuhio Highway, 4 miles west of Hanalei and 2 miles from the end of the road (look for the sign), sits right on the ocean, on 4 grassy acres ringed with ironwood and kumani trees and bordered by a sandy beach that offers excellent swimming and snorkeling in the summer. Camp Naue has two bunkhouses overlooking the beach; each has four rooms with 10 to 12 beds, $12 per bunk. The facilities are coed, with separate bathrooms for men and women. There's no bedding here, so bring your sleeping bag and towels. Also on the grounds is a beachfront pavilion and a campfire area with picnic tables.

You can pick up basic supplies in Haena, but it's best to stock up on groceries and other necessities in Lihue or Hanalei. To reserve a spot, call ☎ 808/246-9090 a few months before your trip. Do *not* e-mail, *do not* send a letter—the Y simply is not set up to answer mail.

Na Pali Coast State Park

Established in 1984, Na Pali Coast State Park takes in a 22-mile stretch of fluted cliffs that wrap the northwestern shore of Kauai between Kee Beach and Polihale State Park. Volcanic in origin, carved by wind and sea, *na pali* (the cliffs), which heaved out of the ocean floor 200 million years ago, stand as constant reminders of majesty and endurance. Four major valleys—Kalalau, Honopu, Awaawapuhi, and Nualolo—crease the cliffs. The only way to see the park is by hiking it, or flying over it in a helicopter. To get to the trail head, follow Hwy. 560. to the end (at MM 10, 7 miles from Hanalei). Park at Haena State Park. Cross the highway—the trail head is well marked on the mauka (mountain) side of the highway.

Hiking. Kalalau Trail winds through this remote, spectacular, 6,500-acre park, ultimately leading to Kalalau Valley. Of all the green valleys in Hawaii (and there are many), only Kalalau is a true wilderness—probably the last wild valley in the islands. The remote valley is home to long-plumed tropical birds, golden monarch butterflies, and many of Kauai's 120 rare and endangered species of plants. The hike into the Kalalau Valley is grueling and takes most people 6 to 8 hours one-way. The park is open to hikers and campers only, on a limited basis, and you must have a permit (though you can hike the first 2 miles, to Hanakapiai Beach, without a permit). See "Getting a Camping Permit, p 510.

Camping. The camping season runs roughly from May or June to September (depending on the site). All campsites are booked almost a year in advance, so call or write well ahead of time. Stays are limited to 5 nights. Camping areas along the Kalalau Trail include **Hanakapiai Beach** (facilities are pit toilets, and water is from the stream), **Hanakoa Valley** (no facilities, water from the stream), **Milolii** (no facilities, water from the stream), and **Kalalau Valley** (composting toilets, several pit toilets, and water from the stream). Generally, the fee for a state park camping permit is $5 per campsite per night, but the Na Pali fee is $10 per campsite per night. You cannot stay more than 5 consecutive nights at one campsite. Keep your camping permit with you at all times.

> *If you want to explore isolated Na Pali Coast State Park you'll either have to hike it or fly over it on a helicopter.*

Flash Floods

When it rains on Kauai, the waterfalls rage and rivers and streams overflow, causing flash floods on roads and trails. If you're hiking, avoid dry streambeds, which flood quickly and wash out to sea. Before going hiking, camping, or sailing, especially in the rainy season (Nov–Mar), check the weather forecast by calling ☎ 808/245-6001.

Kauai's Best Golf Courses

From a funky 9-hole course populated with wild chickens to one of the best courses in the state, Kauai offers a range of options for golfers of all abilities and budgets.

> *The links-style layout of par-72 Poipu Bay Golf Course offers challenging greens and water hazards along with its beautiful vistas.*

Kauai Lagoons Golf Courses. Choose between two excellent Jack Nicklaus-designed courses: the **Mokihana Course** (a links-style course), for the recreational golfer; or the ★ **Kauai Kiele Championship Course,** for the low handicapper (with a mixture of tournament-quality challenge and high-traffic playability). Facilities include a driving range, lockers, showers, a restaurant, a snack bar, a pro shop, practice greens, a clubhouse, and club and shoe rental; transportation from the airport is provided. Hwy. 51, Lihue. ☎ 808/241-5061. www.kauailagoonsgolf.com. Greens fees: $175, $115 for Kauai Marriott guests.

Puakea Golf Course. This Robin Nelson-designed course, formerly a sugar plantation, opened its first 9 holes in 1997 to many kudos; *Sports Illustrated* named it one of the ten best 9-hole golf courses in the U.S. It's now an 18-hole course with lockers, showers, a pro shop, practice greens, a clubhouse, and club and shoe rental. 4150 Nuhou St., Lihue. ☎ 866/773-5554 or 808/245-8756. www.puakeagolf.com. Greens fees: $135; twilight rate (after 2pm) $59.

Wailua Municipal Golf Course. A challenging and very popular municipal course (book tee times a week in advance). Facilities include

pro shop, lockers, practice putting green, driving range, and golf cart rental. There is no restaurant, but a lunch wagon is stationed by the practice putting green. 3-5350 Kuhio Hwy., Lihue, HI 96766. ☎ 808/241-6666. Greens fees: $32 weekdays, $44 weekends; twilight rate (after 2pm) $16 weekdays, $22 weekends; cart rental fee $16.

Kiahuna Golf Club. This par-70, 6,353-yard Robert Trent Jones, Jr.,–designed course is a Scottish-style course with rolling terrain, undulating greens, 70 sand bunkers, and near-constant winds. Facilities include a driving range, practice greens, and a snack bar. 2545 Kiahuna Plantation Dr. (adjacent to Poipu Resort area), Koloa. ☎ 808/742-9595. www.kiahuna-golf.com. Greens fees: $95; twilight rate $65.

Kukuiolono Golf Course. This is a fun 9-hole course in a spectacular location with scenic views of the entire southern coast. You'll see some oddities such as wild chickens, ancient Hawaiian rock structures, and the grave of Walter McBryde, whose family donated this land. Facilities include a driving range, practice greens, club rental, a snack bar, and a clubhouse. Kukuiolono Park, Kalaheo. ☎ 808/332-9151. Greens fees: $9 for the day.

★★ **Poipu Bay Golf Course.** This 6,959-yard, par-72 course with a links-style layout is the home of the PGA Grand Slam of Golf. Designed by Robert Trent Jones, Jr., this challenging course features undulating greens and water hazards on 8 of the holes. The par-4 16th hole has the coastline weaving along the entire left side. Facilities include a restaurant, a locker room, a pro shop, a driving range, and putting greens. 2250 Ainako St. (across from the Grand Hyatt Kauai), Poipu. ☎ 808/742-8711. www.kauai-hyatt.com. Greens fees: $200, $140 Grand Hyatt guests; afternoon play (noon–3pm) $125; twilight rate (after 3pm) $75.

★★ **Princeville Golf Club, Prince Course.** One of the best golf courses in Hawaii. This Robert Trent Jones, Jr.,–designed devil of a course sits on 390 acres molded to allow ocean views from every hole. Facilities include a restaurant, a health club and spa, lockers, a clubhouse, a golf shop, and a driving range. Princeville. ☎ 808/826-5070. www.princeville.com/golf.html. Greens fees: $200, $155 for Princeville resort guests; twilight rate (after 3pm) $70.

Kauai Adventures on Land

Although Kauai is known for its incredible beaches, there are also plenty of things to do on land, from exploring hard-to-reach areas on an all-terrain vehicle to birding to riding a zip-line above the treetops.

> *Kauai's horseback tours can take you through working ranches or past volcanoes and waterfalls.*

All-Terrain-Vehicle (ATV) Tours

Kipu Ranch Adventures. The latest way to explore Kauai's wilderness. Each person is given a four-wheel-drive vehicle resembling an oversize motorcycle. It's not for the weak: Wrestling with an ATV and learning how to steer, shift gears, maneuver over ruts in the dirt, and charge up and down hills takes some instruction and practice. You'll start out with a lesson on flat ground. After about 10 to 15 minutes of pretty easy riding, you'll practice on a very steep hill that has all kinds of ruts and bumps. Once you've passed this tortuous hill test, the rest of the 3-hour tour is a breeze. There are other ATV tours on Kauai, but we recommend this one because of their emphasis on safety and because the tour explores a 3,000-acre private property never before opened to the public. Extending from the Huleia River to the top of the Haupu Mountains, this property has been the filming site for numerous movies (*Jurassic Park, Raiders of the Lost Ark, Outbreak, Six Days and Seven Nights*). The tour provides helmets, safety glasses, snacks, juice, water, fruit, and a stopover at a swimming hole with a swinging rope. Those who would

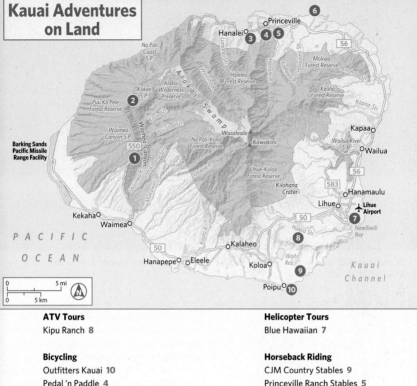

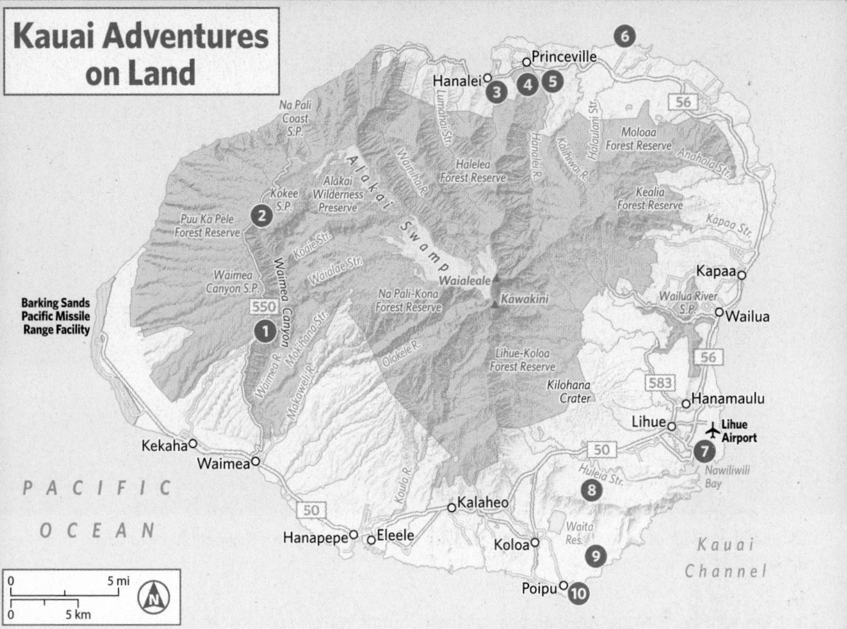

ATV Tours
Kipu Ranch **8**

Bicycling
Outfitters Kauai **10**
Pedal 'n Paddle **4**
Waimea Canyon **1**

Birding
Hanalei National Wildlife Refuge **3**
Kilauea Point National Wildlife Refuge **6**
Kokee State Park **2**

Helicopter Tours
Blue Hawaiian **7**

Horseback Riding
CJM Country Stables **9**
Princeville Ranch Stables **5**

Tennis
Poipu Resort **10**

Ziplining
Outfitters Kauai **10**

rather leave the driving to someone else (and kids ages 6–15) can ride the "mule," a four-wheel-drive Kawasaki that holds up to three passengers. Kipu. ☎ 808/246-9288; www.kiputours.com. $130 adults, $104 seniors (over 65), $75 children 5–15.

Bicycling

There are a couple of great places on Kauai for two-wheeling: the Poipu area, which has wide flat roads and several dirt-cane roads (especially around Mahaulepu); and the cane road (a dirt road used for hauling sugarcane) between Kealia Beach and Anahola, north of Kapaa.

If you are staying in south Kauai, go to **Outfitters Kauai,** 2827A Poipu Rd., Poipu; ☎ 888/742-9887 or 808/742-9667; www.outfitterskauai.com. Bike rentals cost $25 per day. If you are in North Kauai try **Pedal 'n Paddle,** Ching Young Village, Hanalei; ☎ 808/826-9069; www.pedalnpaddle.com. Bike rentals cost $12/day.

⋆ **Outfitters Kauai** (☎ 808/742-9667; www.outfitterskauai.com) offers a fabulous downhill **guided bike tour** from Waimea Canyon to the ocean. The 12-mile trip (mostly coasting) begins at 6am, when the van leaves the shop in Poipu and heads up to the canyon. By the time you've eaten the fresh-baked muffins and enjoyed the coffee, you're at the top of the canyon, just as the sun is rising over the rim—it's a remarkable moment. The tour makes a couple of stops on the way down for

> *Cycling opportunities on Kauai range from the wide roads near Poipu to a downhill tour starting at the top of Waimea Canyon.*

short scenic nature hikes. You'll be back at the shop around 10am. The tour costs $98 per adult, $78 children 12 to 14.

Birding

Kauai provides some of Hawaii's last sanctuaries for endangered native birds and oceanic birds, such as the albatross.

At **Kokee State Park,** a 4,345-acre wilderness forest at the end of Hwy. 550 in southwestern Kauai, you have an excellent chance of seeing some of Hawaii's endangered native birds. You might spot the apapane, a red bird with black wings and a curved black bill; or the iwi, a red bird with black wings, orange legs, and a salmon-colored bill. Other frequently seen native birds are the honeycreeper, which sings like a canary; the amakihi, a plain, olive-green bird with a long straight bill; and the anianiau, a tiny yellow bird with a thin, slightly curved bill. The most common native bird at Kokee is the moa, or red jungle fowl, brought as domestic stock by ancient Polynesians. Ordinarily shy, they're quite tame in this environment.

★ **Kilauea Point National Wildlife Refuge,** a mile north of Kilauea on the North Shore (☎ 808/828-1413; www.fws.gov/kilaueapoint), is a 200-acre headland habitat that juts above the surf and includes cliffs, two rocky wave-lashed bays, and a tiny islet that serves as a jumping-off spot for seabirds. You can easily spot red-footed boobies, which nest in trees, and wedge-tailed shearwaters, which burrow in nests along the cliffs. You may also see the great frigate bird, the Laysan albatross, the red-tailed tropic bird, and the endangered nene. Native plants and the Kilauea Point Lighthouse are highlights as well. The refuge is open from 10am to 4pm daily (closed on Thanksgiving, Christmas, and New Year's Day); admission is $3. To get here, turn right off Kuhio Highway (Hwy. 56) at Kilauea, just after mile marker 23; follow Kilauea Road to the refuge entrance.

Peaceful Hanalei Valley is home to Hawaii's endangered Koloa duck, gallinules, coots, and stilts. The **Hanalei National Wildlife Refuge** (☎ 808/828-1413; www.fws.gov/hanalei) also provides a safe habitat for migratory shorebirds and waterfowl. It's not open to the public, but an interpretive overlook along the highway serves as an impressive vantage point. Along Ohiki Road, which begins at the west end of the Hanalei River Bridge, you'll often see white cattle egrets hunting crayfish in streams.

Helicopter Tours

★★★ **Blue Hawaiian.** The only way to see a large part of Kauai is from the air. Blue Hawaiian has been the Cadillac of helicopter tour companies on Maui and the Big Island for more than a decade, and recently they have expanded their operations to Kauai. I strongly recommend that you try to book with them first. Their operation is first-class, and they use state-of-the-art equipment: American Eurocopter ECO-Star, which reduces noise in the helicopter by 50% and allows 23% more interior room. Plus, the craft has individual business class–style seats, two-way communication with the pilot, and expansive glass for incredible views. The 50-minute flights journey first to Hanapepe Valley, and then continue on to Mana Waiapuna, commonly referred to as "Jurassic Park Falls." Next it's up the Olokele Canyon, then on to the Waimea Canyon, the famed "Grand Canyon of the Pacific." Most of the flight will continue along the Na Pali Coast, before heading out to the Bali Hai cliffs and the pristine blue waters of Hanalei Bay (and the Princeville Resort area). If the weather gods are on your side, then you'll get to see the highest point on Kauai: Mount Waialeale. Your flight will take you right into the center of the crater of Mount Waialeale with its 5,000-foot walls towering above and its 3,000-foot waterfalls surrounding you—something you will remember forever. **3501 Rice St., Lihue. ☎ 800/745-2583 or 808/245-5800. www.bluehawaiian.com. 55-min. tour $230. Harbor Mall staging area; takeoff from the Lihue Airport.**

Horseback Riding

Only in Kauai can you ride a horse across the wide-open pastures of a working ranch under volcanic peaks and rein up near a waterfall pool. No wonder Kauai's *paniolo* (cowboys) smile and sing so much. I recommend the escorted Hidden Valley beach rides: You'll trot over Hidden Valley ranch land, past secluded beaches and bays, along the Haupu Ridge, across sugarcane fields, and to Mahaulepu Beach. It's worth your time and money just to get out to this seldom-seen part of Kauai. I recommend **CJM Country Stables,** 1731 Kelaukia St. (2 miles beyond the Grand Hyatt Kauai Resort & Spa), Poipu (☎ 808/742-6096; www.cjmstables.com), with escorted rides starting at $98; and **Princeville Ranch Stables,** Hwy. 56 (just after the Princeville Airport), Hanalei (☎ 808/826-6777; www.princevilleranch.com), with rides starting at $80.

> *Tear along the treeline on a half-day zipline adventure over waterfalls and valleys.*

Tennis

The **Kauai County Parks and Recreation Department,** 4444 Rice St., Suite 150, Lihue (☎ 808/241-6670), has a list of the nine county tennis courts around the island, all of which are free and open to the public. Private courts that are open to the public include **Grand Hyatt Kauai Resort & Spa,** Poipu (☎ 808/742-1234; www.kauai-hyatt.com), which has four courts, available for $30 an hour; and **Kiahuna Swim and Tennis Club,** Poipu Road (just past the Poipu Shopping Village on the left), Poipu, (☎ 808/742-9533), which has 10 courts renting for $10 per person per hour.

Zip-Lining

Outfitters Kauai. Here's a unique way to see Kauai. The zip-line tour is a half-day adventure combining hiking, swimming, and soaring above the trees in a series of zip-line crossings—you're outfitted with a seat harness and connected to a cable and then launched from one platform to the next, flying over valleys, gulches, and even waterfalls. **2827A Poipu Rd., Poipu. ☎ 888/742-9887 or 808/742-9667. www.outfitterskauai.com. $138 adults, $118 children 7–14.**

Kauai Adventures in the Ocean

Kauai's beauty does not end at the ocean's edge. To really appreciate this incredible island, get out on (or in) the ocean. You can skim over the surface on a boogie board or glide along on a sailboard. Try your luck at fresh- or salt-water fishing, or get up close and personal on a kayak. Or explore life beneath the waves with some snorkeling or scuba diving.

> *Shred the surf or just settle in the sand for the perfect shoreline experience at Kauai's Poipu Beach.*

Body Boarding, Boogie Boarding & Bodysurfing
The best places for bodysurfing and boogie boarding are **Kalapaki Beach** (near Lihue, p 502) and **Poipu Beach** (p 505).

Sailing
★ **Captain Andy's Sailing Adventures.** Captain Andy operates a 55-foot, 49-passenger catamaran out of two locations on the south shore. They offer a variety of cruises, from a Na Pali snorkel- cruise to a Poipu sunset cruise. Kukuiula Small Boat Harbor, Poipu; and Port Allen, Eleele. ☎ 800/535-0830 or 808/335-6833. www.capt-andys.com. Cruises from $69.

Holoholo Charters. This outfitter has taken over several boats and features both swimming/snorkeling sailing charters as well as powerboat charters to the Na Pali Coast. They also provide complimentary shuttle service to and from your hotel. Port Allen, Eleele. ☎ 800/848-6130 or 808/335-0815. www.holoholocharters.com. Tours from $64.

★ kids **Liko Kauai Cruises.** Liko offers more than just a typical whale-watching cruise; this is a 4-hour combination Na Pali Coast tour-deep-sea fishing-historical lecture-whale-watching extravaganza with lunch. It all happens on a 49-

Kauai Adventures in the Ocean

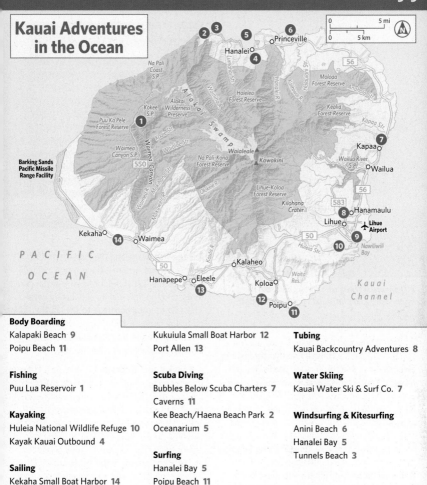

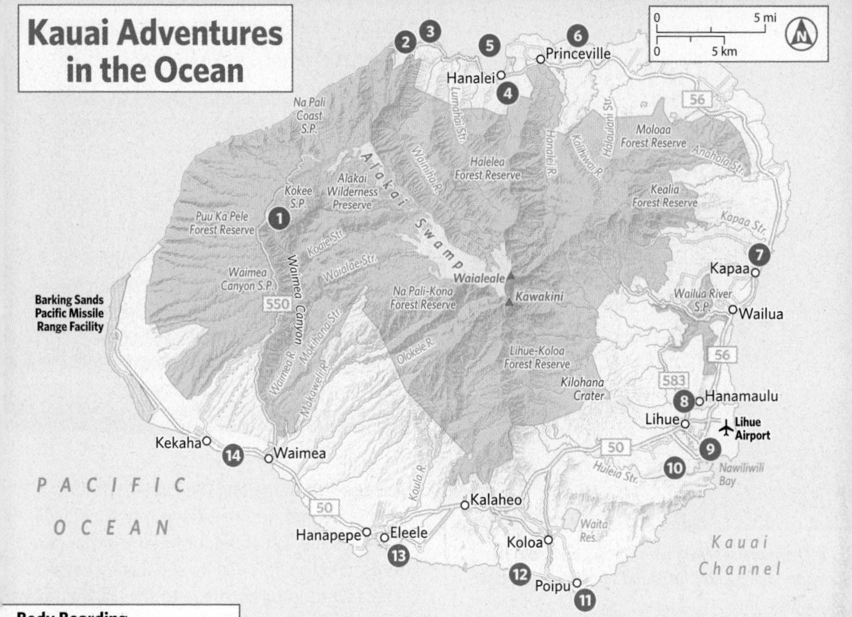

Body Boarding
Kalapaki Beach **9**
Poipu Beach **11**

Fishing
Puu Lua Reservoir **1**

Kayaking
Huleia National Wildlife Refuge **10**
Kayak Kauai Outbound **4**

Sailing
Kekaha Small Boat Harbor **14**
Kukuiula Small Boat Harbor **12**
Port Allen **13**

Scuba Diving
Bubbles Below Scuba Charters **7**
Caverns **11**
Kee Beach/Haena Beach Park **2**
Oceanarium **5**

Surfing
Hanalei Bay **5**
Poipu Beach **11**

Tubing
Kauai Backcountry Adventures **8**

Water Skiing
Kauai Water Ski & Surf Co. **7**

Windsurfing & Kitesurfing
Anini Beach **6**
Hanalei Bay **5**
Tunnels Beach **3**

foot power catamaran (with only 24 passengers). In addition to viewing the whales, you'll glimpse sea caves, waterfalls, lush valleys, and miles of white-sand beaches; you'll also make stops along the way for snorkeling. **Kekaha Small Boat Harbor, Waimea. ☎ 888/SEA-LIKO (732-5456) or 808/338-0333. Fax 808/338-1327. www.liko-kauai.com. 5-hour Na Pali trips (with lunch) $140 adults, $95 children 4–12.**

Fishing

Kauai's **deep-sea fishing** fleet is smaller and less well recognized than others in the islands, but the fish are still out there. All you need to bring are your lunch and your luck. The best way to book a sport fishing charter is through the experts; the best booking desk in the state is ★ **Sportfish Hawaii** (☎ 877/388-1376 or 808/396-2607; www.sportfishhawaii.com). Prices for a shared boat start at $159.

Freshwater fishing is big on Kauai, thanks to its dozens of "lakes," which are really man-made reservoirs. Regardless, they're full of large-mouth, small-mouth, and peacock bass (also known as *tucunare*). The **Puu Lua Reservoir,** in Kokee State Park, also has rainbow trout and is stocked by the state every year. Fishing for rainbow trout in the reservoir has a limited season: It begins on the first Saturday in August and lasts for 16 days, after which you can fish only on weekends and holidays through the last Sunday in September.

> *There are several dive charters on Kauai that can take you to the island's best offshore dive spots.*

Not So Close! They Hardly Know You

In your excitement at seeing a whale or a school of dolphins, don't get too close—both are protected under the Marine Mammals Protection Act. Swimmers, kayakers, and windsurfers must stay at least 100 yards away from all whales, dolphins, and other marine mammals. And yes, visitors have been prosecuted for swimming with dolphins! If you have any questions, call the **National Marine Fisheries Service** (☎ 808/541-2727) or the **Hawaiian Islands Humpback Whale National Marine Sanctuary** (☎ 800/831-4888).

Before you rush out and get a fishing rod, you have to have a **Hawaii Freshwater Fishing License,** available through the **State Department of Land and Natural Resources,** Division of Aquatic Resources, P.O. Box 1671, Lihue, HI 96766 (☎ 808/241-3400; https://www.ehawaii.gov/dlnr/fish/exe/fresh_main_page.cgi). The license is also available through any fishing supply store, like **Lihue Fishing Supply,** 2985 Kalena St., Lihue (☎ 808/245-4930); **Rainbow Paint and Fishing Supplies,** Hanapepe (☎ 808/335-6412); or **Waipouli Variety,** 4-901 Kuhio Hwy., Kapaa (☎ 808/822-1014). A 7-day tourist license is $10. When you get your license, pick up a copy of the booklet *State of Hawaii Freshwater Fishing Regulations.* Another great little book to get is *The Kauai Guide to Freshwater Sport Fishing*, by Glenn Ikemoto, available from **Magic Fishes Press,** P.O. Box 3243, Lihue, HI 96766. If you would like a guide, ★ **Sportfish Hawaii** (☎ 877/388-1376 or 808/396-2607; www.sportfishhawaii.com) has guided bass fishing trips starting at $265 per person for a half-day and $375 for a full day.

Kayaking

Kauai is made for kayaking. You can take the Huleia River into **Huleia National Wildlife Refuge** (located along the eastern portion of Huleia Stream, where it flows into Nawiliwili Bay). It's the last stand for Kauai's endangered birds, and the only way to see it is by kayak. The adventurous can head to the Na Pali Coast, featuring majestic cliffs, empty beaches, open-ocean conditions, and monster waves. Or you can just paddle around Hanalei Bay.

★ **Kayak Kauai Outbound,** a mile past Hanalei Bridge on Hwy. 560, in Hanalei (☎ 800/437-3507 or 808/826-9844; www.kayakkauai.com), has a range of tours for independent souls. The shop's experts will be happy to take you on a guided kayaking trip or to tell you where to go on your own. Guided trips start at $145. Equipment rental starts at $29 for a one-person kayak and $54 for a two-person ocean kayak per day. Kayak lessons are $50 per person per hour.

Scuba Diving

Diving on Kauai is dictated by the weather. In winter, when heavy swells and high winds hit the island, diving is generally limited to the more protected south shore. In the summer it's the opposite. Because the best dives on Kauai are offshore, I recommend going with a **dive charter.** One of the best is **Bubbles Below Scuba Charters,** 6251 Hauaala Rd., Kapaa (☎ 808/822-3483; www.aloha.net/~kaimanu). They specialize in highly personalized, small-group dives with an emphasis on marine biology. The 35-foot dive boat, *Kaimanu,* is a custom-built Radon that comes complete with a hot shower. Two-tank boat dives cost

> *Kayakers paddling through Huleia National Wildlife Refuge have a good chance of seeing endangered Hawaiian birds.*

Ocean Activity Outfitters

Several outfitters on Kauai offer not only equipment rentals and tours but also expert information on weather forecasts, sea and trail conditions, and other important matters for hikers, kayakers, sailors, and all backcountry adventurers. For watersports questions and equipment rental, contact **Kayak Kauai Outbound,** 1 mile past Hanalei Bridge on Highway 560, in Hanalei (☎ 800/437-3507 or 808/826-9844; www.kayakkauai.com), the outfitters' center in Hanalei. They have a private dock (the only one on Kauai) for launching kayaks and canoes. In Kapaa, contact **Kauai Water Ski & Surf Co.,** Kinipopo Shopping Village, 4-356 Kuhio Highway (on the ocean side of the highway), Kapaa (☎ 808/822-3574). In the Kapaa and Koloa areas, go with **Snorkel Bob's Kauai** at 4-734 Kuhio Highway (just north of Coconut Marketplace), Kapaa (☎ 800/262-7725 or 808/823-9433; www.snorkelbob.com); in Koloa, Snorkel Bob's is at 3236 Poipu Rd. (just south of Poipu Shopping Village), near Poipu Beach (☎ 808/742-2206).

$135 ($125 if you book on their website); nondivers can come along for the ride for $80. In summer (May–Sept) Bubbles Below offers a three-tank trip, for experienced divers only, to the "forbidden" island of Niihau, 90 minutes by boat from Kauai ($320, or $275 if you book online). You should be comfortable with vertical drop-offs, huge underwater caverns, possibly choppy surface conditions, and significant currents. You should also be willing to share water space with the resident sharks.

There are a few good **shoreline dive spots** as well. At **Caverns,** a series of lava tubes interconnected by a chain of archways, a constant parade of fish streams by (even shy lion-fish are spotted lurking in crevices), brightly hued Hawaiian lobsters hide in the lava's tiny holes, and turtles swim past. It's best in the winter months, and located off the Poipu Beach resort area. On a calm summer day, the drop-off near the reef at **Kee Beach/ Haena Beach Park** (p 504 and 506) begs for underwater exploration. In summer, when the north Pacific storms subside, the magnificent North Shore opens up. At **Oceanarium,** you'll find a kaleidoscopic marine world in a horseshoe-shaped cove. From the rare (long-handed spiny lobsters) to the more common (taape, conger eels, and nudibranchs), the resident population is one of the more diverse on the island. The topography, which features pinnacles, ridges, and archways, is covered with cup corals, black-coral trees, and nooks and crannies enough for a dozen dives. Located northwest of Hanalei Bay; it's possible to reach from the shore, but getting there by boat is better.

SNORKEL GUIDE PAGE 526

Snorkeling

All you need is a mask, snorkel, fins, and the ability to swim, and you are ready to explore Kauai's underwater world. If you've never snorkeled or are a nervous swimmer, there are plenty of activity providers and resorts with instructions on how to use the equipment. But it's easy: Relax, float over a reef, breathe normally through the snorkel, and explore the tropical environment under the waves.

See "Ocean Activity Outfitters," above, for advice on where to rent snorkel gear.

Surfing

Hanalei Bay's winter surf is the most popular on the island, but it's for experts only. **Poipu Beach** is an excellent spot at which to learn to surf; the waves are small and—best of all—

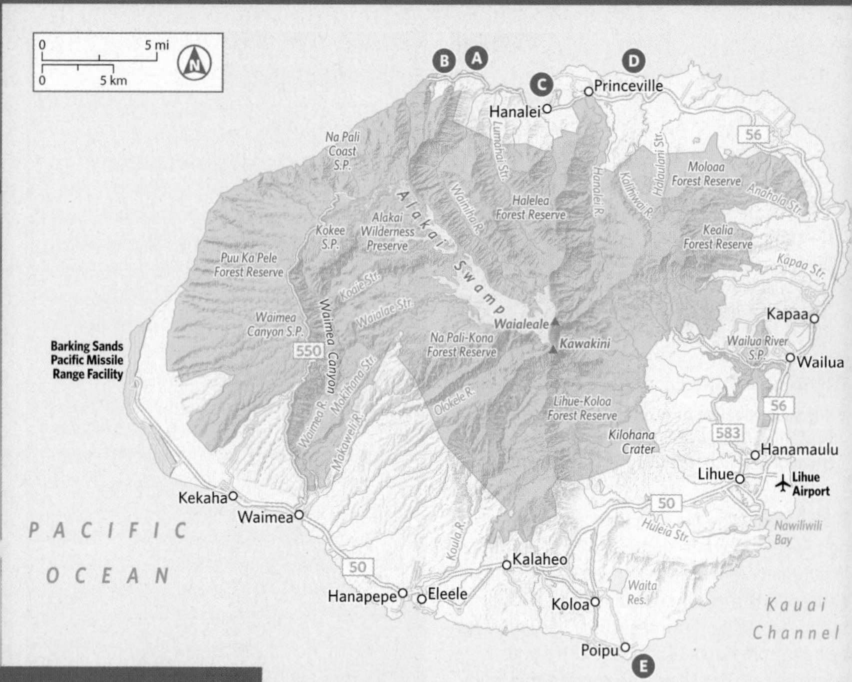

SNORKEL GUIDE

Kauai's Best Snorkeling

A fringed coral reef makes (A) **Tunnels Beach** (p 506) safe for snorkeling. (However, the waters can get rough in winter.) Around the corner is grainy-gold-sand (B) **Haena Beach Park** (p 506), which offers great snorkeling amid clouds of tropical fish in summer (stay out of the water in winter). The bay at beautiful (C) **Hanalei Beach** (p 502) indents the coast a full mile inland and runs 2 miles point to point, with coral reefs on either side and a patch of coral in the middle—plus a sunken ship that belonged to a king, so divers love it. Snorkeling is excellent year-round, especially in summer, when Hanalei Bay becomes a big placid lake. The area known as **Black Pot,** near the pier, is particularly good for swimming, snorkeling, and surfing. The 3-mile-long, gold-sand (D) **Anini Beach** (p 502) is shielded from the open ocean by the longest, widest fringing reef in Hawaii. With shallow water 4 to 5 feet deep, it's also the very best snorkeling spot on Kauai, even for beginners. On the northwest side, a channel in the reef runs out to the deep blue water with a 60-foot drop that attracts divers. Popular (E) **Poipu Beach Park** (p 505) also has great reefs for snorkeling and diving.

Ocean Activity Outfitters

Several outfitters on Kauai offer not only equipment rentals and tours but also expert information on weather forecasts, sea and trail conditions, and other important matters for hikers, kayakers, sailors, and all backcountry adventurers. For watersports questions and equipment rental, contact **Kayak Kauai Outbound,** 1 mile past Hanalei Bridge on Highway 560, in Hanalei (☎ 800/ 437-3507 or 808/826-9844; www.kayakkauai.com), the outfitters' center in Hanalei. They have a private dock (the only one on Kauai) for launching kayaks and canoes. In Kapaa, contact **Kauai Water Ski & Surf Co.,** Kinipopo Shopping Village, 4-356 Kuhio Highway (on the ocean side of the highway), Kapaa (☎ 808/822-3574). In the Kapaa and Koloa areas, go with **Snorkel Bob's Kauai** at 4-734 Kuhio Highway (just north of Coconut Marketplace), Kapaa (☎ 800/262-7725 or 808/823-9433; www.snorkelbob.com); in Koloa, Snorkel Bob's is at 3236 Poipu Rd. (just south of Poipu Shopping Village), near Poipu Beach (☎ 808/742-2206).

nobody laughs when you wipe out. Check with the local surf shops or call the **Weather Service** (☎ 808/245-3564) to find out where surf's up.

Surf lessons are available from $68 for a 1½-hour session, including all-day use of equipment, from **Margo Oberg's School of Surfing,** at the Nukumoi Surf Shop, across from Brennecke's Beach (☎ 808/742-8019). She guarantees that by the end of the lesson, you'll be standing and catching a wave.

Equipment is available for rent (from $5 an hour or $20 a day for "soft" beginner board from **Nukumoi Surf Shop,** across from Brennecke's Beach, Poipu Beach Park (☎ 888/384-8810 or 808/742-8019; www.nukumoisurf.com); and on the North Shore at **Hanalei Surf Co.,** 5-5161 Kuhio Hwy. (across from Zelo's Beach House Restaurant in Hanalei Center), Hanalei (☎ 808/826-9000; www.hanaleisurf.com).

Tubing

Kauai Backcountry Adventures. Back in the days of the sugar plantations, local kids would grab inner tubes and jump in the irrigation ditches, crisscrossing the cane fields for an exciting ride. Today you enjoy an authorized ride through the flumes and ditches of the old Lihue Plantation. Passengers are taken in four-wheel-drive vehicles high into the mountains above Lihue and see vistas generally off-limits to the public. At the flumes, you will be outfitted with a giant tube, gloves, and headlamp (for the long passageways through the tunnels). All you do is jump in the water, and the gentle gravity-fed flow will carry you through forests, into tunnels, and finally to a mountain swimming hole, where a picnic lunch is served. The tour lasts about 3 hours and is appropriate for anyone ages 5–95. ☎ 888/270-0555 or 808/245-2506. www.kauaibackcountry.com.

Water-Skiing

Hawaii's only freshwater water-skiing is on the Wailua River. Ski boats launch from the boat ramp in Wailua River State Park, directly across from the marina. **Kauai Water Ski & Surf Co.,** Kinipopo Shopping Village, 4-356 Kuhio Hwy., Kapaa (☎ 800/344-7915 or 808/822-3574), rents equipment and offers lessons and guided tours. Trips from $76.

Windsurfing & Kitesurfing

Anini Beach is one of the safest beaches for beginners to learn windsurfing. Lessons and equipment rental are available at **Anini Beach Windsurfing and Kitesurfing** (☎ 808/826-WIND 826-9463). Owner Foster Ducker has been teaching windsurfing for nearly a decade. He has special equipment to help beginners learn the sport. A 1-hour lesson is $50 and includes equipment and instruction. If you fall in love with the sport and want to keep going, he'll rent the equipment for $25 an hour or $50 for the rest of the day. For those experienced windsurfers who don't want to cart their equipment halfway around the globe, he will rent windsurfing equipment for $25 an hour or $75 a day. Serious windsurfers should head to **Hanalei Bay** or **Tunnels Beach** on the North Shore.

Ducker is also a certified instructor in kitesurfing; he claims he can get people up and on the water in just one lesson. His introduction to kitesurfing is 5 hours long and costs $400 for one person and $600 for two.

UNDERWATER HAWAII

Scuba and Snorkeling in the Islands BY KATHRYN WILLIAMS

HAWAII'S WARM WATERS make it one of the world's most popular scuba and snorkeling sites. Lava formations, grottoes, shipwrecks, and fringing and barrier reefs are hospitable habitats and a food source for the approximately 680 species of fish that inhabit the waters surrounding the islands. Hawaii's relatively young coral reefs have formed over thousands of years as coral polyps—tiny animals that get their nutrition from photosynthetic microorganisms living in their tissue—excrete stony, calcified exoskeletons.

Hawaii is made up of more than 130 islands and atolls, but the islands of Oahu, Maui, Kauai, and Hawaii (the Big Island) are the most dived. Experienced divers might also enjoy trips to Lanai, Molokai, and Niihau.

What You'll See...

A fringing reef, the most common in Hawaii, can be divided into four zones each home to different fish, coral, and other aquatic organisms. Remember: Coral reefs are living animals and protected by law, as are the endangered species you might see there.

REEF FLAT ZONE
(0–6.5 feet)

Green Sea Turtles

Endangered green sea turtles can be found close to almost any Kona shore. For early Hawaiians *honu* were a source of food, and their shells were used for tools and ornamentation.

Surgeonfish Surgeonfish, also called tang, get their name from the scalpel-like spines near the base of their tails.

Convict Tang A pale white fish with vertical black stripes; the most abundant species in Hawaiian waters.

Cauliflower Coral Often found on or near lava boulders and rock walls, compact and sturdy cauliflower coral is able to withstand strong currents and wave energy.

REEF BENCH ZONE
(6.5–33 feet)

Parrotfish Parrotfish are easy to spot—their fused front teeth protrude like a beak they use to scrape algae from rocks and coral. The coral is digested and excreted by the fish as fine sand. Most of the white sand found in Hawaii is parrotfish waste.

Moray Eels Though they look menacing, moray eels are naturally

shy and docile unless provoked. Unfortunately, some morays that have been fed by divers now associate humans with food and can become aggressive.

Wrasses Wrasses are a diverse family of fish that can change gender from female to male. Some have brilliant coloration that changes as they age. Several types are endemic to Hawaii.

REEF SLOPE ZONE
(33-100 feet)
Butterflyfish
Butterflyfish are among the most

colorful of reef fish. Usually seen in pairs, they can be identified by a dark band through the eye and a spot near the tail resembling an eye, meant to confuse predators.

Sea Urchins At night, seemingly sedentary slate pencil sea urchins venture out from coral reefs on hundreds of tiny, sticky tube feet to feed on algae, seaweed, and the remains of other oceanic organisms.

Sharks Sharks swim at all depths, but in the spring, schools of scalloped hammerhead sharks migrate

from deeper waters to the relative safety of bays, like Kaneohe, to give birth to their young.

RUBBLE ZONE
(below 100 feet)
Black Sea Cucumbers
Black sea cucumbers live on the sandy bottom. If attacked by predators, they will expel their toxic internal organs and regenerate them later.

Scorpionfish Scorpion-

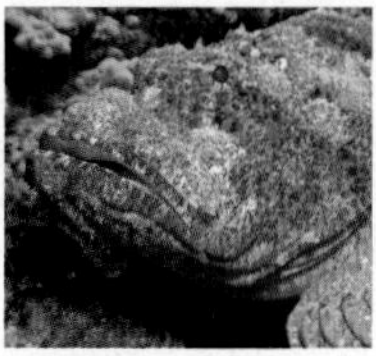

fish hide behind their camouflaged exteriors and ambush their prey, stinging them with venomous spines. You'll usually find them resting on ledges or the ocean floor.

Garden Eels Garden eels live in colonies, burrowing into the sandy ocean floor like

straws. If you don't scare them into their holes, you'll see their heads sticking out as they feed on plankton passing in the current.

Kauai Shopping A to Z

Alohawear

Hilo Hattie LIHUE

Their selection of Hawaii-related items is immense: food, books, CDs, mugs, key chains, T-shirts, and alohawear. They even offer free hotel pickup from Poipu and Kapaa. 3252 Kuhio Hwy. (Hwy. 50) and Ahukini Rd. ☎ 808/245-3404. AE, DC, V. Map p 531.

Art

Kela's Glass Gallery KAPAA

The island's showiest showplace for handmade glass in all sizes, shapes, and prices, with the most impressive selection in Hawaii. Go nuts over the vases and studio glass pieces, functional and nonfunctional. 4-1354 Kuhio Hwy. ☎ 808/822-4527. M, V. Map p 531.

Ola's HANALEI

Sharon and Doug Britt (an award-winning artist) have amassed a head-turning assortment of American and island crafts, including Doug's paintings and the one-of-a-kind furniture that he makes out of found objects, driftwood, and used materials. Lundberg Studio handblown glass, exquisite jewelry, sensational handblown goblets, koa jewel boxes, and many other fine works fill this tasteful, seductive shop. Hwy. 560. ☎ 808/826-6937. AE, MC, V. Map p 531.

Edibles

Banana Joe's KILAUEA

The granddaddy of Kauai's roadside fruit-and-smoothie stands. Banana Joe's has been a Kilauea landmark since 1986. Come for smoothies, fresh fruit, organic vegetables, macadamia nuts, tropical-fruit salsas, jams and jellies, Anahola Granola, and baked goods such as homemade papaya-banana bread. 52719 Kuhio Hwy. (btw. MM 23 & 24 heading north, on the mountain side of the street). ☎ 808/828-1092. Map p 531.

Sunshine Markets MULTIPLE LOCATIONS

The county of Kauai sponsors regular weekly Sunshine Markets throughout the island, featuring fresh Kauai fruits, vegetables, and herbs. The market schedules vary by location; call or check the website for details. ☎ 808/241-6390. www.kauai.gov. Map p 531.

Fashion

Bambulei WAILUA

Bordering the cane field in Wailua next to Caffè Coco (p. 536) is this charming collection of 1930s and 1940s treasures—everything from Peking lacquerware to exquisite vintage aloha shirts and muumuu to dresses, lamps, quilts, jewelry, parrot figurines, and zany salt and

> *You'll find a great selection of local-made crafts at the Kauai Museum.*

Kauai Shopping A to Z

Bambulei 5
Banana Joe's 3
Banana Patch Studio 10
Ching Young Village 1
Coconut MarketPlace 4
Hilo Hattie 6
Kauai Museum 6
Kauai Village 4
Kela's Glass Gallery 4
Kukui Grove Center 6
Ola's 1
Poipu Shopping Village 8
Princeville Shopping Center 2
Sandal Tree 8
Sunshine Markets:
- Hanapepe 10
- Kapaa 4
- Kalaheo 9
- Kekaha 11
- Kilauea 3
- Koloa 7
- Lihue 6

Tropical Flowers by Charles 7
Yellowfish Trading Company 1

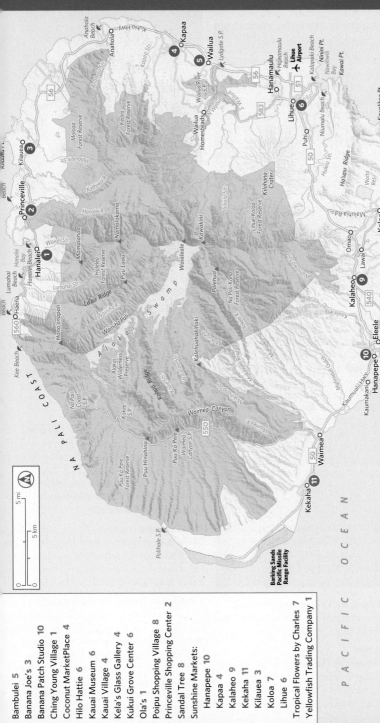

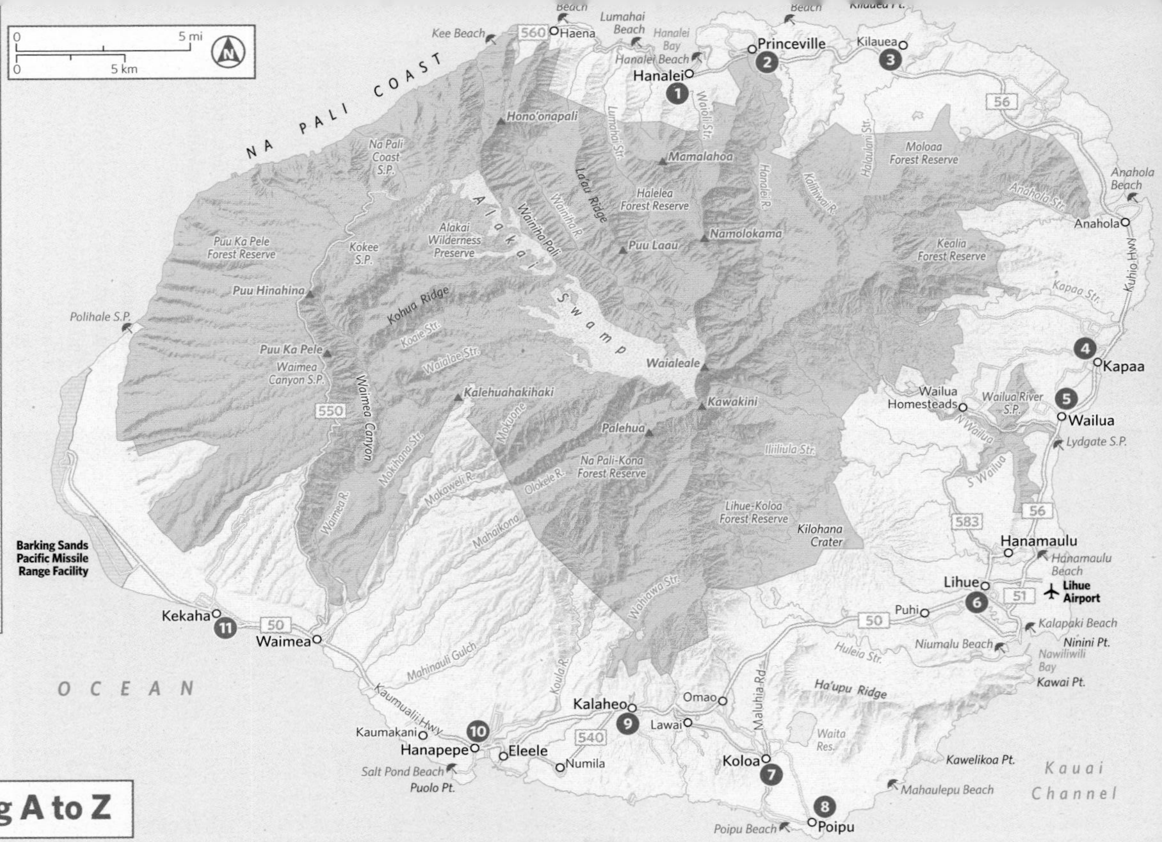

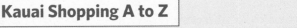

The Ultimate Kauai Souvenir

If you are looking for an inexpensive, easy-to-pack souvenir of your trip to Kauai or gifts for all the friends and relatives back home, check out the **Red Dirt Shirt.** Every T-shirt is hand-dyed and unique. The shirts were the result of a bad situation turned into a positive one. The "legend" is that Paradise Sportswear, in Waimea (☎ 808/335-5670; www.dirtshirt.com), lost the roof of their warehouse during Hurricane Iniki in 1992. After the storm passed, employees returned to the building to find all their T-shirts covered with Kauai's red soil. Before throwing out their entire inventory as "too soiled to sell," someone had an idea—sell the shirts as a Kauai "Red Dirt Shirt." The grunge look was just starting to be popular. Unbelievable as it is, people took to these "dirt" shirts. Fast-forward a couple of decades, and the shirts have numerous outlets on Kauai.

Paradise Sportswear is a true community effort. They employ people who, due to family or disability challenges, prefer to work from home. Their employees take ordinary white T-shirts home and dye the shirts in vats with red dirt collected from valleys on Kauai where centuries of erosion have concentrated red iron oxide into the dirt. It's this red iron oxide that is used in the tinting agent, along with some other organic compounds in the dye solution, that ensure that your dirt shirt will keep its red-dirt color.

The best prices on Red Dirt Shirts can be found at the factory by the Port Allen Small Boat Harbor, open daily 9am to noon and 1 to 4pm. You can watch the silk-screening process or purchase a few shirts from the retail shop, which has sizes from infant to XXXXL. The deals are on the factory seconds and discontinued designs.

pepper shakers. If it's not vintage, it will look vintage, and it's bound to be fabulous. Hwy. 56. ☎ 808/823-8641. MC, V. Map p 531.

Flowers & Leis

Tropical Flowers by Charles KOLOA
The best place to order flowers to be sent home. Charles grows a range of tropical flowers, including some very rare and unusual varieties. His hardy blooms and his skill at packing means that your little bit of Kauai will live for a long, long time. 3465 Lawailoa Lane. ☎ 800/699-7984 or 808/332-7984. www.a-tropical-flower.com. Map p 531.

> *Handmade glass and pottery is available in all shapes and sizes at the renowned Kela's Glass Gallery in Kapaa.*

Hawaiiana Gifts

Banana Patch Studio HANAPEPE
For the best prices on the island for tropical plates and cups, hand-painted tiles, artwork, handmade soaps, pillows with tropical designs, and jewelry, this is the place. Plus, they will pack and ship for you anywhere. 3865 Hanapepe Rd. ☎ 808/335-5944. www.bananapatchstudio.com. Map p 531.

Kauai Museum LIHUE
One of the best places to get made-on-Kauai arts and crafts, from Niihau shell leis to woodwork, lauhala and coconut products, and more. 4428 Rice St. ☎ 808/245-6931. MC, V. Map p 531.

★ **Yellowfish Trading Company** HANALEI
Owner Gritt Benton's impeccable eye and zeal for collecting are reflected in the 1920s to 1950s collectibles: menus, hula-girl nodders, hula lamps, rattan and koa furniture, vases, bark-cloth fabric, retro pottery and lamp bases, must-have vintage textiles, and wonderful finds in books and aloha shirts. Hanalei Center. ☎ 808/826-1227. AE, MC, V. Map p 531.

Niihau Shell Lei: The Island's Most Prized Artwork

Because Kauai is so close to Niihau (the "Forbidden Island," where the public is prohibited), it's the best place in the state to buy the exquisite art form, Niihau shell leis. Nothing can match the craftsmanship of this highly sought-after and highly prized jewelry. Niihau is in the best position to catch the very tiny and very rare shells that roll up from the deep onto the windward shores after a big storm (generally Nov–Mar). When the tiny shells are spotted on a beach, everyone (men, women, and children) on Niihau drops what they are doing and races down to the beach to begin the backbreaking work of collecting these exceptional shells.

The shells are then sorted according to size and color, and only the best are kept. Some 80% of the shells are thrown out because they are chipped, cracked, discolored, or flawed in some way that renders them imperfect. The best shells are the teeny, tiny ones. The best colors are white or the rare gold (the shells can also be yellow, blue, or red).

The shells can be crafted into anything, but leis and necklaces are the most popular items. A necklace may take anywhere from hours to years to complete. Each shell is strung with very small and very intricate knots. The patterns sometimes mimic flower leis, and the length can range from a single-strand choker to a multistrand, 36-inch (or longer) necklace. No two leis are alike. The leis are not cheap; they range from several hundred to several thousand dollars, depending on the length, the shells used, and the intricacy of the work involved.

You can find Niihau shell leis at numerous locations on Kauai. One of our two favorite places is Hawaiian Trading Post, Koloa Road and Kaumualii Highway, in Lawai (☎ 808/332-7404), which carries a range of items from junky souvenirs to excellent Niihau leis. (You have to ask for them to bring out the "good stuff" from the back.) Our other favorite place to buy the leis is at www.niihau.us/leis1.htm, which is owned and operated by Niihau residents.

Shoes

Sandal Tree POIPU
This store is the island's footwear mecca. Grand Hyatt Resort Kauai, 1571 Poipu Rd. ☎ 808/742-2009. AE, MC, V. Map p 531.

Shopping Centers

Ching Young Village HANALEI
Artsy shops, clothing boutiques, and restaurants. 5-5190 Kuhio Hwy. ☎ 808/826-7222. www.chingyoungvillage.com. AE, DC, DISC, MC, V. Map p 531.

Coconut MarketPlace KAPAA
Unique shops (**Elephant Walk** gift shop, **Gifts of Kauai**) mixed with some underwhelming souvenir and clothing shops. Check out **Ship Store Gallery** for an unusual collection of nautical artwork, antiques, and contemporary Japanese art. 848 Hwy. 56. ☎ 808/822-3641. www.coconutmarketplace.com. Map p 531.

Kauai Village KAPAA
You'll find everything from **Wyland Galleries'** trite marine art to Yin Chiao Chinese cold pills and organic produce at **Papayas Natural Foods.** 4-831 Kuhio Hwy. ☎ 808/822-4904. AE, DC, DISC, MC, V. Map p 531.

Kukui Grove Center LIHUE
From K-Mart to Macy's, this center has everything, even a Blockbuster and a Borders and a couple of banks. Beware of the macadamia nut fudge, found only at Kauai Products Store: It's rich, sweet, and irresistible. 3-2600 Kaumualii Hwy. (Hwy. 50) and Old Nawiliwili Rd. ☎ 808/245-7784. www.kukuigrovecenter.com. AE, DC, DISC, MC, V. Map p 531.

Poipu Shopping Village POIPU
Artsy boutiques plus a range of restaurants and entertainment. 2260 Kiahuna Plantation Dr. ☎ 808/742-2823. AE, DC, DISC, MC, V. Map p 531.

Princeville Shopping Center PRINCEVILLE
High-end shops, grocery store, and gas station. 5-4280 Kuhio Hwy. ☎ 808/826-9497. Map p 531.

Kauai Restaurant Best Bets

Best on the Beach
Duke's Canoe Club $$ Kauai Marrriott, Nawiliwili (p 537)

Best Breakfast
Kalaheo Coffee Co & Café $ 2560 Kaumualii Hwy., Kalaheo (p 539)

Best Burger
Duane's Ono-Char Burger $ Kuhio Hwy., Anahola (p 537)

Best for Families
Wailua Family Restaurant $$ 4361 Kuhio Hwy., Wailua (p 543)

Freshest Fish
Tidepool Restaurant $$$$ Grand Hyatt Kauai Resort & Spa, Poipu (p 541)

Best Italian
Dondero's $$$$ Grand Hyatt Kauai Resort & Spa, Poipu (p 536)

Best Luau
Sheraton Kauai $$$$ Poipu Beach (See "A Hawaiian Feast: The Luau," p 541)

> *Gaylord's is my top pick for a special-occasion meal.*

Best Meal under $15
Kilauea Fish Market $ 4270 Kilauea Lighthouse Rd., Kilauea (p 540)

Best Pasta
Pomodoro $$ Rainbow Plaza, Kaumualii Hwy., Kalaheo (p 541)

Best People-Watching
Brennecke's Beach Broiler $$ 2100 Hoone Rd., Poipu (p 535)

Best Pizza
Kilauea Bakery & Pau Hana Pizza $$ Kong Lung Center, Kilauea Rd., Kilauea (539)

Best Splurge
Gaylord's $$$ Kilohana, 3-2087 Kaumualii Hwy., Lihue (p 537)

Best Sushi
Hanamaulu Restaurant $$ 3-4291 Kuhio Hwy., Lihue (p 538)

Most Trendy
Bar Acuda $$$ 5-5161 Kuhio Hwy., Hanalei (p 535)

Best View
The Beach House $$$ 5022 Lawai Rd., Poipu (p 535)

Kauai Restaurants A to Z

★★★ **Bar Acuda** HANALEI *TAPAS* Creative dishes here range from ono escabeche (fresh fish braised in olive oil with burnt garlic and tomato) to grilled rib-eye steak with caramelized shallots ($28). Excellent wine selection. 5-5161 Kuhio Hwy. ☎ 808/826-7081. www.restaurantbaracuda.com. Tapas $6–$28. MC, V. Dinner Tues–Sun. Map p 539.

Barefoot Burgers WAIMEA *BURGERS/SANDWICHES* This roadside burger joint along the highway to Waimea Canyon is a throwback to the 1950s. Burgers galore, plus sandwiches (tuna, BLT, chicken) and hot dogs. Ice cream desserts and espresso drinks round out the menu. 9643 Kaumualii Hwy. ☎ 808/338-2082. Burgers and sandwiches $4.75–$6.75. MC, V. Lunch daily. Map p 537.

★★★ **The Beach House** POIPU *HAWAII REGIONAL* The Beach House remains the south shore's premier spot for sunset drinks, appetizers, and dinner—a treat for all the senses. Come for cocktails or early dinner, when you can still catch the sunset and perhaps see a turtle or two bobbing in the waves. 5022 Lawai Rd. ☎ 808/742-1424. Entrees $20–$34. AE, DC, MC, V. Dinner daily. Map p 536.

★ kids **Brennecke's Beach Broiler** POIPU *AMERICAN/SEAFOOD* This casual restaurant has the best hamburgers on the south shore, excellent vegetarian selections, fresh fish, and a view that's worth a visit alone. What more could you ask for? 2100 Hoone Rd. (across from Poipu Beach Park). ☎ 808/742-7588. www.brenneckes.com. Entrees $13–$40. AE, DC, DISC, MC, V. Lunch and dinner daily. Map p 536.

kids **Brick Oven Pizza** KALAHEO *PIZZA* This quintessential mom-and-pop business has been a Kalaheo fixture for nearly 25 years. The pizza is cooked directly on the brick hearth, brushed with garlic butter, and topped with cheeses and long-simmering sauces. The result: very popular pizza, particularly when topped with fresh garlic and served with Gordon Biersch beer. 2-2555 Kaumualii Hwy. (Hwy. 50). ☎ 808/332-8561. Pizzas $11–$32. MC, V. Lunch and dinner Tues–Sun 11am–10pm. Map p 537.

The charming Caffè Coco has a great selection of vegetarian items, as well as a tempting dessert menu.

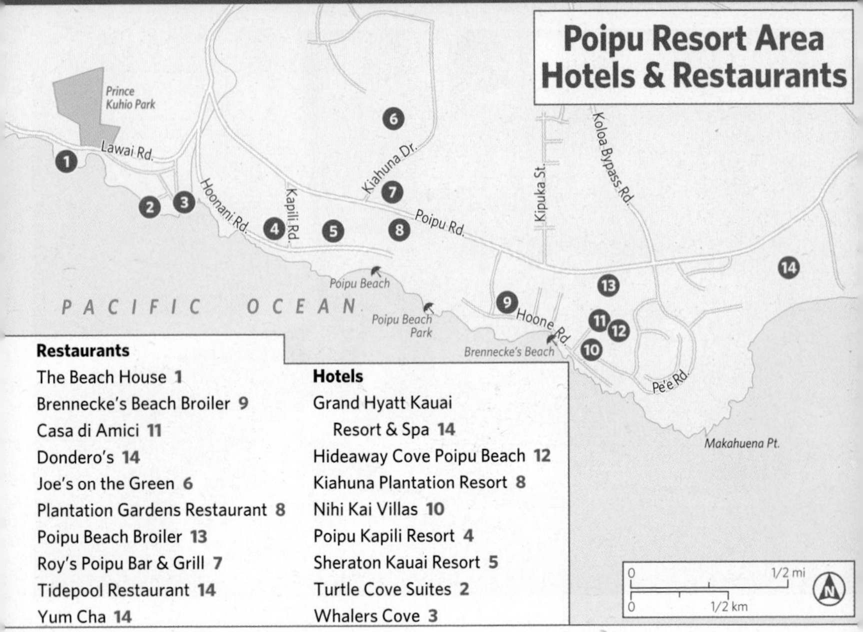

kids **Bubba Burgers** KAPAA *BURGERS*
At Bubba the burger is king, attitude reigns, and lettuce and tomato cost extra. They dish out humor, great T-shirts, and burgers nonpareil, along with chili, fresh fish sandwiches, chicken burgers, and tempeh burgers. 4-1421 Kuhio Hwy. ☎ 808/823-0069. All items less than $9. MC, V. Lunch and dinner daily. Map p 537.

The Bull Shed WAIPOULI *STEAK/SEAFOOD*
The informality and oceanfront location are big pluses, but Kauai regulars also tout the steaks and chops—prime rib, Australian rack of lamb, garlic tenderloin—and the fresh catch. 796 Kuhio Hwy. ☎ 808/822-3791. Entrees $12–$38. AE, DC, DISC, MC, V. Dinner daily. Map p 537.

★★ **Café Portofino** NAWILIWILI *ITALIAN*
This romantic, candlelit restaurant offers authentic Italian cuisine at reasonable prices in a relaxing atmosphere. Appetizers range from ahi (or beef) carpaccio to the house special antipasto (with five different daily choices), and there are a variety of fish, chicken, and beef dishes. But I keep coming back for the wonderful homemade pasta. 3481 Hoolaulea St. ☎ 808/245-2121. Entrees $14–$26. MC, V. Dinner daily 5–9pm. Map p 537.

★★ **Caffè Coco** WAILUA *GOURMET BISTRO*
This gets my vote for the most charming ambience on Kauai, with a backyard shaded by fruit trees and a view of the Sleeping Giant Mountain. The food is excellent, with vegetarian and other healthful delights such as Greek salad, fish wraps, seared ahi with wasabi cream, and an excellent tofu-and-roast-veggie wrap. Service can be, to say the least, laid-back. 4-369 Kuhio Hwy. ☎ 808/822-7990. Entrees $7–$21; specials usually less than $20. MC, V. Lunch Tues–Fri, dinner daily. Map p 537.

★★ **Casa di Amici** POIPU *ITALIAN/INTERNATIONAL*
The memorable Italian food here has strong Mediterranean and cross-cultural influences. You'll find organic greens from Kilauea, several risotto choices (quattro formaggio and smoked salmon are outstanding), panko-crusted tiger prawns, Thai lobster bisque, and some two dozen pasta selections. 2301 Nalo Rd. ☎ 808/742-1555. Entrees $17–$25. DC, MC, V. Dinner daily. Map above.

★★★ **Dondero's** POIPU *ITALIAN*
If you're looking for a romantic dinner either under the stars overlooking the ocean or tucked away at an intimate table, the Grand Hyatt's stellar Italian restaurant is the place for you. It's

Barefoot Burgers **11**
Brick Oven Pizza **9**
Bubba Burgers **2**
The Bull Shed **3**
Caffè Coco **3**
Café Portofino **5**
Duane's Ono-Char Burger **1**
Duke's Canoe Club **5**
Gaylord's **6**
Genki Sushi **4**
Hamura's Saimin Stand **4**
Hanamaulu Restaurant **4**
Hanapepe Café **10**
JJ's Broiler **5**
Kalaheo Coffee Co. & Café **9**
Kalapaki Beach Hut **5**
Pomodoro **8**
Tip Top Café/Bakery **4**
Tomkats Grille **7**
Wailua Family Restaurant **3**
Waimea Brewing Company **11**

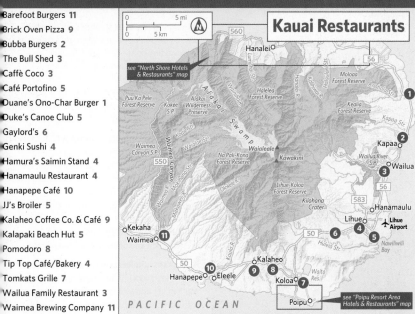

hard to have a bad experience here. Dinners are pricey, but worth every penny. **Grand Hyatt Kauai Resort & Spa, 1571 Poipu Rd. ☎ 808/742-1234. Entrees $22–$42. AE, DC, DISC, MC, V. Dinner daily. Map p 536.**

kids **Duane's Ono-Char Burger** ANAHOLA *HAMBURGER STAND* This roadside burger stand has been serving up hefty, all-beef burgers for generations (and now they offer Boca burgers for vegetarians). Duane's beefy, smoky, and legendary ono-charburgers are served several ways: teriyaki, mushroom, cheddar, barbecue, and the Special, with grilled onions, sprouts, and two cheeses. **On Kuhio Hwy. ☎ 808/822-9181. Hamburgers $4.15–$6.45. MC, V. Lunch and dinner daily. Map above.**

★ **Duke's Canoe Club** NAWILIWILI *STEAK/SEAFOOD* This oceanfront oasis is the hippest spot in town, with a winning combination of great view, affordable menu, attractive salad bar, popular music, and a very happy happy hour. The inexpensive fish tacos are a major attraction, as are the five or six varieties of fresh catch each night. **In the Kauai Marriott Resort & Beach Club, 3610 Rice St., Nawiliwili. ☎ 808/246-9599. Entrees: $6–$13 lunch, $15–$30 dinner. AE, DISC, MC, V. Lunch and dinner daily. Map above.**

Icy-Cold Dessert

Don't leave Kauai until you have tried "shave ice." It's made by shaving a block of ice with an ultra-sharp blade, which results in ice as thin as frozen powder. The shave ice is then saturated with a sweet syrup. (Flavors range from old-fashioned strawberry to such local treats as *li hing mui.*) You'll find shave ice all over the island, from small, hole-in-the-wall stores to vans alongside the road. A few to look for are: **Shave Ice Paradise,** in the Hanalei Center (☎ 808/826-6659); **Hawaiian Blizzard,** a small stand in front of Big Save, in the Kapaa Shopping Center, 4-1105 Kuhio Hwy., no phone; **Halo Halo Shave Ice,** 2956 Kress St., Lihue (☎ 808/245-5094); and **Hawaiian Hut Delights** (which features sugar-free shave ice), 3805 Hanapepe Rd., Hanapepe (☎ 808/335-3781).

★★ **Gaylord's** LIHUE *CONTINENTAL/PACIFIC RIM* This former 1930s plantation manager's estate on a 1,700-acre sugar plantation overlooks rolling lawns and purple mountains. Gaylord's serves American classics (New York steak,

> *Gaylord's has a beautiful former plantation setting, a bumper crop of American classic recipes, and sumptuous desserts.*

rack of lamb, prime rib), and international specials (kalua pork, fajitas) along with pasta, fresh seafood, and lavish desserts. **At Kilohana, 3-2087 Kaumualii Hwy. ☎ 808/245-9593. www.gaylordskauai.com. Entrees: $9–$14 lunch, $19–$42 dinner. AE, DC, DISC, MC, V. Breakfast, lunch, and dinner Mon–Sat; Sun brunch. Map p 537.**

kids **Genki Sushi** LIHUE *SUSHI*
This affordable chain is a great place to take the kids: The sushi is inexpensive, and it's fun to select as it circulates the counter on a conveyor belt. Prices are based on the color of the plate. The sushi is continually made fresh and added to the conveyor belt. **Kukui Grove Shopping Center, 3-2600 Kaumualii Hwy. ☎ 808/632-2450. Sushi plates $1.55–$4.90. MC, V. Lunch and dinner daily. Map p 537.**

Hamura's Saimin Stand LIHUE *SAIMIN*
If there were a saimin hall of fame, Hamura's would be it. It's a cultural experience, a renowned saimin stand where fans line up to take their place over steaming bowls of this Island specialty at a few U-shaped counters. The noodles come heaped with vegetables, wontons, hard-boiled eggs, sweetened pork, vegetables, and several condiment combinations. **2956 Kress St. ☎ 808/245-3271. Most items under $9. No credit cards. Lunch and dinner daily. Map p 537.**

★ **Hanalei Dolphin Restaurant & Fish Market** HANALEI *SEAFOOD* This fish market and adjoining steak-and-seafood restaurant sit on the banks of the Hanalei River. Enjoy the river view as you dine on fresh catch, baked shrimp, Alaskan king crab, chicken marinated in soy sauce, or other tried-and-true dishes. **5-5016 Kuhio Hwy. ☎ 808/826-6113. Entrees $20–$36. MC, V. Lunch and dinner daily. Map p 539.**

kids **Hanamaulu Restaurant** LIHUE *CHINESE/JAPANESE/SUSHI* When passing this restaurant, you'd never know that serene Japanese gardens with stone pathways and tatami-floored teahouses are hidden within. You can dine at the sushi bar or in the teahouse (reservations required). Chop suey, wontons, teriyaki chicken, and sukiyaki (less verve than value) are some of the options in budget-friendly Japanese and Chinese plate lunches. **3-4291 Kuhio Hwy. ☎ 808/245-2511. Entrees $6–$15. MC, V. Lunch Tues–Fri, dinner Tues–Sun. Map p 537.**

★★ **Hanapepe Café** HANAPEPE *GOURMET VEGETARIAN/ITALIAN* Vegtarian cuisine elevated to gourmet status. The menu changes every week, featuring Italian and fresh seafood specialties. There's no liquor license, so if you want wine, bring your own. **3830 Hanapepe Rd. ☎ 808/335-5011. Entrees: $6.50–$13 lunch, $16–$24 dinner. MC, V. Lunch and bakery Mon–Fri, dinner Fri. Map p 537.**

★ **JJ's Broiler** NAWILIWILI *AMERICAN*
Famous for its Slavonic steak (tenderloin in butter, wine, and garlic) and herb-crusted ahi, JJ's is a lively spot on Kalapaki Bay, with open-air dining, stellar views of the bay, and a menu that covers more than the usual surf and turf. Options include coconut shrimp, Manila clams, scallops Florentine, and appetizers that run the gamut from potato skins to wontons. **3416 Rice St., Nawiliwili. ☎ 808/246-4422. Reservations recommended for dinner. Entrees: $10–$15 lunch, $20–$30 dinner. DISC, MC, V. Lunch and dinner daily. Map p 537.**

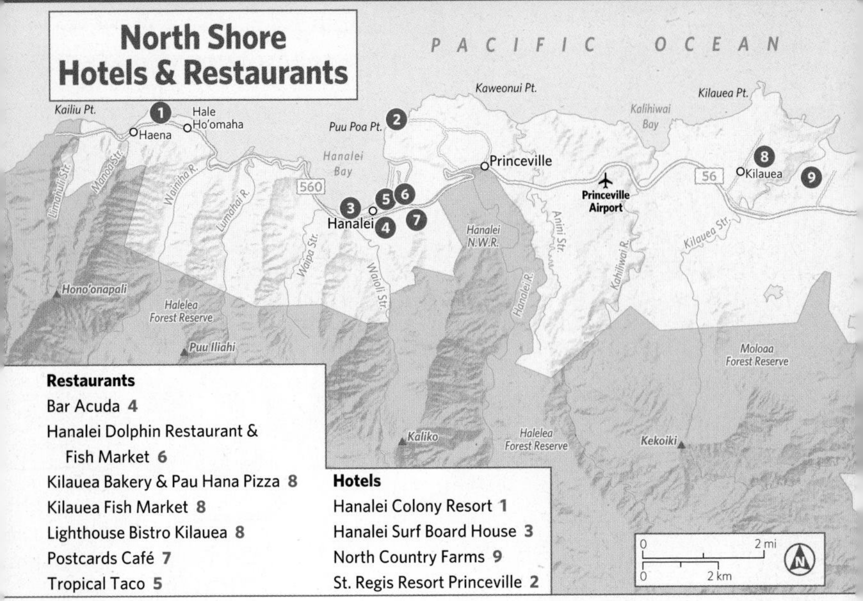

★ **Joe's on the Green** POIPU *AMERICAN* Local residents flock to this eatery for breakfast or for lunch after a round of golf. Breakfasts are a bargain, especially if you go before 8:30am and get the early-bird special for $5.99. I recommend the banana-macadamia nut pancakes. Lunch is popular because of a range of sandwiches (from fresh fish to burgers to a quarter-pound hot dog with sauerkraut), salads (build your own), and desserts. **2545 Kiahuna Plantation Dr., at the Kiahuna Golf Club. ☎ 808/742-9696. Entrees: $4.95–$9.50 breakfast, $5.50–$10.50 lunch. MC, V. Breakfast and lunch daily. Map p 536.**

Kalaheo Coffee Co. & Cafe KALAHEO *COFFEEHOUSE/CAFE* John Ferguson has long been one of my favorite Kauai chefs, and his cafe is a coffee lover's fantasy: Kauai Estate Peaberry, Kona dark roast, Guatemalan French roast, Colombian, Costa Rican, Sumatran, and African coffees—you can visit the world on a coffee bean! The coffeehouse also serves masterful breakfasts (from breakfast burritos to bagels). At lunch the fabulous grilled turkey burgers, fresh-from-the-garden salads, and soup of the day are all winners. **2-2560 Kaumualii Hwy. (Hwy. 50). ☎ 808/332-5858. Most items less than $8. Dinner entrees $16–$27. MC, V. Breakfast and lunch daily. Dinner Wed–Sat. Map p 537.**

kids **Kalapaki Beach Hut** NAWILIWILI *BURGERS* This is basic fare served on paper plates with plastic cutlery at cheap, cheap prices. Breakfasts are hearty omelets, pancakes, and numerous egg dishes. Lunches are heavy on the hamburgers, lots of sandwiches, a few healthful salads, and fish and chips. Very casual—feel free to drop by in your bathing suit. **3474 Rice St. ☎ 808/246-6330. Entrees: $3.75–$6.50 breakfast, $3.95–$6.25 lunch. Breakfast and lunch daily. MC, V. Map p 537.**

★ **Kilauea Bakery & Pau Hana Pizza** KILAUEA *PIZZA/BAKERY* Inventive pizzas include the Billie Holiday, with smoked ono, Swiss chard, roasted onions, Gorgonzola-rosemary sauce, and mozzarella; or the scampi, with tiger prawns, roasted garlic, capers, and cheese. The much-loved bakery puts out guava sourdough, coconut cream-filled chocolate eclairs (yum!), and other fine baked goods. **In Kong Lung Center, Kilauea Rd. ☎ 808/828-2020. Pizzas $11–$30. MC, V. Breakfast, lunch, and dinner daily 6:30am–9pm. Map p 539.**

> *Fresh local delicacies combine with culinary delights from around the world at Roy's Poipu Bar & Grill.*

★ **Kilauea Fish Market** KILAUEA *HEALTHFUL PLATE LUNCH* This is the perfect place to get a picnic takeout lunch or an easy dinner. Coriena Rogers not only has healthful, yummy meals made with just-caught fish but she also has a deli section with fresh fish for those looking to cook it themselves. Vegetarians will be happy with the daily specials. These are some of the best prices on the North Shore. 4270 Kilauea Lighthouse Rd. ☎ 808/828-6244. Most items under $15. MC, V. Lunch and dinner Mon–Sat. Map p 539.

★ **Lighthouse Bistro Kilauea** KILAUEA *CONTINENTAL/PACIFIC RIM/ITALIAN* The ambience is wonderful, with a retro feeling, and the food is excellent, an eclectic selection that highlights local ingredients in everything from fresh-fish tacos and burgers to mac-nut-crusted chicken and four preparations of fresh catch. This is much more elegant than usual lunchtime fare. In Kong Lung Center, Kilauea Rd. ☎ 808/828-0481. Entrees: $5–$11 lunch, $18–$39 dinner. MC, V. Lunch Mon–Sat, dinner daily. Map p 539.

Plantation Gardens Restaurant POIPU *HAWAII REGIONAL CUISINE* Many menu items are fresh Kauai products: seaweed, fish, and shellfish are from local waters, and many of the fruits, herbs, and vegetables are grown on the restaurant premises. The historic architecture includes a generous veranda, koa trim, and Brazilian cherry floors. The property includes koi ponds, shade-giving coconut and kou trees, orchids, bromeliads, and a cactus and succulent garden. In Kiahuna Plantation Resort, 2253 Poipu Rd. ☎ 808/742-2216. Main courses $18–$28. AE, DC, MC, V. Dinner daily. Map p 536.

kids **Poipu Beach Broiler** POIPU *STEAK/SEAFOOD* This casual eatery is the perfect place for sunset pupu—the large appetizer menu includes vegetable summer rolls, sea scallops, seared ahi sashimi, or tender calamari. Lunch is burgers, sandwiches, and salads; dinner entrees include fresh fish, prime rib, grilled sirloin, and baby back ribs. **1941 Poipu Rd. ☎ 808/742-6433. Entrees: $8–$12 lunch, $19–$27 dinner. AE, DC, DISC, MC. V. Lunch and dinner daily. Map p 536.**

★ **Pomodoro** KALAHEO *ITALIAN* Hawaiian hospitality meets European flavors in this warm, welcoming restaurant. Choose from homemade garlic focaccia, homemade mozzarella, chicken saltimbocca, and homemade pastas, as well as veal, chicken, scampi, calamari, and very fresh organic green salads. **In Rainbow Plaza, Kaumualii Hwy. (Hwy. 50). ☎ 808/332-5945. Entrees $14–$24. MC, V. Dinner Mon–Sat. Map p 537.**

★★ **Postcards Cafe** HANALEI *GOURMET SEAFOOD/NATURAL FOODS* The charming plantation-style building that used to be the Hanalei Museum is now Hanalei's gourmet central. Postcards is known for its use of healthful ingredients, fresh from the island and creatively prepared and presented. Great menu, presentation, and ambience—a winner. **On Kuhio Hwy. (at the entrance to Hanalei town). ☎ 808/826-1191. Entrees $15–$28. AE, DC, DISC, MC, V. Dinner daily. Map p 539.**

★★★ **Roy's Poipu Bar & Grill** POIPU *EURO-ASIAN* The signature touches of Roy Yamaguchi are abundantly present in this loud, lively restaurant: an excellent, affordable wine selection; fresh local ingredients prepared with a nod to Europe, Asia, and the Pacific; and service so efficient it can be overbearing. Because appetizers (such as blackened ahi with mustard soy sauce and grilled Szechwan baby back ribs) are a major part of the menu, you can sample Roy's legendary fare without breaking the bank. **In Poipu Shopping Village, 2360 Kiahuna Plantation Dr. ☎ 808/742-5000. www.roysrestaurant.com. Main courses $15–$45. AE, DC, DISC, MC, V. Dinner daily. Map p 536.**

★★★ **Tidepool Restaurant** POIPU *SEAFOOD* A cluster of Polynesian-style thatched bungalows overlook the lagoon in this dreamy, open-air restaurant. The atmosphere would be enough to make you book a table, but the cuisine is outstanding, a definite "do

A Hawaiian Feast: The Luau

The luau usually begins at sunset and features Polynesian and Hawaiian entertainment (from torch juggling to hula). The food always includes *imu*-roasted kalua pork, lomi salmon, dried fish, poke (raw fish cut into small pieces), poi (made from taro), laulau (meat, fish, and vegetables wrapped in ti leaves), Hawaiian sweet potato, sauteed vegetables, salad, and the ultimate taste treat, a coconut dessert called haupia. Most luau will have more common preparations of fish, chicken, and roast beef as well.

The mainstay of the feast is the *imu,* a hot earthen pit in which the pig and other items are cooked. The preparations for the feast actually begin in the morning, when the luau master layers hot stones and banana leaves in the pit to get the temperature up to about 400°F (200°C). The pig, vegetables, and other items are lowered into the pit and cooked all day. The water in the leaves steams the pig and roasts the meat to a tender texture.

One of the larger commercial luau in the island is **Smith's Tropical Paradise Garden Lu'au,** in the Tropical Paradise Gardens on the Wailua River (☎ 808/821-6895 or 808/821-6895; www.smithskauai.com), every Monday, Wednesday, and Friday at 5pm (Mon–Fri in summer). Luau prices are $75 for adults, $30 children 7 to 13, and $19 children 3 to 6.

Recently the **Sheraton Kauai,** Poipu Beach (☎ 808/742-8200), launched the island's only oceanfront luau. The Surf to Sunset Luau is held on Friday, beginning at 5pm with a shell lei greeting and a mai tai. Guests can wander among the local artisans who teach lei-making, lauhala-weaving, and coconut frond-weaving. Cost for adults ranges from $75 for the buffet dinner and entertainment to $87 for premier seating, table service, and professional photos ($38 or $44 children 6–12).

On the south coast, check out **Tihati Production's "Havaiki Nui,"** in the Grand Hyatt Kauai Resort & Spa, 1571 Poipu Rd., Poipu (☎ 800/55-HYATT 554-9288 or 808/742-1234; www.kauai-hyatt.com), every Sunday and Thursday. They have an elaborate buffet and a very professional Polynesian show. The cost is $75 for adults, $65 teens 13 to 20, and $40 children 6 to 12.

> *TOP & BOTTOM Dinner and dessert at Hamura's Saimin Stand. CENTER Gaylord's seafood delights.*

not miss." Their specialty is fresh fish (the signature dish is macadamia nut-crusted mahimahi with a Kahlua, lime, and ginger butter sauce), but they also have juicy steaks and ribs, as well as entrees for vegetarians. Grand Hyatt Kauai Resort & Spa, 1571 Poipu Rd. ☎ 808/742-1234. Reservations recommended. Entrees $22–$48. AE, DC, DISC, MC, V. Dinner daily. Map p 536.

kids **Tip Top Café/Bakery** LIHUE *LOCAL*
This small cafe/bakery (also the lobby for the Tip Top Motel) has been serving local customers since 1916. The best deal is their breakfast: Most items are $5 or under, and their macadamia pancakes are known throughout Kauai. Lunch ranges from pork chops to teriyaki chicken, but their specialty is oxtail soup. For a real treat, stop by the bakery and take something home (we recommend the freshly baked *malasadas*). 3173 Akahi St. ☎ 808/245-2333. Breakfast items under $5; lunch entrees under $6. MC, V. Breakfast and lunch Tues–Sun. Map p 537.

Tomkats Grille KALOA *AMERICAN/GRILL*
Fried appetizers, inexpensive New York steak, rotisserie chicken, seafood salad with fresh catch, and sandwiches and burgers are among the offerings at the Grille, in a serene garden setting in Old Koloa town. Wash down your kalua pork quesadilla or seared poke with a beer—they serve everything from local micro brews to Guinness. 5404 Koloa Rd. ☎ 808/742-8887. Main courses $11–$37. MC, V. Lunch and dinner daily. Map p 537.

★ **Tropical Taco** HANALEI *MEXICAN*
For more than a quarter of a century Roger Kennedy has been making tasty tacos and burritos in Hanalei, including the signature "fat Jack": a 10-inch deep-fried tortilla with cheese, beans, and beef or fish. Roger does warn everyone about his tasty treats: "Not to be consumed 1 hour before surfing!" Roger offers "anything you want to drink, as long as it's lemonade." Hale Lea Building, 5-5088 Kuhio Hwy. ☎ 808/827-TACO (827-8226). www.tropicaltaco.com. Most items under $8. No credit cards. Lunch Mon–Sat. Map p 539.

kids **Wailua Family Restaurant** WAILUA *AMERICAN/LOCAL* The salad bars, efficient service, and family-friendly feeling here are

› *A charming plantation-style building is the picture-postcard setting for a delicious island meal at Postcards Cafe.*

egendary. Seniors get discounts on the huge menu, and there's a special menu for kids. The cross-cultural salad bar includes a Mexican bar, pasta bar, sushi section, homemade soups, and ethnic samplings from Korean, Japanese, Filipino, and Hawaiian traditions. **4361 Kuhio Hwy. ☎ 808/822-3325. Entrees: $6–$8 breakfast, most under $10 lunch, $11–$16 dinner. MC, V. Breakfast, lunch, and dinner daily. Map p 537.**

Waimea Brewing Company WAIMEA *ECLECTIC*
This popular brewery in the Waimea Plantation Cottages is a welcome addition to the dry west side, serving pub fare with a multiethnic twist. Choose from "small plates" (ale-steamed shrimp, taro-leaf-and-goat-cheese dip) or "big plates" (steak with wasabi mashed potatoes, kalbi short ribs, kalua pork). In between are soups, salads, and sandwiches, including fresh catch. The beer is brewed on the premises. **9400 Kaumualii Hwy. ☎ 808/338-9733. Entrees $10–$30. AE, DISC, MC, V. Lunch and dinner daily. Map p 537.**

Yum Cha POIPU *ASIAN*
Come here for a range of Asian dishes at fairly reasonable prices. Small plate appetizers range from chilled summer rolls to a grilled chicken satay. Entrees include Korean beef short ribs, Mandarin chicken, and stir-fried soba noodles. They specialize in a great selection of Chinese loose teas (*Yum Cha* means "drink tea"). **Poipu Bay Golf Course, 1571 Poipu Rd. ☎ 808/742-1515. Entrees $10–$18. MC, V. Lunch and dinner Tues–Sat. Map p 536.**

Kauai Hotel Best Bets

Best Budget Hotel

Garden Island Inn $ 3445 Wilcox Rd., Lihue (p 545)

Kalaheo Inn $ 4444 Papalina Rd., Kahaleo (p 547)

Most Charming B&B

Marjorie's Kauai Inn $$ off Hailima Rd., Lawai (p 548)

Best Club-Level Amenities

Grand Hyatt, $$$$$ 1571 Poipu Rd., Poipu (p 545)

Best Family Condo

Kiahuna Plantation Resort, $$$ 2253 Poipu Rd., Poipu (p 548)

Best Fantasy Resort

Kauai Marriott, $$$$ 3610 Rice St., Lihue (p 548)

Most Historic

Waimea Plantation Cottages $$$ 9400 Kaumualii Hwy., Waimea (p 550)

Best for Kids

Sheraton Kauai $$$$ 2440 Hoonani Rd., Poipu (p 550)

Most Luxurious Hotels

St. Regis Resort Princeville $$$$$ 5520 Ka Haku Rd., Princeville (p 549)

Grand Hyatt $$$$$ 1571 Poipu Rd., Poipu (p 545)

Most Luxurious Condo

Outrigger Waiouli $$$ 4-820 Kuhio Hwy., Kapaa (p 549)

Best Moderate Hotel

Kauai Country Inn $$ 6440 Olohena Rd., Kapaa (p 547)

Best Off the Beaten Path

Kokee Lodge $ Waimea Canyon Dr., Kokee State Park (p 548)

Most Romantic

Turtle Cove Suites $$ P.O. Box 1899, Poipu (p 550)

Most Secluded

Hanalei Colony Resort $$$ 5-7130 Kuhio Hwy., Hanalei (p 545)

Best Service

Grand Hyatt, $$$$$ 1571 Poipu Rd., Poipu (p 545)

Best Spa

Grand Hyatt, $$$$$ 1571 Poipu Rd., Poipu (p 545)

Best Value

Hanalei Surf Board House $$ 5459 Weke Rd., Hanalei (p 546)

Best View

St. Regis Resort Princeville, $$$$$ 5520 Ka Haku Rd., Princeville (p 549)

> *With beautiful lagoons, waterfalls, and fountains, the Kauai Marriott Resort & Beach Club is a virtual water park.*

Kauai Hotels A to Z

★ kids **Aloha Beach Resort** KAPAA
This moderately priced resort captures the feeling of Old Hawaii. Its location right next door to 57-acre Lydgate Beach Park (with Kamalani Playground for the kids) makes it a family-friendly choice. Convenient to restaurants, shopping, and golf. 3-5920 Kuhio Hwy. ☎ 877/997-6667 or 808/823-6000. www.abrkauai.com. 216 units. Doubles $149–$169. AE, DC, DISC, MC, V. Map p 546.

★ **Garden Island Inn** LIHUE
This bargain-hunter's delight is located 2 miles from the airport, 1 mile from Lihue, and within walking distance of shops, restaurants, and a beach just across the street. Spacious island-style rooms and flower-filled grounds. 3445 Wilcox Rd. (across the street from Kalapaki Beach, near Nawiliwili Harbor). ☎ 800/648-0154 or 808/245-7227. www.gardenislandinn.com. 21 units. Doubles $99–$170. AE, DISC, MC, V. Map p 547.

★★★ kids **Grand Hyatt Kauai Resort & Spa** POIPU This is one of Hawaii's best luxury hotels and one of the top-ranked tropical resorts in *Condé Nast Traveler*'s annual readers' poll. The four-story resort, built into the oceanside bluffs, spreads over 50 acres. Spacious, elegant rooms have marble bathrooms and private lanais. It's also home to the **ANARA Spa,** the best spa on Kauai. 1571 Poipu Rd. ☎ 800/55-HYATT (554-9288) or 808/742-1234. www.kauai-hyatt.com. 602 units. Doubles $430–$770. AE, DC, MC, V. Map p 536.

More Hotel Maps

See also "Poipu Resort Area Hotels & Restaurants" (p 536) and "North Shore Hotels & Restaurants" (p 539).

★★ kids **Hanalei Colony Resort** HANALEI
This 5-acre resort has all the magic of the enchanting North Shore: a perfect white-sand beach, lush tropical gardens, fertile jungle, and jagged mountain peaks. Unbelievably spacious units have plenty of room for families. Each has a private lanai, full kitchen, and ceiling fans. The property has a large pool, laundry facilities, and a barbecue and picnic area. No TVs or phones. 5-7130 Kuhio Hwy. ☎ 800/628-3004 or 808/826-6235. www.hcr.com. 48 units. Doubles

> *Tucked between Hanalei Bay and impressive mountain peaks, Princeville's St. Regis Resort enjoys one of the world's most spectacular settings.*

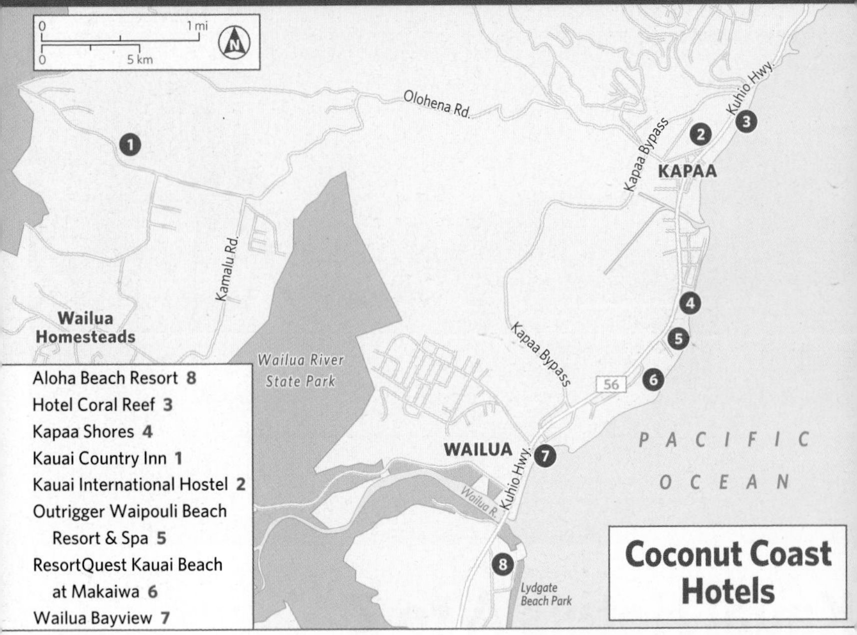

$230–$410 2-bedroom apt. AE, MC, V. Map p 539.

★★ Hanalei Surf Board House HANALEI
Just a block from the beach, these two incredibly decorated studio units are a steal at $195. One studio is filled with whimsical "cowgirl" decor and the other in pure Elvis Presley memorabilia. Both units have kitchenettes, 300-channel televisions, free Wi-Fi access, Bose CD player, DVD, ipod dock, barbecues, and backyard lanais. A 2-minute walk to either the beach or downtown Hanalei. 5459 Weke Rd. ☎ 808/826-9825. www.hanaleisurfboardhouse.com. 2 units. Doubles $195. No credit cards. Map p 539.

★★ Hideaway Cove Poipu Beach POIPU
Just a short walk to a white sandy beach are these gorgeous condominium units in a plantation setting. Amenities are top-drawer. Units have hardwood floors, TV/VCR/DVD, spacious living areas, kitchenettes with the best appliances and granite countertops, and big outdoor lanais with top-of-the-line grills. 2307 Nalo Rd. ☎ 866/849-2426 or 808/635-8785. www.hideawaycove.com. 7 units. Doubles: $170–$195 studio, $210 1-bedroom, $280–$305 2-bedroom, $415–$500 3-bedroom; $720 5-bedroom. AE, DISC, MC, V. Map p 536.

Hilton Kauai Beach Hotel Resort LIHUE
This 25-acre property, now a condo-hotel (a portion of the rooms in the hotel will be available for private ownership), commands a 3-mile stretch of the beach, next door to a top-ranked municipal golf course. Rooms have plush new carpeting, a Balinese-style wood entry door, marble bath and floors, top-of-the-line bedding, and high-speed wireless Internet service. 4331 Kauai Beach Dr. ☎ 800/HILTONS (445-8667) or 808/245-1955. www1.hilton.com. 350 units. Doubles $179–$399. AE, DC, DISC, MC, V. Map p 547.

Hotel Coral Reef KAPAA
This small, older hotel faces a grassy lawn, coconut trees, and a white-sand beach. It's not the Hyatt, but it's a great way for frugal travelers to enjoy the beach. It's within walking distance of shops, restaurants, golf, and tennis, and just 50 yards away from good swimming and snorkeling. 4-1516 Kuhio Hwy. ☎ 800/843-4659 or 808/822-4481. www.hotelcoralreefresort.com. 21 units. Doubles $125–$249. AE, DC, MC, V. Map above.

Inn Waimea WAIMEA
This quaint two-story inn occupies an ideal location in Waimea. It's just a block from the ocean and within walking distance of restaurants

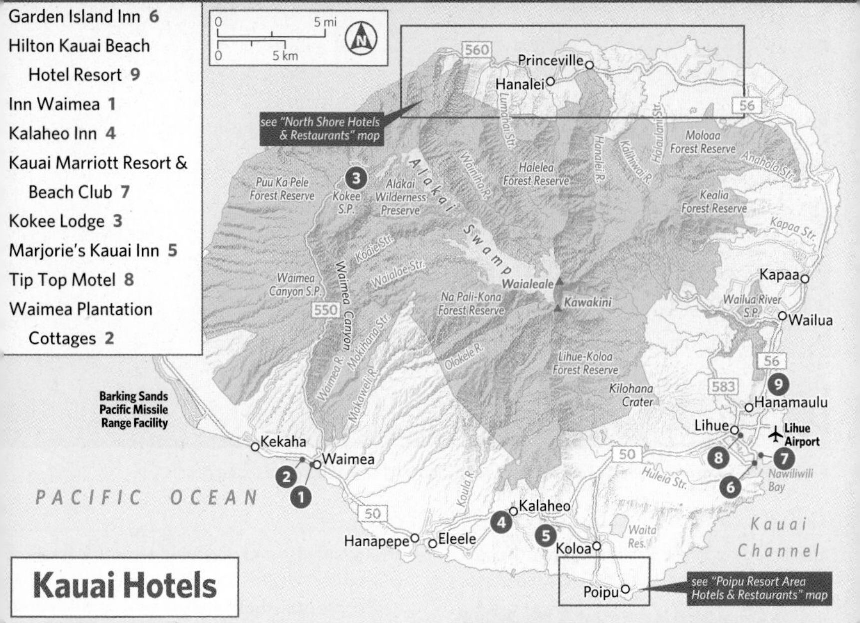

Kauai Hotels

and shops. Each to the suites is uniquely decorated. All of the rooms have coffeemakers, refrigerators, cable TV, ceiling fans, and free high-speed Internet. **4469 Halepule Rd. ☎ 808/338-0031. www.innwaimea.com. 4 units. Double $110. No credit cards. Map above.**

★ Kalaheo Inn KALAHEO

This inn is a 1940s motel totally remodeled in 1999 and converted into comfortable apartment units with kitchens. The friendly owners love families and have a storeroom full of games to keep the kids entertained. They also loan out complimentary beach towels, beach toys, and even golf clubs. **4444 Papalina Rd. ☎ 888/332-6023 or 808/332-6023. www.kalaheoinn.com. 15 units. Doubles: $83 studio, $93–$103 1-bedroom, $133 2-bedroom, $183 3-bedroom w/full kitchen. MC, V. Map above.**

★ Kapaa Shores KAPAA

These apartments are located right on the beach in the heart of Kapaa. All units are in excellent shape and come with fully equipped modern kitchens and large lanais. On-site amenities include a large pool, a tennis court, hot tub, a shuffleboard court, laundry facilities, and barbecues. Golf courses, restaurants, and bars are nearby. **900 Kuhio Hwy. ☎ 800/801-0378 or 808/822-4871. www.kauaiproperties.com. 84 units. Doubles: $115–$160 1-bedroom, $122–$210 2-bedroom. AE, MC, V. Map p 546.**

★★ Kauai Country Inn KAPAA

This slice of paradise, nestled on 2 acres in the rolling hills behind Kapaa, consists of four suites uniquely decorated in Hawaiian Art Deco. You get hardwood floors, kitchen or kitchenette, and your own Macintosh computer with Wi-Fi connection. Everything is top-drawer, from the "rain" shower head in the bathroom to the subzero refrigerator. You're welcome to pick fruit from the trees on the property. ***Beatles fans take note:*** Mike has been collecting memorabilia for decades and has the only private Beatles Museum in the state. **6440 Olohena Rd. ☎ 808/821-0207. www.kauaicountryinn.com. 4 units. Doubles $110–$165 1- and 2-bedroom suites. AE, MC, V. Map p 546.**

Kauai International Hostel KAPAA

Located in the heart of Kapaa, a block from the beach, this hostel provides clean rooms in a friendly atmosphere. There's a very clean kitchen, laundry facilities, a TV, a pool table, and a barbecue area. Just 1 block from the highway, it's within walking distance of shops and restaurants. Airport pickup is available ($15). **4532 Lehua St. ☎ 808/823-6142. www.kauaiinternationalhostel.com. 32 bunk beds, 6**

> *Hideaway Cove offers guests spacious units and high-end amenities close to the beach.*

private rooms. Single $25 dorm room, double $60–$75 private room. AE, MC, V. Map p 546.

★★ kids Kauai Marriott Resort & Beach Club LIHUE Water is everywhere throughout this luxury resort: lagoons, waterfalls, fountains, a 5-acre circular swimming pool, and a terrific stretch of beach. Guest rooms are comfortable, with fabulous views of gold-sand Kalapaki Beach, verdant gardens, and palm trees. The downside: It's just a mile from Lihue Airport, which means you can hear the takeoff and landing of every jet. **3610 Rice St. ☎ 800/220-2925 or 808/245-5050. www.marriott.com/lihhi. 356 units. Doubles $339–$454. AE, DC, DISC, MC, V. Map p 547.**

★★ kids Kiahuna Plantation Resort POIPU One of the best condominium developments in the Poipu area, this complex consists of several plantation-style buildings, loaded with Hawaiian style and sprinkled on a 35-acre garden setting with lagoons, lawns, and a gold-sand beach. Golf, shopping, and restaurants are within easy walking distance. **2253 Poipu Rd. ☎ 800/OUTRIGGER (688-7444) or 808/742-6411. www.outrigger.com. 333 units. Doubles: $265–$499 1-bedroom apt. (sleeps up to 4), $405–$545 2-bedroom apt. (sleeps up to 6). AE, DC, DISC, MC, V. Map p 536.**

Kokee Lodge KOKEE There are two types of cabins here: The older ones have dormitory-style sleeping arrangements (and resemble a youth hostel), while the new ones have two separate bedrooms each. Both styles sleep six and come with cooking utensils, bedding, and linens. The newer units have wood floors, cedar walls, and more modern kitchen facilities. No phones or TVs. The Kokee Lodge Restaurant is open for continental breakfast and lunch every day. **Waimea Canyon Dr., P.O. Box 819. ☎ 808/335-6061. 12 units. Doubles $90. AE, DC, DISC, MC, V. Map p 547.**

★ Marjorie's Kauai Inn LAWAI This quiet property, perched on the side of a hill, is just 10 minutes from Poipu Beach and 5 minutes from Old Koloa Town. It offers stunning views over rolling pastures and the Lawai Valley. Every unit has a kitchenette and lanai. On the hillside is a huge, 50-foot-long swimming pool. Every room is beautiful, but my favorite is the Sunset View Room, with its own hot tub outside and a view that will linger in your memory forever. The inn is not appropriate for families with children. **Off Hailima Rd. ☎ 800/717-8838 or 808/332-8838. www.marjorieskauaiinn.com. 3 units. Doubles $130–$175. No credit cards. Map p 547.**

★ Nihi Kai Villas POIPU This is a great deal, with large units just 200 yards from the beach. It's a 2-minute walk from world-famous Brennecke's Beach Broiler and a block from Poipu Beach Park. On-site amenities include an oceanfront swimming pool, tennis and paddle courts, and a barbecue and picnic area. Within a 5-minute drive are two great golf courses, several restaurants, and loads of shopping. **1870 Hoone Rd. Reservations: c/o Grantham Resorts, 3176 Poipu Rd. ☎ 800/325-5701 or 808/742-2000. Fax 808/742-9093. www.grantham-resorts.com. 70 units. Doubles: $145–$244 1-bedroom, $159–$380 2-bedroom, $300–$625 3-bedroom. DC, DISC, MC, V. Map p 536.**

★ kids **North Country Farms** KILAUEA
In the rolling green hills outside of Kilauea, on a 4-acre organic vegetable, fruit, and flower farm, Lee Roversi and her family have private, handcrafted redwood cottages for rent. The cottages have hardwood floors, large lanai with garden views, compact kitchenettes, and separate bedrooms. The couches in the living rooms turn into two separate beds, so the cottages can easily sleep four, making this a great choice for families. **Kahlili Makai St. ☎ 808/828-1513. www.northcountryfarms.com. 2 units. $150 double with breakfast fixings. No credit cards. Map p 539.**

★★★ kids **Outrigger Waioulí Beach Resort & Spa** KAPAA This luxurious condominium project on 12½ acres is located right on the beach and within walking distance to restaurants and shops. Each unit is furnished with top-of-the-line materials such as granite countertops, stainless steel appliances, full-size Whirlpool washers and dryers, whirlpool tubs, and 37-inch flat-screen TVs. **4-820 Kuhio Hwy. ☎ 800/OUTRIGGER (688-7444) or 808/823-3300. 196 units. Doubles: $215–$245 hotel room, $265–$485 1-bedroom/2-bath, $395–$755 2-bedroom/3-bath. AE, DC, DISC, MC, V. Map p 546.**

★★ **Poipu Kapili Resort** POIPU
This quiet, upscale oceanfront cluster of condos is outstanding in every area. Home-away-from-home comforts include a video and book library, a spacious pool, several barbecues, tennis courts lit for night play, and an herb garden. A golf course is also nearby. The large apartments have fully equipped kitchens, tropical furnishings, ceiling fans, and private lanais. **2221 Kapili Rd. ☎ 800/443-7714 or 808/742-6449. www.poipukapili.com. 60 units. Doubles: $230–$335 1-bedroom apt, $320–$600 2-bedroom apt. MC, V. Map p 536.**

> *Just 2 miles from Lihue's Airport, the Garden Island Inn is surrounded by shops and restaurants and offers beauty at bargain prices.*

★ **ResortQuest Kauai Beach at Makaiwa** KAPAA This property sits on 10½ acres, nestled between a coconut grove and a white-sand beach. The convenient location offers easy access to the North Shore and the Poipu Beach area on the south shore. The large guest rooms have a Hawaiian theme. The property features a new pool, hot tub, day spa, fitness center, tennis courts, jogging paths, and lounge (with nightly entertainment). **650 Aleka Loop. ☎ 866/77-HAWAII (774-2924) or 808/822-3455. www.resortquesthawaii.com. 311 units. Doubles $285–$472. AE, DC, DISC, MC, V. Map p 546.**

★★★ kids **St. Regis Resort Princeville** PRINCEVILLE This just reopened as a St. Regis property (with new pool and a spa). This is one of the world's finest settings, between Hanalei Bay and Kauai's steepled mountains. The building steps down a cliff, with the entrance on the 9th floor, giving you a jaw-dropping

> *One of the St. Regis Resort's luxurious rooms.*

panoramic vista from the lobby. Opulent rooms have lots of extras (my favorite: a liquid-crystal shower window that you can switch from clear to opaque). 5520 Ka Haku Rd. ☎ 800/826-4400 or 808/826-9644. www.princevillehotelhawaii.com. 252 units. Doubles $565–$815. AE, DC, DISC, MC, V. Map p 539.

★★ kids **Sheraton Kauai Resort** POIPU
This Sheraton has the feeling of Old Hawaii and a dynamite location on one of Kauai's best beaches. Recently updated rooms overlook either the tropical gardens or the rolling surf and feature flat-screen TVs and tropical furniture. A golf course is nearby. ***Families, take note:*** Kids eat free with a paying adult at the Shell Restaurant, at both breakfast and dinner. 2440 Hoonani Rd. ☎ 800/782-9488 or 808/742-1661. www.starwoodhotels.com/hawaii. 394 units. Doubles $400–$740. AE, DC, DISC, MC, V. Map p 536.

Tip Top Motel LIHUE
The Tip Top is an institution on Kauai—it's been around for over 75 years. The two-story concrete tile building provides very basic accommodations: twin beds (with solid, hard mattresses), shower, air-conditioning unit in the window, a dresser, and linoleum tile floors. 3173 Akahi St. ☎ 808/245-2333. 30 units. Doubles $70. MC, V. Map p 547.

★★ **Turtle Cove Suites** POIPU
A fabulous location overlooking the stream and ocean. My favorite unit is the 1,100-square-foot oceanfront suite with a full kitchen and private Jacuzzi. All units come with lanais and feature top-of-the-line materials like slate from India, four-poster beds, and marble bathrooms. The property has a swimming pool and Jacuzzi. P.O. Box 1899, Poipu. ☎ 866/294-2733. www.kauaibeachrentals.com. 4 units. Doubles $150–$250. AE, DC, DISC, MC, V. Map p 536.

★ **Wailua Bayview** KAPAA
Located right on the ocean, these spacious one-bedroom apartments offer excellent value. All units have ceiling fans, full kitchens, washer/dryers, and large lanais. Some have air-conditioning as well. On-site facilities include a pool and barbecue area. Restaurants bars, shopping, golf, and tennis are nearby. 320 Papaloa Rd. ☎ 800/882-9007. www.wailuabay.com. 45 units. Doubles $140–$165. AE, DISC, MC V. Map p 546.

★ kids **Waimea Plantation Cottages** WAIMEA
The restored sugar plantation cottages at this beachfront vacation retreat date from the 1880s to the 1930s. The lovely cottages have been transformed into cozy, comfortable guest units with period furniture and fabrics. Each has a furnished lanai and a fully equipped modern kitchen and bathroom; some units are

Enjoy Old Hawaii ambiance when you stay in one of Waimea Plantation Cottages' carefully restored units.

oceanfront. Facilities include an oceanfront pool, tennis courts, and laundry. 9400 Kaumualii Hwy. ☎ 866-77-HAWAII (774-2924) or 808/338-1625. www.waimeacottages.com. 48 units. Doubles: $155–$175 studio with kitchenette, $220–$360 1-bedroom, $275–$425 2-bedroom, $325–$475 3-bedroom, $525 4-bedroom, $800 5-bedroom. AE, DC, DISC, MC, V. Map p 547.

★★ **Whalers Cove** POIPU
These ultraluxury units are first-class all the way, from the koa door at the entry to the ocean view from the master bedroom. The two-bedroom, two-and-a-half-bathroom units have plenty of space and privacy for two couples. These units have it all: a huge deck overlooking the Pacific, top-of-the-line appliances in the kitchen, washer/dryer, and entertainment center. The property itself features an oceanside infinity pool, a whirlpool, and a barbecue area. 2640 Puuholo Rd. Reservations: Grantham Resorts, 3176 Poipu Rd., Koloa, HI 96756. ☎ 800/325-5701 or 808/742-2000. www.grantham-resorts.com. 35 units. Doubles $345–$469 2-bedroom. DC, DISC, MC, V. Map p 536.

The King of Condos

One of the easiest ways to find lodging in the Poipu Beach area is to contact **Grantham Resorts** (which recently sold to Jonathan Parrish), 3176 Poipu Rd., Koloa, HI 96756 (☎ 800/325-5701 or 808/742-2000; fax 808/742-9093; www.grantham-resorts.com), which handles more than 100 "handpicked" rental units for 12 different condo developments, plus dozens of vacation homes, ranging from quaint cottages to elite resort homes.

If you're staying on Kauai for 5 days, ask Grantham Resorts about the **"Frommer's Preferred Guest Discount,"** for large, well-equipped one- and two-bedroom condos, starting as low as $105 a night for one bedroom and $135 for two bedrooms, with garden views, or $145 a night for ocean-view condos (see the review for Nihi Kai Villas).

Kauai Nightlife & Entertainment A to Z

Bars & Cocktail Lounges

Duke's Canoe Club Barefoot Bar NAWILIWILI
Traditional and contemporary Hawaiian music on Friday nights. Kauai Marriott Resort & Beach Club, 3610 Rice St. ☎ 808/246-9599. Map p 553.

Lizard Lounge KAPAA
A real down-home, neighborhood bar with reasonably priced drinks in a relaxing atmosphere. Waipouli Center. ☎ 808/821-2205. Map p 553.

Pau Hana Bar and Grill KAPAA
If you're looking for a bar where local residents go to relax in a casual atmosphere, here's your best bet. Kauai Village Shopping Center, 4-831 Kuhio Hwy. ☎ 808/821-2900. Map p 553.

Poipu Shopping Village POIPU
Free Tahitian dance performances every Tuesday and Thursday at 5pm in the outdoor courtyard. 2360 Kiahuna. ☎ 808/742-2831. Map p 553.

Rob's Good Time Grill LIHUE
A terrific place to have a beer, shoot some pool, watch the big-screen TV, and display you talent at karaoke. This down-home bar isn't fancy, but the crowd is friendly and it's a great place to meet local folks. Rice Shopping Center, 4303 Rice St. ☎ 808/246-0315. Map p 553.

Hula

Coconut MarketPlace KAPAA
The Coconut Coast towns of Wailua, Waipouli, and Kapaa offer sunset torch-lighting ceremonies, music, and other evening entertainment, but the real action is here. Every Wednesday, starting at 5pm, the shopping center features

> *Enjoy a free traditional hula show featuring local performers Wednesday nights at Coconut MarketPlace.*

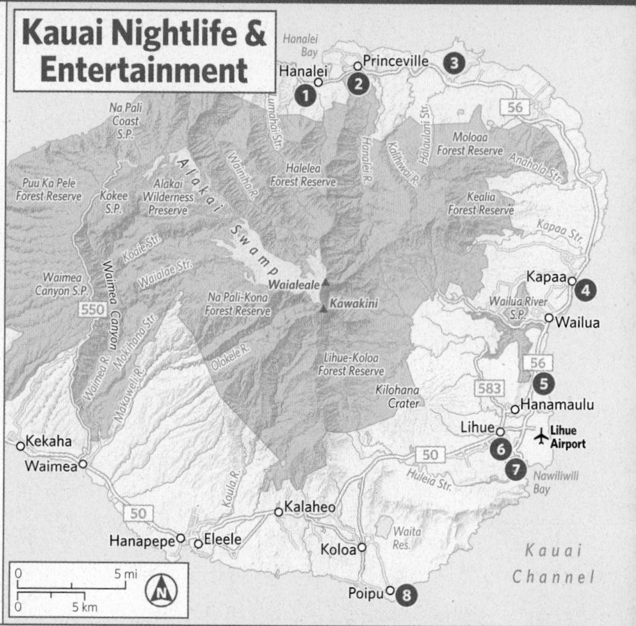

free hula show performed by local residents, anging from troops of tiny dancers who still lon't have their permanent teeth to lithe young vomen and men gracefully performing this anient Hawaiian art to grandmothers who have een dancing for decades. **4-484 Kuhio Hwy. ☎ 808/822-3641. Map above.**

heater & Shows

Hilton Kauai Beach Resort LIHUE

he dinner theater here is currently showing ogers and Hammerstein's *South Pacific* every Monday and Wednesday night. There's also a ightly torch-lighting ceremony and hula show the central courtyard. **4331 Kauai Beach Dr. ☎ 808/346-6500. www.hilton.com. Dinner and how $80 adults, $40 children 12 and under. Map bove.**

Kauai Community Players LIHUE

or arts and culture, local residents flock to he plays put on by the nonprofessional group. ontact them to find out what the latest roduction is and where it will be performed. 's not Broadway (or off-Broadway), but is energetic community theater at its est. **P. O. Box 343. ☎ 808/245-7700. www. auaicommunityplayers.org. Map above.**

Friday Night Is Art Night

Every Friday from 5 to 9pm is **Hanapepe Art Night** in the old plantation community of Hanapepe. Participating galleries take turns being the weekly "host gallery," offering original performances or demonstrations that set the theme for that art night. All the galleries are lit up and decked out, giving the town a special atmosphere. Enjoy a stroll down the streets of quaint, historic Hanapepe town and meet the local artists. Also on Friday night, the **Hanapepe Café** (p 538) is open for dinner from 6 to 9pm and has live music.

Kukui Grove Cinemas LIHUE

This multiplex features the latest films. **Kukui Grove Shopping Center, 4368 Kukui Grove St. ☎ 808/245-5055. Map above.**

Plantation Cinema 1 and 2 KAPAA

This movie theater is convenient to lodgings on the Coconut Coast. **Coconut MarketPlace, 4-484 Kuhio Hwy. ☎ 808/821-2324. Map above.**

Live Music

Hanalei Bay Resort PRINCEVILLE

Music lovers will be thrilled with the Sunday

> *Check out the Friday Night Art Walk in Hanapepe to meet local artists and enjoy special performances.*

Jazz Jam in their **Happy Talk Lounge** from 4 to 7pm and again on Saturday from 6:30 to 9pm. Al Jarreau and Quincy Jones are among those who have stopped by the Sunday Jazz Jam, and the evening crowd has had its share of well-known Hawaiian jammers. On Tuesday evenings from 6:30 to 9:30pm they have live hula5380 Honoiki St. ☎ 808/826-6522. Map p 553.

It Begins with Sunset . . .

Take the time every day to stop and enjoy the sunset. You can watch the big yellow ball descend slowly into the blue waters of the Pacific anywhere, from Poipu to Polihale State Park to Kee Beach to the entire Na Pali Coast. Some insist that the sunset and a mai tai go hand-in-hand. For more information on how to prepare a mai tai, see "The Hawaiian Mai Tai" on p 405.

Hanalei Gourmet HANALEI
This casual spot on the North Shore has live music every night except Monday and Thursday. Old Hanalei Schoolhouse, 5-5161 Kuhi Hwy. ☎ 808/826-2524. Map p 553.

Hukilau Lanai Restaurant KAPAA
Live music Sunday, Tuesday, and Friday, 6:30 to 9:30pm. Kauai Coast Resort, located on the ocean side of Coconut MarketPlace, 520 Aleka Loop. ☎ 808/822-0600. Map p 553.

Keoki's Paradise POIPU
Live music Monday through Friday evenings (call for times), ranging from Hawaiian to contemporary. The cafe menu is available from 11am to 11:30pm. The crowd here is mainly the 21-and-over dancing type. Poipu Shopping Village, 2360 Kiahuna Plantation Dr. ☎ 808/742-7534. Map p 553.

Lighthouse Bistro KILAUEA
Great live music (from flamenco guitar to

Hawaiian) is played during dinner Monday, Friday, and Saturday. **Kong Lung Center, Kilauea Rd. ☎ 808/828-0480. Map p 553.**

The Point POIPU
This oceanside Poipu hotspot features live music Thursday and Saturday with dancing; music ranges from contemporary Hawaiian to good ol' rock and roll. **Sheraton Kauai Resort, 2440 Hoonani Rd. ☎ 808/742-1661. Map p 553.**

Stevenson's Library POIPU
This lounge is the place for an elegant after-dinner drink, with live jazz nightly from 8 to 11pm. Dress in casual resortwear (no tank tops or flip-flops). Sink into comfy, overstuffed chairs, watch fish flit through the big saltwater aquarium, or engage in activities like pool, billiards, or chess. **Grand Hyatt Kauai Resort & Spa, 1571 Poipu Rd. ☎ 808/742-1234. www.kauai-hyatt.com. Map p 553.**

Tahiti Nui HANALEI
If you are looking for a way to experience Old Hawaii, stop by for an exotic drink and "talk story" with the owner, Louise Marston, who actually is from Tahiti. The restaurant/bar is family-friendly and someone always seems to drop in and sing and play music, just like they used to do in the old days. **Hwy. 560 and Aku Rd. ☎ 808/826-6277. Map p 553.**

Luau
See "A Hawaiian Feast: The Luau," p 541.

Sunset Dinner Cruise
Capt. Andy's Sailing Adventure ELEELE
For a romantic evening that will linger in your memory as the highlight of your trip, take the **Na Pali Sunset Dinner,** a 4-hour cruise along the Na Pali Coast. Your evening will include commentary on the history and legends of this coast, great views of the island from out at sea (guests frequently spot turtles), live music, and a sumptuous buffet dinner. The menu includes salads, Teriyaki chicken topped with diced pineapple, Pulehu beef with sautéed mushrooms and onions in garlic sauce, Kaffir lime and lemon rice pilaf, and pineapple bars for dessert. It's best enjoyed during the calm summer months, May to September, but they do have cruises during the winter as well. **Boat leaves from Port Allen Marina Center, 4353 Waialo Rd. ☎ 800/535-0830 or 808/335-6833. www.napali.com. $105 adults, $80 children 2-12.**

> *The Grand Hyatt Resort & Spa's Havaiki Nui Polynesian show on Sundays and Thursdays offers authentic entertainment with a delicious buffet. (See "A Hawaiian Feast: The Luau," p. 541).*

Star-Gazing

Any Kauai beach is great for star-gazing almost any night of the year. Once a month, on the Saturday nearest the new moon, when the skies are darkest, the **Kauai Educational Association for the Study of Astronomy** sponsors a star watch at Waimea Plantation Cottages. For information on the next star watch, contact KEASA, P.O. Box 161, Waimea, HI 96796 (☎ 808/332-STAR (332-7827); www.keasa.org). Video presentations start at 6pm, with star-gazing on the ocean side of the resort to follow.

10

Hawaii's History & Culture

Hawaii: A Brief History

> PREVIOUS PAGE *Most luaus serve meat from a pig roasted in a traditional imu pit.* THIS PAGE *Hawaii's first settlers traveled to the islands via outrigger canoes like the one pictured here.*

The First Hawaiians

Paddling outrigger canoes, the ancestors of today's Hawaiians followed the stars and birds across the sea to Hawaii, "the land of raging fire." They were part of the great Polynesian migration that settled the vast triangle of islands stretching between New Zealand, Easter Island, and Hawaii. No one is sure exactly when they came to Hawaii, but a bone fishhook found at the southernmost tip of the Big Island has been carbon-dated to A.D. 700. An entire Hawaiian culture arose from these settlers.

The "Fatal Catastrophe"

In 1778, a *haole* (white person; literally, one with "no breath") sailed into Waimea Bay on Kauai, where he was welcomed as the god Lono. The man was 50-year-old Capt. James Cook, who had set sail from Tahiti northward across uncharted waters to find the mythical Northwest Passage that was said to link the Pacific and Atlantic oceans. On his way, Cook stumbled upon the Hawaiian Islands quite by chance. He named them the Sandwich Islands, for the Earl of Sandwich, who had bankrolled the expedition.

Overnight, stone-age Hawaii entered the age of iron. Nails were traded for fresh water, pigs, and the affections of Hawaiian women. The sailors brought syphilis, measles, and other diseases to which the Hawaiians had no natural immunity, thereby wreaking havoc on the native population.

After his unsuccessful attempt to find the Northwest Passage, Cook returned to Kealakekua Bay on the Big Island, where a fight broke out over an alleged theft, and the great navigator was killed by a blow to the head. After this "fatal catastrophe," the British survivors sailed home. But Hawaii was now on the sea charts, and traders on the fur route between Canada and China anchored in Hawaii to get fresh water.

Two more sea captains left indelible marks on the islands. The first was American John Kendrick, who in 1791 filled his ship with sandalwood and sailed to China. By 1825, Hawaii's sandalwood forests were gone, enabling invasive plants to take charge. The second captain was Englishman George Vancouver, who in 1793 left cows and sheep. King Kamehameha I sent for cowboys from Mexico and Spain to round up the wild livestock, thus beginning the islands' *paniolo* (cowboy) tradition.

The tightly woven Hawaiian society began to unravel after the death in 1819 of King Kamehameha I, who had united the islands under his rule. One of his successors, Queen Kaahumanu, abolished old taboos and opened the door for religion of another form.

Staying to Do Well

In April 1820, missionaries bent on converting the pagans arrived from New England. The missionaries clothed the natives, banned them from dancing the hula, and nearly dismantled their ancient culture. They also created the 12-letter Hawaiian alphabet, started a printing press, and began recording the islands' history.

Children of the missionaries became the islands' business leaders and politicians, causing

> King Kalakaua hosting a luau for Robert Louis Stevenson, around 1899.

> This early tourism poster promotes Pan American's air service to Hawaii, which began in 1936.

› Hawaii's Royal Crest

ne wag to remark that the nissionaries "came to do ;ood and stayed to do well." n 1848 King Kamehameha III roclaimed the Great Mahele division), which enabled :ommoners and eventually oreigners to own land. In two ;enerations, more than 80% of ll private land was in foreign ands. Sugar planters imorted waves of immigrants to vork the fields.

King David Kalakaua was lected to the throne in 1874. 'his popular "Merrie Monrch" built Iolani Palace in 1882 nd lifted the prohibitions on ne hula and other native arts. For this, he was much loved. He also gave Pearl Harbor to the United States. In 1891 King Kalakaua visited San Francisco, caught a cold, and died in the royal suite of the Sheraton Palace. His sister, Queen Liliuokalani, assumed the throne.

A Sad Farewell

On January 17, 1893, a group of American sugar planters and missionary descendants, with the support of U.S. Marines, overthrew the Hawaiian government and imprisoned Queen Liliuokalani in her own palace, where she later penned the sorrowful "Aloha Oe," Hawaii's song of farewell. The monarchy was dead.

A new republic was established, controlled by Sanford Dole, a powerful sugarcane planter. In 1898, through annexation, Hawaii became an American territory ruled by Dole. His fellow sugarcane planters, known as the Big Five, controlled banking, shipping, and every other facet of economic life on the islands.

Oahu's central Ewa Plain soon filled with crops. The Dole family planted pineapple on its vast acreage. Planters imported more contract laborers. Most of the new immigrants stayed on to establish families and become a part of the islands. Meanwhile, the native Hawaiians became a landless minority.

For nearly a century on Hawaii, sugar was king, generously subsidized by the U.S. government. But the workers eventually went on strike for better wages and working conditions, and the planters found themselves unable to compete with cheap third-world labor costs.

The Tourists Arrive

Tourism proper began in the 1860s. Kilauea Volcano was one of the world's prime attractions for adventure travelers. In 1865 a grass Volcano House was built on the Halemaumau Crater rim to shelter visitors; it was Hawaii's first tourist hotel.

In 1901 W. C. Peacock built the elegant Beaux Arts Moana Hotel on Waikiki Beach, and W. C. Weedon convinced Honolulu businessmen to bankroll his plan to advertise Hawaii in San Francisco. Armed with a stereopticon and tinted photos of Waikiki, Weedon sailed off in 1902 for 6 months of lecture tours to introduce "the beautiful lands of Hawaii." He drew packed houses. A tourism promotion bureau was formed in 1903, and about 2,000 visitors came to Hawaii that year.

The steamship was Hawaii's tourism lifeline. Streamers, leis, and pomp welcomed each Matson liner at downtown's Aloha Tower. Hawaii amused visitors with personal tours, floral parades, and shows spotlighting that naughty dance, the hula.

Beginning in 1935 and running for the next 40 years, Webley Edwards's weekly live radio show, "Hawaii Calls," planted the sounds of Waikiki—surf, sliding steel guitar, sweet Hawaiian harmonies, drumbeats—in the hearts of millions of listeners in the United States, Australia, and Canada.

By 1936, visitors could fly to Honolulu from San Francisco on the *Hawaii Clipper*, a seven-passenger Pan American Martin M-130 flying boat, for $360 one-way. The flight took 21 hours, 33 minutes. Modern tourism was born. The 1941 visitor count was a brisk 31,846 through December 6.

> The devastating attack on Pearl Harbor killed 2,388 people, sank or damaged 21 vessels, and damaged or destroyed 323 military aircraft.

World War II & Its Aftermath

On December 7, 1941, Japanese Zeros came out of the rising sun to bomb American warships based at Pearl Harbor. This was the "day of infamy" that plunged the United States into World War II.

The attack brought immediate changes to the islands. Martial law was declared, stripping the Big Five cartel of its absolute power. Japanese Americans and German Americans were interned. Only young men bound for the Pacific came to Hawaii during the war years. Many came back to graves in a cemetery called Punchbowl.

The postwar years saw the beginnings of Hawaii's faux culture. Harry Yee invented the Blue Hawaii cocktail and dropped in a tiny Japanese parasol. Vic Bergeron created the mai tai, a drink made of rum and fresh lime juice, and opened Trader Vic's, America's first theme restaurant that featured the art, decor, and food of Polynesia. Arthur Godfrey picked up a ukulele and began singing *hapa-haole* tunes on early TV shows. In 1955 Henry J. Kaiser built the Hilton Hawaiian Village, and the 11-story high-rise Princess Kaiulani Hotel opened on a site where the real princess once played. Hawaii greeted 109,000 visitors that year.

Statehood

In 1959 Hawaii became the 50th of the United States. That year also saw the arrival of the first jet airliners, which brought 250,000 tourists to the state. From 1969 to 1971, Waikiki's room count nearly doubled. By 1980, annual arrivals had reached 4 million.

In the early 1980s, the Japanese began traveling overseas in record numbers. Their effect on sales in Hawaii was phenomenal: European boutiques opened branches in Honolulu, and duty-free shopping became the main supporter of Honolulu International Airport. Japanese investors competed for the chance to own or build part of Hawaii. Hotels sold so fast and at such unbelievable prices that heads began to spin with dollar signs.

In 1986 Hawaii's visitor count passed 5 million. Two years later, it went over 6 million. Expensive fantasy megaresorts popped up on the neighbor islands, swelling the luxury market with ever-swankier accommodations.

The visitor count was at a record 6.7 million in 1990 when the bubble burst in early 1991 with the Gulf War and worldwide recessions. In 1992 Hurricane Iniki devastated Kauai. Airfare wars sent Americans to Mexico and the Caribbean. Overbuilt with luxury hotels, Hawaii slashed its room rates, giving middle-class consumers access to high-end digs at affordable prices—a trend that continues as Hawaii struggles to stay atop the tourism heap.

Hawaii was finally back to record-breaking visitor counts (6.9 million) in 2000. Tourism dropped abruptly after September 11, 2001, but visitor arrivals were back up to 6.75 million by 2005. A record number of visitors, some 9 million, came to Hawaii in 2007, but in 2008, the economic downturn saw the closure of ATA and Aloha Airlines (which served Hawaii for 61 years), and the shutting down of all operations (both cattle and visitor accommodations) of Molokai Ranch, the islands' largest employer and landowner.

A Cultural Renaissance

A conch shell sounds, a young man in a bright feather cape chants, torchlight flickers at sunset on Waikiki Beach, and hula dancers begin telling their graceful centuries-old stories. It's a cultural scene out of the past come to life once again—for Hawaii is enjoying a renaissance of hula, chant, and other aspects of its ancient culture.

The biggest, longest, and most elaborate celebrations of Hawaiian culture are the Aloha Festivals, which encompass more than 500 cultural events from August to October.

In 1985, native Hawaiian educator George Kanahele started integrating Hawaiian values into hotels like the Big Island's Mauna Lani and Maui's Kaanapali Beach Hotel. "Ultimately, the only thing unique about Hawaii is its Hawaiianess," Kanahele told the Hawaii Hotel Association. "Hawaiianess is our competitive edge."

Many hotels have joined the movement and instituted Hawaiian programs. No longer content with teaching hula as a joke, resorts now employ a real *kumu hula* (hula teacher) to instruct visitors and have a *kupuna* (elder) take guests on treks to visit *heiau* (temples) and ancient petroglyph sites.

> *The resurgence of the Hula as an art form has been a primary component of Hawaii's cultural renaissance.*

The Question of Sovereignty

The Hawaiian cultural renaissance has also made its way into politics. Many *kanaka maoli* (native people) are demanding restoration of rights taken away more than a century ago when the U.S. overthrew the Hawaiian monarchy. In 1993, President Bill Clinton signed a document stating that the U.S. Congress "apologizes to Native Hawaiians on behalf of the people of the United States for the overthrow of the Kingdom of Hawaii on January 17, 1893, with the participation of agents and citizens of the United States, and deprivation of the rights of Native Hawaiians to self-determination."

But even neo-nationalists aren't convinced that complete self-determination is possible. Each of the 30 identifiable sovereignty organizations (and more than 100 splinter groups) has a different stated goal. In 1993 the state legislature created a Hawaiian Sovereignty Advisory Commission to "determine the will of the native Hawaiian people." The commission plans to pose the sovereignty question in a referendum open to anyone over 18 with Hawaiian blood, no matter where they live. The question still remains unanswered.

A Brief History

EARLY HISTORY

AROUND 250–700 Paddling outrigger canoes, the first ancestors of today's Hawaiians follow the stars and birds across the sea to Hawaii, which they call "the land of raging fire."

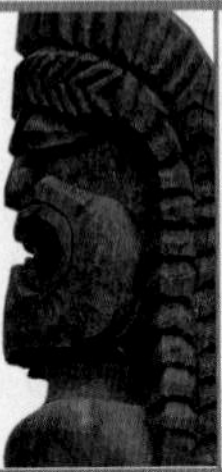

1300

AROUND 1300 At about this time, the transoceanic voyages stop for some reason, and Hawaii begins to develop its own culture in earnest. The settlers build temples, fishponds, and aqueducts to irrigate taro plantations. Sailors become farmers and fishermen. Each island is a separate kingdom. The royal *alii* create a caste system and establish taboos. Violators are strangled. High priests ask the gods Lono and Ku for divine guidance. Ritual human sacrifices are common.

1700

1778 Capt. James Cook (left), trying to find the mythical Northwest Passage to link the Pacific and Atlantic oceans, sails into Waimea Bay on Kauai, where he is welcomed as the god Lono.

1779 On February 14, Cook and four of his crew are killed in Kealakekua Bay on the Big Island.

1782 Kamehameha I begins his campaign to unify the Hawaiian Islands

1800

1804 King Kamehameha I (left) conquers Oahu in a very bloody battle fought the length of Nuuanu Valley and then moves his court from the Big Island to Waikiki.

1810 Kamehameha I unites the Hawaiian Islands under a single leader.

1819 The events of this year change the Hawaiian Islands forever: Kamehameha I dies, and his son Liholiho is proclaimed Kamehameha II; under the influence of Queen Kaahumanu, Kamehameha II orders the destruction of the temples *(heiau)* and an end to the *kapu* system, thus overthrowing the traditional Hawaiian religion. The first whaling ship, *Bellina*, drops anchor in Lahaina.

1823 Missionaries begin arriving from New England, bent on converting the pagan Hawaiians.

1845 King Kamehameha III moves the capital of Hawaii from Lahaina to Honolulu, where more commerce could be accommodated in the natural harbor there.

1848 The Great Mahele is signed by King Kamehameha III, which allows commoners and foreigners to own land outright or in "fee simple," a concept that continues today.

1850 Kamehameha III proclaims Honolulu the capital city of his kingdom. It is still the capital and dominant city of the nation's 50th state.

1882 America's only royal residence, Iolani Palace (left), is built on Oahu.

1885 The first contract laborers from Japan arrive to work on the sugarcane plantations.

1893 On January 17, a group of American sugar planters and missionary descendants, with the support of U.S. Marines, imprison Queen Liliuokalani in her own palace in Honolulu and illegally overthrow the Hawaiian government.

1898 Hawaii is annexed to the United States.

1900

1900 Hawaii becomes a United States territory. The Great Chinatown Fire leaves 7,000 people homeless in Honolulu.

1922 Prince Jonah Kalanianaole Kuhio dies. He was the last powerful member of the royal Hawaiian family.

1927 The first nonstop air flight is made from the mainland to Honolulu.

1941 On December 7, Japanese Zeros bomb American warships based at Pearl Harbor, plunging the United States into World War II.

1959 On March 18, Hawaii becomes the 50th state of the union. The first jet airliners bring 250,000 tourists to the fledgling state.

1967 The state of Hawaii hosts one million tourists.

1990s Hawaii's state economy goes into a tailspin following a series of events: First, the Gulf War severely curtails air travel to the island; then, Hurricane Iniki slams into Kauai, crippling its infrastructure; and finally, sugarcane companies across the state begin shutting down, laying off thousands of workers.

2000

2000 Hawaii welcomes a record-setting 6.9 million visitors.

2006–2009 The Waikiki Beach Walk project (left) transforms an 8-acre area into an oasis of broad sidewalks, tropical foliage, and water features. Eleven hotels are razed, or upgraded, and 90,000 square feet of swank shops and trendy restaurants are added, all linked through pedestrian bridges and connecting walkways.

2007 Another tourism record is set, with some nine million travelers visiting Hawaii.

2008 The global economic downturn hits Hawaii. Real estate values and tourism levels drop. Aloha Airlines goes out of business. Molokai Ranch, the island's largest employer and landowner, shuts down all operations.

The Lay of the Land

The first Hawaiian Islands were born of violent volcanic eruptions that took place deep beneath the ocean's surface about 70 million years ago—more than 200 million years after the major continental landmasses had been formed. As soon as the islands emerged, Mother Nature's fury began to carve beauty from barren rock. Untiring volcanoes spewed forth rivers of fire that cooled into stone. Severe tropical storms, some with hurricane-force winds, battered and blasted the cooling lava rock into a series of shapes. Ferocious earthquakes flattened, shattered, and reshaped the islands into precipitous valleys, jagged cliffs, and recumbent flatlands. Monstrous surf and gigantic tidal waves rearranged and polished the lands above and below the reaches of the tide.

It took millions of years for nature to shape the familiar form of Diamond Head on Oahu, Maui's majestic peak of Haleakala, the waterfalls of Molokai's northern side, the reefs of Hulopoe Bay on Lanai, and the lush rainforests of the Big Island. The result is an island chain like no other—a tropical dreamscape of a landscape rich in flora and fauna.

The Flora of the Islands

Hawaii is filled with sweet-smelling flowers, lush vegetation, and exotic plant life.

> *Banyan tree.*

BANYAN TREES Among the world's largest trees, banyans have branches that grow out and away from the trunk, forming descending roots that grow down to the ground to feed and form additional trunks, making the tree very stable during tropical storms. The banyan in the courtyard next to the old Court House in Lahaina, Maui, is an excellent example of a spreading banyan—it covers ⅔ acre.

BIRDS OF PARADISE These natives of Africa have become something of a trademark of Hawaii. They're easily recognizable by the orange and blue flowers nestled in gray-green bracts, looking somewhat like birds in flight.

BREADFRUIT TREES A large tree—more than 60 feet tall—with broad, sculpted, dark-green leaves, the famous breadfruit produces a round, head-size green fruit that's a staple in the diets of all Polynesians. When roasted or baked, the whitish-yellow fruit tastes somewhat like a sweet potato.

> *Ripe coffee berries.*

BROMELIADS There are more than 1,400 species of bromeliad, of which the pineapple plant is the best known. "Bromes," as they're affectionately called, are generally spiky plants, ranging in size from a few inches to several feet in diameter. They're popular not only for their unusual foliage but also for their strange and wonderful flowers. Used widely in landscaping and interior decoration, especially in resort areas, bromeliads are found on every island.

COFFEE Hawaii is the only state that produces coffee commercially. Coffee is an evergreen shrub with shiny, waxy, dark-green, pointed leaves. The flower is a small fragrant white blossom that develops into ½-inch berries that turn bright red when ripe. Look for coffee at elevations above 1,500 feet on the Kona side of the Big Island and on large coffee plantations on Kauai, Molokai, Oahu, and Maui.

GINGER White and yellow ginger flowers are perhaps the most fragrant in Hawaii. Usually found in clumps growing 4 to 7 feet tall, these sweet-smelling, 3-inch-wide flowers are composed of three dainty petal-like stamens and three long thin petals. Ginger was introduced to Hawaii in the 19th-century from the Indonesia-Malaysia area. Other members of the ginger family frequently seen in Hawaii include red, shell, and torch ginger. Red ginger consists of tall green stalks with foot-long red "flower heads." The red "petals" are actually bracts, which protect the 1-inch-long white flowers. Shell ginger, which originated in India and Burma, thrives in cool, wet mountain forests. These plants, with their pearly white, clamshell-like blossoms, bloom from spring to fall. Torch ginger rises directly out of the ground. The flower stalks, which are about 5 to 8 inches in length, resemble the fire of a lighted torch.

> *Hibiscus.*

HELICONIA Some 80 species of the colorful heliconia family came to Hawaii from the Caribbean and Central and South America. The bright yellow, red, green, and orange bracts overlap and appear to unfold like origami birds. The most common heliconia to spot is the lobster claw, which resembles a string of boiled crustacean pincers. Another prolific heliconia is the parrot's beak: Growing to about hip height, it's composed of bright orange flower bracts with black tips. Look for parrot's beaks in spring and summer.

HIBISCUS The 4- to 6-inch hibiscus flowers bloom year-round and come in a range of colors, from lily white to lipstick red. The flowers resemble crepe paper, with stamens and pistils protruding spirelike from the center. Hibiscus hedges can grow up to 15 feet tall. The yellow hibiscus is Hawaii's official state flower.

> ABOVE *Macadamia nuts.* BELOW *Plumeria.*

MACADAMIA A transplant from Australia, macadamia nuts have become a commercial crop in recent decades in Hawaii, especially on the Big Island and Maui. The large trees—up to 60 feet tall—bear a hard-shelled nut encased in a leathery husk, which splits open and dries when the nut is ripe.

> *Orchid.*

> *Protea.*

MONKEYPOD TREES The monkeypod is one of Hawaii's most majestic trees; it grows more than 80 feet tall and 100 feet across. Seen near older homes and in parks, the leaves of the monkeypod drop in February and March. Its wood is a favorite of woodworking artisans.

ORCHIDS To many minds, nothing says Hawaii more than orchids. The most widely grown variety—and the major source of flowers for leis and garnishes for tropical libations—is the vanda orchid. The vandas used in Hawaii's commercial flower industry are generally lavender or white, but they grow in a rainbow of colors, shapes, and sizes. On the Big Island, don't pass up a chance to wander through the numerous orchid farms around Hilo.

PANDANUS (HALA) Called *hala* by Hawaiians, pandanus is native to Polynesia. Thanks to its thick trunk, stiltlike supporting roots, and crown of long swordlike leaves, the hala tree is easy to recognize. In what is quickly becoming a dying art, Hawaiians weave the *lau* (leaves) of the hala into hats, baskets, mats, bags, and the like.

PLUMERIA Also known as frangipani, this sweet-smelling, five-petal flower, found in clusters on trees, is the most popular choice of lei-makers. The Singapore plumeria has five creamy white petals, with a touch of yellow in the center. Another popular variety, ruba—with flowers from soft pink to flaming red—is also used in leis.

PROTEA Originally from South Africa, this unusual oversize shrub comes in more than 40 different varieties. The flowers of one species resemble pincushions; those of another look like a bouquet of feathers. Once dried, protea flowers will last for years.

SILVERSWORD This very uncommon and unusual plant is seen only on the Big Island and in the Haleakala Crater on Maui. This rare relative of the sunflower family blooms between July and September. The silversword in bloom is a fountain of red-petaled, daisy-like flowers that turn silver soon after blooming.

TARO Around pools, near streams, and in neatly planted fields, you'll see these green heart-shaped leaves, whose dense roots are a Polynesian staple. The ancient Hawaiians pounded the roots into poi. Originally from Sri Lanka, taro is not only a food crop but is also grown for ornamental purposes.

The Fauna of the Islands

When the first Polynesians arrived in Hawaii between A.D. 500 and 800, scientists say they did not find any reptiles, amphibians, mosquitoes, lice, fleas, or even cockroaches.

There were only two endemic mammals: the hoary bat and the monk seal. The hoary bat must have accidentally blown to Hawaii at some point, from either North or South America. It can still be seen during its early evening forays, especially around the Kilauea Crater on the Big Island.

The Hawaiian monk seal, a relative of warm-water seals found in the Caribbean and the Mediterranean, was nearly slaughtered to extinction for its skin and oil during the 19th-century. They're protected

> The Big Island is one of the best places to see such endangered Hawaiian species as the pueo (left), the aeo (top right), and the nene (bottom right).

under federal law by the Marine Mammals Protection Act. If you're fortunate enough to see a monk seal, just look; don't disturb one of Hawaii's living treasures.

The first Polynesians brought a few animals from home: dogs, pigs, and chickens (all were for eating), as well as rats (stowaways). All four species are still found in the Hawaiian wild today.

More species of native birds have become extinct in Hawaii in the last 200 years than anywhere else on the planet. Of 67 native species, 23 are extinct and 30 are endangered.

The aeo, or Hawaiian stilt—a 16-inch-long bird with a black head, black coat, white underside, and long pink legs—can be found in protected wetlands like the Kanaha Wildlife Sanctuary on Maui, the Kealia Pond on Maui, and the Hanalei National Wildlife Refuge on Kauai, which is also home to the Hawaiian duck. Other areas in which you can see protected birds are the Kipuku Puaulu (Bird Park) and the Olaa Rain Forest, both in Hawaii Volcanoes National Park on the Big Island, and at the Goat Island bird refuge off Oahu, where you can see wedge-tailed shearwaters nesting.

Another great birding venue is Kokee State Park on Kauai. Various birds that have been spotted include some of the 22 species of native honeycreepers. Also in the forest is the elepaio, a small gray flycatcher with an orange breast and an erect tail. The most common native bird at Kokee is the moa, or red jungle fowl, a chicken brought to Hawaii by the Polynesians.

To get a good glimpse of the seabirds that frequent Hawaii, drive to Kilauea Point on Kauai's North Shore. Here you can spot red- and white-footed boobies, wedge-tailed shearwaters, frigate birds, red-tailed tropic birds, and the Laysan albatross.

The nene is Hawaii's state bird. It's being brought back from the brink of extinction through strenuous protection laws and captive breeding programs. It can be seen in only three places: at Haleakala National Park on Maui, at Mauna Kea State Park bird sanctuary, and on the slopes of Mauna Kea on the Big Island.

The Hawaiian short-eared owl, the pueo, which grows to between 12 and 17 inches, can be seen at dawn and dusk on Kauai, Maui, and the Big Island. According to legend, spotting a pueo is a good omen.

Hawaii in High & Popular Culture

> *Mark Twain's classic writings offer a great introduction to Hawaiian history*

In addition to reading the books discussed below, those planning an extended trip to Hawaii should check out *Frommer's Hawaii; Frommer's Maui; Frommer's Honolulu, Waikiki & Oahu; Frommer's Kauai; Frommer's Maui Day by Day; Frommer's Honolulu & Oahu Day by Day;* and *Frommer's Hawaii with Kids* (all published by Wiley Publishing, Inc.).

Books: Fiction

The first book people think about is James A. Michener's *Hawaii* (Random House, 1959). This epic novel manages to put the islands' history into chronological order, but remember, it is still fiction and very sanitized fiction, at that. For a more contemporary fictional look at life in Hawaii, one of the best novels is *Shark Dialogue,* by Kiana Davenport (Plume, 1995). The novel tells the story of Pono, the larger-than-life matriarch, and her four daughters of mixed races. Lois-Ann Yamanaka uses a very "local" voice to give stark depictions of life on the islands in her fabulous novels *Wild Meat and the Bully Burgers* (Farrar, Straus, Giroux, 1996), *Blu's Hanging* (Avon, 1997), and *Heads by Harry* (Avon, 1999).

Books: Nonfiction

Mark Twain's writing on Hawaii in the 1860s offers a wonderful introduction to Hawaii's history. A recommended collection is *Mark Twain in Hawaii: Roughing It in the Sandwich Islands* (Mutual Publishing, 1990). For contemporary voices on Hawaii's unique culture, one of the best books is *Voices of Wisdom: Hawaiian Elders Speak,* by M. J. Harden (Aka Press, 1999). Some 24 different *kahuna* (experts) in their fields were interviewed about their talent, skill, or artistic practice. These living treasures talk about how Hawaiians of yesteryear viewed nature, spirituality and healing, preservation and history, dance and music, arts and crafts, canoes, and the next generation.

Books: Flora & Fauna

Because Hawaii is so lush with nature and blessed with plants, animals, and reef fish seen nowhere else on the planet, a few reference books can help you identify what you're looking at and make your trip more interesting. In the botanical world, Angela Kay Kepler's *Hawaiian Heritage Plants* (A Latitude 20 Book, University of Hawaii Press, 1998) is the standard for plant reference. There are great color photos and drawings to help you sort through the myriad species.

The other necessary reference guide to have in Hawaii is a book identifying the colorful fish you will see while snorkeling. The best reference book is John E. Randall's *Shore Fishes of Hawaii* (University of Hawaii Press, 1998). Two other books on reef fish identification, with easy-to-use spiral bindings, are *Hawaiian Reef Fish—The Identification Book* (Blue Kirio Publishing, 1993), by Casey Mahaney, and *Hawaiian Reef Fish* (Island Heritage, 1998), by Astrid Witte and Casey Mahaney.

For everything you need to identify Hawaii's unique birds, try H. Douglas Pratt's *A Pocket Guide to Hawaii's Birds* (Mutual Publishing, 1996).

Books: History

There are many great books on Hawaii's history. One of the best books to start with is David E. Eyre's *By Wind, By Wave: An Introduction to Hawaii's Natural History* (Bess Press, 2000), a vivid description of the formation of the Hawaiian Islands. In addition to chronicling the natural history of Hawaii, Eyre describes the complex interrelationships among the plants, animals, ocean, and people that are necessary.

My favorite books on old Hawaii include *Stories of Old Hawaii* (Bess Press, 1997), by

> *This campy 60s classic will help get you in the mood for your trip.*

Roy Kakulu Alameide, on myths and legends; *Hawaiian Folk Tales* (Mutual Publishing, 1998), by Thomas G. Thrum; and *The Legends and Myths of Hawaii* (Charles E. Tuttle Company, 1992), by His Hawaiian Majesty King David Kalakaua.

The best story of the 1893 overthrow of the Hawaiian monarchy is told by Queen Liliuokalani in her book *Hawaii's Story by Hawaii's Queen Liliuokalani* (Mutual Publishing, 1990).

I love Davianna Pomaikai McGregor's *Na Kua'aina, Living Hawaiian Culture* (University of Hawaii Press, 2007) for so many reasons. It focuses not on the Hawaiian royalty but also on the common people of Hawaii and how they lived. McGregor, a professor of ethnic studies at UH, examines how people lived in rural lands and how they kept the Hawaiian traditions alive. She describes the cultural significance of each area (the island of Molokai; Hana, Maui; and Puna, Hawaii), the landscape, the Hawaiian gods who lived there, the chants and myths about the area, and how the westernization of the area has changed the land and the Hawaiian people.

Film

The following films were made in Hawaii and are about Hawaii. The list of films made in Hawaii but about other places is huge; it includes *Jurassic Park, Joe Versus the Volcano, Bird of Paradise, Karate Kid, Part 2, King Kong* (the 1976 version), *Outbreak, Planet of the Apes* (the 2001 remake), *South Pacific,* and *Raiders of the Lost Ark.* Film buffs visiting Kauai should contact **Hawaii Movie Tours** (☎ 800/628-8432 or 808/822-1192; www.hawaiimovietour.com) to visit several Kauai locations that made it to the silver screen, plus locations from such TV classics as *Fantasy Island* and *Gilligan's Island.*

Blue Hawaii Elvis Presley, Joan Blackman, and Angela Lansbury make this 1961 film a classic, with great music and beautiful Hawaiian scenery from the early 1960s.

50 First Dates This 2003 film stars Drew Barrymore and Adam Sandler in a romantic comedy about a young girl (Barrymore) who has lost her short-term memory in a car accident and who now relives each day as if it is October 13th.

From Here to Eternity Fred Zinnermann's 1953 Oscar winner, set in pre–World War II Hawaii, tells the story of several Army soldiers stationed on Oahu on the eve of Pearl Harbor. The film won Best Picture, Best Supporting Actor (Frank Sinatra), Best Supporting Actress (Donna Reed), and five other awards.

Hawaii George Roy Hill's 1966 adaptation of the James Michener novel features amazing island scenery and stars Julie Andrews, Max von Sydow, and Richard Harris.

> *Tora! Tora! Tora!* *explores the attack on Pearl Harbor from both sides of the conflict.*

Molokai: The Story of Father Damien This 1995 film tells the story of Belgian priest Damien DeVeuster from 1872, the year before his arrival in Kalaupapa, through his years ministering to the Hansen's disease patients at Kalaupapa, until his death at the Molokai settlement in 1889.

Pearl Harbor Michael Bay's 2001 film depicts the time before, during, and after the December 7, 1941, Japanese attack and tells the story of two best friends and the woman they both love.

Picture Bride Japanese director Kayo Hatta presents this 1995 film about a Japanese woman who travels to Hawaii to marry a man she has never met. Beautifully filmed on the North Shore of Oahu and the Hamakua Coast of the Big Island.

Tora! Tora! Tora! This 1970 film tells the story of the Japanese attack on Pearl Harbor as seen from both the American and Japanese perspectives.

Eating & Drinking in Hawaii

> *Fresh local produce forms the foundation of Hawaii Regional Cuisine.*

Hawaii Regional Cuisine

HRC was established in the mid-1980s in a culinary revolution that catapulted Hawaii into the global epicurean arena. The international training, creative vigor, fresh ingredients, and cross-cultural menus of the 12 original HRC chefs have made the islands a dining destination applauded nationwide.

While in Hawaii, you'll encounter many labels that embrace the fundamentals of HRC and the sophistication, informality, and nostalgia it encompasses. Euro-Asian, Pacific Rim, Indo-Pacific, Euro-Pacific, fusion cuisine—by whatever name, Hawaii Regional Cuisine has evolved as Hawaii's singular cooking style. It highlights the fresh seafood and produce of Hawaii's rich waters and volcanic soil, the cultural traditions of Hawaii's ethnic groups, and the skills of well-trained chefs.

Here's a sampling of what you can expect to find on a Hawaii Regional menu: seared Hawaiian fish with *lilikoi* shrimp butter; taro-crab cakes; Pahoa corn cakes; Molokai sweet-potato vichyssoise; Ka'u orange sauce and Kahua Ranch lamb; fern shoots from Waipio Valley; and Hawaiian bouillabaisse, with fresh snapper, Kona crab, and fresh aquacultured shrimp. You may also encounter locally made cheeses and Polynesian imu-baked foods. If there's pasta or risotto on the menu, it could be nori (red algae) linguine with opihi (limpet) sauce or risotto with local seafood served in taro cups.

Plate Lunches & More: Local Food

At the other end of the spectrum is the vast and endearing world of "local food." By that I mean plate lunches and poke, shave ice and saimin, bento lunches and manapua—cultural hybrids all.

A typical **plate lunch** ordered from a lunch wagon might consist of fried mahimahi, "two scoops rice," macaroni salad, and a few leaves of green. Heavy gravy is often the condiment of choice. Like **saimin**—the local version of noodles in broth topped with scrambled eggs, green onions, and sometimes pork—the plate lunch is Hawaii's version of high camp.

Because this is Hawaii, at least a few licks of poi—cooked, pounded taro (the traditional Hawaiian staple crop)—are a must. Other **native foods** include those from before and after Western contact, such as *laulau* (pork, chicken, or fish steamed in ti leaves), kalua pork (pork cooked in a Polynesian underground oven known here as an imu), lomi salmon (salted salmon with tomatoes and green onions), squid luau (cooked in coconut milk and taro tops), poke (cubed raw fish seasoned with onions and seaweed), haupia (creamy coconut pudding), and *kulolo* (steamed pudding of coconut, brown sugar, and taro).

Bento, another popular quick meal available throughout Hawaii, is a compact, boxed assortment of picnic fare usually consisting of neatly arranged sections of rice, pickled vegetables, and fried chicken, beef, or pork.

For dessert or a snack, particularly on Oahu's North Shore, the prevailing favorite is **shave ice,** heaps of finely shaved ice topped with sweet tropical syrups. (The sweet-sour *li hing mui* flavor is a current favorite.) Aficionados order shave ice with ice cream and sweetened adzuki beans plopped in the middle.

The Hawaiian Language

The Hawaiian alphabet, created by the New England missionaries, has only 12 letters: the five regular vowels (a, e, i, o, and u) and seven consonants (h, k, l, m, n, p, and w). The vowels are pronounced in the Roman fashion: that is, *ah, ay, ee, oh,* and *oo* (as in "too")—not *ay, ee, eye, oh,* and *you,* as in English. For example, *hale* is pronounced *hah-lay.* Most vowels are sounded separately, though some are pronounced together, as in Kalakaua: Kah-lah-*cow*-ah.

Some Hawaiian Words

Here are some basic Hawaiian words that you'll often hear in Hawaii and see throughout this book. For a more complete list of Hawaiian words, point your Web browser to www.geocities.com/~olelo/hltableofcontents.html or www.hisurf.com/hawaiian/dictionary.html

aa
rough, crumbling lava

ala
road or path

alii
Hawaiian royalty

aloha
greeting or farewell

halau
school

hale
house or building

haole
white person

hapa
part or half

heiau
Hawaiian temple or place of worship

hookipa
hospitality

imu
an underground oven

kahuna
priest or expert

kamaaina
old-timer

kapa
tapa, bark cloth

kapu
taboo, forbidden

keiki
child

lanai
porch or veranda

lomilomi
massage

mahalo
thank you

makai
a direction, toward the sea

mana
spirit power

mauka
a direction: inland, toward the mountains

moana
the ocean

muumuu
loose-fitting gown or dress

nani
beautiful

ono
delicious

pahoehoe
smooth lava

pali
cliff

paniolo
Hawaiian cowboy(s)

pau
finished, done

pupu
appetizers

wiki
quick

11 The Best Special-Interest Trips

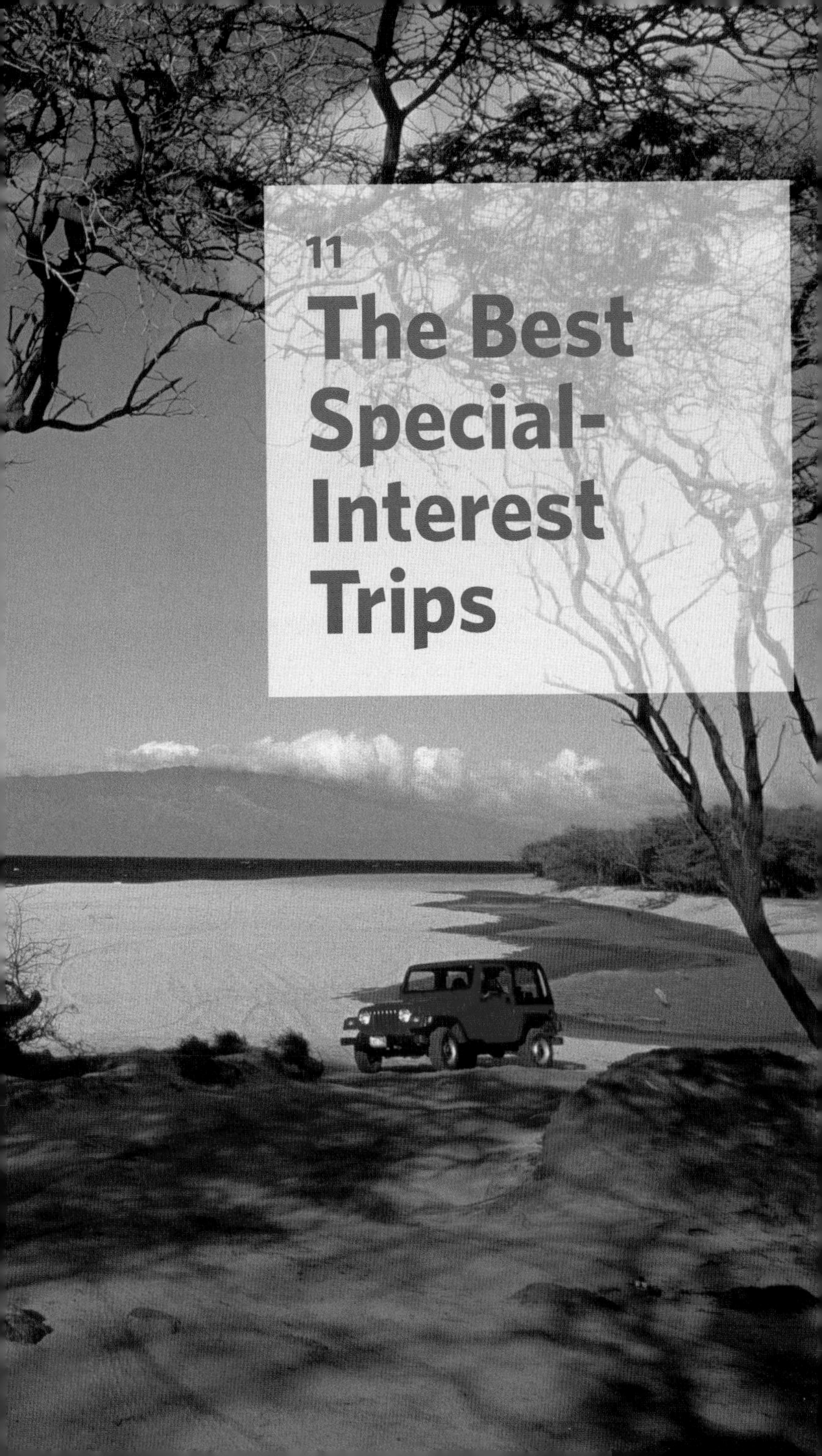

Outdoor Activities A to Z

Here's a brief rundown of the many outdoor activities available in Hawaii. For our recommendations on the best places to go, the best shops for renting equipment, and the best outfitters to use, see the individual island chapters earlier in this book.

Birding

Many of Hawaii's tropical birds are found nowhere else on earth. There are curved-bill honeycreepers, black-winged red birds, and the rare o'o, whose yellow feathers Hawaiians once plucked to make royal capes. When you go birding, take along *A Field Guide to the Birds of Hawaii and the Tropical Pacific,* by H. Douglas Pratt, Phillip L. Bruner, and Delwyn G. Berett (Princeton University Press, 1987). **Kauai** and **Molokai,** in particular, are great places to go birding. On Kauai large colonies of seabirds nest at Kilauea National Wildlife Refuge and along the Na Pali Coast. Be sure to take along a copy of *The Birds of Kauai* (University of Hawaii Press), by Jim Denny. The lush rainforest of Molokai's Kamakou Preserve is home to the Molokai thrush and Molokai creeper, which live only on this 30-mile-long island.

Boating

Almost every type of nautical experience is available in the islands, from old-fashioned Polynesian outrigger canoes to America's Cup racing sloops to submarines. You'll find details on all these seafaring experiences in the individual island chapters.

No matter which type of vessel you choose, be sure to see the Hawaiian Islands from offshore if you can afford it. It's easy to combine multiple activities into one cruise: Lots of snorkel boats double as sightseeing cruises and, in winter, whale-watching cruises. The main harbors for visitor activities are Kewalo Basin, Oahu; Honokohau, Kailua-Kona, and Kawaihae on the Big Island; Lahaina and Maalaea, Maui; Nawiliwili and Port Allen, Kauai; and Kaunakakai, Molokai.

Camping

Hawaii's year-round balmy climate makes camping a breeze. However, tropical campers should always be ready for rain. And remember to bring a good mosquito repellent. If you're heading to the top of Hawaii's volcanoes, you'll need a down mummy bag. If you plan to camp on the beach, bring a mosquito net and a rain poncho. Always be prepared to deal with contaminated water (purify it by boiling, through filtration, or by using iodine tablets) and the tropical sun (protect yourself with sunscreen, a hat, and a long-sleeved shirt).

Hawaiian Trail and Mountain Club, P.O. Box 2238, Honolulu, HI 96804, offers an information packet on hiking and camping throughout the islands. Send $2 and a legal-size, self-addressed, stamped envelope for information. Another good source is the *Hiking/Camping Information Packet,* available from **Hawaii Geographic Maps and Books,** 49 S. Hotel St., Honolulu, HI 96813 (☎ 800/538-3950 or 808/538-3952), for $7. The **University of Hawaii Press,** 2840 Kolowalu St., Honolulu, HI 96822 (☎ 888/847-7377; www.uhpress.hawaii.edu), has an excellent selection of hiking, backpacking,

Activities Desks

If you're unsure of which activity or which outfitter or guide is the right one for you and your family, you might want to consider booking through a discount activities center or activities desk. Remember, however, that it's in the activities agent's best interest to sign you up with outfitters from which they earn the most commission. If an agent tries to push a particular outfitter or activity too hard, be skeptical. Also stay away from activities centers that offer discounts as fronts for timeshare sales presentations. Because their business is timeshares, not activities, they won't be as interested in, or as knowledgeable about, which activities might be right for you.

There are a number of very reliable local activities centers. On Maui your best bet is **Tom Barefoot's Cashback Tours** (☎ 800/ 621-3601 or 808/661-1246; www.tombarefoot.com), 250 Alamaha St., Kahului. On the Big Island, check out the **Activity Connection,** Bougainvillea Plaza Suite 102, 75-5656 Kuakini Hwy., Kailua-Kona (☎ 800/459-7156 or 808/329-1038).

Finally, you can often get discounts yourself by booking via the Internet. Most activities offer from 10% to 25% off their prices if you book online.

> PAGE 572 *Deserted Polihua Beach, on Lanai, is perfect for beachcombing.* THIS PAGE *Molokini might be Hawaii's most famous snorkeling spot, but you can find fantastic opportunities on any of the Hawaiian Islands.*

and bird-watching guides, especially Stuart M. Ball, Jr.'s, *The Hikers Guide to the Hawaiian Islands.*

Camping is generally set up for local residents, and getting a permit off-island can be quite an ordeal. Some permits aren't given out too far in advance, making planning hard. Some agencies want you to show up in person for a permit. If you are interested in camping, see the "Hiking and Camping" section of each island chapter for information on how to obtain a permit:

Hiking

Hiking in Hawaii is a breathtaking experience. The islands have hundreds of miles of trails, many of which reward you with a hidden beach, a private waterfall, an Eden-like valley, or simply an unforgettable view. However, rock climbers are out of luck: Most of Hawaii's volcanic cliffs are too steep and brittle to scale.

Hawaiian Trail and Mountain Club, P.O. Box 2238, Honolulu, HI 96804, offers an information packet on hiking and camping in Hawaii. To receive a copy, send $2 and a legal-size, self-addressed, stamped envelope. **Hawaii Geographic Maps and Books,** 49 S. Hotel St., Honolulu, HI 96813 (☎ 800/538-3950 or 808/538-3952), offers the *Hiking/Camping Information Packet* for $7. Also note that the **Hawaii State Department of Land and Natural Resources,** 1151 Punchbowl St., Honolulu, HI 96813 (☎ 808/587-0300; www.hawaii.gov/dlnr), will send you free topographical trail maps.

The **Nature Conservancy of Hawaii** (☎ 808/537-4508 on Oahu, ☎ 808/572-7849 on Maui, or ☎ 808/553-5236 on Molokai; ☎ 808/565-7430 on Lanai; www.tnc.org/hawaii) and the **Hawaii Chapter of the Sierra Club,** P.O. Box 2577, Honolulu, HI 96803

Fun for Less

Almost any activity you can think of, from submarine rides to Polynesian luau, can be purchased at a discount by using the **Activities and Attractions Association of Hawaii Gold Card,** P.O. Box 598, Makawao, HI 96768 (☎ 800/398-9698 or 808/871-7947; fax 808/877-3104; www.hawaiifun.org). The Gold Card, accepted by members on all islands, offers a discount of 10% to 25% off activities and meals for up to four people. It's good for a year from the purchase date and costs $30.

> *Whether you're an expert kayaker or you've never touched a paddle, there are plenty of great places to glide across the waves in Hawaii.*

Travel Tip

When planning sunset activities, be aware that Hawaii, like other places close to the Equator, has a very short (5–10 min.) twilight period after the sun sets. After that, it's dark. If you hike out to watch the sunset, be sure you can make it back quickly, or take a flashlight.

(☎ 808/538-6616), both offer guided hikes in preserves and special areas during the year. Also see the individual island chapters for complete details on the best hikes for all ability levels.

A couple of terrific books on hiking are Stuart M. Ball, Jr.'s, *The Hikers Guide to the Hawaiian Islands,* published by the University of Hawaii Press, and his book on Oahu, *The Hikers Guide to Oahu,* also from University of Hawaii Press.

Horseback Riding

One of the best ways to see Hawaii is on horseback. Almost all the islands offer riding opportunities for just about every age and level of experience. You can ride into Maui's Haleakala Crater, along Kauai's Mahaulepu Beach, or through Oahu's remote windward valleys on Kualoa Ranch, or you can gallop across the wide-open spaces of the Big Island's Parker Ranch, one of the largest privately owned ranches in the United States. See the individual island chapters for details. Be sure to bring a pair of jeans and closed-toed shoes to wear on your ride.

Kayaking

Hawaii is one of the world's most popular destinations for ocean kayaking. Beginners can paddle across a tropical lagoon to two uninhabited islets off Lanikai Beach on Oahu, and more experienced kayakers can take on Kauai's awesome Na Pali Coast. In summer, experts take advantage of the usually flat conditions on the north shore of Molokai, where the sea cliffs are the steepest on earth and the remote valleys can be reached only by sea. See "Kayaking" in the island chapters for local outfitters and tour guides.

Scuba Diving

Some people come to the islands solely to take the plunge into the tropical Pacific and explore the underwater world. Hawaii is one of the world's top 10 dive destinations, according to Rodale's *Scuba Diving* magazine. Here you can see the great variety of tropical marine life (more than 100 endemic species found nowhere else on the planet), explore sea caves, and swim with sea turtles and monk seals in clear, tropical water.

If you dive, **go early in the morning.** Trade winds often rough up the seas in the afternoon, especially on Maui, so most operators schedule early-morning dives that end at noon. It's usually worth the extra bucks to go with a good dive operator. Check "Scuba Diving" in the island chapters; we've listed the operators that'll give you the most for your money. To organize a dive on your own, I recommend *The Oahu Snorkelers and Shore Divers Guide,* by Francisco B. de Carvalho, from University of Hawaii Press.

Snorkeling

Snorkeling is one of Hawaii's main attractions, and almost anyone can do it. All you need are a mask, a snorkel, fins, and some basic swimming skills. In many places, all you have to do is wade into the water and look down at the magical underwater world. If you don't have your own gear, you can rent it from one of dozens of dive shops and activity booths, discussed in the individual island chapters.

While everyone heads for Oahu's Hanauma Bay—the perfect spot for first-timers—other favorite snorkel spots include Kee Beach on Kauai, Kahaluu Beach on the Big Island, Hulopoe Bay on Lanai, and Kapalua Bay on Maui. Although snorkeling is excellent on all the islands, the Big Island, with its recent lava formations and abrupt drop-offs, offers some particularly spectacular opportunities. Some of the best snorkel spots in the islands—notably, the Big Island's Kealakekua Bay and Molokini Crater just off Maui—are accessible only by boat. For tips on the islands' top snorkel boats, see the "Adventures in the Ocean" section in chapters 5 and 6.

Snorkel Tips

Always snorkel with a buddy. Look up every once in a while to see where you are and if there's any boat traffic. Don't touch anything; not only can you damage coral, but camouflaged fish and shells with poisonous spines may surprise you. Always check with a dive shop, lifeguards, or others on the beach about the area in which you plan to snorkel, and ask if there are any dangerous conditions you should know about.

Snorkel Bob's

Snorkel Bob's (www.snorkelbob.com) lets you rent snorkel gear, boogie boards, life jackets, and wet suits on any one island and return them on another. A basic set of snorkel gear costs $3.50 a day or $9 a week—a very good deal. The best gear is $6.50 a day or $29 a week. If you're nearsighted and need a prescription mask, it's $9 a day or $39 a week.

You can find Snorkel Bob's on **Oahu** at 702 Kapahulu Ave. (at Date St.), Honolulu (☎ 808/735-7944); on **Maui** at 1217 Front St. (☎ 808/661-4421) and 180 Dickenson St. (☎ 808/662-0104) in Lahaina, at Napili Village, 5425-C Lower Honoapiilani Hwy., Napili (☎ 808/669-9603), and in South Maui at Kamole Beach Center, 2411 S. Kihei Rd., Kihei (☎ 808/879-7449); on the **Big Island** at 75-5831 Kahakai St. (off Alii Drive, next to Huggo's and the Royal Kona Resort), in Kailua-Kona (☎ 808/329-0770); and on **Kauai** at 4-734 Kuhio Hwy. (just north of Coconut Plantation Marketplace), in Kapaa (☎ 808/823-9433), and in Koloa at 3236 Poipu Rd., near Poipu Beach (☎ 808/742-2206).

Sport Fishing

Big-game fishing at its best is found off the Big Island of Hawaii at **Kailua-Kona,** where the deep blue waters offshore yield trophy marlin year-round. You can also try for spearfish, swordfish, various tuna, mahimahi (dorado), rainbow runners, wahoo, barracuda, trevallies, bonefish, and various bottom fish like snappers and groupers. Each island offers deep-sea boat charters for good-eating fish like tuna, wahoo, and mahimahi. Visiting anglers currently need no license.

Charter fishing boats range widely both in size—from small 24-foot open skiffs to luxurious 50-foot-plus yachts—and in price—from about $100 per person to "share" a boat with other anglers for a half-day to $900 a day to book an entire luxury sport fishing yacht on an exclusive basis. See the individual island chapters for details. To save money, try

> *There are numerous surfing schools throughout the islands, but it's hard to beat learning on legendary Waikiki Beach.*

contacting the charter boat captain directly and bargaining. Many charter captains pay a 20% to 30% commission to charter-booking agencies and may be willing to give you a discount if you book directly. Also, many boat captains tag and release marlin or keep the fish for themselves (sorry, that's Hawaii style).

Surfing

The ancient Hawaiian practice of *hee nalu* ("wave sliding") is probably the sport most people picture when they think of Hawaii. If you'd like to give it a shot, just sign up at any one of the numerous surfing schools located throughout the islands; see "Surfing" in the island chapters. On world-famous Waikiki Beach, just head over to one of the surf stands that line the sand. These guys say they can get anybody up and standing on a board. If you're already a big *kahuna* in surfing, check the same chapters listed above for the best deals on rental equipment and the best places to hang ten.

Whale-Watching

Every winter, pods of Pacific humpback whales make the 3,000-mile swim from the chilly waters of Alaska to bask in Hawaii's summery shallows, fluking, spy hopping, spouting, breaching, and having an all-around swell time. About 1,500 to 3,000 humpback whales appear in Hawaiian waters each year.

The best time to see humpback whales in Hawaii is between **January and April,** from any island. Just look out to sea. Each island also offers a variety of whale-watching cruises, which will bring you up close and personal with the mammoth mammals; see the individual island chapters for details. I recommend booking a snorkeling cruise during the winter whale-watching months. The captain of the boat will often take you through the best local whale-watching areas on the way.

Windsurfing

Maui is Hawaii's top windsurfing destination. World-class windsurfers head for Hookipa Beach, where the wind roars through Maui's isthmus and creates some of the best windsurfing conditions in the world. Funky Paia, a derelict sugar town saved from extinction by surfers, is now the world capital of big-wave board sailing. And along Maui's Hana Highway, there are lookouts where you can watch the pros flip off the lip of 10-foot waves and gain hang time in the air.

Others, especially beginners, set their sails for Oahu's Kailua Bay or Kauai's Anini Beach, where gentle onshore breezes make learning this sport a snap. See the individual island chapters for outfitters and local instructors.

Food & Wine Festivals & Tours

Oahu

The Flavors of Honolulu, Hawaii's premier outdoor food festival, features small samples from 25 restaurants, entertainment, beer and wine tasting, cooking demos, and a gourmet marketplace. Proceeds go to Abilities Unlimited. At the Civic Center. Call ☎ 808/532-2115. End of June.

Former Honolulu newspaper food critic and chef Matthew Gray has put together **"Hawaii Food Tours."** Matthew preorders the best dishes from a variety of restaurants for each tour. I love the "Hole-in-the-Wall Tour," a lunch tour, from 10am to 2pm, for $99 per person. For information and booking, call ☎ 800/715-2468 or 808/926-FOOD (926-3663), or go to www.hawaiifoodtours.com.

Big Island

The **Great Waikoloa Food, Wine & Music Festival,** Hilton Waikoloa Village, features Hawaii's top chefs (and a few mainland chefs) showing off their culinary talents, wines from around the world, and an excellent jazz concert with fireworks. Not to be missed. Call ☎ 808/886-1234 or visit www.hiltonwaikoloavillage.com or www.dolphindays.com. Mid-June.

Get a behind-the-scenes look at the making of a meal at Merriman's with **Merriman's Farm Visits & Dinner.** Monday through Thursday, a group of 10 leaves Waimea at noon for a 4-hour tour of two farms that sell produce, coffee, and meat to Merriman's, followed by a four-course dinner (salad, fish, meat, and dessert) at the restaurant. The price for the tour and meal is $155. For reservations and information, contact Hawaii Forest & Trail, ☎ 808/331-8505 or www.hawaii-forest.com/adv-farmtour.html.

"Go Local for a Day" is the mantra of **Home Tours Hawaii** (☎ 877/325-5772 or 808/325-5772; www.hometourshawaii.com). Chef Ann Sutherland and her partner, Pat, pick you up in an air-conditioned van and then escort you to private homes in the Kona region for a progressive brunch, prepared by Chef Ann using local products. The 4-hour tour, with transportation, brunch, and a gift bag of local products to take home with you, is $105.

> *Gourmands can let their appetites lead the way at one of Hawaii's many food tours and festivals.*

Maui

Famous wine and food experts and oenophiles gather at the Ritz-Carlton and Kapalua Bay hotels for the **Kapalua Wine and Food Festival.** Formal tastings, panel discussions, and samplings of new releases. Call ☎ 800/KAPALUA or go to www.kapaluaresort.com. End of June or early July.

Some 30,000 people show up at the Lahaina Civic Center for **A Taste of Lahaina**. Sample signature entrees from Maui's premier chefs during this weekend festival, which includes cooking demonstrations, wine tastings, and live entertainment. Call ☎ 888/310-1117 or go to www.mauiinformationguide.com/taste-of-lahaina. Second weekend in September.

300
BEACHWALK

12 The Savvy Traveler

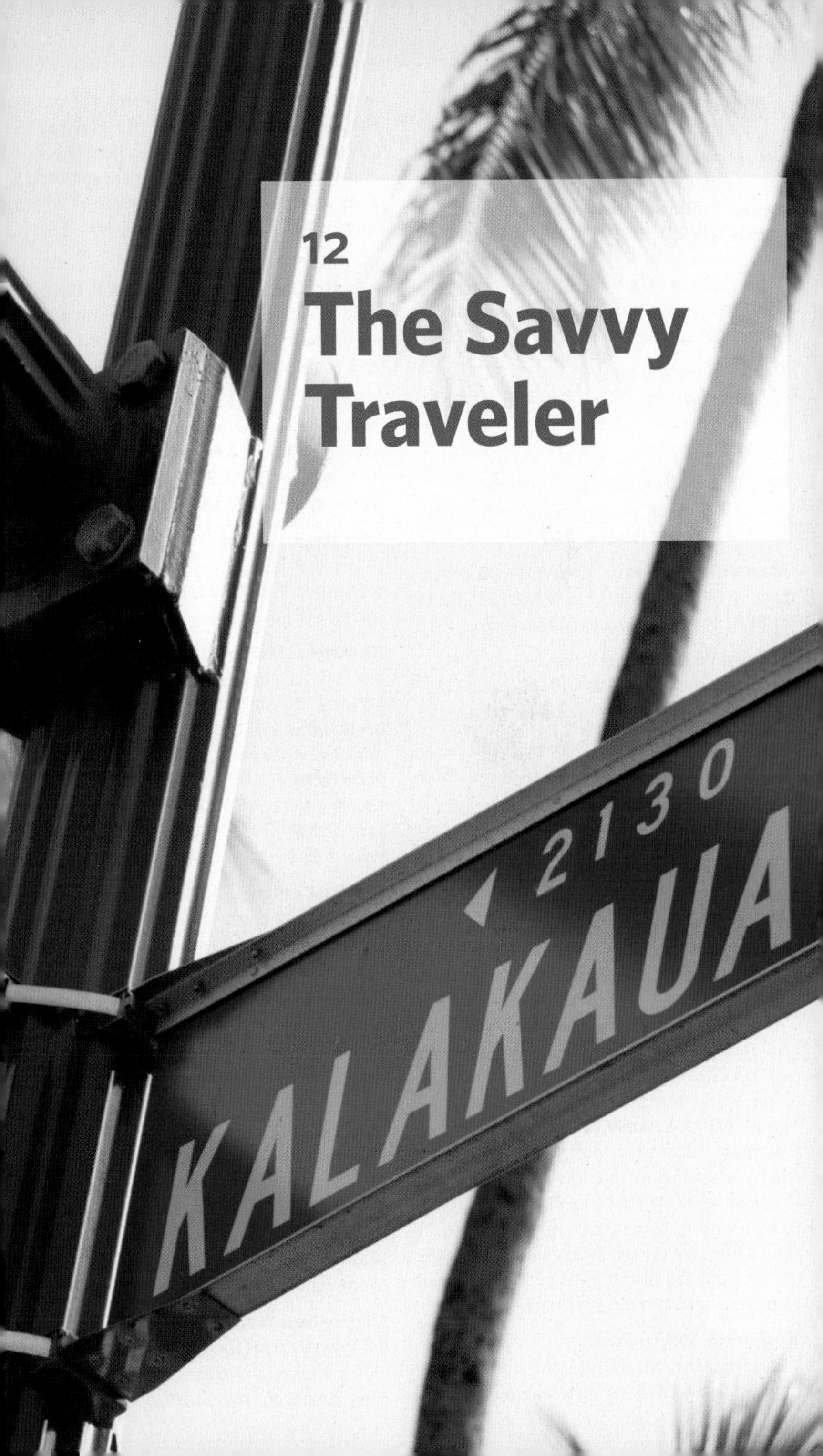

Before You Go

Government Tourist Offices

For information on all the islands, you can contact the **Hawaii Visitors and Convention Bureau (HVCB),** 2270 Kalakaua Ave., Seventh Floor, Honolulu, HI 96815; ☎ 800/GO-HAWAII (464-2924) or 808/923-1811; www.gohawaii.com. Contact information for individual island visitors bureaus are as follows:

Oahu Visitors Bureau, 735 Bishop St., Suite 1872, Honolulu, HI 96813; ☎ 877/525-OAHU (525-6248) or 808/524-0722; www.visit-oahu.com.

Big Island Visitors Bureau, 250 Keawe St., Hilo, HI 96720; ☎ 800/648-2441 or 808/961-5797; www.bigisland.org.

Maui Visitors Bureau, 1727 Wili Pa Loop, Wailuku, HI 96792; ☎ 800/525-MAUI (525-6284) or 808/244-3530; www.visitmaui.com.

Molokai Visitors Association, P.O. Box 960, Kaunakakai, HI 96748; ☎ 800/800-6367 or 808/553-0404; www.molokai-hawaii.com.

Lanai Visitors Bureau, P.O. Box 631436, Lanai City, HI 96763; ☎ 800/947-4774 or 808/565-7600; www.visitlanai.net.

The Best Time to Go

The **high season**—when prices are up and resorts are booked to capacity—generally runs from mid-December through March or mid-April (depending when Easter falls). The last 2 weeks of December in particular are the prime time for travel.

The **off seasons,** when the best bargain rates are available, are spring (mid-Apr to mid-June) and fall (Sept to mid-Dec)—a paradox, since these are the best seasons in terms of reliably great weather. **Summer** isn't the bargain that spring and fall are, but you'll still get better rates than you will in the winter months.

Note: If you plan to come to Honolulu at the end of April, be sure to book way in advance. In Japan there are three holidays in the last week of April, and the islands are especially busy with Japanese tourists during this time.

Festivals & Special Events

Please note that, as with any schedule of upcoming events, the following information is subject to change; always confirm the details before you plan your trip around an event. For an exhaustive list of events beyond those listed here, check http://events.frommers.com, where you'll find a searchable, up-to-the-minute roster of what's happening in cities all over the world.

JANUARY

Rockstar Games Pipeline Pro 2008, Banzai Pipeline, North Shore, Oahu. Competition is judged on the best wave selection and maneuvers on the wave. Call ☎ 732/528-0621. Early January.

PGA Kapalua Mercedes Championship, Kapalua Resort, Maui. Top PGA golfers compete for $1 million. Call ☎ 808/669-2440; www.kapaluamaui.com. Early to mid-January.

Sony Open, Waialae Country Club, Oahu. A $1.2-million PGA golf event featuring the top men in golf. Call ☎ 808/792-9300. Early to mid-January.

Ka Molokai Makahiki, Kaunakakai Town Baseball Park, Mitchell Pauole Center, Kaunakakai, Molokai. Makahiki, a traditional time of peace in ancient Hawaii, is re-created with performances by Hawaiian music groups and hula *halau* (school), ancient Hawaiian games, a sporting competition, and Hawaiian crafts and food. Call ☎ 800/800-6367 or 808/553-3876; www.molokai-hawaii.com. Late January.

Ala Wai Challenge, Ala Wai Park, Waikiki, Oahu. This all-day event features ancient Hawaiian games, like *ulu maika* (bowling a round stone through pegs), *oo ihe* (spear throwing at an upright target), and a ¼-mile outrigger canoe race. It's also a great place to hear Hawaiian music. Call ☎ 808/923-1802; www.waikikicommunitycenter.org. Last weekend in January.

Hula Bowl Football All-Star Classic, Aloha Stadium, Honolulu, Oahu. An annual all-star football classic featuring America's top college players. Call ☎ 800-971-1232; www.hulabowlhawaii.com. Ticket orders are processed beginning April 1 for the next year's game. Mid- to late January.

Chinese New Year, Maui. Lahaina town rolls out the red carpet for this important event with a traditional lion dance at the historic Wo Hing Temple on Front Street, accompanied by ireworks, food booths, and a host of activities. Call ☎ 888/310-1117 or 808/667-9175. Also on Market Street in Wailuku; call ☎ 808/244-3888. On Oahu a big celebration takes place in Chinatown; call ☎ 808/533-3181 for details. January or February; exact date varies.

FEBRUARY

NFL Pro Bowl, Aloha Stadium, Honolulu, Oahu. The National Football League's best pro players square off in this annual gridiron all-star game. Call ☎ 212/450-2000 or 808/486-9555; www.nfl.com. Early February (a week after the Super Bowl).

Wendy's Champions Skins Game at Wailea, Wailea Golf Courses, Maui. Longtime golfing greats participate in this four-man tournament for $770,000 in prize money. Call ☎ 808/875-7450; www.seniorskinswailea.com. Mid-January to early February.

Whale Day Celebration, Kalama Park, Kihei, Maui. A daylong celebration in the park with a parade of whales, entertainment, a crafts fair, games, and food. Call ☎ 808/249-8811; www.visitmaui.com. Early or mid-February.

Waimea Town Celebration, Waimea, Kauai. This annual 2-day party on Kauai's west side celebrates the Hawaiian and multiethnic history of the town where Captain Cook first landed. Top Hawaiian entertainers, sporting events, rodeo, and lots of food are on tap during the weekend celebration. Call ☎ 808/338-1332; www.wkbpa.org/events.html. Weekend after Presidents' Day weekend.

Buffalo's Big Board Classic, Makaha Beach, Oahu. This contest involves traditional Hawaiian surfing, long boarding, and canoe-surfing. Call ☎ 808/951-7877. Depending on surf conditions, it is held in February or March.

MARCH

Kona Brewer's Festival, King Kamehameha's Kona Beach Hotel luau grounds, Kailua-Kona, Big Island. This annual event features microbreweries from around the world, with beer tastings, food, and entertainment. Call ☎ 808/334-1133. Second Saturday in March.

Annual Kona Chocolate Festival, Kona, Big Island. A 3-day celebration of the chocolate (cacao) that is grown and produced in Hawaii. A chocoholic's dream! For information and tickets, call ☎ 808/987-8722; www.konachocolatefestival.com. Mid- to late March.

Ocean Arts Festival, Lahaina. The entire town of Lahaina celebrates the annual migration of Pacific humpback whales with an Ocean Arts Festival in Banyan Tree Park. Artists display their best ocean-themed art for sale, and Hawaiian musicians and hula troupes entertain. Call ☎ 888/310-1117 or 808/667-9175 or visit www.visitlahaina.com. Mid-March.

Prince Kuhio Day Celebrations, all islands. State holiday. Various festivals throughout the state celebrate the birth of Jonah Kuhio Kalanianaole, who was born on March 26, 1871, and elected to Congress in 1902. Kauai, his birthplace, stages a huge celebration in Lihue; call ☎ 808/240-6369 for details. Molokai also hosts a 2-day-long celebration; call ☎ 808/553-3876 to learn more. March 26.

APRIL

East Maui Taro Festival, Hana, Maui. Taro, a Hawaiian staple food, is celebrated through music, hula, arts, crafts, and, of course, food. Call ☎ 808/264-1553; www.tarofestival.org. Varying dates in April.

Annual Ritz-Carlton Kapalua Celebration of the Arts, Ritz-Carlton Kapalua, Maui. Contemporary and traditional artists give free hands-on lessons. Call ☎ 808/669-6200. The 4-day festival begins the Thursday before Easter.

Annual Easter Sunrise Service, National Cemetery of the Pacific, Punchbowl Crater, Honolulu, Oahu. For a century, people have gathered at this famous cemetery for Easter sunrise services. Call ☎ 808/566-1430.

Merrie Monarch Hula Festival, Hilo, Big Island. Hawaii's biggest hula festival features 3 nights of modern *(auana)* and ancient *(kahiko)* dance competition in honor of King David Kalakaua, the "Merrie Monarch" who revived the dance. Tickets sell out by January 30, so reserve early. Call ☎ 808/935-9168; www.merriemonarchfestival.org. The festival takes place the week after Easter.

Hawaii International Film Festival, various locations throughout the state. These cinema festivals with a cross-cultural spin feature filmmakers from Asia, the Pacific Islands, and the United States. Call ☎ 808/528-3456; www.hiff.org. Spring and Fall.

MAY

Outrigger Canoe Season, all islands. From May to September, canoe paddlers across the state participate in outrigger canoe races nearly every weekend. Call ☎ 808/383-7798, or go to www.y2kanu.com for this year's schedule of events.

Annual Lei Day Celebrations, various locations on all islands. May Day is Lei Day in Hawaii, celebrated with lei-making contests, pageantry, arts and crafts, and the real highlight, a Brothers Cazimero concert at the Waikiki Shell. Call ☎ 808/692-5118 or visit www.honolulu.gov/parks/programs/leiday for Oahu events; ☎ 808/597-1888, ext. 232, for the Brothers Cazimero show; ☎ 808/886-1655 for Big Island events; ☎ 808/224-6042 for Maui events; or ☎ 808/245-6931 for Kauai events. May 1.

World Fire-Knife Dance Championships and Samoan Festival, Polynesian Cultural Center, Laie, Oahu. Junior and adult fire-knife dancers from around the world converge on the center for one of the most amazing performances you'll ever see. Authentic Samoan food and cultural festivities round out the fun. Call ☎ 808/293-3333; www.polynesianculturalcenter.com. Mid-May.

International Festival of Canoes, West Maui. Celebration of the Pacific islands' seafaring heritage. Events include canoe paddling and sailing regattas, a luau feast, cultural arts demonstrations, canoe-building exhibits, and music. Call ☎ 888/310-1117; www.mauifestivalofcanoes.com. Mid- to late May.

Memorial Day, National Memorial Cemetery of the Pacific, Punchbowl, Honolulu, Oahu. The armed forces hold a ceremony recognizing those who died for their country, beginning at 9am. Call ☎ 808/532-3720. Memorial Day (last Mon in May).

JUNE

Hawaiian Slack-Key Guitar Festival, Maui Arts and Cultural Center, Kahului, Maui. Great music performed by the best musicians in Hawaii. It's 5 hours long and absolutely free. Call ☎ 808/239-4336 or 808/226-2697; www.slackkeyfestival.com. Late June.

King Kamehameha Celebration, all islands. This state holiday features a massive floral parade, *hoolaulea* (party), and much more. Call ☎ 808/586-0333 for Oahu and Kauai events, ☎ 808/886-1655 for Big Island events, ☎ 808/667-9194 for Maui events, or ☎ 808/553-3876 for Molokai events; hawaii.gov/dags/king_kamehameha_commission. Although King Kamehameha Day is officially June 11, each island celebrates on a different date.

Maui Film Festival, Wailea Resort, Maui. Five days and nights of screenings of premieres and special films, along with traditional Hawaiian storytelling, chants, hula, and contemporary music. Call ☎ 808/572-3456; www.mauifilmfestival.com. Beginning the Wednesday before Father's Day.

King Kamehameha Hula Competition, Neal Blaisdell Center, Honolulu, Oahu. This is one of the top hula competitions in the world, with dancers from as far away as Japan. Call ☎ 808/586-0333; hawaii.gov/dags/king_kamehameha_commission for information. Third weekend in June.

JULY

Makawao Parade and Rodeo, Makawao, Maui. The annual parade and rodeo event have been taking place in this upcountry cowboy town for generations. www.visitmaui.com. July 4.

Fourth of July Fireworks, Desiderio and Sills Field, Schofield Barracks, Oahu. A free daylong celebration, with entertainment, food, and games, ends with a spectacular fireworks show. Call ☎ 808/655-0110.

Hawaii State Farm Fair, Aloha Stadium, Honolulu, Oahu. The annual state fair is a great one: It features displays of Hawaii agricultural products (including orchids), educational and cultural exhibits, entertainment, and local-style food. Call ☎ 808/682-5767; www.ekfernandez.com. Late July or early August.

AUGUST

Hawaii International Jazz Festival, The Hawaii Theatre, Honolulu, Oahu. This festival includes evening concerts and daily jam sessions. Call ☎ 808/941-9974. Early August.

Maui Onion Festival, Whalers Village, Kaanapali, Maui. Everything you ever wanted to know about the sweetest onions in the world. Food, entertainment, tasting, and the Maui Onion Cook-Off. Call ☎ 808/661-4567, or go to www.whalersvillage.com/onionfestival.htm. Early August.

Hawaii State Windsurf Championship, Kanaha Beach Park, Kahului. Top windsurfers compete. Call ☎ 808/877-2111. Early August.

Duke's Ocean Fest Ho'olaule'a, Waikiki, Oahu. Nine days of water-oriented competitions and estivities celebrating the life of Duke Kahanamoku. Events include the Hawaii Paddleboard Championship, the Pro Surf Longboard Contest, a Surf Polo tournament, and Hawaiian Luau (luau is 60 at the door). Call ☎ 808/545-4880; www.dukefoundation.org. Mid-August.

Admissions Day, all islands. Hawaii became he 50th state on August 21, 1959. The state akes a holiday (all state-related facilities are losed) on the third Friday in August.

Hawaiian Slack-Key Guitar Festival, Queen Kapiolani Park Bandstand, Honolulu, Oahu. The best of Hawaii's folk music—slack-key guitar—erformed by the best musicians in Hawaii. Noon to 6pm and absolutely free. Contact ☎ 808/226-2697; www.slackkeyfestival.com. Third Sunday in August.

EPTEMBER

Queen Liliuokalani Canoe Race, Kailua-Kona to Honaunau, Big Island. The world's largest long-istance canoe race takes place over Labor Day weekend, with hundreds participating. Call ☎ 808/334-9481 or visit www.kaiopua.org.

Parker Ranch Rodeo, Waimea, Big Island. This is a hot rodeo competition in the heart of cowboy country. Call ☎ 808/885-7311 or go to www.parkerranch.com. Labor Day weekend.

Hawaiian Slack-Key Guitar Festival, Sheraton Keauhou Bay Resort & Spa, Kona, Big Island. The best of Hawaii's folk music (slack-key guitar) performed by the best musicians in Hawaii. It's 5 hours long and absolutely free. Call ☎ 808/239-4336; e-mail kahokuproductions@yahoo.com. Early September.

Aloha Festivals, various locations statewide. Parades and other events celebrate Hawaiian culture and friendliness throughout the state. Call ☎ 808/391-8714 or visit www.alohafestivals.com for a schedule of events.

Maui County Fair, War Memorial Complex, Wailuku, Maui. The oldest county fair in Hawaii features a parade, amusement rides, live entertainment, and exhibits. Call ☎ 808/242-2721 or visit www.mauicountyfair.com. Late September or early October.

OCTOBER

Ironman Triathlon World Championship, Kailua-Kona, Big Island. Some 1,500-plus world-class athletes run a full marathon, swim 2½ miles, and bike 112 miles on the Kona-Kohala coast of the Big Island. Spectators can watch the action along the route for free. Call ☎ 808/329-0063 or visit www. ironman.com/worldchampionship. The first Saturday in October closest to the full moon.

Hana Ho'ohiwahiwa O Ka'iulani, Waikiki, Oahu. The Sheraton Princess Kaiulani Hotel commemorates the birthday of its namesake, Princess Victoria Ka'iulani with a week of special activities: complimentary hula lessons, lei-making, ukulele lessons, and a children's hula festival. The festival takes place mid-month and admission is free. Call ☎ 808/931-4524.

Hawaii International Film Festival, various locations throughout the state. These cinema festivals with a cross-cultural spin feature film-makers from Asia, the Pacific Islands, and the United States. Call ☎ 808/528-3456; www.hiff.org. Spring and fall.

NOVEMBER

Hawaiian Slack-Key Guitar Festival, Kauai Marriott Resort, Lihue, Kauai. The best of Hawaii's folk music (slack-key guitar) performed by the best musicians in Hawaii. It's 5 hours long and absolutely free. Call ☎ 808/226-2697 or e-mail kahokuproductions@yahoo.com.

Annual Kona Coffee Cultural Festival, Kailua-Kona, Big Island. Celebrate the coffee harvest with a bean-picking contest, lei contests, song and dance, and the Miss Kona Coffee pageant. Call ☎ 808/326-7820; www.konacoffeefest.com for this year's schedule.

Triple Crown of Surfing, North Shore, Oahu. The world's top professional surfers compete in events for more than $1 million in prize money. Call ☎ 808/739-3965; www.triplecrownofsurfing.com. Held between mid-November and mid-December, whenever conditions are best.

DECEMBER

Old-Fashioned Holiday Celebration, Lahaina, Maui. This day of Christmas carolers, Santa Claus, live music and entertainment, a crafts

HONOLULU'S AVERAGE TEMPERATURES & RAINFALL

MONTH	HIGH	LOW	WATER TEMP	RAIN INCHES
January	80	66	75	3.6
February	81	65	75	2.3
March	82	67	76	2.3
April	83	68	77	1.5
May	85	70	79	1.1
June	87	72	81	0.5
July	88	74	81	0.6
August	89	75	81	0.6
September	89	74	81	0.8
October	87	73	81	2.3
November	84	71	79	3.0
December	82	68	76	3.8

fair, Christmas baked goods, and activities for children takes place in the Banyan Tree Park on Front Street. Call ☎ 888/310-1117; www.visitlahaina.com. Second Saturday in December.

Billabong Pro Maui, Honolua Bay at Kapalua Resort, Maui. The final Triple Crown women's surfing contest of the year, bringing together the best of the women's international surfing community. Call ☎ 808/669-2440 or visit www.kapalua.com. Early December.

Festival of Lights, all islands. On Oahu, the mayor throws the switch to light up the 40-foot-tall Norfolk Island pine and other trees in front of Honolulu Hale, while on Maui, marching bands, floats, and Santa roll down Lahaina's Front Street in an annual parade. Molokai celebrates with a host of activities in Kaunakakai; on Kauai the lighting ceremony takes place in front of the former county building on Rice Street, Lihue. Call ☎ 808/523-4385 on Oahu, ☎ 808/667-9175 on Maui, ☎ 808/552-2800 on Molokai, or ☎ 808/828-0014 on Kauai. Early December.

Aloha Bowl, Aloha Stadium, Honolulu, Oahu. A Pac-10 team plays a Big-12 team in this nationally televised collegiate football classic. Call ☎ 808/483-2500. Christmas day.

Rainbow Classic, University of Hawaii, Manoa Valley, Oahu. Eight of the best NCAA basketball teams compete at the Special Events Arena. Call ☎ 808/956-7523. The week after Christmas.

First Light, Maui Arts and Cultural Center, Maui. Major films are screened at this festival (past films have included *The Lord of the Rings: Return of the King, Mystic River, Aviator, Hotel Rwanda,* and many others). Not to be missed. Call ☎ 808/573-3456 or visit www.mauifilmfestival.com. End of December and early January.

Weather

Because Oahu lies at the edge of the Tropical Zone, it technically has only two seasons, both of them warm. The dry season corresponds to summer, and the rainy season generally runs during the winter from November to March. The **year-round temperature** usually varies no more than 9–10°F (–12°C), but it depends on where you are. Oahu's **leeward** sides (the west and south, where Waikiki and Honolulu are located) are usually hot and dry, whereas the **windward** sides (east and north) are generally cooler and moist. If you want arid, sunbaked, desertlike weather, go leeward. If you want lush, often wet junglelike weather, go windward. If you want to know how to pack just before you go, check CNN's online 5-day forecast at www.cnn.com/weather. You can also get the local weather by calling ☎ 808/871-5111.

Useful Websites

www.gohawaii.com: An excellent, all-around guide to activities, tours, lodging, and events by the members of the Hawaii Visitors and Convention Bureau.

www.planet-hawaii.com: Click on "Island" for an island-by-island guide to activities, lodging, shopping, culture, the surf report, weather, and links.

www.visit-oahu.com: Oahu chapter of the state visitors bureau lists activities, dining, lodging, parks, shopping, and more.

www.hawaiian105.com: Local music radio station.

www.geocities.com/~olelo: Hawaiian-language website with easy lessons on Hawaiian and a cultural calendar.

www.honoluluadvertiser.com: Honolulu's daily newspaper with a section on entertainment.

www.honoluluweekly.com: The alternative weekly newspaper, a good source to find out entertainment listings.

www.weather.com: Up-to-the-minute worldwide weather reports.

Getting There

Direct flights are available only to **Oahu,** the **Big Island, Maui,** and **Kauai.** There are no direct flights to **Molokai** and **Lanai.**

Oahu

In **Honolulu,** on Oahu: **United Airlines** (☎ 800/225-5825; www.ual.com) offers the most frequent service from the U.S. Mainland. **American Airlines** (☎ 800/433-7300; www.americanair.com) offers flights from Dallas, Chicago, San Francisco, San Jose, Los Angeles, and St. Louis. **Continental Airlines** (☎ 800/231-0856; www.continental.com) offers the only daily nonstop from the New York area (Newark) to Honolulu. **Delta Air Lines** (☎ 800/221-1212; www.delta.com) flies nonstop from the West Coast and from Houston and Cincinnati. **Hawaiian Airlines** (☎ 800/367-5320; www.hawaiianair.com) offers nonstop flights to Honolulu from several West Coast cities (including new service from San Diego). **Northwest Airlines** (☎ 800/225-2525; www.nwa.com) has a daily nonstop from Detroit to Honolulu.

Airlines serving Honolulu from places other than the U.S. Mainland include **Air Canada** (☎ 800/776-3000; www.aircanada.ca); **Air New Zealand** (☎ 0800/737-000 in Auckland, 643/379-5200 in Christchurch, 800/926-7255 in the U.S.; www.airnewzealand.com); **Air Pacific Airways** (☎ 808/833 5582 in the U.S.; www.airpacific.com); **Continental Air Micronesia** (☎ 800/231-0856; www.continental.com); **Qantas** (☎ 008/177-767 in Australia, 800/227-4500 in the U.S.; www.qantas.com.au); **Japan Air Lines** (☎ 03/5489-1111 in Tokyo, 800/525-3663 in the U.S.; www.japanair.com); **Jetstar** (☎ 866/397-8170, www.jetstar.com) from Sydney; **All Nippon Airways (ANA)** (☎ 03/5489-1212 in Tokyo, 800/235-9262 in the U.S.; www.fly-ana.com); **China Airlines** (☎ 02/715-1212 in Taipei, 800/227-5118 in the U.S.; www.china-airlines.com); **Air Pacific,** serving Fiji, Australia, New Zealand, and the South Pacific (☎ 800/227-4446; www.airpacific.com); **Korean Air** (☎ 02/656-2000 in Seoul, 800/223-1155 on the East Coast, 800/421-8200 on the West Coast, 800/438-5000 from Hawaii; www.koreanair.com); and **Philippine Airlines** (☎ 631/816-6691 in Manila, 800/435-9725 in the U.S.; www.philippineair.com).

The Big Island

The **Kona Airport,** on the Big Island, was the only airport with direct mainland flights when we went to press. Carriers from the mainland include: **American Airlines** (☎ 800/433-7300; www.aa.com); **Delta Airlines** (☎ 800/221-1212; www.delta.com); **Northwest Airlines** (☎ 800/225-2525; www.nwa.com); **U.S. Airways/American West** (☎ 800/428-4322; www.usairways.com); and **United Airlines** (☎ 800/241-6522; www.united.com). The Kona Airport also receives direct overseas flights from Japan on **Japan Airlines** (☎ 800/525-3663; www.japanair.com) and from Vancouver on **Air Canada** (☎ 888/247-2262; www.aircanada.com).

Maui

The following airlines offer direct flights to Maui: **United Airlines** (☎ 800/241-6522; www.united.com); **Hawaiian Airlines** (☎ 800/367-5320; www.hawaiianair.com); **American Airlines** (☎ 800/433-7300; www.aa.com); **Delta Airlines** (☎ 800/221-1212; www.delta.com); **Northwest Airlines** (☎ 800/221-1212; www.nwa.com); and **U.S. Airways/American West** (☎ 800/428-4322; www.usairways.com). Direct flights from Canada include **Air Canada** (☎ 888/247-2262; www.aircanada.com) and **West Jet** (☎ 888/937-8538; www.westjet.com).

Kauai

The only airlines with direct flights to Kauai are **United Airlines** (☎ 800/225-5825; www.ual.com) and **American Airlines** (☎ 800/433-7300; www.aa.com).

Getting Around

Between Islands

If you are unable to get a direct flight to the island of your choice, generally you will be routed to Honolulu, then take an interisland carrier to the island of your choice. At press time the two interisland carriers are: **Hawaiian Airlines** (☎ 800/367-5320 or 808/838-1555; www.hawaiianair.com) and **go!** (☎ 888/IFLYGO2 (435-9462); www.iflygo.com), which offer jet service between Honolulu and the other neighboring islands.

To get to Molokai or Lanai, there are some twin-engine planes that offer daily service:

PW Express (☎ 888/866-5022 or 808/873-0877; www.pacificwings.com/pwexpress), **go!Express** (☎ 888/IFLYGO2, (435-9462); www.iflygo.com), and **Island Air** (☎ 800/323-3345 from the mainland, or 800/652-6541 interisland; www.islandair.com). I must tell you that I have gotten less than sterling service from Island Air; their reservations system has left me stranded in mid-route twice.

Car Rentals

To rent a car in Hawaii, you must be at least 25 years old and have a valid driver's license and a credit card. In the event of an accident, Hawaii law mandates that if you don't have collision-damage insurance, you are required to pay for all damages before you leave the state, whether or not the accident was your fault. Your personal car insurance back home may provide rental-car coverage. Bring your insurance identification card if you decline the optional insurance, which usually costs from $12 to $20 a day. Some credit card companies also provide collision-damage insurance for their customers; check with yours before you rent.

Honolulu is the only city with a "real" public transportation system, but even on Oahu I recommend you rent a car. The bus service is set up for local residents, and many visitor attractions do not have direct routes from Waikiki. The best way to get a good deal on a car rental is to book online. Cars are usually plentiful, except on holiday weekends, which in Hawaii also means King Kamehameha Day (June 10 or the closest weekend), Prince Kuhio Day (Mar 26), and Admission Day (third weekend in Aug). All the major car-rental agencies have offices at the major airports on each island (Honolulu on Oahu, Lihue on Kauai, Kahului on Maui, and Kona and Hilo on the Big Island): **Alamo** (☎ 800/327-9633; www.alamo.com), **Avis** (☎ 800/321-3712; www.avis.com), **Budget** (☎ 800/572-0700; www.budget.com), **Dollar** (☎ 800/800-4000; www.dollar.com), **Enterprise** (☎ 800/325-8007; www.enterprise.com), **Hertz** (☎ 800/654-3011; www.hertz.com), **National** (☎ 800/227-7368; www.nationalcar.com), and **Thrifty** (☎ 800/367-2277; www.thrifty.com). It's almost always cheaper to rent a car at the airport than in Waikiki or through your hotel (unless there's one already included in your package deal).

Tips on Accommodations

Hawaii offers all kinds of accommodations, from simple rooms in restored plantation homes and quaint cottages on the beach to luxurious oceanview condo units and opulent suites in beachfront resorts. Book in advance! Hawaii is NOT the kind of place you want to show up in without a reservation—even sleeping on the beach is illegal.

Hotels

In Hawaii, "hotel" can indicate a wide range of options, from few or no on-site amenities to enough extras to qualify as a miniresort. Generally, a hotel offers daily maid service and has a restaurant, on-site laundry facilities, a pool, and a sundries/convenience-type shop. Top hotels also have activities desks, concierge and valet service, room service, business centers, airport shuttles, bars and/or lounges, and perhaps a few more shops.

The advantages of staying in a hotel are privacy and convenience; the disadvantage is generally noise (either thin walls between rooms or loud music from a lobby lounge late into the night). Hotels are often a short walk from the beach rather than right on the beachfront (although there are exceptions).

Resorts

In Hawaii a resort offers everything a hotel does—and more. You can expect direct beach access, with beach cabanas and lounge chairs; pools and a Jacuzzi; a spa and fitness center; restaurants, bars, and lounges; a 24-hour front desk; concierge, valet, and bellhop services; room service; an activities desk; tennis and golf; ocean activities; a business center; kids' programs; and more.

The advantages of a resort are that you have everything you could possibly want in the way of services and things to do; the disadvantage is that the price generally reflects this. In addition, many resorts charge a mandatory daily "resort fee" for such "complimentary" items as local phone calls and the use of fitness facilities. And don't be misled by a name—just because a place is called "ABC Resort" doesn't mean it actually *is* a resort. Make sure you're getting what you pay for.

Condos

The roominess and convenience of a condo—which is usually a fully equipped, multiple-bedroom apartment—makes this a great choice for families. Condos usually have amenities such as some maid service (ranging from daily to weekly; it may or may not be included in your rate), a pool, and an on-site front desk or a live-in property manager. Condos tend to be clustered in resort areas. There are some very high-end condos, but most are quite affordable, especially if you're traveling in a group.

The advantages of a condo are privacy, space, and conveniences—which usually include a full kitchen, washer and dryer, private phone, and more. The downsides are the lack of an on-site restaurant and the density of the units (vs. the privacy of a single-unit vacation rental).

Bed & Breakfasts

Hawaii has a wide range of places that call themselves B&Bs: everything from a traditional B&B—several bedrooms in a home, with breakfast served in the morning—to what is essentially a vacation rental on an owner's property that comes with fixings for you to make your own breakfast. Make sure that the B&B you're booking matches your own mental picture. Note that laundry facilities and private phones are not always available.

The advantages of a traditional B&B are its individual style and congenial atmosphere, with a host who's often happy to act as your own private concierge. In addition, this is usually an affordable way to go. The disadvantages are lack of privacy, usually a set time for breakfast, few amenities, and generally no maid service. Also, B&B owners usually require a minimum stay of 2 or 3 nights, and it's often a drive to the beach.

Vacation Rentals

This is another great choice for families and long-term stays. "Vacation rental" usually means that there will be no one on the property where you're staying. The actual accommodations can range from an apartment to an entire fully equipped house. Generally, vacation rentals allow you to settle in and make yourself at home for a while. They have kitchen facilities (at least a kitchenette), on-site laundry facilities, and a phone; some also come with such extras as a TV, VCR, and stereo.

The advantages of a vacation rental are complete privacy, your own kitchen (which can save you money on meals), and lots of conveniences. The disadvantages are a lack of an on-site property manager and generally no maid service; often a minimum stay is required. If you book a vacation rental, be sure that you have a 24-hour contact to call if the toilet won't flush or you can't figure out how to turn on the air-conditioning.

Directions—Hawaiian Style

Mainlanders sometimes find the directions given by locals a bit confusing. Seldom will you hear the terms east, west, north, and south; instead, islanders refer to directions as either **makai** (ma-*kae*), meaning toward the sea, or **mauka** (*mow*-kah), toward the mountains. In Honolulu, people use **Diamond Head** as a direction meaning to the east (in the direction of the world-famous crater called Diamond Head), and **ewa** as a direction meaning to the west (toward the town called Ewa, on the other side of Pearl Harbor). Similarly, on Maui, locals might use **Kaanapali** to mean north, or **Lahaina** to mean south.

So, if you ask a local for directions, this is what you're likely to hear: "Drive 2 blocks makai (toward the sea), then turn Diamond Head (east) at the stoplight. Go 1 block, and turn mauka (toward the mountains). It's on the ewa (western) side of the street."

Using a Booking Agency vs. Doing it Yourself

If you don't have the time to call several places yourself to make sure they offer the amenities you'd like, you might consider a booking agency.

A statewide booking agent for B&Bs is **Bed & Breakfast Hawaii** (☎ 800/733-1632 or 808/822-7771; fax 808/822-2723; www.bandb-hawaii.com), offering a range of accommodations from vacation homes to B&Bs, starting at $65 a night. For vacation rentals, contact **Hawaii Beachfront Vacation Homes** (☎ 808/247-3637; fax 808/235-2644; www.myhawaiibeachfront.com). **Hawaii Condo Exchange** (☎ 800/442-0404; www.hawaiicondoexchange.com) acts as a consolidator for condo- and vacation-rental properties.

Surfing for Hotels

In addition to the online travel booking sites **Travelocity, Expedia, Orbitz, Priceline,** and **Hotwire,** you can book hotels through **Hotels.**

com, Quikbook (www.quikbook.com), and **Travelaxe** (www.travelaxe.com).

HotelChatter.com is a daily webzine offering smart coverage and critiques of hotels worldwide. Go to **TripAdvisor.com** or **HotelShark.com** for helpful independent consumer reviews of hotels and resort properties.

It's a good idea to **get a confirmation number** and **make a printout** of any online booking transaction.

Fast Facts

Apartment or Condo Rental

See "Tips on Accommodations", p 588.

ATMs

ATMs are everywhere. You'll find them at most banks, in supermarkets, at Long's Drugs, and in most resorts and shopping centers. **Cirrus** (☎ 800/424-7787; www.mastercard.com) and **PLUS** (☎ 800/843-7587; www.visa.com) are the two most popular networks; check the back of your ATM card to see which network your bank belongs to (most banks belong to both these days).

Babysitting

The larger hotels and resorts offer supervised programs for children and can refer you to qualified babysitters. By state law, hotels can accept only children ages 5 to 12 in supervised activities programs, but they often accommodate younger children by simply hiring babysitters to watch over them. You can also contact **People Attentive to Children (PATCH),** which can refer you to babysitters who have taken a training course on child care. On Oahu call ☎ 808/839-1988; on the Big Island call ☎ 808/325-3864 in Kona or ☎ 808/961-3169 in Hilo; on Maui call ☎ 808/242-9232; on Kauai call ☎ 808/246-0622; on Molokai and Lanai call ☎ 800/498-4145; or visit www.patchhawaii.org.

Banking Hours

Bank hours are Monday through Thursday from 8:30am to 3pm and Friday from 8:30am to 6pm; some banks are open on Saturday.

Bed & Breakfast, Condominium & Vacation Home Rentals

See "Tips on Accommodations", p 588.

Business Hours

Most offices are open from 8am to 5pm. Shopping centers are open Monday through Friday from 10am to 9pm, Saturday from 10am to 5:30pm, and Sunday from 10am to 5 or 6pm.

Car Rentals

See "Getting Around," p 587.

Climate

See "Weather," p 586.

Customs

Depending on the city of your departure, some countries (like Canada) clear customs at the city of their departure, while other countries clear customs in Honolulu. Every visitor older than 21 years of age may bring in, free of duty, the following: (1) 1 liter of wine or hard liquor; (2) 200 cigarettes, 100 cigars (but not from Cuba), or 3 pounds of smoking tobacco; and (3) $100 worth of gifts. These exemptions are offered to travelers who spend at least 72 hours in the United States and who have not claimed them within the preceding 6 months. It is forbidden to bring into the country almost any meat products (including canned, fresh, and dried meat products such as bouillon, soup mixes, etc.). Generally, condiments including vinegars, oils, spices, coffee, tea, and some cheeses and baked goods are permitted. Avoid bringing rice products, as rice can often harbor insects. Bringing fruits and vegetables is not advised, though not prohibited. Customs will allow produce depending on where you got it and where you're going after you arrive in the U.S. Foreign tourists may carry in or out up to $10,000 in U.S. or foreign currency with no formalities; larger sums must be declared to U.S. Customs on entering or leaving, which involves filing form CM 4790. For details regarding U.S. Customs and Border Protection, consult your nearest U.S. embassy or consulate, or **U.S. Customs** (www.cbp.gov).

Dining

With a few exceptions at the high end of the scale, dining attire is fairly casual. It's a good idea to make reservations in advance if you plan on eating between 7 and 9pm.

Electricity

Like Canada, the United States uses 110 to 120 volts AC (60 cycles), compared to the 220 to 240 volts AC (50 cycles) used in most of Europe, Australia, and New Zealand. If your small appliances use 220 to 240 volts, you'll need a 110-volt transformer and a plug adapter with two flat parallel pins to operate them here. Downward converters that change 220 to 240 volts to 110 to 120 volts are difficult to find in the United States, so bring one with you.

Embassies & Consulates

Honolulu has the following consulates: **Australia,** 1000 Bishop St., Penthouse Suite, Honolulu, HI 96813 (☎ 808/524-5050); **Federated States of Micronesia,** 3049 Ualena St., Suite 908,
Honolulu, HI 96819
(☎ 808/836-4775); **Japan,** 1742 Nuuanu Ave., Honolulu, HI 96817
(☎ 808/543-3111); and **Republic of the Marshall Islands,**1888 Lusitana St, Suite 301, Honolulu, HI 96813 (☎ 808/ 545-7767).

Emergencies

Dial ☎ **911** for the police, an ambulance, and the fire department. For the **Poison Control Center,** call ☎ **800/362-3585**.

Event Listings

The best source for listings are the Friday edition of the local daily newspaper, *Honolulu Advertiser* (www.honoluluadvertiser.com); the weekly alternative newspaper, *Honolulu Weekly* (www.honoluluweekly.com); and the weekly shopper, *MidWeek* (www.midweek.com). There are also several tourist publications, such as *This Week on Oahu* (www.thisweek.com).

Family Travel

If you need to rent equipment for kids, try **Baby's Away** (www.babysaway.com). They rent cribs, strollers, highchairs, playpens, infant seats, and the like on Maui (☎ 800/942-9030 or 808/344-2219), the Big Island (☎ 800/996-9030 or 808/322-5158), and Oahu (☎ 800/496-6386 or 808/497-2009). The staff will deliver whatever you need to wherever you're staying and pick it up when you're done.

To locate accommodations, restaurants, and attractions that are particularly kid-friendly, refer to the "Kids" icons throughout this guide. Recommended family travel websites include **Family Travel Forum** (www.familytravelforum.com), a comprehensive site that offers customized trip planning; **Family Travel Network** (www.familytravelnetwork.com), an online magazine providing travel tips; and **TravelWithYourKids.com** (www.travelwithyourkids.com), a comprehensive site written by parents for parents offering sound advice for long-distance and international travel with children. Also look for *Frommer's Hawaii with Kids* (Wiley Publishing, Inc.).

Gay & Lesbian Travelers

The International Gay & Lesbian Travel Association (IGLTA) (☎ 954/630-1637; www.iglta.org) is the trade association for the gay and lesbian travel industry and offers an online directory of gay- and lesbian-friendly travel businesses. For information on gay-friendly business, accommodations, and gay-owned and gay-friendly lodgings in Hawaii, try **Pacific Ocean Holidays,** P.O. Box 88245, Honolulu, HI 96830 (☎ 800/735-6600; www.gayhawaii.com). **The Center** (P.O. Box 22718, Honolulu, HI 96823, mailing address, or 2424 S. Beretania St., between Isenberg and University, Honolulu; ☎ 808/951-7000; http://thecenterhawaii.org), open Monday through Friday 10am to 6pm, and on Saturday, noon to 4pm, is a referral center for nearly every kind of gay-related service you can think of, including the latest happenings on Oahu. Check out their quarterly community newspaper, *Outlook,* on local issues on the gay community in the islands.

Holidays

Federal, state, and county government offices are closed on all federal holidays: January 1 (New Year's Day), the third Monday in January (Martin Luther King, Jr., Day), the third Monday in February (Presidents' Day, Washington's Birthday), the last Monday in May (Memorial Day), July 4 (Independence Day), the first Monday in September (Labor Day), the second Monday in October (Columbus Day), November 11 (Veterans Day), the fourth Thursday in November (Thanksgiving Day), and December 25 (Christmas). Hawaii's state and county offices are also closed on local holidays, including Prince Kuhio Day (Mar 26), King Kamehameha Day (June 11), and Admissions Day (third Fri in Aug).

Other special days celebrated in Hawaii by many people but which involve no closing of federal, state, and county offices are the Chinese New Year (which can fall in Jan or Feb), Girls' Day (Mar 3), Buddha's Birthday (Apr 8), Father Damien's Day (Apr 15), Boys' Day (May 5), Samoan Flag Day (in Aug), Aloha Festivals (in Sept and Oct), and Pearl Harbor Day (Dec 7).

Insurance

For information on traveler's insurance, trip cancellation, and medical insurance while traveling, please visit www.frommers.com/planning.

Internet Access

All major hotels, and even most small B&Bs, have Internet access. Many of them have high-speed wireless, but check ahead of time—access fees can be exorbitant. The best Internet deal in Hawaii are the **public libraries** (www.librarieshawaii.org), which offer free access if you have a library card—you can purchase a 3-month visitor card for $10. **ShakaNet,** Hawaii's largest Wireless Internet Service Provider, has completed the first phase of its free Wireless Waikiki network. Phase I covers a significant portion of Waikiki: roughly Kalakaua Avenue from Liliuokalani Avenue to Queen's Beach in the Diamond Head direction, Liliuokalani Avenue to Kuhio Avenue on the ewa side, and down Kuhio Avenue across Kapiolani Park to Monsarrat Avenue. If you are outside that area, try: **Caffé Giovannini,** 1888 Kalakaua Ave. C-106 (☎ 808/979-2299).

Lost Property

Contact **Travelers Aid International,** Waikiki Shopping Plaza, 2250 Kalakaua Ave, Suite 403-3, Waikiki (☎ 808/926-8274; www.visitoralohasocietyofhawaii.org).

Mail & Postage

To find the nearest post office, call ☎ 800/ASK-USPS (275-8777) or log on to www.usps.gov. In Waikiki, the post office is located at 330 Saratoga Rd. (☎ 808/973-7515). Mail can be sent to you, in your name, c/o General Delivery, at the post office. Most post offices will hold your mail for up to 1 month. At press time, domestic postage rates were 27¢ for a postcard and 42¢ for a letter. For international mail, a first-class letter or postcard of up to 1 ounce costs from 72¢.

Money

Don't carry a lot of cash in your wallet. Many small restaurants won't accept credit cards, so ask upfront if you plan to pay with plastic. Traveler's checks are something of an anachronism from the days before ATMs; American Express (☎ 800/221-7282), Visa (☎ 800/732-1322), and MasterCard (☎ 800/223-9920) all offer them.

Passports

Always keep a photocopy of your passport with you when you're traveling. If your passport is lost or stolen, having a copy significantly facilitates the reissuing process at your consulate. Keep your passport and other valuables in your room's safe or in the hotel safe.

Pharmacies

Twenty-four-hour pharmacies on **Oahu** are: **Longs Drugs:** in Waikiki at 1450 Ala Moana Blvd. (at Atkins Dr.), ☎ 808/941-4433; and in Honolulu at 330 Pali Hwy. (near Vineyard Blvd.), ☎ 808/536-7302; and 2220 South King St., ☎ 808/947-2651.

Other islands: There are no 24-hour pharmacies on the neighbor islands. I recommend Longs Drug Stores (www.longs.com): on **Maui** at 1215 South Kihei Rd., Kihei (☎ 808/879-2033) and in the Maui Mall Shopping Center, 70 E. Kaahumanu Ave., Kahului (☎ 808/877-0068); on the **Big Island** at 75-5595 Palani Rd., Kailua-Kona (☎ 808/329-1632), 111 E. Puainako St., Hilo (☎ 808/595-4508), and 555 Kilauea Ave., Hilo (☎ 808/935-9075); and on **Kauai** at 4-831 Kuhio Hwy., Kapaa (☎ 808/822-4918) and 3-2600 Kaumualii Hwy., Lihue (☎ 808/245-8871).

Safety

Although Hawaii is generally a safe tourist destination, visitors have been crime victims, so stay alert. The most common crimes against tourists are rental-car break-ins. Never leave any valuables in your car, not even in your trunk. Be especially careful at high-risk areas, such as beaches and resorts. Never carry large amounts of cash with you. Stay in well-lit areas after dark. Don't hike on deserted trails or swim in the ocean alone. If you are a victim of a crime, contact the **Visitor Aloha Society of Hawaii** (VASH), Waikiki Shopping Plaza, 2250 Kalakaua Ave, Suite 403-3 (☎ 808/926-8274; www.visitoralohasocietyofhawaii.org).

Senior Travelers

Discounts for seniors are available at almost all major attractions and occasionally at hotels and restaurants. Always inquire when making hotel reservations and especially when you're buying your airline ticket—most major domestic airlines offer senior discounts. Members of **AARP** (☎ 800/424-3410 or 202/434-2277; www.aarp.org) are usually eligible for such discounts. AARP also puts together organized tour packages at moderate rates. Some great, low-cost trips to Hawaii are offered to people 55 and older through **Elderhostel,** 75 Federal St., Boston, MA 02110 (☎ 617/426-8056; www.elderhostel.org), a nonprofit group that arranges travel and study programs around the world. You can obtain a complete catalog of offerings by writing to Elderhostel, P.O. Box 1959, Wakefield, MA 01880-5959.

Smoking

Hawaii has a very strict no-smoking law (no smoking in public buildings, restaurants, bars, retail stores, etc.), and more and more hotels, resorts, condos, and vacation rentals generally do *not* allow smoking in the guest rooms. The majority of bed-and-breakfast units forbid smoking in the rooms. Be sure to check the policy of your accommodations before you book.

Spectator Sports

You've got your choice of **golf tournaments** (☎ 808/792-9300); **Hawaiian outrigger canoe races,** from May to September (☎ 808/383-7798; www.y2kanu.com); and **surfing** (☎ 808/739-3965; www.triplecrownofsurfing.com).

Taxes

The United States has no value-added tax (VAT) or other indirect tax at the national level. Every state, county, and city may levy its own local tax on all purchases, including hotel and restaurant checks and airline tickets. Hawaii state general excise tax is 4%; the city and county of Honolulu adds an additional .005% on anything purchased there. Hotel tax is 11.4%. These taxes will not appear on price tags.

Telephone

For directory assistance, dial ☎ 411; for long-distance information, dial 1, then the appropriate area code and 555-1212. Pay phones cost 50¢ for local calls (all calls on the island of Oahu are local calls). The area code for all of Hawaii is 808. Calls between islands are considered long distance. To make a call to another island you have to dial 1 + 808 + the seven-digit phone number.

Time Zone

The continental United States is divided into **four time zones:** Eastern Standard Time (EST), Central Standard Time (CST), Mountain Standard Time (MST), and Pacific Standard Time (PST). Alaska and Hawaii each have their own zones. Hawaii-Aleutian Standard Time (HST) is 2 hours behind PST. For example, when it's 7am in Honolulu (HST), it's 9am in Los Angeles (PST), 10am in Denver (MST), 11am in Chicago (CST), noon in New York City (EST), 5pm in London (GMT), and 2am the next day in Sydney.

Daylight saving time is in effect from 1am on the second Sunday in March to 1am on the first Sunday in November, except in Arizona, Hawaii, the U.S. Virgin Islands, and Puerto Rico. Daylight saving time moves the clock 1 hour ahead of standard time.

Tipping

Tipping is ingrained in the American way of life. Here are some rules of thumb: In hotels, tip bellhops at least $1 per bag ($2–$3 if you have a lot of luggage), and tip the chamber staff $1 to $2 per person per day (more if you've left a mess). Tip the doorman or concierge only if he or she has provided you with some specific service (like calling a cab). In restaurants, bars, and nightclubs, tip service staff 15% to 20% of the check, and tip bartenders 10% to 15%. Tipping is not expected in cafeterias and fast-food restaurants. Tip cab drivers 15% of the fare, and tip skycaps at airports at least $1 per bag ($2–$3 if you have a lot of luggage).

Toilets

Your best bet is Starbucks or a fast-food restaurant. You can also head to hotel lobbies and shopping centers. Parks have restrooms, but generally they are not very clean and in need of major repairs.

Tourist Offices

See "Government Tourist Offices", p 582.

Index

A

B

C

Q

R

S

T

Y

Z

Accommodations Index

Restaurants Index

Photo Credits

Note: l= left; r= right; t= top; b= bottom; c= center

Cover Photo Credits: Front cover (l to r): © Marco Garcia; © Dana Nadeu/Garden Island Photography; © Bruce Omori. ack cover (t to b): © Marc Schechter/Photo Resource Hawaii/Alamy; © Norma Joseph/Alamy. Cover flap (t to b): © Bettmann/Corbis; © Photo Resource Hawaii/Alamy; © Douglas Peebles Photography/Alamy; © Mark Morgan/ Alamy. Inside front cover (clockwise from tr): © Marco Garcia; © Bruce Omori; © Kristin Mills; © Marco Garcia; © Marco Garcia; © Garden Island Photography/Dana Nadeau. **Interior Photo Credits:** AGE: © Mimi Forsyth/age otostock: p453(br); © Raga Jose Fuste/age fotostock: p484(t); © Reimar Gaertner/age fotstock: p321 (2nd from tl); © Index Stock/age fotostock: pp572-73; © JTB Photo/age fotostock: p104; © Thomas Northcut/ age fotostock: p563(c); © The Print Collector/age fotostock: p453(tl), p562(b); © SuperStock/age fotostock: p321(tl), p424; © Tom Till/age fotostock: pp20-21; © Karl Weatherly/age fotostock: pp234-35; Alamy: © Russ Bishop/Alamy: p226, p451, p495; © blickwinkel/Alamy: p529(bc) © Tibor Bognar/Alamy: p413; © Charles O. Cecil/Alamy: p147(t); © Cornforth Images/Alamy: p567(tr); © Chad Ehlers/Alamy: p300; © Roger Fletcher/ Alamy: p211; © Stephen Frink Collection/Alamy: p529(bl); © Gaertner/Alamy: 150; © Bill Heinsohn/Alamy: p471; © LOOK Die Bildagentur der Fotografen GmbH/Alamy: p512; © Michael Matthews/Alamy: pp580-81; © David L. Moore - Oahu/Alamy: p147(b); © Mark Morgan/Alamy: p528(br); © Douglas Peebles Photography/Alamy: p319, p351(bl), p414-15, p446, p508; © Photo Resource Hawaii/Alamy: p092(l), p148, p200, p250, p255, p321 3rd from tl and tr), p447, p524; © Photos 12/Alamy: p560; © Tom Till/Alamy: p44; © Travel Division Images/ Alamy: p359; © Greg Vaughn/Alamy: p235(tr), p452, p474, p493; © WaterFrame/Alamy: p529(br); © Wendy White/Alamy: p242; Atlantis Submarine: p35, p375(t); Corbis: © Bettmann/CORBIS: p162-63; © CORBIS: 481(bl and r); © Macduff Everton/CORBIS: p74, p163; © Randy Faris/CORBIS: pp320-21; © Robert Holmes/ CORBIS: p321(b); © Amos Nachoum/CORBIS, p529(tr); © Douglas Peebles/CORBIS: piii(t), p73, p78, pp408-09; © Jim Richardson/CORBIS: p260; David Paul's Lahaina Grill: Kent Hwang: p394(r); DoubleTree Alana Hotel: p189; Thomas Dove: p351(tl, tr and br), p567(l); Everett: © Everett Collection: p569(l); Fairmont Kea Lani: p325; Fairmont Orchid: p283, p291; John Fischer: p352; Four Seasons Hualalai, John C. Russell: p280; Four Seasons Lanai, John C. Russell: piv(t), p456; Four Seasons Resort Maui at Wailea: p398; © Marco Garcia: pii(b and c), p8, p12, p19(b), p23, p24-25, p26, p28, p29, p30, p31, p32, p33(t and b), p34 (t and b), p36(t and b), p38, p39, p40, p41(b), p42, p43(t), p72, p76, p77(t and b), p86-87, p88, p90, p91(t and b), p92(r), p94, p96, p97, p101, p103, p106, p107, 108, p108-09, p110, p112, p113, p114, p115(t and b), p116, p117, p118, p120, p121, p122, p123, p124, p125(t and b), p126, p127, p128(t and b), p129, p130(l and r), p131, p134 (t and b), p135, p137, p138, p140, p141, p142, p143, p144, p146, p154, p156, p157(t and b), p158, p159, p160(b), p161, p164, p165, p168, p169, p170, p171, p173, p174, p175, p176, p177, p182(t, b, and 2nd from bottom), p183, p184, p185, p195, p199, p312, p410, p412, p416, p418, p420, p421(l and r), p422, p425, p427, p428 (t and b), p429, p433, p434, p436, p437, p438, p440, p441, p442, p443 p448, p449, p450, p454, p458, p459, p460, p464, p465, p559(bl), p564(l), p565(tl and br), p576; The Garden Island Inn: p549; Getty: David Fleetham: p528-29; Mike Severns: p444-45; Inga Spence: p321 (2nd from tr); David Stubbs: p514; Time & Life Pictures/Getty Images: p453 (2nd from tl); Grand Hyatt Kauai Resort and Spa: p17, p84; Grand Wailea Resort Hotel & Spa: Michael Gilbert: p399; Halekulani Hotel, Courtesy of Halekulani: p188; Hawaiian Waters Adventure Park: p98; Hilton Hawaiian Village Beach Resort & Spa: p182 (2nd from top); Holualoa Inn, wowizowi.com: p285; Hotel Hana-Maui: p348(t), p400; Hotels & Resorts of Halekulani: p193; Alecia Hoyt Photography: p93; The Inn at Volcano, David Warganich, Chalet Kilauea Collection, LP: p287; Iolani Palace, The Hawai'i State Archives: p453(bl), p563(t); © Carla Jalbert: p15, p68, p69, pp296-97, p314, p317, p318, p322, p324(l and r), p334, p336(b), p356, p369, p370, p377, p379, p382, p384(l), p386(b), p405, p566(r); Kaanapali Beach Hotel: p403; Kahala Hotel & Resort: p132, p192; Kapalua Golf Courses: p364; Kauai Marriott Resort: p544; Ki'I Gallery, John Sweitzer: p384(r); Kobal: 20TH CENTURY FOX / THE KOBAL COLLECTION: p569(r); Kona Village Resorts: Courtesy of Kona Village: pv(c), p288, p292, pp556-57; Ko Olina: p151; LaReaux Communications: Hawaii Opera Theatre: p43(b); Steve Lee Las Vegas: p198; Mama's Fish House: p402; Masters of Hawaiian Slack Key Guitar Concert Series: 404; Maui Ocean Center, Darren Jew: p306; Maui Ocean Center: p386(t); Mauna Lanai Bay Hotel & Bungalows: p275; Janice McLaughlin: 528(bl and bc), p529 (2nd from tr); © Kristin Mills: p11, p13, p64, p305, p327, p336(t), p338, p339 (t and b), p340, p344, p354(t), p368, p376, p378, p385; Mutual Publishing, LLC, p568; © Garden Island Photography/Dana Nadeau: piii(b), pv(b), ppx-1, p80, p81, p82, p85, p466-67, p468, p470, p472, p475, p476, p478, p482, p484(b), p486, p48 (l and r), p489, p490, p492, p494, 496 (t and b), p498, p500, p502, p504, p506, p507, p510, p511, p515, p51 p518, p520, p521, p522, p525 (t and b), p526, p530, p532, p534, p535, p538, p540, p542 (t, c and b), p54 p552, p554, p555, p561; © Aaron Nagata: p57(b); The Nature Conservancy: p70; Old Lahaina Luau, p304, p39 © Bruce Omori: piii(c), pix, p13, p19(t), pp46-47, p47, p48, p49, p50, p51, p53, p54, p55, p56, p57(t), p13 pp202-03, p206, p208, p210, p212, p213(t and b), p214, p216, p217, p218, p219, p220, p222, p223, p227, p22 p230, p231, p236, p238, p239(t and b), p243(t), p244, p246(r), p247, p248, p251, p254, p262, p264(l and p265, p266, p268, p270, p272, p273, p274(t and b), p276(t and b), p277, p278, p282, p286, p295, p562(t p564(r), p565(tr), p566(l), p570 , p578, p579; Pacific Stock: Bob Abraham/PacificStock.com: p349; Erik Aeder PacificStock.com: p258; Joe Carini/PacificStock.com: p321 (3rd from tr), p366; Ron Dahlquist/PacificStock.com p61, p224, p310, pp350-51, p354(b); Peter French/PacificStock.com: p10, p261(t); Hawaiian Legacy Archive, PacificStock.com: p235(bl), p453 (3rd from tl and tr), p481(tr), 558, 559(tl and tr); Joss/PacificStock.com p261(b); Ray Mains/PacificStock.com: p301; Ali O'Neal/PacificStock.com: p232; Philip Rosenberg/PacificStock com: p160(t), p233, p259; Greg Vaughn/PacificStock.com: p240, p243(b); Jody Watt/PacificStock.cc p256(b), p257; Paradise Cove Luau: p41(t); Photo Resource Hawaii: © David Franzen/PhotoResourceHaw com: p480; ©Alan Goya/PhotoResourceHawaii.com: p426; © Tor Johnson/PhotoResourceHawaii.com: p36 Pineapple Grill Kapalua: Nina Lee: piv(c), p396; Polynesian Cultural Center: p100; Ken Posney: p548; Merce Richards: p375(b); Roselani: p395; Royal Hawaiian, Starwood Hotels & Resorts Hawai'i: p190; Sandwich Isle Divers: Tim Ewing: p256(t); Sansei Seafood Restaurant and Sushi Bar, Steve Brinkman: p388; Sea Life Park Hawaii: p102; © Ryan Siphers: pii(t), piv(b), p58, p302, p316, p326, p328, p329, p331 p332, p335, p345, p34 p358, p362, p372(b), p373, p374, p387, p390, p392, p394(l); SkyDive Hawaii, Greg Flint: p152; Spa Grande a the Grand Wailea: p313; Starwood Hotels & Resorts Hawai'i: p16, p186, p191, p194, p545, p550; Superstock © age fotostock/SuperStock: p207; © Pacific Stock/SuperStock: pv(t) p14, p246(l), p252, p430, p431, p4 p575; © SuperStock/SuperStock: p562(c); © Agustin Tabares: p62, p65, p66, p298, p330, p342, p348(b); Tril Lanai Ocean Sports: Trilogy Excursions, Maui-Lanai: p60, p67, p308, p372(t), p457; Peter Vitale: p18; © Annett Wagner: p355, p567(br); Waikiki Beach Walk: p563(b); © Waimea Plantation Cottages: 551; Joe West: p462